AF594379

Newman on Doctrinal Corruption

MATTHEW LEVERING

Newman on Doctrinal Corruption

MATTHEW LEVERING

Published by Word on Fire Academic, an imprint of
Word on Fire, Park Ridge, IL 60068

Printed in the United States of America

Cover design, typesetting, and interior art direction by Cassie Pease,
Clark Kenyon, and Rozann Lee

ISBN: 978-1-68578-030-2
Library of Congress Control Number: 2022907604

TABLE OF CONTENTS

ACKNOWLEDGMENTS

This book began with an invitation from the National Institute for Newman Studies to deliver a lecture at a March 2020 symposium. I am especially grateful to Elizabeth Huddleston, Ken Parker, and Bud Marr for this invitation. Although the symposium was shifted to Zoom—its date coincided with the week during which school began to be canceled around the country as the severity of Covid became apparent—I received helpful feedback from the participants. A much-revised version of my paper was published as "Froude, Newman, and Doctrinal Corruption," *Newman Studies Journal* 18 (2021): 24–55. It forms the basis of chapter 2.

In June 2021, I presented a keynote address on "Newman and Döllinger" to a conference entitled Development of Doctrine: Revelation, Magisterium, and Human Reason. This conference was sponsored by the Sacra Doctrina Project and was held at St. Bernard's School of Theology and Ministry in Rochester, New York. I wish to thank the conference organizers, among them Ryan Brady, Brandon Wanless, and Matthew Kuhner. I am indebted to the participants for a number of important and challenging questions and insights.

The manuscript benefited from the corrections and suggestions made by the two readers for Word on Fire Academic, Benjamin King and Andrew Meszaros. I thank them for the care that they put into this labor and for saving me from some significant mistakes. I gratefully incorporated their insights into the book. Ken Parker and Chris Cimorelli of the National Institute for Newman Studies also provided helpful comments on portions of the manuscript.

In moving this book toward publication, the staff members of Word on Fire Academic were a delight to work with. I owe particular thanks to

Brandon Vogt, Jason Paone, and Matthew Becklo. I am thrilled to be part of helping to launch an academic press associated with the work of Bishop Robert Barron. I wish to thank Dan Seseske, who skillfully copyedited the book; Edyta McNichol, who wrote the index and adapted all footnote citations to Word on Fire's in-house style; Madeleine Cook, who proofread the book and caught many typos; and Dr. Marial Corona, who prepared the bibliography. Rozann Lee, Cassie Pease, and Clark Kenyon did exceptional work designing the book and its cover. Christopher Rogers and the library staff at Mundelein Seminary helped me to acquire books, and Mary Bertram has been so supportive of my work in her role as administrative assistant to the Rector of Mundelein Seminary.

My work depends upon the generosity of Jim and Molly Perry, who endowed the chair that I hold at Mundelein Seminary, and whose support has gone far beyond what I could ever have expected. The engine behind my work is my amazing wife, Joy Levering. My life exemplifies the truth of the proverb "He who finds a wife finds a good thing, and obtains favor from the Lord" (Prov 18:22).

I dedicate this book to Elizabeth Huddleston and Alan Mostrom, who helped me so much during my time at the University of Dayton (2009–2013), and who, in their different ways, embody St. John Henry Newman's spirit. May they and their loved ones be blessed!

INTRODUCTION

Recent years have seen the appearance of major studies of Newmanian doctrinal development from various perspectives by such scholars as Andrew Meszaros, Christopher Cimorelli, Stephen Morgan, and Reinhard Hütter, responding in part to current historicist theological trends.[1] In this book, I aim to complement such books from a new angle by highlighting Newman's concerns about doctrinal corruption.[2]

1. See Andrew Meszaros, *The Prophetic Church: History and Doctrinal Development in John Henry Newman and Yves Congar* (Oxford: Oxford University Press, 2016); Meszaros, "John Henry Newman and the Thomistic Tradition: Convergences in Contributions to Development Theory," *Nova et Vetera* 19, no. 2 (2021): 423–468; Christopher Cimorelli, *John Henry Newman's Theology of History: Historical Consciousness, Theological 'Imaginaries,' and the Development of Tradition* (Leuven, BE: Peeters, 2017); Stephen Morgan, *John Henry Newman and the Development of Doctrine: Encountering Change, Looking for Continuity* (Washington, DC: The Catholic University of America Press, 2021); and Reinhard Hütter, "Progress, Not Alteration of the Faith: Beyond Antiquarianism and Presentism. John Henry Newman, Vincent of Lérins, and the Criterion of Identity of the Development of Doctrine," *Nova et Vetera* 19, no. 2 (2021): 333–391. See also Tracey Rowland's forthcoming "John Henry Newman on the Development of Doctrine: A Via Media between Intellectualism and a Voluntarist-Historicism," in a volume edited by Juan Velez (Washington, DC: The Catholic University of America Press, 2022); as well as my chapter on Newmanian doctrinal development—responding to challenges posed by John T. Noonan and others—in my *Engaging the Doctrine of Revelation: The Mediation of the Gospel through Church and Scripture* (Grand Rapids, MI: Baker Academic, 2014), 175–216. In his essay, Meszaros shows both the strengths and the weaknesses of Francisco Marín-Sola's neo-scholastic approach, naming among the strengths the fact that Marín-Sola "affirms without reservation the role that affectivity and connatural knowledge play in the actual development of doctrine" ("John Henry Newman and the Thomistic Tradition," 462). The main weakness is that Marín-Sola exaggerates the logical demonstrability of *every* dogmatic development, not perceiving how much the premises have been shaped in ways that exceed the rules of strict logical demonstration. For her part, Rowland draws heavily upon two insightful essays by Heinrich Fries: "Die Dogmengeschichte des fünften Jahrhunderts im theologischen Werdegang von John Henry Newman," in *Das Konzil von Chalkedon: Geschichte und Gegenwart*, vol. 3, ed. Aloys Grillmeier and Heinrich Bacht (Würzburg: Echter-Verlag, 1954), 421–454; and "Newmans Bedeutung für die Theologie," *Newman-Studien* 1 (Nüremberg: Glock und Lutz Verlag, 1948), 181–199.

2. Jan Hendrik Walgrave holds that councils and popes cannot err in solemn teaching, but he also admits that "the Spirit does not destroy the natural tendencies to deviate in the Christian community as a whole" (Walgrave, *Unfolding Revelation: The Nature of Doctrinal*

In his famous Tract 90, which brought the Tracts to a rather sudden end in 1841 (due to the Anglican bishops' condemnation of the Tract), Newman begins by affirming that an ecclesial "change in theological teaching involves either the commission or the confession of sin; it is either the profession or renunciation of erroneous doctrine, and if it does not succeed in proving the fact of past guilt, it, *ipso facto*, implies present."[3] Newman does not here mean any kind of change. Rather, he means a rupture with solemn doctrine. It is this kind of change that is "either the profession or the renunciation of erroneous doctrine." If the Church were to repudiate one of its solemnly taught doctrines, this would entail that the Church either *has corrupted* or *is now corrupting* the apostolic deposit of faith, a sin indeed.[4]

Today, however, some Catholic theologians toss around the term "development" with little concern about doctrinal corruption. In some circles, the term "development" has come to function like a magician's hat that can unproblematically contain almost anything, even including the occasional (or constant!) rupture of solemnly taught doctrine. In such cases, the notion of an apostolic deposit of faith has faded into the mists, to be replaced by the notion that the Church "develops" doctrine by changing its doctrines to promote a universal religious experience that is expressed differently in every era.

Nothing could be further from Newman's own perspective on

Development [Philadelphia: Westminster, 1972], 383). This point was never far from Newman's mind. See also Walgrave, *Newman the Theologian: The Nature of Belief and Doctrine as Exemplified in His Life and Works*, trans. A. Littledale (New York: Sheed & Ward, 1960). Here Walgrave argues, with religious liberalism in view, that Newman achieved a powerful synthesis: "In avoiding both Scylla and Charybdis, in rejecting neither the logical structure of development nor its vital connection with the whole person, he proved most convincingly the balance and force of his genius" (Walgrave, 299).

3. John Henry Newman, "Tract 90: Remarks on Certain Passages in the Thirty-Nine Articles," in *Tracts for the Times*, ed. James Tolhurst (Notre Dame, IN: University of Notre Dame Press, 2013), 383–475, at 384.

4. See Terrence Merrigan, "Newman and Theological Liberalism," *Theological Studies* 66, no. 3 (2005): 605–621; Edward Short, "Newman and the Liberals," in *Newman and History* (Leominster, UK: Gracewing, 2017), 135–202. See also David Newsome, "Newman and Oxford," in *Newman: A Man for Our Time*, ed. David Brown (London: SCK, 1990), 35–51, at 41.

doctrinal development and the "dogmatic principle," which entails that divine truths are necessarily and adequately, even if imperfectly, expressible in human words.[5] Throughout his career, Newman passionately engaged with questions regarding the doctrinal corruption of the apostolic deposit of faith. Indeed, Newmanian doctrinal development cannot be understood outside this context, so caught up was Newman in responding to concerns about doctrinal corruption brought by some of the preeminent Anglican, Protestant, Catholic, and secular thinkers of the eighteenth and nineteenth centuries.

Bishop Robert Barron aptly associates Newman with the view that "one of the surest signs that the faith is developing properly is that Catholics stubbornly think about the data of revelation."[6] To think in faith about the revealed mysteries is to treasure them as true. When Christians make ontological truth-claims about the revealed mysteries, it follows that these truths can be denied or misunderstood—as happens in doctrinal corruption. It should not surprise us that Newman fully grasped "the difficulty . . . and hazard of developing doctrines" in the above truth-bearing sense, and therefore he applauded the "strong feelings and energetic acts and severe sufferings which age after age have been involved in the maintenance of the Catholic dogmas" against the danger of doctrinal corruption.[7]

Nevertheless, in 1847 Newman's own brother-in-law, James Mozley, published a scathing book-length review of *An Essay on the Development of*

5. See Andrew Meszaros, "Cardinals Newman and Scheffczyk on the Development of Dogma," *Rivista Teologica di Lugano* 25 (2020): 411–437.

6. Robert Barron, *Renewing Our Hope: Essays for the New Evangelization* (Washington, DC: The Catholic University of America Press, 2020), 17. Barron is broadly referencing Sermon 15 in John Henry Newman, *Fifteen Sermons Preached before the University of Oxford between A.D. 1826 and 1843,* ed. Mary Katherine Tillman, 3rd. ed. (Notre Dame, IN: University of Notre Dame Press, 1997).

7. Newman, *Fifteen Sermons Preached before the University of Oxford between A.D. 1826 and 1843*, 327–328. Newman preached this sermon, of course, as an Anglican (or Anglo-Catholic). As Barron observes, "Newman contended that ideas don't exist on the printed page but rather in the play of lively minds, which is to say, in the give-and-take of question, analysis, judgment, and debate" (Barron, *The Priority of Christ: Toward a Postliberal Catholicism* [Grand Rapids, MI: Brazos, 2007], 50).

Christian Doctrine. Mozley's concerns merit our attention at the outset. He argues that Newman has failed to acquaint himself sufficiently with the danger of doctrinal corruption. As a result, Newman has in consequence fallen into the deceitful embrace of Roman Catholicism. According to Mozley, the Anglican Newman rightly valued the development that was characteristic of the earliest Church. What the Catholic Newman fails to see is that, in Roman Catholicism, such "development goes on farther" and engenders a poisonous brew of doctrinal corruption.[8] In Mozley's view, despite Newman's best intentions, his theory amounts to a repurposing of the old religious liberal idea that Christian doctrines such as the Incarnation and the Trinity developed progressively over time—as for religious liberals such doctrines did, namely, out of the original experience of Jesus as a very good man.[9] Even if Newman has in fact not fallen into religious liberalism, Mozley deems that Newman's post-1845 view of Roman Catholic doctrinal development could be plausible only if one ignored the problem of "corruption by excess"—that is, doctrinal corruption by exaggeration within the same "type."[10]

---

8. J.B. Mozley, *The Theory of Development: A Criticism of Dr. Newman's* Essay on the Development of Christian Doctrine (London: Rivington, 1878), 26. This edition is a reprint of Mozley's review, published originally in the *Christian Remembrancer*. Mozley argues that Newman's position runs counter not only to that of Newman's Catholic critic Orestes Brownson but also to that of eminent Catholics such as Nicholas Wiseman and Giovanni Perrone. Mozley sums up the problem with Newman's theory: "It has to convert explanation into growth, new expression into new substance; to raise the definition of a truth,—because it moulds it into mere verbal accuracy,—into truth's rising manhood compared with former infancy, into the plant compared with the seed; it is to be obviously hollow and bombastic. Nor is this all which the new hypothesis [doctrinal development of Roman Catholic doctrine] has to do, for it has to explain away the loud, clear, unanimous assertion of the whole Nicene Church that its doctrine was not a development" (Mozley, 217). The solution, says Mozley, is to follow the Anglican approach of distinguishing between "Nicene doctrines and Roman, between primitive and later" (Mozley, 218). Like other commentators, Mozley also presses the question of what, if anything, Newman deems to belong explicitly to the original apostolic deposit of faith. Newman tried to make this aspect clearer in his 1878 edition.

9. Mozley devotes many pages to challenging Newman's claim that most pre-Nicene Fathers were subordinationists in Christology, a claim that the Anglican Newman had denied.

10. Mozley, 34. Thus, Mozley responds to Newman's discussion of "preservative additions" by remarking, "Whereas then the ordinary charge maintained by English divines against the Roman system is, as we have said, that of exaggeration and abuse in exaggeration, we

I think Newman addresses such concerns about doctrinal corruption far more successfully than Mozley supposes. But the aim of the present book is to place front and center the issue of doctrinal corruption that Mozley identifies and that Newman equally recognizes to be decisive. I explore Newman's responses to five challenges regarding doctrinal corruption, articulated respectively by Edward Gibbon, Richard Hurrell Froude, Francis Newman, Edward Bouverie Pusey, and Johann Joseph Ignaz von Döllinger. Whenever Newman thinks about doctrinal development, he always has the threat of doctrinal corruption in view. This enables his approach to doctrinal development to measure up to the seriousness of the Gospel promise regarding "the truth that abides in us and will be with us forever" (2 John 2).

In our day, as already indicated above, widespread religious liberalism often makes Newmanian doctrinal development seem passé: Newman's claims now appear "conservative." Much theological effort today goes into supporting the secular movement du jour, whether it be sexual, ecological, or socioeconomic; and the notion of enduringly true Catholic doctrine is frequently dismissed as naïve. Andrew Meszaros observes in his study of Newman and Yves Congar, "Contemporary Christian theology—of whatever tradition—is increasingly subject to a relativization of doctrine."[11]

Although the present book will focus with a firmly historical eye on

have here a definition of corruption which excludes exaggeration from its meaning. With such a definition, an arguer of course proceeds with considerable advantage to vindicate the Roman system from all corruption" (Mozley, 36). Mozley's list of exaggerations or corruptions accords with that described by Peter B. Nockles (and thus accords with Newman's own earlier charges against Rome): "In High Church rhetoric, Rome may have been a true church but she was deemed to have abandoned Antiquity by adding to as well as corrupting the Faith with tenets such as Transubstantiation, Purgatory, the Invocation of Saints, devotion to the Blessed Virgin Mary, Indulgences, and obligatory private confession. The necessity of the Reformation, defined as conservative restoration rather than radical departure, was deemed self-evident" (Nockles, "Sources of English Conversions to Roman Catholicism in the Era of the Oxford Movement," in *By Whose Authority? Newman, Manning and the Magisterium*, ed. V. Alan McClelland [Bath: Downside Abbey, 1996], 1–40, at 9–10).

11. Meszaros, *The Prophetic Church*, 240.

Newman and his nineteenth-century context, I am writing as a constructive theologian immersed in today's crisis of doctrine.[12] Rather than distancing me from the historical Newman, this context draws me closer to him and to his view of history. Newman understood that given the active providence of God, human history involves not only "historical depth, change over time, and causal relationships," but also the presence of "a transcendent intelligence that renders historical events as symbols of its will, connecting them according to a system of inner meaning."[13] I share this understanding of history, against the radical historicism that acts like a solvent upon Christian doctrine. Throughout this book, therefore, Newman's theology of history plays a central role.[14]

In notes made while preparing *An Essay on the Development of Christian Doctrine*, Newman urged that his forthcoming book should be read in conjunction with his Anglican Tract 85, "Letters on the Scripture Proof of the Doctrines of the Church" (1838). The main theme of his *Essay* is that true doctrinal development has been sustained in the (Roman) Catholic Church. But one of the *Essay*'s major subplots has to do with

12. Stephen Morgan points out, "In the last thirty years or so, attitudes toward Newman have often been proxies for other theological controversies" (Morgan, *John Henry Newman and the Development of Doctrine*, 11). I think this is because many of the theological controversies with which Newman engaged are very much alive today, and so to write on Newman is unavoidably to take a position with relation to contemporary controversies. Morgan argues, "Under the papacies of St. John Paul II and Benedict XVI, such [Ultramontanist] appeals to authority were deployed in what might be called a more 'conservative' direction, but these appeals were often made without acknowledging the complexity and far-from-univocal voice of tradition. Those whose Ultramontanist instincts served more 'progressive' causes were prone to the same error—especially when claiming the warrant of the early church in support—but did and continue to do so without any serious consideration of the extent to which such innovations and changes are consistent and cohere with the antecedent teaching or practice" (Morgan, 269).

13. James Matthew Wilson, "Doctrinal Development and the Demons of History: The Historiography of John Henry Newman," *Religion and the Arts* 10, no. 4 (2006): 497–523, at 498. I make the same point in my *Participatory Biblical Exegesis: A Theology of Biblical Interpretation* (Notre Dame, IN: University of Notre Dame Press, 2008).

14. See also the three patristic principles shared by Newman and Henri de Lubac and their impact on the theological vocation, as shown in Theresa Marie Chau Nguyen, "Preservation of Type and the Continuity of Patristic Principles in the Legacies of Saint John Henry Newman and Henri de Lubac," *Newman Studies Journal* 17, no. 2 (2020): 22–40.

religious liberalism's impact upon all Christian churches and traditions. In Tract 85, Newman warns that even Christians may soon come to think that the Apostles' proclamation of the Gospel was merely a "historical event occurring eighteen hundred years since, which modified or altered the course of human thought and society"—rather than an event that was "specially divine in its origin, and directly acting upon us."[15] Tract 85 emphasizes that there really has been a divine revelation in Jesus Christ and it is imperative for us to hear and obey its contents. Newman states, "From beginning to end, Scripture implies that God has spoken, and that it is right, our duty, our interest, our safety to believe."[16] No wonder he deems doctrinal corruption of the Gospel to be so serious a threat!

Concerns about doctrinal corruption go back to the New Testament itself. Just to give one example, consider Paul's warning to the Galatians that "there are some who are confusing you and want to pervert the gospel of Christ" by introducing "another gospel" (Gal. 1:7). The same concerns about doctrinal corruption are present in the early patristic writings. For

---

15. John Henry Newman, "Holy Scripture in Its Relation to the Catholic Creed," in Newman, *Discussions and Arguments on Various Subjects*, ed. Gerard Tracey and James Tolhurst (Notre Dame, IN: University of Notre Dame Press, 2004), 109–235, at 232. Newman adds, "This is what the Age is coming to. . . . We know it denies the existence of the Church as a divine institution: it denies that Christianity has been cast into any particular social mould. Well: but this, I say, is not all; it is rapidly tending to deny the existence of any system of Christianity either; any creed, doctrine, philosophy, or by whatever other name we designate it. Hitherto it has been usual, indeed, to give up the Church, and to speak only of the covenant, religion, creed, matter, or system of the Gospel; to consider the Gospel as a sort of literature or philosophy, open to all to take and appropriate, not confined to any set of men, yet still a real, existing system of religion. This has been the approved line of opinion in our part of the world for the last hundred and fifty years; but now a further step is about to be taken. The view henceforth is to be, that Christianity does not exist in documents, any more than in institutions; in other words, the Bible will be given up as well as the Church. It will be said that the benefit which Christianity has done to the world, and which its Divine Author meant it should do, was to give an impulse to society, to infuse a spirit, to direct, control, purify, enlighten the mass of human thought and action, but not to be a separate and definite something, where doctrine or association, existing objectively, integral, and with an identity, and forever, and with a claim upon our homage and obedience" (Newman, 232–233). See also Owen Chadwick, *From Bossuet to Newman*, 2nd ed. (Cambridge: Cambridge University Press, 1987), 129.

16. Newman, "Holy Scripture in Its Relation to the Catholic Creed," 233.

instance, Ignatius of Antioch commands the Trallians to "partake of Christian food exclusively; abstain from plants of alien growth, that is, heresy."[17] Ignatius of Antioch was faced with proto-Gnostic Christian thinkers who argued that Jesus' "suffering was but make-believe."[18] Had this error taken hold in the Church, the truth of the Gospel would have been decimated. Similarly, at the end of the second century, Irenaeus of Lyons combated various Gnostic Christian teachings, including the notion that the female deity Achamoth brought forth the Father, who on the Gnostic view is only "God of everything outside of the Pleroma, being the creator of all animal and material substances."[19]

In the tradition of Paul and the early Church Fathers, Newman cares about doctrinal corruption not due to a narrow dogmatism but out of love for the life-giving "gospel, which you received, in which you stand, by which you are saved, if you hold it fast" (1 Cor. 15:1–2).[20] In Newman's era, the fundamental question for Christians was whether there has been a

---

17. Ignatius of Antioch, "To the Trallians," in *The Epistles of St. Clement of Rome and St. Ignatius of Antioch*, trans. and ed. James A. Kleist (Westminster, MD: Newman Bookshop, 1946), 75–79, at 77.

18. Ignatius of Antioch, 78.

19. Irenaeus, *Against Heresies*, 1.5, in *The Apostolic Fathers, Justin Martyr, Irenaeus*, ed. Alexander Roberts and James Donaldson, vol. 1 of the Ante-Nicene Fathers series (Peabody, MA: Hendrickson, 1995), 315–567, at 322.

20. Against defensiveness, narrowness, and dogmatism, see John Henry Newman, Sermon 14: "Wisdom, as Contrasted with Faith and with Bigotry," in Newman, *Fifteen Sermons Preached before the University of Oxford between A.D. 1826 and 1943*, ed. Mary Katherine Tillman (Notre Dame, IN: University of Notre Press, 1997), 278–311, at 307–308, at 311: "Narrow minds have no power of throwing themselves into the minds of others. They have stiffened in one position, as limbs of the body subjected to confinement, or as our organs of speech, which after a while must learn new tones and affections. They have already parceled out to their own satisfaction the whole world of knowledge; they have drawn their lines, and formed their classes, and have given to each opinion, argument, principle, and purity, its own locality; they profess to know where to find every thing; and they cannot learn any other disposition. . . . They think that any one truth excludes another which is distinct from it, and that every opinion is contrary to their own opinions which is not included in them. . . . Let us ever make it our prayer and our endeavour, that we may know the whole counsel of God, and grow into the measure of the stature of the fulness of Christ; that all prejudice, and self-confidence, and hollowness, and unreality, and positiveness, and partisanship, may be put away from us under the light of Wisdom, and the fire of Faith and Love; till we see things as God sees them, with the judgement of His Spirit, and according to the mind of Christ."

divinely given revelation with concrete cognitive content. Believing that God has spoken in Jesus Christ, and believing that this divine revelation has been faithfully taught in Scripture and handed on by the Church, Newman nevertheless affirmed these truths in a manner that was, in Frederick Aquino's words, "profoundly dynamic, multifaceted, contextual, integrative, and existential."[21] It is clear that Newman's complex arguments in favor of Catholic doctrine "polarize[d] the theological landscape" of his day, both during his Anglican years and after his conversion.[22] But his goal was consistently to help the Church avoid the deformation described by Reinhard Hütter: "Without being rooted in the original deposit of faith, without a constant return to revelation received in scripture and in sacred tradition, the church would cease to be apostolic in its doctrinal substance; she would betray the teaching of the Gospel."[23]

For some, like Newman's brother-in-law Mozley, it may seem that Roman Catholic bishops meeting in council, or the (infallible) pope by himself, have the power to contradict the Gospel's contents at will. Are not bishops merely powerful men who often do not include the laity in their deliberations and who may lack biblical erudition? In his study of the Newman brothers (John and Francis), William Robbins sharpens this question. He argues that the dogma of papal infallibility poses "a cruel dilemma for a Church which has for so long justified authoritarian

21. Frederick D. Aquino, *An Integrative Habit of Mind: John Henry Newman on the Path to Wisdom* (Dekalb, IL: Northern Illinois University Press, 2012), 14.

22. Aquino, 14. Aquino is here warning against how "people from various perspectives employ him [Newman] to support their positions and polarize the theological landscape"—whereas I am pointing out that Newman understood that theological strife was necessary and important (with its inevitable polarization), although theologians must proceed—by God's grace—with charity and humility.

23. Reinhard Hütter, *John Henry Newman on Truth and Its Counterfeits: A Guide for Our Times* (Washington, DC: The Catholic University of America Press, 2020), 129. See also Günter Biemer's emphasis on the subjective dimension of Tradition, in his "Newman on Tradition as a Subjective Process," in *By Whose Authority?*, 149–167, although Biemer's accurate points are diminished by his anti-neo-scholastic polemic; as well as Heinrich Fries, "J.H. Newmans Beitrag zum Verständnis der Tradition," in *Die mündliche Überlieferung*, ed. Michael Schmaus (Munich: Max Hueber Verlag, 1957), 33–122; and Gottlieb Söhngen, *Kardinal Newman: Sein Gottesgedanke und seine Denkergestalt* (Bonn: Götz Schwippert, 1946).

intolerance by claiming unique possession of sacred truth."[24] For Robbins, the only path forward is for a liberal pope to employ solemn papal authority itself to *deny* the truth of the dogma of papal infallibility, thereby bringing to an end all Catholic claims to have faithfully developed doctrine.

While Newman recognizes that authoritarianism can become a temptation for powerful people in the Church, he does not think that the solution is to deny the Church's ability to faithfully hand on divine revelation under the Spirit's guidance. After all, such a solution would only further entrench the notion that Christianity is whatever powerful people make of it. By contrast, Newmanian doctrinal development holds ultimately that not powerful humans but God himself is in charge of the communication of divine revelation. In the course of my study, I will explore Newman's perspective in detail, including Newman's willingness to challenge powerful people both within and outside the Church. His concerns about doctrinal corruption should remind all members of the Church that we are accountable to the Triune God for the way in which we hand on the salvific realities that Jesus Christ wishes his people to know and share in.[25]

The Plan of the Work

My book explores Newman on doctrinal corruption by means of five comparative chapters. Each chapter treats a text from one of Newman's chief dialogue partners and then engages with one or more writings by Newman.

---

24. William Robbins, *The Newman Brothers: An Essay in Comparative Intellectual Biography* (Cambridge, MA: Harvard University Press, 1966), 181.

25. I note here that the eminent Anglican convert Robert Hugh Benson was aided by reading Newman's *An Essay on the Development of Christian Doctrine* not simply by itself, but specifically in conjunction with W.H. Mallock's *Doctrine and Doctrinal Disruption: Being an Examination of the Intellectual Position of the Church of England* (London: Adam and Charles Black, 1900)—though Mallock's book was not nearly at the level of Newman's. See Benson, *Confessions of a Convert* (Notre Dame, IN: Ave Maria, 2016), 68.

Without claiming that Newman says everything that needs to be said, I hope to show that his responses to the challenges posed by the threat of doctrinal corruption remain profoundly instructive.

The first chapter compares Edward Gibbon's *Decline and Fall of the Roman Empire* with Newman's *Essay on the Development of Christian Doctrine*. Notwithstanding their sharp disagreement over Christianity, Gibbon was a major influence on Newman. The second chapter compares a seminal 1833 essay by Richard Hurrell Froude to two works by Newman, *The Via Media of the Anglican Church* and *Essay on the Development of Christian Doctrine*. Froude's anti-Erastian theorizing was crucial in inaugurating the Oxford Movement—even if, going beyond Newman's and Keble's perspective, "Froude advocated the actual supremacy of the Church over the state in a truly theocratic manner."[26] As Newman remarked in looking back upon the Oxford Movement in 1850, the first principle of the Oxford Movement "was ecclesiastical liberty; the doctrine which [the Oxford Movement] especially opposed was, in ecclesiastical language, the heresy of Erastus."[27] Froude

26. J.H.L. Rowlands, *Church, State and Society: The Attitudes of John Keble, Richard Hurrell Froude and John Henry Newman, 1827–1845* (Worthing, UK: Churchman Publishing, 1989), 229. Edward Short observes more broadly regarding English Erastianism, "The Erastian nature of English Christianity was important because it was out of the National Church's subordination to the State that the Broad Church arose, and, in turn, it was out of the non-dogmatical accommodation of the Broad Church that liberalism in religion arose—the conviction, as Newman famously wrote, that 'No theological doctrine is any thing more than an opinion which happens to be held by bodies of men' and 'Therefore . . . no creed, as such, is necessary for salvation'" (Short, "Newman and the Liberals," 142–143, citing Newman, *Apologia Pro Vita Sua and Six Sermons*, ed. Frank Turner [New Haven, CT: Yale University Press, 2008], 260).

27. John Henry Newman, *Certain Difficulties Felt by Anglicans in Catholic Teaching Considered*, vol. 1 (London: Longmans, Green, 1897), 101. Newman explains along lines that identify Froude's position with that of the Movement: "The writers of the Apostolical party of 1833 were earnest and copious in their enforcement of the high doctrines of the faith, of dogmatism, of the sacramental principle, of the sacraments (as far as the Anglican Prayer Book admitted them), of ceremonial observances, of practical duties, and of the counsels of perfection; but, considering all those great articles of teaching to be protected and guaranteed by the independence of the Church, and in that way alone, they viewed sanctity, and sacramental grace, and dogmatic fidelity, merely as subordinate to the mystical body of Christ, and made them minister to her sovereignty, that she might in turn protect them in their prerogatives. Dogma would be maintained, sacraments would be administered,

could be a difficult person to deal with, but Newman benefited from his keen intellectual and spiritual perception.[28]

Third, I compare Edward Pusey's 1865 *Eirenicon* with Newman's book-length response, not least because Pusey was one of the most important interlocutors that Newman had in the course of his lifetime. Fourth, I compare Francis Newman's 1850 autobiographical *Phases of Faith* with Newman's *Apologia Pro Vita Sua*. The impact of Newman's family upon his life and career is something that deserves more attention, building upon such studies as Robbins' *The Newman Brothers* and Edward Short's *Newman and His Family*.[29] Fifth and finally, I compare Johann Joseph Ignaz von

---

religious perfection would be venerated and attempted, if the Church were supreme in her spiritual power; dogma would be sacrificed to expedience, sacraments would be rationalized, perfection would be ridiculed if she was made the slave of the State. Erastianism, then, was the one heresy which practically cut at the root of all revealed truth. . . . Such was the teaching of the movement of 1833. The whole system of revealed truth was, according to it, to be carried out upon the anti-Erastian or Apostolical basis. The independence of the Church is almost the one subject of three out of four volumes of Mr. Froude's Remains; it is, in one shape or other, the prevailing subject of the early numbers of the *Tracts for the Times*, as well as of other publications which might be named. It was for this that the writers of whom I speak had recourse to Antiquity, insisted upon the Apostolical Succession, exalted the Episcopate, and appealed to the people, not only because these things were true and right, but in order to shake off the State" (Newman, 102–103).

28. Sheridan Gilley describes Froude as "arguably the nearest thing that the Oxford Movement possessed to a continental radical of the right, and with his affection for the theocratic medieval Church, [he] could be called the Anglican de Maistre or founder of Anglican Ultramontanism" (Gilley, "The Ecclesiology of the Oxford Movement: A Reconsideration," in *From Oxford to the People: Reconsidering Newman and the Oxford Movement*, ed. Paul Vaiss [Leominster, UK: Gracewing, 1996], 60–75, at 62). For Froude's bullying of his much younger brother James Anthony Froude—in addition to Hurrell Froude's sincere efforts to assist his brother—see Ciaran Brady, *James Anthony Froude: An Intellectual Biography of a Victorian Prophet* (Oxford: Oxford University Press, 2013). In Hurrell Froude's favor, however, stands "the manner in which he bore his sufferings in his last years" (Brady, 67). James Anthony Froude became a strong opponent of Tractarianism in particular and Christianity in general, and Brady cautions that the portraits of Newman found in James Anthony Froude's "Reminiscences of the High Church Revival: Six Letters," *Good Words* 22, nos. 1–6 (January–July 1880), 18–23, 98–102, 162–167, 306–312, and 409–415 are based on little personal contact with Newman, despite Froude's giving the opposite impression.

29. See Robbins, *The Newman Brothers*; and Edward Short, *Newman and His Family* (London: Bloomsbury, 2013), especially chapter 4: "Frank Newman and the Search for Truth." What Short elsewhere says of James Fitzjames Stephen also applies fully to Francis: "For Fitzjames Stephen and so many men like him, the only acceptable course for [John

Döllinger's writings about papal infallibility with Newman's response in his *Letter to the Duke of Norfolk* and its Postscript. Döllinger's depth of engagement with the historical issues involved in the dogma of papal infallibility is second to none. So far as I can tell, scholars have not yet sufficiently addressed the significance of Newman's engagement with Döllinger.[30]

The five chapters span Newman's career. His encounter with Gibbon comes first because he read Gibbon as a young man and continually returned to Gibbon's work over the ensuing decades. Thomas Parker comments, "Together with Locke, Gibbon was Newman's reading during the long vacation of 1818. . . . At first sight so incongruous, the influence of Gibbon upon Newman is often underrated. Yet it was considerable."[31] Gibbon interprets the history of the early Church as a history of doctrinal

---

Henry] Newman after he found the Anglican Church untenable would have been to join Fitzjames Stephen and his friends in honest, foursquare skepticism. In their eyes, that Newman persevered in what they could only regard as groundless credulity was proof of his dishonesty" (Short, "Newman and the Liberals," 143; cf. Newman's brilliant sketch in "Faith and Doubt," in *Discourses Addressed to Mixed Congregations*, ed. James Tolhurst [Notre Dame, IN: University of Notre Dame Press, 2002], 214–237, at 221–222, ending with the line: "When it [the world] sees a Catholic Priest, it looks hard at him, to make out how much there is of folly in his composition, and how much of hypocrisy").

30. Lawrence Poston makes an accurate offhand comment but does not expand upon it: "Here [in *Letter to the Duke of Norfolk*] Newman's rhetorical task was even more complicated than in his response to Pusey, and much more hung on the result. He had to address Gladstone and the Protestants, Manning and the Ultras, and Döllinger and the liberal Catholic adherents on the Continent who still looked to Newman as a potential ally" (Poston, *The Antagonist Principle: John Henry Newman and the Paradox of Personality* [Charlottesville, VA: University of Virginia Press, 2014], 218). Poston is similarly insightful, though brief, with regard to Newman's work in relation to Francis Newman. His remarks are worth quoting: "As Newman was closing his Anglican accounts in *Loss and Gain*, his brother Francis Newman was about to raise dust in another quarter. Both Newman's secession and the irritating air of certainty that pervaded his novel [*Loss and Gain*] had much to do with Frank's timing of his two works, *The Soul, Her Sorrow and Her Aspirations* (1849) and the autobiographical *Phases of Faith* (1850)" (Poston, 152). In a nutshell, Francis is writing against John. Poston suggests that John's *Apologia Pro Vita Sua* is written (in part) against Francis: see Poston, 191–192.

31. Thomas M. Parker, "The Rediscovery of the Fathers in the Seventeenth-Century Anglican Tradition," in *The Rediscovery of Newman: An Oxford Symposium*, ed. John Coulson and A.M. Allchin (London: Sheed & Ward, 1967), 31–49, at 38. See also Edward Short's "Newman, Gibbon and God's Particular Providence," in *Newman and History*, 3–80. Short points out correctly that "for Newman, Gibbon's rationalist history adumbrates the liberalism that he spent so much of his long life opposing. Indeed, in many critical ways, Gibbon helped

corruption, whereas Newman, by 1845, interprets it as a history of doctrinal development. Second comes his encounter with Froude, whom he first met in 1826, and who, more than anyone else, moved Newman in the direction that produced the Oxford Movement. In my view, J.H.L. Rowlands is correct to esteem Froude as "politically and socially the most advanced, sophisticated and penetrating" of the Tractarians.[32] If Newman's friendship with Froude was particularly important in Newman's late twenties and early thirties, then arguably his interactions with his brother Francis grew increasingly important for Newman as his thirties progressed. As Francis was losing his dogmatic faith step by step, Newman was reassessing the Anglican Church but holding ever more firmly to dogmatic Christianity.

When in the early 1840s he began to break with his friend and collaborator in the Oxford Movement, Edward Pusey, Newman underwent the most decisive crisis of his life. After Newman's entrance into the Catholic Church, and especially after the definition of the dogma of Mary's Immaculate Conception by Pope Pius IX, Pusey challenged Newman to explain why this papal action was not clear proof that the case for doctrinal development that Newman had laid out in *An Essay in the Development of Christian Doctrine* was false. In the 1850s and 1860s, Pusey urged Newman to reconsider whether the Catholic Church to which he had converted was, in fact, a blatant corruptor of doctrine.[33] Lastly, in the early 1870s, Döllinger

---

to refine Newman's understanding of the errors of liberalism, which had their roots in the rationalist zeal of the Enlightenment" (Short, 6).

32. Rowlands, *Church, State and Society*, 78. Rowlands points out that "Froude, along with Keble, Newman and Pusey thought that ecclesiastical purity was essential. This does not, however, preclude an acute consciousness, for instance, of the Church's mission to society. Froude, like Pusey, was very aware of the need to Christianise the large industrial towns" (Rowlands, 78). As Rowlands goes on to say, Froude "realised in 1831 that the Church needed a blow-up. Without such a happening it could never right itself. In less emotive language, Froude realised that the position of the Establishment was certainly anomalous. Her rights were there by divine permission alone, as the state had secured by law the endowments which it could not have seized without sacrilege and had encumbered the rightful possession of them by various conditions calculated to bring the Church into bondage" (Rowlands, 79).

33. Newman, of course, had held precisely this viewpoint as an Anglo-Catholic, and so Pusey's concerns would have been no surprise to him.

demanded that Newman draw the line at Vatican I's definition of papal infallibility, since, for Döllinger, this was an evident instance of doctrinal corruption, grounded in historical falsehoods, theological overreach, and sheer power-mongering with no real regard for Scripture or the patristic Church.

In sum, my book follows Newman from his early reading of Gibbon, through the Oxford Movement which for Newman was rooted in his friendship with Froude, to his disagreements with his anti-dogmatic brother Francis, to his break with Pusey and the Anglican Church, and to the ecclesiastical and theological crises surrounding the Catholic Church's dogmatic definitions of Mary's Immaculate Conception in 1854 and papal infallibility in 1870.

Let me now describe the chapters a bit more fully. The first chapter shows that Gibbon presents an idealized portrait of pagan religious toleration. In Gibbon's view, Christianity both extends and worsens Judaism. It worsens Judaism because, despite the (supposed) fact that Jewish Christianity did not at first consider Jesus to be God, Christians soon proclaimed him to be divine in order to attract Gentile converts. Gibbon deems almost all Christian doctrinal disputes to be conflicts over unrealities. Just as Gibbon (having rejected the Catholicism to which he briefly converted as a young man) begins with the hypothesis that the Church has corrupted its doctrine from the outset, so Newman (on the path to embracing Catholicism) begins with the hypothesis that the Church develops but does not corrupt revealed truth.

Both Gibbon and Newman require Christians to confront the available historical facts. Though not philologists themselves, they both show "esteem for hard-core philological scholarship, as well as for the thorough documentation long typical of ecclesiastical history."[34] What differentiates

34. James Turner, *Philology: The Forgotten Origins of the Modern Humanities* (Princeton, NJ: Princeton University Press, 2014), 110. Turner is here discussing Gibbon, not Newman. See also Turner's high praise for Barthold Niebuhr's "revolutionary" philological labor (in his historical research), notable perhaps since Newman drew upon Niebuhr: Turner, 169–170.

them is the way they link the historical facts together and the conclusions they draw. They both set forth hypotheses to account for how the available facts cohere. Their hypotheses are grounded, in part, upon what they deem to be antecedent probabilities. They exemplify the ways in which historical conclusions are affected by the historian's philosophy of history.

In the original 1845 edition of *An Essay on the Development of Christian Doctrine*, Newman provides a lengthy excerpt from *The Decline and Fall of the Roman Empire*, showing how Gibbon organizes his historical data and remarking that while Gibbon's hypothesis is plausible, Gibbon "has not mentioned its hypothetical character" and thereby gives the impression of more historical certitude than is possible.[35] Since Newman was in constant dialogue with Gibbon's *Decline and Fall*, it is appropriate that my first chapter examines Gibbon's and Newman's divergent hypotheses about the early Church, the former favoring corruption, the latter development.

The second chapter has Froude at its center. Due to a series of bills passed by Parliament in the late 1820s and early 1830s, the question arose as to whether a Parliament whose legislators include non-Anglicans can legitimately determine Anglican episcopal appointments or exert influence in any way over intra-Anglican disputes, including doctrinal ones. Once being an Anglican no longer is required for governmental office, it seems that doctrinal indifferentism has been inscribed into the way in which the British government perceives its established Church. On this basis, Froude and Newman feared that Erastianism and Latitudinarianism (or religious liberalism) were coming together in a manner that would result in the doctrinal corruption of the Church.[36] As Richard Hutton remarked in 1891,

35. John Henry Newman, *An Essay on the Development of Christian Doctrine [1845]*, ed. Stanley L. Jaki (Pinckney, MI: Real View Books, 2003), 181.

36. Of course, as Kenneth L. Parker et al. point out, "Erastianism—state intervention in ecclesiastical affairs—had been a source of tension in the Church of England since the sixteenth century," and so Froude and Newman were not the first to discover a problem, even if the situation was new in the sense that now "non-Anglican politicians in parliament exercised authority over the affairs of the Church of England" (Parker and the Contributors, "The Converts and the Council," In *Authority, Dogma, and History: The Role of Oxford Movement Converts in the Papal Infallibility Debates*, ed. Kenneth L. Parker and Michael J. Pahls, [Bethesda,

"Newman's wrath against 'Liberalism,' as for many years afterwards he always called it—identifying as he did Liberalism with Latitudinarianism—was to a very considerable extent a moral contagion caught from Hurrell Froude."[37]

My chapter shows that Newman, in *The Via Media of the Anglican Church*, echoes concerns raised by Froude in 1833.[38] Unlike Froude, however, Newman in the *Via Media* argues that the Roman Catholic Church has fallen into doctrinal corruption by making determinations where none are warranted by Scripture or the Fathers.[39] In *An Essay on the Development*

MD: Academica, 2009], 1–9, at 4). Or as Benjamin O'Connor puts the concerns of Froude, Keble, and Newman: "If parliament was now legislating against Anglican tradition on ecclesiastical and juridical matters, they asked, how long until it voted similarly on doctrinal matters?" (O'Connor, "The Oxford Movement," in *Authority, Dogma, and History*, 9–43, at 13).

37. Richard H. Hutton, *Cardinal Newman* (London: Methuen, 1891), 36; cf. 104–105). Hutton, a theologian, mathematician, professor, journalist, and longtime editor of the *Spectator* who began as a Unitarian and died as a High-Church Anglican (under the influence especially of F.D. Maurice), knew and corresponded with Newman over many years. On their relationship, see Edward Short, *Newman and His Contemporaries* (London: T.&T. Clark International, 2011), 303–334.

38. Yngve Brilioth has shown that Alexander Knox, among others, influenced the Tractarian view of the "via media" between Protestantism and (Roman) Catholicism: see Brilioth, *The Anglican Revival: Studies in the Oxford Movement* (London: Longmans, Green, 1933), 47–53. More recently, this point has been contextualized by David McCready, *The Life and Theology of Alexander Knox: Anglicanism in the Age of Enlightenment and Romanticism* (Leiden, NL: Brill, 2020). Knox collaborated with Bishop John Jebb, most importantly on an Appendix to Jebb's *Sermons on Subjects Chiefly Practical, with Illustrative Notes and an Appendix, Relating to the Character of the Church of England as Distinguished from Other Branches of the Reformation and from the Modern Church of Rome* (London: T. Cadell, 1815). For further discussion of Knox and Jebb, noting the often-critical assessment of their writings that one finds in Newman, Froude, Keble, and Pusey, see Geoffrey Rowell, "'Church Principles' and 'Protestant Kempism,' Some Theological Forerunners of the Tractarians," in *From Oxford to the People*, 17–59, at 38–54. For the important role of Jebb's thought in the controversies of Abbé Jager with the Tractarian Benjamin Harrison and later with Newman, see Louis Allen, "Introduction," in *John Henry Newman and the Abbé Jager: A Controversy on Scripture and Tradition*, ed. Louis Allen (Oxford: Oxford University Press, 1975), 1–32, at 20–29.

39. His trip to Italy and Sicily, however, did persuade Froude that Catholic countries, too, were beleaguered by Erastian troubles, in addition to general immorality and laxity: see *Remains of the Late Reverend Richard Hurrell Froude*, vol. 1, ed. John Keble and John Henry Newman (London: J.G. & F. Rivington, 1838), 293–294. Froude concludes that "the whole

of Christian Doctrine, then, Newman has to defend Roman Catholicism against the charges of doctrinal corruption that he himself put forward only a few years earlier. As a Catholic, Newman also was concerned about maximalist claims regarding papal power.[40] I argue that Newman consistently reminded his fellow Christians that the Gospel must be defended from becoming the toy of powerful people inside or outside the Church.

The third chapter begins with Francis Newman's *Phases of Faith*, which describes his gradual loss of dogmatic faith (he ended up believing only that God exists and loves us). In their teens, both Francis and John Henry Newman converted to Evangelical Anglicanism.[41] Francis, however, came increasingly to connect Christian dogma with biblical literalism, fanatical dogmatism, and scientific and historical absurdity. Francis also experienced painful ill-treatment from John, and in his *Apologia Pro Vita Sua*, John grants the truth of Francis' charges in this regard. The argument of *Apologia Pro Vita Sua* is that dogmatic faith need not lead to dogmatism, and that a sincere quest for truth—which Francis asserts will inevitably culminate in religious skepticism or liberalism—is fully compatible with arriving at a firm dogmatic faith. I note that for the quest for truth to have this outcome, it is necessary that the "sacramental principle" be affirmed.[42] This

Christian system all over Europe 'tendit visibiliter ad non esse.' The same process which is going on in England and France is taking its course everywhere else, and the clergy in these Catholic countries seem as completely to have lost their influence, and to submit as tamely to the state, as ever we can do in England" (Froude, 296).

40. For the diversity of "Ultramontanist" viewpoints in different nations, see *Varieties of Ultramontanism*, ed. Jeffrey von Arx (Washington, DC: The Catholic University of America Press, 1998).

41. For background, see David Newsome, "The Evangelical Sources of Newman's Power," in *The Rediscovery of Newman*, 11–30, at 11–20.

42. James Pereiro helpfully describes what Newman means by a "principle": "Newman's use of the term 'principle' combined both the intellectual and moral dimensions. He conceived principles, within the general literature of the time [Pereiro cites a similar understanding found in contemporaneous books by Christopher Wordsworth and Joseph Fletcher], as the fundamental inner laws ruling the thought and activity of a particular person or institution, growing from deep moral roots and endowed with moral content. Principles lay deeper than doctrines; they are fundamental assumptions or general approaches to reality. They are abstract, general, permanent, more immediately ethical and practical than doctrines. . . . An idea has

principle holds that behind earthly realities stands the presence and causality of God: real history is never separated from God's presence and action.

Against dogmatism, John grants that scientific and historical challenges to Christian beliefs are not easily answered. But he urges all the more that, given the natural skepticism of the human mind, God in giving a revelation would have ensured the presence of an interpreter able to hand on the revealed truth without corrupting it. Toward the end of the *Apologia*, John depicts human rationality as neither frozen nor impeded by a dogmatic Church—as Francis had concluded—but rather as functioning vigorously and creatively due to having an authority (bearing authoritative truths) as a partner. Under the watchful eye of the Church's teaching office, "doctrines must expand, must become explicit where they had been only implicit, must assert themselves under new conditions which shed new light upon them"—and in fact "without such a developing power as this, the primitive teaching, the deposit given once for all, would be a dead formula, and not a living power."[43]

The fourth chapter treats Pusey's *Eirenicon* and Newman's response. In his *Eirenicon*, as noted above, Pusey argues that the Roman Catholic Church's Mariology is proof that Newmanian "development of doctrine" is a false path. For Pusey, claims about "development of doctrine" inevitably lead to doctrinal corruption because such claims embolden the Church to go beyond the limits of the testimony of the Church Fathers. Pusey deems it to be much better to follow the path of the Oxford Movement, adhering only to the doctrines that can be safely demonstrated from Scripture and the witness of the Fathers. In addition, Pusey argues that where Anglicanism highlights Jesus, Roman Catholicism highlights Mary; and he quotes various exaggerated claims about Mary made by Roman Catholic theologians and saints.

In response, Newman contends that, far from being corruptions,

---

its own proper principles in which it lives and develops" (Pereiro, *'Ethos' and the Oxford Movement: At the Heart of Tractarianism* [Oxford: Oxford University Press, 1991], 181).

43. Hutton, *Cardinal Newman*, 164.

Mary's Immaculate Conception and bodily Assumption are scriptural, even if to perceive this fact we must learn from the Fathers (or from Tradition) how to read Scripture.[44] Newman also argues that the Catholic Church's Marian doctrines flow from the Fathers' testimony to Mary as Mother of God and the New Eve. While rejecting the exaggerated Marian piety favored by some English Ultramontanists such as Frederick Faber and exemplified by some Catholic saints, Newman emphasizes that in cultures where Mary is praised, Jesus is worshipped.[45] Regarding doctrinal development, he defends Mary's Immaculate Conception on various grounds, including conservative action upon the past.

Lastly, my fifth chapter focuses on the dogma of papal infallibility (1870) as rejected by Döllinger. I first survey Döllinger's writings, which denounce all post-patristic understandings of the primacy of the bishop of Rome. Far too often, according to Döllinger, an expansion of papal power was supported by faked documents passed off as ancient. He charges Newman with cowardice or ignorance for not speaking out more strongly in the period prior to the dogmatic definition and for not rejecting the Vatican Council's dogma. Without mentioning Döllinger's name, Newman responds to him in his *Letter to the Duke of Norfolk* and its Postscript, while also addressing William Gladstone's concerns.

44. On Newman and the Church Fathers in the context of nineteenth-century (and contemporary) religious liberalism, see the work of the patristics scholar Michael Fiedrowicz, *John Henry Newman und die Kirchenväter: Anti-Liberalismus im Geist der frühen Kirche* (Fohren-Linden, DE: Carthusianus Verlag, 2020).

45. Hutton responds critically: "Surely the real danger of the immense development which the Roman Catholic Church has given to the intercession of the Virgin Mary and the saints, is, that it tends to present to us the wills of beings who in knowledge and limitations are like ourselves, and who are supposed, at least by ignorant people, to be more influenced by our pertinacity of entreaty than God would be, as likely to urge upon God what He would otherwise refuse to do, and to try to impose upon Him by their entreaties their weaker forms of good-will; whereas, what ought to be impressed on the ignorant is, that the more completely any finite being has conformed himself to the will of God, the more resolutely would he refuse to intercede for any favour not intrinsically in harmony with the Divine providence" (*Cardinal Newman*, 182). I note that the worship of Christ without a sense of the prayerful presence of Christ's Mystical Body would be inadequate, since God wills to work out his providence not least through the prayers of the members of the Body of Christ.

Newman makes clear, first, that the patristic period cannot be used as an inflexible standard that must be merely replicated by the Church of all later eras: this is the mistake of antiquarianism.[46] In the patristic period, certainly, the bishop of Rome did not exercise universal governance. But, in Newman's view, this does not mean that continuity with the Church Fathers is lacking in the new dogma. On the contrary, the bishop of Rome's universal governance was always part of Christ's plan for the Church, and the prerogatives claimed by the later popes ensured the continuance of the marks of the patristic Church. The patristic Church understood itself to be one, to have universal jurisdiction, and to be able to hold authoritative and binding councils. The only Church that today plausibly lays claim to these crucial patristic elements is the Roman Catholic Church led by the pope. Given the geographical spread of the Church, such elements could not have been retained if a centralizing papacy had not emerged.

Just as importantly, Newman argues that historical research alone, even when practiced by someone as erudite as Döllinger, cannot stand as the sole determinant of whether a true doctrinal development has occurred. He also rejects the maximalist reading of papal infallibility offered by Döllinger and instead advocates the interpretation offered by the German bishop Joseph Fessler, the secretary general of the council. Fessler's *True and False Infallibility* was translated into English by Newman's close friend and fellow Oratorian Ambrose St. John.[47]

46. See Hütter, *John Henry Newman on Truth and Its Counterfeits*, 133–134: "For ecclesial antiquarianism, all developments beyond some allegedly pure origin or some purportedly undistorted temporally limited expression of the origin are nothing but a fall from the original truth, an amassment of both light and grave corruptions that more and more pollute the clear spring water the further it is carried away from its pristine source. Return to and union with this origin, or at least with the latest state of its authentic expression, is the ultimate goal of ecclesial antiquarianism. *Nota bene*: the ecclesial antiquarian does not oppose the authentic development of doctrine, but rather simulates it. Authentic development, for the antiquarian, is nothing but the latest state of the origin's authentic expression. Anything beyond this state is to be rejected as a corruption of doctrine."

47. See Avery Dulles, *Newman* (London: Continuum, 2002), 94; as well as Joseph Fessler, *The True and the False Infallibility of the Popes: A Controversial Reply to Dr. Schulte*, trans. Ambrose St. John (London: Burns and Oates, 1875).

These five chapters show that concerns about doctrinal corruption stand at the heart of a great deal of Newman's work. As noted above, speaking for (and to) the rising class of educated nonbelievers, Gibbon's *Decline and Fall of the Roman Empire* indicts the whole of Christianity and especially Catholicism on a simple charge: historical research proves that Christianity is built upon repeated doctrinal corruptions. For his part, Froude urges that the Anglican bishops must reject the (newly non-Anglican) State's power over ecclesiastical matters, or else an Erastian religious liberalism or Latitudinarianism will negate the Anglican Church's claim to hand on the true teaching of Scripture in light of the patristic witness.

In his formative Oxford years, then, Newman was attentive to charges of doctrinal corruption. His brother Francis' loss of dogmatic faith in the 1830s intensified these charges, since Francis came to believe that no thinking person—no one who is open to truth wherever it be found—can retain belief in dogmatic Christianity. As a Catholic, moreover, Newman had to answer similar charges regarding doctrinal corruption, now from his erstwhile Oxford Movement compatriot Pusey and his erstwhile anti-Ultramontanist compatriot Döllinger.

The Challenge of Religious Liberalism

Orthodox, Anglican, and Protestant theologians have long believed that the Catholic Church has corrupted doctrine. Jaroslav Pelikan remarks, "Protestants have usually denied both the theological and the historical implications of the claim that the developments of Roman Catholic Christianity have in fact preserved the type or idea. In various ways and with varying degrees of radicalism, Protestants have asserted 'the fall of the Church'" due to Catholic doctrinal corruption.[48] At various points in his career, Martin Luther gave different dates to this decisive fall, but he

---

48. Jaroslav Pelikan, *Development of Christian Doctrine: Some Historical Prolegomena* (New Haven, CT: Yale University Press, 1969), 14.

generally considered it to have taken place in the early medieval period. Other notable Protestant theologians have traced it back to the time of Constantine or even earlier.[49] Similarly, the Orthodox theologian Nikolaos Loudovikos, whose ecumenical erudition and sophistication are exemplary, articulates a standard Orthodox viewpoint when he states (as his own view), "After the great schism, a hierarchic ecclesiological model, clearly prevailing in the West, was gradually invested with the rigid legalistic armor of the Roman spirit, and gave birth to an openly nomocanonical ecclesiology, with the pope as universal jurisdictional monarch on top."[50]

Liberal theology seeks an end to this kind of blame for corrupting doctrine, not however by resolving the issues but by relativizing doctrine itself. In England and the continent, varieties of religious liberalism were already well-known in the eighteenth century. In Germany, Friedrich Schleiermacher's 1799 *On Religion: Speeches to Its Cultured Despisers* influentially denied that religion is a matter of knowledge. On this view, the Christian religion does not involve the kind of knowledge that can be expressed dogmatically. Dogmas are either "merely abstract expressions of religious

49. For Luther, Pelikan relies upon John M. Headley, *Luther's View of Church History* (New Haven, CT: Yale University Press, 1963), 187–192. As an example of the case for a Constantian fall, Pelikan points to Gerrit J. Heering's *The Fall of Christianity: A Study of the Relationship between Christianity, the State, and War*, trans. J.W. Thompson (London: George Allen & Unwin, 1930), but of course many more recent such works could be named. See also the rich discussion of the issues in Jaroslav Pelikan, *The Christian Tradition: A History of the Development of Doctrine*, vol. 5, *Christian Doctrine and Modern Culture (since 1700)* (Chicago: University of Chicago Press, 1989), 227–238, 247–281.

50. Nikolaos Loudovikos, *Church in the Making: An Apophatic Ecclesiology of Consubstantiality*, trans. Norman Russell (Yonkers, NY: St. Vladimir's Seminary, 2016), 115. He argues that the root of the problem is an inadequate appropriation of the insights of the Greek Fathers: "The deep and absolute ontological identification-through-participation-in-uncreated-grace of the Church with Christ in the Spirit, made by the majority of Greek Fathers, still remains foreign to Roman Catholic ecclesiology" (Loudovikos, 114–115). More boldly, the Orthodox ecclesiologist Cyril Hovorun argues that not only is "primacy" "a matter of convenience and agreement between churches" rather than a divine gift, but also that "the church is not hierarchical in its nature. The hierarchical principle is not even its natural property. It was borrowed from outside the church and remains there as its scaffolding. In application to primacy this means that the assumption that primacy belongs to the nature of the church is not correct" (Loudovikos, 128, 141).

intuitions" or else are second-order "free reflections upon original achievements of the religious sense."[51] The notion that Christianity contains enduringly true revelation about divine realities, as propositionally expressed in the New Testament and in the creeds, is foreign to Schleiermacher's understanding of both religion and revelation, although he thinks that time-bound formulations will inevitably arise from the Christian experience of the feeling of absolute dependence.[52]

The liberal Protestant thinker Ernst Troeltsch, writing in 1913, contends that "the essence of Christianity can be understood only as the new interpretations and new adaptations, corresponding to each new situation," and thus, while there is "development" in a sense, neither the Bible nor the Christian creed provides any enduring or universally binding truth-claims.[53] For the liberal Catholic George Tyrrell, a contemporary of Troeltsch's, dogmatic truth-claims are the root of religious intolerance and persecution. Somewhat like Troeltsch, he proposes that the solution is to perceive that Christian dogmas are ever-developing symbols that fit the experiential "laws of nature and of life" and that can be said to be true not due to any ontological reference to Jesus or God, but due to their reference to ever-developing human life and action.[54] John Coulson sums up Tyrrell's

---

51. Friedrich Schleiermacher, *On Religion: Speeches to Its Cultured Despisers*, trans. and ed. Richard Crouter, 2nd ed. (Cambridge: Cambridge University Press, 1996), 48.

52. In a Postscript to Tract 73 ("On the Introduction of Rationalistic Principles into Religion") in Newman, *Tracts for the Times*, 180–243, at 241–243, Newman briefly addresses some points drawn from Schleiermacher's treatise on Sabellianism (*On the Discrepancy between the Sabellian and the Athanasian Method of Representing the Doctrine of the Trinity*), of which Newman possessed a full translation. Newman concludes that Pietism (or "Protestantism") is descending into a rationalistic Sabellianism, but, as Stephen Thomas shows, Newman does not possess a clear understanding of all Schleiermacher's subtleties (see Thomas, *Newman and Heresy: The Anglican Years* [Cambridge: Cambridge University Press, 1991], 136).

53. Ernst Troeltsch, "The Dogmatics of the History-of-Religions School," in Troeltsch, *Religion in History*, trans. James Luther Adams and Walter F. Bense (Minneapolis, MN: Fortress, 1991), 87–108, at 97.

54. George Tyrrell, *Christianity at the Cross-Roads* (London: Longmans, Green, 1910), 236; cf. 225, 230. Tyrrell comments, "The comparatively modern toleration of other religions is, to a large extent, due to the scepticism suggested by the multiplication of sects each claiming to be the one authentic Christianity; and by an increased experience of other religions making the same claims as the Christian Church. This scepticism has been

position (without agreeing with it): "The language of revelation is poetic and, as such, is neither true or false. . . . Thus Tyrrell comes to deny the possibility of there being a demonstratively and reliably *analogical* relation between the forms in which Revelation has been expressed and the language of interpretation. . . . Tyrrell commits himself to a principle, not of development, but of epigenesis."[55]

More recently, Catholic theologians such as Edward Schillebeeckx have sought to measure the truth of Christian dogma in terms of praxis. For Schillebeeckx, "christology derives its authenticity from the concrete praxis of the kingdom of God: the history of Jesus' career must be continued in his disciples; only then is it meaningful to talk of the uniqueness and distinctiveness of Christianity."[56] Meaningful and authentic Christology is found not in articulating the unique being of Jesus himself, but in the liberative praxis of his followers. On this view, the thing that is enduringly true in Catholicism—namely, "the insight of Christian faith that God is

systematically deepened by the comparative study of religion, and by all the causes that have brought dogma into disrepute" (Tyrrell, 229). Positively, Tyrrell proposes that Jesus "desired to supplement and fulfil the necessarily ever-imperfect expressions of the spirit [such as the Jewish Torah and Temple]; to push the letter down to its proper place of subordination and instrumentality; to carry religion to its final phase; to deny the static immutability and perpetuity of the external embodiment of the spirit, and to make it a living and growing organism. . . . Jesus Himself was the great sacrament and effectual symbol of the Divine Life and Spirit. He worked on His disciples, not doctrinally as a teacher of the understanding, but with all the force of a divine and mysterious personal ascendancy, transmitted through every word and gesture. . . . The Spirit of Jesus uttered in the Church, in the Gospel, in the sacraments, is apprehended by His followers, not as a doctrine but as a personal influence, fashioning the soul to its own divine nature. . . . The human frame and mind of Jesus, His local and temporal limitations of thought and knowledge, were but the sacramental elements through which the influence of His Divine Spirit was mediated. To our age He would have spoken differently, but the spirit would have been the same" (Tyrrell, 262, 265–266). For the enthusiastic appropriation of Tyrrell today, see Anthony M. Maher, *The Forgotten Jesuit of Catholic Modernism: George Tyrrell's Prophetic Theology* (Minneapolis, MN: Fortress, 2018); David G. Schultenover, *George Tyrrell: In Search of Catholicism* (Shepherdstown, WV: Patmos, 1981).

55. John Coulson, "Was Newman a Modernist?," in *John Henry Newman and Modernism*, ed. Arthur Hilary Jenkins (Sigmaringendorf, DE: Glock und Lutz, 1990), 74–84, at 76.

56. Edward Schillebeeckx, *Church: The Human Story of God*, trans. John Bowden (New York: Crossroad, 1990), 168.

personally involved with men and women and their history"—is expressed politically, through solidarity with the oppressed.[57]

Arguably the most influential Catholic theologian of the twentieth century, Karl Rahner, while continuing to speak about the "substance of faith," proposed in 1977 that the era of "an evolutive explication and systematizing differentiation of the basic substance of faith" is over.[58] In other words, development of doctrine as Newman understood it has come to an end. This is because the global Church of the present and future will face an "incommensurable and not adequately synthesizable pluralism of present and future horizons of understanding," which will mean that doctrinal formulations in different contexts within the global Church will appear incommensurable and no longer will be reducible to any one formulation or interpretation.[59] Thus, Catholics can no longer expect to be united explicitly by dogmatic faith, beyond the most basic substance of faith in Christ.

Observing the doctrinal divisions among postconciliar Catholics,

57. Schillebeeckx, 170; cf. 169. As Schillebeeckx goes on to say, "The thematization of universal meaning can be accomplished meaningfully only with a practical-critical intention, i.e. in a perspective in which a bit of meaninglessness is done away with, step by step, through human action. The thematization or reflection must thus be supported by a praxis of gradual liberation which will prepare and free the way for total meaning. In other words, total meaning can only come about through historical experiences and commitment; it cannot be speculatively thought out in a theoretical anticipation, precisely because concrete history is a mixture of sense and nonsense. . . . The salvation that is founded in Christ as a promise for all becomes universal, not through the mediation of an abstract, universal idea, but by the power of its cognitive, critical and liberating character in and through a consistent praxis of the kingdom of God" (Schillebeeckx, 175–176; cf. 177–178, 182). On Schillebeeckx, see especially Thomas Joseph White, *The Incarnate Lord: A Thomistic Study in Christology* (Washington, DC: The Catholic University of America Press, 2015), 470–486. White traces Schillebeeckx's perspective back to the influence of M.-D. Chenu: see Chenu's "La raison psychologique du développement du dogme," *Revue des sciences philosophiques et théologiques* 13, no. 1 (1924): 44–51. Chenu goes further—in full accord with the later Schillebeeckx—in his postconciliar "Vérité évangélique et métaphysique wolffienne à Vatican II," *Revue des sciences philosophiques et théologiques* 57, no. 4 (1973): 632–640.

58. Karl Rahner, "Yesterday's History of Dogma and Theology for Tomorrow," in Rahner, *Theological Investigations*, vol. 18, *God and Revelation*, trans. Edward Quinn (New York: Crossroad, 1983), 3–34, at 33. See also Rahner, "Pluralism in Theology and the Unity of the Creed in the Church," in Rahner, *Theological Investigations*, vol. 11, *Confrontations 1*, trans. David Bourke (New York: Seabury, 1974), 3–23.

59. Rahner, "Yesterday's History of Dogma and Theology for Tomorrow," 33.

Rahner called for the immediate unification of the Catholic, Protestant, and Orthodox communions into a new umbrella Church, sharing faith in Christ and the Trinity while retaining their traditionally distinctive doctrines, without these differences obstructing either ecclesiastical unity or sacramental intercommunion.[60] In this approach to ecumenism, which is essentially the same one that Pope Pius XI condemned in his 1928 encyclical *Mortalium Animos*, the various distinctive doctrines carry so little significance for the new umbrella Church's faith that it hardly matters whether they are true or not. In fact, Rahner makes clear that many solemnly taught Catholic doctrines are now discardable, having served a purpose in the past but no longer meeting a need today. It will be enough for future Christians to be united by "the gracious God and the fullness of God's revelation in Jesus Christ," now expressed in pluralistic ways answering to the diversity of places and times.[61]

Whereas his postconciliar religiously liberal view of doctrine diverges sharply from Newman's, Rahner's 1958 "Considerations on the Development of Dogma" stands much closer to Newman. Here, Rahner not only affirms that "the Church as the hearing Church, and hence also as the authoritatively teaching Church, is and must be infallible," but also asserts that "a new dogma must be in accord with the ancient *depositum fidei* on the conceptual level" and thus "there must be an objective connexion between the ancient *depositum* and a newly defined dogma, on principle, and that this connexion must be demonstrable. To renounce this would be to postulate in fact, even though one avoided saying so, new official revelations

60. See Heinrich Fries and Karl Rahner, *Unity of the Churches: An Actual Possibility*, trans. Ruth C.L. Gritsch and Eric W. Gritsch (New York: Paulist, 1985), developing ideas found earlier in Rahner's *The Shape of the Church to Come*, trans. Edward Quinn (New York: Seabury, 1974). See my response—and Joseph Ratzinger's—in my "Introduction: Doctrine and Ecumenism," in *Joseph Ratzinger and the Healing of the Reformation-Era Divisions*, ed. Emery de Gaál and Matthew Levering (Steubenville, OH: Emmaus Academic, 2019), ix–xxvii.

61. Mary E. Hines, *The Transformation of Dogma: An Introduction to Karl Rahner on Doctrine* (Mahwah, NJ: Paulist, 1989), 156.

in the Church which would go beyond the apostolic *depositum*."[62] The approach and implications of his 1958 essay could hardly be further from his 1977 essay, just as Schillebeeckx's theology, too, underwent a profound shift in a religiously liberal direction after the Second Vatican Council.[63]

Many Catholic theologians today explicitly reject Newmanian doctrinal development. The Belgian Catholic theologian Lieven Boeve, to take just one example, has offered an influential account of what is outmoded in

62. Karl Rahner, "Considerations on the Development of Dogma," in Rahner, *Theological Investigations*, vol. 4, *More Recent Writings*, trans. Kevin Smyth (New York: Seabury, 1974), 3–35, at 9, 19. Rahner adds, "Here and there one gets the impression that the search for such rational explanations has been abandoned, wordlessly, and that theologians are ready to renounce such connexions in the theory of dogmatic development. There are various reasons for such defeatism within a rational theology. One proceeds perhaps from the false supposition that such a rationally demonstrable connexion must be able to explain and justify all and everything in dogmatic development. In doing so, one wrongly makes the rational process of explicitation the only element in dogmatic development, which of course it is not. Or one exaggerates the certainty that can be asked of such examples of explicitation" (Rahner, 19–20). Rahner emphasizes, against some of his fellow neo-scholastics (since at this stage he was a neo-scholastic with *Ressourcement* sympathies) but in full accordance with Newman, that there is "a rational certainty which is not properly syllogistic and which cannot be comprised under that head except imperfectly, though no doubt a transposition into such terms is useful and indeed to a certain extent necessary" (Rahner, 21). Rahner concludes his essay with a summation of his purpose that indicates both its boldness and its commitment to the irreversibility (and enduring truth) of Church's solemn doctrinal proclamation of the contents of the apostolic deposit of faith—ending with the sentence "For we know that in such development the faith of the Church remains the same, at one with what it received as the assertion about the absolute revelation of God, which is Jesus Christ our Lord, he who was crucified and rose again" (Rahner, 35).

63. As Mary Hines puts it, Rahner's "thought [on dogma] developed and changed along with the changing church of the volatile period in which he lived and wrote" (Hines, *The Transformation of Dogma*, 1). She concludes her book, "[Rahner] says yes to a future for dogma, but dogma quite differently understood. In fact, because of the past narrow associations of the term dogma, it can be misleading to apply it to faith formulations of the future as Rahner conceives them. It better describes his conception to say that he envisions a continuing and vital role for plural formulations of faith in the contemporary situation. . . . There must continue to be attempts at articulating the experience of God which lies unthematically at the heart of every human existence because that experience bears within itself the dynamism toward articulation. . . . In the world-church of the future we can and should expect no more universal and binding faith articulations. The needs of this church will be better met by provisional and diverse formulations reflecting the concrete situation of a particular place and time. . . . Pastorally speaking the church can no longer expect all its members to appropriate and find helpful all the many and variegated doctrines of the past" (Hines, 155).

Newman's approach. Boeve remarks that in the nineteenth century, "The development of tradition was seen as cumulative, as the elucidation and explication of what was already implicitly known. Confrontations with newness and otherness were considered in this regard to be situations that stimulated further unfolding of the tradition."[64] According to Boeve, after Vatican II, contextualist and historicist Catholic theologians identified the weaknesses of this Newmanian viewpoint. These postconciliar theologians recognized that the "truth" identified in each epoch of the Church's history has been inseparably bound up with its specific context, and also that historically speaking "the idea of a 'Christian Tradition' that had survived unchanged (or 'changed' only in the cumulative sense) down through the centuries was untenable."[65]

For Boeve, then, since each recontextualization changes Tradition and makes it new, one can only speak of a non-cumulative "development" of Tradition. He affirms, of course, that Catholic Christianity has normative texts, longstanding practices, and organizational principles. This history can continue to be affirmed, says Boeve, even while we recognize today that Catholicism has "worked its way through a variety of successive contexts, continually recontextualising along the way. As a result it took on a multitude of different forms that were not always reconcilable with those it had left behind."[66] Boeve suggests that each new context involves doctrinal rupture through a recontextualization that substantially changes the beliefs and practices at the heart of the experience of Catholics.

Since our own era is as historically contextualized as any other era, the result is that what "we encounter in the tradition . . . is always irreducibly encountered within our current frames of interpretation."[67] Do we believe in the same God as did Christians living in the fifth century? Boeve argues

64. Lieven Boeve, *Interrupting Tradition: An Essay on Christian Faith in a Postmodern Context* (Leuven, BE: Peeters, 2003), 21.

65. Boeve, 22.

66. Boeve, 24. Boeve states, "Theology only exists, therefore, as contextual theology, and the development of tradition only as an ongoing process of recontextualisation" (Boeve, 26).

67. Boeve, *Interrupting Tradition*, 32.

that any positive answer to this question requires embracing a version of continuity-as-rupture: "The Christian narrative . . . is to be considered both the same as before and no longer the same. Identity and rupture go hand in hand."[68] But in what does the "identity" consist? Boeve answers that the "inspiration" or "narrative" are the same, as are many of the "images, symbols, rites, narratives, terminology, [and] concepts."[69] What has changed is the way that the community understands these narratives and symbols in the present context.

According to Boeve, the Catholic community now accepts that it is a community of constant doctrinal rupture, even while sharing in the same history as the communities of the past. Today, Catholics perceive that the only way that the "same" Christian community can proceed in time and space is through continual ruptures. Boeve explains, "The discovery of plurality in the Christian tradition (on account of its development) and of the undeniability and indeed legitimacy thereof, is peculiar to our own time."[70] In Boeve's view, we now perceive the irreducible pluralism of Catholic belief, whereas nineteenth-century Catholics such as Newman, working within a different theological paradigm, "only accepted that, at most, *cumulative* development took place, evolution towards more and better."[71] In a nutshell, for Boeve the Church has moved beyond Newman in the sense that Catholics rightly no longer believe in dogmatic judgments that are true in all times and places.

Boeve goes on to fill out his comparison of the pre–Vatican II and post–Vatican II situations. In the nineteenth century and even up to Vatican II, "the Catholic Church formulated its own great anti-modern counter-narrative," which claimed that "the Christian tradition related the

68. Boeve, 34.

69. Boeve, 34.

70. Boeve, 34. He emphasizes "the diverse forms of living and experiencing the Christian tradition (recontextualisations) within the Catholic Church and the multiple contexts in which it finds itself"; and he asserts that "it is often the case that perspectives rejected by one century were valued as orthodox tradition in another" (Boeve, 104–105).

71. Boeve, 35.

true narrative about God, humanity and the world, and this was valid for everyone, past, present and future. This truth was unassailable, revealed and entrusted to humanity in the Bible and the tradition."[72] By contrast, says Boeve, postconciliar theologians sought to integrate the claims of modernity into the received tradition. Boeve compares the two sides: "In the first instance, the tradition as a dynamic process of recontextualisation was abandoned. In the second instance, the tradition as bestower of meaning was neglected."[73]

Boeve's solution consists in rejecting *all* "master narratives," both the anti-modern one and the modern one. Thus he bemoans both "traditionalism" and "*à la carte* religious identity."[74] Against master narratives, he proposes that we Christians should understand ourselves by means of a postmodern "open narrative" which "is conscious of its own historicity, contingency and particularity" and which perceives "its own meaning and truth claims in relation to the claims of other narratives."[75] Against modernity's pure relativism, he holds that an "open narrative" does not require indifference toward the truth-claims of one's own tradition. In his view, one can recognize that one's truth-claims are radically contextualized (i.e., dependent upon one's particular time and place, rather than universalizable as ontologically true) without thereby choosing to distance oneself from these truth-claims.

Specifically, Boeve thinks that when initiated by faith and Baptism into the "Christian tradition," believers can experience the transcendent—the divine—giving them a vocation. This vocation should be understood experientially as a response to "the God who made Godself known in Jesus Christ as the God of love."[76] Like the Christians who have gone before us, we who belong to the Christian tradition are called to go in search of the experiential

72. Boeve, 47.
73. Boeve, 49.
74. Boeve, 58, 61.
75. Boeve, 61.
76. Boeve, 62.

and vocation-oriented truth of Christ, even while we do this in a historically contextualized way that, in the future, will be superseded by further historical recontextualizations. The specificity of our personal narrative should be embraced, not within a "master narrative" of either traditionalism or modernity, but as an "open narrative" that accepts radical particularity and plurality as part of the "continuity" of Christian tradition.[77] Boeve contends that even though our narrative and the Christian tradition as we understand it are radically contingent and particular (given our context-specific location), we can still take them seriously as experiential markers.

Yet can we be confident about the value of our Christian truth-claims if we know that ever-changing recontextualizations will result in radically changed truth-claims among Christians in later times and in other places? Boeve attempts to assuage this Newmanian concern by urging, with Tyrrell and others, that truth is not so much a matter of knowledge as it is a matter of life. On this view, we should judge "truth" experientially—namely, by whether our relationships to others (and to the transcendent) are authentic. He argues that this is the lesson of apophatic theology.[78] Indeed, for Boeve, the more we claim to know God in finite propositions, the less we have understood "the God of the interruptive (grace) event, the God who calls us beyond harsh inflexibility and closedness" and who is revealed in Christ.[79] Through the "continuity" found in our recourse to the narrative of the interruptive Christ, we receive the "potential for fertile (discontinuous) experiences of transcendence."[80]

77. Boeve defines an "open narrative" as follows: "a narrative structure that takes the actual situation of plurality seriously, that has the capacity to make critical judgements, and that offers the means to structure our own personal and collective narratives in an 'open' fashion. . . . This implies the recognition of the fact that life is made up of a multiplicity of narratives and that no single narrative has the right to claim that it can transcend this multiplicity" (Boeve, 92–93).

78. For insight into apophatic theology that cuts against Boeve's claim here, see for example Nonna Verna Harrison, "The Relationship between Apophatic and Kataphatic Theology," *Pro Ecclesia* 4, no. 3 (1995): 318–332.

79. Boeve, *Interrupting Tradition*, 106.

80. Boeve, 107. Most people in Belgium, hearing this kind of thing from theologians, have preferred to renounce Catholicism on the grounds that its core claims are untrue.

By adopting this view of revelation and dogma, Boeve has left far behind Newman's notion of Tradition and doctrinal development, along with Newman's dogmatic principle. Boeve argues that his position is not "relativistic progressivism," because he still grounds himself in a certain kind of continuity—namely, the "Christian open narrative, as a historically and contextually-rooted witness to the ungraspable and unexpected yet hoped-for grace."[81] As we have seen, for Boeve the interruptive grace or fundamental religious experience to which Christianity bears witness in every era cannot be apprehended or articulated in enduringly true propositional judgments. Nor does the Christian tradition unfold, as an ever-growing and secure body of knowledge, the truth of Jesus Christ who reveals the Father by the Holy Spirit. Instead, Catholics must accept that "the ancient words, stories, and deeds that we have inherited require ongoing recontextualisation as the context in which we find ourselves changes."[82] Having chosen to stand in experiential "continuity" with Catholics who have handed on these words and stories before us, we can share their trust in the interruptive grace of Christ in our quest to experience the transcendent.[83]

Boeve concludes that tradition is truly Christian when it testifies to its own rupture, its own inadequacy in the presence of interruptive grace. According to Boeve, this is as it should be, given the fact that "Jesus' indictment of closed narratives and his witness to the God of love have their roots in his *fundamental contemplative attitude*, an openness towards the Other who is revealed in moments of interruption."[84] The key is that Tradition is not "a

---

81. Boeve, 108, 176.

82. Boeve, 178.

83. Boeve states that Christians, in faith, have made "the explicit choice for the Christian narrative as the interpretative framework of our thoughts, words and deeds and thus the specific option for God who has revealed Godself in history as love, *par excellence*, in Jesus of Nazareth, God's interrupter" (Boeve, 179; cf. 115–116). Yet Boeve insists that truth-claims about this God (as revealed in Jesus) can only be tested practically: see Boeve, 181.

84. Boeve, 131; Boeve is here drawing upon Edward Schillebeeckx, *Jesus: An Experiment in Christology*, trans. Hubert Hoskins (New York: Seabury, 1981), 256–268. The disciples' faith-experience is that Jesus has "[shattered] the hegemonic narrative of rejection and death" (Boeve, *Interrupting Tradition*, 134).

unified mass of content" but an experiential journey with and toward the interruptive and unspeakable God. He explains, "Continuity thus takes shape in rupture."[85] Boeve is hardly alone in this view. I could cite many others who make an eloquent case against Newmanian doctrinal development and in favor of something that, they argue, is much more dynamic, historically plausible, and exciting.

In fact, however, once the claim that Christianity is about knowable realities (the real Triune God, Jesus who is the incarnate Son of God, the redemption from sin and death won by Jesus' Paschal Mystery, the transformative power of the seven sacraments, and so on) slips away, Christianity has lost its core and, in hollowed-out form, staggers along attracting little or no interest from our contemporaries. Newmanian doctrinal development, affirmed by Vatican II, is the far better path forward, assuming it remains plausible—as I believe—that Catholicism is not a matrix of doctrinal corruption.

Conclusion

By embracing doctrinal corruption, religious liberalism ultimately leaves little in Christianity worth retaining. Resisting this path, Newman committed himself to defending doctrinal development. Throughout his career, he was concerned about powerful humans—whether politicians or Churchmen—causing "perversions and corruptions of divine truth."[86] As an

85. Boeve, *Interrupting Tradition*, 183, 142. For an analysis of human and Christian speech about God, which is not what Boeve thinks it is, see Thomas Joseph White, *Wisdom in the Face of Modernity: A Study in Thomistic Natural Theology*, 2nd ed. (Ave Maria, FL: Sapientia, 2016). For discussion of various historicizing perspectives (including Boeve's), which he ably contrasts with Newman's "dogmatic principle," see Meszaros, *The Prophetic Church*, 2–10. As Meszaros states the problem to which he (and Newman and Congar, among others) are responding, "With the advent of historical consciousness . . . arises the danger of a historicism according to which, in its Christian variant, the contextuality of doctrinal expressions so obscures any enduring content to be had, that any absolute Christian truth is considered entirely eschatological" (Boeve, 10).

86. Newman, "Tract 71," 179. Newman has in view the (Roman) Catholic Church here; see also his remark in Tract 20 (1833) that the Roman Catholic Church is "infected with heterodoxy; we are bound to flee it, as a pestilence. They have established a lie in the

Anglican, the question of State determination of matters of faith and practice worried him, given that Parliament no longer was confessionally Anglican. In defending the Church of England, he strove to "find which among the Churches had preserved incorrupt the inheritance of primitive doctrine."[87] In the chapters that follow, we will see how this quest led him to the Catholic Church, despite the fact that the early Fathers did not speak about such things as Mary's Immaculate Conception or the infallibility of the bishop of Rome.

How did Newman defend the latter teachings as belonging to the apostolic deposit of faith? Working along Newmanian lines, Reinhard Hütter has laid down a point that is fundamental for any answer—namely, for each real doctrinal *development*, two things must be possible retrospectively: "a persuasively argued demonstration of continuity" and the rejection of a "heterogeneous rupture and corruption of doctrine."[88] The alternative is

place of God's truth; and, by their claim of immutability in doctrine, cannot undo the sin they have committed. They cannot repent. Popery must be destroyed; it cannot be reformed" (Newman, "Tract 20: The Visible Church: Letters to a Friend, No. III," in *Tracts for the Times*, 68–73, at 71).

87. James Pereiro, *'Ethos' and the Oxford Movement*, 183. For Newman, as Pereiro says, "although true developments can be shown to result by logical sequence from given premises, in the majority of cases they are not the fruit of a logical sequence: development follows as a result of the fuller 'realization' of the idea" (Pereiro, 184). This is correct but it does not negate the necessary place of "logical sequence," since divine revelation, assuming it be coherent, cannot ultimately contain both X and its contradictory opposite Y. In the post-1845 editions of his *Essay on the Development of Christian Doctrine*, Newman speaks "of the two fundamental characters of a true development of Christian doctrine: its continuity with previous teaching, and its sharing in the *ethos* of the Primitive or Apostolic Church" (*'Ethos' and the Oxford Movement*, 185). See also Aidan Nichols, *From Newman to Congar: The Idea of Doctrinal Development from the Victorians to the Second Vatican Council* (Edinburgh: T&T Clark, 1990), 1: "The issue of doctrinal development is vital to the justification of specifically Catholic Christian doctrinal insights, *vis-à-vis* the serious objections to these which other historic Christian communities can lodge. . . . This is a matter of defending the Catholic Church against the claim that it has corrupted the Gospel by adding to it elements which are not divinely revealed, being of merely human devising." See also Jay M. Hammond, "The Interplay of Hermeneutics and Heresy in the Process of Newman's Conversion from 1830 to 1845," in *Authority, Dogma, and History*, 45–75, at 62n93.

88. Hütter, "Progress, Not Alteration of the Faith," 384. For the same point, see Guy Mansini, "Saint Thomas and the Development of Doctrine," *Nova et Vetera* 19, no. 2 (2021): 393–422, at 394, where Mansini emphasizes that Newmanian doctrinal development requires

magisterial voluntarism, as though the Catholic Church could continually revise divine revelation in any way that a present pope deemed suitable. In addition to contradicting everything that Newman sought to uphold, such magisterial voluntarism would confirm Protestant and Eastern Orthodox charges of Roman Catholic rationalism and abuse of power vis-à-vis the Gospel of Jesus Christ.[89] It would lead to a Catholic version of religious liberalism that would be all the worse for claiming the support of papal power, ostensibly in the name of ecclesiastical humility but actually in the name of arbitrary ecclesiastical will, through "an overblown, creeping extension of the dogma of papal infallibility."[90]

Of course, some doctrines can be revised or even discarded. Thomas Guarino speaks for Newman when he observes, "Catholic theology has never considered all Christian doctrine, even positions that have been taught over a considerable period of time, to be irreformable. . . . However, such reversals must be clearly distinguished from the annulment of fundamental dogmatic landmarks."[91] These landmarks include everything that

that reason, illumined by faith, must be able to "discern and verify that it really is the one, integral cognitive whole that is exfoliated into the many subsequent doctrinal propositions"—given that without "the one perduring whole of revelation, we have not development but transformation, a self-contradictory plurification of Christian discourse where one age says something different from another." Of course, development requires change; development is not mere repetition.

89. Consider the Evangelical theologian Kevin Vanhoozer's response to my *Was the Reformation a Mistake? Why Catholic Doctrine Is Not Unbiblical*, with a Response by Kevin J. Vanhoozer (Grand Rapids, MI: Zondervan, 2017), 191–231. In his Response, Vanhoozer maintains that the (Roman) Catholic Church is a false and faulty corrupter of the teachings of Jesus Christ and the Apostles.

90. Morgan, *John Henry Newman and the Development of Doctrine*, 275. Morgan argues further, "The key to understanding the voice of living authority for Newman and, perhaps, for the church at this moment, is to conceive of that living authority operating in its proper context: that is, in relation to the development of the idea of Christianity. The idea of Christian was, in Newman's thinking, Christ Himself: God made Man for our Salvation" (Morgan, 276).

91. Thomas G. Guarino, *The Disputed Teachings of Vatican II: Continuity and Reversal in Catholic Doctrine* (Grand Rapids, MI: Eerdmans, 2018), 193. Guarino attends to "the distinction between a proper *profectus* and a destructive *permutatio*," a distinction that continues to have far more purchase than theologians such as Tyrrell, Schillebeeckx, and Boeve have supposed. Guarino treats *Dignitatis Humanae* in this light. On this topic see also his *Revelation and Truth: Unity and Plurality in Contemporary Theology* (Scranton, PA: University

the Church has solemnly taught as contained in Scripture and Tradition. Since these include things that do not appear in Scripture or Tradition in an evident way, questions arise when Catholics insist upon such matters. Ultimately, the issue is whether the Catholic Church has exceeded the limits of divine revelation, or, what is the same, has corrupted rather than developed the apostolic Gospel.

Newman holds that such questions are best resolved through appreciating the reality of doctrinal development, in accordance with the "notes" or "tests" that shed light on the difference between a true development and a corruption. However, the Orthodox theologian Andrew Louth has pointed out that the notion of "doctrinal development" may appear logically to imply that the truths taught by the Church in the fourth century are not actually present in the revelation given in the first century, but instead are the developmental product of the Church. Emphasizing that divine revelation has its fundamental source in Christ's words and deeds as received by the Apostles, Louth warns against giving "the impression of some kind of evolution, with the Church's faith changing and even getting better, as if we in the twenty-first century know the faith more deeply than St Paul."[92] Louth thinks that due respect to Christ and the Apostles requires

---

of Scranton Press, 1993), 158–160. See also Nicholas J. Healy Jr., "*Dignitatis Humanae*," in *The Reception of Vatican II*, ed. Matthew L. Lamb and Matthew Levering (New York: Oxford University Press, 2017), 367–392.

92. Andrew Louth, *Introducing Eastern Orthodox Theology* (Downers Grove, IL: IVP Academic, 2013), 57; for a more appreciative engagement with Newman's views, see Louth's *Discerning the Mystery: An Essay on the Nature of Theology* (Oxford: Clarendon, 1983), written while Louth was still an Anglican. For further discussion, drawing attention to the similar argument of Dumitru Staniloae, "The Orthodox Conception of Tradition and the Development of Doctrine," *Sobornost* 5, no. 9 (1969): 652–662, see Daniel J. Lattier, "The Orthodox Theological Reception of Newman," in *Receptions of Newman*, ed. Frederick D. Aquino and Benjamin J. King (Oxford: Oxford University Press, 2015), 177–194, at 188–190. Lattier argues that Louth's critique of Newmanian doctrinal development is "not necessarily a function of his [Louth's] Orthodoxy, but of principles present in his Anglican works, as well" (Lattier, 190). See also the observation of Jaroslav Pelikan: "Ironically, one of the most impressive cases of development of doctrine in all of church history had been the Byzantine apologia for images in response to the attacks of iconoclasm" (Pelikan, *The Christian Tradition*, vol. 5, 280).

us to admit that the Church must be bound by the apostolic faith. This content is not ours to reshape or augment, though we can clarify and illuminate it. Louth therefore prefers the word "realization" rather than "development."

Louth's concern is relevant to my purposes. For I seek to show that Newman himself consistently maintained quite similar concerns, even while holding that in a real sense the "stream" of Christian knowledge "is more equable, and purer, and stronger, when its bed has become deep, and broad, and full" through doctrinal development.[93] The Anglican Newman used the term "realize" to describe the process of development in an idea. It makes sense from a Newmanian perspective to say that the revealed realities expressed in Scripture are "realized" by Christians in light of Tradition.[94] Newmanian doctrinal development does not entail moving

93. Newman, *An Essay on the Development of Christian Doctrine*, 40. Mansini comments, "This means . . . that we judge the adequacy of *earlier* expressions and the theological success of *earlier* exponents of faith by the measure of the *later* expressions" ("Saint Thomas and the Development of Doctrine," 394). We now know, for instance, that Origen's third-century articulation of the Father, Son, and Holy Spirit, while not to be ignored, is less accurate than that of Athanasius in the fourth century. However, both Origen and Athanasius were participating in the source—divine revelation—and so the metaphor of the stream cannot be taken to mean that the apostolic source (let alone Christ Jesus himself!) is lacking by comparison with later Christianity.

94. See the remarks on "realizing divine truth" in James Pereiro, *Theories of Development in the Oxford Movement* (Leominster, UK: Gracewing, 2015), 45–50. Drawing upon Newman's use of the term, Pereiro describes "realizing" as characteristic of "the existence and growth of proper learning in religious matters," and Pereiro explains further: "This realizing . . . might be granted directly by God's illumination; it might take place while meditating or reading the Scriptures, when, its sense suddenly breaks upon the reader as it had never done before; it might be mediated through a person, introducing another to truths he did not know or helping him understand previously half-understood ones; it might result from the application of principles to particular circumstances or problems. The list is not an exhaustive one. God might choose other avenues to bring about the process of realizing. In any of those ways, the individual in question comes to perceive at the appropriate time, and according to his personal dispositions, new dimensions of already held principles, corollaries of known truths, the path he is to follow, and so on. . . . The moment of 'realizing,' therefore, may also cast a light upon the past, enabling the person in question to perceive the development of his previous opinions into the ones he now holds. He may become conscious of the changes he has undergone, perceive that there is a connexion between his former opinions and his later ones. He may discover that the new truths just perceived had perhaps been with him

beyond the apostolic deposit of faith as communicated in Scripture and Tradition, as though new revelation were being received or parts of revelation could now be rejected. Instead, Newmanian doctrinal development involves a dynamic participation in, or "realization" of, the apostolic deposit, just as our predecessors in faith have done, and in such a manner that a true development "is able to be recognized as such" by believers and allows the Church to express or clarify an aspect of the realities of faith.[95] Christopher Cimorelli describes such ongoing Christian knowing: "Development arises out of participation in the covenantal relationship established and fulfilled in Christ, and particularly in the celebration of the liturgy."[96] The result is real communion between the Church today and the apostolic Church, without supposing that Christians in later centuries

---

long, barely hidden under the surface of his consciousness or the principles he held. Past events are now seen under a new light: some of those not considered relevant at the time may now be perceived as having had a determining influence in leading the person to his present notions; particular decisions which did not seem specially significant when taken now appear as having had momentous consequences" (Pereiro, 48–49). One can see how such "realizing" can be achieved not only by individuals but also by the Church as a whole. Pereiro directs attention to Bernhard Trocholepczy, "Newman's Concept of 'Realizing,'" in *By Whose Authority?*, 136–148. Trocholepczy points out, "Newman included in his fifteenth University Sermon the verse of Luke 2:19: 'Mary kept all these things, and pondered them in her heart' as a short formula for his theory of *realizing*. Mary in her meditative attitude is not only the ecclesial archetype of the development of doctrine. She is also the perfect exemplification of the realizing process in the Church. The decisive elements are: a) to have a heart open to the reality of the divine message; b) to be rooted in good principles" (Trocholepczy, 144).

95. Mansini, "Saint Thomas and the Development of Doctrine," 394: "It is a condition of the possibility of genuine development of doctrine that it be able to be recognized as such. This recognition, of course, is magisterial, but it also engages the *sensus fidei* of all the faithful. Moreover, this ability, while it requires faith, requires also certain *auxilia*, two *auxilia* in fact, namely, metaphysical skill and historical learning."

96. Christopher Cimorelli, *John Henry Newman's Theology of History*, 299–300. Here may be the place to note that in *The Disputed Teachings of Vatican II*, 17—in light of his *Vincent of Lérins and the Development of Christian Doctrine* (Grand Rapids, MI: Baker Academic, 2013)—Thomas Guarino shows that as a (Roman) Catholic, Newman accepts Vincent of Lérins' second rule for doctrinal development, whereas in his Anglican writings Newman emphasized Vincent's first rule (*semper, ubique, et ab omnibus*). For the latter, see for instance Newman's "Tract 71: On the Controversy with the Romanists," in *Tracts for the Times*, 140–179. See also the background in C. Stephen Dessain, "The Reception among Catholics of Newman's Doctrine of Development," *Newman-Studien* 6 (Nüremberg: Glock und Lutz, 1964), 179–191.

know a different entity or know more deeply than did the Apostles. Since Christians of every epoch participate in and "realize" the same divine revelation, there can be "a real and unbroken continuity between 'the religion taught by Christ and his apostles'" and the faith taught by the Catholic Church.[97]

In the year after the publication of *An Essay on the Development of Christian Doctrine*, Newman traveled to Rome to study and to arrange for his future. In Rome from October 1846 through December 1847, he was visited at his lodgings by "cardinals, Roman professors, bishops, and on at least one occasion the pope [Pius IX] himself," who extended a warm welcome that delighted Newman.[98] In 1846, the newly elected pontiff, still considered a liberalizing reformer,[99] had published his first encyclical, *Qui Pluribus*, in which he addressed two contrasting but related errors: the rejection of all Christian doctrines as "fictions of human invention," and the embrace of Christian doctrines as merely the high point of human philosophy.[100] The latter error "import[s] the doctrine of human progress into

97. Terrence Merrigan, "Revelation," in *The Cambridge Companion to John Henry Newman*, ed. Ian Ker and Terrence Merrigan (Cambridge: Cambridge University Press, 2009), 47–72, at 47, 63. For concerns about the term "development" similar to Louth's, though more directly focused on the problem of rationalism, see Hans Urs von Balthasar, *The Office of Peter and the Structure of the Church*, trans. Andrée Emery (San Francisco: Ignatius Press, 1986), 323–324.

98. Kenneth L. Parker and C. Michael Shea, "The Roman Catholic Reception of the *Essay on Development*," in *Receptions of Newman*, 30–49, at 37. In summer 1847, Newman reports with delight in a letter to his sister Jemima that Pius IX was addressing him as "mio caro Signore Newman" (cited in Parker and Shea, 41). Parker and Shea go on to say, "Visits from Perrone and [Giacomo] Mazio on 5 August and Pius IX on 9 August—when Wiseman happened to be there—add further confirmation that Newman's place in Rome was secure and his writings respected. While these private visits by two prominent Roman theologians and the pope are compelling evidence of Newman's acceptance in Rome, an article by Mazio and a lecture by Perrone during this period establish unequivocally the Roman reception of Newman's *Essay*" (Parker and Shea, 41). See Giacomo Mazio, "Liturgia Anglicana," *Annali delle scienze religiose*, 2nd series, 5/13 (July/August 1847): 181–292; and the discussion of Perrone and his lecture in C. Michael Shea, *Newman's Early Roman Catholic Legacy 1845–1854* (Oxford: Oxford University Press, 2017), 163.

99. This perspective would come to an abrupt end after the 1848 revolution and the pope's resultant two-year exile from the Vatican.

100. Pius IX, *Qui Pluribus* 4, papal encyclical, 1846.

the Catholic religion," and this prompts a reply from Pope Pius IX: "Our holy religion was not invented by human reason, but was most mercifully revealed by God; therefore, one can quite easily understand that religion itself acquires all its power from the authority of God who made the revelation, and that it can never be arrived at or perfected by human reason."[101] Pius IX is here responding to the neo-Kantian views of Georg Hermes, not to Newmanian development of doctrine. He adds in his 1856 encyclical *Singulari Quidem*, "We should not conclude that religion does not progress in the Church of Christ. There is great progress! But it is truly the progress of faith, which is not change. The intelligence, wisdom, and knowledge of everybody should grow and progress, like that of the whole Church of the ages."[102]

The question in the mid-nineteenth century was whether not only Catholics, but indeed all Christians have corrupted and distorted the original teaching of Jesus. The dogmas regarding Mary's Immaculate Conception and papal infallibility only intensified this question.[103] The chapters that follow aim to show how seriously Newman took the possibility of doctrinal corruption throughout his career. He recognized that his writings were not the final word on such complex issues, and he recognized that readers working from within a different set of antecedent probabilities will be inclined to deny that he has proven his case. Although I defend Newmanian doctrinal development, my book is not a study of Newman's understanding of development of doctrine per se, since I do not treat issues such as the development of Newman's own theorizing about doctrinal development. My goal instead is simply to reflect with Newman upon the threat of doctrinal corruption as it presented itself to him over the course of his long career of faithful proclamation of the Gospel. In this way, I

101. *Qui Pluribus* 7.

102. Pius IX, *Singulari Quidem* 8, papal encyclical, 1856.

103. See James Gaffney, "Preface," in John Henry Newman, *Roman Catholic Writings on Doctrinal Development*, ed. and trans. James Gaffney (Kansas City, MO: Sheed & Ward, 1997), v–xx, at xvi.

hope to share with St. John Henry Newman in obeying the risen Jesus' commandment: "Go into all the world and proclaim the good news to the whole creation" (Mark 16:15).

Chapter 1

Newman and Gibbon

By the early nineteenth century, as Cyril O'Regan says, "emergent secularity put a newfound stress on history," and it became commonplace to criticize the Catholic Church on the grounds that "no sifting of the evidence could sustain the verdict that Roman Catholicism is in line with the early church. At the very least doctrines, but possibly even creeds, exceed what is given in Scripture and/or in the apostolic period and therefore represent corruptions."[1] Both the Tübingen School and John Henry Newman—not only as a Roman Catholic but also as an Anglican—sought to respond to this line of criticism. The modern critique of Catholicism as a corruption of the early Church has its roots largely in the historical work of sixteenth- and seventeenth-century Protestant controversialists, but it found enduring expression in the writings of the eighteenth-century historian Edward Gibbon. In this first chapter, I will focus on Newman's effort to defend the connection between Catholicism and the earliest Church within a historiographical context framed for English Churchmen by Gibbon.[2]

---

1. Cyril O'Regan, "Newman's Forensic Classic of Development: Its Uniqueness and Its Agon with Gibbon and Surrogates," *International Journal of Systematic Theology* 20, no. 2 (2018): 225–252, at 228–229.

2. For critical and, in part, appreciative reflection on Gibbon, see John Henry Newman, "Letter to T.W. Allies, 3 September 1854," in *The Letters and Diaries of John Henry Newman*, ed. Charles Stephen Dessain, vol. 16 (London, 1965), 244. By comparison with Newman's day (or Gibbon's), the understanding of Christianity possessed today by historians in general is woefully low. See for example the laughable summaries of the Oxford Movement offered respectively by Richard J. Evans (the University of Cambridge's Regius Professor of History, knighted for his scholarship) in his *The Pursuit of Power: Europe 1815–1914* (London: Penguin, 2016), 456–457; and John E. Toews, "Church and State: The Problem of Authority," in *The Cambridge History of Nineteenth-Century Political Thought*, ed. Gareth Stedman Jones and Gregory Claeys (Cambridge: Cambridge University Press, 2011), 603–648, at 632.

Among early-nineteenth-century German historians, Barthold Niebuhr most influenced Newman. An expert on ancient Rome, Niebuhr argued throughout his career that writing ancient history requires a process of formulating and testing hypotheses. Such a process is necessary especially because of the lack of extensive documentary evidence from the ancient world. Leighton Frappell sums up Niebuhr's approach: "Cause-and-effect relationships could not be established directly, since the 'facts' were random and dispersed; the way forward therefore had to be indirect, by the testing of such data as exists against an hypothesis which the historian's intuition . . . recommended as most likely to account for them."[3]

Scholars familiar with Newman's historiography will not be surprised to hear that Newman largely adopted Niebuhr's method, though in his own distinctive fashion.[4] In *An Essay on the Development of Christian Doctrine*, after appreciatively quoting Niebuhr on the idea of development, Newman praises Niebuhr: "Here this sagacious writer recognizes the true principle of historical logic, while he exemplifies it."[5] Later German historians moved away from the hypothesis-and-testing model of historiography and instead

3. Leighton O. Frappell, "John Henry Newman: History and the Two Systems of Providence," *Journal of Religious History* 15, no. 4 (1989): 470–487, at 478.

4. For further discussion of Newman's historical method, see James Matthew Wilson, "Doctrinal Development and the Demons of History: The Historiography of John Henry Newman," *Religion and the Arts* 10, no. 4 (2006): 497–523; Christopher Cimorelli, *John Henry Newman's Theology of History: Historical Consciousness, Theological 'Imaginaries,' and the Development of Tradition* (Leuven, BE: Peeters, 2017); Terrence Merrigan, "The 'Theological Imaginary' in History: John Henry Newman and the Catholic Theological Imagination," *Louvain Studies* 34, no. 2 (2009–2010): 185–208. As Wilson and Cimorelli emphasize, Newman's approach to history includes a typological sensibility, according to which (in divine providence) past realities such as the Arian heresy serve as types of present realities. Wilson comments, "To read history according to only one method—to exclude figural and vertical relations—is to ensure the human condition will be conceivable only within a vertiginous historicism. The transcendent becomes unconscionable to a worldview that perceives the unidirectional, singular progress of time extending to the very limits of consciousness. Typology and other such historiographies and hermeneutics cut across time and text, securing for each a fuller, more profound significance" (Wilson, "Doctrinal Development and the Demons of History," 521).

5. John Henry Newman, *An Essay on the Development of Christian Doctrine*, 6th ed. (Notre Dame, IN: University of Notre Dame Press, 1989), 113.

focused upon critically analyzing and comparing sources. This approach "rendered the method of hypothesis-testing suspect," on the grounds that beginning with a hypothesis often leads to "ignoring unwelcome evidence in pursuit of a theory."[6]

Yet, in Newman's view, it is inevitable that we begin with a hypothesis when studying Church history, whether that hypothesis is shaped by faith or by a secular philosophy of history. In *An Essay on the Development of Christian Doctrine*, Newman puts forward the following initial hypothesis: "In the Church revealed truth is rendered ever-present to mankind, and to this end [the Church] is preserved against substantial doctrinal error, decay or dissolution."[7] At first glance, this hypothesis seems unlikely to be vindicated by any historical method, English, German, or otherwise. After all, the notion that there exists any longstanding human institution that unerringly has developed its "idea" is hardly probable. Why then does Newman, in his hypothesis, eschew even an occasional corruption in solemn dogmatic teaching on faith and morals?

The answer has partly to do with Catholic ecclesiology and its Christian competitors. Newman was aware of four such competitors: Eastern Orthodoxy, Anglo-Catholicism, Protestantism, and Liberal Christianity. In relation to these, Catholic ecclesiology is differentiated perhaps most importantly by the claim to a lack of error in solemn conciliar and papal teaching over nearly two millennia. Consider Pope Pius IX's apostolic letter *Iam Vos Omnes* (1868), which teaches: "No one can contest or doubt that the same Christ Jesus, in order to apply to all human generations the fruits of his redemption, established here on earth, on Peter, his unique Church, which is one, holy, catholic, and apostolic, and that he conferred all necessary power on her so that the deposit of faith might be protected whole and

6. Frappell, "John Henry Newman," 479.

7. Frappell, 472. Frappell emphasizes the difference: "Whereas Niebuhr, working in the science of history, derived his hypothesis from indications in the historical evidence, Newman, in the field of the history of dogma, brought to the construction of his hypothesis the insights of theology, notably that supernatural providence preserved the Church from doctrinal error" (Frappell, 478).

uncorrupted."[8] In faith, Newman—like Vatican II's *Dei Verbum*—believed that Christ did precisely this, establishing the Catholic Church and ensuring that in this Church the whole deposit of faith is handed on faithfully, without doctrinal corruption. If Christ did not do so, then the Catholic Church is untrustworthy as a teacher of the Gospel, and Catholics should convert to one of the other existing versions of Christianity.

Eastern Orthodoxy makes a similar doctrinal claim about its lack of error, but it does not have as long a chain of second-millennium councils, let alone solemn papal teaching, for which to account. In Newman's day, High Church Anglicans defended only the patristic period (and not the whole of it) and the 39 Articles. For their part, Protestants generally affirm that *every* Christian communion corrupts doctrine, at least occasionally, with the result that Christian communities must continually return to Scripture and be corrected insofar as possible. Fourth and finally, liberal Christians hold that the Church's purpose consists in building authentic communities grounded in evolving human religious experience as exemplified by Jesus, which means that all doctrines are malleable as times change.

In *An Essay on the Development of Christian Doctrine*, then, Newman seeks to show the reasonableness of the claim that the Catholic Church has never corrupted doctrine, in light of the other ecclesiological options.[9] He asks whether Catholicism's "utterances have been from time to time so strangely at variance, that we are necessarily thrown back on our own judgment individually to determine, what the revelation of God is, or rather if

8. Pius IX, *Iam Vos Omnes*, in Heinrich Denzinger, *Compendium of Creeds, Definitions, and Declarations on Matters of Faith and Morals*, revised and enlarged and edited by Peter Hünermann with Helmut Hoping, 43rd ed., English edition edited by Robert Fastiggi and Anne Englund Nash (San Francisco: Ignatius Press, 2012), 2997–2999, at 2997.

9. Exaggerating only somewhat (in my view), Frappell argues that "although Newman enunciated his well-known tests of true development, his confidence that under providence a true development of the Christian idea must indeed exist meant that in the last analysis the *Essay* was not an exposition of the theory of development so much as an inquiry into the question, 'where has the development of Christian doctrine been carried out truly and without corruption?'" (Frappell, "John Henry Newman," 477, citing Günter Biemer, *Newman on Tradition* [London: Burns & Oates, 1967], 54).

in fact there is, or has been, any revelation at all."[10] Of course, he is well aware that it seems unpromising to argue that "an institution [i.e., the Catholic Church] teaching a range of doctrines unknown to Christian antiquity might yet be antiquity's sole heir."[11] But in his view, the burden of proof in fact falls upon those who hold that the Catholic Church has corrupted rather than *developed* its doctrine, including doctrines such as the seven sacraments and Mary's Immaculate Conception that do not appear in the first centuries of the Church. Arguing that "the present communion of Rome is the nearest approximation in fact to the Church of the Fathers,"[12] he explains that the Orthodox East, like Anglicanism, lacks the patristic Church's characteristic territorial claim to universality and ability to call a council that can make binding doctrinal claims upon the whole Church.[13]

---

10. Newman, *An Essay on the Development of Christian Doctrine*, 9.

11. Frappell, "John Henry Newman," 472.

12. Frappell, 97.

13. I agree with William J. Abraham that "Newman was much too quick to dismiss the claims of Eastern Christianity" (Abraham, "Revelation," in *The Oxford Handbook of John Henry Newman,* ed. Frederick D. Aquino and Benjamin J. King [Oxford: Oxford University Press, 2018], 304–317, at 316), even though I also agree with the points Newman raises. Given his context in nineteenth-century England (where Orthodox Christians were rare, or else were viewed by Anglo-Catholics as a third "branch" along lines that Orthodox Christians themselves rejected), Newman treats Protestantism and Anglicanism as concrete options in a way that he does not extend to Eastern Orthodoxy. For demonstration of this point, see Newman's *Certain Difficulties Felt by Anglicans in Catholic Teaching Considered*, vol. 1 (London: Longmans, Green, 1897), 392–393. At the same time, Newman was greatly influenced by the Greek Fathers, on which point see Charles Stephen Dessain, "Cardinal Newman and the Eastern Tradition," *Downside Review* 94, no. 315 (1976): 83–98; Ian Ker, *Newman and the Fullness of Christianity* (Edinburgh: T&T Cark, 1993), 83–102—even though I am persuaded by Mark McInroy's critique of Dessain and Ker's exaggerated notions of Newman's "Eastern" emphasis (which Dessain and Ker set against Western "rationalism" in certain all too familiar and misleading ways). See McInroy, "Before Deification Became Eastern: Newman's Ecumenical Retrieval," *International Journal of Systematic Theology* 20 (2018): 253–268, at 263–265. For the argument that Newman relied upon Clement and Origen in the 1830s, then turned against them and focused upon Athanasius in the 1840s, and then finally rehabilitated Origen (and distorted Athanasius) in the 1870s—an argument that I find only partially persuasive—see Benjamin John King, *Newman and the Alexandrian Fathers: Shaping Doctrine in Nineteenth-Century England* (Oxford: Oxford University Press, 2009), 3. King observes that Newman was not a pioneer in his appreciation for the Greek Fathers: "Greek theologians, rather than Latins, were since the seventeenth century the favourites of High Churchmen. . . . Moreover, High Church historians like George Bull, the Bishop of St David's (1634–1710),

Both Eastern Orthodoxy and Anglicanism also lack the office of the bishop of Rome, whose role was already significant by the time of the later patristic period. The ecclesiastical facts on the ground, as well as the antecedent probabilities that should incline believers toward the view that in revealing himself God has ensured that his revelation will be truly communicated across time and space, lead Newman to contend that "the *onus probandi* is with those who assail a teaching which is, and has long been, in possession."[14]

If so, however, is Antoine Arjakovsky correct that Newman "cared little about the historical meandering of truth"?[15] Does Newman simply see the past in accordance with his *a priori* ecclesiastical beliefs? Kenneth Parker, in an essay on Newman's historiography, has drawn attention to the troubles that ensue "when ahistorical metanarratives of the Christian past are pressed too far in an era when historical consciousness is an undeniable component of our intellectual discourse."[16] Parker correctly suggests that at different stages in his early career, Newman fell into ahistorical notions of "changeless continuity" and of "a lost primitive purity" in need of restoration.[17] According to Parker, the Newman of *An Essay on the Development of Christian Doctrine* has exchanged both of these ahistorical notions for a much more suitable "historicized understanding of tradition"—namely, real doctrinal development over the course of history.[18]

---

and William Cave (1637–1713), Chaplain to Charles II, did not discriminate in praising both pre-Nicene and post-Nicene Greek theology, seeing continuity across the first five Christian centuries" (King, 5).

14. Frappell, "John Henry Newman," 120.

15. Antoine Arjakovsky, *What Is Orthodoxy? A Genealogy of Christian Understanding*, trans. Jerry Ryan and Penelope Cavill (Brooklyn, NY: Angelico, 2018), 318. Arjakovsky, however, also has some positive things to say about Newman. Gareth Atkins has correctly noted "Newman's divergence from the approach of writers like Johann Lorenz von Mosheim (1693–1755), whose dispassionate dissection of the controversies of the past . . . so repulsed him [Newman]" (Atkins, "Evangelicals," in *The Oxford Handbook of John Henry Newman*, 173–195, at 179).

16. Kenneth L. Parker, "Historiography," in *The Oxford Handbook of John Henry Newman*, 557–577, at 574–575.

17. Parker, 574.

18. Parker, 575. Owen Chadwick points out that Lord Acton, in private notes, held the opposite view: "Acton once wrote that for Newman the theory of development was a way

But on what grounds can we suppose that Newman's more "historicized" (though not historicist) approach does not still fall into an idealized metanarrative? This question is particularly pressing given Newman's sharp distinction between development and corruption, which, as noted above, sets a very high standard for the Church's doctrine. As Newman puts the matter in his *Essay*, "The one essential question is whether the recognized organ of teaching, the Church herself, acting through Pope or Council as the oracle of heaven, has ever contradicted her own enunciations. If so, the hypothesis which I am advocating [i.e., doctrinal development] is at once shattered."[19]

In light of this question, this chapter examines the historiographical perspective that guides *An Essay on the Development of Christian Doctrine*. I undertake this task by comparing Newman's historical approach with Gibbon's. Certainly, Gibbon never attempted to present himself as merely an objective observer of historical facts; he delighted in demonizing the Roman Catholic Church. But Gibbon does repeatedly present himself as reporting facts that the Catholic Church has obscured or forgotten. Moreover, Gibbon is thoroughly modern in his historiography when he (in O'Regan's words) carefully "neutralizes appeals to revelation and dismisses theological construals of the history of development."[20] For Gibbon as for almost all academic historians today, proper historical consciousness means avoiding

over history, that it enabled him to disregard history" (Chadwick, *From Bossuet to Newman*, 2nd ed. [Cambridge: Cambridge University Press, 1987], 129). Indeed, Chadwick contends that, logically speaking, Newman's efforts in *An Essay on the Development of Christian Doctrine* do not succeed, because in Chadwick's view some Catholic doctrines are indeed unrelated to the divine revelation that closed with the death of the last Apostle, and Newman was unable to square the circle. But Chadwick appreciates that Newman at least staved off anti-historical "obscurantism" among Catholic thinkers by means of his "genuine appeal to history" (Chadwick, 194). See also, for the concerns raised by Anglicans at the time of publication and afterward, Maurice Nédoncelle's "Le développement de la doctrine chrétienne: J.B. Mozley, critique Anglican de Newman," in *Tradition in Lutheranism and Anglicanism*, ed. G. Gassmann and V. Vajta (Minneapolis, MN: Augsburg, 1972), 156–172; and David Nicholls, "Newman's Anglican Critics," *Anglican Theological Review* 47, no. 4 (1965): 377–395.

19. Newman, *An Essay on the Development of Christian Doctrine*, 121.

20. O'Regan, "Newman's Forensic Classic Development," 240.

any notion of divine action, providence, or revelation. Instead, as O'Regan says, Gibbon deems that "the proper writing of history lies in describing the actions, motivations, feelings and thoughts of those to whom revelation was putatively given. . . . The historian has access only to secondary causes and these are historically immanent."[21]

To what degree does Newman's *An Essay on the Development of Christian Doctrine* follow this path of modern historical consciousness? In O'Regan's view, Newman seeks to mount arguments that even a Gibbonite would have to accept, in defense of the claim that the Christian "idea" has developed rather than corrupted.[22] O'Regan aptly comments that in nineteenth-century England (and indeed still today), "Gibbon has set the historiographical terms and one does not have the option of refusing them. Not to play within the parameters of secondary rather than primary causes is not to do history and therefore to deprive oneself of the essential argumentative coin in favor of tradition and the institutional Catholic Church."[23] Yet Newman insists that history is not what Gibbon thinks it is, because history sacramentally manifests God's providential presence and action,

21. O'Regan, 240. O'Regan adds: "Gibbon's stipulations have the advantage of all methodological stipulations, which is to say that they are capable of being embraced by very different—even heterogeneous—groups. In this case, we are speaking of skeptics who agree with Hume that there is little evidence for a God who operates providentially in the universe; strong rationalists who commit to a deistic God as the efficient cause of a world that, for all practical purposes, is governed by more or less mechanical cause and effect; and Christian believers who, cowed into accepting the position that we should stick more or less to naturalistic accounts of Christianity because they have the sanction of reason, still hold that such an account does not rule out individual believers enjoying their own personal conviction about divine providence" (O'Regan, 240).

22. Of course, Newman, like Gibbon, wrote history in part "to change lives in the present" (King, *Newman and the Alexandrian Fathers*, 16).

23. O'Regan, "Newman's Forensic Classic Development," 240. Curtis Adler states of Newman's *An Essay on the Development of Christian Doctrine* that it is "imbued with a spirit of theological polemic rather than of pure historical scholarship" (Adler, "John Henry Newman on Edward Gibbon: Indebted to the Infidel," *Classical Bulletin* 69, no. 1 [1993]: 17–20, at 17). Adler grants, however, that Newman's "polemic intent . . . does not nullify the extensive research," especially patristic research, that gives Newman's work its scholarly weight. Adler also points out that Newman "was indebted for a great deal of his historical knowledge to the most prominent atheistical classicist of the eighteenth century: Edward Gibbon" (Adler, 17).

including in the realm of the Church's doctrinal teaching.[24] Thus Edward Short remarks that "Newman countered Gibbon's account of the rise of Christianity by insisting on the role that God's particular Providence plays in its rise."[25] For Newman, although the historian qua historian must remain within the realm of secondary causes (and cannot simply play the "God" card), there are two different kinds of historians: historians who view events, persons, and so forth as secondary causes (with God as primary, transcendent, and noncompetitive cause), and historians who do not.[26]

---

24. See Nicholas Lash, *Newman on Development: The Search for an Explanation in History* (London: Sheed & Ward, 1975), where Lash discusses Newman's 1841 criticisms of Henry Hart Milman's *History of Christianity*. Lash notes that for Newman, "the only theory or interpretative viewpoint which adequately accounts for the historical phenomena is one that takes into consideration not only the 'outside' but also the 'inside' of the events in question. His fear that Milman's use of his method may encourage a reductionism such as would render the perception of the divine meaning in human history impossible is thus expressed in characteristically 'sacramental' terminology. . . . When the historian's interpretative viewpoint (or 'theory') is not that of christian belief, although he may attempt a 'neutral' stance, prescinding from issues of belief or unbelief, he will in fact inexorably tend to adopt the interpretative viewpoint of unbelief, or at least will too easily be understood to do so" (Lash, 28–29). Unsurprisingly, Milman responded critically to Newman's *An Essay on the Development of Christian Doctrine*: see Milman, "Newman on the Development of Christian Doctrine," *Quarterly Review* 77, no. 3 (1846): 404–465, which charges Newman with historical malpractice.

25. Edward Short, "Newman, Gibbon and God's Particular Providence," in *Newman and History* (Leominster, UK: Gracewing, 2017), 3–80, at 6. See also Terrence Merrigan, "'One Momentous Doctrine Which Enters into My Reasoning': The Unitive Function of Newman's Doctrine of Providence," *Downside Review* 108, no. 373 (1990): 254–281.

26. See John Henry Newman, *The Idea of a University*, ed. Martin J. Svaglic (Notre Dame, IN: University of Notre Dame Press, 1982), 64: "A living dignity of the Established Church wrote a History of the Jews; in which, with what I consider at least bad judgment, he took an external view of it, and hence was led to assimilate it as nearly as possible to secular history. . . . I must conclude that he was simply betrayed into a false step by the treacherous fascination of what is called the Philosophy of History, which is good in its place, but can scarcely be applied in cases where the Almighty has superseded the natural laws, of society and history." Shortly thereafter, Newman sums up his position on the relation of the sciences (including history) to theology: "I have said that, all sciences being connected together, and having bearings one on another, it is impossible to teach them all thoroughly, unless they all are taken into account, and Theology among them. Moreover, I have insisted on the important influence, which Theology in matter of fact does and must exercise over a great variety of sciences, competing and correcting them; so that, granting it to be a real science occupied upon truth, it cannot be omitted without great prejudice to the teaching of the rest. And lastly, I have urged that, supposing Theology be not taught, its province will not simply be

In this light, the present chapter addresses two interrelated questions. First, on what basis do Gibbon and Newman construe the doctrinal history of the early Church as corruption and development, respectively? And second, has Newman—who values modern historical research even while recognizing its limitations in a way that progressivist nineteenth-century historians failed to do[27]—actually avoided an ahistorical metanarrative?

I will begin by examining a selection of texts from Gibbon, focusing on passages that shed light on his view of Catholic doctrine, including some material from his *Memoirs of My Life*.[28] I will then explore Newman's approach to history and doctrinal development, first in his 1841 essay "Milman's View of Christianity"—where Newman emphasizes the necessity of affirming divine providence for an adequate view of the past—and then in his 1845 *An Essay on the Development of Christian Doctrine*.

A final word before proceeding. Brian Young has forcefully maintained that Newman refused to be guided by true historical consciousness. Young remarks, "For Newman, dogmatic religion provided the benchmark by which to judge the origin and progress of Christian history, a position he shared with the juvenile Gibbon, whose readings of the Church Fathers and [Jacques-Bénigne] Bossuet had famously led to his brief conversion to Roman Catholicism."[29] According to Young, Gibbon outgrew his juvenile dogmatism and became a real historian, whereas Newman continued to

neglected but will be actually usurped by other sciences. . . . All branches of knowledge are connected together, because the subject-matter of knowledge is intimately united in itself, as being the acts and the work of the Creator" (Newman, 74–75).

27. Thus the historian John Lukacs remarks, "A little more than a century ago the English historian Lord Acton claimed that historical science had reached a stage when a history of the Battle of Waterloo could be written that would not only be perfectly acceptable to French and British and Dutch and Prussian historians but would be unchanging, perennial, and fixed. Already Acton's great contemporary John Cardinal Newman said that Acton 'seems to me to expect more from History than History can furnish'" (Lukacs, *At the End of an Age* [New Haven, CT: Yale University Press, 2002], 77).

28. For discussion of Gibbon's most productive years (the volumes of his *Decline and Fall of the Roman Empire* appeared from 1776 to 1788), see Patricia Craddock, *Edward Gibbon: Luminous Historian, 1772–1794* (Baltimore, MD: Johns Hopkins University Press, 1989).

29. Brian W. Young, "Gibbon, Newman, and the Religious Accuracy of the Historian,"

pursue an ahistorical ideal. Young adds as further evidence, "Gibbon's conversion to Rome was effected through the reading of historical sources and the assessment of historical arguments; in the case of Newman's conversion, however, dogmatic considerations prevailed over the reading of history."[30] Is this correct about Newman, granting for the sake of argument that Gibbon's conversion actually took place in this way? Or did Newman, during the period of writing *An Essay on the Development of Christian Doctrine*, adopt enough of Gibbon's historiographical methods to be able to justify Catholicism at the bar of "a critical-rationalist historiography that sets aside references to revelation and providence,"[31] while at the same time sharply undermining Gibbon's notion of a providence-less history?

Gibbon's History

Brian Young remarks about Gibbon's early conversions: "The journey from Protestantism to Catholicism and thence to skepticism was . . . a familiar itinerary in the intellectual history of seventeenth- and eighteenth-century Europe."[32] As Young observes, Jean-Jacques Rousseau, too, began as a Protestant before becoming a Catholic, then reverting to Protestantism, and

in *The Victorian Eighteenth Century: An Intellectual History* (Oxford: Oxford University Press, 2007), 70–102, at 86.

30. Young, 86. See also the enumeration of the contents of Newman's library at Littlemore, detailing his extensive collection of primary sources from the patristic period (and from other periods as well, along with Church histories of various kinds), in Thomas S. Bokenkotter, *Cardinal Newman as an Historian* (Louvain, BE: Publications Universitaires de Louvain, 1959), 85–90.

31. Young, "Gibbon, Newman, and the Religious Accuracy of the Historian," 230. Nicholas Lash notes that in *An Essay on the Development of Christian Doctrine*, "the frank recognition that the history of Christianity follows the general 'laws' of historical process is combined with the doctrinal claim that therefore this process is 'proved to have been in the contemplation of its Divine Author' (*Dev* 2.1.8)" (Lash, *Newman on Development*, 29). See also Young, "Gibbon and Catholicism," in *The Cambridge Companion to Edward Gibbon*, ed. Karen O'Brien and Brian Young (Cambridge: Cambridge University Press, 2018), 147–166. According to Young, Gibbon's fundamental problem with Christianity was its ascetic morality; he rejected Christian belief because it cut against "the values of a man of culture and refinement" (Young, 162).

32. Young, "Gibbon and Catholicism," 154.

finally becoming (in his own way) a devotee of natural religion. In his *Memoirs of My Life*, Gibbon depicts another convert-revert-skeptic, William Chillingworth—who also appears frequently in Newman's pages. As a young man, Chillingworth was persuaded to become Roman Catholic by a simple argument based upon the implications of divine revelation, an argument later repeated appreciatively by Newman: "That there must be somewhere an infallible judge, and that the Church of Rome is the only Christian society, which either does or can pretend to that character."[33] After entering the Catholic seminary in Flanders, however, Chillingworth began to doubt, and he returned to England and Anglicanism. He published a book in 1634 titled *The Religion of Protestants a Safe Way to Salvation*, which argued in favor of "the principle that the Bible is our sole judge, and private reason our sole interpreter."[34] In due time, Chillingworth felt himself compelled to reject the Anglican Church's 39 Articles, and ultimately he rejected the doctrine of the Trinity as well, coming to rest either in Socinianism or, perhaps, pure skepticism. As another example of the same phenomenon, Gibbon names the philosopher Pierre Bayle, famous for his philosophical dictionary. Bayle began as a Protestant, and after a short interlude as a Catholic during his university years, his study of physics persuaded him that the doctrine of transubstantiation must be false. He appears to have ended his life as a skeptic.

Gibbon followed a similar path. When he was sixteen, during his time at Oxford, warnings that he heard against Conyers Middleton's *A Free*

---

33. Edward Gibbon, *Memoirs of My Life*, ed. Betty Radice (New York: Penguin, 1984), 87.

34. Gibbon, 87. See William Chillingworth, *The Works of William Chillingworth* (London: A. and J. Churchill, 1704). Regarding *The Religion of Protestants a Safe Way to Salvation*, Peter B. Nockles has this to say: "Newman's judgments on some of the Caroline Divines could be as harsh as any of Froude's in relation to the Reformers. For instance, he was convinced that Laud's friend, William Chillingworth, was the patron of later latitudinarianism, and an 'ultra-Protestant,' on account of his maxim, 'the Bible only, the religion of protestants.' It was in vain that Edward Churton, who was far better conversant with the nuances of Chillingworth's theology than was Newman, argued that 'the doctrine of Chillingworth . . . is good Oxford divinity,' and that Laud had 'something to do with this'" (Nockles, *The Oxford Movement in Context: Anglican High Churchmanship, 1760–1857* [Cambridge: Cambridge University Press, 1994], 131–132).

Inquiry into the Miraculous Powers led him to read both the book and the writings of its opponents. Though no Catholic, Middleton argued that in the first five centuries "most of the leading doctrines of popery were already introduced in theory and practice."[35] The book moved Gibbon halfway toward conversion, and a friend accomplished the rest—along with two books by Bishop Bossuet, *An Exposition of the Doctrine of the Catholic Church* and *The History of the Variation of the Protestant Churches*. Upon hearing what had taken place, Gibbon's horrified father sent him to Lausanne, Switzerland, to be tutored by a Calvinist minister.[36] Reading anti-Catholic materials (including texts written by Catholics themselves, such as Pascal's jibes at the Jesuits), he soon abandoned Catholicism. But "the arguments . . . used to loosen Gibbon's attachment to Roman Catholicism" proved "to be solvents of all religious faith whatsoever."[37]

Thus, by the time he came to research and write his multivolume *The Decline and Fall of the Roman Empire*, Gibbon had long been a religious skeptic with a special animus toward Catholicism. Joseph Levine remarks appreciatively, "The *Decline and Fall* is undoubtedly the most ambitious history of the eighteenth century."[38] The work is ambitious not only because

35. Gibbon, *Memoirs of My Life*, 85.

36. By the nineteenth century, English travel to and residency in Switzerland was commonplace, and indeed Newman achieved a breakthrough in his writing of the *Grammar of Assent* while touring Catholic Switzerland in 1866, as Aidan Nichols recounts as a prelude to comparing Newman and Hans Urs von Balthasar: see Nichols, "Littlemore from Lucerne: Newman's *Essay on Development* in Balthasarian Perspective," in *Newman and Conversion*, ed. Ian Ker (Edinburgh: T&T Clark, 1997), 100–116.

37. David Womersley, "Afterword: A New Gibbon Manuscript," in *The Cambridge Companion to Edward Gibbon*, 219–232, at 225.

38. Joseph M. Levine, *The Autonomy of History: Truth and Method from Erasmus to Gibbon* (Chicago: University of Chicago Press, 1999), 157. Eighteenth- and early nineteenth-century historiography did not come out of nowhere: for its roots in the seventeenth century, see Anthony Grafton, *What Was History? The Art of History in Early Modern Europe* (Cambridge: Cambridge University Press, 2007), which makes clear that historians already recognized that historiography "required the consultation of official archives, the creation of [the historian's] own systematic collection of copies of documents, and the weaving of networks of correspondence" (Grafton, 238). After describing episodes in the "battle between the ancients and the moderns," Grafton observes: "Throughout the later seventeenth and early eighteenth centuries . . . sophisticated scholarly tools multiplied. Elaborate formal

of its vast range, but also because of Gibbon's combining three modes of historiography. Namely, he sought to write an enjoyable and compelling narrative, to make "the past intelligible to enlightened opinion," and to undertake the serious philological and antiquarian research needed to sift fact from fable regarding the past.[39] He strove to "learn the ancient languages and the arcane procedures of paleography, numismatics, and diplomatics, reading the treatises and visiting the practitioners" of antiquarian scholarship.[40] He aimed to avoid hagiographical exaggeration, idealized portraiture, and mere invention.

Eighteenth-century philosophers such as David Hume did not conceal their biases when writing history, but they did at least advocate objectivity. To the approach taken by Hume and his fellow philosophers, Gibbon added greater philological or scholarly appreciation for "documentary evidence and criticism."[41] Gibbon also employed "master narratives" that were familiar at the time, such as the view (drawn from Tacitus) that Rome thrived while it was a republic led by "warrior citizens" and that Rome's downfall came when, having become too big for the warrior citizens to handle, a professional military class took over.[42] Another such "master narrative" was that Christianity caused the demise of Roman religious toleration.

My goal is to determine what counts as "historical" for Gibbon with respect to early Catholicism. Here chapter 15 of the first volume of *The*

---

manuals of diplomatics, palaeography, numismatics, and other fields reached print, and though they hardly put an end to the religious controversies that called many of them into being or stamped out wild speculations, they marked a sea change in historical method" (Grafton, 250–251). Scholarly history replaced history as a rhetorical-philosophical art.

39. Levine, *The Autonomy of History*, 158.

40. Levine, 159–160.

41. Levine, 161. See also J.G.A. Pocock, "An Overview of *The Decline and Fall of the Roman Empire*," in *The Cambridge Companion to Edward Gibbon*, 20–40, at 20–21. Pocock directs attention to Giuseppe Giarrizzo, *Edward Gibbon e la cultura europea del Settecento* (Naples: Istituto Italiano per gli Studi Storici, 1954); and especially Arnaldo Momigliano, "Gibbon's Contribution to Historical Method," *Historia: Zeitschrift für Alte Geschichte* 2 , no. 4 (1954): 450–463.

42. See Pocock, "An Overview of *The Decline and Fall of the Roman Empire*," 21–22.

Decline and Fall of the Roman Empire is particularly important, since Gibbon argues in this chapter that as soon as Christianity came to be, it shared in the tendency toward corruption that belongs to all historical realities.

In treating the early Church, says Gibbon at the outset of his chapter, historical inquiry faces two problems: first, the "scanty and suspicious" character of early Christian portraits; and, second, the fact that "the great law of impartiality too often obliges us to reveal the imperfections of the uninspired teachers and believers of the Gospel," which may cause offense.[43] In light of these problems, Gibbon leaves to theologians their task of proclaiming that a pure revelation has come from God or descended unstained to earth through Christ. Whereas theologians imagine that they can perceive divine revelation in its original transcendent purity, historians discover it in a corrupted condition, which is the condition that for Gibbon it necessarily has if it really is historical. He explains that the historian "must discover the inevitable mixture of error and corruption which she [the Church] contracted in a long residence upon earth, among a weak and degenerate race of beings."[44]

Of course, Gibbon does not really imagine that the pure divine revelation envisioned by theologians ever existed. Rather, Gibbon sees "theology" as operative on an idealized, transcendent (ahistorical) level that is illusory, while "history" operates on the level of real human life. When theologians talk about Christian doctrine (or "Religion") as though it were somehow an incorrupt development from an original, divinely bestowed deposit of faith, theologians are talking about a transcendent ideal that has no grounding in actual human history. The historian must address "the inevitable mixture of error and corruption" because the historian, in contrast to the theologian, is firmly rooted in the actual reality of human life, as opposed to the ethereal realm of ideas.

Investigating why Christianity spread so quickly and successfully

43. Edward Gibbon, *The Decline and Fall of the Roman Empire*, vol. 1 (New York: Alfred A. Knopf, 1993), 487–488.

44. Gibbon, 487–488.

throughout the Roman empire, Gibbon observes that the theological answer is that Christian doctrine was persuasive and God's providence was powerful. He allows this theological answer to stand, so long as it keeps to its ahistorical transcendent plane. In the real world of human beings—the world of "history"—the answer is quite different. Gibbon names five historical reasons why Christianity succeeded, and none of these reasons is complimentary toward Christian revelation. Taken together, the five reasons suggest that Christianity spread because it was sufficiently fanatical, duplicitous, and disciplined to overthrow and ruin a previously healthy and good empire.

Gibbon idealizes the tolerant paganism of the Roman empire, which he thinks produced "religious harmony."[45] Unfortunately, says Gibbon, Judaism did not share this tolerance. He states that in the Roman empire, Judaism spread quite extensively, and Jews became known for "the sullen obstinacy with which they maintained their peculiar rites and unsocial manners."[46] According to him (working along venomously anti-Semitic lines), Jews set themselves up as almost a separate species, and they made clear "their implacable hatred to the rest of human kind."[47] In his view, the Romans, tolerant to a fault, generally protected the religious expression of the Jewish people, thereby nourishing at the heart of the empire a serious threat to the empire's perdurance.[48] Gibbon blames what he deems to be the Jewish people's stubborn and fanatical zeal on their belief in the miracles of the Exodus. He holds that the Jewish people in the early Roman empire gave a "stronger and more ready assent to the traditions of their remote ancestors than to the evidence of their own senses."[49]

Christianity, then, arose from this intolerant, hateful, zealous,

---

45. Gibbon, 489.

46. Gibbon, 489.

47. Gibbon, 489.

48. In this portrait, one sees not only Gibbon's idealizing of Roman paganism but also the virulent anti-Semitism of Gibbon's day. His hatred of the Jewish people here stands as a prelude to his hatred of Catholicism.

49. Gibbon, 491–492.

stubborn, and credulous root. To these supposed Jewish flaws, Gibbon adds one more: in their conquest of the Promised Land, the Jews became a murderous people, committed to obliterating men, women, and children simply because it was the divine will. Even so, Gibbon considers that, due to the Jews' ancestral pride, they never would have spread their faith to other peoples, since they imagined themselves alone to be God's chosen people; and besides, few men would willingly line up to receive circumcision. But Christianity was different. Gibbon deems it equally intolerant, hateful, zealous, stubborn, credulous, and murderous, but he notes that it conceived of the new covenant in Christ as opening up God's people to the whole world. It replaced circumcision with Baptism, and it replaced animal sacrifices with Christ's once-and-for-all sacrifice. It inspired its new converts with a powerful sense of mission to spread the faith. It proclaimed a good, merciful, and loving God who (as Gibbon says with dripping irony) plans to damn to hell any person who refuses to believe the Church's doctrine and be baptized. The result, says Gibbon, was that the arrogant, fanatical intolerance that characterizes Christianity spread quickly through the Roman empire like a poison.

Gibbon gives much attention to the divisions between Jewish and Gentile Christians over the necessity of practicing the Mosaic Law. Had the "Judaizing" Christians won, things would have been radically different. In giving the Law, God never proclaimed it a temporary expedient; and even Christ announced (in Matt. 5:17) that he had not come to make any changes to it. Gibbon mockingly observes that "the industry of our learned divines has abundantly explained the ambiguous language of the Old Testament, and the ambiguous conduct of the apostolic teachers."[50] According to the theologians—and Gibbon echoes them tongue-in-cheek—the allowance for Torah observance among the first Christians "was proper gradually to unfold the system of the Gospel, and to pronounce with the utmost

50. Gibbon, 496.

caution and tenderness a sentence of condemnation so repugnant to the inclination and prejudices of the believing Jews."[51]

Gibbon argues that the Church originally could not determine whether it was Jewish or Christian. Far from having an originally pure doctrinal deposit, the earliest Church was beset by confusion and conflict. Gibbon remarks, "The first fifteen bishops of Jerusalem were all circumcised Jews; and the congregation over which they presided united the law of Moses with the doctrine of Christ."[52] Surely, if the Jerusalem Church cannot lay down the original "standard of orthodoxy," then nothing can.[53] But in fact, Gibbon observes, once Christian churches had been established in major cities such as Corinth and Rome, Jerusalem lost its influence, and the Jewish converts who still practiced the Mosaic Law were soon condemned by their fellow Christians. Eventually, in the mid-second century, the surviving band of Torah-observant Jewish Christians elected a Gentile for their bishop and gave up practicing the Mosaic Law. The few who refused to renounce Torah observance were accused of "the crimes of heresy and schism," under the moniker "Ebionites."[54] So much for unbroken, pure apostolic doctrine!

The Gnostic Christians took things one step further and condemned the Jewish religion and the Old Testament itself. Tongue firmly in cheek, Gibbon describes the Gnostics as "impiously" deeming that the Old Testament God could not be the true God because the Old Testament God is "liable to passion and to error, capricious in his favour, implacable in his resentment, meanly jealous of his superstitious worship, and confining his partial providence to a single people, and to this transitory life."[55] Gibbon presents the Church Fathers as scurrilously concealing the truth about the Old Testament so as to retain it as part of the Christian religion. He

51. Gibbon, 496.
52. Gibbon, 496.
53. Gibbon, 496.
54. Gibbon, 498.
55. Gibbon, 501.

comments, "Acknowledging that the literal sense [of the Old Testament] is repugnant to every principle of faith as well as reason, they deem themselves secure and invulnerable behind the ample veil of allegory, which they carefully spread over every tender part of the Mosaic dispensation."[56] The Church Fathers simply allegorized Judaism away.

Gibbon maintains that the earliest Church was doctrinally very loose, so that contraries could be held within it. Rather than the repository of a pure deposit of faith, it was something of a free-for-all. Gibbon states that in the first decades of Christianity, "the disciples of the Messiah were indulged in a freer latitude both of faith and practice than has ever been allowed in succeeding ages."[57] The eighteenth-century Anglican Latitudinarians (or liberal Christians), in other words, represent the true earliest Church.

In due time, says Gibbon, zealotry, fanaticism, and authoritarian control produced an ever-growing number of heresies, generally arising from devout elites within the Church whose thinking happened to deviate from the line taken by those with the most power. Nevertheless, the various competing groups of Christians were united by their vicious animosity toward the (supposedly) idolatrous pagans of the Roman empire. All Christians, whether "orthodox" or "heretical," joined together in deeming their tolerant and reasonable pagan neighbors to be worshipers of demons.[58] Public life in the Roman empire was suffused with ritual celebrations for the gods, rituals that were not taken overly seriously. Gibbon notes that the Christians fanatically refused to take part in this normal societal life. The Roman

56. Gibbon, 501.

57. Gibbon, 501.

58. For a contemporary study that takes the early Christians to task for their attacks on Greco-Roman paganism, though without mentioning Gibbon, see Luke Timothy Johnson, *Among the Gentiles: Greco-Roman Religion and Christianity* (New Haven, CT: Yale University Press, 2009). Johnson shows that, in terms of religious practices or "modes of religious sensibility" (Johnson, 276), there are broad similarities between Greco-Roman religion and Christianity, but he intentionally (and unfortunately) does not address issues related to the truth of God as distinct from human "religious responses to what is perceived as ultimate" (Johnson, 278).

empire's rituals included ceremonies to greet the new year "with vows of public and private felicity; to indulge the pious remembrance of the dead and living; to ascertain the inviolable bounds of property; to hail, on the return of spring, the genial powers of fecundity; to perpetuate the two memorable eras of Rome . . . ; and to restore . . . the primitive equality of man."[59] With delicious irony, Gibbon observes that the Christians were dead set against all this, and their fanatical and intolerant zeal against the supposed demons won them adherents.

According to Gibbon, Christianity also won adherents by promising life after death, not only of the soul but also of the body. The best the Romans could do was to insist reasonably upon the immortality of the soul. The Jews, for their part, began by denying the immortality of the soul. Eventually, having added Tradition as an authority conjoined to Scripture, the Pharisees managed to affirm both the immortality of the soul and the resurrection of the body. Christ sanctioned these claims by his "authority and example"—although Gibbon passes over the accounts of Christ's Resurrection.[60] Christianity thus managed to promise more than any pagan religion could. No wonder that people converted when they were told that all they had to do was to follow Christ and they would receive eternal bliss.

Gibbon adds that the first Christians expected Christ's imminent return in glory, but this did not happen. He suggests that the grounds for believing in such a hoped-for event cannot bear much scrutiny: "The revolution of seventeen centuries has instructed us not to press too closely the mysterious language of prophecy and revelation."[61] For Gibbon, the promise of Christ's return is an example of theologians living on an idealized level. Many Christians have believed that Christ would come back soon, and this belief gave to their lives a certain urgency and meaning; but it cannot now be taken seriously as a claim about the future. A number of early Church Fathers were Millenarians, but this viewpoint was rejected by

59. Gibbon, *The Decline and Fall of the Roman Empire*, vol. 1, 507.
60. Gibbon, 513.
61. Gibbon, 513.

the later Church Fathers. All, however, agreed that in the future glorious kingdom, "the wisest and most virtuous of the Pagans"—and indeed the great majority of all people who have ever lived—would be "delivered over, without hesitation, to eternal torture."[62] Tongue still firmly in cheek, Gibbon praises those who held this hellish doctrine as possessing a faith "of a much firmer consistence" than the faith of we moderns to whom such notions sound utterly unjust and appalling.[63] Gibbon notes that some Church Fathers, stimulated by supernatural love, were bold enough to hope that, perhaps, a very few pagans such as Socrates might not be subjected to everlasting damnation.

Overall, Gibbon's point is that real history, as opposed to the idealized "Church history" of the theologians, shows that the tolerant pagans of the Roman empire never devised anything as demonically wicked as the Christians, grounded in Judaism, managed to devise. The Romans may have worshiped idols, but not the kind of idols that, in the name of mercy and love, would roast almost the entirety of the human race—created by God—for everlasting eons.

Gibbon makes his accusation clear: at the core of Christianity's "system of love and harmony," there appears to be "a spirit of bitterness."[64] He grants that surely there were some early Christians who were as charitable and meek as they professed to be in their doctrine, but the problem of fanatical doctrine and practice remained. Moreover, although miracles were apparently plentiful, these miracles somehow failed to spare the early Christians many difficulties and miseries; when miracles were really needed, they were absent. Gibbon deems miracles to be part of the idealized history concocted by theologians. In modern England, no one seriously claims that miracles are ongoing. As he says, "Accustomed long since to observe and to respect the invariable order of Nature, our reason, or at least our

62. Gibbon, 517.
63. Gibbon, 517.
64. Gibbon, 518.

imagination, is not sufficiently prepared to sustain the visible action of the Deity."[65] In other words, while in the early Christian centuries people were credulous,[66] today no one believes in actual miracles.

For Gibbon, then, real history shows that there was never a deposit of faith (or divine revelation)—instead, there was an original Jewish Christianity that in due time was proclaimed to be heretical and persecuted mercilessly. Real history shows, too, that early Christianity won converts due to its promise of everlasting glory through bodily resurrection and due to its supposed multiplicity of miracles; and in both regards Gibbon suggests that credulity was the driving factor. The overthrow of Rome's tolerant religion was accomplished under false pretenses.

Let me turn to Gibbon's treatment of three notable early Christian saints and leaders: Athanasius, John Chrysostom, and Cyril of Alexandria. These Church Fathers are notable especially for their contributions to the earliest dogmatic councils of the Church, in which the full humanity and full divinity of Christ were proclaimed and defended. What does Gibbon say about the incarnate Lord's Greek-speaking defenders?

Gibbon prefaces his treatment of Athanasius with an argument that Christian Trinitarian doctrine owes its provenance not to Scripture or Christ but to Plato. According to Gibbon, Plato, pondering the mystery of the deity—and seeking especially to understand how divine simplicity could logically coexist with the multiplicity of the divine ideas—came up with the basic framework of Trinitarian doctrine. Thus Plato reflected upon "the divine nature under the threefold modification—of the first cause, the reason, or *Logos*, and the soul or spirit of the universe."[67] Gibbon claims

65. Gibbon, 523.

66. Gibbon comments: "The primitive Christians perpetually trod on mystic ground, and their minds were exercised by the habits of believing the most extraordinary events. They felt, or they fancied, that on every side they were incessantly assaulted by daemons, comforted by visions, instructed by prophecy, and surprisingly delivered from danger, sickness, and from death itself, by the supplications of the church" (Gibbon, 523).

67. Edward Gibbon, *The Decline and Fall of the Roman Empire*, vol. 2 (New York: Alfred A. Knopf, 1993), 301.

that the Evangelist John derived his Platonism from an Alexandrian Jewish Platonic treatise, the *Wisdom of Solomon*; and Philo's Platonic Judaism also influenced John. Gibbon observes wryly, "The eloquence of Plato, the name of Solomon, the authority of the school of Alexandria, and the consent of the Jews and Greeks, were insufficient to establish the truth of a mysterious doctrine, which might please, but could not satisfy, a rational mind."[68] In Gibbon's view, the (Platonic) Gospel of John was published in order to confute the Jewish Christians in Jerusalem—the purest form of Christian belief—where Jesus was revered "as the greatest of the prophets, endowed with supernatural virtue and power," but certainly not as the pre-existing Logos or divine Son of God.

Gibbon remarks that even Athanasius himself admitted to not understanding the doctrine of the Trinity. Even so, the doctrine of the Trinity became the cause célèbre of the day; uneducated people joined the educated in debating it enthusiastically, because belief in it was supposed to be necessary for salvation. Having conquered the dangerous Sabellian heresy, next up was the equally dangerous Arian heresy, set forth by an "eminent presbyter" of deep "learning and blameless life."[69] Throughout much of the long fourth century, a venomous, back-and-forth battle was waged over the

68. Gibbon, 303. Gibbon's understanding of the Gospel of John, as with much of his understanding of the early Church, has been shown by later historians to be mistaken. Yet the points upon which he seizes continue to be the most notable points of controversy.

69. Gibbon, 310. By contrast, Newman and the High Church Anglican tradition emphasized Arius' personal faults. In this regard, Benjamin John King points out that the seventeenth-century Cambridge Platonist Ralph Cudworth argued that "the substance of God is one and the same, but the persons are three. The unity of the divine persons came from their substance—the substance of the one God or Father—and not from their number. Alternatively, argued Cudworth, since 1215, Catholics have taught numerical unity in which each of the divine persons is the one God. . . . Newman in the 1840s disagrees with Cudworth but expresses his disagreement by citing Edward Gibbon not Cudworth. Gibbon claimed that numerical oneness was stressed by the Latin Fathers (a 'Trinitas' suggesting *one* triad) whereas Greeks stressed what was generic to the three Persons (τριάς suggesting a substance shared among *three*). Newman shares Gibbon's (and Cudworth's) view that the doctrine of generical unity is 'Greek', while differing from Gibbon in thinking that the Greeks also 'taught the doctrine of "a one" or a numerical unity'" (King, *Newman and the Alexandrian Fathers*, 203). One sees here some further background to Michel René Barnes, "De Régnon Reconsidered," *Augustinian Studies* 26, no. 2 (1995): 51–79.

homoousian doctrine. At first, Constantine deemed the whole debate to be a trifling matter; but he later became zealous on Athanasius' side, putting the military force of his empire behind the Homoousians. Constantine's son Constantius did the opposite. In this foolish and befuddling conflict Athanasius distinguished himself—and Gibbon hails him as follows: "Athanasius displayed a superiority of character and abilities which would have qualified him, far better than the degenerate sons of Constantine, for the government of a great monarchy."[70]

Gibbon disarms and deflates this praise at the same time that he offers it. Indeed, in the very same sentence he notes that Athanasius' "mind was tainted by the contagion of fanaticism," and he goes on to say that Athanasius' learning was meager by comparison with his opponent Eusebius of Caesarea's, and his eloquence was much less than that of the Cappadocians.[71] Gibbon grants that Athanasius was a master at understanding human nature, and also that Athanasius' political prudence was second to none. Thanks to Athanasius' artifices, his ecclesiastical opponents typically ended up having their malice exposed, despite their attempts to appear as "mild and devout" followers of Christ.[72] When he had to flee, he took refuge with the "wild, yet submissive fanatics" populating the Egyptian desert as monks.[73] Fanatical violence broke out even in the consecrated domains of the churches themselves, as people battled to the death over the *homoousion*.

After narrating some of the violence, Gibbon comments, "The fierce and partial writers of the times, ascribing *all* virtue to themselves, and imputing *all* guilt to their adversaries, have painted the battle of angels and demons. Our calmer reason will reject such pure and perfect monsters of vice or sanctity."[74] Both sides, says Gibbon, displayed a fanatical

70. Gibbon, *The Decline and Fall of the Roman Empire*, vol. 2, 330.
71. Gibbon, 330.
72. Gibbon, 334.
73. Gibbon, 348.
74. Gibbon, 362.

and murderous "intolerant spirit."[75] He reflects briefly on the tumultuous interval consisting in Julian's attempt to restore paganism to the Roman empire. He deems that the reign of Valentinian restored some order, due to "the firm and temperate impartiality which he uniformly preserved in an age of religious contention," avoiding all "subtle questions of theological debate."[76] Valentinian ensured tolerance for all religious beliefs and practices, and the result was "to soften the manners, and abate the prejudices, of the religious factions," even if fanaticism remained.[77] Valentinian's brother Valens, however, supported the Arians in the Eastern empire, and got himself entangled in theological controversy. During this period, Athanasius died of old age.

Athanasius, then, receives Gibbon's respect as a practical man, even while Gibbon scorns the violent and fanatical debates over the (Platonic) *homoousion*—in Gibbon's view an embarrassment to the real Jesus attested by the first Jewish Christians. By contrast, Gibbon presents John Chrysostom as both impractical and fanatical. Famous for his eloquent preaching style, Chrysostom "was naturally of a choleric disposition. Although he struggled, according to the precepts of the Gospel, to love his private enemies, he indulged himself in the privilege of hating the enemies of God and of the church."[78] For Chrysostom, says Gibbon, these enemies included almost everyone. Chrysostom condemned not only the degenerate rich but also the merely powerful, including the empress; and he added to his list of malefactors the clergy and the monks. Exhibiting a hunger for power, Chrysostom expanded his territorial jurisdiction as archbishop of Constantinople and "deposed thirteen bishops of Lydia and Phrygia" on the excuse that "a deep corruption of simony and

75. Gibbon, 362.

76. Gibbon, 542. See Newman's balanced portrait of Julian—quoting Gibbon, who idealized Julian and his pagan cause—in *The Idea of a University*, 147–149.

77. Gibbon, *The Decline and Fall of the Roman Empire*, vol. 2, 543.

78. Edward Gibbon, *The Decline and Fall of the Roman Empire*, vol. 3 (New York: Alfred A. Knopf, 1993), 349.

licentiousness had infected the whole episcopal order."[79] When faced with a conspiracy against him led by the empress herself, Chrysostom boldly compared the empress to Herodias, who demanded the head of John the Baptist.

Cyril of Alexandria, as portrayed by Gibbon, was fundamentally a thug, even if a fanatically zealous believer. Educated by monks until his mind was filled with "the cobwebs of scholastic theology," Cyril rose to become archbishop of Alexandria (a post that had previously been held by his uncle, Theophilus), which gave him tremendous power over the city.[80] After oppressing the Novatians in his city, he led a violent attack that destroyed and plundered the Jewish synagogues of Alexandria. He either advocated or allowed—Gibbon is not sure—the gruesome torture and murder of the talented young pagan philosopher Hypatia by a Christian mob. Gibbon concludes that "the murder of Hypatia has imprinted an indelible stain on the character and religion of Cyril of Alexandria."[81] Like Theophilus, Cyril in his youth was an opponent of John Chrysostom, and he remained doubtful about Chrysostom's sanctity until it had been universally accepted by the Church. Most notably, Cyril spent many years attacking the sanctity and orthodoxy of Nestorius, the archbishop of Constantinople. Gibbon paints a violent scene: "Ephesus, the city of the Virgin, was defiled with rage and clamour, with sedition and blood."[82] Paganism was better than this!

It is clear that Gibbon is working with historical metanarratives that, when it comes to Christianity (and Roman paganism), are hardly "objective." From his historical sources, Gibbon accentuates certain details that accord with his guiding metanarratives, and later historical research has shown him to be mistaken on some central points. Even so, Gibbon strikes some telling blows against idealized Church history.[83] It seems likely that

79. Gibbon, 350.

80. Edward Gibbon, *The Decline and Fall of the Roman Empire*, vol. 5 (New York: Alfred A. Knopf, 1994), 15.

81. Gibbon, 18.

82. Gibbon, 25.

83. For further background, arguing in favor of Gibbon's approach, see Charlotte

Cyril of Alexandria did some deplorable things and that Chrysostom was imprudent in his denunciations. The extensive conflict and violence between Christians in the early centuries are tragic and embarrassing, as are Christian persecutions of pagans and Jews.

Is an idealized understanding of Church history necessary for defending the theological view that there is a divinely revealed apostolic deposit of faith and that the Church did not corrupt this deposit? Put another way, is Newman's historiography just as biased as Gibbon's, but from the opposite angle? Let me now turn to Newman's historical approach, focusing on two works from the 1840s—when he was moving beyond the historiographical method of his youthful *The Arians of the Fourth Century*—"Milman's View of Christianity" and, most famously, *An Essay on the Development of Christian Doctrine.*

Newman's History

"Milman's View of Christianity"

In "Milman's View of Christianity" (1841), Newman critically engages the liberal Anglican Henry Hart Milman's *History of Christianity, from the Birth of Christ to the Abolition of Paganism in the Roman Empire*. He begins by praising Milman's abilities and by remarking that there is much to learn from Milman's work, just as, says Newman, it is "impossible even for a Gibbon [i.e., an unbeliever] to write an uninstructive history of the Evangelical Dispensation."[84] After this rather faint praise, Newman proceeds to make clear his strong disagreement with Milman's approach. Like Gibbon

Roberts, *Edward Gibbon and the Shape of History* (Oxford: Oxford University Press, 2014).

84. John Henry Newman, "Milman's View of Christianity," in Newman, *Essays Critical and Historical*, vol. 2, ed. Nicholas Schofield (Leominster, UK: Gracewing, 2019), 224–293, at 225. See Henry Hart Milman, *The History of Christianity, from the Birth of Christ to the Abolition of Paganism in the Roman Empire*, 3 vols. (published in two in this reprint) (New York: A.C. Armstrong, 1887). I note that Milman was undeterred by Newman's criticisms and went on to publish *History of Latin Christianity; Including That of the Popes to the Pontificate of Nicholas V*, 9 vols., 4th ed. (London: John Murray, 1867).

but with less excuse, Milman approaches Christianity simply "as a secular fact" and seeks to portray it "as it would appear to a man of the world."[85] Newman considers this approach to be giving away the game at the outset, since if Christian history involves nothing more than what men of the world can grant, Christianity is false to its core.

Newman quotes extensively from Milman's preface, in which Milman separates the task of the theologian from that of the historian. A theologian, says Milman, addresses doctrinal matters pertaining to the relation of God and humanity, while a historian focuses more closely upon the political, institutional, and cultural manifestations of Christianity. The this-worldly effects of Christian faith, rather than the truth of faith, are the province of the historian. When Christianity changes, it is not for the historian to evaluate these changes for their consistency or truth; rather, the historian must simply set forth the facts.[86]

Newman challenges the adequacy of such an approach to Christian history, while also pointing out that Milman does not actually live up to it. Newman grants that the history of the Church unfolds as other history does, with external causes and effects. Yet he insists that undergirding this external system is divine providence, "so that all that exists or happens visibly, conceals and yet suggests, and above all subserves, a system of persons, facts, and events beyond itself."[87] Divine providence employs visible causes to achieve supernatural effects. God uses the things that exist—normal things pertaining to culture, ritual, and political life—in an extraordinary way in divine revelation. For example, all ancient Near Eastern nations had prophets, but none had prophets through whom the Spirit worked as in Israel. Similarly, says Newman, "the kingdom of Christ, though not of this world, yet is in the world, and has a visible, material, social shape."[88] Thus,

85. Newman, "Milman's View of Christianity," 226.

86. As Stephen Thomas says, "Milman's declared aim is to present Christianity purely as a historian, that is, dispassionately, eschewing polemics, considering only the external facts" (*Newman and Heresy*, 157).

87. Newman, 231.

88. Newman, 235.

its history *can* be written as though it were solely this-worldly, even though such a history will fail to understand its true nature. This is what Milman has done. Milman does not deny the presence of the supernatural, but neither does his analysis bring it forward. In general, he simply describes how the Jewish and Christian communities would have appeared to the eyes of the pagan cultures in which they dwelt.

Newman argues that "this external contemplation of Christianity necessarily leads a man to write as a Socinian or Unitarian *would* write."[89] Certainly, Milman notes that Jesus avers that the Son of God has descended and made himself present in Jesus. But for Milman, when describing the events reported in the Gospels, it is enough to say that God has associated himself with human flesh in Jesus, who exemplifies human perfection and whose victory consists in enlightening minds and purifying hearts. In taking an external, historical view, Milman cannot get at Christ's divinity or the uniquely salvific power of the cross. His Christianity is reductive, emphasizing ethics, neglecting the atonement, and failing to adequately articulate the Incarnation. Milman's liberal Christian vision, Newman thinks, fits with his historiographical approach. What Milman gains in assimilating Christianity to other religions, Milman loses in understanding the true supernatural power of Christianity. It is not broadness of mind to associate the Jewish prophets closely with Zoroaster; rather, if the Jewish prophets are what Christians think they are, then the mind is truly broadened by encountering the divine at work in them.

In addition, Newman enumerates numerous places where Milman advances significant theological views, all on the side of liberal (or in some

89. Newman, 242. For further discussion of Newman's meaning here, see Thomas, *Newman and Heresy*, 158–159. As Thomas remarks, Newman grants that "Milman's intention *appears* to be the very reverse of the systematic, his purpose being 'merely' to state 'the *facts* of Christianity.' But Newman is quick to point out that this approach is itself 'a theory of the facts.' This is because the 'principles' which are the 'life' of the facts are omitted. The supernatural, which underlies and sustains the facts, is artificially repressed by a principle of selectivity which amounts to an 'external system' distorting the 'higher and invisible system' of revelation, the inner life of the supernatural which has its own mysterious coherence" (Thomas, 159).

cases Protestant) Christianity, in the course of recounting the facts of the New Testament and the early Church. For example, Milman takes a dismissive view of most miracles. Regarding the doctrinal history of the Church, Milman holds—according to Newman—that "nothing belongs to the Gospel but what originated in it," so that anything that seems to belong to the Gospel but originated elsewhere is not really part of the Gospel.[90] For Newman, to hold such a position is to reject divine providence guiding the creedal formation of the Christian faith. Newman grants that Milman himself may not perceive "the tendency of the line of thought" that he advocates, and indeed some of Milman's own doctrinal beliefs are not in accord with his method.[91] Milman argues that the following elements originate outside the Gospel: Philo teaches a Mediator, the Babylonians teach the existence of angelic hierarchies, Plato teaches a divine Logos, and Zoroaster teaches the resurrection of the body and the restoration of all things. In Newman's view, these correspondences show the existence of seeds of the Word or of a vague general revelation, ensuring that "the philosophies and religions of men have their life in certain true ideas, though they are not directly divine."[92] Newman considers it a sign of divine providence that the Church in every culture is able to draw upon this broad cultural heritage, and to stamp and refine it.

Against Milman's effort to accept only what is original to the Gospel, Newman argues that it should be evident that divine revelation in Israel was "various, complex, progressive, and supplemental of itself," and that the articulation of the deposit of the faith by the Church has followed a similar path.[93] If so, then the effort to track down a Gospel undefiled by prior Jewish or pagan notions is a mistake. As Newman says, those who think otherwise will inevitably be "driven to maintain . . . that the Church's doctrine was never pure"; whereas Newman affirms that divine revelation entails

90. Newman, "Milman's View of Christianity," 273.
91. Newman, 272.
92. Newman, 275.
93. Newman, 277.

solely "a divine promise" to keep "the Church Catholic from doctrinal corruption."[94] Newman adds that Milman likes to use the existence of Jewish or pagan correspondences to argue against the truth of the doctrines that are denied by Protestants, while retaining some doctrines that are held by Protestants even when there are Jewish or pagan correspondences.

Newman deems the inevitable result of this approach to be religious liberalism. Once the specifically Catholic doctrines are ruled out on the grounds of Judaizing and Hellenizing—and once the same principles have been applied to the doctrines held by Protestants—there will be little left but the claim that "revelation" in Christ introduced a certain higher ethical life. The result will be that "Christianity will melt away in our hands like snow; we shall be unbelievers before we at all suspect where we are."[95] As a liberal Anglican version of Gibbon, Milman's approach to history will lead to the conclusion that Christianity does not have deeper divine dimensions such as the forgiveness of sins, the indwelling presence of the Trinity, the gift of the sacraments, the Church as the Mystical Body of Christ, and so on.[96] In such a perspective, Jesus might be valued as a teacher of humanity who manifests the benevolence of the deity, but the dogmatic truth of Christianity will evaporate. Milman tries "to set bounds to his own principle, and to shut the door on innovation, when he has let in as much of it as suited his taste"; but Newman thinks Milman's effort to impose limits will

94. Newman, 277–278.

95. Newman, 287. As Newman sums up: "With a sigh we shall suddenly detect the real state of the case. We shall look at Christianity, not as a religion, but as a past event which exerted a great influence on the course of the world, when it happened, and gave a tone and direction to religion, government, philosophy, literature, manners; an idea which developed itself in various directions strongly, which was indeed from the first materialized into a system or a church, and is still upheld as such by numbers, but by an error; a great boon to the world, bestowed by the Giver of all good, as the discovery of printing may be, or the steam-engine, but as incapable of continuity, except in its effects, as the shock of an earthquake, or the impulsive force which commenced the motions of the planets" (Newman, 287).

96. Stephen Thomas provides further context: "Like that of his fellow Liberal Anglican historians, Milman's relativistic presentation of history, in terms of cycles from childhood, through maturity to decay, with its stress upon the alien quality of the mental worlds of the past, is balanced by belief in the application of a universal standard of morality, as an interpreted fixed point" (*Newman and Heresy*, 160).

not stand logical scrutiny.[97] When the historiography of the Church lacks a sense of divine providence guiding the Church, and when Protestant privileging of pure origins becomes the evaluative touchstone, the result will be the victory of Gibbon's atheism via the path of religious liberalism.

An Essay on the Development of Christian Doctrine

Milman promises a neutral historical approach, focusing like Gibbon upon external facts, even while importing (without being upfront about it) a Protestant principle of primitivism. By contrast, Newman holds that, as Stephen Thomas says, every Catholic "history of dogma has a sacramental quality" because of the supernatural realities hidden under the empirically perceptible things.[98] In *An Essay on the Development of Christian*

97. Newman, "Milman's View of Christianity," 287. Thomas shows that Milman tries to ward off the claims of D.F. Strauss against the New Testament's portraits of Jesus, but Newman clearly thinks Milman's principles are insufficient for accomplishing this purpose. Thomas sums up Milman's approach to the New Testament: "Milman attacks Strauss for describing the gospel-events as 'mythic,' the imaginative creations of early Christian communities. . . . Particularly important is Milman's strong assertion of the physical resurrection of Jesus, as the basis for the doctrine of the immortality of the soul, a position made polemically in contradistinction to his understanding of Schleiermacher" (*Newman and Heresy*, 162–163). Newman therefore concludes his review of Milman's work: "To one set of persons only is he likely to do much mischief, those who just at this moment are so ready to use his main principle for the demolition of Catholic views, without seeing that it applies to the New Testament History and teaching just as well. . . . Let all who carp at the Fathers and deny Tradition, who argue against sacramental influence, who refer celibacy to Gnosticism, and episcopal power to Judaism, who declaim against mysticism, and scoff at the miracles of the Church while at the same time they uphold what is called orthodox Protestantism, steadily abstain from Mr. Milman's volumes" (Newman, "Milman's View of Christianity," 293).

98. Thomas, *Newman and Heresy*, 159. Thomas responds to Newman's critique of Milman: "In Milman's defence, it is difficult to see how else he could have operated—and remain a historian! By contrast, Newman's assertion of the symbolic quality of Christian history seems to have absorbed the other-worldliness of the Alexandrian Platonist Fathers" (Thomas, 159). The assertion that Newman's notion of history is "Platonist" or other-worldly is mistaken; his notion of history is biblically warranted. Indeed, Thomas goes on to say: "Newman is not so much neo-platonic as incarnationalist: his vision of Christian history derives from the two natures of Christ, which, though distinct, are hypostatically united. As A.M. Allchin has pointed out, a theological vision centred upon the Incarnation implies the transfiguration, but not the destruction of, the human. It is this vision, encompassing but going beyond history, that Newman opposes to Milman's 'theory of the facts'" (Thomas, 160). See Allchin, "The Theological Vision of the Oxford Movement," in *The Rediscovery of*

Doctrine, Newman responds more directly to Gibbon's use of historiography to convict the Church of doctrinal corruption. His approach differs from that of his critique of Milman, though he has not changed his mind. Specifically, he examines the early histories of particular Christian doctrines and strives on the basis of the historical facts to show the reasonableness, even from a historian's perspective, of holding that divine providence has been guiding the development of the Christian "idea" in the Catholic Church.[99]

Along lines that Gibbon could accept, the first sentence of *An Essay on the Development of Christian Doctrine* asserts: "Christianity has been long enough in the world to justify us in dealing with it as a fact in the world's history."[100] This "fact" is Christianity as known through its human, external realities. Newman here has in view the modern meaning of "the world's history," according to which miraculous realities are not counted among the acknowledged facts, while the *testimonies* to such realities are counted

Newman: An Oxford Symposium, ed. John Coulson and A.M. Allchin (London: Sheed & Ward, 1967), 50–75, at 54.

99. For discussion of what Newman means when he speaks of an "idea," see Aidan Nichols, *From Newman to Congar: The Idea of Doctrinal Development from the Victorians to the Second Vatican Council* (Edinburgh: T&T Clark, 1990), 49; James Pereiro, *Theories of Development in the Oxford Movement* (Leominster, UK: Gracewing, 2015), 120–123; Nicholas Lash, *Newman on Development*, 46–79 and 94–98. Lash comments with reference to the editions of Newman's text: "In *1845*, the concept of the 'idea' gradually shifts in the course of the argument. In the opening passages 'ideas' are described as those 'habitual judgements' which are 'exercised' on the 'things which come before' the mind (Lash, 30). By the end of the section, the term seems to refer to an objective entity, existing independently of and influencing the minds of men. In *1878*, this shift in meaning is less marked and, throughout the section, the term refers primarily to some objective fact or reality, apprehended as a whole" (Lash, 47). Lash also raises the concern that Newman's view of Scripture inclines Newman to conceive of "the starting-point of the process, the *revelatum*, . . . as an aggregate of divinely authenticated statements" (Lash, 58; cf. 100–102). Lash deems it best to conceive of development (along lines that he attributes to Newman) as "the 'realization'. . . of the ineffable word of God in the life, institutions, worship and belief of a people" (Lash, 59). As Pereiro says, "The Idea . . . does not only reveal itself [as the incarnate Word] in revelation; it also opens the Christian mind to it, and helps the mind 'realize' truth, making possible the mind's progress from notional to real and from implicit to explicit knowledge," toward the goal of the Idea's "full manifestation in the world" (Pereiro, *Theories of Development in the Oxford Movement*, 122–123).

100. Newman, *An Essay on the Development of Christian Doctrine*, 3.

as facts on the grounds that it is clear that the testimony really took place, whether or not the miracle itself took place.

Thus, Newman opens *An Essay on the Development of Christian Doctrine* by suggesting that Christianity be treated for the purposes of his investigation in the way that historians treat "the Spartan institutions or the religion of Mahomet"—presuming in the latter case that the historian is not Muslim and therefore is not drawing upon the specific theological commitments of Muslims.[101] Different historians will begin with different theories or presuppositions about Sparta's guiding ideas and institutions. But all historians—and here Newman means to agree with Gibbon—will have to deal with certain facts about Sparta that historical research has uncovered and demonstrated. These facts remain, whatever theories one builds up from, or brings to, the facts.

Newman describes the kinds of evaluative judgments that scholars make about a particular entity encountered in historical study: "what is its moral and political excellence, what its due location in the range of ideas or of facts which we possess, whether it be divine or human, whether original or eclectic, or both at once; how far favourable to civilization or to literature, whether a religion for all ages or for a particular state of society."[102] Inevitably, historians differ sharply regarding such evaluations. But there are elements about Christianity that cannot be denied by historians. Given that Christianity is a concrete reality that has been embodied in the world, Newman emphasizes that "to know what [Christianity] is, we must seek it in the world, and hear the world's witness of it."[103] Christianity, as a reality in history, limits our freedom to shape it however we might think it should be shaped. We must be conformed to Christianity, rather than it to us.

Newman is aware that many people today act as though "Christianity does not fall within the province of history,—that it is to each man what

101. Newman, 3.
102. Newman, 3.
103. Newman, 4.

each man thinks it to be, and nothing else."[104] Similarly, it may appear that the best that can be done is to bring together the diverse claimants to be "Christianity" by observing that they have some shared core elements. Some consider that the original, pure Christianity has been lost forever, and the only chance is to try to reconstruct it and begin anew (as Gibbon implies with his view of an original Jewish Christianity). Others hold that there has been no "doctrinal corruption," because (as Gibbon also implies, and as does Milman to a lesser degree) the original teachings were in fact "nothing more than a mere assemblage of doctrines and practices derived from without, from Oriental, Platonic, Polytheistic sources, from Buddhism, Essenism, Manicheeism."[105] Others suggest that pure "Christianity" still exists uncorrupted, but only in the hearts of a hidden spiritual elite. Others hold that Christianity was never anything but a human philosophy, a proposal regarding God and human duty toward God—on which view there was never a divine revelation that Christians could "corrupt."

These diverse views of "Christianity" tend to presume either that if there was a divine revelation, it was quickly doctrinally corrupted; or else that there never really was anything particularly meaningful to "corrupt." Given the complexities of human history, Newman appreciates that those who deem there to have been doctrinal corruption have a strong hand. Yet he pushes back against the above views of Christianity. Just as the possibility of corruption should not be neglected, so also the possibility of real development should not be dismissed out of hand. Newman argues that, historically speaking, "the external continuity of name, profession, and communion, argues a real continuity of doctrine."[106] Indeed, he thinks he can show that, in fundamental ways, "as Christianity began by manifesting itself as of a certain shape and bearing to all mankind," it has continued to manifest this shape and bearing over the centuries, up to the present day.[107]

104. Newman, 4.
105. Newman, 4.
106. Newman, 5.
107. Newman, 5.

He refuses to grant the assumption that the entity that calls itself the Catholic Church today (or in "the second, fourth, seventh, twelfth, sixteenth, and intermediate centuries") is not "in its substance the very religion which Christ and His Apostles taught in the first" century.[108] If historians insist upon approaching the Church with an a priori assumption that it is not the Church Christ founded, historians must first provide strong evidence in favor of the assumption.

As Newman knows, historians have attempted to offer just such evidence. Newman quotes Chillingworth in this regard, and he could equally have quoted Gibbon. These authors find Christianity's "doctrines so variously represented, and so inconsistently maintained by its professors" that there is no possibility of digging back to an original Christianity whose doctrine could be deemed normative.[109] According to these authors, there is no unity of the Church Fathers, and the Church of one period is in contradiction with the Church of a later period on the most important matters.[110] For Chillingworth in his *Religion of a Protestant*, the Bible is the only place where the true Christian doctrine can hope to be found; and in order to retrieve this true doctrine, we must rely entirely, not on the later dicta of the Church or of the Church Fathers but on our own judgment—termed "private judgment" by Chillingworth, in a phrase much repeated and deplored by Newman.

Newman responds to this claim that Church history is a morass by making two points. His first point is that the history of Christianity can at least tell us something: "The Christianity of history is not Protestantism. If

108. Newman, 5.

109. Newman, 6.

110. Jaroslav Pelikan largely agrees with the views Newman opposes: "Newman's *Essay* is by no means the only illustration of a romanticism on all sides about the unity of the ancient Church, with many interpreters professing to find there the very same guarantees of unity to which they now point as means for the reunion of Christendom" (Pelikan, *Development of Christian Doctrine: Some Historical Prolegomena* [New Haven, CT: Yale University Press, 1969], 64). Pelikan adds that the unity that did exist in the patristic Church encompassed quite a diversity of theological viewpoints and proceeded without ecclesiastical centralization.

ever there were a safe truth, it is this."[111] He explains briefly why this is so, quoting an earlier writing of his. His second point is that Protestants such as Chillingworth have accurately recognized that there are significant differences—"inconsistencies and alterations"—between the teachings found in different eras of life of the Catholic Church.[112] Historically, the question is what these differences are and what their probable import is.

At this stage, Newman states explicitly that his view of the history of the Church is colored by his belief that God gave a revelation. He notes that some historians (Gibbon, of course, preeminent among them) hold that "Christianity has ever changed from the first and ever accommodates itself to the circumstances of times and seasons"[113]—and these historians reject the notion of divine revelation. Given the inevitable presence of antecedent beliefs shaping a historian's perspective, Newman suggests that historical inquiry entails, at one level or another, formulating a hypothesis about divine revelation that one then tests. As we saw, Gibbon treats as outside the bounds of acceptable historiography any hypothesis or supposition that relies upon believing in the reality of divine action in history. Gibbon instead defends the hypothesis that Christianity is both spurious and worse than Roman paganism.

Newman here recalls his own earlier Anglo-Catholic hypothesis—namely, the notion that the true Christianity must have the full "sanction of primitive times," in other words that there was a pure Christianity up to a certain point, at least through the first four or five centuries.[114] Anglo-Catholics draw this hypothesis from the first part of Vincent of Lérins' definition of what constitutes revealed doctrine: "Christianity is what has been held always, everywhere, and by all."[115] According to this view, what happened was that, due to the growing power of the papacy and

111. Newman, *An Essay on the Development of Christian Doctrine*, 7.

112. Newman, 9.

113. Newman, 10.

114. Newman, 10.

115. Newman, 10. Nockles adds, "As the *catenae patrum* of exponents of the Vincentian rule compiled by Manning in *Tract 78* testified, on this question the Tractarians were following

the split between East and West, the one Christian trunk separated into distinct branches. The trunk contains the incorrupt doctrine, whereas in anything that differentiates the branches there are some corruptions, though not enough to destroy the trunk. This is the Anglican "via media" between Roman Catholicism and Protestantism, and it is the position that Newman advocated in the 1830s.[116]

Against this Anglo-Catholic hypothesis, Newman's hypothesis in 1845 is that there has been true doctrinal development in the (Roman) Catholic Church. In his introduction to *An Essay on the Development of Christian Doctrine*, Newman identifies some historical facts that militate against the Anglo-Catholic hypothesis. He shows, for instance, that the great majority of the early Fathers were subordinationists with respect to the Son, a point he had earlier denied.[117] Of all the early Fathers, only Tertullian affirmed the doctrine of the Trinity in reasonably clear terms, and he did so after becoming a Montanist. Even in the fourth century, Basil of Caesarea

in the footsteps of the Caroline and Nonjuring divines" (Nockles, *The Oxford Movement in Context*, 105).

116. See John Henry Newman, *The Via Media of the Anglican Church*, 3rd ed. (London: Basil Montagu Pickering, 1877). For background to the traditional Anglican understanding of the "via media," see Mark D. Chapman, *Anglicanism: A Very Short Introduction* (Oxford: Oxford University Press, 2006), chapter 3; and see also Sheridan Gilley, "The Ecclesiology of the Oxford Movement: A Reconsideration," in *From Oxford to the People: Reconsidering Newman and the Oxford Movement*, ed. Paul Vaiss (Leominster, UK: Gracewing, 1996), 60–75, at 63–64. See also the discussion of Newman's views in the mid-1830s—pointing out the significance of Newman's exchange with Jean-Nicolas Jager—in Avery Dulles, "Authority in the Church," in *The Cambridge Companion to John Henry Newman*, ed. Ian Ker and Terrence Merrigan (Cambridge: Cambridge University Press, 2009), 170–188, at 173; as well as the discussion of the Newman-Jager exchange in Stephen Morgan, *John Henry Newman and the Development of Doctrine: Encountering Change, Looking for Continuity* (Washington, DC: The Catholic University of America Press, 2021), 118–132; and Thomas, *Newman and Heresy*, 185–190, including Thomas' observation that "Jager shrewdly and ruthlessly pressed this weak point in Newman's argument: the issue of *fundamental error*. If Roman Errors are fundamental, then a branch of the church has failed—and the branch theory falls. But if Rome's errors are not fundamental, why has the Church of England broken with it?" (Thomas, 188). See *John Henry Newman and the Abbé Jager: A Controversy on Scripture and Tradition*, ed. Louis Allen (Oxford: Oxford University Press, 1975).

117. This point had been made by the Evangelical Anglican William Goode against the Oxford Movement's appeal to the authority of the early Fathers: see William Goode, *The Divine Rule of Faith and Practice*, 2 vols. (London: J. Hatchard and Son, 1842).

hesitated to affirm the divinity of the Holy Spirit—not because he disbelieved it, but because the orthodox party was not yet unified on this matter. Newman similarly directs attention to the doctrine of the Eucharist. Anglo-Catholics generally seek to accept (Roman) Catholic teaching on the Eucharist, but Newman contends that "scanty as the Ante-nicene notions may be of the Papal Supremacy, they are both more numerous and more definite than the adducible testimonies in favour of the Real Presence."[118]

He then describes his theory of doctrinal development in a bit more detail. His theory is a working hypothesis that, like the hypotheses of natural scientists, seeks to account for a given range of evidence. Admittedly, the need for such a hypothesis may seem a sign of weakness: Is it not special pleading to argue that what might appear to be arbitrary changes are in fact something entirely regulated? In answer, Newman notes that during the three hundred years of post-Reformation controversies, all sides have combed through history looking for evidence that tells against their opponents. Their combined efforts have put dogmatic truth in doubt, since the adherents of dogma have not yet been able to explain the pattern of the evidence. Some hypothesis or theory is therefore necessary to account for the evidence.

If doctrinal development is Newman's "hypothesis," how does it relate to what Newman calls the "idea" of Christianity? Newman explains that Second Temple Judaism, second-century Gnosticism, and Athenian democracy are all instances of an "idea," embodied in actual persons,

118. Newman, *An Essay on the Development of Christian Doctrine*, 24. Regarding Newman's views as an Anglican, Nockles comments: "Initially, the Tractarians were concerned only to exalt the importance of the sacrament and did not engage in doctrinal speculation. Tractarian antipathy to the doctrine of Transubstantiation was marked, being grounded on a conviction that it represented a form of rationalism. . . . It was only in his *Letter to Dr Faussett* [responding to Faussett's 1838 sermon *Revival of Popery*—itself a response to the publication of Froude's *Remains*] in 1838 that Newman was provoked into a more explicit statement of eucharistic theology. There are hints in this work that, under the influence of Froude's more advanced views, Newman was moving towards acceptance of an 'objective' or 'local' presence, but there is no evidence to suggest that he as yet defined the Real Presence in anything but a spiritual sense" (*The Oxford Movement in Context*, 239).

institutions, and events on the historical stage. A complex idea—for instance the idea of democratic government—unfolds more richly over the passage of time, rather than being already fully expressed at the outset. In Newman's view, therefore, development should be expected in any "idea" worthy of the name. Newman maintains, "Its beginnings are no measure of its capabilities, nor of its scope. At first no one knows what it is, or what it is worth. . . . It seems in suspense which way to go; it wavers, and at length strikes out in one definite direction."[119] An "idea" is essentially a living organism, which grows into a large entity without deviating from the principles it possessed from the outset. Newman here has in view political, logical, historical, ethical, theological, and metaphysical developments; and he gives various examples of each of these.

In this context, Newman quotes a lengthy passage on development from the French historian of European civilization François Guizot, whose fame was at its height in the early 1840s. In the passage quoted by Newman, Guizot reflects upon the development of a religious society. A religious society, he says, must have a particular form of government and particular truth-claims that unite its members. Newman draws from this passage the point that development pertains to Christianity according to eminent contemporary historians such as Guizot. In addition, Newman cites his own reflections on "development" in his fifteenth University Sermon.[120]

---

119. Newman, *An Essay on the Development of Christian Doctrine*, 40.

120. See John Henry Newman, *Fifteen Sermons Preached before the University of Oxford between A.D. 1826 and 1843*, ed. Mary Katherine Tillman, 3rd ed. (Notre Dame, IN: University of Notre Dame Press, 1997), Sermon 15: "The Theory of Developments in Religious Doctrine," 312–351, at 330, 335. He goes on to say: "The question, then, is not whether this or that proposition of the Catholic doctrine is *in terminis* in Scripture, unless we would be slaves to the letter, but whether that one view of the Mystery, of which all such are the exponents, be not there; a view which would be some other view, and not itself, if any one of such propositions, if any one of a number of similar propositions, were not true. These propositions imply each other, as being parts of one whole; so that to deny one is to deny all, and to invalidate one is to deface and destroy the view itself. One thing alone has to be impressed on us by Scripture, the Catholic idea, and in it they are all included" (Newman, 336). Jane Garnett identifies the significant influence of Joseph Butler upon Sermon 15, as

The second chapter of *An Essay on the Development of Christian Doctrine* argues that Christianity—which is a "fact" that "impresses an idea of itself on our minds" and stands as the "subject-matter of exercises of reason"—has developed over time in precisely the ways that Newman's first chapter described an idea developing.[121] Put simply, it takes time for a living idea to disclose its various aspects. Believers' understanding of the content of divine revelation will not be perfect at the outset but will require time to mature and unfold. Since Christianity lives in the world, the articulation of Scripture's teachings will be affected by the particular cultures in which the interpreters live; and Christian principles will be applied in different ways in different societies and under different circumstances.

Newman knows that the (Roman) Catholic Church is charged by Protestants with both adding to scriptural teaching and contradicting scriptural teaching.[122] As Newman points out in response, not only is the principle of "sola scriptura" absent in Scripture, but also other standard Christian doctrines, such as "the lawfulness of bearing arms," cannot easily be read off the text of the New Testament, but require thought and development.[123] Newman observes that "great questions exist in the subject-matter of which Scripture treats, which Scripture does not solve; questions . . . so real, so practical, that they must be answered."[124] One such question is what should constitute the canon of Scripture; another is how Scripture is to be interpreted; another is infant Baptism and the related question of what Baptism accomplishes; another is how Christians are freed of the guilt of their sins

upon all Newman's University Sermons. Her summary is worth citing here: "This elaboration of different ways in which conviction comes, and with it (in matters of faith as well as other contexts) the moral certitude necessary for action served both as a corrective to a naive historical progressivism—to the notion that the faith of a sophisticated nineteenth-century theologian was more profound than that of a first-century peasant—and as a recognition that persuasiveness of argument—whether in the past or the present—grows within a historical tradition the terms of articulation of which themselves change over time" (Garnett, "Joseph Butler," in *The Oxford Handbook of John Henry Newman*, 135–153, at 141).

121. Newman, *An Essay on the Development of Christian Doctrine*, 55.

122. See Newman, 58.

123. Newman, 59.

124. Newman, 60.

committed after Baptism. Furthermore, Scripture itself conditions us to expect doctrinal development, since we find development in prophecies and typologies as the epoch of the Old Testament moves closer to that of the New. As an example, Newman remarks that "the Messianic idea . . . was gradually developed in the minds of the Jews."[125]

Here, Newman's view of history coincides with modern secular views, quite intentionally—though Newman holds that divine action and providence are involved. Just as Newman grants that the idea of the "Messiah" developed over time in ways that secular historians can trace, so also Newman grants that the Wisdom of Solomon and Sirach are books that carry forward Jewish ideas from within a Hellenistic philosophical milieu. He recognizes that these ideas, as developed in Second Temple Judaism, influenced the writings of the New Testament. On this basis, Newman to some degree can accept the secular historian's view of the Bible as consisting in the development of ideas rather than in new revelatory moments—although for Newman this cannot be all that we say, since there actually are new revelatory words and deeds. Where secular historians see merely the work of human tradents, Newman sees not only prophetic inspiration and the work of the incarnate Lord, but also more broadly the guiding hand of the Holy Spirit and thus of divine providence.

As another example of development, Newman examines ancient Israel's understanding of sacrifice. The Torah commands an extensive system of cultic sacrifice of animals; the prophets emphasize the centrality of mercy and righteousness; and finally, Jesus establishes the structure of Christian worship. Newman, like secular historians of his day, sees an interior development here, as God's people move from worship revolving around animal sacrifice to worship that does not include animal sacrifice.[126] Newman adds

125. Newman, 65. See the historical-critical evidence in Joseph A. Fitzmyer, *The One Who Is to Come* (Grand Rapids, MI: Eerdmans, 2007).

126. For pushback against this viewpoint, see Jonathan Klawans, *Purity, Sacrifice, and the Temple: Symbolism and Supersessionism in the Study of Ancient Judaism* (Oxford: Oxford University Press, 2006); see also my chapter on "Temple" in my *Engaging the Doctrine of*

that just as prophetic teachings unfold in a particular direction, so too do statements made by Jesus in the New Testament. An example is the statement "This is my body," which has unfolded in a particular direction within the Church's Eucharistic worship. The point is that the kind of developments that secular historians expect to see are also seen by Christians who examine the history and reception of the biblical texts. Secular history does not perceive the Spirit's guidance or the working of divine providence, let alone the presence of the incarnate Lord or of biblical inspiration, but secular history *does* rightly perceive the development of ideas. For this reason, Christians need not be afraid of secular historiography, even while Christians rightly understand history to be the locus of divine action and providence.

Newman's concern in this part of his book is the *fact* of development, and both secular historians and Christians can agree upon this fact. He provides examples of development after the day of Pentecost: Peter's receiving the command to baptize the Gentile Cornelius; Paul's teachings in his letters; Ignatius of Antioch's articulation of the doctrine of the office of the bishop; the canonization of Scripture. He concludes, "No one doctrine can be named which starts complete at first, and gains nothing afterwards from the investigations of faith and the attacks of heresy."[127] This is not a defect in Christian doctrine, but rather an entailment of Christianity being a living, historical religion. Christians recognize in these post-Pentecost developments the providential work of the Holy Spirit, ensuring that the creed, the canon, and the Church's hierarchical structure are what God wills them to be.

Newman notes that the fully historical and thus developmental character of biblical religion was never hidden. For instance, when God announces to Moses that God will bring his people out of Egyptian slavery, the Bible does not merely go on to say, "This redemption took place."

Israel: A Christian Israelology in Dialogue with Ongoing Judaism (Eugene, OR: Cascade, 2021), 262–321.

127. Newman, *An Essay on the Development of Christian Doctrine*, 68.

Instead, the Bible portrays a detailed historical progression or development. The Bible does not teach doctrine in an abstract way; rather, doctrine stands as intricately connected to a lengthy history, which means that the truth of doctrine cannot be fully systematized but rather is always "full of concealed wonders and choice treasures."[128] For this reason, the interpreters of biblical doctrine cannot repudiate the normal ways in which people gain understanding. Research is required, as interpreters undertake the work of carefully reflecting upon Scripture in its whole and its parts. Just as a field of study is built up within a university community, so are the doctrinal aspects of biblical interpretation built up in the Church. All patristic and medieval doctrines "rest upon definite, even though sometimes obscure, sentences of Scripture."[129] Such post-scriptural developments are an extension of the developments that one finds within Scripture itself.

With respect to a number of the above insights, Newman relies upon the work of the eighteenth-century Anglican theologian and bishop Joseph Butler. The central "analogy" that drives Butler's project is between the natural world and the supernatural dispensation of Christianity. Historians can study the development of Athenian democracy, and historians can study the development of Christianity. The difference between Athenian democracy and Christianity will not be that the latter was doctrinally complete from the outset, but that the Holy Spirit, in God's providential plan, ensures that the development of Christianity does not fall into the kind of corruption that would distort divine revelation. For Butler and Newman, "If the Author of Nature be the Author of Grace, it may be expected that, while the two systems of facts are distinct and independent, the principles displayed in them will be the same, and form a

128. Newman, 71. For the point that Newman should not be depicted as an opponent of "system" or "systematic" thinking, see Mary Katherine Tillman, *John Henry Newman: Man of Letters* (Milwaukee, WI: Marquette University Press, 2015), 303–314.

129. Newman, *An Essay on the Development of Christian Doctrine*, 72.

connecting link between them."[130] For example, although the Incarnation is *sui generis*, the doctrine of mediation is found throughout nature and serves as an analogy for understanding the Incarnation.

According to Newman, therefore, it is appropriate to call the developments of Christianity "natural," at least in the sense that such developments are the kind that can broadly be expected by a historian with regard to a human institution. Since Christianity is a human institution, its history can be studied by historians and can be compared with that of other historical entities. The difference, however, is that God is working in and through this particular institution in order to preserve and unfold divine revelation. What historians perceive to be Christianity's "natural" developments are in fact from eternity "contemplated and taken into account by its Author, who in designing the work designed its legitimate results."[131]

Newman goes so far as to suggest that a Christian historian, if only he or she had sufficiently detailed information and an objective view of the whole, could know precisely what the "natural" and correct developments of the Christian idea are. But he points out immediately that no human can possibly have this kind of detailed view. No Christian historian can have certitude, based simply on historical knowledge, that a particular development is a true one rather than a corruption. History always remains susceptible to divergent interpretations, and it is deeply unpredictable. Besides, the primary interpreters of revelation must be theologians, and their writings (as can be seen from the patristic corpus) respond to a wide variety of occasions and sources, forming a "culture" of the Church. Newman calls this culture "Prophetical Tradition," and he notes that in order to decide upon what constitutes true development, even the vast corpus of "Prophetical Tradition" will be insufficient. There must be certain tests of true development, and there must also be an authoritative interpreter. This interpreter ultimately must be the living Church, guided by the Spirit and infallible in

130. Newman, 85.
131. Newman, 75.

handing on the true Gospel. It must be possible for the Church to distinguish clearly between true and false teaching; otherwise, God's revelation would almost immediately have been distorted, given the many controversies that have arisen in the Church from the outset.

On this basis, Newman defends the Catholic Magisterium in its conciliar and papal forms: "As creation argues continual governance, so are Apostles harbingers of Popes."[132] Even by secular historians, and certainly by Christian historians, the Magisterium can be recognized as a reasonable development. Newman underscores that "the very idea of revelation implies a present informant and guide, and that an infallible one"—and this cannot simply be Scripture, since Scripture is open to various interpretations and does not settle all important matters.[133]

Newman remarks that historians have the task of examining the course taken by societies, including societies such as the Church that are united by certain truth-claims. With respect to such societies, it is reasonable to suppose that an arbiter is needed; without such an arbiter, one will either have a unity that is merely extrinsic (the truth-claims being ignored) or else not unity but division. History shows, moreover, that in actual fact an arbiter did arise in the Church. Here, Newman returns to the notion that Church historians inevitably advance a "hypothesis" that the study of the evidence then either supports or refutes. Gibbon has one such bias, a Catholic another. The characteristic mark of a good history is that it favors the account of the evidence that is "the simplest, the most natural, the most persuasive."[134] With regard to the papal office, then, the theory or hypothesis of doctrinal development is the most natural, since historians should anticipate not only development but also the specific kind of development found in the papacy. Those who claim a divine revelation will naturally need to claim an interpreter capable of settling disputes that arise from Scripture and from the problems of the day.

Of course, Newman recognizes that other theories are possible: for

132. Newman, 86.
133. Newman, 87.
134. Newman, 92.

instance, that the Church has been guided by chance or by Hellenism or by the Antichrist.[135] But he shows the reasonableness of the view that the doctrine of the papacy has developed because of the clear need, in actual history, for an authoritative interpreter of an authoritative revelation. He sums up his twofold argument: first, since Christianity contained truth-claims from the outset, it can be seen to be inevitable that doctrinal development would occur as these truth-claims passed through many minds over many generations. Second, if a revelation has in fact been given, then God will have from the outset "secured it from perversion and corruption"—which entails an infallible interpreter.[136]

This argument, Newman insists, is not a mere theory but flows from history itself. In investigating history, one need not begin, as Gibbon does, with a skeptical bias. Different historians, depending on their views and character, will find different things antecedently probable. The historical evidence will then confirm or refute what one deems probable.[137] If in history one sees extensive "accretions" to the original deposit, the historian can begin by supposing that these *may* be the very developments that one would expect to find in a historical and social religion. The supposition of true doctrinal development over the centuries, in Newman's view, finds further strength when one appreciates the "harmonious order" and "precision" found in the actual

---

135. The notion that the Catholic Church was the Antichrist was still current in Anglicanism in the 1850s and 1860s: see for example Christopher Wordsworth, *Union with Rome: Is Not the Church of Rome the Babylon of the Book of Revelation?* (London: Rivington, 1850), a book which by 1866 was in its fifth edition. Wordsworth became bishop of Lincoln, and, in part due to what Mark D. Chapman calls his "Gallican ideals" and "ecumenical openness to fellow national Catholics" (an openness rooted in shared opposition to the papacy), Wordsworth drafted the Church of England's official response to the Vatican Council and led the way in supporting the "Old Catholics" on the continent: see Chapman, *The Fantasy of Reunion: Anglicans, Catholics, and Ecumenism, 1833–1882* (Oxford: Oxford University Press, 2014), 213–219. See also Robert Fitzsimons, "The Church of England and the First Vatican Council," *Journal of Religious History* 27, no. 1 (2003): 29–46; and the biographical study of John Henry Overton and Elizabeth Wordsworth, *Christopher Wordsworth, Bishop of Lincoln, 1807–1885* (London: Rivington, 1888).

136. Newman, *An Essay on the Development of Christian Doctrine*, 92.

137. See John Henry Newman, *An Essay in Aid of a Grammar of Assent* (Westminster, MD: Christian Classics, 1973), 302–303.

developments.[138] When one contemplates this order, one observes that each doctrine shines light upon the others. One soon realizes that one "must accept the whole or reject the whole; attenuation does but enfeeble, and amputation mutilate."[139]

Furthermore, according to Newman, history gives no evidence of alternative paths of consistent Christian development other than that of the Catholic Church. As noted above, he considers that there are no alternative Christianities that stretch back to the apostolic period in competition with Catholicism. He has in view mainly the contrasts between Catholicism and Protestantism (as distinct from Eastern Orthodoxy), and he moves rather too quickly through the debated issues. His fundamental point is that even non-Catholics recognize Catholicism to be a coherent unity, whereas the various forms of Protestantism are each arguably partial, so that Lutheranism can be complemented by Calvinism and so on. Historians also recognize that the Catholicism of the nineteenth century is the "legitimate heir" of the Catholicism of the medieval and patristic periods.[140] This is so not only on core doctrinal matters but also on practical ones. Athanasius, who fought successive Semi-Arian emperors, would never have agreed to be subservient, in theological or ecclesiastical matters, to any temporal ruler, as is the case in Erastian versions of Christianity such as Anglicanism and the Eastern Orthodox Churches in Newman's day.

Thus, when the evidence of history shows that the Catholic Church has increased its doctrinal affirmations beyond those known to the apostolic generation, there is no need to assume that new doctrinal affirmations are corruptions. Gibbon's skeptical bias is no more the requisite stance of a historian confronted with the Catholic Church's doctrinal history than is the believing stance of a Catholic historian. In fact, the latter has a much better claim to truth, given what we know about development and the doctrinal history of the Church.

---

138. Newman, *An Essay on the Development of Christian Doctrine*, 93.
139. Newman, 94.
140. Newman, 97.

Let me append a brief note drawn from Newman's *Grammar of Assent.* Toward the end of that book, he remarks that Gibbon argued that there are five historical reasons that fully explain the spread of Christianity, and so there is no need for any appeal to divine providence or to anything miraculous or out of the ordinary. The five reasons are the zeal of the first Christians, their promise of a future life, their claim to possess the power to do miracles, their virtuous mode of life, and the structure of the Church. Newman agrees that each of these reasons help to explain Christianity's spread, but he does not agree that it follows that God's role has thereby been disproved. After all, says Newman, how is it that the five causes all came together in Christianity? In fact, Gibbon has not probed deeply enough. Newman asks, "How came a multitude of Gentiles to be influenced with Jewish zeal? How came zealots to submit to a strict, ecclesiastical *régime*? What connexion has a secular *régime* with the immortality of the soul? Why should immortality, a philosophical doctrine, lead to belief in miracles, which is a superstition of the vulgar? What tendency had miracles and magic to make men austerely virtuous?"[141]

To answer these questions, Newman says, Gibbon would have to reopen the issue of whether divine action and divine power (the Holy Spirit) are at the root of the confluence of these characteristics. Furthermore, Gibbon would also have to face the question of whether the characteristics really caused the spread of Christianity. How can it be assumed that these characteristics produced interior conversions? This question is especially pressing when, as Gibbon does, one denigrates the actual characteristics: for example, he deems Christian zeal to be mere fanaticism, and the Christian doctrine of a future life to be mere fear of hell (which is, Newman observes, already dependent on belief in a future life). Newman points out that today neither fanaticism nor fear of hell does much work in effecting conversion, and the pagans certainly did not need Christianity in order to believe superstitiously in miracles. When contemplating Christians' austere

141. Newman, *An Essay in Aid of a Grammar of Assent*, 457–458.

virtue, moreover, Gibbon himself expresses repulsion and tedium. And with respect to ecclesiastical structure, the Church was much looser in the earliest centuries.

Newman proposes therefore that there are other, more probable reasons for Christianity's spread, reasons that depend upon divine action and providence. Christians themselves gave such reasons, and they included faith, hope, and love, as well as "repentance towards God, and faith in Christ."[142] The Jewish people were expecting a Messiah, and the earliest Christian testimony is that the Messiah has come in Jesus of Nazareth. This belief is what, according to the first Christians' own testimony, propelled them zealously into the world and produced many conversions. Why not suppose that the cause of the conversions was the person whom they preached—namely, Jesus? Why not suppose that the Church as the Body of Christ—and the witness of individual believers configured to Christ—brought people to Christ through Christ's own power? Why not suppose that Christ caused the zeal and that the desire for immortality was a desire for everlasting personal communion with Christ? In sum, why not ground the spread of Christianity, not in ordinary historical reasons but in the utterly extraordinary (indeed divine) person of Christ?

As Newman goes on to say, when one consults the early Roman sources regarding the spread of Christianity, they (the Romans) report that the main reason seems to be devotion to Christ and all that follows from real devotion to Christ. The Romans chalked up the firmness of this devotion to an obstinate spirit on the part of the Christians, as well as to the intercession of demons and magic. The early Christians, however, credited it to the powerful and living love of Jesus Christ, and to the indwelling of Christ and his Spirit in believers. As a matter of historical fact, Newman adds, many Christians "felt it an acceptable service to Him who loved them, to confess with courage and to suffer [martyrdom] with dignity."[143] Newman

142. Newman, 462.
143. Newman, 480.

concludes that more plausible than Gibbon's five reasons is the actual power of the Gospel, which, when all is said and done, alone has the "gift of staunching and healing the one deep wound of human nature."[144]

Conclusion

Recall Kenneth Parker's concern, with which I began this chapter, about what happens "when ahistorical metanarratives of the Christian past are pressed too far in an era when historical consciousness is an undeniable component of our intellectual discourse."[145] Reflecting a particular notion of what it means to be "ahistorical," as we saw, Gibbon allows that the theologian may "indulge in the pleasing task of describing Religion as she descended from Heaven, arrayed in her native purity," but the reality of the Christian religion is much more mundane: the historian "must discover the inevitable mixture of error and corruption which she contracted in a long residence upon earth, among a weak and degenerate race of beings."[146] Gibbon holds that the "corruption" began at the very outset when Jewish and Gentile followers of Christ could not agree with one another about obligatory Torah observance. In his view, the earliest Christianity was a Jewish Christianity for which Jesus was a moral teacher or exalted prophet but certainly not the divine Son of the Father. By the time of the Gospel of John, the original Christian idea had, Gibbon insists, been completely corrupted.

In *An Essay on the Development of Christian Doctrine*, Newman does not agree with Gibbon's assessment of the earliest Church, and he draws upon other historians to defend the reasonableness of identifying as true development what Gibbon identifies as mere corruption. At the same time, Newman is working with a theology of history—grounded in divine action

144. Newman, 487. For further discussion of this section of the *Grammar of Assent*, see Short, "Newman, Gibbon and God's Particular Providence," 21–27.

145. Parker, "Historiography," 574–575.

146. Gibbon, *The Decline and Fall of the Roman Empire*, vol. 1, 488.

and providence—that Gibbon rejected as an idealization of the actual messiness of events. According to Parker, three theologies of history or "metanarratives" were present among the participants in the Oxford Movement: "successionism, supersessionism, and developmentalism."[147] In the "successionist" metanarrative, "the Christian truth was received by the apostles from Christ (or the Holy Spirit on the day of Pentecost) and has been preserved by their successors unaltered by time and circumstance."[148]

---

147. Kenneth L. Parker, "Tractarian Visions of History," in *The Oxford Handbook of the Oxford Movement*, ed. Stewart J. Brown, Peter B. Nockles, and James Pereiro (Oxford: Oxford University Press, 2017), 151–165, at 152. Parker adds a fourth metanarrative, "appercessionism," in his "Re-visioning the Past and Re-sourcing the Future: The Unresolved Historiographical Struggle in Roman Catholic Scholarship and Authoritative Teaching," in *The Church on Its Past*, ed. Peter D. Clarke and Charlotte Methuen (Rochester, NY: Ecclesiastical History Society, 2013), 389–416. He defines it as follows: "Appercessionism, unlike the other three metanarratives, does not privilege earlier Christianity, but looks to the heightened consciousness of the current age to critique former Christian teaching and practice, chart a new way forward and reshape Christianity in light of newly realized values" (Parker, 309). I note that depending upon the scope of its critique and the ways in which it reshapes Christianity, "appercessionism" may accord with what Newman meant by religious liberalism (and its corresponding view of history), grounded in the rejection of the dogmatic principle. For his part, Parker links "appercessionism" with the perspective of Acton and ultimately with the perspective of Vatican II. He suggests, mistakenly in my view, that on issues such as birth control and women's ordination, the postconciliar Church has followed the "successionist" metanarrative. For the same four metanarratives, see Parker's "Historical Consciousness and the First Vatican Council: Manning, Döllinger, Newman, and Acton's Uses of History in the Papal Infallibility Debates," in *The Rise of Historical Consciousness among the Christian Churches*, ed. Kenneth L. Parker and Erick H. Moser (Lanham, MD: Rowman & Littlefield, 2013), 89–122. Here, however, Parker's description of the development and appercession metanarratives is somewhat different: "Advocates of development understood truth to be whole and complete in the Logos—Christ—but mediated to the Christian faithful in time; so that deeper and more complete understandings of truth were achieved through the guidance of the Holy Spirit, despite the failures of human leaders and the institutions they controlled. Apper-cessionists . . . understood their age to be one of higher moral consciousness; a position from which they could critique and judge past actions and ideas in light of a new consciousness, which prioritized orthopraxy over orthodoxy" (Parker, 90).

148. Parker, "Tractarian Visions of History," 152. For examples of this perspective among Catholic theologians, see Anthony Kemp, *The Estrangement of the Past: A Study in the Origins of Modern Historical Consciousness* (Oxford: Oxford University Press, 1991), 35–65, although Kemp, working within a historical metanarrative that presupposes God's absence, aims to critique the view (aided by a typological understanding of history) that "God's salvific purpose . . . , like the converging lines in an optical diagram, reaches its focal point at the Incarnation and ever after diverges outward as the Church" (Kemp, 64). I note that when

Although Newman always affirmed the existence (and, in a real sense, the fullness) of the apostolic deposit of faith, Newman consistently held that there have been alterations related to "time and circumstance," though not alterations that have caused the apostolic deposit of faith to fail to be handed on in its integrity.

Parker defines the "supersessionist" metanarrative as follows: "Supersessionism ascribes to ancient Christianity a privileged normative quality, identifies a period—or periods—of corruption or innovation that distorted Christian teaching, and looks to a later era when primitive Christian truth is rediscovered and restored."[149] Although Newman as a Catholic (and while writing *An Essay on the Development of Christian Doctrine*) rejected supersessionism thus defined, nonetheless it is necessary to observe that Newman always ascribed "to ancient Christianity a privileged normative quality." This ascription makes sense, because in fact by the fifth century most of the fundamental Christian doctrinal developments had taken place.[150] There was a privileged, Spirit-guided reception of the Scriptures in the patristic centuries.

Lastly, Parker identifies the metanarrative of "developmentalism" as the one that Newman favors. Parker states, "Developmentalism identifies in early Christianity nascent expressions of doctrinal teaching, yet assumes that organic growth—in human time and experience—results in deeper, more expansive understandings of truth that may take centuries of struggle

---

patristic and medieval authors affirm that the Catholic faith has not been changed but remains the same faith handed on by the Apostles, they are not rejecting every kind of alteration but only a certain kind of alteration. No doubt, however, their consciousness of the historical past differs from that of modern scholars, who have a much larger sense of the differences between the present (in its various instantiations) and particular periods of the past—and who rule out "participatory" dimensions of the past-present-future relationship, grounded in divine providence. For further insight into the patristic-medieval outlook and its openness in certain important respects to a developmental metanarrative (understood in Newmanian terms), see Guy Mansini, "Saint Thomas and the Development of Doctrine," *Nova et Vetera* 19, no. 2 (2021): 393–422.

149. Parker, "Tractarian Visions of History," 152.

150. This becomes apparent in John Anthony McGuckin, *The Path of Christianity: The First Thousand Years* (Downers Grove, IL: IVP Academic, 2017).

and debate to discern."[151] I note that Newman holds that the deepest participation in Christ is that of the Apostles. Scripture is inexhaustibly deep, by contrast to even the greatest works of theology. Even so, guided by the Holy Spirit, the Church advances in understanding the Gospel, as the truth of Christ and salvation is opened up by means of controversies and with the assistance of human culture. This advance has to be understood properly so as to avoid modern notions of progress, since there are various modes of participating in the apostolic deposit.

Parker recognizes all the above, and he also remarks upon the influence had by an Anglo-Catholic figure whom I have not yet mentioned, Samuel Francis Wood, who in 1835 was already setting forth the lineaments of the theory of development of doctrine.[152] It is fascinating to see Newman in 1835–1836 rejecting Wood's proposals, which Wood articulated at some length in dialogue with Newman and with Henry Manning. Also notable is the fact that in an 1839 sermon, the English Catholic priest (later cardinal archbishop) Nicholas Wiseman compared the Christian faith to the mustard seed of Jesus' parable (Matt. 13:31–32) and argued that "the religion of Christ will be found to possess a marvelous power of developing, when proper occasion presents itself, germs of great principles latent within it, adapted to the circumstances in which Providence shall place it."[153]

151. Parker, "Tractarian Visions of History," 152–153.

152. Parker draws upon James Pereiro, *'Ethos' and the Oxford Movement: At the Heart of Tractarianism* (Oxford: Oxford University Press, 2008), Appendix I, 239–250; and Pereiro, *Theories of Development in the Oxford Movement* (Leominster, UK: Gracewing, 2015), 81–104. Parker notes that Henry Manning and especially Charles Marriott—the authors of Tract 78 (1837)—were somewhat more receptive to Wood's ideas than was Newman. See also Michael Peterburs' "Newman and the Development of Doctrine," in *By Whose Authority? Newman, Manning and the Magisterium*, ed. V. Alan McClelland (Bath: Downside Abbey, 1996), 49–78; as well as Stephen D. Lawson, "'To Be Deep in History': The Role of History in the Conversions of John Henry Newman and Erik Peterson," *Newman Studies Journal* 16, no. 2 (2019): 5–33, at 14–15.

153. Nicholas Wiseman, *A Sermon Preached at the Opening of St. Mary's Catholic Church in Derby* (London: James Storer, 1839), 4, cited in C. Michael Shea, "Doctrinal Development," in *The Oxford Handbook of John Henry Newman*, 284–303, at 297–298; for further background, see Paul Asveld, "Newman and Wiseman in the Days of the Oxford Movement," in

Already in 1829, Newman posited that the apostolic deposit of faith contained not only truths explicitly known, but also truths implicitly present (even if not demonstrably so) that are later apprehended by the mind of the Church.[154] Newman in the 1830s moved increasingly in the direction of the theory of development, helped by various debates and discussions, perhaps above all his debate with Abbé Jager.[155] Newman fully embraced doctrinal development in 1843, when he preached his fifteenth and final University Sermon on this theme. Even then, however, he was not completely certain that the Catholic Church had in every case faithfully developed rather than corrupted doctrine. As Michael Peterburs has shown, "Notes in Newman's diaries from this period suggest that it was

---

From Oxford to the People, 286–298. Shea remarks, "Like Möhler a decade earlier, Wiseman argued that understanding the principle of development would help to show that it was vain to look for explicit evidence of specific truths in certain periods of the Church, because the principles often remained latent until circumstances brought them to light. . . . Wiseman directly employed the principle of development to argue for Roman Catholic claims such as the emergence of the hierarchy, the development of public liturgy, and Marian devotion. . . . The language of 'development' and 'corruption' which Wiseman used to delineate true and false expressions of Christian faith was identical to Newman's *Essay*" ("Doctrinal Development," 298; see also Thomas, *Newman and Heresy*, 219–221). Newman had been taking Wiseman seriously since the publication of Wiseman's lengthy *Lectures on the Principal Doctrines and Practices of the Catholic Church* (London: J. Booker, 1836). See also Johann Adam Möhler, *Unity in the Church, or, The Principle of Catholicism Presented in the Spirit of the Church Fathers of the First Three Centuries*, trans. Peter C. Erb (Washington, DC: The Catholic University of America Press, 1996), 167 and elsewhere, as well as Kenneth Parker and Charles [C. Michael] Shea, "Johann Adam Möhler's Influence on John Henry Newman's Theory of Doctrinal Development: The Case for a Reappraisal," *Ephemerides Theologicae Lovanienses* 89, no. 1 (2013): 73–95. See Pereiro, *Theories of Development in the Oxford Movement*, 110–114 on W.G. Ward's 1841–1842 articles in the *British Critic*, which were indebted to Möhler. Pereiro emphasizes the significance of the Tractarian approach to religious knowledge for Newman's understanding of doctrinal development.

154. For this point, see Cimorelli, *John Henry Newman's Theology of History*, 235–237, discussing a letter to his mother written on March 13, 1829. Cimorelli argues that Pereiro's (and thus Parker's) perspective should be augmented by attention to the fact that "Newman had an interest in the transmission and articulation of implicit truths well before even the Oxford Movement" (Cimorelli, 237n288).

155. See Stephen Morgan's argument that Pereiro attempts "to make the contribution of S.F. Wood central to the whole question of the development of doctrine by largely minimizing and making derivative, if not completely eclipsing, Newman's contribution" (Morgan, *John Henry Newman and the Development of Doctrine*, 14).

not until 1844–5 that he was fully convinced that the Catholic Church's so-called 'additions' to the faith were in fact true developments."[156]

Although his view of development developed, as did his view of Christian historiography, Newman's theology of history always had at its center his faith in creation and redemption, in accord with God's providential plan "to gather up all things in [Christ]" (Eph. 1:10). By comparison, Gibbon embraced an agnostic or atheistic philosophy of history, which presumes that in history there have solely been human and natural events, or at least this is all that historians can allow for. I have argued in this chapter that Newman's theology of history does not overdetermine his approach to historical facts in *An Essay on the Development of Christian Doctrine.* Even so, the core argument that he makes on historical grounds (namely, that the Catholic Church has been characterized consistently by doctrinal development rather than doctrinal corruption) is in the end inseparable from his theology of history. Christopher Cimorelli rightly observes that Newman "sought to bolster revealed religion through historical consciousness that

156. Peterburs, "Newman and the Development of Doctrine," 67. See also the details added by Stephen Morgan in *John Henry Newman and the Development of Doctrine*, 227–230. Pereiro finds the core elements of Newman's mature theory of development to be already present in letters from 1840 and 1841, but Newman is still struggling against the Catholic position. For example, in a September 1841 letter, "Newman questioned whether the Church of Rome had authority to vary or add to primitive religion. Rome's ground of defence, according to him, was that the Church did not reveal new truths; it only taught 'developments from germs held in primitive times.' He thought that in some cases—Mary's cult for example—this was trifling with words; the only solid ground for Rome was to 'maintain that the Church has the power of adding new truths to the Apostolic revelation' [something Newman rightly could never accept]" (Pereiro, *'Ethos' and the Oxford Movement*, 177). In a November 1841 letter to his brother Francis, Newman "described his theory of development in twelve numbered propositions, affirming that all systems that have life have a development, without thereby losing their identity. He acknowledged that development might also lead to corruption but affirmed that continuity of temper and principles guaranteed orthodox development and served to distinguish it from a false one. . . . The tenth proposition added that there was no antecedent objection to developments in doctrine, provided that these harmonized with Catholic temper and principles, that the doctrines were consistent with the ideas from which they profess to spring, and that they were professed unanimously by its members" (Pereiro, 183). Pereiro observes that Newman's concept of "realizing"—moving from notional to real knowledge—helped him in coming to appreciate doctrinal "development," as can be seen in Newman's 1843 University Sermon.

did not forget revealed truth" and "sought to organize facts in light of antecedent considerations and probabilities."[157] Newman's historiographical approach meets Gibbon and other modern historians such as Barthold Niebuhr on their own (secular) terrain; namely, that of facts accessible to historical research.[158] But it does so explicitly with much different antecedent probabilities in view, and thereby differs from Milman's approach.

Let me summarize Newman's case. Just as Niebuhr holds on the basis of his historical research that "ideas" develop in history (as for instance the "idea" of Athenian democracy developed over time, though Athens ultimately corrupted it), so Newman holds that Christianity can be seen as an "idea" that develops over time in ways that secular historians can perceive. In his view, the "idea" of Christianity has developed in the Catholic Church along lines that a secular historian could deem reasonable. Yet the secular historian, trained to exclude divine action and divine providence, will assume that the history of the Church must be no different from the history of other institutions, filled not only with wickedness and folly but also with doctrinal corruption. Newman feels free to begin from the opposite assumption about doctrinal corruption (though not about wickedness and folly!) until the facts show otherwise. He does so both on the grounds of his theology of history, and on the grounds that if the Catholic Church is *not* the same Church that Christ founded and that has continued for

157. Cimorelli, *John Henry Newman's Theology of History*, 81, 239. Cimorelli directs attention here to the insights of J.D. Holmes, "Cardinal Newman on the Philosophy of History," *Tijdschrift vor filosofie* 32 (1970): 521–553; and see also Holmes, "Newman, History and Theology," *Irish Theological Quarterly* 36, no. 1 (1969): 34–45.

158. See Mark D. Chapman, "Temporal and Spatial Catholicism: Tensions in Historicism in the Oxford Movement," in *The Shaping of Tradition: Context and Normativity*, ed. Colby Dickinson with Lieven Boeve and Terrence Merrigan (Leuven, BE: Peeters, 2013), 17–26, at 26, where Chapman affirms Newman's openness to historical facts but oddly attributes this to skepticism: "It was probably Newman's inherent scepticism that forced him to change his views: history simply could not be made to yield what he felt it had to yield. In history there simply could not be the degree of probability required for faith: as Wiseman had pointed out, patristic scholarship could not reveal a unity of truth which appeared crucial for faith to flourish. This meant that the Tractarian method, which Pusey continued to hold throughout his long life, was brought into question" (Chapman, 26).

centuries, then this must be shown by the historian rather than merely asserted.[159]

Thus, where Gibbon sees corruption and fanaticism, Newman sees development and truth, but he does not thereby succumb to an idealization of history. He remains committed to seeing and responding to the actual historical evidence. In his approach to the doctrinal history of the Church, he is no more blinded by his faith than is Gibbon by his religious skepticism or Milman by his religious liberalism. Indeed, Newman is arguably much more self-aware about the impact of his antecedent beliefs than either Gibbon or Milman. In the *Essay*, he does not contest modern historical scholarship's focus upon secondary causes, but he avers that there is no historical reason for denying or doubting the existence of a transcendent God who is active in history—and so God cannot be ruled out a priori as an explanation of certain facts or as an influence upon the Church's doctrinal history. Since this is the case, the absence of doctrinal corruption (as distinct from other kinds of ruptures within the history of doctrinal development) is a possible hypothesis, so long as it can be supported by the

159. Cimorelli tests the hypothesis that "John Henry Newman's historical method can be considered critical in that it allows for ongoing dynamism between the three constitutive elements of a historical theory (i.e., evidence, antecedent probabilities, and antecedent considerations)" (*John Henry Newman's Theology of History*, 85), and he concludes that, in *The Arians of the Fourth Century* at least, Newman's elaboration of 'historical connections' cannot be said to correspond with a method of inquiry like the historical-critical, the practitioners of which would establish such connections through identifiable textual influences and philological similarities" (Cimorelli, 169). Yet I note (and Cimorelli goes on to confirm) that in *An Essay on the Development of Christian Doctrine*, as well as in later writings, Newman allows his historiography to deliver bad news for his theology. Cimorelli states that in his *Essay* Newman "challenges readings of the past which lay too much stress on antecedent considerations . . . to the detriment of historical facts" (Cimorelli, 227–228). Regarding Newman's overall project, Cimorelli argues that "his ongoing 'exposure' to the historical record led to shifts, in both his antecedent considerations and (consequently) theories of the church. He was in search of the 'real' church, both in antiquity and in nineteenth-century England, and the historical record was to have a normative say in this regard" (Cimorelli, 183). I note that with respect to the normativity of the results of historical research, the difference between Newman's approach and Döllinger's, which I discuss in chapter 5, requires attention, and indeed Cimorelli is aware that Newman's practice of history has theological dimensions. See also J.D. Holmes, "Newman's Reactions to the Development of Scientific and Historical Criticism in England," *Clergy Review* 64 (1979): 280–290.

historical evidence. Cimorelli aptly concludes, "Newman's view challenges historians to present hypotheses that make better sense of the evidence without distorting the facts."[160]

160. Cimorelli, *John Henry Newman's Theology of History*, 228. Cimorelli adds, "In other words, history must be perpetually allowed to inform and potentially challenge one's hypotheses" (Cimorelli, 228; cf. 242). This is true in one sense, but not in the sense that solemn dogma now becomes subject to endless revision or rupture in light of present or future historical research. Cimorelli helpfully points out in this context, "Newman was elucidating a more historically conscious, and epistemologically humble, position about what can be determined on the basis of historical research *vis-à-vis* revealed religion. He wanted to resist the temptation to expect more of history than it could deliver" (Cimorelli, 229).

Chapter 2

Newman and Froude

In *The Causes of the Corruption of Christianity*, Newman's Protestant contemporary Robert Vaughan expressed great concern about doctrinal corruption. He argues that "with regard to a state of things which Infinite Wisdom has devised, and to which a Supreme and Unalterable Authority is attached, every innovation must be an inroad of corruption, and must partake, according to its extent, of the nature of impiety."[1] Vaughan therefore condemns the Catholic Church for its manifold doctrinal corruptions.

Newman considered positions such as Vaughan's to be ignorant. After all, even the dogmatic definition of the Holy Spirit's full divinity can be termed an "innovation," since the doctrine of one divine nature and three divine persons is not stated as such in Scripture, and the divinity of the Holy Spirit was not taught explicitly even at Nicaea. Nevertheless, although his perspective on Catholicism (Anglo- and, eventually, Roman) was the opposite of Vaughan's, Newman firmly concurred with Vaughan's basic point—namely, his opposition to doctrinal corruption. Like Vaughan, and perhaps even more so, Newman was profoundly sensitive to the ways in which human

1. Robert Vaughan, *The Causes of the Corruption of Christianity*, 2nd ed. (London: Jackson and Walford, 1852), 3. As Sheridan Gilley says, "The stock polemical charge against Rome" was that "Rome had corrupted early Christianity by adding to it new doctrines like those concerning the Virgin or the Papacy," and also given the evident "difference between the New Testament and the highly sophisticated Christological and Trinitarian dogmas of the Nicene and Athanasian Creeds" (Gilley, *Newman and His Age*, 2nd ed. [London: Darton, Longman, and Todd, 2003], 237). Cyril O'Regan adds the point that "for the liberal wing of the Anglican Church doctrines formulated over the centuries are over-claims that lead to fanaticism, which in turn leads to repression and violence" (O'Regan, "Newman's Forensic Classic of Development: Its Uniqueness and Its Agon with Gibbon and Surrogates," *International Journal of Systematic Theology* 20, no. 2 [2018]: 225–252, at 234).

power, inside and outside the Church, can be used to the detriment of the integrity of the Gospel.[2]

The origins of the Oxford Movement shed light upon Newman's sensitivity to the threat posed to Christian doctrine by human power. I devote the first section of this chapter to examining these origins, primarily by surveying Richard Hurrell Froude's 1833 "Remarks on State Interference in Matters Spiritual," reprinted with additions in Froude's posthumous *Remains*. Froude, whose influence upon Newman and the Oxford Movement was immense, contended that Erastianism was paving the way for doctrinal corruption in the Anglican Church and therefore must be excised—although Froude understood himself to be arguing firmly "within the limits of Anglicanism."[3]

In the second and final section of the chapter, I argue that Newman's mature view of doctrinal development arises in significant part from his Anglo-Catholic fear of Erastian-inspired doctrinal corruption. In this section, I begin by exploring Newman's Anglican *Via Media*, and then turn to relevant portions of his *Essay on the Development of Christian Doctrine* and *Certain Difficulties Felt by Anglicans in Catholic Teaching*. I show that Newman's Roman Catholic sense of the importance of the role of the pope and bishops flows partly from his anti-Erastian concerns as an Anglican. Although he is aware (and becomes increasingly aware) that the pope and bishops can exaggerate their power in harmful ways, he thinks that far worse is the interference of the State in matters of doctrine, which should be the preserve of the Church led by the successors of the Apostles.

2. Citing Newman's 1848 novel *Loss and Gain* (ed. Trevor Lipscombe [San Francisco: Ignatius Press, 2012]), Avery Dulles suggests that "in his first years as a Catholic, Newman was inclined to make extreme claims on behalf of the papacy" (Dulles, "Authority in the Church," in *The Cambridge Companion to John Henry Newman*, ed. Ian Ker and Terrence Merrigan [Cambridge: Cambridge University Press, 2009], 170–188, at 179). I am not sure that Newman's claims during this period were "extreme," but they did not have the nuance of his later writings on the topic.

3. Pierre Gauthier, "Richard Hurrell Froude's Influence on Newman and the Oxford Movement," in *From Oxford to the People: Reconsidering Newman and the Oxford Movement*, ed. Paul Vaiss (Leominster, UK: Gracewing, 1996), 255–268, at 267. See also R.W. Church, *The Oxford Movement: 1833–1845* (London: Macmillan, 1891), 49.

Let me briefly offer some background to the relationship of Froude and Newman before proceeding. Peter Nockles has rightly observed, "It is impossible to overestimate the personal magnetism exerted by the ascetical and anti-establishment [i.e., anti-Erastian] Hurrell Froude on Newman's theological and spiritual evolution."[4] Froude took appreciative notice of Félicité de Lamennais' Ultramontanist, anti-Gallican movement, which demanded

4. Peter B. Nockles, "The Oxford Movement," in *The Oxford Handbook of John Henry Newman*, ed. Frederick D. Aquino and Benjamin J. King (Oxford: Oxford University Press, 2018), 7–27, at 9. I agree with Nockles that "the political dimension to the origins and formation of the Oxford Movement had a theological and spiritual rationale. . . . The Movement as championed by Newman was counter-revolutionary in the context of a reaction to the challenge of 'Liberalism' and the Whig government's interference in matters ecclesiastical. . . . What was primarily at stake for Newman was the spiritual integrity of the Church" (Nockles, 11). In his *The Oxford Movement in Context: Anglican High Churchmanship, 1760–1857* (Cambridge: Cambridge University Press, 1994), 53, Nockles similarly remarks, "The Oxford Movement represented an anti-Erastian, moral protest against the apparently popular notion that the Church of England was but a human establishment, subservient to the material and secular interests of the state." Nockles warns, however, that "some of the Tractarians, especially Froude and Newman, did much to perpetuate a historical misrepresentation of Orthodox [High Church] teaching on church and state. Increasingly, in Tractarian polemic, 'Erastianism' . . . became a 'catch-all' rhetorical device" (Nockles, 55). Nockles argues that later scholars have been caught up in this (alleged) exaggeration, as for instance J.R. Griffin, "The Anglican Politics of Cardinal Newman," *Anglican Theological Review* 55, no. 10 (1973): 434–443. According to Nockles, "The pre-Tractarian High Church identification with monarchy always had both an important theological basis and practical religious application. It drew as its scriptural source of inspiration the text of Isaiah 49, v. 23: 'And Kings shall be thy nursing fathers, and their queens thy nursing mothers.' The text was interpreted to justify an understanding of the Royal Supremacy that was consciously anti-Erastian" (*The Oxford Movement in Context*, 57). Reverence for the Royal Supremacy (which strikes me as inevitably Erastian) was the default position of John Keble, but Froude moved him in a more radical direction—as J.H.L. Rowlands shows in *Church, State and Society: The Attitudes of John Keble, Richard Hurrell Froude and John Henry Newman, 1827–1845* (Worthing, UK: Churchman Publishing, 1989), 85–90. For Keble's later position, in which the influence of Froude is still strongly present, see his *The State in Its Relation with the Church: A Paper Reprinted from the "British Critic," October, 1839* (London: James Parker, 1869). Keble is reviewing and responding to William Gladstone's *The State in Its Relation with the Church*, 3rd ed. (London: John Murray, 1839), a full-throated defense of the Establishment and of Erastianism as the path forward. For discussion of Gladstone's book, John E. Toews, "Church and State: The Problem of Authority," in *The Cambridge History of Nineteenth-Century Political Thought*, ed. Gareth Stedman Jones and Gregory Claeys (Cambridge: Cambridge University Press, 2011), 603–648, at 633–634. Toews notes that "Gladstone's tendency to merge the state and church was also present in the 'liberal' or 'Broad Church' wing of post-Coleridgean church reformers," including F.D. Maurice and Connop Thirlwall (Toews, 634).

that the French State give up its thoroughgoing control of the French Church. Nockles observes, "The parallel between Lamennais' call to the French clergy in 1829 to exert 'the liberty of your ministry' and Newman's message to the Anglican clergy in *Tract 1* in 1833, 'magnify your office,' is clear enough. Lamennais demanded a free Church in a free State, and the logic of Tractarian anti-Erastianism points in the same direction."[5] Froude and Newman were insisting upon the reclamation of the Anglican Church's self-governance, even if they were not pushing for democratization of the State.[6] In "Remarks on State Interference in Matters Spiritual," Froude

5. Peter Nockles, "'Church and King': Tractarian Politics Reappraised," in *From Oxford to the People*, 93–123, at 93; see also Nockles, "Newman and Early Tractarian Politics," in *By Whose Authority? Newman, Manning and the Magisterium*, ed. V. Alan McClelland (Bath: Downside Abbey, 1996), 79–111. For Nockles, far from supporting the political liberalism favored by de Lamennais, "Tractarianism signalled no 'farewell to Toryism' as such, but represented the spiritual refashioning and reapplication of a sacred political creed" ("'Church and King,'" 115; "Newman and Early Tractarian Politics," 101); "The uncompromising anti-Erastianism of the *Tracts for the Times* was not . . . tantamount to political radicalism, any more than the anti-Erastianism of the Nonjurors had been" ("Newman and Early Tractarian Politics," 99). After a period in which de Lamennais' teachings received papal favor due to his Ultramontanism, Pope Gregory XVI condemned de Lamennais' teachings in two encyclicals, *Mirari Vos* (1832) and *Singulari Nos* (1834), and de Lamennais renounced Catholicism.

6. Further evidence of this connection—though in polemical terms—is found in the short letter of de Lamennais' disciple Le comte de Montalembert (Charles Forbes René de Troyon), *A Letter Addressed to a Rev. Member of the Camden Society, on the Subject of Catholic Literary Societies, on the Architectural, Artistical, and Archaeological Movements of the Puseyites* (Liverpool: Booker, 1844), 8, speaking about the Church of England: "Was there ever a Church, except perhaps the Greco-Russian since Peter I, which has so basely acknowledged the supreme right of the secular power?" For discussion see Jeremy Morris, "'Separated Brethren': French Catholics and the Oxford Movement," in *The Oxford Movement: Europe and the Wider World 1830–1930*, ed. Stewart J. Brown and Peter B. Nockles (Cambridge: Cambridge University Press, 2012), 203–220, at 207–209. Morris notes, "Comparison of royal domination of the Anglican and Russian Orthodox Churches was a common trope of Catholic polemic" (Morris, 208n29). Morris argues that by the 1850s, Montalembert had altered his viewpoint on the Anglican Church, so as to appreciate its strengths (especially the work of the Oxford Movement) and to encourage the Catholic Church in England to embrace the traditions and customs of the English. See Charles de Montalembert, *The Political Future of England*, 2nd ed. (London: John Murray, 1856).

draws significantly upon de Lamennais for his insistence that the Church of England must now be free of State interference in spiritual matters.[7]

For almost ten years, until his death in 1836, Froude was Newman's closest friend.[8] Newman himself fully recognized Froude's influence upon him. He replied in 1850 to a correspondent who proposed writing a history of the Oxford Movement, "You cannot, of course, do anything in the way of an account of the Oxford Movement without going to Froude's *Remains*."[9] On the one hand, the *Remains* are more medieval and political than were either the Oxford Movement or Newman himself, and the *Remains* also show Froude's unique dislike of the English Reformers.[10] On the other hand, the *Remains* contain many of the most important ideals and principles of the Oxford Movement, above all the critique of Erastianism. Froude taught Newman and Keble that Christians who shared the "Apostolic *ethos* would pay allegiance to no human establishment, but only to the Church Catholic."[11]

In 1837, a year after Froude's death and some years after de Lamennais'

7. The connection between Froude and de Lamennais is also explored by, among others, Christopher Dawson, *The Spirit of the Oxford Movement* (London: Sheed & Ward, 1933), 59–65; and W.G. Roe, *Lamennais and England: The Reception of Lamennais's Religious Ideas in England in the Nineteenth Century* (Oxford: Oxford University Press, 1966), 93–124, especially 96–106.

8. See Guy Nicholls, *Unearthly Beauty: The Aesthetic of St John Henry Newman* (Leominster, UK: Gracewing, 2019), 26–28.

9. "Letter to J. M. Capes, 23 August 1850," in *The Letters and Diaries of John Henry Newman*, vol. 14, *Papal Aggression; July, 1850 to December, 1851*, ed. Charles Stephen Dessain (London: Thomas Nelson, 1963), 49; cited in Ciaran Brady, *James Anthony Froude: An Intellectual Biography of a Victorian Prophet* (Oxford: Oxford University Press, 2013), 68. See also James Pereiro, *Theories of Development in the Oxford Movement* (Leominster, UK: Gracewing, 2015), 56–57, where Pereiro discusses Samuel Francis Wood's concurrence with Newman's high estimation of Froude's role in the Oxford Movement, including through Froude's exemplification of the Movement's "ethos."

10. For discussion, see Rowlands, *Church, State and Society*, 112–120.

11. Pereiro, *Theories of Development in the Oxford Movement*, 60. Pereiro completes this sentence with: "and to the great principle of Catholicism: the universal consent of the primitive and true Church, the certain witness of God's divine truth and will" (Pereiro, 60). I note that Froude's focus on the Fathers was much less than Newman's and Keble's, but Froude too appealed to the Church of the Fathers.

excommunication, Newman published "Fall of De la Mennais."[12] Here Newman criticizes both English Whigs and French Papists for their Erastianism, and he contrasts France's abusive Erastianism with the comparative gentleness of English Erastianism. In its central arguments, however, the essay stands as a tribute to Froude and an expression of Newman's conviction that Froude had been correct from the outset, including in his refusal to take any solace in the Royal Supremacy.[13] Channeling Froude, Newman directs attention to the English State's "various successful encroachments" upon the rights of the Church of England, and he observes with biting sarcasm that at least Anglican bishops are "appointed, not by pagans [as the Turkish ruler appoints the head of the Greek Orthodox Church in Constantinople], but only by schismatics, latitudinarians, profligates, socinians, and infidels."[14]

For Newman as for Froude, James Pereiro's words apply: "The danger they [the Tractarians] dreaded was that the day might come when the State, without destroying the established Church, would corrupt it and, under the pretence of the usefulness of a profession of religion, would construct a national religion, and use it for its own purposes."[15] In Newman's *Apologia Pro Vita Sua*, he traces his anti-Erastianism both to Froude and to his Oxford teacher Richard Whately, who from a Whig perspective favored a form of disestablishment in the 1820s. But Froude in particular articulated the

12. This essay was reprinted, with an appended Note, as "Fall of De la Mennais," in John Henry Newman, *Essays Critical and Historical*, vol. 1 (London: Longmans, Green, 1897), 138–178.

13. Keble always held that "the Royal Supremacy was essentially not Erastian" (Rowlands, *Church, State and Society*, 229; cf. 104–111), whereas Froude perceived from the outset that it was Erastian, at least in practice. According to Rowlands, Newman finally lost all hope for the Royal Supremacy in 1836 and moved in Froude's direction, though without advocating theocracy. Rowlands states, "After Froude's death on 26 February, 1836 Newman hoped earnestly, as he informed Keble on 6 March, that it would be granted him to receive Froude's mantle. After so much procrastination and diffidence, Newman realised that the Royal Supremacy, far from benefiting the interests of the Church and University against an infidel Parliament, was inimical to both. It was unashamedly Erastian" (Rowlands, 111).

14. Newman, "Fall of De la Mennais," 140.

15. James Pereiro, *'Ethos' and the Oxford Movement: At the Heart of Tractarianism* (Oxford: Oxford University Press, 2008), 102.

problem along the lines to which Newman came to adhere.[16] As Newman recalls in his *Apologia*: "With Froude, Erastianism,—that is, the union (so he viewed it) of Church and State,—was the parent, or if not the parent, the serviceable and sufficient tool, of liberalism. Till that union was snapped, Christian doctrine could never be safe."[17]

Froude on the Erastian Threat of Doctrinal Corruption

In the period 1828–1833, the religious reforms proposed and passed by Parliament caused alarm to many Anglicans. Scholars debate whether this alarm had primarily political or primarily theological roots, but all agree that the Oxford Movement met a clear need at the time among a significant segment of Anglicans.[18] The proximate cause of the Oxford Movement was the Irish Church Temporalities Act of 1833, which significantly reduced the number of bishoprics and instituted some changes regarding Church-owned lands. Although it was this Act that prompted John Keble to preach his sermon "National Apostasy," Keble's sermon articulated a position that he, along with Newman and especially Froude, had been developing for some years—namely, that the English State was in the process of

16. See John Henry Newman, *Apologia Pro Vita Sua* (New York: Doubleday, 1989), 134–135.

17. Newman, 155.

18. For the argument that England's *ancien régime* collapsed in the early 1830s, thereby providing a strong stimulus to the Oxford Movement, see J.C.D. Clark, *English Society 1688–1832: Ideology, Social Structure and Political Practice during the Ancien Régime* (Cambridge: Cambridge University Press, 1985), as well as the discussion of Clarke's thesis in Stephen Thomas, *Newman and Heresy: The Anglican Years* (Cambridge: Cambridge University Press, 1991), 59–62. Thomas argues that "Newman's primary task" was a political one, namely, to convince the public that a breach had occurred; and on this basis Newman could then "re-examine the nature of the Church in relation to the ancient past and *reconstruct*, in a contested context, an ecclesiology and a theology, in a sophisticated bid for his countrymen's assent" (Thomas, 61–62). For background to the Whigs (often liberal Anglicans) who were understandably put off by the Oxford Movement, see Richard Brent, *Liberal Anglican Politics: Whiggery, Religion, and Reform, 1830–1841* (Oxford: Clarendon, 1987); as well as David De Giustino, "Finding an Archbishop: The Whigs and Richard Whately in 1831," *Church History* 64, no. 2 (1995): 218–236.

radically altering its commitments toward the Church of Christ (the Anglican Church). As Benjamin O'Connor says of "National Apostasy," "At the core of Keble's argument was the claim that the Church of England was a truly apostolic successor, whose operations should not and could not be overtaken or controlled by the government."[19]

This view of the Church of England was shared by few Whigs, who generally favored State support of religious pluralism and opposed the political power of bishops. Like the other founders of the Oxford Movement, Keble abhorred and feared the influential ideas of the eighteenth-century Anglican bishop William Warburton, author of *The Alliance between Church and State*, which combined a strong Whig Erastianism with Latitudinarianism.[20] Evangelical Anglicans likewise opposed Warburton's theological views, but "High Church" viewpoints—for example on Baptism or on the bishops as successors of the Apostles—differentiated the Oxford Movement from the Evangelical Anglicanism of such great figures as William Wilberforce. Frank Turner argues that the Oxford Movement was "a nineteenth-century religious experiment intended to counter the eighteenth-century evangelical religious experiment and all that had flowed therefrom."[21] Yet like Evangelical Anglicans, the leaders of

19. Benjamin O'Connor, "The Oxford Movement," in *Authority, Dogma, and History: The Role of the Oxford Movement Converts in the Papal Infallibility Debates*, ed. Kenneth L. Parker and Michael J.G. Pahls (Bethesda, MD: Academica, 2009), 9–43, at 16. For further background to "National Apostasy" and the development of Keble's thought, including his political thought regarding care for the poor, see Rowlands, *Church, State and Society*, 46–59.

20. See William Warburton, *The Alliance between Church and State: Or, the Necessity and Equity of an Established Religion and a Test Law Demonstrated*, 4th ed. (London: A. Millar and J. and R. Tonson, 1766). For discussion of Warburton's ideas, see John Keble, "Unpublished Papers of Bishop Warburton" (a book review originally published in the April 1841 issue of the *British Critic*), in Keble, *Occasional Papers and Reviews* (London: James Parker, 1877), 108–147.

21. Frank M. Turner, *John Henry Newman: The Challenge to Evangelical Religion* (New Haven, CT: Yale University Press, 2002), 158. I agree with Turner that Newman, like the other Tractarians, was opposed to much within Evangelical Anglicanism, though (*pace* Turner) religious liberalism (joined to Erastianism) was the primary opponent of the Oxford Movement—and the promotion of the true Gospel and the true Church of Christ was the primary constructive purpose.

the Oxford Movement were concerned to promote a living faith in the true Gospel, on the grounds that "only truth is capable of shaping man into the likeness of Christ, which is the object of man's sanctification."[22] Keble's "National Apostasy" therefore took particular aim (in James Pereiro's words) "at the dominant national *ethos*" whose "symptoms" were "growing indifference" and "following the rule of public opinion rather than the rule of truth"—that is, religious liberalism.[23]

22. Pereiro, *Theories of Development in the Oxford Movement*, 146. Yngve Brilioth pointed out some time ago that "a direct connection existed between Tractarianism and Evangelicalism. . . . The Tractarians were in great measure recruited from Evangelicals" (*The Anglican Revival: Studies in the Oxford Movement* [London: Longmans, Green, 1933], 43); and this view has been seconded by various studies, including David Newsome, *The Parting of Friends: The Wilberforces and Henry Manning* (London: John Murray, 1966), and Owen Chadwick, "The Mind of the Oxford Movement," in his *The Spirit of the Oxford Movement: Tractarian Essays* (Cambridge: Cambridge University Press, 1990), 1–53, at 18, as well as more recent work. For Brilioth, however, the fact that persons converted from Evangelicalism to Oxford-Movement Anglicanism and then to Catholicism can partly "be explained by the fact that the pendulum of human life, when once set going, has an innate tendency to swing to the utmost extreme" (Brilioth, 43). See also Brilioth, *The Anglican Revival* and his *Three Lectures on Evangelicalism and the Oxford Movement* (Oxford: Oxford University Press, 1934); and most recently Peter B. Nockles, "The Oxford Movement and Evangelicalism: Parallels and Contrasts in Two Nineteenth-Century Movements of Religious Revival," in *Perfecting Perfection: Essays in Honour of Henry D. Rack*, ed. Robert Webster (Cambridge: James Clarke, 2016), 233–259. For contemporaneous Evangelical critiques of the Oxford Movement, see Peter Toon, *Evangelical Theology, 1833–1856: A Response to Tractarianism* (London: Marshall, Morgan, and Scott, 1979) and Grayson Carter, *Anglican Evangelicals: Protestant Secessions from the Via Media, c. 1800–1850* (Oxford: Clarendon, 2001).

23. Pereiro, *'Ethos' and the Oxford Movement*, 102; for the role of "ethos" in Newman's depiction of early patristic heresies, see also Thomas' *Newman and Heresy*, 27. Here may be the place to note that Keble, in the 1840s, chose to remain an Anglican on the grounds (summarized by Pereiro) that "the right *ethos* tilted the balance toward the Church of one's baptism: given the complexity of the question, remaining in the Church of one's baptism was more in accordance with humility and self-distrust" (*'Ethos' and the Oxford Movement*, 224). Thomas finds a version of this view of "ethos" in Newman's May 1829 sermon "Religious Faith Rational," which appears in an edited form in Newman's *Parochial and Plain Sermons* (San Francisco: Ignatius Press, 1987), 121–128, and which argues that in faith "we obey God primarily because we actually feel His presence in our consciences bidding us obey Him" (Newman, 127). For further background, see John Henry Newman's appreciative 1846 essay "John Keble," in Newman, *Essays Critical and Historical*, vol. 2, ed. Nicholas Schofield (Leominster, UK: Gracewing, 2019), 499–536, and the background to Keble's situation after 1845 provided by Edward Short, *Newman and His Contemporaries* (New York: T.&T. Clark International, 2011), 65–76.

Prior to the Irish Church Temporalities Act, the 1832 Reform Act removed the selection of members of Parliament from the hands of the landed gentry, expanded the ranks of voters, and bestowed new Parliamentary seats upon the larger cities. These things mattered because the Anglican Church relied upon the patronage of the landed gentry and was weak in the cities. Thus, the Reform Act seemed likely to produce a Parliament that would have less interest in protecting traditional Anglican orthodoxy. Moreover, in 1828 Parliament passed the Sacramental Test Act, repealing the Test Act of 1673 and the Corporation Act of 1661. Although these latter two Acts had not been enforced for some time, they still served a symbolic function in requiring that elected members of corporations and all civil and military officeholders take the Oath of Supremacy and Allegiance and receive communion in the Anglican Church. And in 1829, Parliament passed the Catholic Relief Act, ensuring that Catholics could freely hold office in government and serve in Parliament.[24]

In short, the British government no longer considered membership in the Anglican Church to be necessary for most high offices. This stance seemed to undermine the very notion of a national Church. Newman, Froude, and Keble reasonably feared that it presaged doctrinal changes, given that popular opinion (the determining factor in Parliamentary elections) was tending in a religiously liberal direction. Anglicans who reverenced the Royal Supremacy—the monarch's oath to nourish and guide the Anglican Church—feared that Parliament might take over entirely. Piers Brendon describes this concern: "A Parliament disaffected by Dissenters and Roman Catholics and pushed in a revolutionary direction by popular representation would not hesitate to usurp totally the Crown's ecclesiastical patronage and take over its role as head of the Church."[25]

24. See Piers Brendon, *Hurrell Froude and the Oxford Movement* (London: Paul Elek, 1974), xv, which provides further context: "The repeal of the Test and Corporation Acts did little more than ratify what annual acts of indemnity had already been achieving. The Duke of Wellington had only allowed Roman Catholic emancipation because he feared civil war in Ireland."

25. Brendon, xv.

Brendon adds an additional factor: behind the reforms of 1828–1833 stood eighteenth-century Whig policies favoring Latitudinarianism in the Anglican Church. In the seventeenth century, England had suffered through numerous religious conflicts that threatened the fabric of the nation, and so "the men of the eighteenth century were pleased to welcome a period of toleration, latitudinarianism and laxity on the part of the Establishment."[26] But the result was the Methodist movement and eventual schism, leading to a further weakening of Anglicanism. Brendon deems that in the eighteenth century, "By acknowledging its Erastianism and accepting its eclecticism the [Anglican] Church had become a reliable moral policeman instead of a potentially subversive force."[27]

Froude perceived this situation acutely, and it was especially his arguments that inspired his friends Keble and Newman to raise the alarm. In both Keble and Newman, what J.H.L. Rowlands calls "the spirit of Froude" came to the surface in 1833 and indeed throughout the 1830s.[28] Thus, in a letter written while visiting Rome with Froude, on April 16, 1833, Newman complains that the British Crown has "become but a Creature of an Infidel Parliament."[29] He calls upon faithful Anglicans to demand recognition of the bishops' independence from the State, precisely as Froude urged.

According to Frank Turner, Froude introduced Newman "to his radical Catholic views of the English Church as an apostolic foundation," in addition to his anti-Erastianism.[30] Already in 1829, Newman had broken with

26. Brendon, xiii.

27. Brendon, xiv. On Methodism, Brendon remarks sympathetically: "There were voices which tried to rouse the Church from its lethargy, the most insistent and influential, of course, being that of John Wesley. The impetus of Methodism, however, was so great that, after Wesley's restraining hand had been removed in 1791, it quickly broke away from the Church of England. It is a sad but true fact that schism (and not oecumenicalism) invariably signals a new birth of religious vigour just as *odium theologicum* is a symptom of strength and not weakness in a church" (Brendon, xiv).

28. Rowlands, *Church, State and Society*, 89.

29. John Henry Newman, Letter to Walter John Trower, 16 April 1833, in *The Letters and Diaries of John Henry Newman*, vol. 3, ed. Thomas Gornall and Ian Ker (Oxford: Oxford University Press, 1979), 293, cited in Turner, *John Henry Newman*, 149.

30. Turner, *John Henry Newman*, 127. See the excellent treatment of Newman's

Whately and Hawkins and joined instead with Froude to oppose the reelection of Robert Peel as a member of Parliament representing Oxford. Peel had not kept his promise to support the Establishment but instead had supported Catholic political rights.[31] Newman and Froude supported an Evangelical Anglican who was more firmly committed to the privileges of the Anglican Church.[32] Around the same time, Newman promoted the bishops' independence from the State in letters to his sisters and mother, in which he bemoaned the spirit of "latitudinarianism, indifferentism, republicanism, and schism, a spirit which tends to overthrow doctrine, as if the fruit of bigotry."[33]

I note that in Turner's view, Newman and Froude were at this time "angry" men marked by "intemperance of spirit and violence of language" and committed to an "extreme" theological position.[34] Keble fares no better;

Evangelical years in Thomas L. Sheridan, "Justification," in *The Cambridge Companion to John Henry Newman*, 98–117, at 98–104.

31. Newman later brilliantly critiqued Peel's religious worldview in his 1841 "The Tamworth Reading Room," in *Discussions and Arguments on Various Subjects*, ed. Gerard Tracey and James Tolhurst (Notre Dame, IN: University of Notre Dame Press, 2004), 254–305. For background, see David P. Delio, *'An Aristocracy of Exalted Spirits': The Idea of the Church in Newman's* Tamworth Reading Room (Leominster, UK: Gracewing, 2016), including Delio's instructive discussion of Peel's tenure as a member of Parliament from Oxford, and Newman's opposition to Peel's re-election, at 17–26; as well as Nockles, "'Church and King,'" 96–97. Delio recognizes that the fears about the relationship of Church and State shared by many of those who opposed Peel in 1829 blossomed into the Oxford Movement in 1832–1833, as the opponents of Peel "increasingly believed that an Erastian State could no longer be a trusted ally for the Church" (*'An Aristocracy of Exalted Spirits,'* 27).

32. Yet as Geertjan Zuijdwegt remarks, "After the Peel debacle, Newman remained on cordial terms with Whately and his circle right up to Whately's departure for Dublin in 1831" (Zuijdwegt, "Richard Whately," in *The Oxford Handbook of John Henry Newman*, 196–216, at 199). Froude, too, retained warm feelings for Whately. Things changed in 1833 with the events that inaugurated the Oxford Movement, but already in 1827, as Zuijdwegt shows, Newman had begun to separate himself theologically from Whately (specifically on Trinitarian doctrine), and he continued along this path with increasing firmness in the next few years.

33. John Henry Newman, Letter to his mother, 13 March 1829, in *The Letters and Diaries of John Henry Newman*, vol. 2, ed. Thomas Gornall and Ian Ker (Oxford: Oxford University Press, 1979), 130, quoted in Turner, *John Henry Newman*, 128. See also Newman's sermon "The Self-Wise Inquirer" (October 1830), in *Parochial and Plain Sermons*, 137–144, where he concludes by depicting the sad progress of a (Lockean) religious liberal.

34. Turner, *John Henry Newman*, 164. Turner suggests, on very slim grounds, that both

he seems to Turner to have become "a person of narrow, angry, and extreme opinions" who by the early 1830s had lost the "keener intellect, more moderate temper, and famously sweet disposition" of his younger years.[35] I do not share Turner's viewpoint. Trying to explain psychologically the shift that he has identified, Turner notes that Froude's father, an Anglican archdeacon, had been subject to popular abuse following the Reform Act; and Keble, too, was from a conservative clerical family. For his part, Newman had been humiliated by his father's financial collapse and eventual bankruptcy and, in Turner's opinion, had a deep-seated need for status. These claims seem a stretch, since there is plentiful evidence that all three men were motivated by concern about the truth of the Gospel. If one must go to an extreme, it makes better sense of the evidence to join Rowlands in praising Keble as "never intemperate, let alone unkind, unfair or unscrupulous."[36]

Froude and Newman were motivated by homosexual repression (see Turner, 430). For similar suggestions, see Geoffrey Faber, *Oxford Apostles: A Character Study of the Oxford Movement* (London: Faber and Faber, 1933); and Rune Imberg, "Who, Then, Was Dr. Newman?—The Man and the Myth," in *From Oxford to the People*, 198–202, at 199–200—as well as the exasperation expressed by Stanley L. Jaki, *Newman's Challenge* (Grand Rapids, MI: Eerdmans, 2000), 146. More broadly, see Rune Imberg, *In Quest of Authority: The "Tracts for the Times" and the Development of the Tractarian Leaders, 1833–1841* (Lund, SE: Lund University Press, 1987). Like Turner, Chapman, and others, Imberg holds that "Newman was, in fact, a sceptic who found refuge in the claims of authority proclaimed by the Roman Catholic Church" ("Who, Then, Was Dr. Newman?," 201)—a claim that Newman repeatedly denied, as for example in his 1871 response to "those more than friendly critics of mine, who, in their perplexity to find a motive sufficient for my becoming a Catholic, attribute the step in me personally (without any warrant, I think, from anything that I have said or written) to a desire for a firmer ground of religious certitude, and a clearer view of revealed truth than is furnished in the Church of England" ("Note on Essay X," in *Essays Critical and Historical*, vol. 2 [London: Longmans, Green, 1895], 74–111, at 75; Newman is making the point that he became Catholic because he discerned that the Catholic Church was the true Church, not out of a desire to ward off skeptical thoughts). A rich account of Newman's conversions and his affective maturation is found in Walter E. Conn, *Conscience and Conversion in Newman: A Developmental Study of Self in John Henry Newman* (Milwaukee, WI: Marquette University Press, 2010). For an assessment of Turner's work and its reception, see Eamon Duffy, "The Reception of Turner's Newman: A Reply to Simon Skinner," *The Journal of Ecclesiastical History* 63, no. 3 (2012): 534–548.

35. Turner, *John Henry Newman*, 72.

36. Rowlands, *Church, State and Society*, 87.

Quite rightly, Turner emphasizes that the early nineteenth-century Church of England was fast losing parishioners to the Baptists, Methodists, and even Roman Catholics, and this situation was a serious cause for concern. Educated persons increasingly did not take Anglicanism seriously, thereby weakening the prestige of the clergy among the gentry, to whom clergymen often owed their positions. In a rapidly urbanizing nation, most of the clergy were stationed in sparsely attended rural parishes. It followed that Anglican clergy more and more depended upon the State for their income and status. In this context, the Irish Church Temporalities Act seemed to bode ill for State support in the future; by abolishing bishoprics and redistributing monies, it "seemed a prelude to the general spoliation of the English Church."[37] For Turner, it follows that the Oxford movement was primarily an outgrowth of social and economic self-interest. He maintains, "In *Tract 1*, dated September 9, 1833, Newman issued a clarion call for the reasserting of social authority on the part of Church of England clergy and directly addressed the innermost fears of those clergy lacking formal protections for their individual status."[38]

Turner's reading of Newman's "clarion call" is misleading. Indeed, even he admits that the first Tracts (written by Newman) actually emphasized a *theological* point—namely, the Church of England was worth defending not because of any intrinsic link to the State but because of its apostolic descent and its faithful handing on of the doctrines and practices of the

37. Brendon, *Hurrell Froude and the Oxford Movement*, xvi. Brendon provides helpful context, remarking that some reformers at this time "talked in terms of more draconian measures such as the confiscation of Church property and disestablishment. The Church made a feeble effort to pre-empt the reformers by diverting some of the revenues of the opulent chapter of Durham Cathedral to found the University, by a few picayune pieces of ecclesiastical legislation and by setting up a commission of enquiry composed of safe men. Such delaying tactics might have worked but for the Established Church's Achilles' heel—Ireland. There all the ecclesiastical abuses complained of by Lord Henley in England were multiplied. The situation was aggravated by the fact that since 1829 the impoverished Roman Catholic population had grown increasingly reluctant, especially in the face of attempts at coercion to pay their tithes and support the alien Church. The Whigs' solution was the Temporalities Bill (1833)" (Brendon, xvi).

38. Turner, *John Henry Newman*, 169.

Apostles in its teachings and sacraments. Along with the Roman Catholic Church and the Eastern Orthodox Church—both of which, for Newman in 1833, were corrupted in far more significant ways than was the Anglican Church—the Anglican Church was in Newman's view a branch of the now divided one, holy, catholic, and apostolic Church. In Tract 1, Newman urges his readers to insist upon the bishops' status as successors of the Apostles and upon the dignity of priests and deacons as possessors of sacramental power.[39]

These points make a claim about what it means for the Church to be in line with the apostolic Church; they seek "to bring the Church to a realisation of her own nature as a divine institution and, as such, a body essentially independent of state control."[40] The Tracts' content differs from Evangelical Anglicanism, but they share with Evangelicalism a strong spiritual fervor. Besides, as Brendon notes, "By the 1830s the Evangelical revival within the Church of England had lost momentum. The spiritual impulse which had inspired the Clapham Sect and its allies seemed to be waning. The most famous Evangelical [Anglican] leader, William Wilberforce, died in 1833."[41] It seems fair to say that the Tracts were motivated not primarily by economic interests or psychological motives, but by a sincere attempt (in Benjamin O'Connor's words) "to defend the theological and historical tradition of the Church of England . . . so it would not fold in the face of the Erastian challenge."[42]

During their trip to Italy in 1833, Newman and Froude paid close attention to the developing situation in England. Perhaps most notably, Keble wrote them about a plan broached by Thomas Arnold, who once had been a close friend of Keble but who, having lost faith in the Trinity, now thought that he could perceive (along religiously liberal lines) "an

39. See Turner, 171.

40. Brendon, *Hurrell Froude and the Oxford Movement*, xvi–xvii.

41. Brendon, xiv. Newman mentored William Wilberforce's sons, three of whom eventually became Catholic.

42. O'Connor, "The Oxford Movement," 19.

immanent historical development towards an ethical society in the history of the state," so that "once the spiritual community of the church was internalised as the conscience of the nation . . . the church would become superfluous, or would simply become the real substance of the political order, now characterised as a 'Christian Kingdom.'"[43] A position more widely separated from that of Keble, Froude, and Newman could hardly be imagined. In his pamphlet, Arnold called for reforming "the Church to avoid the disaster of disestablishment," but Keble deemed his reform proposal to be far worse than disestablishment could ever be.[44] Arnold sought to redefine the Church of England on the grounds that "the Church, as it now stands, no human power can save."[45] In his view, Anglican churches should now open their doors to other religious bodies, so that as much of England's populace as possible would be able to enter into the Anglican communion—thus preserving a truly State Church while bringing to an end any serious State Church concern about doctrinal differences.

In a letter from Rome, Newman condemned Arnold's plan as epitomizing religious liberalism. With sarcasm, Newman remarks in his letter that Parliament could strengthen Arnold's proposed "reform" by passing an

43. Toews, "Church and State," 634.

44. Ian Ker, *John Henry Newman: A Biography* (Oxford: Oxford University Press, 1988), 66. See Thomas Arnold, "Principles of Church Reform" (originally published in 1833, including a Postscript responding to critics), in *Miscellaneous Works of Thomas Arnold, D.D.*, ed. A.P. Stanley (London: B. Fellowes, 1845), 73–130. Arnold sums up in his Postscript: "The substance of what I endeavoured to show was this,—that a Church Establishment is one of the greatest national blessings; that its benefits have been lessened, and are now in danger of being forfeited altogether, by its being based on too narrow a foundation, and being not so much the Church of England, as of a certain part of the people of England; and that in order at once to secure it from destruction, and to increase its efficiency as an instrument of national good, it should be made more comprehensive in its doctrines, its constitution, and its ritual. . . . I have supposed it impossible to include at present the Roman Catholics, the Quakers, and the Unitarians: it may be, that other bodies of Dissenters whom we might be willing to admit, would themselves object to the union, and would prefer their present independence. . . . But if the Establishment were to set its doors widely open, do we doubt that within fifty years the great mass of the dissenting population would gladly enter them?" (Arnold, 118–119).

45. Quoted in Brendon, *Hurrell Froude and the Oxford Movement*, xv, from A.P. Stanley, *The Life and Correspondence of Thomas Arnold D.D.* (London: Ward & Lock, 1846), 253. For discussion of Arnold's views, see also Brilioth, *The Anglican Revival*, 86–91.

Act decreeing two Sundays per week, thereby ensuring that each religious body would be able to meet at the Anglican parish church on a "Sunday" morning. He further adds that the Jews and Muslims could meet at the reconstituted Anglican parish on Friday and Saturday mornings, respectively.[46] His point is that Erastianism, in its openly post-confessional form, can lead only to new triumphs of pluralism in which Christian doctrine will go by the wayside.

Writing from Naples to H.A. Woodgate, Newman sets forth the anti-Erastian vision that he and Froude would implement on their return to England. He urges Woodgate "to join the brotherhood of those who wish a return to the primitive state of the Church, when it was not a mere instrument of civil government, which it approaches to be now."[47] In Newman's view, the evident problem with the Church now being "a mere instrument of civil government" is that such a Church cannot hope to communicate faithfully the Gospel of Jesus Christ. Froude, too, emphasized that the Anglican Church risks doctrinal collapse (in a Latitudinarian or liberal direction) unless it unbinds itself from the State—at least through the bishops reasserting their unique privilege to oversee doctrine and Church discipline as successors of the Apostles.

James Pereiro has shown that the concept of "ethos" had a particular importance for Keble, Froude, and Newman. Pereiro states, "Froude absorbed the concept of *ethos* from Keble, refined it further and made it central to his vision of the intellectual and religious life, developing at length the relationship between character and opinions, especially in the religious sphere."[48] Froude was already writing about this relationship in 1827. Inquiring into how errors in belief could prevent someone from inheriting the kingdom of God, Froude reasoned that this could only be possible if

46. See Ker, *John Henry Newman*, 66, quoting "Letter to R. F. Wilson, March 18, 1833," in *The Letters and Diaries of John Henry Newman*, vol. 3, 257–258.

47. Quoted in Ker, *John Henry Newman*, from *The Letters and Diaries of John Henry Newman*, vol. 3, 300.

48. Pereiro, *'Ethos' and the Oxford Movement*, 99.

the assent to the truths of faith partly comes through a movement of will. If we habituate ourselves to good actions and our wills are good, we will find ourselves assenting internally to the doctrines of faith.[49] Furthermore, "a moment arrives inevitably when one becomes responsible for adhering to error" or else chooses the truth.[50] No doubt, attention is needed here both to the role of grace and to the possibility of invincible ignorance. On these latter counts, Newman eventually moved beyond Froude.[51]

For my purposes, the point is a simple one: Froude and Newman, along with Keble, were motivated in 1833 not primarily by desire for power or status, but by sincere anti-Erastian concerns and by belief in the

49. Although Froude's position here has its distinctive characteristics, Nockles points out that the emphasis on holiness and asceticism found among the Tractarians accords broadly with some seventeenth- and eighteenth-century High Church spirituality, such as the influential eighteenth-century work of William Law (who even established a religious community of vowed women in 1761 in an attempt to revive religious orders—something that Pusey also later did). At the same time, however, a significant part of High Church or Orthodox Anglicanism cautioned against such spirituality as unsuitable enthusiasm, characteristic of Methodists or Roman Catholics rather than of true Anglicans. See Nockles, *The Oxford Movement in Context*, 184–190. Nockles grants that "the representatives of High Churchmanship with which the rising Tractarians had contact in the later 1820s and early 1830s, and which Newman witheringly satirised as 'condescending and pompous,' stiff and 'priggish,' were arguably more deserving of the 'High and Dry' label than their eighteenth-century predecessors" (Nockles, 197). Nockles links Tractarian spirituality with "Hutchinsonian" spirituality, and he shows that eighteenth-century High Church Anglicans were contending against "the Evangelical emphasis on an inward, sensible perception of the Holy Spirit as test of faith"—and the Tractarians concurred in this "dislike of the Evangelical tendency to regard subjective feelings as a test of truth" (Nockles, 195, 199).

50. Pereiro, *'Ethos' and the Oxford Movement*, 100. For Froude, part of having a good will involves not relying upon our own private judgment in matters of divine revelation, but rather receiving divine revelation obediently from God as mediated by the Church. Pereiro explains that for Froude, "there are as many different prejudices and opinions as there are different turns of mind and different moral histories. People, whether they are conscious of it or not, are likely to be prejudiced to some degree in the examination of evidence, inclined to underrate and neglect some while overrating and overemphasizing others. The fact that they may not be conscious of those prejudices only makes their influence more pervasive and determining. On the basis of this theory Froude criticized the Protestant principle of private judgement" (Pereiro, 101).

51. In his Roman Catholic years, Newman believed that Protestants and even unbelievers could be saved, given the likelihood that many of them were invincibly ignorant about Catholicism, and also given (in the case of Protestants) the many blessings received from Baptism, reading Scripture, and so forth.

importance of apostolic doctrine in fostering the path to sanctity. In their view, the doctrinal content of the Gospel matters.

Whereas many commentators present Keble as the main influence upon Froude, it will be clear that I agree with those commentators who perceive that Froude was also a major influence upon Keble. Keble encouraged Froude's piety, while "Froude inspired Keble to think beyond Tory High Churchmanship."[52] Peter Nockles rightly remarks with Keble in view, "Froude's influence on the attitude of other Tractarian leaders to establishment was potent."[53]

The extent of Newman's debts to Froude has been noted by many scholars, as well as by Newman himself in the *Apologia*. Yet these debts have perhaps been best shown by Brendon in his *Hurrell Froude and the Oxford Movement*. Some of the debts may be attributed to similar worldviews from childhood. Newman resonated with the fact that "from childhood Froude's mind had been impressed with the mysterious coexistence

---

52. Short, *Newman and His Contemporaries*, 27. Short devotes an instructive chapter to "John Keble and the Crisis of Tractarianism." For an account of the "High Church" Anglicanism that provided context for the Oxford Movement, see Peter Nockles, *The Oxford Movement in Context*. Even Nockles admits that "an element among the Orthodox [High Church] undoubtedly considered themselves primarily as servants of the establishment," although he shows that many held that establishment "was by no means essential to the church's existence" (Nockles, 62, 65). Nockles insists upon "the coherence of pre-Tractarian High Churchmanship," while surveying "the painful breach that came to separate old High Churchmen and Tractarians" (Nockles, 19, 21). Nockles directs attention to such works as F.C. Mather, *High Church Prophet: Bishop Samuel Horsley (1733–1806) and the Caroline Tradition in the Later Georgian Church* (Oxford: Oxford University Press, 1992); J.C.D. Clark, *English Society, 1688–1832: Ideology, Social Structure and Political Practice during the Ancien Régime*; and Elizabeth A. Varley, *The Last of the Prince Bishops: William Van Mildert and the High Church Movement of the Early Nineteenth Century* (Cambridge: Cambridge University Press, 1992).

53. Nockles, *The Oxford Movement in Context*, 82. Nockles notes that while Keble remained "haunted by the spectre of a separation between church and state," nevertheless "in private correspondence Keble began to sound more like Froude, eschewing compromise and even threatening dramatic gestures," such as threatening to refuse to take the Oath of Supremacy (Nockles, 83). As Nockles says, "there were limits to Froude's influence on Keble. For Keble, it was Hooker, albeit with the addition of his own gloss . . . who remained a sure guide on church-state matters" (Nockles, 83).

and interpenetration of the spiritual and the material universes."[54] Brendon names three foundational connections between Froude's ideas and Newman's, although the influence of Keble is also present here: "a deep commitment to the quest for holiness, a belief in the immanence of the spiritual world and a mistrust of reason as an alternative to faith and obedience."[55]

When Froude and Newman met in 1826, Newman was still under the joint influences of Whately and Evangelicalism. Brendon demonstrates that, by 1828, "Froude's theological views . . . began, by a gradual process of osmosis, to permeate Newman's consciousness."[56] Brendon notes that Froude had strong political interests as well as theological ones, as Turner also highlights. Froude opposed the Reform Act of 1832 with bellicose words, since he thought it favored the Latitudinarians and Dissenters by taking power away from the gentry.[57] At the same time, however, Froude increasingly took a sharp line against Erastianism as such, aided by historical studies of Henry II's conflict with Thomas à Becket and of Cardinal Pole's opposition to Henry VIII. Brendon sums up, "The solution to the ecclesiastical problem of Froude's own day seemed to be to counter the designs of the Whigs by cutting the Church away from the State and putting it beyond their jurisdiction."[58]

Was Froude, then, the true leader in 1833? All historians can agree (as did Newman) with Brendon's affirmation that "the force of his personality

54. Brendon, *Hurrell Froude and the Oxford Movement*, 90.

55. Brendon, 91. See also the portrait of Keble—more negative than I think warranted, but still generally appreciative—offered by Owen Chadwick in his "The Limitations of Keble," in Chadwick, *The Spirit of the Oxford Movement*, 54–62.

56. Brendon, *Hurrell Froude and the Oxford Movement*, 93.

57. Paul Vaiss observes that, influenced by Froude, "Newman's last university sermon for 1832 has a decidedly political turn. He firmly denounces the new spirit of the age which was manifest in the events surrounding the failure of the Reform Bill in 1831 and the unprecedented torrent of abuse it unleashed against the bishops of the Church of England who had voted against it. Newman reasserts the duties of obedience and the sacred character of the priesthood" (Vaiss, "Newman's State of Mind on the Eve of His Italian Tour," in *From Oxford to the People*, 203–222, at 213).

58. Brendon, *Hurrell Froude and the Oxford Movement*, 112.

gave him remarkable sway over Newman's mind at this time."[59] But Brendon denies that Froude ever was the leader of the Oxford Movement, even in its nascent stages. Here he agrees with Newman's *Apologia Pro Vita Sua*, which assigns the primary (practical) leadership role to Keble. Nevertheless, Froude's ideas and boldness shaped the early direction of the movement in every way. It was he who insisted upon a "radical Apostolical gospel" with the goal of renewing Anglicanism in an anti-Erastian way, before doctrinal corruption could take root.[60]

In light of the above background, let me now survey Froude's "Remarks on State Interference in Matters Spiritual," published, in its original form, at the very outset of the Oxford Movement in 1833. I will here examine the expanded version that Newman and Keble printed in their *Remains of the Late Reverend Richard Hurrell Froude*.[61] As Yngve Brilioth observes, "Froude saw more clearly than others at an early date how the Liberal reforms of 1828 and 1829 removed the very pillars of the English Church Constitution."[62]

Froude begins this lengthy article by referring to "the recent changes which have taken place in our political constitution."[63] He argues that, taken together, the repeal of the Test and Corporation Acts and the passage of Roman Catholic emancipation, along with the 1832 Reform Act, have done away with Parliament's ability to act as an "Ecclesiastical Legislature"

---

59. Brendon, 127.

60. Brendon, 128.

61. The *Remains* proved quite controversial and alienated many who had previously supported the Oxford Movement. Ciaran Brady comments, "Though it has inevitably been associated with Newman, the origins of the idea that Hurrell's unpublished papers should serve as his memorial can be traced to the Froudes themselves, and to the archdeacon and brother William in particular" (Brady, *James Anthony Froude*, 65). Nevertheless, as Brady goes on to say, "Newman, Keble, and the Froudes fully expected to provoke outrage and controversy with the *Remains*, and when the first volumes appeared in March 1838 the storm they had hoped for duly broke" (Brady, 66).

62. Brilioth, *The Anglican Revival*, 203–204. For discussion of Froude's "Remarks on State Interference in Matters Spiritual," see Brilioth, 204–205.

63. Richard Hurrell Froude, "Remarks on State Interference in Matters Spiritual," in Froude, *Remains of the Late Reverend Richard Hurrell Froude*, vol. 2, ed. John Keble and John Henry Newman (London: J.G. & F. Rivington, 1839), 184–269, at 184.

in addition to acting as a civil legislature.[64] Classical Anglican theologians such as Richard Hooker (1554–1600) had argued that Parliament, as an explicitly Anglican body, represented the laity in the determination of the appointment of bishops and in other ecclesiastical functions. Froude emphasizes that now that Parliament is no longer explicitly Anglican, the traditional argument no longer works.

According to Froude, what is at stake here is nothing less than the status of "Christ's Holy Catholic and Apostolic Church."[65] Englishmen err if they think that ecclesiastical changes made in Parliament have simply to do with the English Church. It is the (Anglican) Catholic Church, the Church of Jesus Christ, that is at issue. Rather than attacking the establishment of the Anglican Church directly, Froude simply registers a warning: England has already entered into "a new system of Ecclesiastical Polity," since the old system in which an all-Anglican Parliament had oversight is no more.[66]

For Froude, the question now is to what degree the newly organized Parliament still has a right of governance over the internal workings of the English Church. Again, he grants that Parliament would have such a right if it were composed entirely of Anglicans. But non-Anglicans are not, or at least should not be, in a position to deliberate in a determinative way about the good of the Anglican Church. If members of Parliament have rejected the doctrines and communion of the Anglican Church, then they are inevitably the opponents or enemies of that Church.

Describing the persons whose authority over the Church he is contesting, he notes that while they may number among themselves Jews, Independents, Socinians, and atheists, they are best described on the whole as "latitudinarians"—that is, as religious liberals who do not care about Anglican doctrine as such.[67] Instead, they care about politics, and specifically

64. Froude, 185.
65. Froude, 186.
66. Froude, 186.
67. Froude, 189.

about peace and order. If the achievement of these political ends requires doctrinal compromises, this does not bother them.

True Anglicanism, Froude argues, cannot proceed on the basis of compromise with "dissenters [i.e., non-Anglican Christians] and latitudinarians."[68] And in fact, the recent changes in the English Constitution automatically entail changes for the English Church's constitution. Heretofore, Parliament had received its ecclesiastical role because Parliament was Anglican; but today the role that "had been reposed by our Apostolical predecessors on a power internal to the Church" (Parliament as an Anglican body) has been handed over to a power external to the Church (Parliament as a non-Anglican body).[69] The successors of the Apostles can delegate their authority to committed Anglicans, but they cannot do so to those who reject communion with the Anglican Church and who are thereby separated from full communion with the Apostles.

Froude hammers home this point repeatedly. If a non-Anglican political body has the power to nominate Anglican bishops, then something has gone awry. The government, headed by the Prime Minister, no longer needs to be comprised of Anglicans. It follows that the government is now intrinsically indifferent with regard to doctrine. Since the Anglican Church remains tied to the State, the principle of religious liberalism (doctrinal indifferentism) has been inscribed into the Anglican Church. A "latitudinarian government"—a government that has adopted the principles of religious liberalism—cannot be trusted with preserving the integrity of a doctrinal Church.[70]

Froude argues that the right to choose bishops never belonged to the

68. Froude, 191.

69. Froude, 192. For background to the Tractarian teaching on apostolic succession and the sacrament of Holy Orders, see Nockles, *The Oxford Movement in Context,* 151–152, which emphasizes that the Tractarian position went well beyond that of most High Churchmen and adopted the Nonjuring position of William Law. Nockles directs attention to an 1842 sermon by Edward Hawkins in which the latter makes this point in response to the Tractarians.

70. Froude, "Remarks on State Interference in Matters Spiritual," 195.

English government per se; the English Church allowed the English government to have this right, so long as the English government was exclusively Anglican. Now that it is not, the Church must insist upon its right to its own internal governance. The Church may not give up these sacred rights, bestowed on it by Christ, simply to preserve a peaceable or privileged relationship with the State. Froude recognizes that he will be accused of being a radical, a zealot, an "ultra." In response, he tells his conservative (High Church) critics, "By standing still you become a party to revolution."[71] The shift from an Anglican Parliament deciding on Church matters to a non-Anglican Parliament deciding on Church matters is nothing short of revolutionary.

Froude points out that Richard Hooker was the one who laid down the originally justifiable principle on these matters. In Hooker's view, the role of Parliament is to represent the consent of the laity to the laws devised by the Church, since the consent of the governed is part of the promulgation

71. Froude, 196. As Brilioth puts it, the political reforms of these years "banished Hooker's Church ideal for ever to the fairy regions of the theoretic ideal" (*The Anglican Revival*, 95). In Nockles' view, however, "the portrait of the conservatism and immobility of [High Church] attitudes to establishment presented by Froude, and Newman in his *Apologia*, was exaggerated. At this date, apart from the exception of Froude himself, inner differences between the two sides had scarcely surfaced. Not only were the Tractarians still imbued with elements of the 'Church and King' mentality, but the [High Church Anglicans] also were alive to the implications of the constitutional revolution of 1828–33" (Nockles, *The Oxford Movement in Context*, 79). As an example of the latter, Nockles cites Godfrey Faussett's 1834 Bampton Lectures. Nockles also adds that in "Remarks on State Interference in Matters Spiritual"—which, as Nockles points out, became Tract 59—Froude somewhat hid his radical rejection of establishment, and "sought to persuade rather than provoke the old High Churchmen" (Nockles, 80). Nockles concludes, "In reality, Froude's church-state ideal was not the constitutionalism of Hooker or even the Laudian theocracy of the Caroline Divines. Rather, it found its model exemplified by that unqualified ecclesiastical supremacy over the civil power in all capacities, symbolised by Becket and the twelfth-century church dictating to monarchs. Whereas old High Churchmen condemned the late medieval church's claim to spiritual dominion over the secular power as championed by Hildebrand, Froude's perspective was diametrically opposite. . . . To the dismay of old High Churchmen, Froude's brand of anti-Erastianism actually led him to identify with the anti-church and -state views of the Puritans in their struggle with 'High Church' episcopal opponents such as Whitgift and Bancroft. Froude privately even faulted Laud and the Caroline Divines on this point" (Nockles, 81–82).

of a law. Parliament functions as a "synod of the laity of the Church of England," just as Convocation is a synod of the clergy.[72] Obviously, Parliament cannot function as a lay synod if Parliament includes a significant number of non-Anglicans. Hooker allows Parliament a role in internal Church matters only if Parliament stands as a lay synod—and Parliament no longer does so.

In 1592, in a law to which Hooker gave approval, Parliament under Queen Elizabeth approved imprisoning anyone who obstinately refused to participate in Anglican worship by receiving communion. If someone convicted of this crime continued to refuse to worship as an Anglican, he was to be sent into exile; and if he dared to return from that exile without confessing Anglican faith, he was to be executed. Froude does not defend this law, but he notes that it certainly served the purpose of identifying the Anglican Church with the English Commonwealth. Although laws such as this one were changed, the identification of Church and commonwealth remained in place *de iure* until the recent reforms. Now that the identification between Church and commonwealth has been formally severed, the basis upon which Parliament validly oversaw internal Anglican matters no longer exists. In sum, says Froude, "our *civil* legislature is no longer qualified, as it formerly was, to be our *ecclesiastical* legislature."[73]

---

72. Froude, "Remarks on State Interference in Matters Spiritual," 198. Froude writes in all capital letters the words that I have quoted. In a November 1834 letter to Keble, however, Froude criticized Hooker. Citing this letter, James Pereiro remarks, "Erastianism was Froude's most serious charge against the Reformers, and he viewed it as the mainspring of their many other errors. Even Hooker came in for criticism because of his idea of a lay synod exercising powers within the Church: the notion was unecclesiastical and Whig" (Pereiro, *'Ethos' and the Oxford Movement*, 187). For Keble, who in 1836 published an edition of Hooker's works, Hooker merited praise especially for his sacramental doctrine. Brilioth comments that in Keble's introduction to this edition, Keble sought "to explain and modify Hooker's freer [by comparison to the Oxford Movement's] conception of Church government, especially the significance of the episcopate and its necessity" (*The Anglican Revival*, 123).

73. Froude, "Remarks on State Interference in Matters Spiritual," 207. Nockles remarks in response that Christopher "Wordsworth appealed to both Hooker and Burke against the Tractarian notion drawn from the later Nonjurors that church and state were two distinct societies only accidentally brought into a condition of union, and in favour of the contrary notion that they represented an organically unified single entity" (*The Oxford Movement in*

Yet it remains the case that the monarch must be an Anglican. Can the monarch simply assume all the duties that he or she once shared with Parliament? Froude answers that with regard to public acts, England's monarchs are in fact no longer independent of Parliament. The English monarch cannot, under the constitutional system (of Froude's day), resist the will of Parliament for very long. After all, the king first resisted the government's will regarding the Reform Act in 1832, but when the government proceeded to resign in protest, the king found himself unable to form another government and had to give way.[74] The point is that if the king actually were to assert himself on behalf of Anglican truth, he would not succeed if Parliament opposed him. Thus, appeal to the monarch as the representative of the laity—as the "lay synod" that Hooker deemed Parliament to be—is not feasible today.[75]

Froude recognizes that he may seem too negative about governmental power, which, according to Romans 13, has been ordained by God. In reply, Froude distinguishes between the power given by Christ to the State and the power given by Christ to the Church, in Matthew 16 and elsewhere. The latter power is "independent and essentially greater" than the State power, and it is "derived through the Successors of the Apostles from Christ Himself."[76] Regarding the distinction between Church and State, Froude has recourse to Gibbon's account of the early Church, after Christianity became the religion of the Roman Empire. The Church was never controlled by the emperor. The bishops insisted upon their rights in defining matters of doctrine

Context, 87). For William Gladstone, Nockles adds, "To advocate disestablishment would be to cut off many from possible means of salvation. This would be the real 'national apostasy'" (Nockles, 88).

74. For discussion of this event, see David Cannadine, *Victorious Century: The United Kingdom, 1800–1906* (London: Penguin, 2017), 159–160.

75. For background, see Zuijdwegt, "Richard Whately," 200–201. To Newman's great dismay, Whately (as Archbishop) argued in the House of Lords that the king has no right to interfere with parliamentary matters even when they bear upon the Church. For Newman, in Zuijdwegt's words, this meant that Whately "was disloyal to the Church: he had parried an attack—levelled by a brother bishop—on a Whig measure encroaching on the rights of his Church" (Zuijdwegt, 201).

76. Froude, "Remarks on State Interference in Matters Spiritual," 214.

and morality. The bishops were elected by the people and by the clergy, although "the Bishops could refuse to ordain an unworthy candidate."[77]

Froude thinks that since the fourteenth century at least, the pope has grasped too much power, overshadowing the right of the Christian people to elect the bishops. The pope has stolen not the power of the monarchs or Parliamentarians but rather the power of the Christian people to choose the successors of the Apostles. For Froude, the power claimed by the medieval popes over *kings* is not the problem, since such power merely replicates the bishops' power in the patristic era, even if the patristic bishops refrained from using that power against the emperor. Froude surveys fourteenth-century instances in which the English kings attempted to wrest control of the election of the archbishop of Canterbury from the monks of Canterbury and from the pope. In all such instances, the kings failed.

Turning to a textual analysis of the Acts that since Henry VIII have regulated the appointment of Anglican bishops, Froude demonstrates that their import is the following: "The rights of the whole Church of England, and of every individual member of it, laity, clergy, and Bishops, are surrendered unconditionally to one person,—the King."[78] This is highly problematic, but

77. Froude, 217.

78. Froude, 241. Nockles points out that Pusey, by contrast, retained a strong adherence "to the ideal of sacral monarchy as a bulwark of the church," and Pusey continued to hold this view even in the face of the Gorham Case of 1850 (Nockles, *The Oxford Movement in Context*, 75), see also Nockles' "Pusey and the Question of Church and State," in *Pusey Rediscovered*, ed. Perry Butler (London: SPCK, 1983), 255–297, especially his explanation on 287 of why for Pusey the outcome of the Gorham Case "did not warrant strictures against the whole ancient system of appellate royal jurisdiction as *per se* erastian." Newman, too, was a royalist for theological reasons in the early 1830s. Nockles states, "Newman's royalism was expressed in a passionate appeal to the crown [in 1833–1834] to use her Supremacy to defend the church against ministerial thralldom" (*The Oxford Movement in Context*, 76). Nockles, however, thinks Newman's position was shaky from the outset: "By 1836, Froude had induced Newman altogether to abandon his belief in the Royal Supremacy. Yet, already by the autumn of 1833, Newman's ambivalence towards the Church's traditional political props was evident" (Nockles, 77). Importantly, Nockles shows that "the contrast between Newman's theoretical defence of establishment in 1883–4 and the tone of his articles on 'The Convocation of the Province of Canterbury' in the *British Magazine*, 1834–5, is marked. In the latter, Newman reproduced, albeit toned down, Froude's earlier polemic against the constitutional basis of the Henrician settlement itself. Having only a year previously been prepared to make the Act

what is to be done? Froude responds that, with regard to members of other religious bodies, "a growing feeling has for a long time prevailed against all legislative interference with the freedom of conscience, and that more particularly on the subject of religion."[79] In his view, this trend should now be extended to the Anglican Church itself: the legislature should not interfere in the Church's internal matters. Here Froude distances himself from those who argue for disestablishment on other grounds. Put simply, why should he support abolishing the laws that recognize the true Church of Jesus Christ (the Anglican Church) to be the Church of the whole of England? Even if these laws have fallen into disrepair, it remains the case that such laws serve the common good by recognizing publicly the true Church.

Nevertheless, if the renunciation of State protection is the only way to ensure that State interference ceases, then disestablishment is necessary—and Froude implies that this situation has come to be. Anglicans must ensure that a liberal, non-Anglican Parliament (whether in 1833 or in the future) is not allowed to corrupt the doctrine of the true Church of Christ. What is at stake is nothing less than the ability of "Christ's Holy Catholic and Apostolic Church"[80] to proclaim the true Gospel.

John Henry Newman on Doctrinal Corruption

Let me now examine how Newman pushes Froude's concerns further. The central issue for both men is the threat of doctrinal corruption. As an

of Settlement the basis of his stand, for the first time, Newman now actually questioned in print the legitimacy of the Church's apparent surrender of juridical power to the state in 1534 as well as in 1689. . . . Far from being a temporary abuse to which the Church of England had been occasionally subject in her history, Newman already now regarded 'Erastianism' as her essential, natural condition. As he told Pusey in 1836, 'the English Church subsists in the state and has no internal consistency to keep it together.' This was doctrine subversive not merely of Hoadlyite principles but those of old High Churchmanship itself" (Nockles, 85, citing John Henry Newman to E.B. Pusey, 24 January 1836, in *The Letters and Diaries of John Henry Newman,* vol. 5, ed. Thomas Gornall [Oxford: Oxford University Press, 1981], 214).

79. Froude, "Remarks on State Interference in Matters Spiritual," 242.

80. Froude, 186.

Anglo-Catholic, Newman, like Froude, held that the Roman Catholic Church had in fact corrupted doctrine. In what follows, therefore, I first examine Newman's effort, in his 1837 *The Via Media of the Anglican Church* (also titled *Lectures on the Prophetical Office of the Church*), to show that the Anglican Church has not corrupted doctrine whereas the Roman Catholic Church has done so, even if not so far as to be a heretical Church rather than a real branch. As a second step, I attend to his explanation in his *Essay on the Development of Christian Doctrine* and *Apologia Pro Vita Sua* of the reasons why he changed his mind. I also briefly examine some remarks from his 1850 work *Certain Difficulties Felt by Anglicans in Catholic Teaching*, in which Newman, now a Catholic, condemns the Anglican Church as fatally Erastian.

In his *Apologia Pro Vita Sua*, Newman recalls that in his controversies as a leader of the Oxford Movement, he acted upon three principles. For my purposes in this chapter, the first of these principles is most significant. Namely, Newman grounded himself on what he calls "the principle of dogma," and at every step he sought to critique "the anti-dogmatic principle and its developments."[81] If the assent of faith does not unite us cognitively with divine realities, then it is worthless. For this reason, dogma has a high importance, since it mediates our connection with the realities that God reveals to us in Christ.

Avoiding Doctrinal Corruption as an Anglican

Given the central role of dogma, it is clearly imperative to avoid doctrinal corruption. Newman as an Anglo-Catholic strives to show that the Anglican Church has avoided it. As he says in his introduction to *The Via Media of the Anglican Church*, it is necessary to advance "a correct theory of the duties and office of the Church Catholic. . . . Rome supplies a doctrine, but

81. Newman, *Apologia Pro Vita Sua*, 163. For Newman's broad use of the term "principle" (focusing on *An Essay on the Development of Christian Doctrine*)—and for a critical appraisal, which I find persuasive only in part—see Nicholas Lash, *Newman on Development: The Search for an Explanation in History* (London: Sheed & Ward, 1975), 73–74, 106–109.

. . . an untrue one."[82] For Newman, the Roman Catholic Church has corrupted ecclesiological doctrine, and his goal is to ensure that the Church in England does not do so. In a letter to Hugh James Rose written in May 1836 while he was working on the *Via Media*, Newman remarks, "I cannot love the 'Church of England' commonly so designated—its very title is an offence . . . for it implies that it holds, not of the Church Catholic but of the State."[83] He fully embraces Froude's anti-Erastianism, and he is highly sensitive to the charge that Anglicanism is a "mere political religion."[84]

In Tract 41, published in 1834, Newman responded to a query about his plans for the renewal of the Church of England. He states, "I would do

---

82. John Henry Newman, *The Via Media of the Anglican Church*, 3rd ed., vol. 1 (London: Basil Montagu Pickering, 1877), 7. I do not cite the first edition of this work, since I generally prefer to cite Newman's final versions. For "old High Churchmen," as Nockles observes, "the Roman and Greek churches were 'true' in terms of order but in their modern form they were 'corrupt' in terms of doctrine" (*The Oxford Movement in Context*, 162; cf. 169–170 for High Churchmen who "used the common 'apostolical foundations' of the two churches as the basis for a proposed reunion," if the Church of Rome "renounced her later corruptions and returned to her supposedly 'primitive' condition"). A number of "old High Churchmen" held to a "distinction between Rome as metaphysically a 'true' church in its foundation, and as apostate and anti-Christian in its later teaching" (Nockles, 177).

83. John Henry Newman, Letter to Hugh James Rose, May 23, 1836, in *The Letters and Diaries of John Henry Newman*, vol. 5, 301–304, cited in Eamon Duffy, *John Henry Newman: A Very Brief History* (London: SPCK, 2019), 9.

84. Newman, *The Via Media of the Anglican Church*, 10. For the outworking of this fear, see Jay M. Hammond, "The Interplay of Hermeneutics and Heresy in the Process of Newman's Conversion from 1830 to 1845," in *Authority, Dogma, and History*, 45–75. Hammond notes that in 1839, "Newman detected the three aspects of liberalism in his own thought. First, he recognized that the *via media* was an intellectual compromise culpable of rationalism. Second, he realized that his individualistic use of antiquity in constructing the *via media* was an abuse of private judgment. Third, Augustine's phrase *securus judicat orbis terrarum*, revealed to Newman that he was guilty of ecclesiological error because he was cut off from the ancient Catholic Church" (Hammond, 68). By contrast, as Nockles remarks, the High Churchman William Palmer (of Worcester, not of Magdalen) "was supremely untroubled by Wiseman's application of St Augustine's *orbis terrarum* dictum. Palmer confidently resorted to the traditional Anglican view that it was the Roman and not the English church that was schismatical. For Palmer, as for the Caroline Divines, the Church of Rome had separated from the communion of the Eastern as well as the British churches" (*The Oxford Movement in Context*, 181). See Palmer's highly critical response to Newman's *An Essay on the Development of Christian Doctrine*: William Palmer, *The Doctrine of Development and Conscience Considered in Relation to the Evidence of Christianity and of the Catholic System* (London: France & John, 1846).

what our reformers in the 16th century did. . . . They kept the creeds as they were, but they *added* protests against the corruptions of faith, worship, and discipline, which had grown up round them."[85] At present, he thinks, the corruptions that threaten the Anglican doctrinal edifice have to do with "erastianism and latitudinarianism."[86] Erastianism and Latitudinarianism raise the issue of whether the Christian faith, as doctrinally expressed, is fundamentally what powerful people choose to impose.

These issues were especially pressing for Newman in the mid-1830s because, in his view, "Protestantism and Popery are real religions; no one can doubt about them; they have furnished the mould in which nations have been cast: but the [Anglican] *Via Media*, viewed as an integral system, has never had existence except on paper."[87] In his view at the time, existing "on paper" was not so bad, since the "paper" consisted in the writings of many of the greatest Anglican divines. Nevertheless, he deems that "it still remains to be tried whether what is called Anglo-Catholicism, the religion of Andrewes, Laud, Hammond, Butler, and Wilson, is capable of being professed, acted on, and maintained on a large sphere of action and through a sufficient period."[88]

---

85. John Henry Newman, "Tract 41: Via Media II," in *Tracts for the Times*, ed. James Tolhurst (Notre Dame, IN: University of Notre Dame Press, 2013), 116–128, at 119. For discussion of Tract 41 and a critical assessment of its arguments, see Thomas, *Newman and Heresy*, 185.

86. Newman, "Tract 41: Via Media II," 119.

87. Newman, *The Via Media of the Anglican Church*, 16. For Newman's constructive purpose here, see Christopher Cimorelli, *John Henry Newman's Theology of History: Historical Consciousness, Theological 'Imaginaries,' and the Development of Tradition* (Leuven, BE: Peeters, 2017), 202–203.

88. Newman, *The Via Media of the Anglican Church*, 17. See also Sheridan Gilley's conclusion: "There was . . . a paradox about the Tractarian insistence that the bishops were the successors of the Apostles and the Angels of the Churches when some of the bishops did not believe this themselves; though this was no more paradoxical than the movement's insistence that their Protestant clerical brethren were, whatever their opinions, really Catholic priests. Confronted, however, with Protestant or liberal bishops, the Anglo-Catholic clergy defied them with gusto. . . . The result was that having begun by reclaiming the doctrine of the Church, the Anglo-Catholics ended up believing in every doctrine of the Church except the doctrine of the Church. In effect, they lacked a convincing living authority" (Gilley, "The Ecclesiology of the Oxford Movement: A Reconsideration," in *From Oxford to the People*,

Newman grants that *if* the Anglican Church, like the Roman Catholic Church, has corrupted divine truth—that is, if the Anglican Church has ever committed itself formally to doctrines other than what is contained in Scripture and the Fathers—then it would be better to be outside the Church's institutional structures. Yet one of the divinely revealed truths in Scripture is the authority of the Church, precisely as an institutional reality. Therefore, the Protestant solution of *sola scriptura* does not work. Instead, Newman thinks, it is necessary to examine closely "Church authority, Tradition, the Rule of Faith, and the like."[89]

In this task, Newman's concern is to show that the Anglican Church is not fundamentally a creature of powerful human beings, but rather is Christ's true Church. This concern about power is not limited to Newman or to Anglo-Catholics. Joseph Ratzinger, for instance, describes in 1964 his dismay about the popular reception in Germany of the Second Vatican Council's ongoing work: "The impression grew steadily that nothing was now stable in the Church, that everything was open to revision. More and more the Council appeared to be like a great Church parliament that could

60–75, at 67–68). In his critical study of the Oxford Movement, which he faults for condemning the High Church tradition, Nockles grants that Newman in the period 1834–1837 developed a significant knowledge not only of the Caroline Divines but also of some eighteenth century High Churchmen. In Nockles' view, however, the problem was that Newman sought to systematize where no system could be imposed: "For Newman wished the Church of England literally to represent the church of antiquity in doctrinal fullness if she was to compete with the Church of Rome. Yet Newman was seeking the impossible. Caroline divinity, however blended, harmonised and supplemented, could never have fulfilled his expectation" (*The Oxford Movement in Context*, 130). Nockles is indebted to Stephen W. Sykes, "Newman, Anglicanism and the Fundamentals," in *Newman after a Hundred Years*, ed. Ian Ker and Alan G. Hill (Oxford: Clarendon, 1990), 353–374. See also Kenneth L. Parker, "Newman's Individualistic Use of the Caroline Divines in the *Via Media*," in *Discourse and Context: An Interdisciplinary Study of John Henry Newman*, ed. Gerard Magill (Carbondale, IL: Southern Illinois University Press, 1993), 33–42.

89. Newman, "Tract 41: Via Media II," 12. For background, colored by the *Ressourcement* movement (the book was originally published in German in 1961), see Günter Biemer, *Newman on Tradition*, trans. and ed. Kevin Smyth (London: Burns and Oates, 1967). In general, Biemer quotes Anglican and Roman Catholic texts by Newman without distinguishing them. Biemer argues that with regard to tradition, Newman's "decisive insights, theories and advances were products of his Anglican period" (Biemer, 64).

change everything and reshape everything according to its own desires."[90] If the content of faith is simply what powerful humans happen to decree at any particular moment, then this hardly seems like a divine revelation. If powerful leaders in one generation reverse what was solemnly held to be divine revelation by earlier generations—and if this process continues with further ruptures and reversals over the centuries—it is clear to everyone that mere arbitrary power is in the driver's seat.

The Anglican Newman does not shrink from stating the problem in its full Froudean urgency: "It may be argued that the Church of England, as established by law, and existing in fact, has never represented a doctrine at all or been the development of a principle, has never had an intellectual basis; that it has been but a name, or a department of the state, or a political party, in which religious opinion was an accident, and therefore was various."[91] The Anglican Newman denies all this, but he also fears it. Accounting for the doctrine of the Church of England, he explains that it arises from the Bible's authoritative divine revelation. Anglican doctrine is measured by Scripture. He remarks in this vein, "All Protestant sects of the present day may be said to agree with us and differ from Roman Catholics, in considering the Bible as the only standard of appeal in doctrinal inquiries. They differ indeed from each other as well as from us in the matter of their belief; but they one and all accept the written word of God as the supreme and sole arbiter."[92]

Yet Newman differs from Evangelical Anglicans, as well as from Protestants, in affirming that God established the Church as the Spirit-guided interpreter of divine revelation. The early Church functioned as this interpreter, and its doctrine, he thinks, remains intact in the nineteenth-century Anglican Church.[93] Against the Evangelical belief in the Bible's perspicacity,

90. Joseph Ratzinger, *Milestones: Memoirs 1927–1977*, trans. Erasmo Leiva-Merikakis (San Francisco: Ignatius Press, 1998), 132.

91. Newman, *The Via Media of the Anglican Church*, 18.

92. Newman, 26.

93. Thus, in response to Newman's *An Essay on the Development of Christian Doctrine*—a response that Newman himself might have made a few years earlier—the Anglican William

the Anglican Newman emphasizes that "the Bible is not so written as to force its meaning upon the reader; no two Protestant sects can agree together whose interpretation of the Bible is to be received; and under such circumstances each naturally prefers his own;—his own 'interpretation,' his own 'doctrine,' his own 'tongue,' his own 'revelation.'"[94] Therefore, the lack of a visible authoritative Church would profoundly undercut any claim to have received divine revelation. Faced with a wide variety of individual interpretations of Scripture, people could be excused for concluding that Christian doctrine is unimportant and unreal—that what matters instead is respecting the right of each individual to have his or her own opinions. This was the position of the religious liberals or "Latitudinarians" in the Anglican Church, and Newman rejects this position.

As evidence of Roman Catholic doctrinal corruption, Newman in the *Via Media* argues that some Roman Catholic doctrines can be found neither in Scripture nor in the Fathers.[95] These doctrines, such as Transubstantiation, universal papal jurisdiction, and the seven sacraments, cannot belong to Tradition but must be inventions of the later Church. In a sharply critical manner, Newman concludes that Roman Catholics' "professed Tradition is not really such," but rather "it is a Tradition of men" and is "not

Archer Butler argued that Newman's theory of development merely admits that the Church of Rome does not accept patristic authority: Newman's theory of doctrinal development "*is* in reality . . . a plain *surrender* of the claims of Romanism to satisfactory evidence from antiquity" (Butler, *Letters on Romanism in Reply to Mr. Newman's* Essay on Development, ed. Thomas Woodward [Cambridge: Macmillan, 1854], 16). Butler's book is a collection of his lengthy and erudite Letters (responding to Newman's book) published in the *Irish Theological Quarterly*, which after Butler's death were collected and published in one volume.

94. Newman, *The Via Media of the Anglican Church*, 27.

95. According to Aidan Nichols, Newman offers what now stands as "the classic case against Catholicism" as a corruptor of divine revelation (Nichols, *From Newman to Congar: The Idea of Doctrinal Development from the Victorians to the Second Vatican Council* [Edinburgh: T&T Clark, 1990], 1). For more recent arguments that (Roman) Catholicism has corrupted divine revelation, see for example R.P.C. Hanson and Reginald H. Fuller, *The Church of Rome: A Dissuasive*, 2nd ed. (London: SCM Press, 1960); Laurent A. Cleenewerck, *His Broken Body: Understanding and Healing the Schism between the Roman Catholic and Eastern Orthodox Churches* (Washington, DC: Euclid University Consortium Press, 2007); and Kenneth J. Collins and Jerry Walls, *Roman but Not Catholic: What Remains at Stake 500 Years after the Reformation* (Grand Rapids, MI: Baker Academic, 2017).

continuous" with the teaching of the Apostles.[96] As Newman puts the matter with his characteristic eloquence, "Romanism may be considered as an unnatural and misshapen development of the Truth; not the less dangerous because it retains traces of its genuine features, and usurps its name, as vice borrows the name of virtue."[97]

According to Newman in *Via Media*, Anglicanism succeeds where Roman Catholicism has failed because Anglicanism professes the true Catholic doctrines but not the corruptions that beset the Roman branch of the Church. The test for this claim is the Church Fathers, to whom Newman appeals in arguing that Roman Catholic doctrine is "substantial Truth corrupted."[98] At the same time, Newman in *Via Media* also argues that the corruption that has infected Roman Catholicism has spared its core principles and doctrines. Corruption has tainted Roman Catholicism especially in its popular practice and its "ecclesiastical policy," which he lumps together under the title "Popery."[99] Within Roman Catholicism, he argues, the most corrupted doctrine is that of the scope of the Church's authority.

---

96. Newman, *The Via Media of the Anglican Church*, 37.

97. Newman, 41. For further discussion of Newman's *Via Media*, see the illuminating analysis in Thomas, *Newman and Heresy*, 193–198. Thomas argues, "An immediate asymmetry arises in Newman's treatment of the two extremes to which the 'Via Media' is equally opposed. The two distinct polemical strategies, against Rome and against popular Protestantism, necessitate two different methods of placing heresy. That against Protestantism *extends* the definition of heresy to cover rationalism crypto-infidelity. That against Rome *restricts* it to denial of the fundamentals and castigates her for unwarrantably extending her criterion of heresy to her additions to the fundamentals" (Thomas, 193). For the notion of fundamental doctrines in play in the *Via Media*, although Newman in this work does not use the traditional Anglican term "fundamentals" (since it had come under attack from Abbé Jager as well as from Froude), see also Pereiro, *Theories of Development in the Oxford Movement*, 76–80.

98. Newman, *The Via Media of the Anglican Church*, 43. As James Pereiro points out, Jager in 1835 had "denied that developing truth meant inevitably changing it: prophets and doctors could comment and develop the mysteries of religion while preserving the same doctrine, the same sense, and the same judgement—the signs of true development, as indicated by Vincent of Lerins. In so doing they could give more force and greater scope to Apostolic Tradition. This was what the Fathers had done in their time, and the Church continued doing so at present" (*Theories of Development in the Oxford Movement*, 80–81). Pereiro concludes that Newman in 1845, in *An Essay on the Development of Christian Doctrine*, takes up Jager's arguments from a decade earlier.

99. Newman, *The Via Media of the Anglican Church*, 45.

Roman Catholicism, as he construes it, prioritizes not Scripture and the Fathers, but rather the Church and its infallibility. This is an act of grave presumption, as though the Church were more important than the Word of God received by the Apostles.

According to Newman in the *Via Media*, the Roman Catholic Church has violated Vincent of Lérins' principle that the Church must adhere to what has been taught "always, everywhere, and by all."[100] Since Vincent of Lérins knew nothing about the pope's supposed universal authority, it follows that "the Pope's supreme authority in matters of Faith, is no Catholic or Apostolic truth."[101] While claiming to be in continuity with the Church of the Fathers, the Roman Catholic Church refuses to allow the Fathers to be the touchstone for the truth of doctrine and thus for the proper interpretation of Scripture. As a consequence, the Roman Catholic Church has set itself against the apostolic Church.

Newman states in his *Via Media* that Roman Catholics' "boasted reliance on the Fathers comes to this,—to identify Catholicity with the decrees of Councils, and to admit those Councils only which the Pope has confirmed."[102] This is mere papalism, not true Catholicism—which is why Newman links the papacy to the Antichrist. He sharply criticizes the ways that Roman Catholics exceed the doctrinal content that can be traced to Scripture and the early Fathers. For example, transubstantiation and certain Mariological teachings *may* be true, but the Fathers (let alone Scripture) do not permit us to say. Therefore, the Church cannot teach the truth of these matters infallibly. The Anglican Newman advises that not all matters need to be decidable by the Church. If the Fathers have not spoken clearly about a particular matter, then God has willed for divine revelation to be incomplete in this respect, and the Church must accept this situation. Newman gives examples from the New Testament where Jesus willingly allows his followers to be in the dark. He concludes, "According to its *theory*, the

100. Newman, 51.
101. Newman, 55.
102. Newman, 57.

[Roman Catholic] Church professes to know only what the Apostles knew, to have received just what they delivered, neither more nor less. But in fact, she is obliged to profess a complete knowledge of the whole Dispensation, such as the Apostles had not."[103] Roman Catholic insistence upon solving every question through new councils or papal teachings has led the Roman Catholic Church into doctrinal corruption.

In the *Via Media*, Newman gives some further examples of Roman Catholic doctrinal corruption. For instance, he questions the Roman Catholic position on when the forgiveness of sins takes place and through what sacramental instruments. He is unsure about whether there actually is a sacrament of penance that forgives all post-baptismal sins.[104] He is also unsure about the number of the sacraments, and about whether the Eucharistic sacrifice heals venial sins. He is unsure about Purgatory, and he is even more unsure about papal indulgences and the treasury of merits. He firmly denies that the bishop of Rome has the status of a universal bishop—that is, a bishop with universal jurisdiction.[105] The doctrines taught by the Roman Catholic Church on such matters are corruptions of the true faith.

---

103. Newman, 89.

104. Note that Newman believed in frequent confession even prior to his entrance into the Catholic Church: see Ian Ker, *Newman on Vatican II* (Oxford: Oxford University Press, 2014), 127. See also the High Church and Tractarian background provided by Nockles, *The Oxford Movement in Context*, 248–256. Nockles contrasts Pusey's negative view of the sacrament of Penance in 1836 with his advocacy of frequent confession in 1845. Pusey ultimately concluded that "Anglican neglect of confession since the Reformation was a sign of the Church of England's spiritual malaise" (Nockles, 251).

105. See Newman, *The Via Media of the Anglican Church*, 183–184. As Shaun Blanchard remarks—with Vatican I's solemn affirmation of the pope's universal jurisdiction in view: "The debate over papal infallibility is the most famous aspect of Vatican I. . . . Nevertheless, *ex cathedra* exercises of papal infallibility are, at least in the opinion of the majority of modern Catholic theologians, extremely rare. It is the pope's universal and supreme jurisdiction—formulated explicitly against the ecclesiology of Febronius and the Synod of Pistoia—that cast a far longer shadow over the life of the church from 1870 until today. Despite what one believes about the frequency or rarity of infallible papal teachings, it is the jurisdictional supremacy of the pope (and when this jurisdiction is exercised via the Roman Curia) that is the much more important reality for contemporary Catholic life, at every level" (Blanchard, "Settling Old Scores: *Pastor Aeternus* as the Final Defeat of Early Modern Opponents of Ultramontanism," *Newman Studies Journal* 17, no. 1 [2020]: 24–51, at 49).

Besides, although all Roman Catholics uphold the infallibility of the Church, they cannot agree upon where to locate it. Some place it in the pope teaching *ex cathedra*, others in the pope teaching with a council, others in a council alone. Roman Catholics do not even fully agree among themselves about which councils or which parts of councils are ecumenical and binding.[106]

Newman is certain that God has revealed himself and that there must be an authoritative interpreter of the revelation. This interpreter must be the Church, and certainly not the State. But the true interpreter cannot be a Church that oversteps its proper limits and becomes an instrument of doctrinal corruption. He remarks, "Not only is the Church Catholic bound to teach the Truth, but she is ever divinely guided to teach it; her witness of the Christian Faith is a matter of promise as well as of duty; her discernment of it is secured by a heavenly as well as by a human rule. She is indefectible in it."[107] This indefectible Catholic Church, he argues in the *Via Media*, exists today, as Christ's guarantee assures us that it must be. It is the Anglo-Catholic Church. As a credible branch of the original undivided Church, the Anglican Church holds fast to the whole truth given by Christ to the Apostles.[108] The Anglican Church can no longer set forth dogma, since it is only one of the three divided branches. This situation is unfortunate, but it is not fatal, because the doctrinal content of Christ's Gospel has been sufficiently and authoritatively set forth in Scripture and the Fathers.[109]

106. See Newman, *The Via Media of the Anglican Church*, 124.

107. Newman, 190.

108. See also, for a work authored by an "old High Churchman" (not a Tractarian), Richard William Jelf's January 1842 sermon published as *Via Media, or the Church of England Our Providential Path between Romanism and Dissent* (Oxford: John Henry Parker, 1842).

109. Ker remarks that for the Anglican Newman "no development of doctrine was any longer possible in any branch of the divided Church" (*Newman on Vatican II*, 48). Ker argues, "Far from denying doctrinal development in the early undivided Church, Newman merely held that 'the right' to do so by any branch of the divided Church was 'suspended'" (Ker, 48). As noted above, however, in the mid-1830s Newman pushed back against "development of doctrine" as he later understood it. For Newman's understanding of Scripture and doctrine in his *Via Media*, see Benjamin John King, *Newman and the Alexandrian Fathers: Shaping Doctrine in Nineteenth-Century England* (Oxford: Oxford University Press, 2009). King

Avoiding Doctrinal Corruption as a Roman Catholic

In his *Apologia Pro Vita Sua*, Newman recounts how he changed his mind on these matters. He highlights the year 1839 as the starting point of his doubts about the argument of his *Via Media*. Specifically, when he examined the grounds on which the Monophysite controversy played out in the 420s, he found that if the choices were the authority of the early Fathers (Anglo-Catholicism), the authority of Rome (Roman Catholicism), or the authority of Scripture alone (Protestantism), then "the Church of the *Via Media* was in the position of the Oriental communion, Rome was, where she now is; and the Protestants were the Eutychians."[110] To his confusion,

describes Newman's distinction in *Via Media* between "essentials" (Apostolic Tradition) and "secondary teachings" (Prophetical Tradition), a distinction that, King thinks, allowed Newman to give a place to something like doctrinal development: "While he [Newman] considers the essentials of doctrine found in scripture and the creeds to be written and fairly fixed in content, secondary teachings (levels of interpretation, secrets, customs) are mainly oral and embodied. An interpretation of the relation of Father to Son, such as the Nicene Creed's definition that they are consubstantial (*homoousios*), is thus a secondary 'explanation' of the primary tradition that God is three persons in one. . . . Newman wanted the faith to be fixed in essentials, but also rich and creative rather than dry and logical" (King, 34–35). In addition, Newman in *Via Media* identified a place for the Rule of Faith: As King puts it, "*Scripture* requires the Rule of Faith in order to be interpreted rightly and *tradition* requires the Rule to ensure that the doctrines taught are those found in scripture" (King, 37). See also the discussion of the distinction between Apostolic and Prophetical Tradition in Thomas, *Newman and Heresy*, 190; as well as, for a Tractarian argument regarding the Apostolic Tradition as a fact accessible to history, Henry Manning's *The Rule of Faith: Appendix to a Sermon*, 2nd ed. (London: J.G.F. and J. Rivington, 1839).

110. Newman, *Apologia Pro Vita Sua*, 217. Jay Hammond explains the background: "In his [unpublished] Monophysite papers, he discovered that the church did not settle matters simply by referring to an immutable deposit of Truth; rather, the church itself was the authority that defined the orthodox rule of faith. . . . Far from being antagonistic, apostolicity-faith-belief and catholicity-church-development were intrinsically interconnected" (Hammond, "The Interplay of Hermeneutics and Heresy in the Process of Newman's Conversion from 1830 to 1845," in *Authority, Dogma, and History*, 45–75, at 67). King somewhat downplays the impact upon Newman in 1839 of his research into the Monophysite controversy—see King, *Newman and the Alexandrian Fathers*, 49–50, 162–166—on the grounds that "the connection that Newman claims to have seen . . . between the Donatist-Anglican analogy and Monophysitism, hardly appears in Newman's work at the time" (162). King is indebted to Stephen Thomas, *Newman and Heresy*, 204–205, 221. Thomas grants, however, that "it is . . . possible, in the light of Newman's autobiography, retrospectively to discern in the 1839 papers the stirrings of a profound unease, which only some years subsequently developed into a method of describing heresy, a ghostly, but nevertheless genuine, memory

as a branch. Just as concerns about doctrinal corruption were at the center of the *Via Media*, so too these concerns stand at the center of *An Essay on the Development of Christian Doctrine*. Newman describes his task as one of determining "whether on the one hand Christianity is still to represent to us a definite teaching from above, or whether on the other its utterances have been from time to time so strangely at variance, that we are necessarily thrown back on our own judgment individually to determine, what the revelation of God is, or rather if in fact there is, or has been, any revelation at all."[114]

As noted in my first chapter, in *An Essay on the Development of Christian Doctrine* he argues that if there has truly been a revelation, then doctrinal development is what we should expect. When Christ communicated divine revelation to his Apostles, he did not give them a set of abstract propositions to write down. Since Christ did not do this, he must have anticipated that their minds would work upon what he had taught them. Christ must also have anticipated that as the Church spread throughout the world, it would "vary in its relations and dealings towards the world around it," since even unchanging principles "require a very various application according as persons and circumstances vary, and must be thrown into new

114. John Henry Newman, *An Essay on the Development of Christian Doctrine* (Notre Dame, IN: University of Notre Dame Press, 1989), 9. I cite the final 1878 edition of this work. For the 1845 edition, see John Henry Newman, *An Essay on the Development of Christian Doctrine [1845]*, ed. Stanley L. Jaki (Pinckney, MI: Real View Books, 2003). Owen Chadwick compares the 1845 edition to the final edition of 1878, and he concludes: "A few changes were dictated because in odd places it was patent that the writer of the original essay was still, half-consciously, an Anglican. He excised one or two unfortunate analogies, passages which the recent course of ecclesiastical history had rendered misleading, a passage of temporary interest and now hardly intelligible to the inexpert reader, or historical concessions which he knew to be impermissible to a Roman Catholic. None of these alterations affected the thought of the *Essay*. . . . He added new paragraphs asserting the place of reason and of logic in development: but he retained almost all the language which rejected the view that development is only logical inference. The 1878 edition is no more compatible than the 1845 edition with the theories of the logicians" (Chadwick, *From Bossuet to Newman*, 2nd ed. [Cambridge: Cambridge University Press, 1987], 190–191). See also the similar comparative conclusions found in Gerard McCarren, "'Tests' or 'Notes'? A Critical Evaluation of Criteria for Genuine Doctrinal Development in John Henry Newman's *Essay on the Development of Christian Doctrine*" (Ph.D. Dissertation, The Catholic University of America, 1999).

shapes according to the form of society which they are to influence."[115] Thus, Christ must have expected ongoing doctrinal development, conditioned in part by historical and cultural circumstances.[116]

Newman is aware of the argument that all the more important doctrinal developments (such as the doctrine of the Trinity) are evident from Scripture and the Fathers, and the rest cannot be labeled *de fide*. In the *Via Media*, as noted above, he argued along such lines. But in 1845, he observes not only that the second- and third-century Church Fathers were often subordinationists,[117] but also that Christians disagree about which doctrines are the most important. Given that Scripture can be shown to be "not adapted or intended" to serve as a catechism, and the Fathers cannot meet this need either, it follows that we must either assume constant doctrinal corruption—in which case skepticism will win the day—or else "revert to that living and present Guide" that has "been so long recognized as the dispenser of Scripture, according to times and circumstances, and the

115. Newman, *An Essay on the Development of Christian Doctrine*, 58.

116. Commenting on Newman's 1840 "The Catholicity of the Anglican Church," in *Essays Critical and Historical*, vol. 2 (London: Longmans, Green, 1895), 1–73, at 13–14, Stephen Thomas draws attention to "two passages on doctrinal development, where he dismisses what, after 1843, became his own distinctive position. . . . He invites us to imagine the Apostles as 'implicit Tridentines,' or behaving in a way even remotely to suggest that they believed in Purgatory or the intercession of Our Lady" (Thomas, *Newman and Heresy*, 222). Newman's purpose is to expose the absurdity of this. As Thomas continues (still summarizing Newman's position on these pages of his 1840 essay): "The Romanist concept of developing articles of faith is 'all very well in the abstract,' but becomes absurd *in concreto*: he demands of the Romanist, 'did he or did he not hold that St Peter could give indulgences to shorten the prospective sufferings of the Corinthians in purgatory?'" (Thomas, 222). Thomas points out in response that in *An Essay on the Development of Christian Doctrine*, Newman makes clear that real doctrinal development unfolds in response to historical circumstances and requires time, so that the absurdity is more apparent than real. Thomas adds that "even in 1840, the appeal to what is or is not imaginable seems strained, almost desperate: 'we cannot imagine an Apostle saying and doing what Romanists say and do; can they imagine it themselves?' This is hardly the point. In any case, Newman's *own* sense of what *is* imaginable—'We can imagine them administering extreme unction or wearing copes'—calls attention to the arbitrariness of this criterion" (Thomas, 222).

117. This point had been made by the Evangelical Anglican William Goode against the Oxford Movement's appeal to the authority of the early Fathers: see William Goode, *The Divine Rule of Faith and Practice*, 2 vols. (London: J. Hatchard and Son, 1842).

arbiter of all true doctrine and holy practice to her children."[118] This "living and present" arbiter is the Church led by the bishops and the pope. In support of this Roman Catholic viewpoint is not only the fact that the Catholic Church actually exists and functions as an authoritative arbiter, but also that "a revelation is not given, if there be no authority to decide what it is that is given."[119]

Recall that Froude in 1833 was centrally concerned with the implications of having the Anglican Church controlled, in its doctrine and practice, by an essentially non-Anglican or liberal State. As we have seen, in 1837 Newman's *Via Media* addressed this issue by proceeding as though the State has no real authority whatsoever, since the Anglican Church has taught only what is found in Scripture and the Fathers, and all the doctrines that need to be taught are present in the patristic period. In 1845, however, the question of a living authority was foremost on Newman's mind, since he had become aware that the patristic witness, though crucial, cannot suffice for the Church's guidance. Newman emphasizes that if divine revelation has been given, then surely "it has been provided with means for impressing its objectiveness on the world," both in the past and in the present.[120] After all, the contents of divine revelation will "make distinct impressions on different minds, and issue in consequence in a multiplicity of developments, true, or false, or mixed."[121] This process will never cease so long as history lasts. Since the different "impressions" inevitably include some false ones, the Church must be gifted with a living authority that keeps the Church united in the truth of divine revelation; otherwise, there

118. Newman, *An Essay on the Development of Christian Doctrine*, 88. Duffy observes—in my view correctly, though I add the caveat that Newman's understanding of "history" was always a providence-governed one—that "Newman was the first great theologian not merely to grasp the importance of the questions posed for faith by the fact of historical flux, but to insist that an acknowledgement of the historical contingency of much of Christian teaching and institutions was compatible with firmly held orthodox belief, with the acceptance of dogma" (Duffy, *John Henry Newman*, 11).

119. Newman, *An Essay on the Development of Christian Doctrine*, 89.

120. Newman, 89.

121. Newman, 89.

will be a chaos of division and doctrinal corruption. Newman remarks, "Scripture will be read in contrary ways. . . . Philosophy, taste, prejudice, passion, party, caprice, will find no common measure, unless there be some supreme power to control the mind and to compel agreement."[122]

Faced with this fact, one might simply decide that doctrinal agreement is unnecessary, so that the Church can solemnly teach one thing today and the opposite tomorrow without imperiling its mission. This is the solution proposed by religious liberalism, but it destroys any real claim to have received a divine revelation with actual content. The only viable alternative to religious liberalism is that there is in fact a living authority able to teach the truth universally and accurately about the contents of the Gospel. As Newman puts it, "There can be no combination on the basis of truth without an organ of truth."[123]

Here Newman adds that as a historical matter it goes almost unchallenged that "the Roman Catholic communion of this day is the successor and representative of the Medieval Church" and that "the Medieval Church is the legitimate heir of the Nicene."[124] Anglicans, Protestants, and Eastern Orthodox think the Roman Catholic Church is the corruptor rather than the heir of the pre-Nicene Church. But Newman maintains that the difficulty is more notional than real. As we have seen, he thinks that if Athanasius or Ambrose came back to life, they would identify the Roman Catholic Church, over against all other claimants, as the Church of Christ, since the Catholic Church alone possesses an ability to call councils and to make universal claims, and also because the Catholic Church alone possesses the Roman See with its acknowledged primacy.

Newman grants that his view of the Catholic Church as a bulwark against doctrinal corruption would be falsified if it could be shown that a solemn teaching of the Church has been contradicted, equally solemnly, by a later Church teaching. If such doctrinal corruption were actually found,

122. Newman, 90.
123. Newman, 90.
124. Newman, 97.

says Newman, then Christians would ultimately be pressed back upon the principle of private judgment, a principle that Newman (as an Anglican and as a Roman Catholic) argues is indefensible both in practice and theologically, because private judgment deprives the assent of faith of its character as an acceptance of divine teaching.[125] Newman allows that there are conditions under which his claims about doctrinal development could be shown to be false, due to the presence of doctrinal corruption.[126] With respect to how to distinguish development from corruption, he sets forth and defends seven "notes" for authentic development that are capacious enough

125. For Newman's writings on private judgment (indebted to Froude) at various stages of his career, see Newman, *The Via Media of the Anglican Church*, 128–188, including a sharp critique of the post-patristic papacy; Newman, "Private Judgment," originally published in 1841 when Newman was in shock due to the rejection of Tract 90, in Newman, *Essays Critical and Historical*, vol. 2 (London: Longmans, Green, 1895), 336–374; Newman, *An Essay on the Development of Christian Doctrine*, 4–8.

126. Lash argues that Newman does not really open his theory to falsification: "Are not some of the assumptions on which the *Essay* rests such as to prevent, in the event, any proffered fact or set of facts from having this devastating effect? Newman is one of a long line of catholic theologians whose commitment to the antecedent improbability of the church's ever having radically 'changed its mind' is so powerful that even the most uncomfortable facts are fitted into the framework of a cumulative, irreversible 'view' of doctrinal history" (Lash, *Newman on Development*, 33–34). In my view, however, Newman's theory could certainly be falsified—and indeed many Catholic theologians today propose changes that they explicitly recognize would falsify Newman's theory. Here I may also note Cimorelli's argument for drawing together "the asymptotic, propositional-historical model of tradition-development" and "a non-linear model of tradition-development" marked by "participation and narrativity" in order to arrive at a "relational-developmental model of doctrine" (Cimorelli, *John Henry Newman's Theology of History*, 309). Cimorelli is particularly concerned to show that the Church's doctrinal teaching is not a static, strictly unchanging body of propositions, even though these doctrines are indeed enduring truths. As he shows, doctrinal development in one area may enrich (and thus in a certain way change) the Church's understanding of prior dogmatic teachings. Yet there is also the danger of making history itself the fundamental norm to which "development" is answerable, so that "it is only through the act—indeed, the 'practice'—of historical work that one can perceive the progress of authentic developments in the church's life" (Cimorelli, 273). What here needs to be articulated more clearly is twofold: a deeper place for ontology (judgments about the being of things) in dogmatic formulations, and more reflection upon the possibility of doctrinal corruption. These cautions need not entail falling into a merely propositional, ahistorical view of dogma.

to accommodate real change while not being so capacious as to be open to any kind of change.[127]

Newman's "notes" take their starting point from identification of what "corruption" involves. Only a living entity can "corrupt"; and an "idea" that corrupts does so when core elements of the original "idea" are rejected or reversed. If the Catholic Church once admitted that a particular dogma was in error, then the whole of the Church's dogmatic system would crumble because there would be no way to trust the Church's teaching authority. In this light, Newman's seven "notes" seek "to discriminate healthy developments of an idea from its state of corruption and decay."[128] By depicting Christianity both as an "idea" and as an organic entity, he strives to show that Christianity's doctrinal growth or development will have the marks that can be found in other human, historical realities that are developing rather than corrupting.[129] As Reinhard Hütter observes, for Newman we should expect to find plentiful (even radical) change, but in accordance with an underlying, intelligible continuity: "Authentic change is a function

---

127. Ker points out, "Newman did not think that you could apply the notes and prove by logical demonstration that a particular change was a development or a corruption. However, that did not mean that one could not be certain by applying the notes that a change was a corruption or a development. For, as he was to put it in his *Essay in Aid of a Grammar of Assent*, there are 'many truths in concrete matter, which no one can demonstrate, yet everyone unconditionally accepts.' There certainty can be reached by what Newman calls 'the cumulation of probabilities,' the '*assemblage* of concurring and converging probabilities.' . . . In Newman's view, then, the seven notes or tests, when all or most of them point towards corruption or development, may indeed be sufficient to justify certainty that a particular change is a corruption or development" (Ker, *Newman on Vatican II*, 42–43). Ker disagrees here with Peter Hinchliff, *God and History: Aspects of British Theology 1875–1914* (Oxford: Clarendon, 1992), 44.

128. Newman, *An Essay on the Development of Christian Doctrine*, 171. Citing Newman's final Oxford University Sermon, Ker observes: "The 'Catholic idea' may seem impersonal, but the 'idea' of course is of the person of Christ" (Ker, *Newman on Vatican II*, 112).

129. Doctrine takes shape within distinct historical contexts, in response to specific historical pressures or controversies. Andrew Meszaros states in this regard, "The connection between the historical causes of doctrine and the mystery of God, then, *at the very least*, on the most basic level, is the creative activity of God working *through* authentically *created (historical) causes*, which, in turn, somehow condition, shape, or modify Church teaching" (Meszaros, *The Prophetic Church: History and Doctrinal Development in John Henry Newman and Yves Congar* [Oxford: Oxford University Press, 2016], 224).

of the ongoing identity of meaning, of faithfulness to the principles given in the one single and selfsame deposit of faith."[130]

Let me now turn to Newman's critique of Erastianism in his 1850 *Certain Difficulties Felt by Anglicans in Catholic Teaching*. In his view in 1850, the Movement of 1833 had anti-Erastianism as its first principle. Above all, the Oxford Movement believed that "dogma would be maintained, sacraments would be administered, religious perfection would be venerated and attempted, if the Church were supreme in her spiritual power; dogma would be sacrificed to expedience, sacraments would be rationalized, perfection would be ridiculed if she was made the slave of the State."[131] In 1850, Newman argues that the role of Parliament and the monarch in the Anglican Church was in fact never justified, even before Parliament welcomed non-Anglican members. He states that the Anglican Church is and always has been "an Establishment, a department of Government, or a function or operation of the State."[132] Put simply, the present Anglican

130. Reinhard Hütter, *John Henry Newman on Truth and Its Counterfeits: A Guide for Our Times* (Washington, DC: The Catholic University of America Press, 2020), 142. As Newman makes clear in the *Essay on the Development of Christian Doctrine*, it matters that dogmas are *intelligible* expressions of saving mysteries: they are "supernatural truths irrevocably committed to human language, imperfect because it is human, but definitive and necessary because given from above" (Newman, *An Essay on the Development of Christian Doctrine*, 325).

131. John Henry Newman, *Certain Difficulties Felt by Anglicans in Catholic Teaching*, vol. 1 (London: Longmans, Green, 1897), 102.

132. Newman, 6. I note that Newman delivered these lectures at the height of, and partly in response to, English anti-Catholicism, which was linked especially to the return of an English Catholic hierarchy in 1850, with Cardinal Wiseman as the Archbishop of Westminster. For background, see D.G. Paz, *Popular Anti-Catholicism in Mid-Victorian England* (Stanford, CA: Stanford University Press, 1992), 8–12, focused on the 1850–1851 "Papal Aggression" controversy. As Paz points out, Newman suffered from popular anti-Catholicism in the Achilli case of 1852, in which Newman was found guilty of criminal libel even though the evidence—as "all but the most credulous anti-Catholics had come to realize"—was firmly in Newman's favor (Paz, 14). For discussion see John Cornwell, *Newman's Unquiet Grave: The Reluctant Saint* (London: Continuum, 2010), 117–121—a biography whose general seriousness and value are not reflected by its title. See also, for the complexities of English anti-Catholicism in a domain where "liberal Catholics" such as Newman could be (at least after 1860) sympathetic to the majority English viewpoint, C.T. McIntire's *England against the Papacy 1858–1861: Tories, Liberals, and the Overthrow of Papal Temporal Power during the Italian Risorgimento* (Cambridge: Cambridge University Press, 1983). McIntire shows that "anti-Catholic, especially anti-papal, convictions explicitly motivated the principal English

Church is the creature of the present set of powerful people in the State and society; and, when that set changes, the Anglican Church of the future will change.[133] On this view, the Anglican Church is not rooted in interiorized principles of Scripture and Tradition, and, lacking a divinely guided Magisterium, it has no doctrinal integrity as such.

Newman is severe toward his former Church. He asks what accounts for the specificity of Anglican doctrine and polity; and his answer is, decisions of the State. For example, he deems that the Anglican Prayer Book, when all is said and done, is the fruit of "an Act of Parliament of two centuries ago."[134] He denies that the structures of Anglicanism are sufficient to preserve orthodoxy in doctrine, if and when political pressures are brought to bear from the opposite direction. Political rulers will not worry much about doctrinal corruption, since power is what they primarily care about. He concludes that the Anglican Church, unlike the Roman Catholic Church, cannot legitimately hold itself to be strictly bound "by what it said and did formerly."[135] If the Anglican Church were to contradict one of its own previous solemn teachings, this would not be a fatal breach, since no Anglican teaching is thought to derive from an infallible body of bishops communicating the truth of the Gospel. With respect to the heresies of the day, therefore, he thinks the Anglican Church "will be able to resist them,

diplomats and statesmen in their diplomatic action concerning Italian affairs," and "these men [including both Disraeli and Gladstone] could rest upon the near universal support of the non-Catholic English population" (McIntire, 224). At 30–31, McIntire discusses the 1850–1851 burst of English anti-Catholicism, which he describes as a "'no-popery' panic" and which was led by the prime minister himself (Lord John Russell).

133. In the context of criticizing the Tractarians, Nockles grants that "popular Anglicanism, as manifest in the tradition of 'Church and King' riots from Sacheverell to Priestley, which Hurrell Froude and other Tractarians wanted to reestablish, had never been primarily theological" (*The Oxford Movement in Context*, 327).

134. Newman, *Certain Difficulties Felt by Anglicans in Catholic Teaching*, vol. 1, 8. Nockles points out that already in the 1830s, both Newman and Froude were critical of the Prayer Book: see *The Oxford Movement in Context*, 221–222. Nockles adds, "The logical result of the Tractarians' devotional motivation in extolling the Breviary at the expense of the Prayer Book was Pusey's systematic policy in the 1840s of republishing 'adapted' Roman Catholic devotional works" (Nockles, 224).

135. Newman, *Certain Difficulties Felt by Anglicans in Catholic Teaching*, vol. 1, 8.

while the State gives the word," but "unable, when the State forbids it."[136] Since the State pays the bills, it will call the shots: "That which determines [the Anglican Church's] existence will determine its voice."[137]

Newman in 1850 recognizes that the English State is Parliament, not the monarch. Therefore, the ultimate ruler of the Anglican Church is English popular opinion, on which the membership of Parliament depends. Whatever eminent Anglican divines may say, English popular opinion is Protestant or else it is liberal. For Newman, the reliance of Protestantism on private judgment means that it inevitably tends toward religious liberalism.

Regarding a recent controversy over the Anglican baptismal service (the Gorham Case), in which it was decided by the State that the baptismal service's words in favor of baptismal regeneration are not doctrinally binding, Newman deems that the reasonable explanation is that "the Nation, which imposes the document, imposes its sense."[138] The English nation is not bound by doctrinal Tradition, and therefore doctrinal corruption will be the result. Newman describes the situation with a rhetorical flourish: "By the breath of [the nation's] mouth it had, as a god, made

136. Newman, 8.

137. Newman, 8. Newman argues that the founders of the Oxford Movement "did not understand that the Established Religion [Anglicanism] was set up in Erastianism, that Erastianism was its essence, and that to destroy Erastianism was to destroy the religion. The movement, then, and the Establishment, were in simple antagonism from the first, although neither party knew it; they were logical contradictories; they could not be true together; what was the life of the one was the death of the other. The sole ambition of the Establishment was to be the creature of Statesmen; the sole aspiration of the movement was to force it to act for itself" (Newman, 105).

138. Newman, 23. Nockles shows that this controversy had a long background: "The sacrament of baptism notoriously divided Orthodox and Evangelicals in the pre-Tractarian era. The exposition of the doctrine of baptismal regeneration by Richard Mant, Richard Laurence and Christopher Bethell in the 1810s was made in the context of the anti-Calvinist controversy spearheaded by the Orthodox and directed against Evangelicals. This Orthodox apologetic provoked a vigorous Evangelical response from Thomas Scott and others and was a factor in the Evangelical secession from the Church of England in 1815 known as the 'Western Schism.' The seceders who adhered to the Calvinist notions of indefectible grace and election denied baptismal regeneration outright as unscriptural. While most Evangelicals regarded baptism as little more than an initiation into the visible church, Scott and others readily conceded that baptism was at least a sign of regeneration as laid down in Article 23" (*The Oxford Movement in Context*, 229).

Establishment, Articles, Prayer-Book, and all that is therein, and could by the breath of its mouth as easily and absolutely unmake them again, whenever it was disposed."[139] No matter what doctrinal Tradition or the Church Fathers or the baptismal service's own words might clearly mean, the State (and the nation) can do away with this meaning whenever convenient to do so. There is nothing to stop the State, or the English nation, from imposing a new interpretation upon its own creation. As Newman sums up, naming notable Anglican divines: "Hooker, Taylor, Bull, Pearson, Barrow, Tillotson, Warburton, and Horne, names mighty in their generation, are broken and wrecked before the power of a nation's will. One vessel alone can ride these waves; it is the boat of Peter, the ark of God."[140]

The anti-Erastian concerns about doctrinal corruption that motivated the Oxford Movement and that are articulated by Froude, therefore, continued to set the tone for Newman. As a Catholic, he both criticized the Erastian doctrinal corruption that he now believed to be characteristic of the Church of England and sought to justify the Roman Catholic Church as offering an anti-Erastian alternative, based upon a magisterial authority that guides doctrinal development, in accordance with Scripture and Tradition, under the guidance of the Holy Spirit, preserving the Church of Christ from doctrinal corruption.

Conclusion

In *The Oxford Conspirators*, Marvin O'Connell depicts Hurrell Froude as fundamentally apolitical, despite his concerns about the English State: "To him the crucial issue went beyond political categories to the supernatural, where Acts of Parliament have no relevance."[141] By contrast, the politicians who passed the reforms (and who did so for good reasons) expected the

139. Newman, *Certain Difficulties Felt by Anglicans in Catholic Teaching*, vol. 1, 23.

140. Newman, 25.

141. Marvin R. O'Connell, *The Oxford Conspirators: A History of the Oxford Movement 1833–45* (London: Macmillan, 1969), 20.

Church of England to represent the interests of the English nation. O'Connell describes the Anglican Church of the early 1830s as characterized by the old "idea that the civil and ecclesiastical communities should be convertible,"[142] which by this time was no longer practicable given the rise of religious dissenters such as Methodists and Quakers and the need for Catholics and non-Christians (including atheists) to have a political voice.[143] For Froude, joined by Newman and Keble, the question was what would happen to the Anglican Church if it retained the "administrative control of the Church by the state."[144] As we have seen, Froude argued that the answer was clear: religious liberalism and doctrinal corruption would flow from such Erastianism.[145]

---

142. O'Connell, 35.

143. O'Connell remarks aptly, "The impact of [John] Wesley's fervent, selfless crusade [beginning in 1728] is hard to overestimate. He left behind him an organized Methodist Church, whose adherents at the time of his death (1791) numbered in the tens of thousands. He breathed new life into the other dissenting and nonconformist sects, which increasingly adopted his system and method, while still maintaining their individual identities. And as far as the Established Church was concerned, though Wesley's fervor perplexed and finally eluded her, she felt his influence profoundly. Her genuinely Protestant character, lethargic from generations of indifference and disuse, awoke with a start. . . . There arose within the Anglican Communion those fathers of the Victorians, the Evangelicals, who were to give a new and noble meaning to the phrase Low Church, and who included in their ranks at one time or another not a few of the nineteenth century's greatest names: Macaulay, Gladstone, Newman, Manning and Wilberforce. . . . The influence of Wesley upon Wilberforce and indeed upon all the Evangelicals was deep, but they achieved what Wesley had failed to achieve, the rescue of the Established Church from the indifferentism and rationalism which had disfigured her through most of the eighteenth century" (O'Connell, 46).

144. O'Connell, 42.

145. Consider for example the way in which the Anglican Church's 1857 sanction of remarriage after divorce was handled politically by Parliament, as discussed in G.I.T. Machin, *Politics and the Churches in Great Britain 1832 to 1868* (Oxford: Clarendon, 1977), 285–289; along with Machin's discussion of "Protestantism, patriotism, and Erastianism" (Machin, 285). For the Gorham Case of 1848–1850, see Machin, 202–208. See also the responses to the Gorham Case penned by E.B. Pusey, *The Royal Supremacy Not an Arbitrary Authority, but Limited by the Laws of the Church, of Which the Kings Are Members* (Oxford: J.H. Parker, 1850); and William E. Gladstone, *Remarks on the Royal Supremacy, as It Is Defined by Reason, History, and the Constitution* (London: John Murray, 1850). Nockles remarks, "For most old High Churchmen and many moderate Tractarians, the Gorham Judgment represented an unacceptable constitutional innovation amounting to a usurpation of the church's inherent spiritual office, but it did not touch or compromise the church's spiritual essence. . . . Pusey

For his part, Newman held that religious liberalism involves "the relativizing of truth claims in the name of tolerance" with the result that Christian doctrine, unmoored from the Church's teaching office (which Christ sustains through his Spirit), becomes a matter of "political manipulation and endless struggle for power."[146] Newman was well aware that powerful people will easily be tempted to nullify unpopular religious doctrines. This point holds both for powerful laity and for powerful clergy, and so once doctrine is perceived to be a mere toy of the powerful, doctrine is in danger. The solution, in Newman's view, is to keep front and center the fact of divine revelation and the properly ecclesial—Spirit-guided—status of solemn doctrine, which must be preserved by the Church precisely as a condition of being properly developed.

As an Anglican, the danger that Newman perceived was the emergence of a Parliament in which non-Anglicans and Anglican religious liberals predominated, with the resultant power to alter doctrine—something that Latitudinarian laity and clergy already desired. As a Catholic, Newman found a somewhat similar problem in Ultramontanism. In the latter context, Newman called for the faithful as a whole, as a witness to the enduring faith of the Church rather than merely as a separate power source or

---

and Keble, for all their sense of the practical abuses of establishment, now ranged themselves with old High Churchmen in insisting that the Reformation statues had never intended the state to act as a judge in matters of Christian doctrine, and that the Church's doctrine remained exactly as it had before. . . . For Gladstone, it was merely the latter-day illegitimate extension of state interference after 1832 that needed to be checked" (*The Oxford Movement in Context*, 95–96). Nockles admits that for other High Churchmen, such as William Maskell, the Gorham Case revealed (in a manner that compelled conversion to Rome) that "ultimate jurisdiction in spiritual matters had always lain with the crown ever since the Reformation" (Nockles, 98). For further background, see Perry Butler, *Gladstone: Church, State and Tractarianism. A Study of His Religious Ideas and Attitudes, 1809–1859* (Oxford: Oxford University Press, 1982).

146. Delio, *'An Aristocracy of Exalted Spirits,'* 150. See also Robert Peel, *An Inaugural Address Delivered by the Right Hon. Sir Robert Peel, Bart. M.P., President of the Tamworth Library and Reading Room on Tuesday, 19th January, 1841*, 2nd ed. (London: James Bain, 1841); as well as Wendell V. Harris, "Newman, Peel, Tamworth, and the Concurrence of Historical Forces," *Victorian Studies* 32, no. 2 (1989): 189–208.

democratic polity, to be consulted in matters of doctrine.[147] While adhering to the pope's infallibility when solemnly teaching *ex cathedra*, Newman as a Catholic regularly insisted that "the Pope cannot, by virtue of his infallibility, reverse what has always been held."[148] As a Catholic, then, he continued to distrust mere power, and, indeed, "his distinguishings and hesitations proved unpalatable to those who conceived [ecclesiastical] life in para-military fashion as a series of decisions crisply made and decisively executed."[149]

The Catholic theologian Gavin D'Costa has recently maintained that there can be radical "non-doctrinal discontinuity" and even in a certain sense "doctrinal novelty," but what there cannot be in the Catholic Church is doctrinal discontinuity in the sense of rupture of solemn teaching.[150] As will be clear by now, this is Newman's position regarding doctrinal development and corruption. In the speech that he gave upon his elevation to the cardinalate, Newman remarked, "For thirty, forty, fifty years I have resisted to the best of my powers the spirit of liberalism in religion. . . . Liberalism in religion is the doctrine that there is no positive truth in religion. . . . It is inconsistent with any recognition of any

147. See John Henry Newman, *On Consulting the Faithful in Matters of Doctrine*, ed. John Coulson (Lanham, MD: Sheed & Ward, 2006).

148. John Henry Newman, *A Letter Addressed to His Grace the Duke of Norfolk on Occasion of Mr. Gladstone's Recent Expostulation*, in Newman, *Certain Difficulties Felt by Anglicans in Catholic Teaching Considered*, vol. 2 (London: Longmans, Green, 1896), 171–378, at 377.

149. G. Egner (a pseudonym for P.J. Fitzpatrick), *Apologia Pro Charles Kingsley* (London: Sheed & Ward, 1969), 208. Egner contrasts the Anglican Church of Newman's day positively with the Catholic Church, on the grounds that the latter possessed a more nefarious and "much more efficient machinery of suppression," and also possessed "no variegated structures for the expression of opinion"—so that "the convenience and consistency of those in power has too often in practice been put above the demands of intellectual honesty" (Egner, 206). The last-named charge holds, I fear, for almost any institution; and in the Catholic Church, despite Egner's claims, a great deal of divergent opinions came to light even in the repressive periods of the nineteenth- and early-twentieth centuries.

150. Gavin D'Costa, "Between Doctrine and Discernment: The Question of the Jewish People and the Development of Doctrine Arising from Vatican II," in *The Past, Present, and Future of Theologies of Interreligious Dialogue*, ed. Terrence Merrigan and John Friday (Oxford: Oxford University Press, 2017), 64–80, at 64.

religion, as *true*."[151] Newman connects "liberalism in religion" with the belief that doctrinal corruption is inevitable and welcome. He recognizes that if rupture in solemn teaching actually took place, then Catholic truth-claims would at bottom be mere power-plays.

The current trend among Catholic theologians in favor of at least occasional ruptures in solemn teaching sometimes appears under the mantle of

151. John Henry Newman, "Biglietto Speech," 1879, available at http://www.newmanreader.org/works/addresses/file2.html. In this speech, Newman has a particular eye toward the movement to ground political society upon a toleration of all religions that allows for no preference toward any particular religion as true; but his meaning here is broader than the relationship of Christianity and political life. Owen Chadwick offered the following well-known, but misleading, comment in 1983: "In the Rome of 1879 to say that Newman stood for the fight against liberalism caught popularity, for at that moment of history the word stood for the vices of the Italian government as it maltreated the Pope. But Newman did not use such a word to gain applause. He believed this about himself. And he was under a delusion about himself" (Chadwick, *Newman* [Oxford: Oxford University Press, 1983], 71). Chadwick accurately points out that Newman was a "liberal Catholic" in the sense of being sympathetic to political liberalism and to religious toleration, but Chadwick adds regarding religious liberalism that Newman "made various not quite compatible statements"—because Newman, while opposing religious liberalism, also opposed an anti-historical spirit (Chadwick, 73). But Newman saw more deeply than Chadwick into the nature of religious liberalism, which extends well beyond a mere commitment to historical and scientific research. See also Newman's "Note A.: Liberalism," appended to his *Apologia Pro Vita Sua*, ed. Charles Frederick Harrold (New York: Longmans, Green, 1947), 259–269, where Newman comments: "Liberty of thought is in itself a good; but it gives an opening to false liberty. Now by Liberalism I mean false liberty of thought, or the exercise of thought upon matters, in which, from the constitution of the human mind, thought cannot be brought to any successful issue, and therefore is out of place. Among such matters are first principles of whatever kind, and of these the most sacred and momentous are especially to be reckoned the truths of Revelation. Liberalism then is the mistake of subjecting to human judgment those revealed doctrines which are in their nature beyond and independent of it, and of claiming to determine on intrinsic grounds the truth and value of propositions which rest for their reception simply on the external authority of the Divine Word" (261). Newman goes on to differentiate the religious liberalism of Oxford in the 1820s from the fully developed religious liberalism, amounting to open rejection of Christian doctrine, of the late nineteenth century; and on 266–268 he adds a list of eighteen principles of the "liberalism" of Oxford in the 1820s and 1830s that he opposed at the time, a list that accords with the stance of Whately and Hampden and that includes Erastian claims as well as some precepts of political liberalism. Importantly, he concludes: "I need hardly say that the above Note is mainly historical. How far the Liberal party of 1830–1840 really held the above eighteen Theses, which I attributed to them, and how far and in what sense I should oppose those Theses now, could scarcely be explained without a separate Dissertation" (Newman, 269).

radical *kenosis*, breaking through the barriers of past ecclesiastical modes of thought and life and doing so in the name of repudiating the prideful and presumptuous claim to "orthodoxy" or to what men of the past have supposed to be orthodoxy. But as I have underscored above, doctrinal rupture favors the people who possess the power to make the rupture. The corruption of doctrine reveals doctrine to be a mere human thing, not God's own word. No doubt, there will be multiple breaks and leaps in the historical course of development of doctrine. But unless these breaks and leaps manifest real doctrinal continuity (and thus identity along Newmanian lines) in the interpretation of the apostolic deposit of faith, then the will of powerful people—whether popes or committees of laity—cannot lay claim to "developing" doctrine. Doctrinal corruption always bears the mark of the will to power.

In the midst of his book-length critique of Newman's anti-liberalism, Robert Pattison states, "Newman devoted his life to a failed crusade against Arians, Socinians, and liberals."[152] Rather predictably, Pattison portrays Newman as clinging desperately to "the assurance that true interpretations exist in the first place."[153] Indeed, for Pattison, Newman's conversion to Catholicism was merely the product of his desperate dogmatism, his absurd demand "that the world contain a single imperishable oracle of truth."[154] Pattison sums up Newman as a fanatical egotist for whom the truth of his own logic was all that mattered.[155] Since religious liberalism in fact

152. Robert Pattison, *The Great Dissent: John Henry Newman and the Liberal Heresy* (Oxford: Oxford University Press, 1991), 144.

153. Pattison, 162.

154. Pattison, 163; cf. 186. See also the similar viewpoint of Andrew Martin Fairbairn, who corresponded with and debated Newman, in his *Catholicism: Roman and Anglican*, 2nd ed. (London: Hodder & Stoughton, 1899). Short comments that Newman's thirty-three volumes of letters are "indispensable because they show like nothing else what animated Newman's life, which was not only love of God but love of neighbor—a love which won over even the captious Fairbairn, whose last letter to Newman was a letter of thanks" (*Newman and His Contemporaries*, 20–21). Fairbairn was thanking Newman for sending him a copy of Newman's latest reply in their public debate.

155. Pattison is joined in this regard by Frank Turner's *John Henry Newman*. With Turner in view, Eamon Duffy grants that the *Apologia Pro Vita Sua* should not be taken as a strict

conquered British society and today defines most Western societies and many Christian communions, Newman can appear to have been a failure—a fact that Newman himself understood and that, according to Pattison, did not bother him much because he believed that the apocalyptic defeat of the liberal Antichrist would not occur prior to a civilizational tribulation.[156]

In my view, Pattison has misread Newman. As a Catholic, Newman's willingness to challenge powerful Churchmen suggests that he was hardly driven to repress and destroy all questioning voices.[157] His commitment to

---

autobiography, while adding that "recent attempts to interpret it as a brilliant confidence trick concealing his true opinions, seem crassly wrong-headed" (Duffy, *John Henry Newman*, 16). Edward Short shows that the view that Newman embodies a "closeted skepticism" is already present in Fairbairn's *The Place of Christ in Modern Theology* (London: Hodder & Stoughton, 1893), 203, and in Connop Thirlwall, *Letters Literary and Theological of Connop Thirlwall*, ed. John J.S. Perowne and Louis Stokes (London: Richard Bentley & Son, 1881), 261. See Short's "Newman, Superstition and the Whig Historian," in *Newman and History* (Leominster, UK: Gracewing, 2017), 83–115, at 94–95. In light of Tract 85, Stephen Thomas argues that in the late 1830s Newman was experiencing a crisis of skepticism brought on by the fact that "he found his position inadequate to an ever-increasing, erosive, inner criticism" (*Newman and Heresy*, 202). Thomas frames his account of Newman's conversion to Catholicism by stating, "He feared the despair of scepticism: he yearned for authority and wholeness" (Thomas, 202).

156. For Newman's apocalyptic rhetoric in the years 1833–1837, see Thomas, *Newman and Heresy*, 55–58; as Thomas concludes, "if Newman may, in some sense, himself be described as 'radical,' or even on occasions 'subversive,' this was not in a democratic direction. He rather appears to have imbibed the Romantic reactionary spirit of his beloved friend, Hurrell Froude" (Thomas, 57). For his part, Pattison fears that in our day liberalism itself (and liberal societies) will become dogmatically intolerant, thereby repudiating the openness to "heresy" and difference that, on this view, separates liberal societies from the fanatical and repressive societies of the past.

157. Indeed, despite Newman's consistent and forceful critique of liberalism in religion, his insistence upon historical nuances and his decentralized account of doctrinal development opened him to the charge of latent liberalism. This fact indicates that something important is missing from Pattison's interpretation. For discussion, see for example Stephen Bullivant, "Newman and Modernism: The *Pascendi* Crisis and Its Wider Significance," *New Blackfriars* 92, no. 1038 (2011): 189–208. For the argument that Newman can be understood as a "liberal Catholic" in his time and place (even though he remained completely committed to the dogmatic principle, so he was never religiously liberal), see Ambrose Mong Ih-Ren, *The Liberal Spirit and Anti-Liberal Discourse of John Henry Newman* (Bern: Peter Lang, 2011), especially 112 and 117; Josef L. Altholz, *The Liberal Catholic Movement in England: The "Rambler" and Its Contributors, 1848–1864* (London: Burns & Oates, 1962), especially

the dogmatic principle was not a sign of desperation or dogmatism. Instead, like Christians through the centuries, Newman believed that God has given a intelligible revelation of himself in and through Jesus Christ, and this revelation has been handed down faithfully in the Church guided by the Holy Spirit. The process involves doctrinal continuity, but it also involves reform and creativity in new contexts. Newman never understood belief in true doctrinal development to be equivalent to the claims that opponents must be repressed, ecclesiastical authorities are always correct, change is impossible, and intellectual advances have no place. On the contrary, he believed that much was still to be learned—just not along lines that negate prior solemn judgments regarding faith and morals.

Thus, as Ambrose Ih-Ren points out, "Although Newman criticised liberalism for its anti-dogmatic principle, he was against dogmatism. In his Oxford University sermon on 'Wisdom as Contrasted with Faith and with Bigotry,' dogmatism is characterised as bigotry, the application of narrow principles."[158] With Newman, I note that the truth communicated by divine revelation expands the mind and heart, rather than locking the mind and heart into a defensive narrowness. What is known in and through divine revelation is a salvific and transformative truth, salutary for human

chapter 6; and Hugh A. MacDougall, *The Acton-Newman Relations: The Dilemma of Christian Liberalism* (New York: Fordham University Press, 1962), although, as MacDougall notes, after Newman's *Letter to the Duke of Norfolk* (or, at least, after Newman accepted the cardinalate), Acton turned sharply against Newman as a morally dishonest defender of the indefensible—on which see also Owen Chadwick, *Acton and History* (Cambridge: Cambridge University Press, 1998), 115–138, especially 124–136. Stephen Thomas remarks with some justification, "The mind-set of ultramontanism was hostile to criticisms made even on patristic grounds. Newman found himself to be a liberal with Roman Catholicism; actually delated to Rome for heresy without his knowledge in 1859, he was regarded by Mgr Talbot as 'the most dangerous man in England.' Suspected, marginalised, cut off from the forum provided by his beloved Oxford, his attitude towards heretics, or those suspected of covert heresy, softened. . . . Always professing the most humble obedience to authority, he was often nevertheless regarded by his superiors much as he had himself regarded the latitudinarian Hampden: as a man of dangerous tendencies" (Thomas, *Newman and Heresy*, 5).

158. Ih-Ren, *The Liberal Spirit and Anti-Liberal Discourse of John Henry Newman*, 116; cf. Mary Katherine Tillman, "Newman: The Dialectic of 'Liberalism' and 'Conservatism,'" *Josephinum Journal of Theology* 9, no. 2 (2002): 181–195.

beings to know and believe, even though it is also a deeply challenging and often resisted truth. It is not the kind of truth that, when meeting resistance, requires bludgeoning resisters. It is a truth that, in a cruciform sense, is willing to "fail" in order to make manifest the self-surrendering love that is the source of all reality.

This is the particular character of divine revelation's "apocalyptic" irruption, its true "rupture." Ultimately, Christ's cross—not pride or domination on the part of those who hold power—is divine revelation's distinguishing mark, confirmed by his Resurrection; and this is the mark, too, of doctrinal development that is faithful to the Gospel. Hierarchical authority need not be domination, since Christ himself is the Church's Head to whom all members must be obedient, and since the practice of lived obedience (including to ecclesiastical authorities in proper contexts) serves the formation of humility. By comparison, doctrinal corruption, however winsomely dressed in modern or democratic garb, "puts people at the mercy of those in power."[159]

159. Ih-Ren, *The Liberal Spirit and Anti-Liberal Discourse of John Henry Newman*, 169. Ih-Ren is here comparing Newman's Biglietto Speech (May 12, 1879) with Joseph Ratzinger's homily to the College of Cardinals on April 18, 2005, as well as Newman's homily "The Infidelity of the Future" (October 2, 1873).

Chapter 3

Newman and Francis Newman

Timothy Larsen has argued that in the England of the late nineteenth century, the situation was better for Christianity than is often imagined by scholars today. As he says, "The nineteenth-century crisis of faith is a motif that has become vastly overblown. . . . When the Victorian landscape is painted, doubt is frequently exaggerated and faith dwarfed. Too often, the crisis of faith is present as the most important thing to be said about religion and the Victorians."[1] It is not that there were no crises of faith or that deistic or atheistic movements did not gain traction. But they were still outliers, and Christian faith generally thrived in Victorian England. Indeed, Larsen suggests that more notable than the examples of prominent Victorian Christians who permanently lost their faith are the examples of prominent Victorian Christians who, having lost their faith and become leaders in the Secularist movement, ended up reconverting to Christianity.[2]

The standard books in the field of Victorian studies proceed as though Christianity was dead or dying among most thinking people. Sally Mitchell remarks along these lines, "Most thoughtful Victorians who lived through

1. Timothy Larsen, *Crisis of Doubt: Honest Faith in Nineteenth-Century England* (Oxford: Oxford University Press, 2006), 1. Larsen notes that some others have recognized this problem: see for example Hugh McLeod, *Religion and Society in England, 1850–1914* (New York: St. Martin's, 1996), 259.

2. For background to the Secularist movement, see the works of George Jacob Holyoake, who coined the term "secularism" in 1851 and who edited *The Reasoner* from 1846 to 1861. See for example Holyoake's *Rationalism: A Treatise for the Times* (London: J. Watson, 1845) and *The Principles of Secularism*, 3rd ed. (London: Austin, 1870); as well as *Christianity and Secularism: Report of a Public Discussion between Rev. Brewin and G.J. Holyoake* (London: Ward, 1853). Holyoake was a good friend of Francis Newman.

the middle years of the century experienced a crisis of faith."[3] General overviews of the period treat religion under headings such as "Post-Christian Days" and "A Non-Dogmatic Affirmation of General Kindliness" and "Natural Science and the Decline of Religion" and "Religion and Doubt."[4] Larsen observes that early-nineteenth-century religious movements are today generally understood as mere preparations for the loss of faith in the latter part of the century. Owen Chadwick published a book in 1975 with the title *The Secularization of the European Mind in the Nineteenth Century*.[5] Even worse is the title given by A.N. Wilson to his book arguing that the Victorians abandoned Christian faith: *God's Funeral*.[6]

For my purposes, one book to which Larsen draws attention stands out. Titled *More Nineteenth Century Studies: A Group of Honest Doubters*, it contains a chapter on Francis Newman, brother of John Henry Newman. Particularly noteworthy is its claim, quoted by Larsen: "The spiritual history of Francis was in no way exceptional, as John's was; what happened to him happened to so many in the nineteenth century that his life-story may be said to conform to the standard pattern."[7]

---

3. Sally Mitchell, *Daily Life in Victorian England* (Westport, CT: Greenwood, 1996), 246; cited in Larsen, *Crisis of Doubt*, 3.

4. See the following books (all cited by Larsen): Donald Read, *England 1868–1914* (London: Longman, 1979); Thomas William Heyck, *The Peoples of the British Isles: A New History*, 3 vols. (Belmont, CA: Wadsworth, 1992); Clayton Roberts and David Roberts, *A History of England*, vol. 2, *1688 to the Present* (Englewood Cliffs, NJ: Prentice-Hall, 1991).

5. See Owen Chadwick, *The Secularization of the European Mind in the Nineteenth Century* (Cambridge: Cambridge University Press, 1975), cited in Larsen, *Crisis of Doubt*, 8.

6. See A.N. Wilson, *God's Funeral* (New York: W.W. Norton, 1999), cited in Larsen, *Crisis of Doubt*, 9.

7. Basil Willey, *More Nineteenth Century Studies: A Group of Honest Doubters* (London: Chatto & Windus, 1956), 12, cited in Larsen, *Crisis of Doubt*, 7. Larsen denies that loss of faith was "the standard pattern" for Victorians, but he recognizes, of course, that a crisis of faith was part of the experience of a number of Victorians. He argues that "the Victorian crisis of faith was actually a by-product of the religiosity of the Victorians and, in particular, the influence of evangelicalism. The Victorians themselves frequently discussed and wrote about the crisis of faith. Many of them did this because they prized faith so much and therefore feared and cared about its loss. Their discussions and reading should not be seen as a measure of the extent of the crisis, but rather as a measure of the extent of their concern" (*Crisis of Faith*, 10). See also Michael Rechtenwald, *Nineteenth-Century British Secularism: Science, Religion and Literature* (New York: Palgrave Macmillan, 2016); as well as John W. Burrow,

I accept Larsen's argument that Francis Newman's loss of faith was not "the standard pattern" for educated Victorians. Nevertheless, Francis' autobiographical work *Phases of Faith* does indeed reflect a well-traveled intellectual path for Evangelicals who began to doubt their faith.[8] Larsen credits Frank Turner for showing how "evangelical expectations shaped the stories of those who lost their faith, such as how their notion of deconversion was modelled on the evangelical idea of conversion."[9] As a notable example of this genre, *Phases of Faith* had a significant impact upon other Christians who lost their faith in mid-century England.[10] Thus, Larsen classes Francis Newman alongside George Eliot and Leslie Stephen as major Victorian "loss-of-faith figures."[11] Whereas in the eighteenth century the skeptic was expected to conceal his or her doubts from the uneducated, in the nineteenth century the Evangelical-turned-skeptic was expected to be open about his or her situation.

In the 1830s, John Henry Newman already sensed that the progression

---

A Liberal Descent: Victorian Historians and the English Past (Cambridge: Cambridge University Press, 1983).

8. See also James Anthony Froude's novel *The Nemesis of Faith* (London: John Chapman, 1849), whose deep opposition to Christianity led Francis Newman first to criticize it and then to praise it in letters to Froude (Hurrell Froude's younger brother). For discussion, see Ciaran Brady, *James Anthony Froude: An Intellectual Biography of a Victorian Prophet* (Oxford: Oxford University Press, 2013), 134–164; and for further background on James Anthony Froude's perspective as a historian, see Short's "Newman, Superstition and the Whig Historian," in *Newman and History* (Leominster, UK: Gracewing, 2017), 83–115, at 101–102, treating Froude's *Lectures on the Council of Trent* (London: Longmans, Green, 1896).

9. Larsen, *Crisis of Faith*, 11, citing Frank Turner, "The Victorian Crisis of Faith and the Faith That Was Lost," in *Victorian Faith in Crisis: Essays on Continuity and Change in Nineteenth-Century Religious Belief*, ed. Richard J. Helmstadter and Bernard Lightman (London: Macmillan, 1990), 9–38.

10. See Larsen, *Crisis of Faith*, 87, 154. Erik Sidenvall observes that for some observers, the result of Francis Newman's loss of faith and John Henry Newman's conversion to Catholicism was one and the same: "The Scottish *Bulwark* drew its readers' attention to the fact that Francis W. Newman had published, just a year before John Henry Newman defended his new ecclesiastical domicile, an autobiographical narrative—*Phases of Faith* (1850)—revealing an intellectual journey that had taken a different turn. But as the writer dryly remarked, 'Satan does not care much whether men become Papists or infidels'" (Sidenvall, *After Anti-Catholicism? John Henry Newman and Protestant Britain, 1845–c. 1890* [London: T&T Clark International, 2005], 30).

11. Larsen, *Crisis of Faith*, 235.

described in Francis' *Phases of Faith* would become the predominant path of modern times, at least in England. Well before Francis and John respectively wrote their autobiographical *Phases of Faith* (1850) and *Apologia Pro Vita Sua* (1864), John wrote to Francis in 1840 about Francis' gradual rejection of Christianity: "I think your reasonings are irresistible, grating certain latent principles which you all along assume. And since I anticipate that these will be generally assumed by the coming age, as they are in great measure already, I am prepared for almost a downfall of Christianity for a time."[12] In a similar vein, thirty-six years later, John wrote to his sister Jemima that Francis' rejection of Jesus' divinity was not mere personal eccentricity but "a spiritual epidemic, which, in one shape or another, is going abroad."[13]

It seems likely that Francis Newman's path was dramatized by John in various writings, although some other associates of John (such as Blanco White) followed a similar path. In *Grammar of Assent* (1870), John notes that "when . . . we are told that a man has changed from one religion to

12. John Henry Newman, Letter to Francis Newman, 22 October 1840, as quoted in Ian Ker, *John Henry Newman: A Biography* (Oxford: Oxford University Press, 1988), 199. John Henry Newman has hope for a future renewal of Christianity in England (and elsewhere), however: "Latitudinarianism is an unnatural state; the mind cannot long rest in it; and especially if the fact of a revelation be granted, it is most extravagant and revolting to our reason to suppose that after all its message is not ascertainable and that the divine interposition reveals nothing. The more scepticism abounds, the more is a way made for the revival of a strong ecclesiastical authority; Christianity arose in the beginning, when the popular religions had lost their hold upon the mind. So strongly do I feel this, that averse as the English people are to Romanism, I conceive that did their choice lie in the mere alternative they would embrace even Romanism rather than acquiesce in absolute uncertainty" (Letter to Francis Newman, 22 October 1840, quoted in Ker, *John Henry Newman*, 200).

13. John Henry Newman, Letter to Jemima [Newman] Mozley, in *The Letters and Diaries of John Henry Newman*, vol. 28, ed. Charles Stephen Dessain and Thomas Gornall (Oxford: Oxford University Press, 1975), 121, quoted in Ann Margaret Schellenberg Richardson, "Brothers," in *The Oxford Handbook of John Henry Newman*, ed. Frederick D. Aquino and Benjamin J. King (Oxford: Oxford University Press, 2018), 70–89, at 85. Louis Bouyer is correct that for Newman, who emphasized both the mysterious and the deeply personal character of divine revelation, "belief, therefore, and fully definite belief, is a *sine qua non* of any faith that is not just pretense or self-deception. A man must know in what or in whom it is he believes: to have a relationship he must know its object" (Bouyer, *Newman's Vision of Faith* [San Francisco: Ignatius Press, 1986], 202).

another, the first question which we have to ask, is, have the first and second religions nothing in common?"[14] He then briefly sketches three Protestants, one of whom converts to Catholicism, one to Unitarianism, and one to unbelief. The one who converts to Catholicism does so because of his "real assent" in faith to divine revelation in the incarnate Lord Jesus Christ, an assent that leads him on toward the fullness of Catholic faith. The one who converts to Unitarianism does so because his fundamental principle was always private judgment, and when his studies persuaded him that the affirmations of Nicaea do not "follow by logical necessity from the text of Scripture," he became a simple humanitarian believing in one God.[15] Newman is likely here describing Francis.[16]

Similarly, Newman's description of the unfolding of the principle of private judgment in his *An Essay on the Development of Christian Doctrine* (1845) may arise from his assessment of his brother's journey. Beginning with private judgment, says Newman, "Lutheranism" ends with rationalism, "a sort of philosophical Pietism."[17] Again, when he discusses in *The Idea of a University* the view of God that characterizes the "spirit of the age," he argues that many educated people today mean by "God" only a deist entity responsible for cosmic order. He concludes that such a God is certainly not the personal, loving, judging God of Christian faith, but rather is a God who "is not difficult for any one to conceive, not difficult for any one to endure" because such a God would be fundamentally irrelevant to

14. John Henry Newman, *An Essay in Aid of a Grammar of Assent* (Westminster, MD: Christian Classics, 1973), 245.

15. Newman, 246. Newman here emphasizes the intellectual journey away from faith, but it is also the case, as Edward Short observes, that "in Frank's opposition to the doctrines of Christianity, Newman came to see the psychology of apostasy, with all its characteristic contempt for the miraculous and the traditional" (Short, *Newman and His Family* [London: Bloomsbury, 2013], 143). Short adds that Francis "thought his brother a sectarian fanatic" (Short, 143).

16. Indeed, of the three brothers Newman, John became a Catholic, Francis a Unitarian, and Charles an unbeliever.

17. John Henry Newman, *An Essay on the Development of Christian Doctrine*, 6th ed. (Notre Dame, IN: University of Notre Dame Press, 1989), 193.

actual human life and history.[18] He again likely has Francis' viewpoint in mind.[19]

Francis was four years younger than John. In their teens, the two brothers converted to Evangelicalism under the influence of their classics master Walter Mayers. When Francis followed John to Oxford, Francis entered Worcester rather than Trinity; and after earning a rare double first at Oxford, Francis was elected a Fellow of Balliol College in 1826. Francis had been put off by John's turn toward Anglo-Catholicism, and Francis instead became heavily involved in a small Evangelical group later known as the Plymouth Brethren. By 1833, however, Francis no longer held that "Jesus was Jehovah."[20] Although in 1840 he still called himself a Christian, he rejected almost all Christian doctrine, and in 1876—when his wife Maria (a Christian) died—he formally became a Unitarian.

Drawing upon William Robbins' 1966 book *The Newman Brothers: An Essay in Comparative Intellectual Biography*, Ann Richardson has remarked that Francis' *Phases of Faith* "is tempting to contrast with John's *Apologia*" because "while John's faith relied upon cumulative probabilities, cumulative improbabilities refined Francis' faith through disbelief."[21] In this chapter, I will explore this comparison.[22] In their theological autobiographies,

18. John Henry Newman, *The Idea of a University*, ed. Martin J. Svaglic (Notre Dame, IN: University of Notre Dame Press, 1982), 28.

19. Francis got the last word (a generally negative one), publishing *Contributions Chiefly to the Early History of the Late Cardinal Newman* (London: Kegan Paul, 1891) after John's death.

20. Richardson, "Brothers," 75.

21. Richardson, 75; see William Robbins, *The Newman Brothers: An Essay in Comparative Intellectual Biography* (Cambridge, MA: Harvard University Press, 1966), 137. Robbins compares Francis' and John's personal histories and writings, and, while recognizing John's brilliance, he generally sides with Francis. He sums up Francis' personality as follows: "Keenness of intellect, purity of character, and kindliness of disposition—these qualities in Frank were offset by the lack of a sense of humour, or of proportion, and by a deficiency in imagination that explains phrases like 'curious literalness' used of him even by his friend Martineau" (Robbins, 97). Robbins finds John to be arrogant and peevish, and he concurs in the charge that John's conversion was due to an underlying profound skepticism and need for religious authority (see Robbins, 119–122).

22. I note that Philip C. Rule has intriguingly compared Newman's *Apologia Pro Vita Sua* with Samuel Taylor Coleridge's 1818 autobiography *Biographia Literaria*. Rule argues

when treating of divine revelation and its mediation, how do Francis and John depict the Church's dogmatic tradition and how do they conceive of doctrinal corruption?

Francis Newman's *Phases of Faith*

In the work of Francis Newman, the issue of whether the Church's doctrine is true is front and center, because Francis' quest is for a true creed. Although *Phases of Faith* is in a certain sense autobiographical, its purpose is not to set forth the entirety of Francis' personal history, but rather, as he observes in the third person in his preface, "The progress of his *creed* is his sole subject, and other topics are introduced either to illustrate this or as digressions suggested by it."[23] His subtitle tells the tale: *Passages from the History of My Creed.* The first four chapters trace his evolving creed or set of doctrinal beliefs. These chapters treat the following topics: "My Youthful Creed"; "Strivings after a More Primitive Christianity"; "Calvinism Abandoned"; and finally, "The Religion of the Letter Renounced." The final four chapters then draw the lessons of the demise of dogmatic Christianity. In chapters 5, 6, and 7, he explains why dogmatic Christianity has no future. The reasons are as follows: "Faith at Second Hand Found to Be Vain"; "History Discovered to Be No Part of Religion"; and "On the Moral Perfection of Jesus." The titles of chapters 5 and 6 are clear enough, but the title of chapter 7, "On the Moral Perfection of Jesus," can be misleading. In this chapter, having defeated dogmatic Christianity in the previous chapters, he defeats a then-current version of liberal religiosity by showing that Jesus was not a sinless man.

Lastly, in his chapter 8—titled "On Bigotry and Progress"—he further

that both books "are written not only to give the reader a tour of the mind that produced certain writings but also to edify readers by drawing them into the penetralia of a human spirit on its journey to infinite Spirit" (Rule, *Coleridge and Newman: The Centrality of Conscience* [New York: Fordham University Press, 2004], 67).

23. Francis Newman, "Preface to the First Edition," in Francis Newman, *Phases of Faith, or, Passages from the History of My Creed*, 2nd ed. (London: Watts, 1907), 7.

attacks dogmatic Christianity in its Protestant, Anglican, and Catholic forms, and he mounts an argument for true religious progress. True religion, he argues, should contain only two doctrines: that God exists and that God desires human perfection. True religion will do away with all other doctrines and with all anathemas, except (inevitably) for the anathematizing of dogmatic religion. It will combine the best of Christianity—namely, the warm heart and tender compassion exhibited by many Christians—with the best of the modern educated world. Thanks to the "activity of intellect, untiring pursuit of truth, and strict adherence to impartial principle which the schools of modern science embody," dogmatic Christianity can be pruned of its dogma and, as a newly spiritual religion, can begin to make real progress.[24] Freed from dogmatic falsehoods, a truly universal religion will emerge that "will lay aside disputes of words, eternal vacillations, mutual illwill and dread of new light, and will be able without hypocrisy to proclaim 'peace on earth and goodwill towards men,' even towards those who reject its beliefs and sentiments concerning 'God and his glory.'"[25]

Francis holds that historians have shown through critical research methods that the Church Fathers built their doctrinal formulations upon misunderstandings of the scriptural texts or else simply invented practices (such as the episcopacy and the priesthood) that would have been quite foreign to Jesus and his first followers. Dogmatic Christianity having been fatally undermined by historical-critical research into the Bible and the Church, it is now necessary to rebuild Christian intellectual life and Christian institutions by listening to the historians.[26] Francis still sees a significant place for "Christianity" insofar as, in his view, Christian spiritual

24. Newman, *Phases of Faith*, 125.

25. Newman, 125.

26. For work along these basic lines, see the essays in *Essays and Reviews*, 2nd ed. (London: John W. Parker and Son, 1860); and see Harvey Hill, "Historical Consciousness and the Controversy over *Essays and Reviews*," in *The Rise of Historical Consciousness among the Christian Churches*, ed. Kenneth L. Parker and Erick H. Moser (Lanham, MD: University Press of America, 2013), 123–140.

writers never paid much attention to doctrine anyway, but rather focused on divine love (or at least did so in their better moments). Thus, he remarks that "for devotional aids, for pious meditations, for inspiring hymns, for purifying and glowing thoughts, we still have to wait upon that succession of kindling souls, among whom may be named with special honour David and Isaiah, Jesus and Paul, Augustine, à Kempis, Fénelon, Leighton, Baxter, Doddridge, Watts, the two Wesleys, and Channing."[27] These inspiring chroniclers of spiritual experience should not be allowed, however, to impose any sort of doctrinal creed. As Francis concludes, "We must needs look to historians, to linguists, to physiologists, to philosophers, and generally to men of cultivated understanding, to gain help in all those subjects which are preposterously called *theology*."[28]

Thus, dogma, in its literal sense at least, should now be swept away, so as to be replaced by the pure interior experience of divine love, an experience that externally will bear fruit in works of love toward humankind. The vicious fights caused by doctrinal differences will fade away. Francis sums up his perspective: "Religion was created by the inward instincts of the soul; it had afterwards to be pruned and chastened by the sceptical understanding."[29] The final fight will be with those who cling to their doctrinal religions and who imagine all other people, especially skeptics, to be wrong. The new religion envisioned by Francis will "combine the tenderness, humility, and disinterestedness that are the glory of the purest Christianity, with that activity of intellect, untiring pursuit of truth, and strict adherence to impartial principle which the schools of modern science embody."[30]

How did Francis, by his own account, arrive at this progressive religion, freed from the bigotry of doctrinal certitude? As Alfred Benn comments, Francis' 1850 book "was not his first contribution to liberal religious thought. In 1844, he had published *A Plea for Catholic Union*, proposing to

27. Newman, *Phases of Faith*, 125.
28. Newman, 125.
29. Newman, 125.
30. Newman, 125.

build the Church of the future on a purely ethical basis. It was followed, in 1847, by *A History of the Hebrew Monarchy* . . . and by a manual of constructive Theism, called *The Soul*, in 1849."[31] In these books, two of which I will briefly discuss below, Francis demonstrated that from "Evangelical Biblicism . . . he had gone forward to a religion of reason and personal experience."[32]

In chapter 1 of *Phases of Faith*, Francis introduces us to "My Youthful Creed." He describes beginning to read the Bible at eleven years old and being converted at age fourteen, accepting a strict Evangelical (or Reformed Anglican) creed. He learned and believed in the doctrines of election, saving faith, the inerrancy of Scripture, sabbath observance, and so on. Bishop Howley confirmed him in the Anglican Church at age sixteen, and he had learned his catechism well.[33] He fully affirmed the 39 Articles of the Anglican Church and "looked on them as a great bulwark of the truth."[34] At Oxford, however, he found that generally the teachers and students were skeptical of doctrine.

Early in his time at Oxford, he had his first doctrinal disputation. He and a friend disagreed about whether a *twofold* imputation of Christ's saving work is needed. The friend thought that the only thing needed for salvation is to receive Christ's atoning sufferings. There is no need also to receive Christ's righteousness or good works. After studying Romans 3–4 with care, Francis changed his mind and came to agree with his friend. Francis recalls this as "my first effort at independent thought against the teaching of my spiritual fathers."[35]

A second doctrinal challenge affected him more deeply. A skeptical

31. Alfred W. Benn, "Introduction to the Present Reprint," in Newman, *Phases of Faith*, 11–14, at 11.

32. Benn, 11.

33. For background to Howley, see James Garrard, "Archbishop Howley and the Oxford Movement," in *From Oxford to the People: Reconsidering Newman and the Oxford Movement*, ed. Paul Vaiss (Leominster, UK: Gracewing, 1996), 269–285.

34. Newman, *Phases of Faith*, 16.

35. Newman, 16.

fellow student mocked the notion that Christ's actual flesh and bones were glorified. How can one conceive of a human body (with its blood, guts, passions, fragile bones, and so on) being "glorified"? Francis defended this article of Anglican faith, but he later recalled Jesus' own teaching that flesh and blood will not inherit the kingdom. This led him to wonder whether the Anglican doctrine was ill-expressed.

A third step was equally significant: he found his strict Sunday sabbath observance challenged, and when he sought in Scripture some proof that Sunday should be treated in accordance with the Old Testament's laws about the sabbath, he could find no proof. When he discussed this with his Evangelical friends, he was greatly disappointed by their inability to respond cogently in defense of their belief. Influenced by the Oxford scholar John Davison, he became acquainted with the view of the Old Testament as bearing witness to progressive religious development.[36] He came to agree with this view of the Old Testament, and the result was a significant change in his perspective. He explains, "The systematic use of the Old Testament by the Puritans [Evangelical or Reformed Anglicans], as if it were 'the rule of life' to Christians, I saw to be a glaring mistake, intensely opposed to the Pauline doctrine."[37]

More doctrinal crises followed. An Oxford teacher argued that Christ's atoning work should be believed in but could not be given a rational explanation—since it seems to make no sense that one man's death on a cross could atone for all sins. Even if one grants that Christ's death was a perfect act, its value can hardly be applied to others so that their sins are washed away. Francis was shaken by this argument, but he continued to believe in

36. See John Davison's 1824 *Discourses on Prophecy, in Which Are Considered Its Structure, Use, and Inspiration* (Oxford: J.H. and J. Parker, 1861); as well as Davison's *An Inquiry into the Origin and Intent of Primitive Sacrifice, and the Scripture Evidence Respecting It* (London: John Murray, 1825). For background (from a different perspective of course, but with great—though not unalloyed—appreciation), see John Henry Newman's 1842 essay "John Davison," in Newman, *Essays Critical and Historical*, vol. 2, ed. Nicholas Schofield (Leominster, UK: Gracewing, 2019), 445–494.

37. Newman, *Phases of Faith*, 17.

the truth of the doctrine of substitutionary atonement. He then was swept up in a controversy over infant Baptism. It seemed clear to him that Scripture does not justify infant Baptism in any way, and yet it is an Anglican doctrine and practice. Again, he was disappointed by the inability of his Evangelical Anglican friends to defend their faith cogently.[38] He could have turned to his brother John, but, as he notes, he already distrusted John for his High-Church views. Francis had disagreed with John about the episcopacy, and John's stern response had greatly offended Francis. He recalls, "I distinctly felt that his arguments were too fine-drawn and subtle, often elaborately missing the moral points and the main points, to rest on some ecclesiastical fiction."[39]

Thus, as he pushed forward in his doctrinal inquiries, he felt that he had to count upon his own reasoning rather than that of any adviser. In this process, while reading the work of an Evangelical theologian, he came to realize that Trinitarian doctrine rested simply upon assertions: in one sense God is one; in another sense God is three; but we can have no understanding of how both claims can be true. Even then, however, he persisted in believing in the Trinity.

Francis almost refused to sign the 39 Articles (necessary for taking his degree from Oxford) over the issue of infant Baptism. In the end, he managed to persuade himself to sign, but he certainly did not believe the Article about infant Baptism. Since he did not believe in this doctrine, he felt that he could not become an Anglican priest. He also could not accept the Anglican teaching that Baptism causes the regeneration of the soul. Inquiring with his Evangelical Anglican friends, he asked them how they dealt with the words of the Anglican baptismal service that imply baptismal

38. For the baptismal controversies that shook the Anglican Church in the 1810s, going so far as to contribute to some Evangelicals leaving the Church of England in what was called the "Western Schism"—and for High Church and Tractarian viewpoints and controversies through the 1850s on the topic of Baptism—see Peter B. Nockles, *The Oxford Movement in Context: Anglican High Churchmanship, 1760–1857* (Cambridge: Cambridge University Press, 1994), 228–235.

39. Newman, *Phases of Faith*, 19.

regeneration. They offered him three ways of dealing with these words, but he found these ways to be "mere shifts invented to avoid the disagreeable necessity of resigning their functions."[40] His friends regularly baptized infants but did not believe in the baptismal regeneration promised by the words of the liturgical service.

As a result, Francis came to feel that Anglican doctrine and practice were mired in irreconcilable contradictions. But he found that anyone who complained of such contradiction was immediately shouted down by both sides, Low Church and High Church.[41] The standing of bishops became a particular flash point for him. The study of history indicated to him that Anglican bishops had all too often been mere pawns of the State. They had failed to support Wesley or Wilberforce, and they had opposed the Missionary and Bible Societies. Besides, the notion that the State should appoint the bishops is antithetical to the apostolic age. He rejected the argument that the State or the Crown now represents the laity, who in the third and fourth centuries voted in episcopal elections. There is an evident difference between the laity electing their bishops and the State appointing them. In addition, he meditated critically upon the fact that the Anglican ordination service suggests that the bishop has the power to bestow upon the ordinand "the power to forgive or retain sins," which young Francis deemed to be a popish absurdity.[42]

In the midst of these doctrinal doubts, Francis began to read historical studies of the New Testament. These led him to think that Paul makes more

40. Newman, 21.

41. I note the following point from Nockles, *The Oxford Movement in Context*, 32: "An Evangelical in the pre-Tractarian era was not a Low Churchman. As [J.] Gascoigne has shown, the epithet 'Low Church' was not levelled at Evangelicals prior to 1833. The term was confined to the Latitudinarian school associated with Benjamin Hoadly and Francis Blackburne. . . . It was only from the 1840s onwards that Evangelicals in the Church of England came to acquire the label 'Low Church' from Tractarian polemicists, though it would appear that by that date Evangelicals did not appear to resent the label; one of its earliest uses in this sense dates from 1835, when an Evangelical pamphleteer appeared proud to adopt the title 'Low Churchman.'"

42. Newman, *Phases of Faith*, 23.

doctrinal sense than do the Gospels, which often rely upon metaphor and typology. As he recalls, at this time he did not have access to the German historical criticism that could have taken (and later did take) him much further. During this time, he also read the Church Fathers but found them unimpressive. He concluded that it is much better to rest doctrine upon the New Testament than upon anything produced during the patristic period, including Church councils. Correspondingly, he came increasingly to think that it is necessary to base one's faith and life solely upon the Bible and to separate Christianity from the power of the State. He could not be an Anglican minister and had no sympathy with Anglicanism; but he found Quaker attempts to rid the New Testament of the sacraments of Baptism and the Lord's Supper to be impossible exegetically, and he was not impressed by the Dissenters who spoke at the Bible Society. He was also questioning the training in "Christian Evidences" that he had received at Oxford, in particular with respect to the relationship of natural and revealed religion.

Francis, at this stage, sympathized with the apocalyptic fervor present in the New Testament—the expectation of the early Christians regarding the imminent fiery destruction of the world and the return of Christ. From this apocalyptic perspective, using the mind for earthly purposes is not worthwhile, since Christ is coming soon. Why spend thirty years studying natural science, for example, if in thirty-five years Christ returns and all earthly works come to naught? In this viewpoint, adopted during this period by Francis, it is mere unbelief that prompts a politician (for instance) to plan for the welfare of future generations. In reaching these conclusions, Francis exhibited the influence of John Nelson Darby, who scorned worldly wisdom of any kind (as distinct from biblical wisdom) and who taught the total depravity of fallen man.[43]

On a trip to the Middle East for missionary purposes, however, Francis

43. For a fuller portrait of Darby in relation to Francis Newman, see Short, *Newman and His Family*, 173–174, 184–185. For Darby's furious response to *Phases of Faith*, see John Nelson Darby, *The Irrationalism of Infidelity: Being an Analysis of "Phases of Faith"* (London:

began to separate himself from Darby and the Plymouth Brethren—a separation that advanced quickly on his return to England. When he attempted to read the Gospel of John with a clear eye, he found that its Christology was subordinationist ("The Father is greater than I": John 14:28), unless one pretended that Christ meant that his Father was greater than his (Christ's) humanity, a point too obvious to need Christ to articulate it. Francis discovered that Scripture does not teach the Trinity in the sense of coequal divine Personhood.[44] Moreover, his sense deepened that the Trinitarian Creed is intrinsically polytheistic. He concluded that only God the Father is the true God, just as Paul (in Francis' view) implies in 1 Corinthians 8 when Paul distinguishes the "one God" from the "one Lord."

By this time, Francis was almost thirty—and John was commencing his Tractarian career. John had rather brutally cut off relations with Francis due to Francis' "sectarian" activities with the Plymouth Brethren. After his discovery that the New Testament taught one God (the Father) rather than a Trinity, Francis felt that he had no choice but to follow his conscience regarding the plain meaning of Scripture, insofar as he could discern it. To his dismay, he discovered that even his most firmly "biblicist" friends held tacitly to extra-scriptural creeds with regard to the Trinity.

Looking back from the perspective of 1850 (some seventeen years later), he cries out sorrowfully, "Oh, dogma! dogma! how dost thou trample under foot love, truth, conscience, justice! Was ever a Moloch worse than thou?"[45] Mere doctrinal differences tore apart his deepest familial and

Groombridge & Sons, 1853). See also Isabel Giberne Sieveking, *Memoirs and Letters of Francis W. Newman* (London: Kegan Paul, 1909).

44. Thomas Arnold had a similar realization in 1819, which is described by Frank M. Turner: "Thomas Arnold . . . in 1819 found himself unable to assent to the damnatory clauses of the Athanasian Creed or to clarify for himself certain aspects of the doctrine of the Trinity. His particular problem was the not unfamiliar one of reconciling elements of those doctrines to the letter of Scripture itself, a process made all the more difficult by English Unitarians who denied the doctrine of the Trinity on the basis of Scripture" (Turner, *John Henry Newman: The Challenge to Evangelical Religion* [New Haven, CT: Yale University Press, 2002], 72).

45. Newman, *Phases of Faith*, 37. See also Francis Newman, *The Soul, Its Sorrows and Aspirations: An Essay Towards the Natural History of the Soul, as the True Basis of Theology* (London: George Manwaring, 1849).

friendship bonds. Dogma, in Francis' experience, perverts charity. He therefore emphasizes that spirituality and spiritual kinship, not intellectual propositions, should be what unites Christians. When Christians focus on defending particular doctrines, Christians forget about love and are at one another's throats.

Of course, Francis recognizes that many doctrines had united him with his former friends prior to his rejection of the Trinity, even though they had believed themselves to be united by personal experience of the Spirit and by charity. For example, they were united by belief in Christ's atoning work, and they were united by belief in Jesus as the Son of God. When he followed Scripture by subordinating the Son to the truly divine Father, he still held to Christ's atoning work and Sonship.

The experience of being cut off from the Plymouth Brethren due to his rejection of the doctrine of the Trinity led Francis not only to anger about dogma but also to a sense that he could no longer trust anyone who had not shared this experience of being cast out as a heretic. In addition, he now became wary of the authority of the Bible itself. He began to face up to its many passages that, on the surface at least, conflict with one another. No longer did he give the Bible the benefit of the doubt. Gradually, he began to see that many biblical doctrines were morally questionable, among them the doctrines of election, prevenient grace, original sin, the atonement, and everlasting punishment. These doctrines, in various ways, call into question the goodness and justice of God.

Being attacked and vilified as a heretic by his friends freed him from his "Calvinism." In opposition to dogma and bigotry, he came to value real striving for moral excellence—wherever it is found—along with belief in a God who is actually good and loving. He discovered that he preferred reason and common sense to blind faith in the truth of the Bible.

Even as a biblicist, he had always abhorred the doctrine of Romans 9 that God loves some and hates others; such a God could not be just or good. He now discovered a Unitarian book against the doctrine of everlasting punishment that made the point that the Greek word αἰώνιος means not "everlasting" but "for a long time."[46] As a result, he perceived that he need not believe in an eternal hell. He awakened fully to the moral depravity of the doctrine of everlasting punishment, which imagines that the wicked choice of a ten-year-old child can merit everlasting punishment and which supposes that a finite sin can merit an infinite penalty. According to "orthodoxy," he now saw, the devil turns out to be the real victor, since Christ manages to save only a minority. He also found that people who believe that their fellow humans will be damned due to lack of correct beliefs are more likely to be cruel and malignant toward those who do not share their beliefs. Hell-believing Christians think that while they will be blessed forever, their neighbors will justly be cursed and miserable forever, without this affecting the joy of the blessed. Francis now understood that this is not "good news" (Gospel) but a scandal! It would be better that humankind had never existed than that God could have created people for this outcome. Francis came to believe that when confronted with Scripture's testimony, we must judge its truth by the only measure we have—namely, conscience or common sense. If it fails this test on a particular point, it cannot be true on that point.

Francis recalls that during this time he focused less on scriptural authority per se than on comparing Calvinism with Unitarianism, and he found the latter to be much preferable even on biblical grounds. He recalls how he reflected upon the fourth-century controversies and found the Semi-Arian position to be much more compelling (even as an account of the Nicene Creed) than the Athanasian position, until he eventually became Arian in his view of Christ. Examining himself, he found himself no better morally for having accepted the logic of subordinationist Christology. He concluded that one's dogma, on arcane points at least, does not affect one's morality. It is not the number of gods, but whether one's gods are

46. For a response to a recent version of this claim, see Michael Pakaluk, *Mary's Voice in the Gospel according to John* (Washington, DC: Regnery, 2021), 301–313.

good or cruel that affects morality. He also recalls how he came to reject the notion of the cross as vicarious punishment for our sins and to reject the doctrine of original sin or the spiritual perversion of humanity. Humans are frail, but not more so than supposedly sinless Adam was. Although he continued to consult Scripture, he found himself growing apart from some central teachings of Paul, who had previously been his favorite biblical author.

Discussing theology with a Unitarian, he found that the Unitarian had a higher view of Christ's sinless humanity than he did. The notion that Jesus was sinless goes against all common sense regarding what we know of actual men. Francis realized that he did not particularly admire Jesus' words and deeds as narrated by the Gospels; instead, his religion had always been one of ideas, a "Pauline" religion. Although he deemed many Unitarian beliefs admirable, he disagreed with their conception of Jesus. Thus, he did not merely move from Calvinist dogma to Unitarian dogma; on the contrary, he moved away from dogma itself. He kept only the "dogma" that the one God, who is infinitely good, loves us.

The fourth chapter of *Phases of Faith*, titled "The Religion of the Letter Renounced," describes the reasons why he turned away from the Bible as an authority. The first reason was that God, in the Bible, regularly sanctions or commands sinful actions, such as commanding Abraham to sacrifice his son or approving (through the prophetess Deborah) the deadly trickery and lying of Jael.[47] The second reason was the repeated contradictions in the Bible, as for example those found in the genealogies of Jesus in Matthew and Luke. He notes errors such as that of Gamaliel in Acts 5, where Gamaliel (or Luke) indicates that Judas of Galilee came after Theudas. Even prior to reading German historical criticism, he realized that the two creation accounts come from different hands, and therefore Moses is not the author

47. See also Francis Newman, *On the Defective Morality of the New Testament* (Ramsgate, UK: Thomas Scott, 1867). This particular Thomas Scott (1808–1878) was an ex-Catholic whose publishing house strove against Christianity.

of the whole Pentateuch. He also rejected the Genesis account of the origin of death and of pain in childbirth.

On the basis of science, he determined that all humans are not descended from an Adam and Eve who lived around six thousand years ago, thereby undermining Paul's teaching about Christ the New Adam. Likewise, science disproves the historicity of Noah's flood as a worldwide deluge; and, besides, all species of animals—requiring distinct climates and distinct foods—could not hope to coexist and survive for a year on a boat. In addition, he observed that the New Testament authors freely apply snippets from the prophetic literature to Jesus—snippets that in their original context clearly have quite a different application. Francis concluded that "not one quotation in ten is sensible and appropriate."[48] Science also indicates that many diseases attributed by the Gospels to demonic possession are in fact physiological in origin, thereby undermining many of Jesus' miraculous healings.

On closer inspection, Francis perceived many legendary elements in the Gospels and Acts, such as the details about Jesus' temptation, Joseph's dreams, Herod's massacre of children, the magi and the star, the tribute money from the fish's mouth, Peter's walking on water, and Israel's heroes coming out of their graves after Jesus' death. Francis perceived even more legendary elements in the Old Testament, including the notion that God specially loved the trickster Jacob. In his reading of the Old Testament, he was increasingly instructed by German historical criticism, which exposed the various sources of the Pentateuchal text, not only the Jehovistic and Elohistic sources, but also ancient Hebrew poetry that (as in the case of Joshua 10's miracle of the sun standing still) has been misunderstood literalistically. He read with profit Johann David Michaelis' *On the New Testament*, W.M.L. De Wette's *Introduction to the Canon of Scripture*, and numerous other German studies. Attending to the story of the discovery of the book of the Law by King Josiah, he reasoned that it is illogical that such

48. Newman, *Phases of Faith*, 63.

a sacred legal code could have been entirely lost and forgotten; much more logical is the theory that the book of the Law was compiled under Josiah or somewhat later, even if its sources are older.[49]

With respect to the New Testament, scholarly study convinced him that Paul did not write Hebrews and that the book of Revelation is not a prophecy but a political speculation about a catastrophe soon to occur to the Roman Empire. With respect to the Old Testament, he became persuaded that the Song of Songs is merely an instance of secular love poetry. He came to doubt the value of the Hebrew canon, given that it contains books such as Ruth, Esther, and 1 and 2 Chronicles whose spiritual value seemed minimal to him. His doubts about the truth of the Old Testament's historical books and about the truth of the synoptic Gospels and Acts firmly convinced him to take his stand elsewhere than biblical authority.

When he encountered friends who, despite the above evidence, clung to their dogmas, he began "to doubt whether, after all, there is much love of truth even among those who have an undeniable strength of religious feeling."[50] He bemoaned the "sham science" by which scholars sought to defend Mosaic authorship of the Pentateuch, even when they understood the weightiness of the evidence against it.[51] He realized that he could only ground his love of God upon an equal love of truth, since God is truth. Indeed, all who love God and love truth are united spiritually as brothers, no matter how much their doctrines may differ. Not creed but this interior religious disposition is what unites God's "true apostles."[52] On this basis, he reassessed his relationship to his brother John: he should not reject John (at this time still an Anglican) merely because John's creed tended toward popery. He gained an admiration for the spiritual yearning

49. This point is elaborated in Francis Newman's *A History of the Hebrew Monarchy*, 3rd ed. (London: N. Trübner, 1865).

50. Newman, *Phases of Faith*, 59.

51. Newman, 67.

52. Newman, 59.

present in John's quest for freedom from a stagnant religion (Anglicanism), misdirected though John's quest was.

Francis continued to embrace Christ, especially as preached by Paul, as his Teacher and Lord. He continued to believe in the Resurrection of Christ in this period. However, as time went on, he came to question Christianity still more deeply. He tells this story in chapter 5, "Faith at Second Hand Found to Be Vain." In this new phase of his journey, he began to question whether modern people can trust the reports of ancient people indebted to ancient thought patterns. Paul, for example, thinks it reasonable to argue in allegorical or typological terms and not to attend to questions of historicity. Paul does not provide his congregations with a wealth of historical data justifying his belief in Jesus as the risen Messiah. This fact should raise a serious doubt in modern minds: "How, then, can it be pretended that we have, or can possibly get, the means of assuring ourselves that the Apostles held correct principles of evidence and applied them justly, when we are not able to interrogate them?"[53] If Christ wanted us to believe in his Resurrection, then he should have provided the kinds of historically accessible proofs that modern reasoners can accept. Likewise, Christ should have produced clear proofs justifying actions that would not be tolerated in modern society—such as his driving people out with whips or his calling the leaders of his people a brood of vipers. We are not justified in simply taking the Evangelists' word that Jesus was justified in such actions, given that there is a real possibility that he was merely a fanatic.

One can see how such viewpoints could sweep away the last scraps of admiration for Jesus and Paul on the part of Francis, especially since Francis ruled out any appeal to "the obedience of faith," which he deemed blind faith. If faith is needed—if demonstrative proof is not present—then this must be because Christ and the early Christians did not offer enough evidence. Francis knows that Christians speak of faith as a supernatural assent, a gift of God, but he thinks this is almost surely a mere papering over of the

53. Newman, 71.

deficiency of the evidence. For those who wish to rely upon the Church's testimony, such as his brother John, Francis points out that in practice this often means relying upon scurrilous, power-hungry, and lying clergy. An uneducated person cannot be expected to be able to see through the machinations of the clergy, but an educated person will be able to do so. If the answer is to rely upon the Bible, how is it that the early Christians, possessed of the Bible, ended up in the clutches of popery? Indeed, says Francis (echoing Gibbon and others), the first Jewish Christians soon found their religion "polluted by the heathenism and false philosophy around it."[54] The spread and growth of Christianity, Francis argues, do not bear supernatural marks but rather can be fully explained by natural occurrences, and especially by Constantine's highly political calculation to side with the Christians. Francis observes that, today, "the whole influence which Christianity exerts over the world at large depends on the political history of modern Europe."[55]

Thus, Francis was further stimulated in his sense that it is not the external Church or Bible but the inward spiritual experience that matters. His fight against dogma did not lead him to idealize Christian ethics as some religious liberals did. As he points out, Paul's view of women is on a lesser moral level than that of modern Germans, who are aware—as Paul was not—of the many contributions made by a marriage of equality to the social order. The New Testament also privileged virginity in an unreal way. Some aspects of the New Testament's moral teaching have proven beneficial, but not to such a degree as to be deemed supernatural. Slavery is another case in point: the New Testament generally assumes it without criticizing it. Why did not the Apostles (or Christ himself) take up the anti-slavery line followed by Quakers? Francis knows the usual excuses that are given, but he denies their applicability. The point is that modern "social freedom" has derived somewhat from the Bible, but more fully from liberal thinkers not tied to the scriptural letter.

54. Newman, 76.

55. Newman, 78.

Christians who claim that Christianity must be supernatural because many Christians today reject slavery must account for the fact that Christians have in fact used Christianity to justify such things as "the assumed right of the popes to carve out the countries of the heathen and bestow them with their inhabitants on Christian powers."[56] Moreover, biblical morality encouraged the superstitions that led to many innocent women being burned or otherwise tortured as witches, and, even worse, biblical morality did not ensure basic toleration for other religions, with the result that people even today are punished "in body, purse, or station for not being Christians or not being orthodox."[57]

Francis next turns his attention back to the truth (or lack thereof) of Scripture, the foundation of "orthodox" dogma. The application to Jesus of prophecies such as Isaiah 53 he finds to be "essentially dishonest," because the prophet did not have Jesus in mind.[58] Likewise, the Old Testament prophecies quoted in Acts 13 to show the truth of Jesus' Resurrection clearly have no such application. Many of Jesus' own prophecies did not take place in the way he predicted (due to his imminent eschatology), and the prophecies that corresponded to things that actually happened were likely composed by the Evangelists after the event (for example, the destruction of the Temple). The Old Testament is full of political prophecies that failed to occur. The Gospel of John's promotion of Jesus' (subordinate) divinity is clearly a later invention, unknown to the synoptics. The Evangelist John must have invented Jesus' raising of Lazarus or else this

56. Newman, 83. Francis notes that some of the respondents to his first edition argued that "a man must not be freed [from slavery] until we have ascertained his capacity for self-rule" (Newman, 83). As he rightly replies, "This is indeed a tyrannical assumption. . . . Men are not to have their human rights until we think they will not abuse them! . . . Abolitionists have no thought of exempting men from the penalties of common law if they transgress the law; we only desire that all men shall be equally subjected to the law and equally protected by it. It is truly a strange inference that, because a man is possibly deficient in virtue, therefore he shall not be subject to public law, but to private caprice. . . . Truer far is Homer's morality, who says that a man loses half his virtue on the day he is made a slave" (Newman, 83–84).

57. Newman, 85.

58. Newman, 85.

momentous event would have been reported in the earlier Gospels. In the end, none of the Gospels can be trusted historically. Francis reached these conclusions, he tells us, well before reading David Strauss' definitive book.[59]

Whereas previously Francis had loved Paul above all else, he now found that Paul's credulity in the matter of speaking in tongues showed that Paul could not be trusted as a witness to the reality of Jesus' Resurrection. Paul could rather easily be deceived, despite his evident brilliance. Paul, moreover, "shows total unconcern to the human history and earthly teaching of Jesus."[60] Rather than meeting with the Apostles and questioning them with historically minded keenness to discern whether Jesus really rose from the dead, Paul simply trusted the vision that he saw. Paul does say that five hundred people witnessed the risen Jesus at one time; but Paul gives us no additional information about the credibility of their testimony, and nowhere else in the New Testament is this astounding piece of information discussed. Since Paul was attempting to persuade Jews and Gentiles to believe in Jesus as the Christ, why did Paul not line up each one among the five hundred and write down their testimonies verbatim, with historical rigor?

In the end, as Francis observes, "the Christ with whom Paul held communion was a risen, ascended, exalted Lord, a heavenly being, who reigned over archangels, and was about to appear as judge of the world."[61] Certainly

---

59. Strauss' book first appeared in 1835. For a translation of the fourth German edition, see David Friedrich Strauss, *The Life of Jesus Critically Examined* (Philadelphia: Fortress, 1972). Francis Newman's contemporary and fellow ex-Evangelical, Marian Evans (the novelist George Eliot), was the first English translator. For Strauss' mixture of skeptical historical criticism and Hegelian conviction, see Darrell Jodock, "D.F. Strauss's *Life of Jesus*, F.C. Baur, and Modern Historical Consciousness," in *The Rise of Historical Consciousness among the Christian Churches*, ed. Kenneth L. Parker and Erick H. Moser (Lanham, MD: University Press of America, 2013), 65–88. Jodock shows how Baur critiques and builds upon Strauss. Much more skilled in historical-critical research than was Strauss, Baur was similarly committed to the Hegelian notion that the "dynamics of historical development" can be shown to be "consistent with theological assertions about God and God's work," once the latter have been de-supernaturalized (Jodock, 83).

60. Newman, *Phases of Faith*, 90.

61. Newman, 90.

Paul was sincere and spiritually profound, but he also was credulous and reliant upon visions and prophecies. The Jerusalem Christians did not trust Paul because he added his own spin to the Gospel. Looking back on Paul from the perspective of historical criticism, Francis deems his testimony to be unlikely to have much connection with Jesus as he actually existed. And the other Apostles—the members of the eleven other than perhaps Peter—wrote nothing about the incredible experience of seeing a risen, glorified dead man. Even Peter only wrote about a "spiritual" resurrection (1 Pet. 3:18). Thus, Francis' faith in the doctrine of Jesus' Resurrection collapsed utterly.

In his sixth chapter, "History Discovered to Be No Part of Religion," Francis maintains that at least the New Testament is spiritually edifying. In this sense, it does not matter that the New Testament cannot be trusted to deliver historical facts; it can be trusted to deliver spiritual uplift (even if mixed, at times, with spiritual imperfections). The New Testament became even more spiritually edifying to Francis when, after some research, he realized that the doctrine of the "devil" has no real biblical basis. Francis in his mid-thirties still had some remnants of belief that Jesus might have had a God-given mission to edify us and teach us about our immortal existence after death. But a little research led Francis to reject both the notion that Jesus was the "Messiah" (he subjects the various supposed "Messianic" prophecies to a withering critique) and the notion that humans have an immortal destiny. Jesus' favorite title for himself, "Son of Man," is based upon a reading of Daniel 7; and this Danielic prophecy—related as it is to political events followed quickly by the eschatological judgment—can easily be shown to be unfulfilled and false. Besides, even if this were not so, an inherently murky ancient history can form no plausible foundation for modern-day beliefs. And without a trustworthy revelation from a divine Messiah, life after death has no plausibility, since the philosophical arguments for the immortality of the soul are less than persuasive.

These considerations brought Francis' dogmatic career to a final end.

He still believed, as noted above, that God exists and loves us. But this belief does not require belief in the Bible or in Christianity. Rather, it is the spiritual, experiential truth upon which both the Bible and Christianity are ultimately based. Now freed from every doctrinal system, Francis reports that his love for his fellow humans has been expanded, since previously he focused his love only or mainly on his fellow Christians.[62] He reports that he is much less egotistical or self-centered, since he is no longer focused upon saving his own eternal soul. He reports that he is no longer fanatically unworldly, since he no longer believes that human history is about to come to an end. He reports that his mind is much freer to embrace truth and to follow his conscience, now that he does not have to twist himself into knots interpreting and obeying an authoritative Bible. In his chapter "On the Moral Perfection of Jesus," he succinctly explains what he means by holding that "no sort of perfection" is possible to real human beings—especially

62. For further discussion, see Francis Newman's *A Plea for Catholic Union: Essays towards a Church of the Future as the Organization of Philanthropy* (London: J. Chapman, 1854). Edward Short comments that this was "a prophetic title considering how many Christian churches have reinvented themselves as philanthropic associations in the wake of the collapse of their theological pretensions" (Short, *Newman and His Family*, 150). Short shows that for Francis in his *Catholic Union*, "the catholicity proclaimed by the Church of Rome should not be abandoned but appropriated for an improved, creedless faith" (Short, 150). A similar proposal is made in Francis Newman, *Theism, Doctrinal and Practical; or Didactic Religious Utterances* (London: John Chapman, 1858). Francis wrote *Theism, Doctrinal and Practical* in verse. Along lines characteristic of religious liberalism, he reduces "faith" to an inward intuition, grounded in conscience, that provides access to God's providence—that is, to the moral order, and to an assurance that God loves human beings (see for example Newman, 64–67). Francis strongly affirms that God "is a Spirit and is Moral and absolutely commands Virtue," and he also holds it to be reasonable (though not demonstrable) to think that virtuous persons will live forever with God (Newman, 73, 75). A year before the publication of Charles Darwin's *The Origin of Species*, Francis also discusses as likely the emergence of the human species from non-rational hominids, since this idea was of course widespread prior to the publication of Darwin's arguments regarding natural selection. John Henry Newman, too, had no problem with Darwinian theory—on this point see John Cornwell, *Newman's Unquiet Grave: The Reluctant Saint* (London: Continuum, 2010), 234–236—but John (grounded by the doctrine of original sin, as well as by his keen sense of reality) did not hold to Francis' doctrine of human progress.

to persons possessed internally of "forces of great intensity, the harmonising of which is a vast and painful problem."[63]

Lastly, in his chapter "On Bigotry and Progress," he rehearses the demise of his biblical and dogmatic faith, and he makes a case for what he calls "religious reform" or "religious progress."[64] He sees himself as in the vanguard of progress, and he holds that "the law of God's moral universe, as known to us, is progress."[65] Just as Jesus threw off the strict "ceremonialism" of his contemporaries, so he, Francis, has thrown off biblicism and dogmatism. The result, he hopes, is a breakthrough in freedom, truth, and tolerance, away from the cruel chains of bigotry, ignorance, and persecution. He hopes to have shown that people "are unjust and utterly unreasonable in expecting thoughtful men to abide by the creed of their ancestors."[66] In this regard, he has some particularly sharp words for "Romanists" (such as his brother John), who insist upon obedience to the Church against all "inward judgment."[67] He notes that Protestants are self-contradictory, however, in criticizing the Romanists for taking such a position while, in practice, taking a comparable position themselves. In his view, it is this self-contradiction among Protestants that makes a full-blown conversion to Romanism—which at least is consistent—attractive to some perceptive, but misguided, persons.[68]

What does John Henry Newman have to say on these matters? He, too,

63. Newman, *Phases of Faith*, 104.

64. Newman, 121.

65. Newman, 121.

66. Newman, 123.

67. Newman, 123.

68. He adds: "But nothing of this ought to be allowed to blind us to the truly spiritual and holy developments of historical Christianity; much less make us revert to the old Paganism or pantheism which it supplanted. The great doctrine on which all practical religion depends—the doctrine which nursed the infancy and youth of human nature—is 'the sympathy of God with the perfection of individual man.' Among pagans this was so marred by the imperfect characters ascribed to the Gods, and the dishonourable fables told concerning them, that the philosophers who undertook to prune religion too generally cut away the root by alleging that God was mere intellect and wholly destitute of affections. But happily among the Hebrews the purity of God's character was vindicated; and with the growth of conscience in the highest minds of the nation the ideal image of God shone brighter and brighter" (Newman, 124).

was concerned about bigotry, especially after he became a Catholic in 1845 and experienced the extent of anti-Catholic bigotry in England. He, too, was concerned about clergy abusing their power. He was well aware, moreover, of the contradictions or ambiguities in Scripture that Francis mentions and that, for Francis, partly caused the evaporation of his belief in every dogma but that of God's existence and love for us.

In Tract 85 (1838), John pressed the point that even central doctrines such as the Trinity are not clearly or without ambiguity taught in Scripture. Bible Protestantism, John argues in this Tract, is inconsistent: it faults Anglo-Catholicism for accepting doctrines that Scripture does not clearly teach while, at the same time, accepting just such doctrines itself. Indeed, every dogma has some scriptural passages that tend against it. The point that the Creed is not explicitly found on Scripture's surface does not invalidate the Creed in John's view; rather, it helps us to perceive more clearly what purpose Scripture actually serves. Scripture, though inspired, is historically and humanly composed just as are other ancient texts, and it is not intended to be a handbook of propositions to be believed. It requires, for its proper understanding, to be read spiritually and creedally. It contains ambiguities and problems throughout.[69]

In sum, John and Francis agreed in their awareness of the humanness and occasional obscurity of Scripture, while disagreeing in their conclusions about what this means for the credibility of dogmatic faith. Does John simply obviate all difficulties by demanding blind and bigoted faith in whatever the Church says, as Francis suggests? Having surveyed Francis' history of his own gradual rejection of dogma, let me now turn to John's history of his coming to embrace fully the dogmas of the Catholic Church. John's *Apologia Pro Vita Sua* defends the view that the Church's dogma, far from being the mass of corruption that Francis perceives, is the true and salutary expression of divine revelation in history. John also defends himself

69. For discussion of Tract 85, later republished as "Holy Scripture in Its Relation to the Catholic Creed," see Ker, *John Henry Newman*, 160–162.

against Francis' charge—which Francis stated openly in his 1891 *Contributions Chiefly to the Early History of the Late Cardinal Newman*—that John "seems never to have known what it is to search after truth. How else could he be ignorant that the searcher after truth seeks for evidence, and constantly sacrifices Prepossessions and his own Will in the search?"[70]

John Henry Newman's *Apologia Pro Vita Sua*

Newman frames his *Apologia* as a response to Charles Kingsley, who had accused him of not caring for the truth as much as he should (an accusation identical with the accusation made against John by Francis).[71] Although the *Apologia* does respond to Kingsley, J.M.I. Klaver aptly reminds us that

70. Francis W. Newman, *Contributions Chiefly to the Early History of the Late Cardinal Newman* (London: Kegan Paul, 1891), 57, cited in Short, *Newman and His Family*, 141–142. On the margins of a letter that Francis wrote to him on August 6, 1845, John wrote: "That I could be contemplating questions of Truth and Falsehood never entered into his imagination!" ("Letter to J. H. Newman, 6 August 1845," in *The Letters and Diaries of John Henry Newman*, vol. 10, *The Final Step; 1 November 1843–6 October 1845*, ed. Francis J. McGrath [Oxford: Oxford University Press, 2006], 745, cited in Short, *Newman and His Family*, 207).

71. Edward Short points out that the same charge was brought against Catholics by Bishop Shute (of Durham) in the early nineteenth century, and received an incisive reply from the Catholic historian John Lingard in his *Remarks on a Charge Delivered by the Bishop of Durham to the Clergy of His Diocese* (London: Keating & Brown, 1807). See Short, "Newman, Superstition and the Whig Historian," 103–104. For Kingsley's anti-Catholicism, see Michael Wheeler, *The Old Enemies: Catholic and Protestant in Nineteenth-Century English Culture* (Cambridge: Cambridge University Press, 2006), 105–110; for a sympathetic treatment of Kingsley, see Owen Chadwick, *The Spirit of the Oxford Movement: Tractarian Essays* (Cambridge: Cambridge University Press, 1990), 105–134. J.M.I. Klaver accentuates the point that Newman's *Apologia* is not a "true autobiography" or even a "spiritual autobiography," and he praises Frank Turner's scholarship in reassessing "Newman's person from a psychological and sexual point of view" (Klaver, "The *Apologia*," in *The Oxford Handbook of John Henry Newman*, 454–474, at 466, 468). Klaver suggests that the often negative reception of Turner's book demonstrates Catholic theologians' desire to protect (and conceal) Newman. Nockles argues that "Newman's *Apologia* is not accurate or balanced history" (*The Oxford Movement in Context*, 2), and he makes plausible criticisms regarding Newman's account of the bishops' condemnation of Tract 90 (see Nockles, 295), but I think the *Apologia* can be shown to be largely accurate in the points that it makes—even while it leaves much out and is colored by and focused on Newman's perspective.

"numerous early reviewers [of the *Apologia*] discerned parallels between John and Francis Newman's search for religious truth."[72]

In answer to Kingsley's charges, Newman says what he might have said to Francis—and what he did say to Francis privately. Newman explains to Kingsley that, quite often, "minds in different states and circumstances cannot understand one another."[73] After all, different minds have trouble with different things. Some people cannot easily understand poetry and must have its deeper meanings explained to them. Some people cannot understand the more complex arguments and demonstrations of philosophy. Some people, reading English law, might come away with the faulty notion that the queen is infallible.

Now, it is clear, says Newman, that Kingsley has such a mind as to fail to be able to understand Newman's writings; and, moreover, "to be stone-blind to his ignorance."[74] Newman functions in Kingsley's mind simply as a representative of a Church—the Catholic Church—that through the machinations of sly and crafty theologians, manages to hold many common people in thrall to dogmatic nonsense. To profess Catholic dogma requires, in Kingsley's view, either being "a knave or a fool."[75] Kingsley supposes that Newman has fallen into a mere "simple credulity," and, in thrall to Rome, has rejected common sense (the basic instinct of truthfulness) and replaced it with crafty logic that weaves complex and high-sounding webs in order to justify dangerous dogmatic nonsense.[76] The highly intelligent Newman has become "a self-made idiot, one who has drugged and abused himself into a shameless depravity; one, who, without any misgiving or remorse, is guilty of drivelling superstition, of reckless violation of

72. Klaver, "The *Apologia*," 469.

73. John Henry Newman, *Apologia Pro Vita Sua* (New York: Doubleday, 1989), 98. For textual background, which I do not take up here (since, as I normally do in this book, I use the final edition), see Martin J. Svaglic, "The Revision of Newman's *Apologia*," *Modern Philology* 50, no. 1 (1952): 43–49.

74. Newman, *Apologia Pro Vita Sua*, 98.

75. Newman, 99.

76. Newman, 99.

sacred things, of fanatical excesses, of passionate inanities, of unmanly audacious tyranny over the weak."[77] For Kingsley (and for Francis), this is what believing in Catholic dogma does to an intelligent person who attempts to employ his or her intelligence on behalf of Catholic dogma and practice. Catholic dogma is filled with falsehood, and a defender of it commits himself in every way to falsehood.

Responding to some of Kingsley's sharper attacks, Newman points out that Kingsley has associated Newman with the popular English view of the Catholic casuist, willing to equivocate and to speak with "economy" (i.e., to deceive). If Kingsley is to be believed, Newman is so shifty that any attempt of his to respond to Kingsley's slurs must be seen as yet further sleights-of-hand by a cunning Catholic. Newman directs attention here to the fact that when we interpret someone's words, we often do so "by our antecedent impressions."[78] In his *Grammar of Assent*, written six years later, Newman explains more fully what he means. Here, the point is that the plausibility of Catholicism—of which, for Kingsley, Newman is the representative—often depends upon people's "antecedent impressions" of what Catholicism is.

Newman expresses the hope that his readers will keep in mind that he has long been in the public eye, and, far from hiding his true thoughts, he has consistently and openly spoken out, often to his own cost. He insists that in the dogmatic domain—the domain of his Catholicism (and prior to that the domain of his Anglo-Catholicism)—he "has never given his name or authority to proofs which he thought unsound, or to testimony which he did not think at least plausible."[79] Indeed, as he says, he has cared so much for truth that he freely gave "up much that he loved and prized and could have retained, but that he loved honesty better than name, and Truth

77. Newman, 100. I note that Kingsley in 1853 authored a popular novel attacking patristic Christianity (and specifically Cyril of Alexandria) on these grounds, in light of Cyril's promotion of the murderous assault against the pagan philosopher Hypatia: see Charles Kingsley, *Hypatia, or New Foes with an Old Face* (London: John W. Parker, 1853).

78. Newman, *Apologia Pro Vita Sua*, 109.

79. Newman, 110.

better than dear friends"—namely, his Oxford position and Tractarian colleagues.[80]

Like Francis, Kingsley holds that Newman, in embracing Catholic dogma, had to abandon his reason and submit blindly to Church authority. In putting matters this way, I am reading the *Apologia* through the lens of *Phases of Faith*. As we have seen, Francis holds that in the quest for truth, the rejection of dogma will prevail; and Francis repeatedly suggests that John's embrace of dogma was a noble-minded delusion made due to a psychological need to obey. In defending himself against Kingsley's charges, John seems likely to have had in mind his brother's similar charges.

With reference to his conversion to Catholicism, John states in his *Apologia*: "For twenty years and more I have borne an imputation"—namely, of untruthfulness, slyness, self-deception, blind glorification of the Catholic Church, and opposition to Scripture.[81] In his *Apologia*, he aims primarily to answer the charge of untruthfulness. The untruthfulness that he specifically has in view is whether, as an Anglo-Catholic, he was really the whole time an intentional agent of Roman Catholicism. Was the Tractarian movement really just a Roman plot against the English? In answering this charge, however, he aims to produce something like a *Phases of Faith*—although he does not mention Francis' book—insofar as he intends to do the following: "I will draw out, as far as may be, the history of my mind; I will state the point at which I began, in what external suggestion or accident each opinion had its rise, how far and how they were developed from within, how they grew, were modified, were combined, were in collision with each other, and were changed."[82] Put simply, he intends to show how his doctrinal ideas developed, and he intends to show that his embrace of Catholic doctrine was not made out of a blind desire to attach himself to the Catholic Church, let alone due to "fraud and the sophistries of the

80. Newman, 112.
81. Newman, 112.
82. Newman, 123.

schools," but on reasonable and good grounds.[83] The more he followed truth, and the more he understood Scripture, the more he found both fulfilled in the Catholic Church's doctrine and practice. In other words, the discovery of doctrinal development, not doctrinal corruption, is the fruit of a reasonable mind's inquiry into Christianity.

Newman begins at the beginning, with his school days and youthful imagination. His first school, he assures us, had no Catholic ideas whatsoever. At age fourteen, he "read Paine's Tracts against the Old Testament, and found pleasure in thinking of the objections which were contained in them. Also, [he] read some of Hume's Essays; and perhaps that on Miracles."[84] Already, then, he was fairly well versed in the historical objections to the truth of Scripture (and thus to the truth of dogma as well).

It was at age fifteen, under the guidance of Walter Mayers, that John first "fell under the influences of a definite Creed and received into [his] intellect impressions of dogma."[85] Joined by Francis, he became an Evangelical Anglican. During this time, he read two books that led him in contrasting directions. The first was the Evangelical Anglican Joseph Milner's work of early Church history, which gave him an enduring love of the Church Fathers; the second was a 1754 book by another Evangelical Anglican, Bishop Thomas Newton, on biblical prophecy that led him for many years to believe that the pope was the Antichrist.[86] As an undergraduate at Oxford, still very much an Evangelical (as he was until the late 1820s), he was influenced by the writings of the Evangelical Anglican Thomas Scott.[87] In

83. Newman, 123.

84. Newman, 127.

85. Newman, 127.

86. For the latter, see Thomas Newton, *Dissertations on the Prophecies, Which Have Remarkably Been Fulfilled, and at This Time Are Fulfilling in the World*, 2 vols. (New York: William Durell, 1794). Gareth Atkins observes, "By the 1860s apocalypticism had become associated with outré millennialists, but fifty years earlier anti-papal readings of prophecy remained central to mainstream Anglican apologetics" (Atkins, "Evangelicals," in *The Oxford Handbook of John Henry Newman*, 173–195, at 177).

87. For the view that Newman's Evangelical Anglican period lasted until 1826, and in certain ways even longer, see Atkins, "Evangelicals," 180–185. Turner likewise suggests that Newman's Evangelicalism lasted longer than some readers might suppose from his *Apologia*:

his *Apologia*, Newman writes the following: "What . . . will strike any reader of Scott's history and writings, is his bold unworldliness and vigorous independence of mind. He followed truth wherever it led him, beginning with Unitarianism, and ending in a zealous faith in the Holy Trinity."[88] This sentence of John's responds implicitly both to Francis' opposite journey and to Francis' claim that independent and objective questing for truth will necessarily lead to rejection of Christian doctrine. Newman credits Scott for giving him two developmental maxims: "'Holiness before peace,' and 'Growth is the only evidence of life.'"[89]

In his Evangelical period, John compiled a list of scriptural proofs for various doctrines, with his own annotations. He also combed through the Athanasian Creed and listed the scriptural texts in favor of each creedal proposition. Although Newman credits Evangelicalism with giving him an Augustinian sense of the "doctrine of the warfare between the city of God and the powers of darkness," he notes that William Law's classic book on

---

see Turner, *John Henry Newman*, 115. Turner portrays Newman as artful, deceitful, double-dealing, and ambitious.

88. Newman, *Apologia Pro Vita Sua*, 128. Newman is here referring to Scott's autobiographical *The Force of Truth: An Authentic Narrative* (London: G. Keith and J. Johnson, 1779). Scott was best known for his biblical commentaries, and *The Force of Truth* has a strongly Evangelical and Methodist tenor. He had lost his faith in the Trinity due to his admiration for John Locke's emphasis on reasonable religion, but even during this period he retained a strong appreciation for Scripture. For the argument that Scott's account of his conversion significantly influenced the first chapters of Newman's *Apologia Pro Vita Sua*, see Linda H. Peterson, *Victorian Autobiography: The Tradition of Self-Interpretation* (New Haven, CT: Yale University Press, 1986), 95–103. Without denying this possibility, I note that Francis Newman's *Phases of Faith* is more similar stylistically to Scott's account—though following the opposite path, as a chronicle of losing Evangelical faith. Peterson adds the point that the reason the *Apologia Pro Vita Sua* is not structured through allusions to biblical figures and events may be that such biblical allusions were standard for "evangelical spiritual autobiography," from which Newman distanced himself (Peterson, 105). See also Lothar Kuld, "Evangelical Patterns of Conversion in Newman's Autobiographical Writings," trans. Michael Payant, in *By Whose Authority? Newman, Manning and the Magisterium*, ed. V. Alan McClelland (Bath: Downside Abbey, 1996), 112–122, which argues that the parallels between the *Apologia* and Scott's *The Force of Truth* are even more extensive than Peterson recognizes.

89. Newman, *Apologia Pro Vita Sua*, 128. On Scott's Evangelical Anglican influence on Newman, see Atkins, "Evangelicals," 175–176. In 1821, Newman attended the memorial service for Scott held at the influential Evangelical Anglican parish St. John's Chapel, Bedford Row, in London, a five-minute walk from Newman's family home.

the life of holiness did the same.[90] Regarding heaven and hell, he remarks that he accepts the existence of hell but has "tried in various ways to make that truth less terrible to the reason"—as he does later in *Grammar of Assent*—thus showing himself to be well aware of the concerns raised by Francis.[91]

Among his mentors and friends in his early years as a Fellow at Oriel College, Newman names four men as most important—three of whom were later dismayed by his public critique of the views of the liberal Anglican Renn Dickson Hampden, when the latter was nominated in 1836 to be Regius Professor of Divinity.[92] Hampden eventually had his revenge,

90. Newman, *Apologia Pro Vita Sua*, 129.

91. Newman, 129. For succinct background to Newman's Evangelical period, which in certain ways extended into the 1830s, see Vincent Ferrer Blehl, "Newman's Conversion of 1845: A Fresh Approach," in *By Whose Authority?*, 123–135, at 126–128. See also Geertjan Zuijdwegt's *An Evangelical Adrift: The Making of John Henry Newman's Theology* (Washington, DC: The Catholic University of America Press, forthcoming), although this book was not published in time for me to employ it.

92. See John Henry Newman, *Elucidations of Dr. Hampden's Theological Statements* (London: J.H. Parker & Messrs. Rivington, 1836), especially his summary on 53, cited in Short, "Newman and the Liberals," 193–194; and see also the correspondence between Hampden and Newman in 1835–1836 contained in *John Henry Newman: A Portrait in Letters*, ed. Roderick Strange (Oxford: Oxford University Press, 2015), 87–89, 92. On 23 June 1835, Hampden charged Newman—joined to Henry Wilberforce and others—with "dissimulation, and falsehood and dark malignity" (*John Henry Newman*, 87), to which Newman replied the next day. In a letter of 14 February 1836, Newman replied to another letter from Hampden, pointing out that "since you state in your pamphlet that an Unitarian holds 'the *whole* revelation' *as holding* 'the basis of divine facts' (vid Observ. pp. 13–19) you surely do deny that 'the truths of the Trinity and Incarnation' are 'revealed'" (Newman, 92). Helpful context has been provided by Geertjan Zuijdwegt, "Richard Whately," in *The Oxford Handbook of John Henry Newman*, 196–216, at 209–211. As Zuijdwegt shows, Hampden's *Observations on Religious Dissent* (Oxford: J.H. Parker, 1834) was a restatement of Whately's theological principles. Zuijdwegt comments, "Given the similarity between the theological principles of Whately and Hampden, Newman's virulent rejection of Hampden's principles, only two weeks after his final letter to Whately, comes as no surprise. Like Whately, Hampden stressed the identity of revelation with Scripture, along with its purely economical and practical character, and applied these principles to a political controversy" ("Richard Whately," 210). Zuijdwegt rightly warns against treating "Newman's critique of Hampden in isolation from his theological development away from Whately. The lack of such an integrated theological perspective is at its worst in Frank Turner's ascription of 'Newman's furious rivalry with Hampden' to personal frustration as much as to theology" (Zuijdwegt, 211). For a similarly insightful defense of Newman's critique of Hampden, see Roderick Strange, "Newman and

responding in print to Newman's *An Essay on the Development of Christian Doctrine* by branding Newman a corruptor of doctrine. Hampden states in his book review, "The Church possessed from the first the knowledge of the Truth as it is in Jesus, as fully as it does now; and . . . the labour of subsequent ages has not added to, or cleared up, or worked out, the original Doctrine, but only counteracted attempts to vary and corrupt it."[93]

The four Oriel scholars whom Newman credits most for his intellectual growth are Richard Whately, Edward Hawkins, Joseph Blanco White, and William James. Newman praises all of them, in addition to apologizing for provocations over the years against Whately, who sharply opposed Newman's Anglo-Catholic turn.[94] From Whately, the young Newman received

Hampden," in *John Henry Newman and Modernism*, ed. Arthur Hilary Jenkins (Sigmaringendorf, DE: Glock und Lutz, 1990), 29–40. For further perspectives, see Marvin R. O'Connell, *The Oxford Conspirators: A History of the Oxford Movement 1833–45* (London: Macmillan, 1969), 191–206; Peter Nockles, "'Lost Causes . . . and Impossible Loyalties': The Oxford Movement and the University," in *The History of the University of Oxford*, vol. 6, *Nineteenth-Century Oxford*, Part 1, ed. M.G. Brock and M.C. Curthoys (Oxford: Clarendon, 1997), 195–267; George Herring, *What Was the Oxford Movement?* (London: Continuum, 2002), 57; and Tod E. Jones, *The Broad Church: A Biography of a Movement* (Lanham, MD: Lexington Books, 2003), 83. Along Turner's lines, see Klaver's argument that Newman's "behaviour to Hampden" was "far from honest" (Klaver, "The *Apologia*," 470); and Nockles expresses himself similarly (describing Hampden as "a bogeyman for the Tractarians as much for the qualified support for the admission of Dissenters that he expressed in his *Observations on Dissent* (1834) as for his apparently 'Socinianizing' but unreadable Bampton lectures of 1832") in Nockles, "The Oxford Movement in an Oxford College: Oriel as the Cradle of Tractarianism," in *The Oxford Movement: Europe and the Wider World 1830–1930*, ed. Stewart J. Brown and Peter B. Nockles (Cambridge: Cambridge University Press, 2012), 11–33, at 21–22. See also Thomas Arnold's sharp attack, "The Oxford Malignants and Dr. Hampden," *Edinburgh Review* 63, no. 127 (1836): 225–239, well discussed in O'Connell, *The Oxford Conspirators*, 204–205.

93. Renn Dickson Hampden, "The Work of Christ and the Work of the Spirit" (1 November 1846), in *Sermons Preached before the University of Oxford, in the Cathedral of Christ Church, from 1836 to 1847* (London: B. Fellowes, 1848), 462–463, cited in Benjamin J. King, "The Protestant Reception of the *Essay on Development*, 1845–1925," in *Receptions of Newman*, ed. Frederick D. Aquino and Benjamin J. King (Oxford: Oxford University Press, 2015), 9–29, at 12. Hampden links Newman's approach with the notion of doctrinal development in Möhler's *Symbolism*, which Hampden disliked.

94. Ker terms Whately a "Latitudinarian in theology" (*John Henry Newman*, 19), even if Whately's contributions to certain aspects of Newman's religious epistemology should not be underestimated. For the latter see Whately, *Elements of Rhetoric*, 2nd ed. (Oxford: John

a volume that persuaded him of the truth of the doctrine of baptismal regeneration; and Whately later (in 1827) cautioned him when, due to Newman's then-preference for the pre-Nicene Fathers, he seemed to be moving in an "Arian" direction.[95] From Hawkins and White, he learned to anticipate the attack that was to come later in the century against Scripture's veracity, and to adopt a looser account of biblical inerrancy and a more historically informed sense of biblical inspiration.[96] From Hawkins, he also

Murray, 1828). As another significant teacher, Newman elsewhere mentions Pusey's mentor Charles Lloyd of Christ Church—later Bishop of Oxford—who emphasized "authoritative doctrine and tradition" (Ker, *John Henry Newman*, 20; see also Benjamin John King, *Newman and the Alexandrian Fathers: Shaping Doctrine in Nineteenth-Century England* [Oxford: Oxford University Press, 2009], 9 for Lloyd's interest in the Greek Fathers); and Newman in the 1830s had frequent recourse to Martin Routh's compendium of patristic texts (for Routh's influence on Newman, see Thomas M. Parker, "The Rediscovery of the Fathers in the Seventeenth-Century Anglican Tradition," in *The Rediscovery of Newman: An Oxford Symposium*, ed. John Coulson and A.M. Allchin [London: Sheed & Ward, 1967], 31–49, at 45–46). For further background to the "Noetic circle," see Yngve Brilioth, *The Anglican Revival: Studies in the Oxford Movement* (London: Longmans, Green, 1933), chapter 6.

95. See the explanatory remarks in Stephen Thomas, *Newman and Heresy: The Anglican Years* (Cambridge: Cambridge University Press, 1991), 14–18. For Whately's eccentric Trinitarian theology, see Zuijdwegt, "Richard Whately," 202–206. Whately inclined toward Sabellianism and held that the doctrine of the three distinct divine persons has to do with the economy of salvation but not necessarily with the immanent Godhead. Zuijwegt argues, "What troubled him in Newman's sermon was not so much that it appeared to depict the Son as inferior to, and therefore less divine than, the Father [since Newman said the opposite in the sermon]. Rather, Whately questioned the whole enterprise of understanding the names Father, Son, and Spirit as corresponding to real relational distinctions in the Godhead" (Zuijdwegt, 203). However, King holds that Newman in this period really did exhibit the subordinationist tendencies (influenced by the pre-Nicene Alexandrians) of High-Church theologians such as Bishop Bull.

96. Eamon Duffy describes Newman's perspective on these matters: "In Tract 85, written while he was still an Anglican, Newman had used the fact of the fallibility of historical and factual material in the Bible as an argument in favour of tradition and the authority of the Church, and he remained alert to the problems for faith posed by biblical criticism. In 1865 he had been visited at the Oratory by the liberal Anglican Dean Stanley of Westminster, and they had discussed these issues. Newman told Stanley he had recognized the multiple authorship of the Pentateuch from his first reading of Genesis in Hebrew. . . . Newman then went on to 'play the "Devils' Advocate" against the story of David in the Books of Samuel, saying that it seemed 'more like a poem than any other part of the Bible.' And while Newman appeared to Stanley to be worried about applying this kind of 'dissolving criticism' to the Gospels, he admitted to Stanley that, 'I seem to myself to see this same compilatory character in the Gospels: not a regular history, but biographical anecdotes strung together.' But Newman

gained an appreciation of Tradition, and from James, an appreciation for apostolic succession.[97] Hawkins, later joined by Whately, showed Newman that Scripture "was never intended to teach doctrine, but only to prove [or verify] it, and that, if we would learn doctrine, we must have recourse to the formularies of the Church; for instance to the Catechism, and to the Creeds."[98] Lastly, Whately taught Newman to value the visible, corporate existence of the Church and to hold an anti-Erastian line on Church polity. For Whately, the State should support the Church but has no right to interfere in spiritual matters; in this sense, "Church and State should be independent of each other."[99]

In his telling, then, these Oxford mentors separated John from the Evangelicalism or Bible Christianity to which Francis continued to adhere.[100] In this period, too, John began to read the work of Joseph Butler, who emphasized the existence of "a visible Church, the oracle of truth and a pattern of sanctity," as well as "the historical character of Revelation" and the significance of probabilities in guiding assent.[101] Butler urged attention to the

considered all this was a problem for Protestants rather than Catholics" (Duffy, *John Henry Newman: A Very Brief History* [London: SPCK, 2019], 72–73).

97. Hawkins delivered his University Sermon on Tradition on May 31, 1818, during Newman's undergraduate years. Peter Nockles points out, "Hawkins's *Noetic* friends, Whately and Arnold, were alarmed at the propaganda use which the Tractarians in the 1830s made of Hawkins' sermon *The Use and Importance of Unauthoritative Tradition* (1819). . . . After Keble's sermon extolling oral Tradition in 1836, Hawkins decided to follow Arnold's advice and to rewrite *Unauthoritative Tradition*. The result was a new sermon, *The Duty of Private Judgment* (1838) and a series of Bampton Lectures in 1840 which, to the dismay of some Tractarians, subtly modified the original argument" (*The Oxford Movement in Context*, 109–110).

98. Newman, *Apologia Pro Vita Sua*, 132. For Hawkins' influence, see also Ker, *John Henry Newman*, 22.

99. Newman, *Apologia Pro Vita Sua*, 134. See Richard Whately, *Letters on the Church* (London: Longman, Rees, Orme, Brown, and Green, 1826), published anonymously. For further discussion, see David De Giustino, "Disconnecting Church and State: Richard Whately's Ideas in the 1830s," *Albion* 35, no. 1 (2003): 53–70; Brilioth, *The Anglican Revival*, 84–85.

100. Ker credits as well Newman's work at the Curate of St. Clement's, a working-class parish, beginning in July 1824.

101. Newman, *Apologia Pro Vita Sua*, 132.

analogies between natural revelation and supernatural revelation, as a way of apprehending the truth of the latter.[102]

In the above five figures (including Butler), most of the foundations for John's Christian worldview are found. The contributions of these scholars suggest why John did not follow Francis in reading Scripture against Trinitarianism and why John never felt the shock over scriptural ambiguities that led Francis to distrust divine revelation as a whole. In this foundational period, John was shaped by Oxford teachers who leaned toward liberal Anglicanism. Apologetically, his trust in Christian claims was buttressed by Butler's strategy of anticipating analogies from natural religion (or natural revelation). Through the work of Thomas Scott, he obtained an appreciation for Trinitarian doctrine and its intelligibility.

None of these figures were "Catholicizers."[103] Against Kingsley's charge that Newman was a Catholic agent within the Anglican Church, Newman shows that his basic theological standpoints came to him from Anglicans. Yet Newman also says that in turning away from Evangelicalism, he was by the mid-1820s "drifting in the direction of liberalism"—along Whately's lines—allowing his theological work to be guided by (rationalistic) cleverness.[104]

---

102. See Joseph Butler, *The Analogy of Religion*, in *The Works of Joseph Butler, LL.D.*, new ed. (London: William Tegg, 1867), 1–200. For an excellent succinct discussion of Butler's work, see Jane Garnett, "Joseph Butler," in *The Oxford Handbook of John Henry Newman*, 135–153. She identifies an extraordinary range of ways in which Butler influenced Newman.

103. For further evidence of this, see Richard Whately, *The Errors of Romanism Traced to Their Origin in Human Nature* (London: B. Fellowes, 1830). Among other things, Whately's book condemns Roman Catholic superstition, fraud, and claims regarding the Church's infallibility. As Zuijdwegt remarks, "Newman knew that his manner of relying on patristic authority and his intellectual approach to the Trinity were condemned in *Errors of Romanism* as 'inseparably connected' with superstition" ("Richard Whately," 208). Whately's book appeared in multiple editions, including one in 1845.

104. Newman, *Apologia Pro Vita Sua*, 135. Newman seemingly has Whately's theology in view here. Defending the Oriel of the early- and mid-1820s, Frank Turner notes that Oriel had "a genuine sympathy for evangelicals, ignored by historians but clearly recognized by Newman himself. In his autobiographical memoir he recalled that religiously the Oriel fellowship stood as 'neither high Church nor low Church' but as 'a new school' marked by 'its spirit of moderation and comprehension'" (Turner, *John Henry Newman*, 115–116). Ker quotes the same passage from *Apologia Pro Vita Sua*, remarking that "there was the 'atmosphere'

Fortunately, during this time he had gained the friendship of Edward Pusey, and by 1826 he came to know Richard Hurrell Froude.[105] As we have seen above, the impact of the latter was profound. Stephen Thomas notes that Froude, in 1827, wrote an essay titled "On the Connexion between a Right Faith and Right Practice; on the Ethos of Heresy."[106] This short essay, influenced by Froude's mentor John Keble, argues that right practice must be present in order to sustain correct faith, and vice versa; in theological matters, it is not the head alone that can suffice. This emphasis on "ethos" spoke to Newman, as did many of Froude's opinions.

In 1828, Froude brought Newman together with Keble, who in 1827 had published his collection of liturgical poems, *The Christian Year*.[107] Newman describes how Keble solidified the foundations noted above, while strengthening Newman's movement away from liberal Anglicanism.[108] Keble's impact had to do primarily with religious epistemology, deepening Newman's ability to assent to Christian doctrine. Indebted to Butler, Keble

---

of the Oriel Common Room, which was 'neither high Church nor low Church, but . . . characterized by its spirit of moderation and comprehension.' Its leading lights, figures like Copleston, Whately, John Davison, Edward Hawkins, and Thomas Arnold, were objects of suspicion to 'the old unspiritual high-and-dry, then in possession of the high places of Oxford,' who 'pronounced them unsafe.' Like other Evangelicals, Newman was 'grateful for that liberality of mind which was in such striking contrast with the dominant high-Church'" (Ker, *John Henry Newman*, 21–22).

105. Ker notes that Pusey was elected a Fellow of Oriel the year after Newman, and at first "Newman was impressed by his religious seriousness, but regretted his lack of sympathy for Evangelicalism" (Ker, *John Henry Newman*, 19).

106. Thomas, *Newman and Heresy*, 25.

107. For discussion of *The Christian Year*, see Brilioth, *The Anglican Revival*, 71–75.

108. See also Newman's "Note A.: Liberalism," appended to his *Apologia Pro Vita Sua*, ed. Charles Frederick Harrold (New York: Longmans, Green, 1947), 259–269 [I cite this edition only for this Note, since my other edition of the *Apologia* does not contain this Note], at 262: "Now and then a man of note appeared in the Pulpit or Lecture Rooms of the University, who was a worthy representative of the more religious and devout Anglicans. . . . Among these especially may be mentioned Mr. John Miller, of Worcester College, who preached the Bampton Lecture for the year 1817. But, as far as I know, he who turned the tide, and brought the talent of the University round to the side of the old theology, and against what was familiarly called 'march-of-mind,' was Mr. Keble. In and from Keble the mental activity of Oxford took that contrary direction which issued in what was called Tractarianism."

underlined the "sacramentality" of reality: "the doctrine that material phenomena are both the types and the instruments of real things unseen."[109] Keble also enriched Butler's doctrine of cumulative probabilities by emphasizing that "it is not merely probability which makes us intellectually certain, but probability as it is put to account by faith and love"—so that our certitude comes in fact from the divine "Object, received in faith and love, which renders it reasonable to take probability as sufficient for internal conviction."[110] For Keble, one assents to God speaking in Christ from personal "knowledge of the speaker" and "from love of him."[111]

Here one sees not only an important influence upon Newman's *Grammar of Assent* but also a second set of foundations that enabled John to proceed very differently from Francis in assessing matters such as the New Testament's use of Old Testament prophecies and typologies or the New Testament's testimonies to Christ's Resurrection.[112]

However, Newman did not think that Keble's perspective, as such, went far enough. Arguably, much of Newman's work over the rest of his life sought to complete it. He remarks that Keble's perspective "was beautiful and religious, but it did not even profess to be logical."[113] Describing how he sought to advance Keble's line of thought, John looks back upon his writings on miracles and doctrinal development and, in the process, anticipates the *Grammar of Assent* he would complete six years later. I will not summarize the whole perspective he adumbrates at this juncture of the *Apologia*, but his view is essentially that the certitude that we possess in matters of natural or revealed theology comes from "an *assemblage* of concurring and converging probabilities."[114]

109. Newman, *Apologia Pro Vita Sua*, 139.

110. Newman, 139.

111. Newman, 140.

112. Newman's apologetics bears affinity with Hans Urs von Balthasar's *Love Alone Is Credible* and with Pierre Rousselot's and Bernard Lonergan's emphasis on the "eyes of faith." See my discussion of these figures in my *Did Jesus Rise from the Dead?* (Oxford: Oxford University Press, 2019), chapters 5 and 6.

113. Newman, *Apologia Pro Vita Sua*, 140.

114. Newman, 140.

Guided by Froude and Keble, Newman revised his mode of defending miracles, on which he had written an essay in 1826 under the influence of Whately and Evangelicalism.[115] In the course of the 1830s, Newman came to believe that what we should look for in assessing the historicity of a particular miracle is greater or lesser probability, rather than simply holding that some miracles must be accepted and others rejected on theological grounds. Influenced also by his early reading of Milner's *History of the Church of Christ*,[116] Newman opened up a place for postbiblical miracles on the grounds of the ongoing outpouring of the grace of the Holy Spirit.

Newman reports that his *close* friendship with Froude began in 1829. As noted above, Froude "professed openly his admiration of the Church of Rome" and "delighted in the notion of an hierarchical system, of sacerdotal power and of full ecclesiastical liberty."[117] Froude is the first firmly Catholicizing voice that Newman presents in the *Apologia*. The basic lines of Newman's dogmatic and philosophical thought were, on Newman's telling, already set; but at the same time, Newman does not minimize Froude's impact. Clearly, Froude strengthened Newman's appreciation for Church Tradition, and Froude celebrated numerous Roman Catholic viewpoints, such as the Real Presence of Christ in the Eucharist, the value of consecrated virginity, and the frequency of miracles through the ministrations of the saints.

Newman recalls that Froude was interested in historical inquiry, but

---

115. Newman's mature view of miracles stood in opposition to Whately's viewpoint. Zuijdwegt notes that Whately, in his *Easy Lessons on Christian Evidences* (London: John W. Parker, 1838) and *Remarks on Some Causes of Hostility to the Christian Religion* (Dublin: Milliken and Son, 1838), contended that "the Tractarian deference to the doctrinal authority of the (early) Church undercut the rational basis of Christian faith, because it obfuscated the distinction between the supernatural message of Scripture—validated by miracles—and the questionable teachings of ecclesial tradition, which lacked such verification" (Zuijdwegt, "Richard Whately," 212).

116. See especially the first (of four) volumes: Milner, *History of the Church of Christ*, vol. 1, *The First Three Centuries*, 4th ed., rev. Isaac Milner (London: T. Cadell and W. Davies, 1812). For discussion, see John D. Walsh, "Joseph Milner's Evangelical Church History," *Journal of Ecclesiastical History* 10, no. 2 (1959): 174–187.

117. Newman, *Apologia Pro Vita Sua*, 143.

not in theology per se. Froude did not read the Fathers or study the councils of the Church. He was not bothered that Newman believed the pope to be the Antichrist, because Froude (in Newman's telling) could not believe that Newman actually meant it. Summing up, Newman identifies three areas in which Froude unwittingly influenced him toward Roman Catholicism: Froude gave him a new appreciation for the Church of Rome, for the Real Presence, and for Marian devotion.

In 1828, Newman read the Church Fathers chronologically, and in 1830, he began research for the book that was published as *The Arians of the Fourth Century*. Recollecting this period, he suggests that it was partly from the seventeenth-century Anglican bishop George Bull that he got the idea that "Antiquity [the patristic era] was the true exponent of the doctrines of Christianity and the basis of the Church of England."[118] At this time, Newman enthusiastically championed the Alexandrians: Clement, Origen, and Athanasius. In Clement and Origin, he found the deep sense of

118. Newman, 145. For insight into Bull's work and Newman's use of it, see especially Thomas, *Newman and Heresy*, 173–176, 246, including Thomas' point that "Bull brought to Newman's attention the most formidable extant scholarly challenge to the static concept of orthodoxy, in the Jesuit historian, Denys Pétau's (Petavius') account of early Church doctrine. . . . Particularly controversial was his argument that Arianism was no new invention, but that it came straight out of earlier orthodox Fathers' subordination of the Son to the Father" (173). Thomas sums up Bull's viewpoint: "In defending the pre-Nicene Fathers, Bull stolidly presents the Church's understanding of the *revelatum* as always having been the same: 'orthodoxy' is fixed and immutable, no new ideas or developments being possible. When confronted with heresy, the Church always knew what orthodoxy was—it had a clear idea of it—although it may, initially, have been stuck for the best way of putting it into *words*. This sharp distinction between on the one hand, words or terms, and, on the other, things, ideas, or realities was all-pervasive in Bull as the main means of reconciling the Fathers' variations with a fixed and static orthodoxy" (Thomas, 173–174). For further background, see Ralph H. Broker, *The Influence of Bull and Petavius on Cardinal Newman's Theory of the Development of Christian Doctrine* (Rome: Gregorian University Press, 1938); James Pereiro, *Theories of Development in the Oxford Movement* (Leominster, UK: Gracewing, 2015), 93–94; as well as George Bull, *A Defence of the Nicene Creed, out of the Extant Writings of the Catholic Doctors Who Flourished during the Three First Centuries of the Christian Church* (London: J. Parker, 1851). Thomas shows that the spread of Socinianism in nineteenth-century England owed something to the Petavian-style historical arguments of the seventeenth-century German defender of Arius (and friend of Spinoza) Christopher Sandius, author of the *Nucleus Historiae Ecclesiasticae* (Cologne: J. Nicolas, 1676).

"sacramentality" that he had found in Keble and also in Butler. Behind created nature, behind the world that we see around us, stand the purposes, dispensations, and actions of God. Newman describes the Alexandrian exegetical and philosophical perspective to which he gravitated: "Nature was a parable: Scripture was an allegory: pagan literature, philosophy, and mythology, properly understood, were but a preparation for the Gospel."[119]

It is unlikely that John is mounting here a direct critique of Francis' path in *Phases of Faith*. Nevertheless, one can see here a much greater range of resources for addressing Francis' concerns about the historical credibility of the New Testament. For John, the New Testament authors, with their love of typology, have entered into the true inner depths of history. Although he admires modern historians, he thinks that they have missed these depths to their detriment.[120] John's way of understanding history has room for divine dispensations, such as God's choosing of his people Israel. He also finds that doctrinal development is at work in Scripture: "first one disclosure and then another, till the whole was brought into full manifestation."[121] On this view, even in the New Testament "room was made for the anticipation of further and deeper

---

119. Newman, *Apologia Pro Vita Sua*, 146. See also Charles F. Harrold, "John Henry Newman and the Alexandrian Platonists," *Modern Philology* 37, no. 3 (1940): 279–291. Further background is provided by Benjamin King, who contends that "in *An Essay on the Development of Christian Doctrine* (1845), Newman reassessed the position of Origen and began to place his former hero outside of orthodoxy" (*Newman and the Alexandrian Fathers*, 184). The result, King argues along lines that I disagree with, is a notion of "development of doctrine" that is "less open to historical dynamism": "Newman's 'development' is shorthand for the triumph of Athanasian orthodoxy—an orthodoxy which, in the way he presents it, allows little room for complexity or dynamism. Cyril among Greeks and Augustine among Latins are portrayed not as enriching a tradition but as merely reiterating the teaching of Athanasius" (King, 185–186; cf. 199–200). King emphasizes areas in which Newman misreads or distorts Athanasius' writings, and King complains that "in *Development of Christian Doctrine* on the one hand Newman showed how the earlier epoch could lead to the later; on the other hand he criticized the earlier by those later standards" (King, 216–217).

120. For the New Testament's typological resonances, see Richard B. Hays, *Echoes of Scripture in the Gospels* (Waco, TX: Baylor University Press, 2016); Hays, *Echoes of Scripture in the Letters of Paul* (New Haven, CT: Yale University Press, 1989).

121. Newman, *Apologia Pro Vita Sua*, 146.

disclosures, of truths still under the veil of the letter, and in their season to be revealed."[122]

I note that Francis' worldview can perceive the corrosive impact that the theory of evolution has upon the six-thousand-year literal biblical timeframe, but it lacks the imagination to see the deeper developmental reality that the Bible reveals. With their appreciation for Christ the Teacher and for the spiritual senses of Scripture, the Alexandrians could illumine this deeper reality.

Newman reports that at this time, he held that the entire material universe was caused and governed by God through the mediation of the angels. On this view, not only God stands behind the material creation, but so also does the spiritual or angelic creation. In the mid-1830s, Newman also believed that the distinctive spirits of nations and institutions were indebted to guardian angels who mingled themselves with humankind.

Newman goes on to say that in the early 1830s, anti-Erastianism and doctrinal corruption became central matters because Parliament formally renounced Anglican requirements for office and began to address ecclesiastical reforms. As we have seen, the question was whether the Church of England would now come fully under the control of liberal governmental leaders. Fearing this outcome, Newman and his friends argued that the early Church, with its bishops willing to endure persecution from the State, was the model to which the contemporary Church should conform. Newman states in the *Apologia*, "If Liberalism once got a footing within [the Anglican Church], it was sure of the victory in the event. . . . Reformation principles were powerless to rescue her."[123] He recalls that he became "fierce" against all of the "instruments" and "manifestations" of Liberalism, and he makes clear that he acted in some ludicrous and overly

122. Newman, 146.

123. Newman, 149. Newman considered that Evangelical Anglican principles, grounded in the individual reader of Scripture, logically led to liberalism.

polemical ways.[124] As he says in self-mocking tones, "I began to think that I had a mission."[125] Newman is describing the early days of the Tractarian movement. A week after Newman returned home from his tour of Italy and Sicily (Francis returned home at the very same time from his trip to Persia with the Brethren), Keble preached his sermon "National Apostasy" on July 14, 1833.[126]

Among the young men who gathered to the cause, there were significant disagreements about how to proceed. Hugh James Rose and William Palmer were more traditionally "High Church," a party disparagingly characterized by Froude as the "Z's." A central point of difference was how radical to be with respect to the Establishment, but all agreed that the advantages of the Establishment were substantial.[127] To stir up public opinion, Newman spearheaded the publication of a series of Tracts written by individuals rather than (as Palmer desired) under the aegis of a steering committee, and these Tracts became widely known. In the *Apologia*, he recalls that the main purpose of the Tracts was to uphold "that

124. Newman, 151.

125. Newman, 152.

126. The import of this sermon is contested, as in the following remark (which I find exaggerated) by Owen Chadwick, in his "Introduction" to *The Mind of the Oxford Movement*, ed. Owen Chadwick (London: Adam & Charles Black, 1960), 11–64, at 33–34: "Newman kept the day of Keble's assize sermon upon *National Apostasy* (*14* July *1833*) as the day when the Oxford Movement began. Yet that sermon is untypical of the movement as it later developed. . . . The sermon is more akin to the sermons of high churchmen in Queen Anne's reign, than to the high churchmanship of Hurrell Froude or Newman. It is high churchmanship with regard to the State and dissent, a claim to retain the rightful privileges of the Establishment, and less markedly the type of high churchmanship which asserted the independent and divine status of the Church, whether the Church was established or disestablished. The sermon collected no disciples, raised no party-standard, asserted nothing but what other high churchmen were saying through the country. The importance of the sermon to the Movement was only in its signal within Newman's mind." More broadly, see the background given by Marvin O'Connell, *The Oxford Conspirators*, 3–63. After setting forth the political context, O'Connell discusses the situation of the Church of England in 1832, as well as the situation of the University of Oxford and the deadly pro-Reform riots that followed upon the original defeat (due to the bishops in the House of Lords) of the Reform Act.

127. See J.H.L. Rowlands, *Church, State and Society: The Attitudes of John Keble, Richard Hurrell Froude and John Henry Newman, 1827–1845* (Worthing, UK: Churchman Publishing, 1989), 91.

primitive Christianity which was delivered for all time by the early teachers of the Church, and which was registered and attested in the Anglican formularies and by the Anglican divines."[128] Rejecting both religious liberalism and Evangelical principles, the Tracts maintained that "the Apostolical form of doctrine was essential and imperative, and its grounds of evidence impregnable."[129]

In the *Apologia*, Newman criticizes his overconfidence and zealotry in the early years of the Oxford Movement. He refuses to defend his behavior toward others during this period. He accuses himself of "sport," by which I assume he means doing whatever was necessary to win, as though he were engaged in a game.[130] He accuses himself of a certain deviousness or willingness to use other people as unconscious instruments of his ideas, despite knowing of their disagreement. Thirdly, he accuses himself of deliberately trying to make fools out of people who disagreed with him in public, and, at times, of speaking with irony rather than plainly. Although he emphasizes that he never employed arguments with which he secretly disagreed, he admits to coming close to this with Tract 15, written mainly by someone else and lightly rewritten by Newman. He states firmly about himself in these years: "This absolute confidence in my cause, which led me to the imprudence or wantonness which I have been instancing, also laid me open, not unfairly, to the opposite charge of fierceness in certain steps which I took, or words which I published."[131]

By "fierceness" he means rash words advocating, for instance, learning

128. Newman, *Apologia Pro Vita Sua*, 159.

129. Newman, 160.

130. Newman, 160.

131. Newman, 161. For discussion of Newman's "public penitence" here, or at least his "half-penitential explanation," see Owen Chadwick, "A Consideration of Newman's *Apologia Pro Vita Sua*," in *From Oxford to the People*, 163–185, at 169–170. Chadwick adds the point that part of the interest of Newman's *Apologia* is that instead of denouncing his past teachers and associates as heretics—which was then a normal way for Catholics to treat non-Catholic Christians and vice versa—Newman "writes as though past and present are friends; and he writes it in such a way that the reader feels no incompatibility and no incongruity. Never before had a convert to the Roman Catholic Church written about his past with such generosity to Protestants" (Chadwick, 177).

to hate or cultivating a certain kind of "bigotry." He advocated the death penalty for heresiarchs. Looking back on such words, he apologizes, while also remarking that he never had the consistency of true zealots: "I think the sight of a Spanish *auto-da-fe* would have been the death of me."[132] He admits to arrogant and legalistic attitudes. He also apologizes, though without using the phrase "I apologize," for his treatment of his brother Francis during this period. He does not blame Blanco White for the latter's dismay at his behavior. Newman quotes from a text written by White in 1839, in which White blames Newman for persecuting Hampden and for consigning White, who in 1835 had rejected Anglicanism and become a Unitarian,[133] to everlasting perdition. Newman does not contest these charges,

---

132. Newman, *Apologia Pro Vita Sua*, 162.

133. Stephen Thomas devotes a chapter each to Hampden and White, in relation to Newman. Regarding Hampden and Newman, he first notes the similarities: "Just as Newman, quite radically, had re-asserted patristic heresiology, so Hampden proposed an equally radical re-interpretation of traditional formulae. Both were attempting to re-draw the boundary-lines in the highly contested atmosphere following the Reform Act" (*Newman and Heresy*, 76). Thomas then provides a brief sketch of the differences: "Hampden . . . extends the scope of 'rationalism' and 'systematisation' to the doctrines themselves of Christian Antiquity, which he opposes to scriptural 'fact': 'The only ancient, only Catholic truth is the Scriptural fact.' Moreover, while Newman accepted the *insufficiency* of language to describe the depth of divine realities, by calling it *economic*, he nevertheless saw words as, in some sense, containing, or participating in, the realities they inadequately describe—the economy rooted in the mystery. But Hampden was radically anti-propositional: for him, it seems, all verbal formulations are dangerous scholasticisms of revelation" (Thomas, 77). Hampden rejected orthodox Trinitarian doctrine (and doctrine about divine being and causality) as beyond the power of the human mind. Keble had the same reaction to Hampden's theology as did Newman, as shown in Rowlands, *Church, State and Society*, 60–62. White became a Unitarian in 1835, in the midst of Newman's struggle with Hampden, and, just as Hampden was a disciple of Whately, so "White had thrown in his lot with the liberals under the patronage of Whately" (Rowlands, 80). For Newman, therefore, "White could be used as a 'beacon': by comparing the teaching of a frank Unitarian with that of Hampden, liberalism could be shown up for the crypto-Socinianism that it was" (Rowlands, 81). For further background, see Joseph Blanco White, *Observations on Heresy and Orthodoxy* (London: J. Mardon, 1835), which describes his renouncing Anglicanism in favor of Unitarianism; and see also *The Life of the Rev. Joseph Blanco White, Written by Himself, with Portions of His Correspondence*, 3 vols., ed. John Hamilton Thom (London: J. Chapman, 1845). Further details appear in Martin Murphy, *Blanco White: Self-Banished Spaniard* (New Haven, CT: Yale University Press, 1989); and *Memorials of Renn Dickson Hampden, Bishop of Hereford*, ed. Henrietta Hampden (London: Longmans, Green, 1871), to which Newman responded positively in a letter to Henrietta

although he does contest a further charge—that he cut off social relations with White during this time.

I mention this section in which Newman grants that his zeal became arrogance and led him to mistreat others in part because White (in his 1839 book) touches upon the very point raised by Francis repeatedly, as Newman well knew. As quoted by Newman, White stated in 1839: "Such is the venomous character of orthodoxy. What mischief can it create in a bad heart and narrow mind, when it can work so effectually for evil, in one of the most benevolent of bosoms, and one of the ablest of minds, in the amiable, the intellectual, the refined John Henry Newman!"[134] By 1864, Newman had had much painful experience with "orthodoxy" as expressed in a "narrow mind" (and even in a "bad heart"). Certainly his battles with Frederick Faber, for instance, counted for him under the rubric of such experience. Newman in 1864, then, can be read as agreeing with White that "orthodoxy" can indeed, when exaggerated, be made "narrow."

Yet in this section of the *Apologia*, Newman certainly does not mean to repudiate the core *principles* for which he fought in this period. He names two principles as fundamental for his whole life's work: the truth of dogma and the truth of the sacraments as causes of grace. A third principle for which he fought in the Tractarian movement was one that he later renounced: the view that the pope is the Antichrist and that Catholic devotions to Mary and the saints are unchristian.

Newman remarks, "From the age of fifteen, dogma has been the fundamental principle of my religion: I know no other religion; I cannot enter into the idea of any other sort of religion; religion, as a mere sentiment, is

---

Hampden. Thomas sums up White's position in 1835, which reflected Whately's influence: "Blanco White held that the Bible only is the source of all religious truth, but that the only *certain* conclusions we can draw are those assimilable in sense experience. The 'facts' of the Bible are, in the latter sense only, objective. This is pure Hampden. However, in this assessment of the nature of doctrine, Blanco goes a little further—far enough, Newman of course argued, to show the 'consequences' and legitimate 'inferences' touching Hampden's similar theology" (*Newman and Heresy*, 82).

134. Newman, *Apologia Pro Vita Sua*, 163.

to me a dream and a mockery. As well can there be filial love without the fact of a father, as devotion without the fact of a Supreme Being."[135] Dogma makes possible an assent to revealed realities that operate in the world. If the core of Christianity were not expressible in universally valid doctrinal propositions, then Christians could have religious feelings, but they would lack true knowledge of God and Christ. Thus, Newman warns strongly against "the anti-dogmatic principle and its developments."[136] He comments, "Even when I was under Dr. Whately's influence, I had no temptation to be less zealous for the great dogmas of the faith, and at various times I used to resist such trains of thought on his part, as seemed to me (rightly or wrongly) to obscure them."[137] Regarding the truth of dogma, Newman held not only religious liberalism to be a threat, but also in its own way Evangelicalism, insofar as the latter rejects many dogmas and leaves a weakened foundation for the dogmas that it retains (*sola scriptura*).

The dogmatic ground of the Church's unity in faith entails a second principle, which Newman describes as the "sacramental principle." This principle has to do with the earthly mediation of transcendent divine realities. As noted above, the sacramental principle entails that behind every earthly thing stands the power and presence of God, hidden mystically or "sacramentally." The Church and its sacraments, such as Baptism and the Eucharist, manifestly exhibit this principle—but all things, as revealing in some fashion the divine Creator or Redeemer, conform in their fashion to this rule of mediation. Christopher Cimorelli aptly comments upon "just how extensive was Newman's sacramental view of reality, in which the entire visible world [and all of history], in some manner, attests to revelation."[138] The sacramental principle as intrinsic to Christianity rests, Newman thinks, both upon Scripture (Acts and the Pauline letters are

135. Newman, 163–164.

136. Newman, 163.

137. Newman, 164.

138. Christopher Cimorelli, *John Henry Newman's Theology of History: Historical Consciousness, Theological 'Imaginaries,' and the Development of Tradition* (Leuven, BE: Peeters, 2017), 44.

particularly significant) and upon the witness of Ignatius of Antioch and, indeed, the witness of the Church up to the present day. In 1833, Newman had in view especially the Anglican ordination service and baptismal service.[139] The necessity of the Church in the mediation of grace is paired by Newman with the necessity of the Church in the mediation of the Gospel through dogma.[140]

Newman sums up the consistency with which he has upheld these two principles: "While I am now as clear in my acceptance of the principle of dogma, as I was in 1833 and 1816, so again I am now as firm in my belief of a visible Church, of the authority of Bishops, of the grace of the sacraments, of the religious worth of works of penance, as I was in 1833."[141] This makes clear how intertwined are the dogmatic and sacramental principles, so that logically speaking it is difficult to believe in dogma (as Francis tried to do) without believing in a sacramental Church.

Newman goes on to describe how conversations with Froude, and his own experiences in Italy, gradually made him less opposed to the Church of Rome. In 1832–1833, however, he still held that the Council of Trent was the time when the Church of Rome took on the mantle of the Antichrist. Indeed, in the *Apologia* he recalls that he held a version of this view until

139. See also E.B. Pusey's Tracts 67–69 (1835), which he published the next year in one volume as *Scriptural Views of Baptism* (London: J.G. and F. Rivington, 1836).

140. Nevertheless, as Benjamin King shows, Newman in the early 1830s had in general a negative view of the Anglican episcopacy, which he associated with Erastianism and theological unseriousness. See King, *Newman and the Alexandrian Fathers*, 71–75. For background regarding the "sacramental conception of the Church" that "is at the heart not only of the Oxford Movement and of Newman's idea of the Church, but also of that other movement which derives even more directly from [Samuel Taylor] Coleridge and is associated with F.D. Maurice," see John Coulson, *Newman and the Common Tradition: A Study in the Language of Church and Society* (Oxford: Clarendon, 1970), 39. Coulson observes, "Coleridge's account of the Church seems to imply that we do not meet it in the sacramental sense directly, but as it is embodied in the nation, which is not merely the context of the Church, but its external form, and in which it is realized" (Coulson, 40). In light of Vatican II's *Lumen Gentium* and *Gaudium et Spes*, Coulson proposes that Newman and Maurice push forward and enrich this understanding of the Church in relation to the world (the State). Coulson focuses upon how the Church's relationship to society is implied by its sacramental constitution, and upon how this works when society is no longer explicitly Christian.

141. Newman, *Apologia Pro Vita Sua*, 166.

around 1843. During the Oxford Movement, he consistently attacked the Church of Rome and "popery." He felt confident in his appeal to the Church Fathers as the basis of Anglicanism, and he believed that this appeal would not lead him to Roman Catholicism. It is relevant here that Newman credits Pusey with the Oxford Movement's success: it was Pusey who "at once gave to us a position and a name. Without him we should have had no chance, especially at the early date of 1834, of making any serious resistance to the Liberal aggression."[142] Newman is full of praise for Pusey, while observing that Pusey was never near to conversion to Rome but rather was always a strong advocate for Anglo-Catholicism. Similarly, Newman's concerns regarding Evangelical Anglicanism were not such as to lead him to suppose that Anglo-Catholicism and Evangelicalism could not be bridged. He points out that he attempted just such a bridge in his *Lectures on Justification*, which argues that Anglicans (including Evangelical Anglicans) follow Melanchthon rather than Luther with regard to the meaning of justification by faith alone.[143]

142. Newman, 173.

143. See Newman, 183. For Evangelical, High Church, and Tractarian views on justification, see Nockles, *The Oxford Movement in Context*, 256–269. Nockles provides insight into the context and reception of Newman's work: "The publication of Knox's controversial essay *On Justification* (1810) in the *Remains* first made the subject one of renewed theological dispute. Knox's views were identified with those of the Schoolmen and Tridentine Fathers and deemed to be anti-Protestant. The partial identification by the Tractarians with Knox's views on Justification ensured that this Evangelical response soon came to be directed at themselves. Newman's debate with Samuel Wilks, the editor of the *Christian Observer* in 1837 focused on their differences over Justification. . . . Newman used the debate with Wilks as a basis for an exploration of the whole subject in his *Lectures on Justification* (1838). . . . In his *Lectures*, Newman seemed to blend two rival systems, the Protestant and the Roman Catholic, when he maintained that whereas Justification was the application of Christ's merits to the individual, it was an inward gift lodged within us by the Spirit. Newman insisted that his own doctrine of the righteousness of Christ, while not 'imputed' to the believer in the external, forensic Lutheran sense, yet differed from the 'inherent righteousness' that constituted the Roman Catholic view. Newman preferred the notion of an 'adhered righteousness' which depended 'wholly and absolutely upon the Divine indwelling.' . . . Newman retained a Protestant element in his schema by making God's pardon of the sinner precede his regeneration, whereas Roman Catholics inverted this. Moreover, his emphasis on the indwelling righteousness of Christ in the believer derived not only from the Greek Fathers but also from the writings of the Saxon Reformer Andreas Osiander" (Nockles, 261–263). See also George Stanley

It was the 39 Articles that, in the end, caused great difficulties for John, as also, in quite a different context and much earlier, for Francis. John reports in the *Apologia* that he long had full confidence in the 39 Articles. In the 1830s, he viewed the Articles in accordance with the Via Media that, drawing upon classical Anglican divines, he outlined in his *The Via Media of the Anglican Church*. But when in 1841, in Tract 90, he put into writing his view of the Articles in light of his increasing Roman Catholic sympathies, he found his new perspective caused a firestorm. In Tract 90, he distinguished between three realities: the Catholic dogma of the patristic period, the Roman dogma found in later periods (such as the Council of Trent), and the popular beliefs and practices fostered by Rome. He argued that the Articles affirm the whole of the patristic Catholic teaching, allow for much of the Roman teaching of later periods, and reject most of the Roman popular beliefs and practices.[144] In making these claims, he sought to defend—in accord with the notion of three "branches" of the Church

---

Faber, *The Primitive Doctrine of Justification Investigated: Relatively to the Several Definitions of the Church of Rome and the Church of England: and with a Special Reference to the Opinions of the Late Mr. Knox, as Published in His Remains with an Appendix, Containing among Other Matters, a Notice of Mr. Newman's Lectures on Justification*, 2nd ed. (London: R.B. Seeley and W. Burnside, 1839); and James Bennett, *Justification as Revealed in Scripture, in Opposition to the Council of Trent and Mr. Newman's Lectures* (London: Hamilton & Adams, 1840). Nockles shows that Newman's position on justification is close to that of Bishop Bull in his *Harmonia Apostolica*.

144. Newman's effort in Tract 90 to affirm the Council of Trent's teachings in relation to the 39 Articles invited criticism from his fellow Anglicans as well as from Roman Catholics; for the latter, see Nicholas Wiseman, *A Letter Respectfully Addressed to the Rev. J.H. Newman upon Some Passages in His Letter to the Rev. Dr. Jelf* (London: C. Dolman, 1841). Nockles comments, "Newman's argument—that only the 'Romish' and not the 'Tridentine' versions of particular Roman Catholic doctrines had been condemned in the Articles—entailed a degree of historical inaccuracy and special pleading as to dates and chronology" (*The Oxford Movement in Context*, 138). In Nockles' view—and I think this is probably correct—Newman aimed to go further in Tract 90 than Pusey supposed in Pusey's *The Articles Treated on in Tract 90 Reconsidered and Their Interpretation Vindicated* (Oxford: J.H. Parker, 1841). Nockles emphasizes, "For old High Churchmen, *Tract 90*, even with the gloss provided by Pusey, entailed a dangerous misapplication of a legitimate principle. The church's formularies were being tried by a merely private judgment as to what was and was not antiquity. The very ambiguity of Newman's use of the word 'Catholic' gave a superficial plausibility to the central argument of *Tract 90*" (*The Oxford Movement in Context*, 139; cf. 282–284, 294–300).

(Anglican, Roman, and Orthodox)—a maximal accommodation of the Articles to the dogmatic teaching of the Roman Catholic Church. In his view, this goal was not far from that of the authors who composed the Articles, since they were mainly concerned to reject the papacy and to unite the Catholics and Protestants in England under the Anglican banner. Thus, they were happy at points to resort to ambiguous language which all sides could interpret in their own direction. Newman's idea was to take advantage of this ambiguity or elasticity in order to show that the 39 Articles can be affirmed while still affirming most Roman Catholic doctrines.[145]

In defense of his approach, Newman in the *Apologia* argues that in interpreting Scripture, all theologians inevitably do what he does in Tract 90 with the Articles. He states, "Every theology has its difficulties; Protestants hold justification by faith only, though there is no text in St. Paul which enunciates it, and though St. James expressly denies it; . . . they deny that the Church has a divine mission, though St. Paul says that it is 'the Pillar and ground of Truth.'"[146] In his view, as noted above, Scripture was never intended by God to be a catechetical textbook, but rather was always intended to be the Church's book, filled with rich truth ascertainable by the Church under the Spirit's guidance. He emphasizes that "every creed has

145. Nockles criticizes Tract 90 for occasionally citing Caroline Divines in a "far-fetched and disingenuous" way (*The Oxford Movement in Context*, 132), but Newman never claims to be representing all the expressed views of each Caroline Divine whom he cites, and he openly engages in what Nockles criticizes as "selectivity of citation" (Nockles, 133). Even more sharply, Nockles criticizes Frederick Oakeley (who also became Roman Catholic in 1845) for the same practice. See Oakeley, *The Subject of Tract XC Examined* (London: J.G.F. and J. Rivington, 1841). As Nockles notes, "In their Charges [against Tract 90], various High Church bishops refuted Tractarian 'patristic fundamentalism' by appealing directly to the teaching of seventeenth-century Anglican divines and their Orthodox successors such as Waterland" (*The Oxford Movement in Context*, 134). He also cites numerous Evangelical Anglican respondents to the Tractarians, who, as he says, "did not neglect the value of patristic or earlier Anglican testimony in attempting to turn the tables on the Tractarians" (Nockles, 135). By 1845, Newman too had reached the conclusion that the Caroline Divines were not sufficient. For further background, see Nockles, "Newman, Tract 90 and the Bishops," in *John Henry Newman: Reason, Rhetoric and Romanticism*, ed. David Nicholls and Fergus Kerr (Bristol, UK: Classical, 1991), 28–87.

146. Newman, *Apologia Pro Vita Sua*, 195.

texts in its favour, and again texts which run counter to it."[147] Unlike Francis, this does not bother John, since after his Evangelical period he never held that all Christian doctrine was intended to be proved by Scripture.[148] Scripture, for John, is not a sole source or fountain of doctrine, but an authoritative witness that corroborates or verifies doctrine, which the Church (not Scripture per se) teaches.

After the publication of Tract 90, the resulting outrage required Newman to resign his place in the Oxford Movement and to end the Tracts. Within his own Oriel College, Edward Hawkins as Provost "conducted an inquisition of fellowship candidates on their attitudes to religious parties and opinions, insisting that candidates completely repudiate Tract 90's interpretation of the Articles."[149] I will skip over the process of reasoning that began in the summer of 1839 and that eventually, in 1845, led Newman into the Catholic Church.[150] But it is important to note that in his *Apologia*,

147. Newman, 195. As an example, in a footnote on page 195, John states: "For instance, let candid men consider the form of Absolution contained in that [Anglican] Prayer Book, of which all [Anglican] clergymen, Evangelical and Liberal as well as high Church, and (I think) all persons in University office declare that 'it containeth *nothing contrary to the Word of God*.' I challenge, in the sight of all England, Evangelical clergymen generally, to put on paper an interpretation of this form of words, consistent with their sentiments, which shall be less forced than the most objectionable of the interpretations which Tract 90 puts upon any passage in the Articles."

148. On this point see especially his powerful Tract 85 (originally published in 1838): John Henry Newman, "Holy Scripture in Its Relation to the Catholic Creed," in Newman, *Discussions and Arguments on Various Subjects*, ed. Gerard Tracey and James Tolhurst (Notre Dame, IN: University of Notre Dame Press, 2004), 109–235. In this regard, Newman's position differs sharply from that of Whately and Hawkins.

149. Nockles, "The Oxford Movement in an Oxford College," 22. Nockles adds that "Richard Church's refusal to disavow Tract 90 or to refrain from lecturing on the Articles prompted Hawkins to remove him from his Oriel tutorship after much agonising" (Nockles, 22).

150. After quoting a lengthy passage that he published in 1840 against Roman Catholics who tried to convert Anglicans, Newman has the following to say, which I quote here as a sign of his ability to perceive his own faults: "No one ought to indulge in insinuations; it certainly diminishes my right to complain of slanders uttered against myself, when, as in this passage, I had already spoken in condemnation of that class of controversialists, to which I myself now belong" (*Apologia Pro Vita Sua*, 229). See also Newman's 1846 response to critics of his conversion, in his "John Keble," in Newman, *Essays Critical and Historical*, vol. 2, ed. Nicholas Schofield (Leominster, UK: Gracewing, 2019), 499–536, at 502–506. Newman

Newman grants, "I am far of course from denying that every article of the Christian Creed, whether as held by Catholics or by Protestants, is beset with intellectual difficulties; and it is simple fact that, for myself, I cannot answer those difficulties."[151] He knows well the various objections that are raised from various quarters; his dogmatic faith is not an arrogant dogmatism. Nevertheless, the difficulties do not refute the dogmas. As he puts it, "Many persons are very sensitive to the difficulties of religion; I am as sensitive as any one; but I have never been able to see a connexion between apprehending those difficulties, however keenly, and multiplying them to any extent, and doubting the doctrines to which they are attached."[152]

But when difficulties multiply, is it not reasonable to become skeptical? Why not follow the path laid down by Francis? John was upheld in part by his antecedent beliefs about God's presence and purposes in history, and about Christ's Church as the divinely guided interpreter of the Gospel. Thus, though many difficulties encompass the doctrine of transubstantiation, Newman believed it "as soon as I believed that the Catholic Roman Church was the oracle of God, and that she had declared this doctrine to be part of the original revelation."[153] In Newman's view, the purpose of

grants, "Never was there a case of conversion, except under the influence of extraordinary inspiration, which might not have proceeded more holily, more wisely, more religiously than it did—never a case which did not present an opportunity of criticism, to those who had the heart, or felt it a necessity, or thought it a duty, to criticize. . . . Good friends, you have not far to seek; *habetis confitentem reum*; he pleads guilty; he has given up a fellowship or a living, or he has forfeited an inheritance, or ruined the prospects or present provision of wife and children, or damaged his reputation for judgment or discernment; he has cheerfully made himself a scoff, submitted himself as a prey to the newspapers, has made himself strange to his brethren; and besides and amid all this, it is true, he has said a strong word he had better not have said—or uttered a sarcasm—his successive disclosures have not severely kept time with the growth of his misgivings,—he has spoken to those with whom he should have been reserved, and has been silent where he should have spoken; at times he has not known where he stood, and perhaps promised what he could not perform. Of his sacrifices he thinks and says nothing; what he does know and does painfully think of, is in substance just that which you so rhetorically urge against him, yes, and before you urge it. His self-scrutiny has preceded your dissection of him" (Newman, 504–505).

151. Newman, *Apologia Pro Vita Sua*, 317.

152. Newman, 317.

153. Newman, 318.

private judgment in matters of divine revelation is to identify where the Church is, because God wills to communicate the Gospel through the Church, in and through which we receive the Scriptures. We may and do use our reasoning powers to contemplate the divine mysteries, but we cannot hope to resolve all difficulties thereby—even if we can resolve many difficulties. For example, regarding the doctrine of the Trinity, Newman receives it from the Church interpreting Scripture in the Tradition. Newman recognizes that "my abstract idea of three is simply incompatible with my idea of one"; but, in accord with Augustine and Aquinas, he holds that there must be a sense in which three and one can both be applied to God without contradiction.[154] To believe reasonably in development rather than corruption is not the same as having a proof for everything.

Newman gives another example in addition to transubstantiation and the Trinity. Like Francis, he is sure of God's existence, a point that he defends philosophically in the *Grammar of Assent*.[155] If God exists, however, why is human life so full of sin, division, and chance—the seeming blindness and purposelessness of history? Newman notes that if he did not already believe in God on other grounds, the miserable condition of the

154. Newman, 318.

155. Newman's arguments in what follows may bear upon some reflections in his 1835 Tract 73, "On the Introduction of Rationalistic Principles into Religion," in Newman, *Tracts for the Times*, ed. James Tolhurst (Notre Dame, IN: University of Notre Dame Press, 2013), 180–243. This Tract contains a critique of Thomas Erskine's bestselling *Remarks on the Internal Evidence for the Truth of Revealed Religion* (Edinburgh: Waugh and Innes, 1821). Stephen Thomas summarizes the salient points, "Erskine's view of the moral imperative as an existential encounter between God and Man resembles Newman's argument from conscience to the existence of God. Moreover, like Erskine, Newman was repelled by the rather glib reliance upon miracles as proofs, as his remarks upon William Paley's apologetic show. Newman, however, restricts his moral proof to natural theology, that is, to proving God's existence. He saw Erskine as wrong in applying his moral proofs to revelation. Erskine seemed to Newman to be arguing that human reason, with its sense of right and wrong, could form a judgment about the truth of revelation" (Thomas, *Newman and Heresy*, 110–111). Newman's emphasis in this section of the *Apologia* on the difficulty even of knowing God, let alone the contents of revealed theology, on the basis of human reason recall his Tractarian emphasis against religious rationalism. In addition, it is noteworthy that Erskine implies not only that revelation must be reasonable, but also that the test for this is whether revelation (for example the revelation of the Trinity) is morally useful.

world would turn him into "an atheist, or a pantheist, or a polytheist."[156] Again, it is not that he fails to recognize the reasonableness of the proofs of God's existence. He does so, but the world still strikes him as godless. As he puts it with his typical eloquence, to consider "the greatness and littleness of man, his far-reaching aims, his short duration, the curtain hung over his futurity, the disappointments of life, the defeat of good, the success of evil, physical pain, mental anguish, the prevalence and intensity of sin, the pervading idolatries, the corruptions, the dreary hopeless irreligion . . .—all this is a vision to dizzy and appal."[157] Humans can know that God exists, and can know that the Christian doctrine of God is true, while still being unable to solve all the difficulties. If one appeals to original sin as the answer for why the world is as it is, this doctrine too possesses some irresolvable mysteries.

Given this situation, God's revelatory action must counter the tendency of the fallen human mind toward skepticism, indeed, toward "atheism in one shape or other."[158] Newman is not a skeptic; his point here is to show that belief in doctrine is not a rationalistic dogmatism that requires one first to resolve all problems, as the human mind wants to do. In sending Christ, Newman says, God counters the tendency to skepticism in matters beyond empirical proof by establishing a Church "invested with the prerogative of infallibility in religious matters."[159] Scripture cannot alone stem the tendency of the human mind toward skeptical rationalism, divinely inspired though Scripture be. Newman remarks, "Experience proves surely that the Bible does not answer a purpose, for which it was never intended. . . . A book, after all, cannot make a stand against the wild living intellect of man, and in this day it begins to testify, as regards its own structure and contents, to the power of that universal

156. Newman, *Apologia Pro Vita Sua*, 319.
157. Newman, 320.
158. Newman, 321.
159. Newman, 323.

solvent, which is so successfully acting upon religious establishments."[160] This solvent is the fallen human mind, now acting through empirical historical inquiry. It seems likely that John has Francis' powerful mind in view here, as well as Gibbon's and Blanco White's, as John reflects upon the "immense energy of the aggressive intellect."[161] By ensuring the doctrinal fidelity of the Church, God ensures the existence of a voice, joined to his revelation, that is strong enough to counterbalance the narrow dogmatisms of the skeptical human mind.

It is reasonable, in other words, to move in precisely the opposite direction that Francis moves, assuming, as Francis himself does, *that God exists and loves humankind.* The standard charge against Catholicism is that it takes human minds prisoner.[162] Catholicism's accusers hold that it

---

160. Newman, 322.

161. Newman, 323.

162. John Coulson argues that Newman here is responding to Pope Pius IX's *Tuas Libenter*, which appeared in March 1864, causing consternation to Lord John Acton, Döllinger, and others of Newman's acquaintance. *Tuas Libenter* cracked down on the kind of historical scholarship favored by Döllinger, and on April 10, 1864, Acton wrote to Newman asking him to respond implicitly to the encyclical in his *Apologia*. See Coulson, "The *Apologia* Revalued," in *Newman: A Portrait Restored. An Ecumenical Reevaluation*, ed. J. Coulson, A.M. Allchin, and Meriol Trevor (London: Sheed & Ward, 1965), 27–61, at 50–51. Whereas Coulson sees Newman as bravely defending his "liberal Catholic" friends, G. Egner contends that "Newman's attitude to ecclesiastical authority was far closer than is generally admitted to that of conservative Roman Catholics of his day" (Egner, *Apologia Pro Charles Kingsley* [London: Sheed & Ward, 1969], 172). I think both Coulson and Egner can be correct here. I note, however, that Egner's book—like a number of others—presents Newman as a skeptic (in Egner's case, a "Cartesian" or idealist skeptic) who converted to Rome largely in order to secure epistemological certitude regarding religious matters (a certitude that he had already sought in the same way in the Anglican Church). I have made clear above how mistaken I hold this viewpoint to be, since in my view it pays no attention to Newman's theology of faith as an assent to God revealing. Egner goes on to say, "Had Newman ever had to face a profound disagreement with the teaching authority of the Roman Church, his verdict on its intellectual effects might well have been different" (Egner, 175–176). However, here the question is what is meant by "a profound disagreement," since Newman of course had various disagreements with the *Syllabus of Errors*, the wisdom of defining papal infallibility, and so on. Newman did not reach the point of thinking that a rupture in solemn doctrine had occurred, and the possibility cannot be ruled out that the reason Newman never reached that point is because the Holy Spirit preserved the Church from fundamentally distorting divine revelation.

turns its adherents into either interiorly rebellious hypocrites or mechanical repeaters of whatever Church authorities say. Newman answers that on the contrary, Catholicism frees the intellect to be what it should be, by upholding the mind in certain fundamental truths, given to us by Jesus Christ and constituting "the Apostolic *depositum* of faith."[163] Given the intensity of fallen humanity's tendency to rebel against the truth of God, God through Christ and the Spirit gives fallen humanity a Church that is able to withstand this tendency. Sacramentally, the Church communicates the restoration that the Church proclaims dogmatically. In our fallen condition, our desire is to be our own pope, to break from every authority, including God's. The Church therefore calls us to be reborn in grace, and to submit ourselves to being instructed by the ongoing apostolic community through which Christ speaks and of which Christ is the head. Our intellect must be "reconsecrated" to God.[164]

As Newman sees it, there is a divine revelation that has been given, healing and elevating our minds and hearts to apprehend the truth of God and his love for humankind. The proper response to this revelation of merciful divine love and Trinitarian life is, as Paul says, the obedience of faith. Setting aside our pride, we assent to what is proclaimed to us by Christ the Healer through his Church, in Scripture as authoritatively interpreted within Tradition. Newman personally makes this assent in full, inclusive of doctrinal developments: "I believe the whole revealed dogma as taught by the Apostles, as committed by the Apostles to the Church, and as declared by the Church to me. I receive it, as it is infallibly interpreted by the authority to whom it is thus committed, and (implicitly) as it shall be, in like manner, further interpreted by that same authority till the end of time."[165]

By humbling human minds under the authority of an infallible Church, does God thereby cut off free human inquiry, so that Catholic minds are deadened and frozen? History suggests the opposite, says Newman. Not

163. Newman, *Apologia Pro Vita Sua*, 327.
164. Newman, 325.
165. Newman, 327.

only is the Church's infallibility limited to faith and morals—and limited by the truths to which the Church must be accountable, both truths of nature and revealed truths—but also, in fact, the human intellect thrives in its "duel" with authority.[166] Private judgment or reasoning seeks to understand what has been defined by the Church, and in this quest Christian minds both understand more and, inevitably, err in certain respects, requiring the action of the Church's authority to stimulate human reasoning yet further along the path of truth. Newman calls this an "incessant noisy process" that bespeaks anything but frozen deadness; it is the refinement of "the raw material of human nature" in the quest to know God and God's ways.[167] He underlines that the Church's authority extends solely to what God has included in natural and supernatural revelation, and so no doctrine can be imposed upon the believer that differs in kind from, or contradicts, what has previously been given and made known. Continuity must be the rule even in radical development: "The new truth which is promulgated, if it is to be called new, must be at least homogeneous, cognate, implicit, viewed relatively to the old truth."[168]

Newman grants that the Church, in matters of discipline—for instance, banning books, silencing theologians, and so on—can err and abuse its power. Even with regard to matters of discipline, he thinks the Church has usually been proven to be correct; but he is far from denying that Church leaders are sinners who can and do abuse their power in particular cases. Regarding the relationship of the Church to natural science, Newman celebrates the latter: "We live in a wonderful age; the enlargement of

166. Newman, 328. For related reflections, see John Henry Newman, *The Idea of a University*, "Discourse IX: Duties of the Church Towards Knowledge," 161–181; and his 1854 lecture "A Form of Infidelity of the Day," in *The Idea of the University*, 286–303.

167. Newman, *Apologia Pro Vita Sua*, 329.

168. Newman, 329–330. He gives the example of the dogma of the Immaculate Conception. It has grounds in Mary's fullness of grace and in the Church Fathers' general reluctance to ascribe sinfulness to Mary. Medieval theologians such as Bernard and Thomas Aquinas came right to the edge of the doctrine, but they could not see how to square it with the doctrine of redemption; this difficulty was addressed by John Duns Scotus and by others in the centuries leading up to the definition.

the circle of secular knowledge just now is simply a bewilderment, and the more so, because it has the promise of continuing, and that with greater rapidity, and more signal results."[169]

Newman adds that he does not intend to criticize people "who look towards the discoveries of the age, certain or in progress, as their informants."[170] For many people, "liberalism" stands merely for "the educated lay world."[171] Newman recognizes that scientists and historians proceed sincerely with their investigations, following the evidence. It ill behooves the Catholic Church to fear or blame "those who pursue secular facts, by means of the reason which God has given them, to their logical conclusions."[172] While he sympathizes with those fearful believers who face scientific or historical evidence "that Christianity or that Scripture is untrustworthy"—especially since some scholars who find such evidence have an antipathy toward religion, sometimes due to "soreness or annoyance occasioned by the acrimony or narrowness of apologists for religion"[173]—Newman strives to show that dogmatic Christianity need not be intellectually narrow or fearful.

In the face of challenges raised by particular scientific or historical studies, the problem is twofold for Catholic thinkers who might wish to respond. First, it is unclear which of the hypotheses will stick and which will be superseded by further discoveries—even while it is clear that real intellectual progress is being made. Second, Church authorities are not yet appreciative of the kind of reasoning that will be necessary to respond to

169. Newman, 335.

170. Newman, 335.

171. Newman, 335.

172. Newman, 336. Benjamin King argues that by 1860, "Newman's shift to a fuller engagement with theological science came at the expense of his former openness to natural science" (King, *Newman and the Alexandrian Fathers*, 57). I think King is mistaken in this regard. King is correct, however, that "concerning the accuracy of events portrayed in the Bible, Newman thought that because the post-Nicene Fathers tended to interpret the Old Testament figuratively, they were more helpful in the face of historical-critical challenges than the pre-Nicene interpreters who were trying to defend the literalism of the Old Testament against Marcion" (King, 61).

173. Newman, *Apologia Pro Vita Sua*, 336.

the problems.[174] The latter point does not surprise Newman, because advances in reasoning come typically from individual theologians, not from Rome. He therefore has no doubt that the Church will be able to respond to the challenges brought by historical and scientific breakthroughs. This task will take time and will require the scientific and historical studies to congeal further, so that the Church is not responding to hypotheses that are soon superseded. A proper response will assimilate the true achievements without undermining the Church's sacramental and dogmatic principles.

The sacramental principle denies the reasonableness of a notion of "history" stripped of divine presence, divine action, and divine purposes. Given a properly sacramental understanding of history, the unfolding of history need not be feared by Catholics—even the messy historical path that characterizes the history of Scripture and of the Church. Nor is spiritual exegesis or typological exegesis an embarrassment in the face of supposedly more "scientific" historical study, because all hinges upon what "history" actually is.[175] For its part, the dogmatic principle insists that the source of Christianity is not mere humans but God; and it also asserts that humans, in speaking about religious experience, can know (even if not exhaustively) divine realities.

---

174. Ian Ker comments that in this part of the *Apologia*, Newman is attempting, "with pointed examples from church history, to show, as against the authoritarianism of the Ultramontanes . . . how important theology is for the life of the church" (Ker, "What Kind of Book Is the *Apologia*?," in *From Oxford to the People*, 186–197, at 196).

175. Peter Nockles shows that the love of typology shared by Newman, Keble, and Pusey is also found in earlier (Hutchinsonian) High Churchman: see Nockles, *The Oxford Movement in Context*, 207–208. He directs attention to the Hutchinsonian William Jones' *A Course of Lectures on the Figurative Language of Holy Scripture, and the Interpretation of It from Scripture Itself* (London: G.G.G. and J. Robinson, 1789), as well as to Pusey's unpublished 1836 manuscript *Lectures on Types and Prophecies of the Old Testament* (on which see David Jasper, "Pusey's 'Lectures on Types and Prophecies of the Old Testament,'" in *Pusey Rediscovered*, ed. Perry Butler [London: SPCK, 1983], 51–70). John Hutchinson's rather strange theories about Scripture—in response to Newtonian physics—had numerous advocates in the Oxford of the 1750s, and these theologians favored "a ritualist and sacramental churchmanship" (*The Oxford Movement in Context*, 211).

Conclusion

John Henry Newman's response to his brother Francis rests upon a notion of "history" that is contested, as John recognized. Is history really "sacramental" in Newman's sense? Is it reasonable to see history as a creature of God, as imbued and teleologically governed (despite human sinfulness) by divine presence and action? Francis grants the existence of a God who loves us. For John, once one grants the existence of such a God—which in John's view generally (in this fallen world) requires faith, even though there are valid proofs of God's existence—then it is reasonable to understand "history" along lines sharply different from those posited by an atheist.

Owen Chadwick describes the situation faced by John: "Here is a man who was brought up to revere the Bible; and who then learnt to see the Bible through the eyes of the early Church and the early Christian Fathers. . . . And then he finds himself in a world of modernity—with critical history, and challenges to the texts of the Bible, and suspicion of miracles."[176] In this world, Francis renounced Christianity and argued that the best Christian insights into morality and the spiritual life can be preserved without dogmatic belief, simply by valuing the religious intuition that arises from our inner wells (conscience). By contrast, John's solution spoke to those who, "even if they were Liberals in politics or humane studies . . . wanted the truth about God and his revelation."[177]

---

176. Chadwick, "A Consideration of Newman's *Apologia Pro Vita Sua*," 178.

177. Chadwick, 179. For Chadwick, however, the *Apologia Pro Vita Sua* boils down to the following argument: "In this sceptical world of the middle nineteenth century, where everyone's ideas were at sea, the authority of Rome was the only reliable safeguard against the dissolvents of Liberalism, when that word is taken in its sense to mean that religious truth was not to be found. It was the purpose of his [John Henry Newman's] argument to show, Rome or nothing; either accept authority, or find yourself in scepticism" (Chadwick, 179). In my view, Newman's position certainly is that the (Roman) Catholic Church is the one, holy, catholic, and apostolic Church founded by Christ; but Chadwick exaggerates matters by his stark polarities, as though for Newman nothing good is to be found outside the (Roman) Catholic Church, or as though Newman in the 1860s imagined that the "dissolvents of Liberalism" would never challenge Catholicism. Chadwick is correct, however, about Newman's kill-or-cure form of argumentation: for Newman Anglicanism is but a half-way house

Can John's sacramental understanding of human history stand against Francis' historicist view of revelation, Jesus, and the Bible? For Ernst Troeltsch (writing in 1898) and for most historians today, as noted above, nothing that involves divine action or presence can rightly be called "history." Troeltsch holds that "critical historiography" can know only "ordinary, secular history."[178] The historical method to which he adheres—and which was already anticipated by Gibbon—has three rules. First, history allows only for "judgments of probability," and so any attempt to move from history to faith's certitude involves a breach with history. Second, history makes its judgments of probability on the basis of whether today there are regularly occurring events that are analogous to the events asserted to have taken place in the past, and so miracles are by definition unhistorical. Third, everything in history is a united set of correlative causes, and so anything that claims to be a divine inbreaking (not comprehensively explicable in terms of natural causes) is unhistorical.

When Francis tries to assess the historical value of the biblical texts, he sometimes draws upon German biblical scholars shaped by rules like Troeltsch's. Let me underline, however, that the skepticism toward biblical narratives that is encouraged by these rules is not dismissed by John as useless. On the contrary, John, from his Oriel days onward, held to a view of Scripture as historically conditioned in such a way that it includes various genres and various kinds of human errors. Well versed in the difficulties and genres of ancient history, John knew that skepticism is not unwarranted, and much can be learned by testing scriptural texts against archeological, scientific, and philological evidence. His view of Scripture was always

to either Catholicism or atheism, Protestantism tends toward liberalism, and liberalism toward infidelity. While individuals along this spectrum hold onto much that is true and good, such individuals are occupying an incoherent zone of existence: private judgment, carried out to its *logical* (not always historically actual) conclusion, terminates in atheism. Where Chadwick exaggerates, I think, is when he makes it sound as if, for Newman, there can be no implicit principle of authority at play in a devout Anglican or Protestant.

178. Ernst Troeltsch, "Historical and Dogmatic Method in Theology," in Troeltsch, *Religion in History*, trans. James Luther Adams and Walter F. Bense (Minneapolis, MN: Fortress, 1991), 11–33, at 21.

Alexandrian—open to spiritual exegesis—and he saw Scripture as a whole through the light of faith in Christ and in accord with the Church's divinely guided interpretation and liturgical proclamation.

Yet although John was able to learn from skeptically inclined historical investigation of scriptural texts, he did not accept the limitations that Troeltsch or earlier historicist thinkers imposed upon what counts as "historical." For John, it is much less reasonable to suppose that nothing exists other than what we can perceive with our senses than to suppose that there is a transcendent cause and purpose in all things, including in the intimate details of a person's life. After all, both suppositions are philosophical ones. The historian who proceeds in accord with Troeltsch's rules for what counts as historical does not obtain these rules from any necessity *within history itself*, and so the rules merely exhibit a philosophical decision that should be contested.

As we have seen, John holds firmly to the "sacramental principle" that "the exterior world, physical and historical, [is] but the outward manifestation of realities greater than itself."[179] This does not mean that the exterior world is a mere veil, uninteresting to theological minds. On the contrary, Newman's work is everywhere peppered with concrete historical events and case studies. God the Redeemer is present and active in the exterior world, including through the Incarnation of Christ and through the "sacrament" of Christ's Body the Church.[180]

Frank Turner is correct when he states that for John in the 1830s, "Francis epitomized the religious impulses of Protestantism gone awry and embodied the pursuit of scriptural religion unencumbered by the restraints or aided by the guidance of the church with its creeds and articles."[181] Yet,

179. Newman, *Apologia Pro Vita Sua*, 145–146.

180. On the Church as "sacrament," see Benoît-Dominique de La Soujeole, *Introduction to the Mystery of the Church*, trans. Michael J. Miller (Washington, DC: The Catholic University of America Press, 2014), chapter 10.

181. Turner, *John Henry Newman*, 229. By the 1840s, the brothers were corresponding again on intimate details. In August 1845, Francis urged John, who by then considered the Anglican Church to be a sect, to form a new body of Anglicans. Francis warns that if John

by 1864, it had become clear that the issues separating Francis and John were broader than Francis' carrying forward of the principle of private judgment, associated by John with Evangelicalism and religious liberalism, and broader even than Francis' rejection of dogma per se. As John insists in his *Apologia*, the dogmatic principle has to be joined to the sacramental principle: the two are inseparable. If one can see one's way to holding that the all-loving God is "sacramentally" present behind and in history, then not only will the "dogmatic principle" regarding the Spirit's guidance of Christ's Church make sense, but also the natural skepticism of the fallen human mind will be tempered in historical inquiry, without thereby causing the historical inquirer to fall into the arrogant dogmatism of claiming to have mastered all problems and difficulties.[182]

---

converts to Rome, he will lose most of his influence and be little esteemed by his new co-religionists. As Turner comments on this 1845 correspondence, "Francis . . . fully comprehended the difficulty that John might encounter with Roman Catholic episcopal authority" (Turner, 615). Turner suggests that John gave serious consideration to starting a new body of Anglicans, even though in his response to Francis' letter, John dismisses the idea. John later recorded his feeling that Francis had in 1845 not been able to enter sympathetically into John's situation, in which theological matters, not practical ones, were paramount.

182. Turner overlooks the "sacramental principle" in describing John's intellectual conflict with his brother in the 1830s, with the result that John seems to be merely an advocate of blind faith. John's richly textured understanding of history is missing, at least, in Turner's description of John's "call to obedience" and authoritarian understanding of "the church as a body teaching through its creeds" (*John Henry Newman*, 228). In this section of his book, Turner presents John as motivated strongly by personal ambition to dominate both at Oxford and within his own family.

Chapter 4

Newman and Pusey

Hans Urs von Balthasar has articulated both the extraordinary greatness of the Blessed Virgin Mary and the temptation felt by theologians in certain eras to exaggerate that greatness. On the side of greatness, Balthasar recognizes Mary as the Mother of God, as the representative of all humanity in speaking her *fiat*, and as the New Eve or type of the Church in cooperating with her Son for the redemption of the world. On the side of exaggeration, Balthasar remarks that "as early as the late Byzantines and in the twelfth century in the West," embarrassing forms of Marian theological discourse emerged.[1] He cites eminent saints and teachers in whose work "Mary's universal intercession is heightened to a quasi-divine 'omnipotence,' which is hers because the Son, who was obedient to her for so long on earth, remains obedient to her in heaven. This omnipotence can even break ultimate decrees issued by the Son; it is an 'almighty power of mercy' that stands over against the Son's almighty justice and wrath."[2] On the ground that Mary is Theotokos, some saintly authors have made her "eternal and celestial, . . . a cocreator of the world, together with God, 'supplementing the Trinity.'"[3] Some authors have concluded that we can "attain divine grace 'more quickly' through her than through her Son, who is preoccupied with justice."[4]

As Balthasar knows, such exaggerations have produced "a stumbling block, understandably, for Protestants"—and so has Pope Pius IX's 1854

1. Hans Urs von Balthasar, *Theo-Drama: Theological Dramatic Theory*, vol. 3, *The Dramatis Personae: The Person in Christ*, trans. Graham Harrison (San Francisco: Ignatius Press, 1992), 312–313.

2. Balthasar, 313.

3. Balthasar, 314.

4. Balthasar, 314–315.

declaration of the dogma of the Immaculate Conception of Mary.[5] With regard to the dogma, at issue is both the truth of the dogma and the authority of the pope to proclaim it. Mary's Immaculate Conception, as specifically defined by the dogma, seems to be clearly taught neither in Scripture nor in the patristic period nor even in the high Middle Ages. Augustine did not directly teach the Immaculate Conception; no early council affirmed it; and Thomas Aquinas denied it. Although the doctrine has biblical and patristic grounds, these are contested.[6] Karl Barth is hardly alone in deeming that the dogma (and "Mariology" as a whole) "is an arbitrary innovation in the face of Scripture and the early Church" and, furthermore, that "where Mary is 'venerated,' where this whole doctrine with its corresponding devotions is current, there the Church of Christ is not."[7]

Moreover, upon the promulgation of the dogma of Mary's Immaculate Conception, the Orthodox East—having long celebrated Mary liturgically and theologically as utterly holy and perfectly spotless—protested against it. Laurent Cleenewerck remarks, "Since 1854, no Orthodox Council has formally condemned the teaching in itself but there can be no doubt that Eastern Orthodoxy rejects the unilateral proclamation of this dogma and the Papal ban on continuing the discussion on this complex matter."[8] Drawing upon Kallistos Ware's *The Orthodox Church*, Cleenewerck notes that the problem is not the identification of Mary as "all-holy" and "immaculate," but rather is the effort to specify what precisely this means (for example, with regard to the doctrine of original sin) and to define it

5. Balthasar, 315.

6. For further discussion of the biblical and patristic grounds, see my "Mary and Grace," in *The Oxford Handbook of Mary*, ed. Chris Maunder (Oxford: Oxford University Press, 2019), 289–302.

7. Karl Barth, *Church Dogmatics*, vol. 1, *The Doctrine of the Word of God*, Part 2, trans. G.T. Thomson and Harold Knight, ed. G.W. Bromiley and T.F. Torrance (Peabody, MA: Hendrickson, 2010), 143.

8. Laurent A. Cleenewerck, *His Broken Body: Understanding and Healing the Schism between the Roman Catholic and Eastern Orthodox Churches* (Washington, DC: Euclid University Consortium Press, 2007), 400. See Timothy Ware (Bishop Kallistos of Diocletia), *The Orthodox Church* (London: Penguin, 1997), 259–260.

dogmatically.[9] Metropolitan Hilarion Alfeyev writes, "The Theotokos' holiness, her lack of involvement in sin and the passions, is one of the leitmotifs of patristic preaching and of treatises dedicated to the Theotokos. The idea that the Most Holy Theotokos could partake in any kind of sin is deeply foreign to Eastern patristic tradition."[10] But Metropolitan Hilarion goes on to reject the dogma of the Immaculate Conception, due not least to its dependence upon an Augustinian understanding of original sin; although he equally rejects St. Ignatius Brianchaninov's denunciation of the dogma as incompatible with Mary's need for a Redeemer. Paul Evdokimov seems to adopt Brianchaninov's position, arguing that the "dogma sets the Virgin apart, removes her from the common destiny of mankind; it presents the possibility of being freed from original sin earlier than the Cross, by means of grace alone. In this case, in order for the Redemption to take place, it was necessary that it should already have happened."[11] Even so, Evdokimov does not ascribe any kind of sin to Mary. On the contrary, he argues: "Although she is of Adam's race, the Virgin is guarded from any personal impurity, all evil being rendered powerless to affect her by the successive purifications of her ancestors, by the special operation of the Spirit and by her outstanding act of free will."[12]

Thus, it is clear that a part of the history of controversy among Christians is controversy over Mary's sinlessness. Even when Catholics and Orthodox fundamentally agree about Mary's holiness, there is a sharp divide about the dogma. It would seem that the dogma also separates post 1854 Catholics from earlier Catholics, since many great saints, including Aquinas (as noted above), rejected it in the form defined by Pope Pius IX.

---

9. Cleenewerck, in *His Broken Body*, 404, goes on to cite approvingly a statement by Clark Carlton, *The Truth* (Salisbury, MA: Regina, 1999), 164: "The Orthodox Church only dogmatizes that which is essential to man's salvation. The Church does not dogmatize matters of opinion (*theologoumena*)."

10. Metropolitan Hilarion Alfeyev, *Orthodox Christianity*, vol. 2, *Doctrine and Teaching of the Orthodox Church*, trans. Andrew Smith (Yonkers, NY: St. Vladimir's Seminary, 2012), 481.

11. Paul Evdokimov, *Orthodoxy*, trans. Jeremy Hummertone, trans. rev. Callan Slipper (Hyde Park, NY: New City, 2011), 157.

12. Evdokimov, 157.

In view of such concerns about the 1854 Marian dogma—among other concerns, chiefly having to do with Catholic Marian devotions—Edward Pusey published *An Eirenicon, in a Letter to the Author of "The Christian Year"* in 1865.[13] Though addressed to his friend and fellow Oxford Movement leader John Keble, Pusey's *Eirenicon* was in fact a reply to Henry Manning's 1864 pamphlet *The Workings of the Holy Spirit in the Church of England, a Letter to the Rev. E.B. Pusey.*[14] Manning, who in 1865 became the Archbishop of Westminster, was a convert to Catholicism who had in his early years belonged to the Oxford Movement. According to the Catholic Manning, the Church of England has no valid Orders, cannot be deemed a true Church, and is a source of religious liberalism. Manning therefore called upon Anglicans to convert to Catholicism.

In response to Manning's pamphlet, Pusey's *Eirenicon* takes a firm line. Pusey devotes over one hundred pages to criticizing Catholic Marian piety, and he makes particular reference to the dogma of the Immaculate Conception. Mark Chapman has well described Pusey's overall perspective: his "interest was in the explicit and *de fide* teachings of the undivided apostolic church, and of witnesses to the apostolic teaching in later generations. . . . There was little room for a theory of development in Pusey's writing."[15]

13. E.B. Pusey, *An Eirenicon, In a Letter to the Author of "The Christian Year"* (London: John Henry and James Parker, 1865). The full title is *The Church of England a Portion of Christ's One Holy Catholic Church, and a Means of Restoring Visible Unity. An Eirenicon, In a Letter to the Author of "The Christian Year."*

14. For background—including the fact that Manning was responding indirectly to Newman's appreciative words about the Anglican Church in his *Apologia Pro Vita Sua*—see Vincent Ferrer Blehl, "Newman and the Church of England," in *By Whose Authority? Newman, Manning and the Magisterium*, ed. V. Alan McClelland (Bath: Downside Abbey, 1996), 41–48, at 43–45. See also Michael J.G. Pahls, "Canterbury's Rejoinder: Pusey, Gladstone, and the Neo-Ultramontanism of Manning," in *Authority, Dogma, and History: The Role of the Oxford Movement Converts in the Papal Infallibility Debates*, ed. Kenneth Parker and Michael J. Pahls (Bethesda, MD: Academica, 2009), 115–128; Mark D. Chapman, *The Fantasy of Reunion: Anglicans, Catholics, and Ecumenism, 1833–1882* (Oxford: Oxford University Press, 2014), 73–77.

15. Chapman, *The Fantasy of Reunion*, 70–71; for the same point, see Chapman, "Temporal and Spatial Catholicism: Tensions in Historicism in the Oxford Movement," in *The Shaping of Tradition: Context and Normativity*, ed. Colby Dickinson with Lieven Boeve and Terrence Merrigan (Leuven, BE: Peeters, 2013), 17–26, at 25. In *The Fantasy of Reunion*,

Through its focus on the explicit testimony of the Fathers and its insistence that the Church cannot go beyond this testimony, Pusey's mode of rejecting the dogma of Mary's Immaculate Conception posed a crucial challenge to Catholics with regard to doctrinal corruption.

In January 1866, John Henry Newman published a book-length reply to Pusey's *Eirenicon*.[16] Newman used the opportunity to criticize, if only in

---

Chapman points out that Pusey's emphasis on the Fathers, far from being innovative, can be found already in the work of the sixteenth-century bishop and theologian John Jewel: see Jewel, *The Works of Bishop John Jewel*, ed. R.W. Jelf (Cambridge: Cambridge University Press, 1845–1850), 4 vols. For confirmation of this point, see Peter B. Nockles, *The Oxford Movement in Context: Anglican High Churchmanship, 1760–1857* (Cambridge: Cambridge University Press, 1994), although Nockles observes that "pre-Tractarian High Churchmen valued the Fathers primarily because their witness followed immediately after the period of Revelation. The early Fathers were deemed more likely to know the apostles' views of scriptural truth, and their real meaning, than modern commentators. . . . For the Tractarians, however, this was merely the starting point. In their hands, antiquity became an absolute standard and final court of appeal, rather than as with most old High Churchmen, merely a corroborative testimony to the truth of the Church of England's formularies and the teaching of her standard divines" (113–114). In making this case, Nockles draws upon the viewpoint of A.P. Perceval, and Nockles makes clear how strongly he stands with the High Churchmen against the Tractarians, whom he connects negatively with the Nonjurors. Nockles sums up the view of the High Churchmen: "The Church was no slave to antiquity. Having made her own authoritative appeal, with its results enshrined in her formularies, this appeal could not be overturned or questioned by any subsequent exercise of private judgment by individuals, however learned. Therefore, even on 'open questions' the Church's mind should be respected" (Nockles, 123). For his part, Pusey retained respect for the English Reformers but held that the Church Fathers provide the ultimate doctrinal standard.

16. I employ the version of this text published in *A Letter Addressed to the Rev. E.B. Pusey, D.D., on Occasion of His Eirenicon* found in Newman's *Certain Difficulties Felt by Anglicans in Catholic Teaching Considered*, vol. 2, new ed. (London: Longmans, Green, 1896), 1–170. For background, remarking that "Newman and Pusey displayed an openness and trust which allowed them to engage with one another on a quite different level from Manning's sort of polemics," see Mark D. Chapman, "Ecumenism, Mariology, and the Papacy," in *The Oxford Handbook of John Henry Newman*, ed. Frederick D. Aquino and Benjamin J. King (Oxford: Oxford University Press, 2018), 355–372, at 359. Chapman briefly reports on the friendly exchange of private letters between Pusey and Newman that prepared the way for Newman's public response. Chapman, however, makes the exaggerated claim that "for Newman, the Catholic religion was so expansive that potentially almost anything could be included, since in the end it might turn out to be a matter of faith" (Chapman, 361). In *The Fantasy of Reunion*, too, Chapman offers what seems to me to be the exaggerated claim that "Newman displays a completely different understanding of the role of reason in religion from Pusey," and Chapman deeply misunderstands Newman's position: "Newman's principle of development produced a volatility in his account of faith: everything taught by somebody accorded

passing, Manning and other Ultramontanists such as Faber and Ward.[17] Most importantly, he sought to show why the dogma of Mary's Immaculate Conception is a doctrinal development rather than a corruption. Despite the fact that Newman had some sharp words for Pusey, Pusey was not offended by Newman's response—although in later writings Pusey does defend his *Eirenicon* against Newman's charge that it is unfair and harsh.[18] Newman's *A Letter to the Rev. E.B. Pusey, D.D., on His Recent Eirenicon* seems to have caused more offense to Manning and his Ultramontanist friends than to Pusey.

In what follows, after surveying Pusey's critique of the dogma of Mary's Immaculate Conception in his *Eirenicon*, I first examine Newman's various discussions of the Blessed Virgin Mary in his *An Essay on the Development of Christian Doctrine*, the book that James Lisowski has rightly identified as "the crucial text for understanding the emergence of Newman's mature Mariology."[19] I then take up Newman's *A Letter to the Rev. E.B. Pusey, D.D., on*

a high degree of authority, he held, had to be accepted as if it were true until proved otherwise, since it was potentially part of the faith, even though as yet undefined" (*The Fantasy of Reunion*, 97, 99; however, see 116 for Pusey's movement in 1870 toward a position on doctrinal development more similar to Newman's actual position, though Chapman on 118 identifies the key difference: "For Pusey, even though he admitted the theoretical possibility of further ecumenical councils, Catholicism was essentially a fixed and limited body of truth which had been defined by the early church. It was unlikely that it would be open to further development"). For a sympathetic Catholic response to Pusey (from an Anglican convert to Roman Catholicism who participated in the Bonn ecumenical conference of 1874 chaired by Ignaz von Döllinger), see Henry N. Oxenham, *Dr Pusey's Eirenicon Considered in Relation to Catholic Unity: A Letter to the Rev. Father Lockhart* (London: Longmans, Green, 1866). For a sharp critique of Pusey's *Eirenicon* from an Anglican perspective, see Archer Gurney, *'Visible Unity': The Price to Be Paid for It. A Letter to Christopher Wordsworth D.D., Archdeacon of Westminster, from Senex, on Reading Dr Pusey's Eirenicon* (London: Hatchard, 1865).

17. Faber had died in 1863. I should also note that Ward's Ultramontanism went further than Manning's. On this point see Hudson Russell Davis, "William George Ward, the *Dublin Review* and Neo-Ultramontanism," in *Authority, Dogma, and History*, 129–155. Note, too, that Ward eventually retracted the "extreme view of infallibility that characterized his *Dublin Review* editorship but not before it became a deep point of contention between him and other Catholic thinkers" (Davis, 147). See Ward, *Essays on the Church's Doctrinal Authority* (London: Burns & Oates, 1880).

18. For this point, see Ian Ker, *John Henry Newman: A Biography* (Oxford: Oxford University Press, 1988), 588; Chapman, *The Fantasy of Reunion*, 86–90.

19. R. James Lisowski, "A Fitting Glory: Newman and Mariology," *Newman Studies*

His Recent Eirenicon. Newman's response to Pusey offers important insight into his view that the Catholic Church's Mariology favors his theory of doctrinal development rather than exemplifying doctrinal corruption.[20] For his part, Pusey left no doubt about his own viewpoint when, reading Newman's *Letter*, he noted in the margins: "[Newman] has indeed made the best of the case he can for a doctrine which has absolutely no respectable account whatever to give of itself at the bar of antiquity and which depends altogether on the fiat of the present Pope."[21]

Problems with Catholic Teaching on the Virgin Mary and Her Immaculate Conception according to Pusey's *Eirenicon*

The section of the *Eirenicon* that especially interests me in this chapter begins with Pusey's response to Manning's central query: "By whom does God the Holy Ghost speak? By the Roman Church? or by the Eastern? or by the Anglican?"[22] Pusey answers that the Spirit speaks through all three; all three are branches of the true Church, even if all three at present have gotten some things wrong (not yet *fatally* wrong, however). Divine revelation ended with the Apostles' generation. The Church transmits the divine revelation given by Christ to the Apostles. Since the generation of the Apostles

---

Journal 15, no. 2 (2018): 21–38, at 26.

20. For further background to the relationship of Newman and Pusey, see Edward Short, *Newman and His Contemporaries* (London: T&T Clark International, 2011), chapter 3. Short comments, "What is most striking about the *Letter to Pusey* is how much of it is a reaffirmation of principles first enunciated in Newman's King William Street lectures [his 1850 lectures *Certain Difficulties Felt by Anglicans in Catholic Teaching*]. In both compositions, Newman grounded his case for Catholicism in the Fathers and urged Pusey and the Tractarians against trying to imagine themselves a branch church" (Short, 130). For background to Pusey's work and influence, see the essays in *Edward Bouverie Pusey and the Oxford Movement*, ed. Rowan Strong and Carol Engelhardt Herringer (London: Anthem, 2012) and Leighton Frappell's "'Science' in the Service of Orthodoxy: The Early Intellectual Development of E.B. Pusey," in *Pusey Rediscovered*, ed. Perry Butler (London: SPCK, 1983), 1–33.

21. Cited in Chapman, *The Fantasy of Reunion*, 96–97. Chapman goes on to contrast, misleadingly, Pusey's "Catholicism of the Word" with Newman's "Catholicism of devotion" (Chapman, 99).

22. Pusey, *An Eirenicon*, 84.

did not write everything down in Scripture, the Church hands on some things that are not explicitly in Scripture but nothing that is contradictory to it. In the first centuries, the whole Church was able to gather in council and to determine the most decisive things; whereas at present, and since the parting of ways between East and West, holding a council of the universal Church is not possible. Still, Pusey argues that discerning the universal understanding of the Church remains possible, just as it was during the first three centuries when the Church in the Roman empire was under persecution and could not hold a universal council, as distinct from local synods that were then received by the whole Church in due time.

Some matters of faith must be decided with dispatch, whereas others pertain to faith but do not need to be decided with any speed. According to Pusey, the question of Mary's Immaculate Conception belongs to the latter category. It festered in the Roman Catholic Church for hundreds of years. Even during the Reformation crisis, the dispute over Mary's Immaculate Conception was not decided by the Roman Catholic Church. The question, then, is why the Roman Catholic Church moved in 1854 to determine the matter dogmatically.

Pusey notes that the answer cannot be that a massive controversy had arisen. In the mid-nineteenth century, the controversies among the schools over this matter, once fierce indeed, had died down. The Catholic world was not demanding a resolution. What produced the dogmatic definition was simply the desire on the part of the Roman Catholic Church "to obtain the favour of the Blessed Virgin towards the Church of Rome by doing honour to her."[23] Pusey implies that this was not much of a reason. The humble Virgin Mary did not need the Roman Catholic Church to stir up a hornet's nest of controversy and further divisions with the Orthodox and Anglican Churches, simply in order to bestow her favors upon the Roman Catholic Church.

Pusey grants that the Roman Catholic Church, like the Orthodox and

23. Pusey, 91.

Anglican Churches, is built upon Scripture and the infallible determinations of the universal councils of the early Church. But for some reason, says Pusey, the Roman Catholic Church persists in taking strong stands on various matters that are disputed among the three branches of the universal Church. For example, the papacy's claims about itself do not, in the view of the Orthodox and the Anglicans, square with the early Church's understanding of patriarchates. Similarly, the denial of the cup to the laity, the practice of papal indulgences, and the question of whether a priest must officiate for a marriage to be valid are all matters where the Roman Catholic Church differs from the Orthodox and the Anglicans. The Roman Catholic Church has tried to determine these matters once and for all, sometimes by flatly contradicting her own centuries-old practice. Other points of dispute include Marian doctrines such as that she is the mediatrix of all graces and that she was immaculately conceived.

Pusey holds that now is not the time to try to define such matters, not only because portions of the universal Church are thereby offended, but also because these matters are not clearly set forth in Scripture. Given the rise of religious liberalism, the last thing the Church should do is to act as though what Scripture teaches is not determinative. Having experienced the costliness of religious liberalism as an Anglican, Pusey cautions his Roman Catholic brethren to be careful: "There have appeared already among Roman Catholics symptoms of a tendency to hold cheaply by Holy Scripture, as being comparatively unimportant to them, who have the authority of an infallible Church, forgetting that the authority of the Church depends upon Holy Scripture."[24] If the leaders of the Roman Catholic Church charge ahead doctrinally without feeling a great need to be guided firmly by Scripture, religious liberals inside the Roman Catholic Church will eventually use the same approach to separate the Church from clear scriptural teachings, by claiming that the Holy Spirit can guide the Church to contradict something that Scripture teaches.

24. Pusey, 95.

Again, Pusey does not deny that the Roman Catholic Church has the right and duty, as well as the ability, to teach its flock when controversies arise, by setting forth "formally the truth of all Holy Scripture, as given by inspiration of God, which has been presupposed by all, everywhere, at all times, from the first."[25] Even if Roman Catholics, Orthodox, and Anglicans cannot get together in a universal council, it is still possible for each branch to receive the truth of a local council held by one of the branches. This happened frequently in the early Church. Besides, there is a great deal of infallible doctrine—defined by the universal councils of the early Church—that needs defending and that is professed today by Roman Catholics, Orthodox, and Anglicans alike. When the three branches solemnly agree regarding (non-dogmatically defined) matters that pertain to salvation, such as the inspiration of Scripture, these matters can be taken as infallibly defined. If, however, one branch solemnly defines something and the other two branches refuse to receive it, then it remains a contested opinion, not an infallible teaching.

Pusey is certain that the Churches at present are divided more over practical matters and lesser issues than over fundamentals. He directs attention here to devotions and practices that have the Virgin Mary at their center. In Roman Catholic devotional life, and in the teachings of eminent saints and doctors of the Roman Catholic Church, he finds that often Mary's "intercession is held to be co-extensive with [Christ's]," and, even more, that an appeal to Mary is presented as necessary for accessing Christ's intercession, even if God certainly *could* grant grace without Mary's intercessory role coming into play.[26] According to some notable Roman Catholic authors, no person can be saved without Mary's intercession, and every person who earnestly turns to Mary and begs for her intercession will be saved. Some Roman Catholic authors propose that whereas God's justice is stern, Mary's mercy in interceding for sinners leads God to overlook his

25. Pusey, 95.
26. Pusey, 101.

justice and to save them. Such authors contend that God relies upon Mary's mercy, which is omnipotent in the order of grace.

Pusey singles out Jean-Jacques Olier for particular attention. In one of his writings, Olier asserts that we are too unworthy to go to Jesus directly; Jesus wants us instead to come to him through his saints, and above all through the Virgin Mary. Pusey deems this to be "unintentional heresy."[27] Olier has overlooked the ascended Christ's constant intercession with his Father on behalf of sinners. Pusey finds another Roman Catholic writer who argues that Jesus' wrath against sin requires that Mary first appease Jesus before he can hear our prayer. Still others claim that mercy belongs to Mary, and justice to God. They contrast God's cold justice with Mary's pity and love—the compassionate love of a mother as distinct from the anger of a just father. Sentiments like these are indeed opposed to Christian faith. Even the Eucharist, where Jesus directly meets us, is seen by some Roman Catholics as requiring Mary's mediation. Pusey remarks that, as a result, "in Southern India and Ceylon, our [Anglican] Churches are called by the natives 'Jesus-Churches;' the Roman Catholic Churches 'Mary-Churches.'"[28]

Pusey describes his own experience with Roman Catholics who write to him, urging him to pray for the grace to convert to Roman Catholicism. Typically, they suggest that he pray for the help of Mary, not for the help of Jesus. Furthermore, Roman Catholics tend to petition Mary to give directly that for which they are praying. Mary appears as the one who makes the decision to give what we request in prayer, whereas in fact only God can make this decision. Similarly, Mary appears as the one who confers life. Thus, all too often in Catholic devotion, Mary is imagined to be capable of doing what only God can do. For penances, Catholics are encouraged to recite Marian prayers, rather than to pray to Jesus. Pusey comments, "Nothing which seems to interfere with exclusive trust and

27. Pusey, 104.
28. Pusey, 107.

reliance on Jesus will, without some great revolution, gain hold of the hearts of the English people."[29]

He finds that the Marian system of piety is neither a legitimate development of doctrine nor a legitimate set of practices. Its exaggerations and disturbing falsehoods lead to a focus on Mary's mediation. It is Jesus who is the one Mediator, but this is hardly reflected in Roman Catholic piety. The Roman Catholic Church has become entangled in a pastoral dilemma of its own making: if people who believe that everyone who appeals to Mary will be saved are told that this is not a *de fide* teaching of the Roman Catholic Church, their whole faith might be undermined.[30]

In Pusey's view, the exaggerated Marian piety of Roman Catholic believers seems likely to spread itself insidiously throughout Roman Catholic doctrine. He hopes he is wrong, but he fears the rise of Marian doctrines whose impact will be "incalculable."[31] Here he remarks upon the viewpoint of Frederick Faber of the London Oratory, an Oxford Movement convert to Roman Catholicism who long was a thorn in Newman's side. In a preface to a new edition of a book by St. Louis Grignon de Montfort, Faber looks forward to a coming "Age of Mary" and seems to place Jesus and Mary on the same level, in addition to placing Mary and the Holy Spirit on the same level.[32] Faber thinks that English people, denied access to Mary, are perishing for that reason. If the English were to devote themselves to Mary, then, says Faber, the Christian faith would thrive in England. For Pusey, this seems completely wrongheaded, since it implies that Marian devotion is essential to salvation, even more essential than devotion to Christ. Pusey observes that reading Faber gives one the impression that Jesus will not be "willing to hear us, unless we seek a Mediatrix with Him,

29. Pusey, 111.

30. On Pusey's desire for the Roman Catholic Church to explain clearly what is and what is not *de fide*, see Roderick Strange, "Reflections on a Controversy: Newman and Pusey's 'Eirenicon,'" in *Pusey Rediscovered*, 332–348, at 335–340.

31. Pusey, *An Eirenicon*, 116.

32. Pusey, 116.

who is to dispose Him to hear us."[33] This is indeed offensive, and Pusey concludes that if Roman Catholics were taught devotion to God and Jesus (rather than constantly being pointed toward Mary), there would be many more saints in Roman Catholic countries.

All this is simply Pusey's preparation for turning to his fundamental concern, the dogma of the Immaculate Conception. He recalls how downcast Anglo-Catholics were when they heard about Pope Pius IX's preparations for declaring such a dogma. Anglo-Catholics knew that the immediate fruit of the dogma would be to increase division between Roman Catholics, on the one hand, and Orthodox and Anglicans, on the other. Even more importantly, they knew the dogma would divide the Roman Catholic Church of today from the Catholic Church of the patristic era, in which such a dogma was not contemplated. He reiterates that the reason for defining the dogma was not any controversy that needed resolution. Pope Pius IX went ahead because he sought to glorify God by giving appropriate glory to God's creature Mary, and thereby to enhance the Church with fresh gifts of God's favor. He quotes from Pius IX's encyclical of 1849, where Pius IX voices his hope that through Mary's intercession, God will cease from scourging his Church under the lash of the tumults of recent decades. Pius IX recalls that God has willed for all graces to come through Mary. Italian and French bishops voiced the same sentiments, hoping that the dogmatic praise of Mary as Immaculate "would establish the truth, restore peace, destroy heresy."[34]

These bishops, Pusey notes, were motivated also by a desire to see the pope demonstrate the truth of papal infallibility, by solemnly defining matters of doctrine on his own. Pusey bemoans the fact that there was no episcopal council, even if the pope did ask each bishop to give his opinion. In Pusey's view, this approach placed the bishops in an untenably subservient role. Besides, the opinion of the bishops was not really deemed necessary:

33. Pusey, 119.
34. Pusey, 124.

"What advice could any individual give to one, who, as all believed, was to give an inspired decision, to reject which was, they held, to reject God?"[35] In retrospect, the outcome was predetermined, and the individual bishops could hardly have dared to challenge the pope. No wonder, says Pusey, that many bishops simply remained silent rather than answering Pius IX's inquiry. By contrast, at a council even one bishop, and certainly a minority of bishops, can have an influence on the final language of a decree, as compromise is sought. In 1854, the bishops who did dare to disagree were not even mentioned by Pope Pius IX in promulgating the dogma. In fact, there was dissent even from some Italian bishops, including the bishops of Mondovì, Viterbo, Urbino, Ancona, Cervia, Otranto, Perugia, and (to a certain extent) Milan. Pusey remarks that the Portuguese bishop of Iaca urged that Salamancan theologians be first allowed to survey the patristic testimonies to Mary's holiness; the Mexican bishop of Chiapo openly "oppose[d] the decision, as being unsupported by any clear testimony from Scripture, or from Tradition"; and the Italian bishop of Ventimiglia demurred on the ground that Scripture does not clearly teach Mary's Immaculate Conception. In inspired Scripture, said the bishop of Ventimiglia, the Holy Spirit chose that Mary's "holy origin should remain hidden."[36]

Pusey goes on to fill in still more background. The Jesuit theologians in Dublin and the professors at Maynooth generally doubted the wisdom of defining the dogma; the apostolic vicars of Scotland cast doubt upon it; "the Archbishops of Paris and Rouen wrote earnestly to deprecate any decision, as did the Bishops of Coutances and Evreux; Chartres was anxious; Annecy, Meaux, Carcassonne doubted. The Archbishop of Rheims, with the Bishops of Soissons, Amiens, Beauvais, Blois, wished the decree to be softened so as to leave those who disbelieved it free from the note of

35. Pusey, 125. After publishing his response to Pusey's *Eirenicon*, Newman considered publishing a second reply to Pusey—this time on the topic of papal infallibility—but in the end decided against it. See John R. Page, *What Will Dr. Newman Do? John Henry Newman and Papal Infallibility, 1865–1875* (Collegeville, MN: Liturgical, 1994), 23–28.

36. Pusey, *An Eirenicon*, 129.

heresy."[37] Pusey goes on in this vein for some time, observing that the Austrian, German, and Swiss bishops were, in general, even more doubtful. Even the archbishop of Munich could not recommend defining the dogma. Hardly any American bishops replied. Had there been a local council in France, Pusey thinks the doubts of the archbishops of Paris and Rouen would have carried the day. He contrasts this with the suggestion of unanimous support found in Pope Pius IX's letter promulgating the dogma. He also quotes some bishops who wrote back in support, but in highly exaggerated and doctrinally troubling language, such as "Glorify the Mother of God that the Mother of God may glorify thee" and so forth.[38]

At this stage, Pusey returns to bemoaning the notion that the Virgin Mary is the mediatrix of all graces, standing between Christ and the Church. Jesus Christ commanded his followers to beseech the Father *in his name*, and it is solely through the merits of Christ, interceding with the Father, that we receive salvation and all corresponding gifts. Pusey complains that whereas Anglicans say, "God will bring it about," Roman Catholics tend to say, "Mary will bring it about." He also suggests that the hoped-for benefits of the dogmatic definition have not materialized. Among the benefits were to be the destruction of heresies, universal peace, conversion of non-Christians, and the conquest of the devil. He expresses deep concern that, if the way to gain favor with God is thought to be to proclaim a Marian dogma, then all sorts of Marian dogmas will follow, with further divisive results. All this is likely to be done, he says, by future popes rather than by councils, further deepening the suspicion that something is gravely awry and that the Vatican has become far too dominant.

In addition, Pusey notes that prior to the definition, theologians distinguished between active and passive conception. The former involves the conception of a person's body (via procreation); the latter involves the infusing of the soul, which was thought to happen a few weeks after

37. Pusey, 130.
38. Pusey, 138.

conception. This meant that it would have been possible for only the "passive conception" to be immaculate: the body could have been conceived in sin but then cleansed by God so as to receive the soul purely. As Pusey observes, "Probably the distinction was altogether wrong," but even so, some bishops advocated—in response to the pope's request for their opinion—that Mary's Immaculate Conception should be defined in such a way as to apply to the passive conception but not the active one.[39] In the end, these bishops, who might be counted as encouraging the definition, were not listened to, and the definition spoke simply of the first moment of her conception.

Even more seriously, Pusey doubts whether the Council of Trent's standards for doctrinal development were upheld by the new dogma. He grants that "the principle of the Council of Trent was maintained in words, that the faith must be contained in Scripture or in continuous tradition from the Apostles."[40] While maintained in words, however, this principle was not maintained in reality. The dogma of Mary's Immaculate Conception is taught clearly neither in Scripture nor in Tradition. Scripture says absolutely nothing about Mary's conception in the womb of her mother. The Church's Tradition is not clear on the matter, given that many Doctors of the Church either did not know of or else firmly rejected the doctrine in the form that Pope Pius IX defined it. These sobering facts were overcome, suggests Pusey, by appeal to the doctrine of the infallibility of the ordinary Magisterium (though he does not use that phrase). Pope Pius IX relied upon the principle "that the Church being incapable of erring, any thing taught throughout the Church, though not defined by any authority, or representing any thing beyond the opinion of the actual clergy, was necessarily true."[41] According to this principle, God would never have allowed his Church to celebrate liturgically the Immaculate Conception for centuries, if the doctrine were not in accord with reality. Since the whole Roman

39. Pusey, 147.
40. Pusey, 148.
41. Pusey, 148.

Catholic Church had long celebrated this feast, it must be true, even if Scripture and the patristic tradition did not teach it. This makes the practice and belief of the Church of Rome to be a guarantee that a particular opinion must have always belonged to divine revelation, no matter how clearly the opinion is absent from Scripture and the Fathers.

As Pusey notes, defenders of the proposed dogmatic definition took refuge in a high view not only of the Roman Catholic Church's inability to err in cases where it had long implied the truth of something, but also in a high view of the papal office. He points out, "To those who believed [in] the personal infallibility of the Pope, the fact that he pronounced any thing to be true was to be a proof that it had been always taught."[42] But in Pusey's view, this too is implausible, not least because of Honorius' heretical formal letter. He thinks that the Roman Catholic Church has fallen into the temptation of exaggerating its competence. Why could not God have allowed the Roman Catholic Church to err in matters of opinion over the centuries, and why suppose that the pope, in solemn pronouncements on faith and morals, must be correct? Much better to have a lower view of the Roman Catholic Church and a higher view of Scripture and the teachings of those closest to the Apostles—namely, the Church Fathers.

Pusey predicts that the next dogma to be defined will be the dogma of Mary's Assumption, which rests upon the self-same grounds as that of her Immaculate Conception. If she was without sin, then she would not owe the penalty of death, or at least would not undergo bodily corruption. Pusey's basic complaint is that here again, what Anglicans apply to Jesus is applied by Catholics to Mary (as well as to Jesus). Jesus was sinless; so must Mary have been. Jesus rose from the dead; so must Mary have done. Jesus is Mediator; Mary must be Mediatrix. Many bishops, in responding to Pius IX, proclaimed her also to be "Co-Redemptrix." Pusey quotes a number of bishops in this regard, and he also points to the work of numerous theologians, from one of whom he draws a lengthy quotation insisting that Mary

42. Pusey, 149.

uniquely shares in all of Christ's titles except those pertaining directly to the hypostatic union. Roman Catholic theologians even hold that in going to the cross out of obedience, Christ obeyed not only his Father but also his mother Mary, who was so merciful that even if the Father had *per impossibile* withheld his consent, Mary would have begged her Son to die for our salvation.

Pusey expresses outrage that Roman Catholic authors are so willing to place Mary at the center of faith and are willing even to claim that Mary was superior to God in the sense of being superior to Christ in his humanity, as mothers are superior over their sons. Mary's role has been inflated beyond all bounds, clearly derogating from what Scripture and the Fathers attribute to Christ. Whereas Scripture and the Fathers proclaim Christ the Redeemer, Roman Catholic theologians now proclaim the Co-Redemptrix Virgin Mary, who was fully redeemed well before Christ's work of redemption. Again, the point is that "it seems to be a part of this system, to parallel the Blessed Virgin throughout with her Divine Son, so that every prerogative which belonged to Him by nature or office should be in some measure imputed to her."[43] Christ is the image of the Father, and the image of his mother. Christ offered himself in sacrifice for the salvation of all; Mary at the foot of the cross offered her Son in sacrifice for the salvation of all. The condign merits of Christ are related to the congruous merits of Mary. Mary is in some way present in the Eucharist. No one comes to God but through Jesus; and no one comes to Jesus but through Mary. When a person receives the Eucharist, Mary should be in the person's soul to help the soul receive her Son. When Mary is in a person's soul, the Holy Spirit fills that soul. Pusey takes all this from a representative volume of Catholic Mariology.

Indeed, in this Marian system, Jesus, having chosen Mary to be his mother and partner, has given her a unique share in all his privileges. Mary herself is the center of creation. If we are servants (or slaves) of Jesus, then we are servants (or slaves) of Mary. Pusey pushes back: "Plainly [Christ]. . .

43. Pusey, 161.

not His creature [Mary], is the Centre of creation."[44] Some Roman Catholic authors have actually gone so far as to proclaim Mary as "the Complement of the Trinity."[45]

Pusey adds that this Marian system still seems to be "developing," being preached and urged by countless priests and bishops—and, if so, then this very fact shows what a danger "development of doctrine" is, with its logical entailments growing ever more absurd and offensive.[46] As the system develops, it becomes insufficient to believe that Jesus is truly present (Body, Blood, Soul, and Divinity) in the Eucharist; Mary must be there too. Cornelius à Lapide, the great biblical commentator, already held this doctrine. Faber held it as well, on the basis, in part, of a mystical revelation given to St. Ignatius of Loyola. In doctrinal development, Pusey asks, are mystical revelations (which are notoriously contradictory) now to play a role? If St. Bridget of Sweden's mystical revelation serves as a doctrinal support of Mary's Immaculate Conception, why not St. Ignatius' mystical revelation as a support for a future dogma on Mary's real presence in the Eucharist? Why not a dogma that teaches, as Faber believed, that the blood shed by Jesus on the cross was actually, by a miracle, precisely the blood Jesus received from Mary?

Pushing toward an argument *ad absurdum*, Pusey is here challenging the very notion of development of doctrine as a plausible mode of preserving Christian truth. He notes that one recent non–Roman Catholic author, caustically surveying the scene, judges that soon the Our Father will be joined by a new prayer: "Our Lady, who art in heaven . . ." For Pusey, as noted above, the far better path is to adhere to Scripture and the Fathers.

Pusey's purpose, therefore, is to attack the whole notion of the development of an "idea"—Newmanian development of doctrine—by considering the present growth and flowering of the Marian system, which carries many Roman Catholics into what amounts to a religion of Mary. The dogma of

44. Pusey, 166.
45. Pusey, 167.
46. Pusey, 168.

the Immaculate Conception is like the tip of the iceberg regarding the doctrinal "development" (i.e., corruption) to come. Roman Catholics may claim to oppose, and even utterly to reject, the notion that those who receive the Eucharist receive Mary as present in the Eucharist. So Roman Catholics today may claim; but many saints and doctors, beginning with Bernard of Clairvaux, utterly rejected the doctrine of the Immaculate Conception on the grounds that Mary required a Redeemer—and yet here the dogma is, proclaiming that Mary was fully redeemed at her conception, obviously well before Christ shed his blood on the cross. To make matters worse, in proclaiming this dogma, Pope Pius IX called for an increase in Marian piety, thereby no doubt spurring even further excesses and exaggerations, all to the detriment of the worship of Jesus Christ as the Lord of history, the one Mediator, and the supreme embodiment of divine mercy.

Pusey asks: Can this "development" or, in actuality, this corruption be stopped? He thinks it will be extremely difficult for the Roman Catholic Church to stop, now that it has embarked upon this course by proclaiming a dogma that inevitably undermines the redemption of all humanity by Christ's shedding his blood on the cross. Now that the Roman Catholic Church has shown itself willing to take this step, and to do so through the action of the pope (thereby showing its commitment to papal infallibility), what is to stop further corruption? Pusey remarks, "The tendency of every decisive act, moreover, both in a body and in an individual, is to produce other similar acts."[47]

A deep doctrinal corruption is setting in, Pusey fears. Each future pope will be able to dogmatize whatever he wishes regarding the Marian system. Future popes will send the faithful to Mary, when Jesus requires the faithful to be sent to Jesus for salvation. Pusey quotes de Montfort's insistence that in order to go to Jesus, people must first go to Mary; Jesus will intercede for his people but only if Mary asks him. Implicitly critiquing Newman's notion of development as the unfolding of an "idea," Pusey emphasizes, "The

47. Pusey, 181.

human mind is narrow, and easily filled with one thought, especially when that thought relates to one's all."[48] Frankly, the whole of Christian doctrine is corrupted when Jesus is feared and when Mary, not Jesus, becomes the merciful and compassionate intercessor. The supposition that Jesus would repel any supplicant is profoundly at odds with the Gospel. Besides, in Roman Catholic authors there is already grave confusion regarding the status of prayer and praise to Mary. Some authors argue that since Jesus is in Mary, worship directed toward Mary is in a certain sense acceptable; honoring Mary means honoring her Son, and so one can hardly go too far.

No doubt, for such authors, there still remains a theoretical difference between the adoration due to God and the adoration due to Mary; only God can be given worship in the strict sense. Practically speaking, however, many Roman Catholics devote themselves assiduously not to God or Jesus, but to Mary. De Montfort argues firmly against any check to Marian devotion, and the whole Roman Catholic Church seems to be following him. Among Roman Catholic theologians and leaders, says Pusey, "there seem to be now those only who are silent, or who intensify the devotion to the Blessed Virgin."[49] In response to Pope Pius IX's query prior to defining the dogma, some Austrian and German bishops dared to speak up and remind the pope that many Catholics in their lands hardly believe the Trinitarian and Christological doctrines at the core of the Gospel—and thus it is an unpropitious time to add a pious belief, quite difficult to demonstrate, to the list of core dogmas necessary for salvific faith. But no one listened to these bishops.

Thus, Pusey thinks there is strong reason to fear that the Roman Catholic Church, overrun by an offensive Marian system and by the unchecked individual authority of the bishop of Rome, is in the midst of a deeply corruptive movement away from Scripture and the Fathers, all in the name (although Pusey leaves this implicit) of "development of doctrine." Pusey

48. Pusey, 182.
49. Pusey, 188.

concludes his book by attacking the Ultramontanists, who seem to have turned the belief in the pope's "preservation from error" into a belief in the pope's "Divine perpetual inspiration."[50] The claims made by Pope Pius IX's *Syllabus of Errors* suggest that the documents promulgated by Pius IX have such binding authority as to make Pius IX "the perpetual Prophet of the Church," with every papal writing now having a weight comparable to Scripture itself.[51]

While disagreeing with Archbishop Manning's Ultramontanism, Pusey agrees with him—though with sorrow rather than gladness—that "the declaration of the Immaculate Conception of the Blessed Virgin as revealed truth, is calculated to be full of consequences, as entailing the transmutation of other 'pious opinions' about her into truths necessary to salvation."[52] This is what happens when, imagining oneself to be developing doctrine, one goes headlong down the path of doctrinal corruption, replacing Jesus with Mary, and replacing Scripture, bishops, and councils with the pope of the day, ignoring how the current pope and the new Marian dogma have transformed into heretics many earlier popes and Doctors of the Church. Pusey comments, "Faber anticipated 'an Age of Mary,' in comparison to which all previous devotion to her should be slight. Archbishop Manning anticipates a new era, in which the Pope should continually be declaring new matters of faith, to be believed without the authority of Scripture or

50. Pusey, 326.

51. Pusey, 328. For W.G. Ward's view—in an 1867 public controversy with the Birmingham Oratorian Henry Ignatius Dudley Ryder—that all papal documents are infallible in which the pope deliberately addresses all Catholics in any matter related to doctrine (even if specifically having to do with politics or history), see Page, *What Will Dr. Newman Do?*, 33–36. At issue was, in part, whether the *Syllabus of Errors* and the encyclical *Quanta Cura* carried binding dogmatic weight. Newman forwarded to Pusey some of Ryder's writings against Ward. For helpful background to the Syllabus and to the infallibility debate—placing both in the context of the broader politics of the day—see Nicholas Atkin and Frank Tallett, *Priests, Prelates and People: A History of European Catholicism since 1750* (Oxford: Oxford University Press, 2003), 101–141, including the discussion of the role of Count Charles de Montalambert, who argued at an 1863 conference of "liberal Catholics" that "the Church in any particular country should no longer depend upon state power and financial wherewithal to sustain its activities" (Atkin and Tallett, 134–135).

52. Pusey, *An Eirenicon*, 328.

tradition, on his sole authority."[53] Pusey wonders: Is this a harbinger of the final coming of the Antichrist? If it is—and even if it is not—he concludes by urging that all people from every branch who hold to the true Catholic faith, now under siege in every land (by liberal Christians and by atheism), should come together under one banner, Jesus Christ.

Newman's Response to Pusey

In his *Essay on the Development of Christian Doctrine*, originally published in 1845, Newman argued—as Pusey well knew in 1865—that "from the nature of the human mind, time is necessary for the full comprehension and perfection of great ideas; and . . . the highest and most wonderful truths, though communicated to the world once for all by inspired teachers, could not be comprehended all at once by the recipients."[54] For a powerful "idea" to unfold fully in the minds of its recipients, much time is required. Newman makes this point into a foundation of his theory of doctrinal development. At first, the "idea" will meet with confused responses; gradually, as judgments accumulate via thought and controversy, settled teachings will arise that form a "body of thought" that is "in substance what that idea meant from the first, its complete image as seen in a combination of diversified aspects, with the suggestions and corrections of many minds, and the illustration of many experiences."[55] Newman concludes that the desire to go directly to the source—to reject all later development so as to be secure in the original expression of the idea—will not work because, as history suggests, an idea stands forth as "more equable, and purer, and stronger, when its bed has become deep, and broad, and

53. Pusey, 333–334.

54. John Henry Newman, *An Essay on the Development of Christian Doctrine*, 6th ed. (Notre Dame, IN: University of Notre Dame Press, 1989), 29–30. I cite the 1878 final edition, as is my practice in this book. Since my arguments regarding Newman on doctrinal corruption are fundamentally theological rather than historical, it seems appropriate to employ his final editions.

55. Newman, 38.

full."[56] The reality named by the idea must be contemplated from various angles and by an array of minds, and must be tested in controversy to prove its solidity. According to Newman, therefore, "If Christianity is a fact, and impresses an idea of itself on our minds and is a subject-matter of exercises of the reason, that idea will in the course of time expand into a multitude of ideas . . . connected and harmonious with one another."[57]

Clearly, Pusey is throwing this argument back at Newman with regard to the dogma of Mary's Immaculate Conception, in light of the Marian practices and devotional language of the Roman Catholic Church. Pusey strives to show that Roman Catholicism, having become entangled in a corrupt idea—or two corrupt ideas, when one adds in the unchecked papacy—is developing this idea to the hilt. On this view, Roman Catholic Mariology promotes a whole system of dogmatic corruption, undermining the most central truths of the Christian faith.

Newman, for his part, is well aware in *An Essay on the Development of Christian Doctrine* that many of his Anglican friends will suppose "that what I have called developments in the Roman Church are nothing more or less than what used to be called her corruptions."[58] He discusses the Virgin Mary three times in the *Essay*. The first time is in chapter four, where he briefly offers some instances of what he has in mind by "development," in service of his argument that from the outset the Church's "teaching looked towards those ecclesiastical dogmas, afterwards recognized and defined, with (as time went on) more or less determinate advance in the direction of them."[59] Here Newman grants that prior to the fifth century, there was not

56. Newman, 40.

57. Newman, 55.

58. Newman, 170.

59. Newman, 122. For further discussion of Newman's reflections on the Virgin Mary in *An Essay on the Development of Christian Doctrine*, see Lisowski, "A Fitting Glory," 26–35. See also three broader studies cited by Lisowski: Robert M. Andrews, *Apologia Pro Beata Maria Virgine: John Henry Newman's Defence of the Virgin Mary in Catholic Doctrine and Piety* (Dublin: Academic, 2017); Peter Gittens, *Mary More or Less: Anglican and Catholic Mariology of John Henry Newman* (Saarbrucken, DE: Scholar, 2013); Nicholas Gregoris, *'The Daughter of Eve Unfallen': Mary in the Theology and Spirituality of John Henry Newman* (Mount Pocono,

a "public and ecclesiastical recognition" of Mary's place; but in the fifth century, a controversy arose as to whether Mary was the Mother of God or God-bearer, "Theotokos."[60] The dogmatic affirmation of this title inaugurated the ecclesiastical recognition of Mary's exalted dignity, although the vision of Revelation 11–12, in Newman's view, already exhibits the dignity of Mary—"a woman clothed with the sun, with the moon under her feet, and on her head a crown of twelve stars" (Rev. 12:1). Newman argues that to praise Mary has always been to praise her Son, since her exaltation derives entirely from her status as the one chosen and prepared to be his mother. Furthermore, already in the early Fathers (from Origen onward) Mary had been called Theotokos. Newman recites the various praises given to her by the Church Fathers, and these praises are great indeed.

Newman's seven notes for true development, as distinct from corruption, are preservation of type, continuity of principles, power of assimilation, logical sequence, anticipation of its future, conservative action upon its past, and chronic vigor.[61] Newman next treats the Virgin Mary when discussing the fifth note, anticipation of its future. He observes that already in second-century Fathers, such as Justin Martyr and Irenaeus, Mary's status as the New Eve had been indicated. From this status come many of the later doctrines regarding her unique cooperation in her Son's work and her

PA: Newman House, 2003). As Andrews puts it, "For Newman's thesis on development to succeed, it was clear that the place of the Virgin Mary within Catholic history would have to be shown to be a true development and not a corruption" (*Apologia Pro Beata Maria Virgine*, 43).

60. Newman, *An Essay on the Development of Christian Doctrine*, 145.

61. Newman lists these somewhat differently in his 1845 edition, where he also calls them "tests" rather than "notes." C. Michael Shea provides the 1845 list: "1) the discernment of a continuity of doctrinal type, 2) a continuity of underlying principle, 3) the power of assimilation in new contexts, 4) early anticipation, 5) logical sequence, or elaboration, 6) additions occurring for the preservation of other doctrines or principles, and 7) chronic (meaning 'long-term') continuance" (Shea, "Doctrinal Development," in *The Oxford Handbook of John Henry Newman*, 284–303, at 289). Aptly, Shea emphasizes that "Newman's tests for distinguishing developments from corruptions in Christianity did not serve as demonstrations. Rather, the tests functioned more as 'heuristics'" (Shea, 290; citing Chau Nguyen, "Encountering Truth: Newman's Theological Method in *An Essay on the Development of Christian Doctrine*," *Newman Studies Journal* 8, no. 1 [2011]: 40–55).

unique preparation for such cooperation. The symbolism of the New Eve is present in Revelation 11–12's portrait of the "woman" who is at enmity with the serpent and who is the mother of the Messiah. Tertullian, too, depicts Mary as the New Eve. Gregory of Nyssa describes a vision of Mary, in glory, discoursing with the Evangelist John and obtaining a favor from him. Gregory of Nazianzus tells the story of a Christian woman praying (efficaciously) to receive the intercession of Mary. Thus, the Church Fathers recognized Mary as the exalted Mother of God and the New Eve, participating in the redemptive work of her Son and interceding for the faithful. All the later Church's Marian doctrines and pious practices flow from these attributes of Mary.

The third and final place where Newman mentions Mary in *An Essay on the Development of Christian Doctrine* is in his chapter on the sixth note, conservative action upon its past. Here he anticipates a large part of Pusey's 1865 concern: "It has been anxiously asked, whether the honours paid to St. Mary, which have grown out of devotion to her Almighty Lord and Son, do not, in fact, tend to weaken that devotion" by exalting a mere creature and turning attention away from Christ.[62] He answers that on the contrary, if one fails to exalt Mary as Theotokos, one will weaken the worship of Christ. In his view, this can be shown from the situation of nineteenth-century Europe. The religious liberalism that minimizes Christ's divinity is most successful not in countries where Mary is honored but in countries where Mary is not honored. In Roman Catholic piety, Newman argues, Mary is treated affectionately as one would treat a mere creature, though an exalted one; whereas Christ is treated with the awe due to God, though a God who is most loving and gracious. In this regard, he compares the *Dies Irae* with the *Stabat Mater*, and he compares the Breviary's services for the Feast of

62. Newman, *An Essay on the Development of Christian Doctrine*, 425. Robert Andrews comments on this third place where Newman discusses Mary in *An Essay on the Development of Christian Doctrine*: "The section was entitled: 'Devotion to the Blessed Virgin' in the 1878 edition and, though untitled in the 1845 edition, similarly deals with the sixth test of an authentic development (preservative additions or, as in 1878, conservative action upon the past)" (Andrews, *Apologia Pro Beata Maria Virgine*, 53).

the Holy Trinity with the Breviary's services for the Feast of the Assumption. He contends that in traditionally Protestant countries, Christ is often treated as an excellent man without being treated with the awe due to God. The point is that veneration of Mary does not in actual fact promote discounting Christ.

Newman insists, too, that although Marian devotion abounds in Roman Catholicism, Mary is not given primacy. As an example, he gives Ignatius of Loyola's *Spiritual Exercises*, which discusses Mary only in a few places, and does so in relation to Christ. Another example along the same lines comes from a sampling of Roman Catholic devotional books, where—unless the book is solely about Mary—Jesus holds the central place, though Mary (and her Immaculate Conception) receives occasional mention.[63] In the devotional books that are focused on Mary, she appears as the highest creature, and, while highly exalted, she stands infinitely below God. She participates in the good things of her Son, but she only participates, as creatures do. Her merit is congruous, not condign like her Son's. Her unique cultus flows from the fact that the Incarnation took place in her womb, rather than any dignity specifically of her own. Newman concludes that the Church's Marian teaching conserves its Christological dogma, by illumining rather than undermining "the divine glory of her Son."[64]

Clearly, Pusey was not satisfied with these explanations (if he read them), and indeed they are rather cursory—due partly to the fact that Newman had so much else to treat in his *Essay on the Development of Christian Doctrine*. Besides, much changed in the decade after Newman's conversion to Roman Catholicism in 1845. No doubt after the 1854 declaration

63. For background, see Andrews, *Apologia Pro Beata Maria Virgine*, 57–58, highlighting the role of the Irish Catholic priest Charles William Russell in sending Newman these books and in encouraging Newman to rethink his view of Catholic Marian devotion in the early 1840s. In his *Apologia Pro Vita Sua*, Newman credits Russell for being instrumental in his conversion. The Anglican Newman shared Pusey's concerns about Roman Catholic Mariology, and it was Russell who helped him through it. See Ambrose Macaulay, *Dr Russell of Maynooth* (London: Darton, Longman, and Todd, 1983), 65–98.

64. Newman, *An Essay on the Development of Christian Doctrine*, 436.

of the dogma, Pusey felt quite justified in calling upon Newman to explain himself more fully or else to admit that the Roman Catholic Church was sliding down the slope of doctrinal corruption.[65]

In his 1866 *A Letter Addressed to the Rev. E.B. Pusey, D.D., on Occasion of His Eirenicon*, Newman does not retract his earlier viewpoint. He opens his *Letter* by thanking Pusey for his ecumenical outreach, which Newman takes as a sign that Pusey (joined by the many Anglo-Catholics who esteem Pusey's views) deeply yearns for the "union of Christendom after its many and long-standing divisions."[66] He assures Pusey that he respects Pusey's sincere conscience in not becoming Roman Catholic and that he is glad that Pusey has enumerated the difficulties that, in Pusey's view, press against the claims of the Roman Catholic Church. At the same time, he finds that

---

65. Newman, of course, does not hold to the notion of three branches of the Catholic Church, and so he speaks not of "Roman" Catholics but simply of "Catholics." See also Pusey's *Is Healthful Reunion Impossible? A Second Letter to the Very Rev. J.H. Newman, D.D.* (London: James Parker, 1870), which focuses on further issues, such as justification, Purgatory, the canon of Scripture, and especially the doctrinal errors and contradictions made by popes (in view of the Catholic Church's movement toward the dogma of papal infallibility). On pages 331–337 Pusey strongly defends himself against the charge of polemic in his *Eirenicon*. He repeats his fundamental charge: "Where we should expect to find the Name of Jesus, we find Mary, or, at the best, Jesus and Mary, as joint, although in a disparate degree, dispensers of graces—He, as having them in Himself to give; His Mother, as being entrusted or delegated by Him to give them. If we complain of this, we are (at least by foreign ecclesiastics) frankly told of the 'exaggeration' of the 'livres de piété.' . . . Why, in the books of your communion, does the Blessed Mother of God so often stand where we should expect to find her Son?" (Pusey, 332–334). A year earlier, Pusey had published his *First Letter to the Very Rev. J.H. Newman, D.D., In Explanation Chiefly in Regard to the Ever-Blessed Theotokos, and the Doctrine of Her Immaculate Conception* (London: James Parker, 1869). Here, at great length, he defends and clarifies his concerns about the dogma of the Immaculate Conception, focusing on patristic testimony but also including many medieval and more recent thinkers; and he also defends his citation of (and concerns about) Roman Catholic Marian devotional texts. His concern about the dogma has to do not with the proposition that Mary was perfectly sanctified in her mother's womb but with the view that Mary was conceived strictly without original sin. For discussion of these two *Letters* to Newman, see Chapman, *The Fantasy of Reunion*, 100–130; and Robert Harvie Greenfield, "'Such a Friend to the Pope,'" in *Pusey Rediscovered*, 162–184, at 178–180.

66. Newman, *A Letter Addressed to the Rev. E.B. Pusey, D.D., on Occasion of His Eirenicon*, 1.

Pusey's *Eirenicon* is not especially irenic. He compares it to an olive branch discharged "from a catapult."[67]

Newman observes that, in holding that all doctrine is contained in Scripture, Anglicans do not differ from Catholics—or at least not from Newman. Certainly, not all doctrine can be adequately *proven* from Scripture without the assistance of Tradition, but this does not mean that the doctrines are not in Scripture. In fact, with the assistance of Tradition, it may be proven that all Catholic doctrine is in Scripture. Nevertheless, says Newman, Pusey's own view of doctrine is untenable. For example, in order to hold to the doctrines of the Trinity and of the Incarnation, one needs a firm notion of doctrinal development, as a glance into the pre-Nicene Fathers will show. Moreover, the purpose of doctrinal development is not to depart from the Fathers but to explain and complete them, including with regard to the Virgin Mary.[68]

Newman challenges Pusey's heavy citation of Faber's Marian texts, as though Faber were an authority. Likewise, Pusey seems to rely on W.G. Ward to judge the meaning of papal infallibility, despite the fact that Ward, too, is no weighty theologian. As Newman says, although these two men are English, "they are in no sense spokesmen for English Catholics."[69] He names a set of English Catholics from the previous generation who had (or have) a claim to speak for English Catholics, and he notes that none of them advocated exaggerated views of Mary or the papacy.

Entering into his discussion of Catholic Marian doctrine, he first

67. Newman, 7.

68. Chapman aptly remarks that "there was a crucial difference between Newman and Pusey over precisely what Newman meant by 'explaining' and 'completing' the teachings of the Fathers. After all, for Pusey, doctrine was already complete in the teachings of the Fathers. . . . [Pusey] was well able to grasp the doctrine of the Second Eve as a pious opinion. His problem, however, was whether the Immaculate Conception which it was seeking to illustrate could be regarded as a necessary requirement of faith rather than simply a pious opinion" ("Ecumenism, Mariology, and the Papacy," 362–363; cf. Chapman, *The Fantasy of Reunion*, 102).

69. Newman, *A Letter Addressed to the Rev. E.B. Pusey, D.D., on Occasion of His Eirenicon*, 23.

insists upon the distinction between doctrine and devotional practice.[70] The reason for this is simple: Catholics may believe in something while varying in the degrees and tones of the devotion by which they give expression to that belief. Catholics all must believe in the Eucharist, but not all must belong to the confraternity of the Precious Blood. There will be differences in religious sensibility. Second, Newman sets forth the fundamental Catholic doctrines about Mary.[71] In addition to being Mother of God, she is, according to the Church Fathers, the New Eve. Just as Eve collaborated with Adam, so does the New Eve collaborate with the New Adam. He cites numerous Fathers in this vein, beginning with Justin Martyr. All underscore that Mary is not simply a "physical instrument" but an intelligent cause (through her *fiat*) in the event of the Incarnation. She does not merely give birth to Christ; she also is exalted in sanctity so as to cooperate in the event. Eve, who fell, cooperated in destructive evil; the New Eve, who was holy, cooperated in salvific good. Indeed, through Eve came death, whereas through the New Eve came life. This is a high doctrine of Mary indeed, and Newman finds it already in the earliest Fathers, who are echoed by the later Fathers. They teach that "the Blessed Virgin had a real meritorious co-operation . . . in the reversal of the fall."[72]

On this foundation, Newman draws inferences about Mary's sanctity and dignity. Anglicans and Catholics agree that Eve was created in a wondrous grace; she was not a sinner prior to her fall. What then about Mary? Newman asks rhetorically: "Is it any violent inference, that she, who was to co-operate in the redemption of the world, at least was not less endowed with power from on high, than she who, given as a helpmate to her husband, did in the event but co-operate with him for its ruin?"[73] If Eve was created in grace, then it is reasonable to suppose that Mary received even

70. See Strange, "Reflections on a Controversy," 341.

71. For a helpful summary of Newman's approach here, see Hilda Graef, *Mary: A History of Doctrine and Devotion* (Notre Dame, IN: Ave Maria, 2009), 365–369.

72. Newman, *A Letter Addressed to the Rev. E.B. Pusey, D.D., on Occasion of His Eirenicon*, 43.

73. Newman, 45.

greater grace. Newman interprets the angel's greeting as more than an expression of external favor. Mary truly was "full of grace" (Luke 1:28 RSV-CE). These reflections suggest to Newman a simple inference: Mary was no more stained by sin than Eve was. Mary was and is immaculate.

In this way, he insists that Mary's condition of marvelous, graced sanctity is firmly grounded in Scripture and the Fathers. Yet Newman is aware that a significant problem remains, and he puts it clearly: "How does this enable us to say that she was conceived without *original sin*?"[74] Newman addresses this problem by arguing that much hinges upon one's doctrine of original sin.[75] According to the Catholic perspective, "original sin" is not in us as an actual fault; rather, our being in a state of "original sin" denotes the state to which the fall from grace has reduced all progeny of Adam and Eve.

---

74. Newman, 47. Andrews points out that Newman's bishop, William Ullathorne, in 1855 published a popular defense of the dogma of the Immaculate Conception (Ullathorne, *The Immaculate Conception of the Mother of God: An Exposition* [London: Richardson & Son, 1855]). Andrews speculates that it may have been "because of Ullathorne's book—and of Newman's approval of it—that Newman did not, during the 1850s, publicly respond to the controversy himself" (Andrews, *Apologia Pro Beata Maria Virgine*, 65). Andrews adds that in responding to Pusey's *Eirenicon* on the topic of Mary's Immaculate Conception, Newman mainly reprised what he had said earlier in private writings, among them the following: Letters to Arthur Osborne Alleyne, 30 May 1860 and 15–17 June 1860; and Letter to William Wilberforce, 9 December 1860, in *The Letters and Diaries of John Henry Newman*, vol. 19, ed. Charles Stephen Dessain (London: Nelson, 1969), 346–347, 361–370, 437–438; and "The Memorandum on the Immaculate Conception," dating from the early 1850s and possibly composed for Robert Isaac Wilberforce, first published in *Meditations and Devotions of the Late Cardinal Newman*, ed. William P. Neville (London: Longmans, Green, 1893), 115–126. Andrews surveys the contents of this Memorandum at some length. Newman's central argument in the Memorandum, as in his reply to Pusey, is that Mary is the New Eve and therefore possesses the holiness of Eve prior to Eve's fall. See also Francis J. Friedel, *The Mariology of Cardinal Newman* (New York: Benziger, 1928), 107.

75. Pusey emphasizes this issue in his *First Letter to the Very Rev. J.H. Newman, D.D.*, 404–409. Pusey supports a viewpoint that he finds in Pope Innocent III, according to which original sin existed in Mary "in the cause" (namely, her parents' act of sexual intercourse, marked by concupiscence), so that "there was not only something from which she had to be 'preserved,' but something also which was to be removed from her inchoate being" (Pusey, 408). For appreciative discussion of Pusey's *First Letter to the Very Rev. J.H. Newman, D.D.*, see Chapman, "Ecumenism, Mariology, and the Papacy," 363–367; and for a brief discussion of Newman's private letters responding to Pusey (June 9, July 4, and September 12, 1869), in which Newman reiterated his position and argued that Pusey could have benefited much from Ullathorne's book, see Chapman, *The Fantasy of Reunion*, 111–114.

It is accurate to say that Mary shares in this state: she is among those who need restoration. The difference is that she receives the restoration that she needs precisely at her conception—because God remits her debt and pours forth his grace upon her "for the sake of Him who was to redeem her and us upon the Cross."[76] This is to prepare her by grace to be the New Eve, and it is done solely in view of the saving work of the New Adam, which is applied to her in advance. She is singled out not because of anything in herself but because of her relation to her Son, from whom all grace comes. Although she belongs to the fallen children of Adam, then, she herself does not bear original sin, because God's grace intervenes in light of the economy of Christ. She is among Adam's fallen children because had it not been for this special grace she would have been conceived in original sin. Her restoration by grace at the instant of her conception ensured that she was "full of grace" and could act in every way as the New Eve.[77]

Newman observes that the Catholic Church long delayed defining the dogma of Mary's Immaculate Conception because Catholics were divided about what such a dogma would mean for Mary's status as a child of fallen Adam. Many Catholics in the centuries prior to the dogmatic definition feared that if Mary were deemed to have been immaculate from conception, this would mean "that the Blessed Virgin did not die in Adam, that she did not come under the penalty of the fall, that she was not redeemed, that she was conceived in some way inconsistent with the verse in the *Miserere* Psalm."[78] But the doctrine of the Immaculate Conception does not mean any of these things. In fact, Mary was redeemed, she was conceived in the normal way, and she died (or at least the belief that she died is not inconsistent with the dogma). The Immaculate Conception simply means that she had the fully restorative and elevating grace of the Holy Spirit from

76. Newman, *A Letter Addressed to the Rev. E.B. Pusey, D.D., on Occasion of His Eirenicon*, 48.

77. For further discussion, see Gregoris, *'The Daughter of Eve Unfallen'*; Andrews, *Apologia Pro Beata Maria Virgine*, 85–93.

78. Newman, *A Letter Addressed to the Rev. E.B. Pusey, D.D., on Occasion of His Eirenicon*, 49.

the very outset; the Spirit dwelt fully within her, as a fully redeemed creature, in view of her Son.

Newman adds that the centuries-long debate over the doctrine never implied that most Catholics thought Mary's life was marked by actual fallen concupiscence or sin. He cites Augustine's refusal to number Mary among sinners, which, although Augustine had purposes in view other than a dogmatic definition, still should impress us. As Newman knows, some Fathers—notably Basil, John Chrysostom, and Cyril of Alexandria—thought she sinned venially. But this was a minority position.

Yet did Mary in fact do much of anything, other than give birth to Jesus and raise him as a mother should? Newman comments in this regard, "The only question is, whether the Blessed Virgin had a part, a real part, in the economy of grace, whether, when she was on earth, she secured by her deeds any claim on our memories."[79] For Newman, this can only be a rhetorical question. After all, Mary pondered the mystery of her Son's birth and destiny; she interceded with her Son on behalf of the wedding guests at Cana; she prayed and wept at the foot of the cross. No wonder she proclaimed that "from now on all generations will call me blessed" (Luke 1:48). When people recollect Mary's actual "position in the gospels" and "what that position imports," they will be amazed not that Mary receives so much veneration but that she generally receives much less than befits her dignity.[80]

Even if the dogma of the Immaculate Conception has scriptural and patristic grounds, it may seem that the same cannot be said for Mary's Assumption. Recognizing that this question will not be far from the minds of his readers, Newman addresses it. He argues that Mary's Assumption is justified scripturally on the basis of Revelation 11–12, even if it cannot be proven scripturally without the aid of Tradition. He points out that recourse to the aid of Tradition characterizes Anglicans such as Pusey as well. At various places in the Gospel of John and the Book of Revelation, Mary

79. Newman, 52.
80. Newman, 53.

appears simply as "woman." In Revelation 11, a serpent is added to the mix, making the allusion to Mary as the New Eve quite clear. This is not an abstract or merely poetical allegory; rather, Scripture is typologically teaching us something about the concrete, actual Mary. In Revelation 12:5, the "woman" gives birth to "a male child, who is to rule all the nations with a rod of iron." This "woman" may signify more than Mary (for example, Israel), but Mary certainly is signified here. This same "woman" is linked with imagery that indicates she is fully in heaven with her son: "God's temple in heaven was opened, and the ark of his covenant was seen within his temple. . . . A great portent appeared in heaven: a woman clothed with the sun" (Rev. 11:19–12:1).[81]

Newman next turns to the ground of Mary's dignity in her stature as "Theotokos," as per the dogmatic definition of the Council of Ephesus. Why, he asks, should it be surprising that the *Mother of God* should receive the blessings of an Immaculate Conception and a glorious Assumption so as to prepare for and to share in the victory of her Son? Surely the title "Mother of God" is far more striking than either of these blessings, and far more striking, too, than Catholic devotional names such as "Mother of mercy." Newman reviews in detail the patristic testimony to this title, beginning with Origen. As Newman puts it, "No wonder if [the later Fathers'] language should become unmeasured, when so great a term as 'Mother of God' had been formally set down as the safe limit of it."[82] In other words, language has quite a ways to go if the title "Mother of God" is its outer limit. He provides numerous examples of seemingly exaggerated Marian praise from the Fathers, from the fourth century onward. The Fathers, he shows, are the root of contemporary Catholic Marian devotion.

Pusey shares with Newman the belief in the intercession of the saints

81. For Pusey's view that Revelation 11–12 does not function as Newman thinks, see Pusey, *First Letter to the Very Rev. J.H. Newman, D.D., In Explanation Chiefly in Regard to the Ever-Blessed Theotokos, and the Doctrine of Her Immaculate Conception*, 44–45. See also my *Mary's Bodily Assumption* (Notre Dame, IN: University of Notre Dame Press, 2015).

82. Newman, *A Letter Addressed to the Rev. E.B. Pusey, D.D., on Occasion of His Eirenicon*, 65.

and the belief that Mary is most exalted among the saints and thus most powerful in intercession. Newman emphasizes that the Church Fathers certainly did not think that when holy Christians died, they stopped praying for their fellow Christians. He offers biblical evidence for this belief, including Hebrews 12:23, which proclaims that the New Jerusalem already contains not only Jesus and the angels, but also "the spirits of the righteous made perfect." In his view, the very fact that the author of Hebrews considers it a blessing to have come to "the spirits of the righteous made perfect" means that these saints must still care for their brethren on earth. All of God's friends constantly prayed to God on behalf of others during their earthly lives. After their death, these people continue to be God's friends—and continue to pray on behalf of others. Newman concludes that Mary's role can be no other than "perpetual intercession for the faithful militant."[83] She intercedes for those who appeal to her.

This role of Mary was already known, Newman says, to the Fathers. He repeats the story that he had mentioned in *An Essay on the Development of Christian Doctrine*, regarding a vision of Mary instructing the Evangelist John to reveal the truth of godliness to a particular person (who became a great saint). According to Gregory of Nyssa, Gregory Thaumaturgus received this vision of Marian intercession in the third century. The Anglican Bishop Bull affirmed the veracity of this story, and Newman employs it to suggest a basis for later devotion to Mary as the destroyer of heresies—since Mary is depicted as illuminating Gregory Thaumaturgus' mind. Whether the story is true or not, Newman has no trouble affirming that Mary intercedes with her Son to assist the illumination of the saints and doctors.

Newman underlines the importance of adducing these patristic testimonies prior to moving on to the more flowery language of the medieval period onward. It was the Fathers who provided the key titles: "Mother of God, Second Eve, and Mother of all Living, the Mother of Life, the Morning Star, the Mystical New Heaven, the Sceptre of Orthodoxy, the

83. Newman, 73.

All-undefiled Mother of Holiness."[84] These patristic titles already are much more than Protestants are willing to hold; and, if Catholics offer further titles, as Catholics do, it can be shown that the patristic titles justify them. Moreover, in judging devotion, one cannot proceed as though one were judging doctrinal faith. Devotion is rooted in affection, and affection allows for words of endearment that are sometimes exaggerated but may still be appropriate in the circumstances. Besides, it must be granted that, by contrast to the intellectual refinements required by highly educated persons, "the religion of the multitude is ever vulgar and abnormal; it ever will be tinctured with fanaticism and superstition, while men are what they are."[85] Of course, even the educated and refined views of theologians can cause great problems, as theologians attempt to use logic to solve unfathomable mysteries.

Having made these arguments, Newman reiterates his fundamental insight: "When once we have mastered the idea, that Mary bore, suckled, and handled the Eternal in the form of a child, what limit is conceivable to the rush and flood of thoughts which such a doctrine involves? What awe and surprise must attend upon the knowledge, that a creature has been brought so close to the Divine Essence?"[86] It will not be *more* awe than that provoked by the Incarnation, since the latter is the reason for the awe about Mary's motherhood; and yet it will be significant awe.

Against any possible misunderstanding, Newman avers that no Catholic says that Mary can act as God within and upon our souls; no Catholic says that we are children of Mary in the same way that we are children of the Father; no Catholic says that the priest acts in the person of Mary when confecting the sacrament of the Eucharist. Catholics recognize Jesus' absolute (and infinite) preeminence over his mother. No one supposes that Jesus intercedes for us in the same way that Mary does. Jesus is God; Mary is solely a creature, infinitely less than God. But there is something

84. Newman, 78.
85. Newman, 81.
86. Newman, 83.

extraordinary nonetheless about the mere creature Mary. As Newman points out, people even admire and praise the queen of England; how much more does Mary deserve praise, since Mary is by far the greatest mere creature. Athanasius spells out the reason: "Man is God, and God is man" and "in Mary they meet," so that "in this sense Mary is the centre of all things," not as the center herself but as the one in whom Jesus Christ literally dwelt.[87] Given what God has done in her, all Christians should praise Mary—and she joyfully intercedes for all Christians in humble love.[88]

As noted above, Newman grants that Catholic devotions to Mary can become, and have become in particular times and places, excessive and exaggerated. Newman firmly repudiates the offensive statements that Pusey adduces from Catholic authors, including from some Catholic saints.[89] According to Newman, however, if Pusey were truly to accept the testimony

---

87. Newman, 87.

88. In *First Letter to the Very Rev. J.H. Newman, D.D., In Explanation Chiefly in Regard to the Ever-Blessed Theotokos, and the Doctrine of Her Immaculate Conception*, Pusey gladly affirms that "we could not love too much *her*, from whom Jesus vouchsafed to receive a mother's care, who loved Him, the All-Holy and her Redeemer too, as no other mother could love her son; whom He loved with a Divine, but also with Deified human love; love, with which no other son could love his mother. The love of the mother and Son were essentially different from all other love, because He was her Son after the Flesh, but also Almighty God. And that same love must continue on now, only that her God-enabled power of love, in the beatific vision of His Godhead, must be unspeakably intensified" (Pusey, 430–431). He reiterates that "it is not the amount of love for the mother of the Redeemer and our God (how could it be?), but the mode of its expression, to which any of us [Anglo-Catholics] have objected" (Pusey, 431).

89. See David Brown, "Pusey as Consistent and Wise: Some Comparisons with Newman," *Anglican and Episcopal History* 71, no. 3 (2002): 328–349, at 336–337: "Newman's response [to Pusey's *Eirenicon*] in terms of a natural excess in devotional piety can scarcely be judged adequate, given the fact that many of the statements Pusey quotes [regarding the dignities of Mary] come from those who have been canonised, and so in effect what Pusey appears to have shown is that the problem runs very much deeper than Newman allows. Even those defined as saints can seriously err, and so far from greater definition securing a deeper spirituality it can in fact contribute towards further corruption. The canonised examples of wrong turns are already there to hand." Newman grants that saints can seriously err. Perhaps notably, the saints who promoted the exaggerations about Mary come from before the definition of the dogma, and since that time there have been far less such exaggerations. But there is no doubt that "greater definition" can in certain cases produce corruption, as for instance in Eutyches' effort to uphold the teachings of the Council of Ephesus.

of the Church Fathers—as Pusey intends to do—then it would become apparent to Pusey that the real differences between Anglo-Catholics and Roman Catholics regarding Mary are negligible. Besides, Pusey greatly admires the Orthodox, and the Orthodox are even more excessive in their Marian devotions than are Catholics. Catholics have nothing comparable to the Orthodox prayers to the Theotokos in the midst of the Eucharistic liturgy.

As he did in *An Essay on the Development of Christian Doctrine*, Newman denies that the exaggerated devotion to Mary of some Catholics has caused the Catholic Church to lose hold of Jesus Christ. He notes that in this regard Pusey implies much but proves nothing. On the contrary, Catholic devotion to Mary, and doctrinal recognition of her privileges, has demonstrably gone hand in hand with retaining faith in Jesus. It may be that Catholic churches are filled with Marian devotion, but, even more, they are filled with adoration of Jesus in the Holy Eucharist. He responds to Pusey's observation that Catholic churches are named the "Mary Church" by pointing out that this may arise from lack of familiarity with Catholic practice: participation in daily Mass often takes place in the morning, whereas at the High Mass believers tell their rosary beads. To any knowledgeable observer, it is clear enough that Catholics worship Christ, not Mary. Pusey insinuates the opposite by quoting a number of lesser figures, including some saints, in their most exaggerated language and without giving adequate explanation and context. For instance, the devotional notion that no one is saved without Mary's intercession may simply mean that Mary intercedes for all who are saved, which is not unreasonable given the configuration of her will to Jesus'. Likewise, various saints mentioned by Pusey as exaggerated devotees of Mary were known even more for their flowery zeal for Jesus.

Newman adds that the Italian devotional spirit is not the English one. The English, including English Catholics, are much more tempered in their language—with the exception of Faber.[90] English Catholic devotional books bear out Newman's point. Very occasionally, in a set of prayers called the *Raccolta*, composed in Italian and Latin but sometimes employed in England, there are some stronger statements, such as one regarding Mary being born in our souls; but Newman points out that Paul says similarly strong things about his own relation to his churches, without undermining his preaching of Jesus Christ.

Expressing deep dismay about some of the Marian devotional language cited by Pusey, Newman rejects it as strongly as Pusey does. Even so, he finds that Pusey exaggerates somewhat. For example, when Mary's prayer is called "omnipotent," Newman notes that in one sense this must be rejected, but in another sense Jesus himself promised that our prayer, when united to him, would accomplish works greater than his. Insofar as her prayers are in accord with Jesus' omnipotent will, her prayers are unfailingly answered. Even the notion that no one can be saved without devotion to Mary—which certainly is false as a general rule—may be true in particular times and places when rejection of Mary goes hand in hand with rejection of her Son. Furthermore, popes themselves have at times intervened against Marian excesses; and Newman cites three eminent Jesuit theologians (Canisius, Petavius, and Raynaudus) who have identified and condemned Marian excesses. Raynaudus goes out of his way to condemn vigorously the notion that the blood of Christ is purely Mary's own blood. Newman concludes this section by offering a list of Marian devotional notions cited by Pusey that Newman himself has no hesitancy in condemning as opposed to Catholic faith, beginning with the notions that "the mercy of Mary is infinite" and that "God has resigned into her hands His omnipotence."[91] Pusey has found real excesses, but Newman makes clear that they are simply excesses, not Catholic doctrine or acceptably Catholic beliefs.

As Newman says, if a critic were to cite all the more fervid things to be

90. See Andrews, *Apologia Pro Beata Maria Virgine*, 82–83.

91. Newman, *A Letter Addressed to the Rev. E.B. Pusey, D.D., on Occasion of His Eirenicon*, 113.

found in Anglican sermons and tracts about the threat of hell and were to mistake this for the Anglican doctrine or the general Anglican viewpoint, Pusey would hardly think this procedure fair. Likewise, Pusey has not been fair to the Catholic position. To rectify this, Newman proposes that he and Pusey resort together to the patristic testimony to the New Eve, the Mother of God.

Conclusion

In Pusey's view, the doctrinal corruption of the Roman Catholic Church is exemplified by Pope Pius IX's decision in 1854 to promulgate the dogma of Mary's Immaculate Conception. The Roman Catholic Church, acting as though it is developing doctrine, is corrupting doctrine. According to Pusey, the Roman Catholic Marian system lacks a sufficient ground in Scripture or Tradition, as attested by those closest to the Apostles, the Church Fathers.

In responding to Pusey in 1866, Newman explains again what he means by doctrinal development. Above all, he really does mean continuity with the teachings of the Church Fathers, and he equally insists that Catholic doctrines are and must be grounded in Scripture. The importance of the Fathers' privileged doctrinal reception of the apostolic testimony needs underlining here, at a time when Catholic systematic theologians are perhaps less aware of the patristic witness than at any other time in the history of the post-patristic Church. If the Catholic Church's doctrine and practice today are not recognizably in continuity with the Church of the Fathers, then something has gone awry. Of course there will be differences—otherwise there would be no real development—but in core elements there must remain a basic "fidelity to type."[92] Patristic Christianity will have a central

92. Newman, *An Essay on the Development of Christian Doctrine*, 173. See also Reinhard Hütter, "Progress, Not Alteration of the Faith: Beyond Antiquarianism and Presentism. John Henry Newman, Vincent of Lérins, and the Criterion of Identity of the Development of Doctrine," *Nova et Vetera* 19, no. 2 (2021): 333–391.

place, not set against Scripture but as the period in which the Church's fundamental doctrinal understanding of the scriptural witness was forged.

To my mind, Newman successfully defends the dogma of Mary's Immaculate Conception against the charge that it has deviated from the patristic (and biblical) testimony. There has been doctrinal development, not corruption. Even so, Newman for obvious reasons never claims that the Church Fathers were unanimous in proclaiming Mary to be sinless (as we have seen, they were not) or that the Church Fathers who taught that Mary was the New Eve thereby drew out the implication that Mary was preserved radically from all sin, including original sin. Newman accepts that the papal definition of the dogma not only proceeded along unusual lines (as a *papal* definition), but also specified matters along lines that many great Catholic theologians over the centuries did not agree with. For Newman, doctrinal development cannot be gauged simply by reference to theologians' logic, even though logical arguments for continuity are important. The key is to be able to make clear connections between Mary as presented by the dogma and Mary as presented by Scripture and the Church Fathers. This is what Newman succeeds in doing. Mary is the New Eve, and therefore Mary has received a grace that, in light of her Son, renders her not less than Eve prior to Eve's sin, but greater: she is "full of grace" and "blessed . . . among women" (Luke 1:28, 42 RSV-CE).

For Newman, it pertains to the task of the Church's theologians and Magisterium to reflect upon what it means for Mary to be the New Eve and Mother of God. In reflecting upon the extent of Mary's gifts, the Church learns how to praise God for what he has done for Mary, all in light of her Son. Mary proclaims in her Magnificat, "From now on all generations will call me blessed; for the Mighty One has done great things for me, and holy is his name" (Luke 1:48–49). Newman makes clear that the Church's reflection upon Mary—not only by theologians but in the liturgical and prayerful experience of believers—belongs to the Church's reflection on Jesus Christ and the plan of salvation, since Mary's grace as New Eve is not for herself but is so that she can fully embrace her mission as Mother of God for the sake of all that God wills to accomplish.

For Pusey, this all may be fine so long as what results is a pious opinion; but Newman sees no reason that the Catholic Church need proclaim only pious opinions. After all, the Church proclaimed Mary as Theotokos at the Council of Ephesus, not merely as a pious opinion, but as a dogmatic truth intended to aid believers in reflecting upon human cooperation by God's wondrous grace in the saving mysteries of Christ. Newman insists that the ongoing Church, guided by the Holy Spirit, must be able to continue to do what it did in the patristic era—namely, develop doctrine, while avoiding doctrinal corruption.

Chapter 5

Newman and Döllinger

We have now reached the final chapter of this book. When Newman was in his late sixties, on July 18, 1870, the First Vatican Council approved the Dogmatic Constitution *Pastor Aeternus*. In *Pastor Aeternus*, Pope Pius IX and the council fathers teach that "according to the gospel evidence, a primacy of jurisdiction over the whole Church of God was immediately and directly promised to the blessed Apostle Peter and conferred on him by Christ the Lord."[1] *Pastor Aeternus* goes on to argue from Tradition, citing the Fourth Council of Constantinople, the Second Council of Lyons, and the Council of Florence. The Fourth Council of Constantinople affirms the necessity of remaining in communion with the See of Rome, which has always preserved Catholic doctrine unblemished. The Second Council of Lyons states, "The holy Roman church possesses the supreme and full primacy and principality over the whole catholic church."[2] The Council of Florence confirms this primacy even more strongly: "The Roman pontiff is the true vicar of Christ, the head of the whole church and the father and teacher of all Christians; and to him was committed in blessed Peter, by our lord Jesus Christ, the full power of tending, ruling and governing the whole church."[3]

According to *Pastor Aeternus*, the popes have consistently ensured that the Church has only defined doctrines that are in accord "with sacred scripture and the apostolic traditions" and that are not, by contrast, "some new

1. *Pastor Aeternus* (First Dogmatic Constitution on the Church of Christ), ch. 1, in *Decrees of the Ecumenical Councils*, vol. 2, *Trent to Vatican II*, ed. Norman P. Tanner (Washington, DC: Georgetown University Press, 1990), 811–816, at 812; translation slightly altered.

2. Cited in *Pastor Aeternus*, ch. 4, 815.

3. Cited in *Pastor Aeternus*, ch. 4, 815.

doctrine."[4] Sustained by the Holy Spirit, the popes have never corrupted doctrine. Instead, their work has served to "religiously guard and faithfully expound the revelation or deposit of faith transmitted by the apostles," due to the papacy having received from God a "gift of truth and never-failing faith" which preserves the Church in all epochs "from the poisonous food of error" and nourishes the Church "with the sustenance of heavenly doctrine."[5]

Solemnly, *Pastor Aeternus* defines as a dogma of the Church, in accord with Scripture and Tradition and for the purpose of the salvation of souls, the following:

> When the Roman pontiff speaks *ex cathedra*, that is, when, in the exercise of his office as shepherd and teacher of all Christians, in virtue of his supreme apostolic authority, he defines a doctrine concerning faith or morals to be held by the whole church, he possesses . . . that infallibility which the divine Redeemer willed his church to enjoy in defining doctrine concerning faith or morals.[6]

The pope, therefore, does not depend upon a council, or upon the reception of the faithful, in order to proclaim an enduring and universally binding truth about the contents of the revealed deposit of faith. *Pastor Aeternus* proceeds to anathematize, or to separate from the communion of the Catholic Church, anyone who knowingly and stubbornly denies the dogma of papal infallibility.

Yet what if this new dogma itself is a doctrinal corruption, whether because it is false, or because it exceeds what the Church has the authority to identify with certitude as pertaining to the deposit of faith? This was the question that exercised Johann Joseph Ignaz von Döllinger. A Catholic

4. *Pastor Aeternus*, ch. 4, 816.
5. *Pastor Aeternus*, ch. 4, 816.
6. *Pastor Aeternus*, ch. 4, 816.

priest, Döllinger was an eminent German Church historian who was close friends with his former student the English political theorist Lord John Acton, and who also developed a lifelong friendship with William Gladstone, whom he first met in 1845.[7] Döllinger and Newman met when the former was in England visiting Acton in the 1850s, and they maintained a sympathetic correspondence.[8] In 1853, Döllinger wrote the preface to the German edition of Newman's *Lectures on the Present Position of Catholics in England.* By the late 1850s, they were both known as public opponents of Ultramontanism. Although they differed in their view of the patristic era and on various matters of historical and theological opinion,[9] their paths

---

7. For further background, see especially Owen Chadwick, *Acton and History* (Cambridge: Cambridge University Press, 1998), 139–203; Helmut Steinsdorfer, "Gladstone—gehörte mit Lord Acton zum Döllinger-Kreis," *Internationale Kirchliche Zeitschrift* 90, no. 2 (2000): 123–131; and Michael Chandler, "The Significance of the Friendship between William E. Gladstone and Ignaz von Döllinger," *Internationale Kirchliche Zeitschrift* 90, no. 2 (2000): 153–167. The relationship of Gladstone, Acton, and Döllinger receives attention in Damian McElrath, *The* Syllabus *of Pius IX: Some Reactions in England* (Louvain, BE: Publications Universitaires, 1964), 220–232. On Döllinger's English friends and correspondents (including Pusey and Newman), see also Victor Conzemius, "Ignaz von Döllinger und die Viktorianische Kirche," in *Kirche, Staat und Gesellschaft im 19. Jahrhundert. Ein deutsch-englischer Vergleich*, ed. Adolf M. Birke and Kurt Kluxen (Munich:1984), 121–152; and Angela Berlis, "Ignaz von Döllinger and the Anglicans," in *The Oxford Movement: Europe and the Wider World 1830–1930*, ed. Stewart J. Brown and Peter B. Nockles (Cambridge Cambridge University Press, 2012), 236–248. John W. O'Malley's *Vatican I: The Council and the Making of the Ultramontane Church* (Cambridge, MA: Harvard University Press, 2018), 17, contains a photo taken in 1879 that shows Acton, Gladstone, Döllinger, and others relaxing at Acton's villa in Tegernsee, Bavaria—indicative of the depth of their friendship. During the Vatican Council, Acton was in close contact with both Döllinger and Gladstone.

8. See Ian Ker, *John Henry Newman: A Biography* (Oxford: Oxford University Press, 1988), 470; and see also Victor Conzemius, "Lord Acton, Ignaz von Döllinger und John Henry Newman: Lebenssituationen und Kirchenkonflikte," *Newman-Studien* 12 (Nüremberg: Glock und Lutz, 1988): 83–102; and Kenneth L. Parker, "Historical Consciousness and the First Vatican Council: Manning, Döllinger, Newman, and Acton's Uses of History in the Papal Infallibility Debates," in *The Rise of Historical Consciousness among the Christian Churches*, ed. Kenneth L. Parker and Erick H. Moser (Lanham, MD: Rowman & Littlefield, 2013), 89–122. See also Chadwick, *Acton and History*, 126, reporting that "when Döllinger talked about Newman he talked about him with a laugh like a sneer." Ranging more broadly, see Claus Arnold, "Newman's Reception in Germany: From Döllinger to Ratzinger," *Newman Studies Journal* 18, no. 1 (2020): 5–23.

9. Kenneth Parker observes that Döllinger, having begun as an Ultramontanist, by the late 1850s had become "a passionate advocate of the febronian supercessionist metanarrative"

diverged sharply only on April 17, 1871, when Archbishop Gregor von Scherr of Munich—who himself had spoken against defining the dogma—excommunicated Döllinger for repudiating the dogma as a corruption of the truth of faith.[10]

Prior to the day when the dogma was defined by the Vatican Council, Döllinger worked with all his strength to persuade the bishops to vote against the proposed dogma. His concerns enjoyed a good deal of support. Especially in the United States and northern European nations such as Germany and Austria, bishops were worried that the teaching would scandalize Protestants by seeming to confirm that Catholics give to the pope an authority that belongs only to Christ. In addition, a number of French Catholic bishops held to a Gallican perspective favoring the prerogatives of the distinctive national churches. Döllinger put the situation in the sharpest possible terms, accusing "the Jesuits and the pope himself of preparing an 'ecclesiastical revolution.' A papal seizure of power was planned that, he warned, would undermine the bishops' authority and create a papal dictatorship."[11]

(Parker, "Historical Consciousness and the First Vatican Council," 90). Parker defines "supercessionism" as follows: "Supercessionists divided history into three periods: an age when truth was known in its 'primitive' purity; an era of corruption and innovation; and a dawning epoch when 'primitive' truth was recovered and restored, freed of the detritus of the middle age" (Parker, 89–90).

10. Döllinger was not alone in rejecting the dogma, of course. Owen F. Cummings notes, "Although no bishop left the church [in response to Vatican I], a number of theologians were excommunicated or left the church of their own accord. The German theologian Johann Friedrich left and with his followers formed the schismatic group known as the Old Catholics" (Cummings, *John Henry Newman and His Age* [Eugene, OR: Cascade, 2019], 130). For further background to the emergence of the Old Catholic movement—which received support from the *Kulturkampf*, but which then became caught in the resultant political and ecclesiastical quandaries—see Thomas Albert Howard, *The Pope and the Professor: Pius IX, Ignaz von Döllinger, and the Quandary of the Modern Age* (Oxford: Oxford University Press, 2017), 178–213. See also, for the persecution of Catholics in Italy in the period after the council, John Cornwell, *Newman's Unquiet Grave: The Reluctant Saint* (London: Continuum, 2010), 197: "processions and outdoor services were banned, communities of religious dispersed, Church property confiscated, priests conscripted into the army."

11. David I. Kertzer, *Prisoner of the Vatican: The Popes' Secret Plot to Capture Rome from the New Italian State* (Boston: Houghton Mifflin, 2004), 26. Kertzer's book focuses on the

Döllinger's career has recently been thoroughly explored by the Protestant historian Thomas Albert Howard, an expert on the religious history of nineteenth-century Germany. As Howard makes clear, the conflict between Pope Pius IX and Döllinger did not originate in the push to define the dogma of papal infallibility.[12] Rather, it had already become a fierce conflict by the early 1860s. In an 1863 lecture titled "On the Past and Present of Catholic Theology," delivered at a major German Catholic intellectual assembly, Döllinger advocated a set of positions that Pope Pius IX, and the theologians who most closely advised him, found to be troubling.[13] Among other things, Döllinger sought to replace the preeminence of scholastic theology with a new preeminence of historical-exegetical theology. He called for (in Howard's words) "prophetic resistance from theologians . . . in the court of public opinion" to assist in accomplishing this theological shift.[14]

In response to Döllinger and to the assembly as a whole, Pope Pius IX in December 1863 addressed an apostolic letter, *Tuas Libenter*, to Archbishop von Scherr. In *Tuas Libenter*, Pius IX defends the scholastic Doctors of the Church and warns against the danger of rationalism.[15] Not

political situation, with Italy in the process of being unified by Garibaldi (deposing various Catholic monarchs in the process) and with the Papal States on the verge of being lost.

12. See Howard, *The Pope and the Professor*, 5.

13. For the text of this lecture, see Johann Finsterhölzl, *Ignaz von Döllinger* (Graz, AT: Verlag Styria, 1969), 225–263; as well as Döllinger, "Die Vergangenheit und Gegenwart der katholischen Theologie," in Döllinger, *Kleinere Schriften: Gedruckte und Ungedruckte*, ed. Franz Heinrich Reusch (Stuttgart, DE: J.G. Cotta'schen Buchhandlung, 1890), 161–196. For further discussion, see Howard, *The Pope and the Professor*, 102–110.

14. Howard, *The Pope and the Professor*, 105. Howard reports, "Since the Council of Trent, Döllinger felt that the Church had relied uncritically on the heritage of Thomas Aquinas and medieval speculative philosophy. It had done so at the expense of developing an exegetical-historical theology, which . . . he traced back to the Anatolian school in antiquity and which Protestant humanists had developed since the sixteenth century, marrying it in more recent times to the spirit of modern scholarly inquiry (*Wissenschaft*), which Döllinger greatly valued. Scholastic theology was not without abiding value, he made clear, but its exponents were limited by their Aristotelian-philosophical method; without embracing biblical criticism and historical scholarship they possessed only one eye of theology, when in fact two were necessary for the task at hand" (Howard, 105–106).

15. Howard notes that *Tuas Libenter* "was followed by a papal edict of July 5 [1864] that regulated the nature of theological conferences, mandating stricter supervision from the hierarchy and the vetting of participants to ensure orthodoxy" (Howard, 110). In May 1864

surprisingly, some of the propositions formally condemned in 1864 in Pius IX's *Syllabus of Errors* echo Döllinger's proposals. For instance, the *Syllabus of Errors* condemns as rationalism the view that "human reason with only historical training can, by means of its natural powers and principles, come to a true understanding of all, even the more obscure dogmas, provided only that such dogmas be proposed to reason as its object."[16] The *Syllabus of Errors* also condemns the claim that "the method and principles according to which the ancient Scholastic Doctors treated theology are by no means suited to the necessities of our times and to the progress of the sciences."[17]

The viewpoint advocated by Döllinger and his colleagues may seem to be merely a nineteenth-century instance of *ressourcement*, moving beyond the scholasticism of his day.[18] In certain ways it was such—but it was also

Pope Pius IX told a friend of Döllinger's "that he was unsettled by some of Döllinger's recent writings, but that he would gladly receive Döllinger at any time for a private audience" (Howard, 113).

16. Cited from Heinrich Denzinger, *Compendium of Creeds, Definitions, and Declarations on Matters of Faith and Morals*, revised and enlarged and edited by Peter Hünermann with Helmut Hoping, 43rd ed., English edition edited by Robert Fastiggi and Anne Englund Nash (San Francisco: Ignatius Press, 2012), §2909. Howard observes that "the 'Syllabus,' which amounted to a compendium of previous condemnations, cited *Tuas libenter* directly in articles 9–14, which focused on errors of 'moderate rationalism,' and in articles 22 and 33, which focused on 'errors concerning the Church and her rights.' Articles 11, 12, and 13 appeared aimed directly against Döllinger and the Munich Congress" (*The Pope and the Professor*, 111).

17. Denzinger, *Compendium of Creeds, Definitions, and Declarations on Matters of Faith and Morals*, §2913.

18. For this reading, see Kenneth L. Parker, "Re-visioning the Past and Re-sourcing the Future: The Unresolved Historiographical Struggle in Roman Catholic Scholarship and Authoritative Teaching," in *The Church on Its Past*, ed. Peter D. Clarke and Charlotte Methuen (Rochester, NY: Ecclesiastical History Society, 2013), 389–416, at 398. In "Historical Consciousness and the First Vatican Council," however, Parker is much more attuned to Döllinger's boldness. In the 1860s, as Parker states in this latter essay, "While Dollinger imbibed the confidence of German historians in the objectivity of their scholarly project, he also took on historiographical assumptions that had been alien to his earlier [Ultramontanist] work"—so that Döllinger ended up adopting traditional German Protestant views of the papacy, while asserting "a scientific objectivity common among German historians of his era" as though "historical facts required no interpretation. The historian need only present them to the public—for history spoke through them" ("Historical Consciousness and the First Vatican

much more. Döllinger held that Catholic dogma's intelligibility must now be judged by objective expert historians. Here, historical methods and historical experts, not the eyes of faith and the Church's Magisterium, become the final interpreter or arbiter of Catholic truth. Howard remarks in his *Religion and the Rise of Historicism*, "As theology diminished in the university setting, so did the plausibility of worldviews legitimated by religious presuppositions."[19] By the mid-nineteenth century in Germany, it had become widely accepted that if Catholic teachings are to be defended, they must be defended by historians whose expertise the modern world accepts, rather than by dogmatic theologians who lack historical expertise. Furthermore, in the view of Döllinger and his peers, the condition of Italian intellectual and ecclesiastical life was at an embarrassingly low ebb. At the time, it seemed clear that the intellectual standard-bearers of the future were German thinkers.

For Newman, as we have seen, historical research mattered a great deal.[20] Although not himself a historian in the sense of undertaking original

Council," 97–98). Parker quotes from Döllinger's 1863 lecture as reported by Acton: "Germany is henceforward the home of Catholic theology. No nation has cultivated so successfully the sciences which are the eyes of theology, viz. history and philosophy" (Döllinger, "Die Vergangenheit und Gegenwart der katholischen Theologie," 184, quoted in Parker, "Historical Consciousness and the First Vatican Council," 98, citing John Acton, "Munich Congress," *The Home and Foreign Review* 4 [1864]: 209–244, at 232–233).

19. Thomas Albert Howard, *Religion and the Rise of Historicism: W.M.L. de Wette, Jacob Burckhardt, and the Theological Origins of Nineteenth-Century Historical Consciousness* (Cambridge: Cambridge University Press, 2000), 20.

20. This point makes it strange that "there is no mention of history as a science, or indeed as a subject for special study, in any of the eight Discourses on 'The Scope and Nature of University Education'" (Aubrey Gwynn, "Newman and the Catholic Historian," in *A Tribute to Newman: Essays on Aspects of His Life and Thought*, ed. Michael Tierney [Dublin: Browne and Nolan, 1945], 279–306, at 292). Gwynn registers the point that Newman's "'Discourses' show no appreciation of the change that was coming over the study of history in France and Germany" (Gwynn, 293). Yet, although there was "no Professor of History on the list of Professors submitted for approval to the Irish Hierarchy in 1854," nevertheless "T.W. Allies . . . appears on this list as Reader on the Philosophy of History; and James Stewart appears as Professor of Ancient History"—and when the aged Newman was asked about what he would do if he were pope, he replied that he would organize commissions to investigate such subjects as "biblical criticism, and the history of the early Church" (Gwynn, 292, 306).

archival research, Newman in *An Essay on the Development of Christian Doctrine* makes ample use of historical research and his own patristic erudition. As noted above, Newman strongly affirms that Christianity "fall[s] within the province of history" and thus has a determinate form rather than being "to each man what each man thinks it to be, and nothing else."[21] Nevertheless, he does not conclude from this fact that the validity of a Catholic dogma depends upon a historically erudite judgment of the dogma's reasonableness. Although he is confident that the Church's dogmas are historically defensible, he anticipates that there will inevitably be some loose ends, as distinct from airtight historical demonstrations that render supernatural faith unnecessary.

Let me pause here to note that the issue of historical research's relationship to dogmatic faith was central to the Catholic religious liberalism (or "Modernism") that emerged in force less than three decades after Döllinger's excommunication in 1871. For Alfred Loisy, Newman himself provides the path down which a Catholic religious liberalism should travel. Loisy argues that Newman's *An Essay on the Development of Christian Doctrine* can be employed, with certain adjustments, in support of the view that no enduringly true apostolic deposit of faith exists, but rather there is only religious experience that evolves in every age and that is expressed (dogmatically) and practiced (sacramentally) in ever new forms in the Church.

In his seminal 1898 article "Le développement Chrétien d'après le cardinal Newman," published under the name "Firmin," Loisy separates Newman's theory of doctrinal development from Newman's concerns regarding doctrinal corruption of the apostolic deposit of faith.[22] Loisy argues that Newman "did not lay enormous stress on [doctrine's] first beginnings. It was the principle of development itself which he wanted to see accepted

21. John Henry Newman, *An Essay on the Development of Christian Doctrine*, 6th ed. (Notre Dame, IN: University of Notre Dame Press, 1989), 4.

22. The notion of doctrinal corruption drops out entirely in the account (all too representative of contemporary historiography) of Catholic Modernism given by Nicholas Atkin and Frank Tallett, *Priests, Prelates and People: A History of European Catholicism since 1750* (Oxford: Oxford University Press, 2003), 160–161.

and, for him, the precise determination of what properly belonged to the primitive foundations of Christianity, or to the earliest layers of Christian development, was secondary."[23] Loisy adds tellingly, along lines which Newman certainly did not share, that "difficult as they may be to establish with certainty, these historical details are unimportant from the religious point of view."[24] Loisy also emphasizes that Christianity's "primitive foundations" or "earliest layers" are in fact already developments in the sense that Christianity was simply a development within Second Temple Judaism. One can see the connections with Newman's *Essay* here, but Newman makes clear that Christ taught and did many things that belong to the apostolic deposit of faith. Because he believed in a divine revelation characterized by enduringly true cognitive content, Newman was concerned about doctrinal corruption, whereas for Loisy doctrine should be always changing (and rupturing) in order to keep up with ever-changing religious experience.

In fact, Loisy's notion of doctrinal "development" exemplifies the religious liberalism that Newman so ardently opposed.[25] If, as Loisy thought,

23. Alfred Loisy, "The Development of Christianity According to Cardinal Newman," in *Prelude to the Modernist Crisis: The "Firmin" Articles of Alfred Loisy*, trans. Christine E. Thirlway, ed. C.J.T. Talar (Oxford: Oxford University Press, 2010), 3–16, at 9.

24. Loisy, 9.

25. Marvin R. O'Connell denies that "Loisy in any measure falsified or distorted Newman's views or failed to distinguish them clearly from his own" (O'Connell, *Critics on Trial: An Introduction to the Catholic Modernist Crisis* [Washington, DC: The Catholic University of America Press, 1994], 179). Like O'Connell, Aidan Nichols takes Loisy's essay on Newman largely at face value (*From Newman to Congar: The Idea of Doctrinal Development from the Victorians to the Second Vatican Council* [Edinburgh: T&T Clark, 1990], 85–87), as does Nicholas Lash, who claims, "The enthusiastic summary and critique of the *Essay* which Loisy wrote in 1898 was lucid and balanced. . . . To accuse Loisy of deliberately distorting Newman's thought, simply because his own concerns were significantly different, and because he only took over from Newman those aspects of his thought which seemed helpful to him, is unjust" (Lash, *Newman on Development*, 147; cf. the same conclusion in Lash, "Newman and 'A. Firmin,'" in *John Henry Newman and Modernism*, ed. Arthur Hilary Jenkins [Sigmaringendorf, DE: Glock und Lutz, 1990], 56–74, although Lash is aware of the differences between the two). For a better reading, see Keith Beaumont, "The Reception of Newman in France at the Time of the Modernist Crisis," in *Receptions of Newman*, ed. Frederick D. Aquino and Benjamin J. King (Oxford: Oxford University Press, 2015), 156–176, at 167: "The way in which Loisy applied Newman's principle of development to the Church shows a radical difference between the ideas of the two men. . . . Where Newman seeks to articulate change or

Jesus was a Jewish fanatic whose dreams of the imminent kingdom were false—if the notion that Jesus is divine is simply the product of trying to translate the term "Messiah" into an idiom comprehensible and attractive to Gentiles—does Catholicism have a future? Loisy answers yes, but only if and when the Catholic Church allows historians to relativize the Church's dogma.[26]

For Loisy's contemporaries Pierre Batiffol and Marie-Joseph Lagrange, the answer to Loisy's concerns is a better use of historical-critical methodology and a richer understanding of what Newman has actually accomplished in his *Essay*.[27] Batiffol engages Loisy from the perspective of Newman, thus responding to Loisy's turning Newman into a religious liberal. Specifically, Batiffol argues that if the Gospel's content was the imminent kingdom, whereas the Church is what actually arose from Jesus' preaching, then there is no "continuity of type" in the doctrinal development that occurred. As Batiffol says, this does not bother Loisy, because Loisy "does not have the same theory of development as Newman had."[28] For Loisy, Jesus' Gospel was a "living faith"; the Gospel of the early Christians was likewise a "living faith." The emphasis for Loisy is on "living," not on any shared content of "faith." According to Loisy, the early Christians soon realized that Jesus' kingdom was not arriving, and thus Jesus' own faith was erroneous. But the living impulse found an appreciative Hellenistic audience once the notion of the Messiah was translated into that of a

innovation and permanence of identity, Loisy simply sees development in terms of *adaptation to changing circumstances* and of *logical necessity*."

26. See Alfred Loisy, "The Development of Christianity According to Cardinal Newman," 3–16; as well as Loisy, *The Gospel and the Church*, trans. Christopher Home (London: Isbister, 1903).

27. For a critique of Batiffol and Lagrange's responses to Loisy, arguing (quite mistakenly in my view) that Batiffol and Lagrange were actually much closer to Loisy than they admitted, see Christoph Théobald, "L'exégèse catholique au moment de la crise moderniste," in *Le monde contemporain et la Bible*, ed. Claude Savart and Jean-Nöel Aletti (Paris: Beauchesne, 1985), 387–439.

28. Pierre Batiffol, "The Gospel and the Church," in *Defending the Faith: An Anti-Modernist Anthology*, ed. and trans. William H. Marshner (Washington, DC: The Catholic University of America Press, 2017), 27–37, at 33–34.

god. Batiffol challenges these claims on a number of grounds, and he deems it inevitable that for Loisy, as for religious liberalism, Christianity is "historical in its origins and in all its successive expressions; it is subject to a law of development by which its formation is explained and its future is predicted. Being thus analogous to all the religions that have turned up in past history, Christianity is . . . nothing more than an ephemeral and symbolic expression of the unknowable."[29]

In early 1903 Marie-Dominic Lagrange published *La méthode historique: Surtout à propos de l'Ancien Testament*, and in the same year Lagrange published a lengthy review essay in the *Revue biblique* on Loisy's *L'Évangile et l'Église*.[30] Like Batiffol, Lagrange notes that for Loisy, it is clear that Jesus, the historical man, had no notion of being divine; the latter was a later theological development that, though legitimate theologically, is not grounded in the Jesus of history. In Loisy's view, Jesus understood himself solely as intended by God to be the Messiah, the "vicar" on God's behalf for the purpose of bringing about the imminent kingdom, which did not appear. Nevertheless, Loisy contends that the Christian doctrines of Jesus' divinity and the kingdom are not "false" because, when these doctrines are understood as referring to religious experience, it is true that the revelation of God takes place in and through humanity, and this was Jesus' primary message. As Lagrange makes clear, Loisy is making a theological case not for Catholicism but for religious liberalism.[31] While Loisy presented himself as

29. Batiffol, 28. Batiffol links Loisy's *L'Évangile et l'Église* to a 1900 volume by Henri Margival, *Essai sur Richard Simon. La critique biblique au XVIIe siècle* (Geneva: Slatkine Reprints, 1970), to which Batiffol had devoted a review essay in *Bulletin de littérature ecclésiastique*. Batiffol also draws the connection to Loisy's Firmin articles. For further background, siding with Loisy and Margival, see C.J.T. Talar, "Rehabilitating Richard Simon, Legitimating Alfred Lisy," in *The Rise of Historical Consciousness among the Christian Churches*, 47–64.

30. See Marie-Joseph Lagrange, *La méthode historique: Surtout à propos de l'Ancien Testament* (Paris: Victor Lecoffre, 1903); Lagrange, "Review of Alfred Loisy, *L'Évangile et l'Église*," trans. William H. Marshner, in *Defending the Faith*, 38–70. See also Bernard Montagnes, *Le père Lagrange (1855–1938). L'exégèse catholique dans la crise moderniste* (Paris: Cerf, 1995), which has appeared in English as *The Story of Father Marie-Joseph Lagrange: Founder of Modern Catholic Bible Study* (New York: Paulist, 2006).

31. Lagrange remarks that the solution is not to get rid of historical-critical biblical

opposed to Auguste Sabatier's liberal Protestant *De la vie intime des dogmes et de leur puissance d'évolution* (1890), in fact he was assimilating Newman's work to Sabatier's.[32]

Although he had not read Newman's *Essay*,[33] Maurice Blondel's

scholarship, and he points out: "Too often, theologians have considered exegesis and history to be noisy rivals, without realizing that by eliminating them they would destroy their own foundations. . . . Before we elucidate the agreement between Suarez and St. Thomas over the question *utrum in Christo sit unum esse*, it would be a good idea to teach them how one establishes the divinity of Christ from the sources of Christian revelation" (Lagrange, "Review of Alfred Loisy, *L'Évangile et l'Église*," 49). Lagrange affirms that there is "dogmatic development" in the New Testament, but Loisy misunderstands and exaggerates it.

32. See Auguste Sabatier, *De la vie intime des dogmes et de leur puissance d'évolution* (Paris: Fischbacher, 1890). See also Guy Mansini, "Experience and Discourse, Revelation and Dogma in Catholic Modernism," *Nova et Vetera* 17, no. 4 (2019): 1119–1143. Mansini also examines the essays written by Loisy after *L'Évangile et l'Église* and published in 1904 as *Autour d'un petit livre* (Paris: Picard, 1904). For Loisy, as Mansini says, faith is separate from "whatever it was that Jesus of Nazareth factually communicated," and correspondingly, "Jesus of Nazareth need not be the incarnate Son of God in order for the Church with religious meaning to declare him so" ("Experience and Discourse, Revelation and Dogma in Catholic Modernism," 1122–1123).

33. Andrew Meszaros comments (with reference to Blondel's teacher Léon Ollé-Laprune, who died in 1898 and who was influenced by Newman's *Grammar of Assent*): "Blondel would have become acquainted with Newman's thought first and foremost through his reading of Ollé-Laprune's *De la certitude morale*. Later, however, he would make the acquaintance of Henri Brémond, who, as a young Jesuit, was finishing his Tertianship in Aix and attending Blondel's lectures. A friendship between Brémond and Blondel ensued, out of which Blondel's acquaintance with Newman deepened. In 1900 Blondel was reading Newman's sermons and in 1904, the same year he published his famous essay 'Histoire et dogme,' he read the first of Brémond's *Newman* trilogy on doctrinal development, a 'grande joie' for Blondel" (Meszaros, *The Prophetic Church: History and Doctrinal Development in John Henry Newman and Yves Congar* [Oxford: Oxford University Press, 2016], 31). For further discussion, see Maurice Nédoncelle, "Newman et Blondel. La théologie des développements doctrinaux," *Newman-Studien* 6 (Nüremberg: Glock und Lutz, 1964), 105–122; C.J.T. Talar, "Newman and the 'New Apologetics,'" *Newman Studies Journal* 6, no. 2 (2009): 49–56; Jan Hendrik Walgrave, "'Real' and 'Notional' in Blondel and Newman," in *John Henry Newman and Modernism*, 142–156. Walgrave comments astutely, "The final conclusion, as I see it up to now, is that real knowledge which, according to both Newman and Blondel, is a process of progressive realization, growing in the case of religion towards a deeper and more vivid sense of God's reality or presence in the union of love . . . takes precedence over a mere notional assent and is conditioned by faithful personal action. . . . However . . . the indispensable doctrinal content cannot but be an unreformable creed, gradually ripened and articulated in the mind of the Church, whereas, according to any form of truly liberal theology, the indispensable doctrinal clothing or conceptual expression is subject to substantial change and may take any suitable form in conformity with the synchronical or diachronical differences in

intervention in the debate in the early 1900s is also significant here. Blondel grants that scholastic apologetics has for too long neglected historical research and has minimized historical complexity. But he finds that Loisy's historicism goes to the opposite extreme by ignoring the complexity of dogma itself, which is rooted in spiritual realities that are perceived only in their external manifestations by historians.[34]

Responding to Loisy, Blondel remarks that if the "development" is in fact the attainment, through Christianity, of the height of religious experience—and if this "development" was unknown to Jesus himself, bound as he was to his Jewish imminent eschatology—then Jesus did not know his Father but rather merely gestured toward the ineffable.[35] Loisy's perspective thus turns Catholicism on its head; Jesus is no longer really the Savior in any serious sense. As Blondel puts it, Loisy's project "involves, in the name of history, a revolution in the manner of defining the relations which obtain between Catholic dogma and the Christian fact, between the believer and the Church, between Christ and God."[36] At the same time, Blondel emphasizes that doctrinal development's continuity is not simply chronological or logical, but must also be organic and spiritual,

cultural setting. These two positions are in principle irreconciliable. I definitely take my stance with Newman and Blondel" (Walgrave, 156). See also, for the misleading character of Henri Brémond's studies of Newman, B.D. Dupuy, "Newman's Influence in France," in *The Rediscovery of Newman: An Oxford Symposium*, ed. John Coulson and A.M. Allchin (London: Sheed & Ward, 1967), 147–173.

34. See Maurice Blondel, *History and Dogma*, trans. Alexander Dru, in *The Letter on Apologetics* and *History and Dogma* (Grand Rapids, MI: Eerdmans, 1994), 219–287.

35. See Blondel, *History and Dogma*, 261.

36. Blondel, 261. On Blondel's relation to Loisy, let me direct attention also to O'Connell, *Critics on Trial*, 288–298; Peter Henrici, "Blondel und Loisy in der modernistischen Krise," *Communio: Internationale katholische Zeitschrift* 16, no. 6 (1987): 513–530; and Michael A. Conway, "Maurice Blondel and *Ressourcement*," in *Ressourcement: A Movement for Renewal in Twentieth-Century Catholic Theology*, ed. Gabriel Flynn and Paul D. Murray (Oxford: Oxford University Press, 2012), 65–82, at 73–75. Friedrich von Hügel defended Loisy against Blondel's critique: see von Hügel, "Du Christ éternel et de nos christologies successives," trans. Henri Bremond, *La quinzaine* 58 (1904): 285–312. For correspondence that exhibits Blondel's differences with Loisy, see *Au coeur de le crise moderniste. Le dossier inédit d'une controverse. Lettres de Maurice Blondel, Henri Bremond, Friedrich von Hügel, Alfred Loisy*, ed. René Marlé (Paris: Aubier, 1960).

in such a way that no historian (located in the midst of history) can *prove* its existence or validity.

These controversies three decades after Vatican I are helpful for understanding the disagreement between Döllinger and Newman. Unlike Loisy, for Döllinger the truth of patristic doctrine is not in doubt.[37] Yet much like Loisy, Döllinger insists that the historian has the responsibility for determining what is compatible with Catholic faith. The task of the Church historian is "to figure out what [is] true in the tradition and what [is] not."[38] On this view, the objective Catholic historian in the modern age should have the independence and authority "to adjudicate the truth of tradition."[39] But how is it that historical science can have authority to determine the real truths of the Catholic faith, given that these truths are supernatural and have been left in the care of the successors of the Apostles? Is the truth of dogma now ascertainable to those immersed in historical-critical research rather than to those immersed, in faith, in the intelligibility of the divine revelation given in Christ?

Lord Acton accurately remarked that Döllinger "set the university in the place of the hierarchy" and "judge[d] church matters by a law which

37. Howard sums up Döllinger's position as of 1860, when Döllinger published (in German) *The First Age of Christianity and the Church*, 4th ed., trans. Henry Nutcombe Oxenham (London: Gibbings, 1906): Döllinger "argued that while the Church develops and matures over time, apostolic Christianity functions as a normative benchmark. Although the development of Christianity through the ages might surpass 'the simple outlines and primitive forms of thought and life in the Apostolic age,' it can never 'transcend . . . the original fullness of its being,' but must develop according to an 'internal law,' set in place at the beginning" (*The Pope and the Professor*, 90, citing Döllinger, *Christentum und Kirche in der Zeit der Grundlegung*, 2nd ed. [Regensburg: G.J. Manz, 1868], iv).

38. Howard, *The Pope and the Professor*, 224.

39. Howard, 224. Howard adds that the tension between academic theologians and ecclesiastical authorities hardly began with Döllinger, even if "in contrast to the views of his medieval and early modern forebears, his outlook bore witness to the historicization of European thought in the nineteenth century and with it the ascendancy of German *Wissenschaft*. This revolution in 'historicism' . . . had many intellectual and cultural implications, but it was perhaps most acutely felt in theology" (Howard, 223). Howard also points out that under Pope Leo XIII, numerous efforts were made to reconcile Döllinger to the Roman Catholic Church, but without success.

was not given from the altar."[40] Acton was not unsympathetic to this approach, since, infuriated by the Vatican Council, he saw "behind the dogma of Infallibility an immoral state of mind, a kind of theological Machiavellianism."[41] Indeed, in an 1864 essay affirming Döllinger's Munich lecture and challenging Pope Pius IX's *Tuas Libenter*, Acton maintains, "God's handwriting exists in history independently of the Church, and no ecclesiastical exigence can alter a fact. The divine lesson has been read; and it is the historian's duty to copy it faithfully without bias and without ulterior views."[42]

---

40. John Emerich Edward Dalberg Acton, "Döllinger's Historical Work," *English Historical Review* 5 (1890): 700–744, at 729, 734; cited in Howard, *The Pope and the Professor*, 224. For Döllinger, as Howard points out, the historian need not assent to what the Church teaches, if, in conscience, he knows that the Church has fallen into an error. Howard mistakenly supposes that "Döllinger's actions . . . accord well with Thomas Aquinas' teaching on conscience" (*The Pope and the Professor*, 226).

41. Roland Hill, *Lord Acton* (New Haven, CT: Yale University Press, 2000), 319. Kenneth Parker comments similarly that the controversies of the 1860s left Acton with "moral outrage and a deeply held belief in the objectivity of historical analysis, especially with regard to theological ideas. His apper-cessionist tendencies convinced him that the historian is not only the truest guarantor of theological truth, but must also function as moral judge of those who have used and abused power" ("Historical Consciousness and the First Vatican Council," 90). Indeed, Acton eventually had a falling out with Döllinger because he felt that Döllinger was not severe enough toward those who had publicly affirmed or defended the dogma. Acton's final assessment of Döllinger is summed up by Owen Chadwick: "Döllinger, according to Acton, was an intelligent and perspicacious man who was not even in the second rank for narrative or description. He was not good at suspending judgement, and sometimes said more than he could be sure of. He suffered from a premature certitude. He could impart knowledge better than learning. Nobody ever learnt from him the mechanism by which history is written. He had a wide-ranging learning, the erudition of centuries. He was grave and unimpassioned. He preferred books full of information. He preferred books not to raise real problems. He was not an innovator and made little use of the new archives. . . . He could not be shaken out of the belief that the religion of history was Catholicism. His conversation was worth far more than all his twenty-five books" (*Acton and History*, 201–202).

42. John Acton, "Conflicts with Rome," *Home and Foreign Review* 4 (1864): 667–690, at 676, cited in Parker, "Historical Consciousness and the First Vatican Council," 107. As Parker says, Acton "made a public submission to the *council* but maintained an internal dissent from the *dogma*" ("Historical Consciousness and the First Vatican Council," 111). Parker concludes, "Acton maintained his absolute conviction that the historian must remain the final arbiter in the quest for Christian truth. . . . To break free, history must be the final arbiter in theological disputes. Only the scientifically trained historian could competently pass judgment in these matters" (Parker, 107). Parker argues that Acton's moral liberalism,

Unsurprisingly, Newman took a keen interest in such issues, and he considered it important to distinguish and defend his own position. He does so in his *A Letter Addressed to His Grace the Duke of Norfolk on Occasion of Mr. Gladstone's Recent Expostulation*, the final 1875 edition of which includes an important Postscript in response to Gladstone's published response to Newman. While the *Letter to the Duke of Norfolk* is a reply to Gladstone's attack on the dogma of papal infallibility, its final 1875 edition is also—even more notably—a reply to Döllinger, who had assisted Gladstone.[43] One purpose of the present chapter is to suggest that Catholics today, in thinking about history and dogma (and thus about doctrinal development and corruption), should follow Newman's approach, not Döllinger's.[44]

---

combined with his historical research, was what moved him to challenge Catholic doctrines (preeminently papal infallibility); but I note that in the nineteenth century, religious liberalism and moral liberalism often joined hands. At the heart of Acton's shift, I think, was the historicist rationalism that Acton adopted vis-à-vis Catholic doctrinal mediation of divine revelation.

43. John R. Page comments in his summary of Newman's *Letter to the Duke of Norfolk*, "Newman turned next to Gladstone's charge that the Roman Church in enacting the definition of papal infallibility had repudiated the history of the Church, especially the history of the first centuries. Newman was aware that this was the position of Döllinger, and his circle and he knew of Döllinger's strong influence on Gladstone's views. Unlike Manning, who had attacked Döllinger bitterly in his first response to Gladstone [i.e. his brief letter to *The Times* of 7 November 1874], Newman wrote of the great Munich scholar with restraint, and even sympathy. He could not, as he had shown since the time of the council, accept Döllinger's view of Church history" (Page, *What Will Dr. Newman Do? John Henry Newman and Papal Infallibility, 1865–1875* [Collegeville, MN: Liturgical, 1994], 311). I should add that issues of papal authority had long been part of Newman's dialogue with Pusey—see especially Pusey's *Is Healthful Reunion Impossible? A Second Letter to the Very Rev. J.H. Newman, D.D.* (London: James Parker, 1870). Thus, although Newman's response to Gladstone is also a response to Döllinger, it is correct to say, as Roderick Strange does, that "Newman eventually continued to reply to Pusey, almost ten years later, when he responded to Gladstone's views about authority and the papacy in his *Letter to the Duke of Norfolk*" (Strange, *Newman 101: An Introduction to the Life and Philosophy of John Cardinal Newman* [Notre Dame, IN: Ave Maria, 2008], 104).

44. Kenneth L. Parker and C. Michael Shea rightly criticize Döllinger on the grounds that he "employed a supersessionist metanarrative to argue that the Pseudo-Isidorian Decretals had tainted all Catholic teaching on papal authority since the ninth century" (Parker and Shea, "The Roman Catholic Reception of the *Essay on Development*," in *Receptions of Newman*, 30–49, at 45). Parker notes that Döllinger's "evidence—analyzed through the prism of

Let me note at the outset that in summarizing Döllinger's historical claims, I will not attempt to sift and evaluate them for accuracy. In fact, since Newman considers most of Döllinger's historical points to be irrelevant to the non-maximalist view of papal infallibility taught by the council, he chooses to answer Döllinger mainly on other grounds.[45] Namely, after granting that papal infallibility and universal jurisdiction were unknown in the early Church, he argues that it is reasonable to hold that Christ willed that his Church, in spreading around the globe, would move from governance by a set of patriarchs ruling over apostolic Sees (with the bishop of Rome exercising a primacy) to a much more centralized governance by an infallible pope as the promised successor of Peter.[46]

---

contemporary historical standards—was copious and 'objectively' convincing" to the professional historians of his day ("Historical Consciousness and the First Vatican Council," 112). Acton, like Döllinger, was deeply disappointed when the "minority bishops" who had opposed the definition moved toward accepting it: see Acton's pamphlet *Sendschreiben an einen deutschen Bischof des Vaticanischen Concils* (Nördlingen: Beck, 1870), to which Bishop Ketteler responded in *Die Minorität auf dem Concil. Antwort auf Lord Actons Sendschreiben an einen deutschen Bischof des Vaticanischen Concils* (Mainz: 1871); see Damian McElrath, *Lord Acton: The Decisive Decade 1864–1874* (New York: Humanities, 1970), 228–239. For a critique of the acquiescence of the minority bishops, written by an excommunicated theologian and Old Catholic leader, see Johann Friedrich, *Die Wortbrüchigkeit und Unwahrhaftigkeit deutscher Bischöfe. Offenes Senschreiben an W.E. Freiherr von Metteler in Mainz* (Constance: 1873). See also, for the French situation (among other things), Margaret O'Gara's *Triumph in Defeat: Infallibility, Vatican I, and the French Minority Bishops* (Washington, DC: The Catholic University of America Press, 1988).

45. Döllinger was not placated by the dogmatic definition, even though it was not as maximalist as he had feared. Howard reports: "To Friedrich von Schulte, a canon lawyer in Prague and future Old Catholic leader, Döllinger wrote that the new definition of Infallibility was 'positively monstrous'" (Howard, *The Pope and the Professor*, 154).

46. The viewpoints of Newman and Döllinger have rarely been compared in an extensive way, but an exception is Wolfgang Klausnitzer, *Päpstliche Unfehlbarkeit bei Newman und Döllinger: Ein historisch-systematischer Vergleich* (Innsbruck: Tyrolia, 1980). See also the background on Döllinger (and other German scholars who agreed with his position on papal infallibility) in August Franzen, *Die katholisch-theologische Fakultät Bonn im Streit um das Erste Vatikanische Konzil* (Cologne: Böhlau, 1974); and Franz Xaver Bischof, *Theologie und Geschichte: Ignaz von Döllinger in der zweiten Hälfte seines Lebens. Ein Beitrag zu seiner Biographie* (Stuttgart, DE: Kohlhammer, 1997). For further discussion from various perspectives, see Avery Dulles, "Newman on Infallibility," *Theological Studies* 51, no. 3 (1990): 434–449; Francis Sullivan, "Newman on Infallibility," in *Newman after One Hundred Years*, ed. Ian Ker and Allan Turnbull (Oxford: Clarendon, 1990), 419–446; Kristin M. Colberg, "'Not Undone,

Johann Joseph Ignaz von Döllinger

On March 19, 1870, Döllinger wrote the following to Newman: "In my opinion, and probably in yours too, the situation of the catholic Church has not been more dangerous in the last four centuries than it is at present. At such a time the true sons and friends of the church ought to be communing together."[47] Döllinger goes on to express irritation that Newman has gone silent. In Döllinger's view, if Newman chooses to offer no public warning against the looming dogmatic definition of papal infallibility—if Newman refuses to do all that he can publicly to prevent such a dogma—then Newman is sinning gravely. As Döllinger says, "Your silence becomes a snare for thousands."[48]

Although Döllinger was not aware of it, Newman had written a letter to William Ullathorne—his bishop—on January 28, 1870, and the letter had become public. In this letter, Newman argued that councils should be called to address heresies and real crises, whereas the current council at the Vatican had no reason requiring its gathering. Newman tells Ullathorne, "I look with anxiety at the prospect of having to defend decisions, which may be not difficult to my private judgment, but may be most difficult to maintain logically in the face of historical facts."[49] The historical facts that he has in view are "the store of Pontifical scandals in the history of 18 centuries, which have partly been poured out, and partly are still to come."[50] Far from

but Completed': John Henry Newman and the Reception of Vatican I," *Newman Studies Journal* 17, no. 1 (2020): 5–23. Colberg directs attention to Newman's Letter to Robert Whitty, April 12, 1870, in *The Letters and Diaries of John Henry Newman*, vol. 25, ed. Charles Stephen Dessain and Thomas Gornall (Oxford: Oxford University Press, 1973), 93–95, in which Newman argues strongly for the inopportuneness of the proposed dogma. For exhaustive background to the Council, see Klaus Schatz, *Vaticanum I, 1869–1870*, 3 vols. (Paderborn, DE: Schöningh, 1992–1994).

47. Johann Joseph Ignaz von Döllinger, Letter to John Henry Newman, 19 March 1870, in *The Letters and Diaries of John Henry Newman*, vol. 25, 84.

48. Döllinger, 84.

49. John Henry Newman, Letter to Bishop William Ullathorne, 28 January 1870, in *The Letters and Diaries of John Henry Newman*, vol. 25, 18–20, at 18.

50. Newman, 19.

being constant beacons of light, the popes have included among their number many depraved individuals, who have said and done deplorable things. At the same time, Newman makes clear in his letter that he is prepared to assent to a dogma of papal infallibility. He states, "If it is God's will that the Pope's infallibility should be defined . . . I shall feel I have but to bow my head to His adorable, inscrutable Providence."[51]

In a March 15 letter to the editor of the newspaper *The Standard* (which had startled Newman by making public the contents of his letter to Ullathorne), Newman makes his stance even clearer. On the one hand, he affirms his opposition to those who are leading the movement toward the dogmatic definition. He states, "I deeply deplore the policy, the spirit, the measures of various persons, lay and ecclesiastical, who are urging the definition of that theological opinion."[52] But on the other hand, he firmly disavows the notion that any Church historian, who is neither the pope nor a member of the episcopacy, has the authority to determine whether a particular doctrinal formulation accords with the deposit of faith and therefore is a development rather than a corruption. He concludes, "I have a firm belief, and have had all along, that a Greater Power than that of any man or set of men will over-rule the deliberations of the Council to the determination of Catholic and Apostolic truth, and that what its Fathers eventually proclaim with one voice will be the Word of God."[53]

---

51. Newman, 19. Newman concludes the letter by briefly describing his recently completed *Grammar of Assent*. For further background to Newman's position on papal infallibility before and after the dogmatic definition, see J. Derek Holmes, "How Newman Blunted the Edge of Ultramontanism," *Clergy Review* 53 (1968): 353–362; Holmes, "Cardinal Newman and the First Vatican Council," *Annuarum Historiae Conciliorum* 1, no. 2 (1969): 374–398. See also James Pereiro, *Cardinal Manning: An Intellectual Biography* (Oxford: Clarendon, 1998), 260–261, where Pereiro notes Archbishop Victor Dechamps' *L'Infaillibilité et le Concile Général* (Paris: Magnin, 1869), a moderate Ultramontanist work that Newman praised highly in an 1869 private letter (and that reflected Dechamps' behind-the-scenes relationship with Pius IX, which Newman would not have known about). Newman's approval of a moderate Ultramontanist doctrine of papal infallibility, of course, does not mean that he approved of dogmatically defining such a doctrine.

52. John Henry Newman, Letter to the Editor of the *Standard*, 15 March 1870, in *The Letters and Diaries of John Henry Newman*, vol. 25, 54–55.

53. Newman, 55.

A statement could hardly be clearer than that—and so no wonder Newman delayed for three weeks in answering Döllinger's letter of March 19. When Newman did reply, on April 9, his reply deeply disappointed Döllinger, who now understood that Newman would accept the council's decision when it came.[54]

A year later, when Döllinger was on the verge of excommunication, Newman received a letter from the Anglican churchman Alfred Plummer, detailing the ultimatum that had been given to Döllinger by Archbishop von Scherr. In answer, Newman bemoans the treatment that Döllinger had received, but then immediately adds the following: "I must say on the other hand I neither can take Dr Dollinger's view of it, nor do I enter into the reasons which are contained, as you report them in his Reply."[55] In explaining his demurral, he appeals to his *An Essay on the Development of Christian Doctrine*, published twenty-six years earlier. He recalls that in that book, he defended the Catholic doctrine of the papacy as grounded in Matthew 16 and elsewhere, even though the papacy (in the way that modern Catholics understand it) did not emerge before the fourth or fifth century or even, in certain respects, before the medieval period. In Döllinger's view, the recent council has erred fatally because it has misinterpreted Scripture, against the interpretations given by the Church Fathers. In response, Newman insists that the infallibility of solemn conciliar teaching rests not upon correct

54. See John Henry Newman, Letter to Johann Joseph Ignaz von Döllinger, 9 April 1870, in *The Letters and Diaries of John Henry Newman*, vol. 25, 85. See also Newman's 1867 response to Alexander Penrose Forbes (Bishop of Brechin in the Scottish Episcopal Church, and a protégé of E.B. Pusey), in which Newman affirms what later became the dogma while still considering it inopportune to define the dogma. For discussion see Mark D. Chapman, "Ecumenism, Mariology, and the Papacy," in *The Oxford Handbook of John Henry Newman*, ed. Frederick D. Aquino and Benjamin J. King (Oxford: Oxford University Press, 2018), 355–372, at 367; as well as the extensive discussion of Forbes—a close friend of both Pusey and Gladstone, and a friend of Döllinger as well—in Mark D. Chapman, *The Fantasy of Reunion: Anglicans, Catholics, and Ecumenism, 1833–1882* (Oxford: Oxford University Press, 2014), chapters 5–7.

55. John Henry Newman, Letter to Alfred Plummer, 3 April 1871, in *The Letters and Diaries of John Henry Newman*, vol. 25, 308–310, at 308.

exegesis but rather upon God's divine guarantee that a council's solemn decision will not go wrong, even if its reasoning might.

Newman emphasizes that God cannot permit the Church "to *go wrong* in the truths of revelation"; or to put the same point in positive terms, even though the Church may err in exegesis or in the historical investigations by which the Church arrives at a doctrine, "she has this security, that, *in order* to fulfil her office, her *outcome* is always true in the matter of revelation."[56] Thus the solemn teaching of a true council does not ultimately rely for its truth upon anything that historians can uncover—even though historians, exegetes, and theologians will necessarily advise the council prior to its teaching. The solemn teaching of a council is sure to be true because God ensures it, not because of human beings.

It follows that Newman—even if he had agreed with Döllinger's historical claims, which he did not—differed sharply from Döllinger's view that an erudite historian has the competence to reject a council's solemn teaching on historical grounds, given the Holy Spirit's guidance of the Church in council. For Newman, the real questions in this case can only be whether the Vatican Council is a true ecumenical council and whether its teaching is solemn and definitive. On both these counts, Newman answers yes.[57] Of course, this determination still leaves the precise scope of its teaching to be interpreted by theologians and by the Church. Newman predicts that a later council will complete the Vatican Council's teaching. As he writes to Dollinger, "The late definition does not so much need to be undone, as to

56. Newman, 308.

57. Newman delayed during the summer and fall of 1870 to make a final judgment on the council, which at the time he thought would soon resume (in fact it never did resume, due to political instability inclusive of the loss of the Papal States). Newman wanted to see not only what the continuation of the council would bring, but also whether the minority bishops would affirm the dogma—as in fact they did. See Colberg, "'Not Undone, but Completed,'" 15–19. Colberg concludes, "Newman's hermeneutic underscores that within the Christian tradition councils are not endlessly revisable suggestions, nor are they fossils disconnected from history and a wider theological context" (Colberg, 23).

be completed. It needs *safeguards* to the Pope's possible acts—explanations as to the matter and extent of his power."[58]

According to Döllinger, Newman's standpoint was an exemplification of historical ignorance. Döllinger complained to Gladstone in 1875, "Whole stretches of Church history and the history of European culture are unknown to him, as the darkest Africa. There is no other way of explaining his naïve and daring assertions."[59] Döllinger admired Gladstone's *The Vatican Decrees in Their Bearing on Civil Allegiance*, and he not only deprecated Newman's *Letter to the Duke of Norfolk* but also assisted Gladstone in replying to Newman in *Vaticanism*.[60] For Döllinger in 1875, it was clear that Newman was a victim of "historical-theological weakness," since his "insights into Church history are too scanty, and with his theory of development he transplants Darwinism into religion, except that where Darwin lets the ape develop into Caucasian man, in Newman's case in contrast man gradually degenerates into ape."[61] What historical evidences, then, does Döllinger bring forward to justify his rejection of the dogma of papal infallibility?

58. John Henry Newman, Letter to Alfred Plummer, 3 April 1871, 310. For further discussion of Newman's correspondence with the Anglican Plummer in the early 1870s—often touching upon Döllinger, whom Plummer visited relatively frequently—see Page, *What Will Dr. Newman Do?*, 209–213.

59. Döllinger to William Gladstone, 17 February 1875, *BL, add., 44,140*/348–349 (German), quoted in Short, "Newman, Superstition and the Whig Historians," in *Newman and History* (Leominster, UK: Gracewing, 2017), 83–115, at 85.

60. Although Gladstone visited Munich and Döllinger in September 1874, his letters to Döllinger and to Newman from 1874–1875 attest that Döllinger did not aid him in the writing of *The Vatican Decrees in Their Bearing on Civil Allegiance*, although of course many of Gladstone's arguments had been anticipated by Döllinger in earlier writings with which Gladstone was well acquainted. See McElrath, *The* Syllabus *of Pius IX*, 225–226. McElrath discusses Gladstone's correspondence with Döllinger while writing *Vaticanism*, which appeared in late February 1875.

61. Döllinger to Lady Blennerhasset, 20 February 1875, in *Ignaz von Döllinger Briefwechsel mit Lady Blennerhassett, 1865–1886*, ed. Victor Conzemius (Munich: Beck, 1963–1981), vol. 4, 597–598 (German), quoted in Hill, *Lord Acton*, 270. I note that in a letter to Professor Michelis, 1 May 1879, excerpted in *Declarations and Letters on the Vatican Decrees 1869–1887*, 122–123, Döllinger speaks much more positively of Newman as one "who stands so high bove the Roman *vulgus praelaticum* in intellect and knowledge" (Döllinger, 122).

In 1869, on the eve of the council and on the basis of a series of articles produced earlier that year, Döllinger published *The Pope and the Council* under the pen name "Janus," a book whose purpose was to investigate "by the light of history"—and indeed to "protest based on history"—the doctrine of papal infallibility whose definition was known to be one of the purposes of the coming council.[62] Döllinger paints the doctrine in grim terms indeed. The doctrine, he contends, is the fruit of minds "whose ideal of the Church is an universal empire spiritually, and, where it is possible, physically, ruled by a single monarch,—an empire of force and oppression."[63] He argues that for a millennium—since around the year 845—the papacy has stood as "a disfiguring, sickly, and choking excrescence on the organization of the Church, hindering and decomposing the action of its vital powers, and bringing manifold diseases in its train."[64] If this is his

62. Johann Joseph Ignaz von Döllinger, *The Pope and the Council* (Boston: Roberts Brothers, 1870), xiii. For further background, see Howard, *The Pope and the Professor*, 132–138. Howard observes, "To say the work created a sensation is an understatement" (Howard, 135). The Archbishop of Munich, Gregor von Scherr, was among those who were so alarmed by the public support for "Janus" among educated German Catholics that he joined in a private letter to Pius IX expressing "concern about the consequences of defining Papal Infallibility for the Church in Germany—quite possibly tearing it asunder" (Howard, 136). The book was placed on the Index on November 30, 1869. For a contemporaneous scholarly critique of the book by a university colleague of Döllinger's, see Josef Hergenröther, *Anti-Janus: An Historico-Theological Criticism of the Work Entitled "The Pope and the Council,"* trans. J.B. Robertson (New York: Catholic Publishing Society, 1870). See also the approach taken by Pusey's *Is Healthful Reunion Impossible?* and the discussion of the latter work (and its reception) in Chapman, "Ecumenism, Mariology, and the Papacy," 367–370 and Chapman, *The Fantasy of Reunion*, 115–129. Chapman notes that Pusey, completely disgusted (like Chapman himself) by the council, "changed the title of his third Eirenicon for all subsequent editions to *Healthful Reunion, as conceived possible before the Vatican Council*" ("Ecumenism, Mariology, and the Papacy," 370).

63. Döllinger, *The Pope and the Council*, xv.

64. Döllinger, xviii. Pusey would have largely agreed, though in much gentler terms. Besides, Pusey held (in the words of Mark Chapman) that "there was already sufficient certainty contained in the teachings of the undivided [patristic] Church, to which the nineteenth century could add nothing" (Chapman, "Ecumenism, Mariology, and the Papacy," 369), especially since a council convened by one branch (Rome) of the Church could not be a binding and authoritative council. Cardinal Manning's response to "Janus" is well summed up by James Pereiro, *Cardinal Manning: An Intellectual Biography* (Oxford: Clarendon, 1998), 258: "Janus' spirit was a curious sort of revived Donatism, pointing to the human errors of

view, no wonder he has strong fears about the doctrine of papal infallibility!

Döllinger recognizes that he will be accused of being radically anti-papal.[65] In response, he argues that he is simply well versed in the history of the distortions that have afflicted the office of the papacy, as befits the man who in 1863 authored *Fables Respecting the Popes in the Middle Ages*.[66] He knows that Christ willed an office of primacy in the Church, and he holds that this office rightfully belongs to the bishop of Rome.[67] In his

Popes and bishops as clear disclaimers of their assumed prerogatives, such abuses being the clear signs of the erroneous character of the principle."

65. It is worth noting Döllinger's growing political involvement in Germany in the 1840s and 1850s, including his 1848 speech to Parliament in which he argued Catholics should "form a 'national German Church,' replete with 'a national synod' and a 'head.' To be sure, this national church would be linked to Rome in a spirit of unity and loyalty, but not in fearful subservience" (Howard, *The Pope and the Professor*, 87). Karl Adam made the same proposal at the height of his involvement with Nazi ecclesiastical politics in the 1930s—but I note that Döllinger strongly defended the Jewish people against Christian anti-Semitism, including in a well-known 1881 speech. Howard shows that his nationalistic perspective moved Döllinger in an anti-papal direction, understandably so in some respects. On his visit to Rome in 1857, Döllinger had an audience with Pope Pius IX, in which Döllinger had to kneel thrice as he made his way across the room toward the pope, whose foot Döllinger then had to kiss.

66. See Johann Joseph Ignaz von Döllinger, *Die Papst-Fabeln des Mittelalters. Ein Beitrag zur Kirchengeschichte* (Munich: J.G. Cotta, 1863); translated by Alfred Plummer as *Fables Respecting the Popes in the Middle Ages: A Contribution to Ecclesiastical History* (London: Rivingtons, 1871). For discussion, see Howard, *The Pope and the Professor*, 124–128. As Howard says, "Belief in the therapeutic power of historical knowledge to purify the Church from errors and misconceptions grew in Döllinger's mind as his *Fables of the Popes* gained recognition (and notoriety) in the 1860s" (Howard, 127).

67. Thus, the Swiss Catholic theologian August Bernhard Hasler, taking up the mantle of Döllinger, arguably goes further than Döllinger insofar as he lacks (to say the least) the latter's regard for the Church Fathers. See Hasler, *How the Pope Became Infallible: Pius IX and the Politics of Persuasion*, trans. Peter Heinegg (Garden City, NY: Doubleday, 1981). Hans Küng wrote a laudatory introduction to Hasler's book, which may thus be read in conjunction with Küng's *Infallible? An Unresolved Enquiry*, trans. John Bowden, rev. ed. (New York: Continuum, 1994), which also pays little attention to the Fathers. But the conclusions of both Hasler and Küng would have pleased Döllinger. Küng is among the many contemporary Catholic theologians who treat "a fallible magisterium" as "an opportunity. Could not the *Church of the future* cope with its errors more easily in this way?" (Küng, 268). Although Küng continues to speak of "the truth of the gospel" and of "the indestructibility, the indefectibility, of the Church of Jesus Christ in truth" (Küng, 268), it is unclear to me on what grounds he could claim to know the contents of such "truth" prior to the eschaton. In his

view, however, the papacy has long been hell-bent upon inflating itself, with the result that the Catholic faith has steadily been losing adherents.

Döllinger argues that the emergence of the monarchical papacy—as distinct from the primacy of the bishop of Rome—in the early medieval period was an unmitigated disaster. Its fruit has been nothing less than "the splitting up of the previously united Church into three great ecclesiastical bodies, divided and at enmity with each other."[68] It is the inflated papacy that is to blame for the Catholic Church's separation from Orthodox and Protestant Christians. Beginning in the early medieval period, the early Church's office of primacy came to be distorted into a "despotic rule of an absolute monarch" in the person of the pope.[69]

Since the ninth century, Döllinger thinks, the privileges that have accrued to the popes have been illegitimate. He grounds this claim upon history, arguing that only the privileges enjoyed by the bishop of Rome in the patristic period can have legitimacy. The patristic Church is the measure, and the task today must be to return the papacy to the form that it had then. In the patristic period, the precise form taken by the bishop of Rome's primacy was somewhat fluid; it varied according to the "concessions of the particular local Churches."[70] But the honor of primacy did not then mean that a council had to go along with a pope's wishes—certain aspects of the Council of Chalcedon being an example of such conciliar freedom.

Döllinger argues that the doctrine of papal infallibility, in a maximal form, was first advanced at the end of the sixteenth century. Eschewing the laborious doctrinal processes found in the early Church, an infallible pope can enforce his doctrinal will once and for all merely by signing his name to a decree written up by a member of the Curia. Given that

view, the "*persistence of the Church in truth, despite all errors*" can be found "in the Christian message and the great Catholic tradition" (Küng, 269), but the grounds for identifying any particular contents in this "message" as "truth" are unclear.

68. Döllinger, *The Pope and the Council*, xxi.

69. Döllinger, xxi.

70. Döllinger, xxii.

solemnizing the doctrine of papal infallibility would destroy efforts to reunite separated Christians and would "cripple all intellectual movement and scientific [i.e., scholarly] activity in the Catholic Church," Döllinger hopes that a formal dogmatic definition can be averted through a powerful movement of public opinion.[71]

After a critique of the *Syllabus of Errors*, Döllinger examines the roots of Ultramontanism, which he defines as the view either that the pope *is* the Church, or that the Church is the slave of the pope.[72] According to the Ultramontanists, the pope stands in the place of Christ vis-à-vis the faithful. Döllinger comments wryly, "It is but one step from this to declare the Pope an incarnation of God."[73] He warns that if the Ultramontanists get their way at the council, the national churches will become Roman in every

71. Döllinger, xxvi.

72. Jacob W. Wood has aptly remarked in this regard, "In one sense, *Pastor Aeternus* seemed to canonize the ultramontanist understanding of the pope. However, while *Pastor Aeternus* did certainly canonize many of the elements of an ultramontanist understanding of the papacy, it did not canonize the ultramontanist system as a whole, nor therefore did it canonize the centrality of the papacy *as understood* by that system. It might have done so, if the Franco-Prussian War had not broken out; both drafts for the Second Constitution on the Church described the Church in terms akin to Suárez, and so made clear the place of the pope within the Church as an absolute monarch along the lines of temporal monarchs. But the untimely interruption of the Council Fathers proved, perhaps by God's Providence, to have been unexpectedly timely; there was yet an opportunity for the development of an alternative way of recognizing the centrality of the papacy in the Church"—namely as found in communion ecclesiology and *Lumen Gentium*: "For de Lubac, the Church is not Suárez's ecclesial nation-state, brought together by the sole monarch of divine right, nor yet is the Church a Jansenist collection of states brought within the Church and yet so vitiated by sin that they remain yet alien from one another. It is, rather, a *communion* of people, whose desires have been healed by grace, and who therefore freely and willingly enter into communion with the one God in one ecclesial community. *Lumen Gentium* elaborated on that ecclesiology of communion. It grounded the unity of the Church not in the pope *qua* Vicar of Christ but in the unity of the three persons of the Trinity, into a participation of which the Church is drawn as the Body of Christ by the Holy Spirit. The pope has his place in the unity of this body; *Lumen Gentium* reaffirms that he is the focal point of Christian unity. But he does not exercise that office as an imposition on Christian freedom, an absolute sovereign imposed upon unwilling subjects" (Wood, "The Five-Hundredth Anniversary of the Reformation: A Catholic Perspective," in *Reformation Observances: 1517–2017*, ed. Philip D.W. Krey [Eugene, OR: Cascade, 2017], 69–93, at 86, 89–90).

73. Döllinger, *The Pope and the Council*, xxvi.

aspect; all Catholics in every nation will have to become "clerico-Italian."[74] Once the pope becomes infallible (through the new dogma), the pope will proceed to define infallibly that he has no limits whatsoever in his teaching authority. The Vatican will then mint a slew of new dogmas, all of them unheard of in the patristic era, and all of them requiring the assent of the faithful on pain of excommunication and damnation. There will be no need for any further councils: bishops will gather simply for a canonization of a pope and other such events. In this dystopian future, theology will be reduced to the task of determining whether this or that doctrine has been defined infallibly by a pope. Every comma of papal bulls will be scrutinized. Scripture and Tradition will no longer be of interest, since "a telegraphic message to Rome will get an answer in a few hours or a few days, which becomes an axiom and article of faith."[75]

The historical fact, says Döllinger, is that popes contradict one another and even contradict themselves, despite their supposed oracle-like infallibility. Thus, papal infallibility (in the maximalist version that he envisions) is easily falsifiable as a matter of history. For this reason, theologians will be kept busy figuring out ingenious ways to harmonize clearly contradictory papal statements. The statements by popes that contradict the Church's doctrines "will have to be twisted into agreement, so as to show that their heterodox or mutually destructive enunciations are at bottom sound doctrine; or, when a little has been subtracted from one dictum and added to the other, are not really contradictory, and mean the same thing."[76]

Döllinger argues that all the real historical data point firmly away from papal infallibility. In his view, however, the Jesuits have shown a disconcerting ability to distort Church history in favor of the dogma. Against their misinformation, he offers a list of papal contradictions that in his view make the doctrine of papal infallibility to be impossible for a reasonable person to hold. Two early popes, for example, held that in order for infants

74. Döllinger, 35.
75. Döllinger, 40.
76. Döllinger, 41.

to go to heaven, they must receive not only Baptism but also the Eucharist—a position anathematized by the Council of Trent. He draws attention to the crises that ensued when, due to simony, the validity of the ordination of bishops and priests began to be doubted—crises that arose from a misunderstanding of the sacrament of Holy Orders on the part of the popes. He cites a case where Pope Celestine III claimed that the marriage bond is dissolved if one spouse falls into heresy, a position that later popes rejected.[77] He notes that Pope Nicolas II, in 1059, forced Berengar to affirm (along lines that were later deemed heretical) that in receiving the Eucharist, the communicant touches and breaks Christ's body in a sensible way. Pope Innocent III declared that the bond of the bishop to his diocese is more indissoluble than the bond between husband and wife, and he further declared that he, the pope, had the power to loosen this bond, by divine authority.

Döllinger recalls numerous other papal teachings that he finds troubling, including various papal teachings in the late medieval controversy with the Spiritual Franciscans. Pope John XXII rejected the clear teachings of his predecessors and reversed his own teaching on the topic of evangelical poverty. Döllinger comments succinctly, "What Nicolas III. and Clement V. had solemnly commended as right and holy, their successor branded, as solemnly, as noxious and wrong."[78] The result was the burning at the stake of at least 114 Spiritual Franciscans, on charge of heresy, in the mid-fourteenth century. Later popes reversed course and resumed papal ownership of Franciscan property. In a similar vein, Döllinger remarks upon Pope Eugenius IV's 1439 decree or confession of faith that, in the name of the Council of Florence, contained a number of dubious propositions. Pope Eugenius IV defined the form of confirmation and the form of penance along lines that would mean that both sacraments fell into disuse for a millennium. Either Pope Eugenius' decree is true—with dire pastoral

77. Döllinger, 45.
78. Döllinger, 48.

consequences—or else, says Döllinger, the doctrine of papal infallibility must be false. Döllinger goes on to mock the papal bull of Pope Sixtus V by which he imposed a standard edition of the Bible to be used by all Catholics under pain of excommunication. The edition turned out to be rife with errors caused by Pope Sixtus himself. To fix the situation, Pope Sixtus persuaded Robert Bellarmine to mislead the public in a preface to a new edition.

If an infallible pope is, by Christ's will, "the pillar and exclusive organ of Divine truth, without whom the Church is like a body without a soul . . . unable to determine any point of faith," then, asks Döllinger, why did the Holy Spirit not tell the Church about this important fact for well over a millennium? Without gainsaying the truth of papal primacy, Döllinger states, "None of the ancient confessions of faith, no catechism, none of the patristic writings composed for the instruction of the people, contain a syllable about the Pope, still less any hint that all certainty of faith and doctrine depends on him."[79] In Döllinger's view, it is ridiculous to proclaim such a doctrine in 1870 as though it were part of the apostolic deposit of faith. In one case where the bishop of Rome did speak out against an early heresy—namely, in 262 against Sabellianism—almost no one paid attention; in fact, we know of this Roman synod only through fragments cited by Athanasius. In another third-century dogmatic dispute, with regard to re-baptism and the validity of heretical baptism, Pope Stephen intervened, but without effect. In the Arian crisis, Pope Sylvester took little part. Later in the fourth century, Pope Julius "pronounced Marcellus of Ancyra, an avowed Sabellian, orthodox at his Roman Synod; and [Pope] Liberius purchased his return from exile from the Emperor by condemning Athanasius, and subscribing an Arian creed."[80] Bishop Hilary of Poitiers and others responded by condemning Pope Liberius as an apostate and a heretic. In the fifth century, Pope Innocent condemned Pelagius' views, but Pope Zosimus

79. Döllinger, 53.
80. Döllinger, 56.

sympathized with them and had to be sternly corrected by the Council of Carthage.

The point is that in the patristic period, the popes not only did not exercise universal jurisdiction but also, at times, fell into lamentable errors. Certainly Augustine knew of no doctrine of papal infallibility. The first dogmatic writing by a pope to be approved by both East and West was Leo's Tome, but only after the Council of Chalcedon had carefully vetted it. Pope Vigilius went back and forth regarding the writings of Theodoret and his colleagues (the "Three Chapters"). When Pope Vigilius reversed himself and approved them as orthodox, he was condemned and excommunicated by the Fifth Ecumenical Council, to which he then humbly submitted (thereby changing his mind once more). The result was schism: "Whole National Churches—Africa, North Italy, Illyria—broke off communion with the Popes, whom they accused of having sacrificed the faith and authority in the Council of Chalcedon by condemning the Three Chapters."[81] Pope Honorius I favored Monotheletism; and when Pope Martin later condemned Monotheletism as a heresy, the eventual result was the Ecumenical Council of Constantinople in 680, where Honorius was "condemned for heresy in the most solemn manner."[82] Döllinger notes that some eminent Jesuits have attempted to discredit the acts of this council as spurious, but their view has been proven wrong. During the reign of Charlemagne, the pope exercised no effective authority even over the Western bishops, who ignored the pope without thinking twice about it.

Döllinger highlights ten salient points from the patristic era, again without denying papal primacy:

- the popes did not convene the councils;
- the popes did not preside at the councils (with two exceptions);

81. Döllinger, 60.
82. Döllinger, 60.

- the councils' decisions did not require the approval of the popes;
- no pope ever promulgated doctrine directly on behalf of the whole Church;
- no pope had legislative or juridical power over the whole Church;
- the power of the keys was deemed to belong to all bishops rather than solely to the pope;
- the pope could not universally excommunicate a person or a national Church from communion with the whole Church;
- the popes did not succeed in rejecting the limitations imposed by the sixth Nicene canon;
- Pope Gregory the Great rejected the notions that the pope "has the plenitude of power" and that "from him all power [in the Church] is derived";[83]
- some national Churches had no relationship at all with the pope, without this affecting their status as Catholic Churches.[84]

83. Döllinger, 68.

84. Döllinger is not naïve about the expansion of papal power during the later patristic period, although he cleaves to the goodness of the patristic period. For a study focusing upon Leo the Great and Gregory the Great and emphasizing the expansion of papal power, see George E. Demacopoulos, *The Invention of Peter: Apostolic Discourse and Papal Authority in Late Antiquity* (Philadelphia: University of Pennsylvania Press, 2013). Demacopoulos argues that his own monograph "forces us to reconsider the traditional narratives of the early papacy. . . . There is little denying the papal efforts to present Petrine authority in a 'totalizing' fashion—not only the completeness of Peter's authority, but a vision in which all Christian meaning flows from Peter and his heirs. While it may be true that many of the claims to total authority (whether dogmatic, ecclesiological, legal, or otherwise) were in no way based on actualized or actualizable authority at the time they were offered, the discourse of primatial ecclesiastical authority fit within the discursive parameters of the age and therefore became an important rhetorical and polemical feature of all subsequent papal and Petrine narratives. . . . In the end, the success of papal actors in harnessing the Petrine topos to their own ends lay in their capacity to invent and perpetuate an epistemic horizon for Christian teaching and Christian leadership through the careful articulation of a Petrine legacy that was tied directly to the city of Rome and, most importantly, to the Roman bishop, 'Peter's heir.' To the extent that the development and control of discourse can be seen as a key to social power, then the papal expansion and promotion of the Petrine discourse along self-interested lines should certainly be seen as one of the critical factors that contributed to the papacy's ascendancy over other power structures in Western Europe in the later Middle Ages" (Demacopoulos, 169–171). In a notable study, too, Steven A. Schoenig has shown how Gregory the Great, in his dealings with the English, set in motion what became (during the Carolingian period)

Döllinger concludes that the current notion of the papacy is a grave distortion of the original, valid understanding of the primacy of the bishop of Rome. The doctrine of papal infallibility represents the apogee of a false second-millennium development (or, more precisely, corruption). Döllinger sums up his vision of how things should be, a vision much at odds with the post-Tridentine papacy: "Without prejudice to its agreement with the Church Universal in all essential points, every Church manages its own affairs with perfect freedom and independence and maintains its own traditional usages and discipline. . . . The Church is organized in dioceses, provinces, patriarchates . . . with the bishop of Rome at the head as first Patriarch."[85] Papal primacy suffices to serve the Church's needs; papal monarchy—increasingly common after Trent—is a false and deleterious corruption. When a controversy breaks out, it is not the pope but a council that must make the final decision about what pertains to the true deposit of faith.

Comparing the patristic period to the medieval one, Döllinger observes that whereas the Cappadocians wrote nothing about the papacy and Augustine wrote only one sentence in his vast corpus about the primacy of the bishop of Rome, Thomas Aquinas and almost all who came after him treated the papacy at some length. The only early Father who has anything truly significant to say about the pope is Irenaeus, and he does not defend anything like the modern papacy, even while he supports Roman primacy. In the mid-sixth century, Pope Pelagius I identified the Apostolic Sees (including Alexandria, Antioch, and Jerusalem along with Rome) as the foundation of Catholic unity in Christ. No heretic in the patristic period was reproached for rejecting the authority, let alone the infallibility, of the pope. In interpreting such passages as Matthew 16:18 and John 21:17—notable in later papal apologetics—no Church Father applied these passages to the bishop of Rome as uniquely the successor of Peter. According to the Church

---

the formal papal gift of the pallium—a highly effective tool in increasing papal power. See Schoenig, *Bonds of Wool: The Pallium and Papal Power in the Middle Ages* (Washington, DC: The Catholic University of America Press, 2016).

85. Döllinger, *The Pope and the Council*, 69.

Fathers, Luke 22:32 applies solely to Peter's own faith, and certainly not to an infallibility possessed by later bishops of Rome. Döllinger comments, "The first to find in [Luke 22:32] a promise of privileges to the Church of Rome was Pope Agatho in 680, when trying to avert the threatened condemnation of his predecessor, Honorius, through whom the Roman Church had lost its boasted privilege of doctrinal purity."[86] The council condemned Honorius anyway.[87]

Döllinger therefore finds that the notion of papal infallibility—like many things about the papacy of the second millennium—contradicts the Church's own commitment, explicitly stated since Pope Pius IV, "never to interpret Holy Scripture otherwise than in accord with the unanimous consent of the Fathers."[88] Papal infallibility rests upon biblical passages that the Fathers themselves interpreted in a manner quite the opposite from that of the advocates of papal infallibility. A pope or a bishop who supported papal infallibility on the basis of any of these scriptural texts would be breaking his own vow to be faithful to the Tridentine profession of faith.

How did the post-patristic popes justify claiming so much power? Döllinger argues that the key to the answer is a ninth-century forgery, the Isidorian decretals, which purported to contain numerous patristic-era testimonies to the papacy.[89] Behind the Isidorian decretals was a concerted

86. Döllinger, 75.

87. Emmett O'Regan is at work on a dissertation at Trinity College Dublin that, among other things, argues that Honorius never actually subscribed the doctrine of Monothelitism. I thank O'Regan for sharing his noteworthy chapter with me.

88. Döllinger, 76.

89. Yves Congar and others have shown—without excusing the forgers—that these forgeries were often grounded in real testimonies to the papacy: see for example Yves Congar, "Saint Thomas Aquinas and the Infallibility of the Papal Magisterium (*Summa Theologiae*, II-II, q. 1, a. 10)," *The Thomist* 38, no. 1 (1974): 81–105, at 97. For background, lacking the clarification made by Congar, see Eamon Duffy, *Saints and Sinners: A History of the Popes*, 4th ed. (New Haven, CT: Yale University Press, 2015), 98–99: "Charlemagne had organised the Frankish church under archbishops, subordinating the ordinary diocesan bishops to their 'metropolitans.' The Frankish bishops resented this extended metropolitan control, and the royal domination of the Church which it often mediated. Around the year 850 there appeared in France an elaborate forgery, allegedly the work of the early seventh-century Spanish scholar Isidore of Seville, but in fact designed as a very contemporary weapon against the authority

effort to preserve the independence of bishops by greatly expanding the power of the pope. From the Isidorian decretals, as taken up by Pope Nicolas I and his successors, two principles emerged: the need for a council's pronouncements to be confirmed by the pope, and the claim that the pope possesses the fullness of power in the Church and alone is bishop of the universal Church. Döllinger grants that "if the Pope is really the bishop of the whole Church, so that every other bishop is his servant, he, who is the sole and legitimate mouth of the Church, ought to be infallible."[90] But the pope is not really the universal bishop; this is a mere invention of pseudo-Isidore. Some scholars argue that the situation described by pseudo-Isidore was legitimately developing anyway. In fact, says Döllinger, the development prior to pseudo-Isidore was itself based on earlier forgeries.

Döllinger goes on to show how the doctrine of papal infallibility emerged with increasing strength after a pause due to the disgraceful corruption of the Roman Church of the ninth and tenth centuries. Pope Gregory VII worked assiduously to inflate papal power. Discussing Gregory VII and his collaborators, Döllinger remarks that today "it is difficult, if not impossible, to distinguish where involuntary delusion merged into conscious deceit," but, at best, they were reckless inventers and mythologizers.[91] They claimed to be mere servants of the constant tradition of the Church, whereas in fact they were advancing newly invented fictitious claims.

of lay rulers and of metropolitan archbishops. These 'False Decretals' of 'Pseudo Isidore' were made up of a series of letters of early popes, all forged, a further series of papal letters from the time of Sylvester I to that of Gregory II, some of them spurious and many of them garbled, and a large collection of canons of councils, mostly authentic: the *Donation of Constantine* was also included. The point of the whole immense collection was to establish that the papacy was the real source of power in the Church, the Pope sharing his authority with the bishops [not the metropolitans or archbishops] at large as his vicars. . . . The role of the papacy as the fountain of all jurisdiction in the Church, even that of councils, already widely accepted, gradually became axiomatic." Duffy goes on to point out the influence of Pope Nicholas I (858–867), whose "understanding of papal jurisdiction coincided closely with that of the False Decretals, which he had probably read. He considered that no synod or council had binding force unless approved by him, that no bishop might be deposed without his agreement, and that all his decisions as Pope had the force of law" (Duffy, 100).

90. Döllinger, *The Pope and the Council*, 77.

91. Döllinger, 84–85.

Gratian codified all of this for them and added some fictions and distortions of his own. Gratian promoted papal supremacy through such impious nonsense as the doctrine that "as Christ submitted to the law on earth, though in truth he was its Lord, so the Pope is high above all laws of the Church, and can dispose of them as he will, since they derive all their force from him alone."[92] Aquinas and the other medieval theologians built doctrinally upon Gratian.[93]

Pope Gregory VII and his followers also began to pretend that the popes had been men of great personal sanctity. In cases where the sins of a pope could not be ignored, they argued (falsely attributing the claim to St. Boniface) that a pope cannot be judged by anyone else in the Church, unless the pope falls into heresy. They also got rid of national synods and allocated to the pope the right of excommunicating anyone. Gregory VII himself seems to have believed that Eastern Christians awaited their cues from him, and he might even have marched upon Constantinople in 1074 had he not busied himself instead with "plunging Germany and Italy into a religious and civil war."[94]

Where Gregory VII led, Innocent III went further, especially in placing

---

92. Döllinger, 121.

93. Döllinger, 122. For a much more sober portrait—but broadly to the same effect—see the concise summation by Geoffrey Barraclough, *The Medieval Papacy* (New York: W.W. Norton, 1979), 96, 104.

94. Döllinger, 93. Here Döllinger is referring, quite unfairly, to the Investiture Conflict. For a contemporary historical overview of Pope Gregory VII's reform pontificate—written from the perspective of secular historiography—see Brett Edward Whalen, *The Medieval Papacy* (New York: Palgrave Macmillan, 2014), 96–105. Whalen remarks that Gregory VII's "view of the papacy and his own role in the Church can be seen at a glance in the so-called *Dictatus Papae*. . . . Written in 1075 for an unclear purpose and never circulated, it made stark, point-by-point claims for the authority of Saint Peter's successors. A few of its statements included the claim that 'only the Roman Pontiff may rightly be called universal,' that 'he alone can depose or restore bishops,' that 'he may depose emperors,' and that 'he may be judged by no one.' It also flatly stated that 'someone not in concord with the Roman Church may not be held catholic'" (Whalen, 98). See also the richly nuanced overview by Barraclough, *The Medieval Papacy*, 80–95; as well as the (in my view justified) praise given to Pope Gregory VII in John Henry Newman's 1841 essay "Reformation of the Eleventh Century," in Newman, *Essays Critical and Historical*, vol. 2, ed. Nicholas Schofield (Leominster, UK: Gracewing, 2019), 294–377.

the papacy (and the Church) above the State and its courts.[95] Just as the soul rules over the body, so the pope rules over all States; and just as the Church alone has a divine right, so the pope is the possessor of all rights and is the one to whom all must be subject. In this period, "Vicar of Christ" superseded "Vicar of Peter." Pope Gregory IX deemed the pope to have full and free reign over everything in the whole world. Pope Boniface VIII's *Unam Sanctam* rejected any independent role for the State; the pope must govern everything. Bishops became mere figureheads in many respects. The popes used their power to keep Germany in submission to France while they dwelt in Avignon.

According to Döllinger, with Rome so dominant and with all things of importance settled in Rome, "religious disease and decay" set in, as the pastoral care of dioceses faltered.[96] By 1327, the ban and interdict had placed half the Christian world in a condition of excommunication. The popes freely employed violence to secure their ends. Councils and synods became mere occasions to rubber-stamp already prepared papal documents. Pope Leo X's Bull *Pastor Aeternus* strung together various fictions from pseudo-Isidore and elsewhere to lend a false patristic weight to Leo X's insistence upon full papal control over councils. Döllinger concludes, "It is a psychological marvel how this unnatural theory of a priestly domination, embracing the whole world, controlling and subjugating the whole of life, could ever have become established."[97]

Döllinger adds some discussion of the deplorable ignorance exhibited by the Roman clergy, along with the popes' control over what little education there was, by means of subservient religious orders. He discusses the displacement of bishops by the pope-controlled College of Cardinals and Curia. He argues that there is no justification for the role of the cardinals;

95. For further background to the medieval period, see for instance Brian Tierney, *The Origins of Papal Infallibility, 1150–1350: A Study of the Concept of Infallibility, Sovereignty and Tradition in the Middle Ages* (Leiden, NL: Brill, 1972); Congar, "Saint Thomas Aquinas and the Infallibility of the Papal Magisterium," 81–105.

96. Döllinger, *The Pope and the Council*, 143.

97. Döllinger, 148.

Christ established only successors of the Apostles—namely, bishops. The Curia gained the hatred of the whole world by changing the Church into a court marked by greed and fueled by bribery.

There is much more in Döllinger's book, including details about the post-Tridentine march over three centuries toward the dogma of papal infallibility. But I think I have said enough to exhibit the main lines of Döllinger's case. For Döllinger, not only are the claims of the post-patristic papacy built upon a pack of lies, but also the post-patristic papacy is the greatest cause of Christian division. While believing that Christ willed to give the bishop of Rome a certain primacy, Döllinger sees the last one thousand years of Church history as largely a record of Catholic depravity, at least in Rome and Italy. He blames Luther's opponent Cajetan for the most odious doctrine of all: "Thomas of Vio or Cajetan was the first to maintain Papal Infallibility in its fullness. . . . Cajetan was a type of that class of sycophantic Court divines afterwards stigmatized by Caraffa and the other compilers of the memorial of 1538, as deceivers of the Pope through their doctrine of absolute supremacy, and as authors of the corruption and dissolution of the Church."[98] Döllinger takes some hope from the theologians of the second millennium who continued to maintain that a pope could teach false doctrine, including the theologian who became Pope Adrian VI. Some theologians, too, continued to insist upon the authority of councils over popes. Unfortunately, says Döllinger, the growing dominance of the Jesuits, who appropriated Cajetan's doctrine, had a sinister impact due to their

98. Döllinger, 304–305. Döllinger devotes somber attention to Pope Paul IV's 1558 Papal Bull *Cum ex Apostolatus officio*. He summarizes its teaching: "The Pope, by virtue of his absolute authority, can depose every monarch, hand over every country to foreign invasion, deprive every one of his property, and that without any legal formality, and not only on account of dissent from the doctrines approved at Rome, or separation from the Church, but for merely offering an asylum to such dissidents, so that no rights of dynasty or nation are respected, but nations are to be given up to all the horrors of a war of conquest. And to all this is finally subjoined the doctrine, that all official and sacramental acts of a Pope or Bishop, who has ever—say twenty or thirty years before—been heretically minded on any single point of doctrine, are null and void" (Döllinger, 312). Döllinger attends with equal or greater alarm to Pope Urban VIII's 1627 Papal Bull *In Coena Domini*.

understanding of obedience. The main culprit was Bellarmine, whose intellectual and moral probity Döllinger repeatedly questions.[99]

Let me now turn to some of Döllinger's shorter writings immediately before and after the dogmatic definition. In October 1869, he published in his own name "Considerations for the Bishops of the Council Respecting the Question of Papal Infallibility," reprising some of the materials he had published anonymously as "Janus" and also some of the materials in his *Fables Respecting the Popes in the Middle Ages.*[100] Here again Döllinger takes as his rhetorical target a maximalist definition of papal infallibility. He states, "Should the infallibility of the popes be proclaimed . . . it would be impossible to suppose that a pope had ever set up a principle that was reprehensible from a moral point of view, that he had ever issued an immoral decision, or instituted a proceeding that contradicted Christian ethics."[101] As an example, he asserts that the definition of papal infallibility as a dogma would ensure that the Inquisition, and every law about it ever promulgated by popes, would be beyond criticism. Every statement of every papal bull, no matter how contradictory or absurd, would have to be affirmed as infallibly true. Döllinger insists again upon the "historical untenableness" of the proposed dogma by the standard of any "scientific test."[102]

---

99. Döllinger states, "Bellarmine further developed the ideas of Cajetan, in which he generally concurs, but he rejects decisively Cajetan's hypothesis of an heretical Pope being deposed *ipso facto* by the judgment of God. An heretical Pope is legitimate so long as the Church has not deposed him. If Cajetan said the Church was the handmaid of the Pope, Bellarmine adds that whatever doctrine it pleases the Pope to prescribe, the Church must receive; there can be no question raised about proving it; she must blindly renounce all judgment of her own, and firmly believe that all the Pope teaches is absolutely true, all he commands absolutely good, and all he forbids simply evil and noxious. For the Pope can as little err in moral as in dogmatic questions. Nay, he goes so far as to maintain that if the Pope were to err by prescribing sins and forbidding virtues, the Church would be bound to consider sins good and virtues evil, unless she chose to sin against conscience" (Döllinger, 317–318). See also Christian D. Washburn, "Three Sixteenth-Century Thomist Solutions to the Problem of a Heretical Pope: Cajetan, Cano, and Bellarmine," *The Thomist* 83, no. 4 (2019): 547–588.

100. For discussion, see Howard, *The Pope and the Professor*, 137.

101. Johann Joseph Ignaz von Döllinger, "Considerations for the Bishops of the Council respecting the Question of Papal Infallibility," in *Declarations and Letters on the Vatican Decrees, 1869–1887*, ed. F.H. Reusch (Edinburgh: T.&T. Clark, 1891), 1–32, at 22.

102. Döllinger, 27. Howard quotes a typical claim made by Döllinger in this regard:

On January 19, 1870, the contours of the proposed dogma received clearer shape through an address authored by participants in the council in which the foundational principles of the proposed dogma were laid out. Döllinger responded in print on January 21. First, pointing out that the address limits papal infallibility to words directed by the pope to the whole Church, he remarks that, in fact, prior to the late thirteenth century, the popes never directed their words to the whole Church. Thus, the popes for the first thirteen centuries had no notion of their supposed "infallibility"; and, indeed, history shows that this understanding of infallibility did not emerge until 1562. Second, he observes that the address contends that the constant tradition of the Church has held that the popes' dogmatic decisions are unalterable. He responds that history shows that the councils freely evaluated the popes' dogmatic decisions, accepting some and rejecting others. Third, the address claims that at the Second Council of Lyons, the Latin and Greek participants agreed that the pope is the final arbiter of doctrinal controversies. He replies that, historically speaking, this is incorrect. Fourth, the address distorts the Council of Florence, as Döllinger argues at length.[103]

"Döllinger made a characteristic appeal to the authority of scholarship: 'It may be asserted that all theologians who combine comprehensive historical knowledge [*umfassende Geschichtskenntniß*] with biblical and patristic erudition have rejected the new doctrine of Papal infallibility'" (*The Pope and the Professor*, 137, citing Döllinger, "Erwägungen für die Bischöfe des Conciliums über die Frage der päpstlichen Unfehlbarkeit," in *Briefe und Erklärungen über die Vaticanischen Decrete, 1869–1887* [Munich: C.H. Beck, 1890], 1–28).

103. See Döllinger, "A Few Words on the Address Presented to the Pope by Certain Members of the Vatican Council, Urging Him to Declare His Own Infallibility," in *Declarations and Letters on the Vatican Decrees, 1869–1887*, 33–45. For discussion, see Howard, *The Pope and the Professor*, 144–146. Howard explains the controversy about Florence: "In the majority bishops' view, the decrees of this Council demonstrated that the Greek representatives in Florence had recognized a form of papal primacy in addition to conciliar authority. But for Döllinger, the decrees were the result of later interpolations (and these resting on earlier forgeries), because the evidence suggested, in his view, that the Greeks were only prepared to consent to an understanding of Infallibility when the Roman See acted in conjunction with and, in fact, simply expressed the will of the entire Church as made known in conciliar decisions. Because the final Latin conciliar texts seemed to gainsay the Greeks' intentions, Döllinger was even willing to dispense with the Council or Florence as a recognized ecumenical council" (Howard, 145). Howard adds that in fact, "Döllinger's analysis of the

In response to the plan for the Vatican Council set forth by five papal legates on March 9, Döllinger states in another article: "The Present Roman Synod is thus the first in the history of the Church in which instructions as to procedure have been made to the assembled fathers beforehand, without their having any share whatever in the matter."[104] Newman is aware of this concern and rejects it on historical grounds. But Döllinger's main concern, of course, is the actual dogma under consideration, and he argues that "a Council only makes dogmatical decrees on things which were already universally believed in the Church as being testified by the Scriptures and by tradition, or which are contained as evident and clear deductions in the principles that have been already believed and taught."[105] For Döllinger, papal infallibility is testified to neither by Scripture nor Tradition, and so the proposed dogma can only be a grave corruption of the deposit of faith. He warns, "Should . . . the infallibility of a single individual be put in the place of the freedom from error of the whole Church as formerly believed and taught, this is no development nor explanation of what was hitherto implicitly believed, nor is it a deduction that follows with logical accuracy, but simply the very opposite of the earlier doctrine."[106]

What, then, was the reaction of Döllinger to the actual defined dogma? Put simply, he was outraged and did everything he could to oppose it. As he makes clear in a letter to Archbishop von Scherr on January 29, 1871, he cannot accept that popes have the ability, on their own, to teach Catholic doctrine infallibly, because his knowledge of the patristic period shows him the opposite. He promises the Archbishop that he will strive to read all

Council of Florence had betrayed the fact that he had not taken into consideration some of the most recent scholarship on the topic" (Howard, 145).

104. Döllinger, "The New Order of Business in the Council, and Its Theological Significance," in *Declarations and Letters on the Vatican Decrees, 1869–1887*, 46–64, at 47. Later in the same essay, Döllinger argues along similar procedural lines: "All theologians make it a condition of the ecumenical character of a Council that perfect freedom should prevail at it—freedom of speech and freedom of voting" (Döllinger, 61).

105. Döllinger, 56.

106. Döllinger, 57. Döllinger adds the claim that the proposed dogma "is foreign to the conscience of the faithful and appears to them as an innovation" (Döllinger, 58).

the Catholic defenses of the new dogma in order to see whether he might be persuaded that the dogma really is "warranted by the Scriptures and by tradition."[107] He explains that the issue, for him, is a historical one having to do with the accuracy of his previous historical studies against such an understanding of papal primacy and authority. If his historical studies are accurate, then the dogma is a corruption. Thus, he tells the Archbishop that he will have to be satisfied on historical grounds. Otherwise, he will not be able to submit publicly to the new dogma in good conscience.

Pope Leo XIII and other Church leaders later wished (as did Newman) that Archbishop von Scherr had not compelled Döllinger to take a public position but had instead granted Döllinger's wish to study the matter assiduously without further comment. But Archbishop von Scherr, due partly to Döllinger's influential position in German Catholicism and in theological circles throughout much of Europe, believed that he had to insist upon a resolution.[108]

In Döllinger's final response to the Archbishop, dated March 28, 1871, he refused to give assent to the dogma of papal infallibility.[109] He explains his refusal to do so on five grounds, most of which we have seen above. The first is the vow taken by all Catholic clergy to interpret Scripture according to the unanimous mind of the Church Fathers, given that the Church Fathers did not interpret the relevant biblical texts—Matthew 16:18, John 21:17, and

107. Döllinger, "Döllinger to Archbishop von Scherr (January 28, 1871)," in *Declarations and Letters on the Vatican Decrees, 1869–1887*, 74–77, at 75.

108. For background that shows why Archbishop von Scherr reached this conclusion—and that explores the intense tensions between the archbishop and the theology faculty of the University of Munich (a faculty that included both Johann Friedrich and Döllinger, neither of whom accepted the dogma)—see Howard, *The Pope and the Professor*, 157–164.

109. Howard notes that this was an open letter, "soon published in newspapers the world over" (*The Pope and the Professor*, 161). Döllinger was seeking publicity, and he got it. Howard states, "The letter created a sensation. Liberals, Protestants, and dissenting Catholics immediately hailed Döllinger's 'declaration' as an act of momentous courage. The liberal Bavarian minister to Florence, Wilhelm von Dönniges, called it a 'historically great' event, inspiring to the educated classes throughout Europe. The *Rheinischer Merkur* editorialized that Döllinger's declaration was an 'incontrovertible witness to the truth, a stumbling block' for Jesuits and ultramontanes everywhere. Soon, letters of support and 'solidarity addresses' poured into Döllinger's residence from near and far" (Howard, 161).

Luke 22:32—to be about the papacy and its authority. The second is that even if the dogmatic definition does not say so, the bishops in their interpretations of the dogma have been asserting the universality or near-universality of belief in papal infallibility across the centuries, and this claim regarding Tradition can be demonstrated to be historically false.[110] Third, the bishops who voted in favor of the dogmatic definition at the Vatican Council were misled by the forgeries and distortions that for centuries served to buttress papal claims to power. Fourth, it can be historically demonstrated that earlier councils, as well as earlier popes, have solemnly defined and delimited the extent of papal power and authority along lines contradicted by the dogmatic proclamation of the Vatican Council. Fifth, the Vatican Council's decrees are opposed to the constitutions of many European nations, including Bavaria,[111] since the dogmatic definition (in Döllinger's view) makes papal bulls such as *Unam Sanctam* and *Cum ex Apostolatus Officio*, along with the *Syllabus of Errors*' condemnation of political liberalism, to be infallible.[112]

---

110. Döllinger, "Döllinger to Archbishop von Scherr (March 28, 1871)," in *Declarations and Letters on the Vatican Decrees, 1869–1887*, 82–104, at 84.

111. One can here see the roots of some liberal German Catholic support for Otto von Bismarck's *Kulturkampf*. See Michael B. Gross, *The War against Catholicism: Liberalism and the Anti-Catholic Imagination in Nineteenth-Century Germany* (Ann Arbor, MI: University of Michigan Press, 2004). On the *Kulturkampf* more broadly, including its lesser instantiations in other European nations, see Nicholas Atkin and Frank Tallett, *Priests, Prelates and People: A History of European Catholicism since 1750* (Oxford: Oxford University Press, 2003), 141–154; as well as Manuel Borutta's "Anti-Catholicism and the Culture War in Risorgimento Italy," in *The Risorgimento Revisited: Nationalism and Culture in Nineteenth-Century Italy*, ed. Silvana Patriarca and Lucy Riall (London: Palgrave Macmillan, 2012), 191–213.

112. Döllinger states in his letter of March 28: "The new Vatican doctrine confers on the pope the attribute of *the whole fulness of power* (totam plenitudinem potestatis) over the whole Church as well as over every individual layman,—a power which is at the same time to be truly episcopal and again specifically papal, which is to include in itself all that affects faith, morals, duties of life, and discipline, and which can, without any mediation whatever, seize and punish, bid and forbid every one, the monarch as well as the labouring man. The wording is so carefully chosen that there remains for the bishops absolutely no other position and authority than that which belongs to papal commissaries or plenipotentiaries" ("Döllinger to Archbishop von Scherr (March 28, 1871)," 91–92; cf. 102: "As he has become infallible, he can, at any moment, with the one little word 'orbi' (thereby addressing the whole Church), make every statute, every doctrine, and every postulate, an infallible and irrevocable article of faith."

As Döllinger goes on to say, a number of his colleagues have submitted to the dogma without being able intellectually to affirm it. Döllinger refuses to follow this path; he must be "convinced by evidences and facts."[113] Given his erudition and his conviction that faith cannot contradict reason, he must be shown historical evidence that assuages his concerns, or else he must be allowed to reject the dogma—and Catholics who follow his lead should also be allowed to reject the dogma. He calls upon Archbishop von Scherr to involve men of "scientific training" in a commission that might study the reasonableness of the dogma; and he asks for a conference to be held on the matter, presided over by the Archbishop and reviewing all the historical facts.[114] He urges that a government official be in attendance at the conference as an impartial witness, and that the minutes of the conference be published. By means of such a conference, he says, the clergy and the laity can be assured that the proper "scientific investigation and establishment of tradition" has been undertaken; and, if "the most eminent German historians" refute him through "historical proofs," he promises to subject himself to their judgment.[115]

Thus, in his view, the relevant question is whether his "reasoning is critically and historically correct or not."[116] For if his historical conclusion is correct, then the fact is that the new dogma is a corruption by which "the episcopate of the ancient Church is . . . dissolved in its inmost being."[117] The pope has become, in reality, the sole successor of the Apostles. Döllinger insists that the dogma has maximalist implications: "In future every Catholic Christian when asked why he believes this or that, can and may give but the one answer: I believe or reject it because the infallible pope has bidden it to be believed or rejected."[118]

113. Döllinger, 87.
114. Döllinger, 86.
115. Döllinger, 90.
116. Döllinger, 91.
117. Döllinger, 92.
118. Döllinger, 100–101. In ringing tones, Döllinger concludes: "As Christian, as theologian, as historian, as citizen, I cannot accept this doctrine. I cannot do so as a Christian, because it is incompatible with the spirit of the gospel, and with the lucid sayings of Christ and the apostles. . . . I cannot do so as a theologian, because the whole genuine tradition of

In response, Archbishop von Scherr, "fearful of a widening schism in his diocese" and aware of the Vatican's stance that prominent dissenters should be ecclesiastically disciplined,[119] published a pastoral letter on April 2, 1871. In this public letter, he maintains that what is at stake is whether a Catholic, for reasons of his own, may reject a dogma of the Church—in this case a dogma solemnly taught by an ecumenical council. If dogmas could be rejected or assented to by each Catholic as he or she discerns—or if it were granted that only councils that proceeded in a scholarly and unimpeachable manner count as true councils—then private judgment would reign. Believers would not receive the faith through the mediation of the Church, but rather would receive only those teachings that make sense to them. For von Scherr, Döllinger's position explicitly "sets historical investigation above the Church. The decisions of the Church are given over to the ultimate and final judgment of historians, while the divinely ordained teaching office in the Church is done away with, and all Catholic truth questioned."[120] If Döllinger's viewpoint were allowed to stand, says von Scherr, a historian's judgment would replace the Church's apostolic Magisterium, because every doctrine would be subjected (retrospectively for all previously defined dogma) to the conclusions of historical research.

the Church stands irreconcilably opposed to it. I cannot do so as a historian, because, as such, I know that the persistent endeavours to realise this theory of a universal sovereignty has cost Europe streams of blood, distracted and ruined whole countries, shaken to its foundations the beautiful organic edifice of the constitution of the older Church, and begotten, nursed, and maintained the worst abuses in the Church. Finally, I must reject it as a citizen, because, with its claims on the submission of States and monarchs and the whole political order of things to the papal power, and by the exceptional position claimed by it for the clergy, it lays the foundation for an endless and fatal discord between the State and the Church" (Döllinger, 103).

119. Howard, *The Pope and the Professor*, 162. Howard notes that prior to excommunicating Döllinger on April 17, von Scherr reached out to King Ludwig II of Bavaria. Although King Ludwig had repeatedly (and personally) supported Döllinger, when von Scherr met with the King and warned him about the growing potential of schism in Bavaria, the King made clear that he would not intervene.

120. "Archbishop von Scherr's Pastoral Letter," in *Declarations and Letters on the Vatican Decrees, 1869–1887*, 105–110, at 107.

John Henry Newman

Two letters to the editor authored by Newman and published in September 1872, in *The Times* and *The Guardian* respectively, can serve to indicate the differences between Newman and Döllinger in their responses to the dogmatic definition. Most importantly, Newman rejects a maximalist interpretation of the dogma. Against the notion that the pope can now make whatever he wants to be infallible truth, Newman points out in his letter of September 9 to *The Times*: "No Pope can make evil good. No Pope has any power over those eternal moral principles which God has imprinted on our hearts and consciences."[121] Against the charge that the popes have acted with great wickedness and impunity, Newman does not deny it but instead observes: "Infallibility is not impeccability."[122] The charism of papal infallibility does not depend upon the holiness of the pope, let alone upon the holiness of his assistants or associates. And the charism of papal infallibility does not give the pope free reign: other standards exist besides the pope's solemn and formal declarations, and the pope's statements can be measured by these divinely given standards.

Newman's letter of September 12 to *The Guardian* responds to criticism brought against Newman by an Anglican who had converted to Catholicism in 1845 and reverted to Anglicanism in 1858. The gist of the criticism was that Newman, while intellectually in the same position as Döllinger, chose to submit his intellect in blind faith to things that he knew to be both untrue

121. John Henry Newman, Letter to the Editor of *The Times*, 9 September 1872, in *The Letters and Diaries of John Henry Newman*, vol. 26, ed. Charles Stephen Dessain and Thomas Gornall (Oxford: Clarendon, 1974), 163–164, at 163. John Page remarks, "Newman's first reaction on reading the definition of papal infallibility was almost one of relief. It was moderate enough. The promoters of extravagant views had not won out" (Page, *What Will Dr. Newman Do?*, 193). Page notes that Newman nevertheless wrote down in his diary not only reasons for accepting the dogma but also, on the other side, possible reasons for not accepting it immediately, above all the "lack of a moral unanimity among the bishops" (Page, 194)—which was soon resolved by the formal adherence to the dogma on the part of the bishops who had resisted it.

122. Newman, Letter to the Editor of *The Times*, 9 September 1872, 164.

and deleterious. In Newman's words, his critic held "that I [Newman] have all along considered the doctrine of the Pope's Infallibility to be contradicted by the facts of Church history, and that, though convinced of this, I have in consequence of the Vatican Council . . . forced myself by some unintelligible quibbles to fancy myself believing what really after all in my heart I could not and did not believe."[123]

In response to this criticism, Newman quotes from his "Discourse on University Education," given in 1852 in Dublin. There he remarks that the pope has, and ever has had, an infallible authority when formally and solemnly teaching.[124] By quoting this discourse from twenty years earlier, Newman clarifies that he, as a Catholic, always believed in papal infallibility—and thus it was not the question of truth that pained him about the council's push toward a definition of this dogma.

In a draft of his letter of September 12, Newman had quoted a telling passage from Lecture XI of his *Certain Difficulties Felt by Anglicans in Catholic Teaching*, published in 1850 and addressed to his erstwhile colleagues in the Oxford Movement. There he had affirmed the necessity of assenting, in faith, to a dogma even if one does not yet understand it. He distinguishes in Lecture XI between a "material faith"—mere habitual faith, received through the culture and the family—and a "formal faith"—namely, an assent to God revealing. A person with mere "material faith," he argues, will have a faith that "has neither the character nor the reward of that grace-implanted, grace-sustained principle, which believes, not merely because it was so taught in the nursery, but because God has spoken; not because there is no temptation to doubt, but because there is a duty to believe."[125] Real faith requires an

123. John Henry Newman, Letter to the Editor of *The Guardian*, 12 September 1872, in *The Letters and Diaries of John Henry Newman*, vol. 26, 166–168, at 166–167.

124. Newman goes on to explain why this text did not appear in the second edition (1859) of his *The Idea of a University*.

125. John Henry Newman, *Certain Difficulties Felt by Anglicans in Catholic Teaching*, vol. 1 (London: Longmans, Green, 1897), 350.

interior assent to God not on the basis of one's own ratiocination, but because it is God who speaks.[126]

According to Newman in Lecture XI, when the Church defines a dogma in a solemn fashion, the difference between material faith and formal faith is often exposed. Persons whose faith has rested upon their surrounding culture or upon their own ideas will not be able to accept the dogma if the dogma cuts against what they have rested their faith upon. Their rejection of the dogma will reveal that they never had faith (in its proper sense) at all. Their faith always rested, for its validity, upon their own minds rather than upon God speaking. Newman adds that "whenever a new definition of doctrine is promulgated by the competent authority," the human tendency is to resist it as a *novum*.[127] He compares such resistance to the acceptance of the dogma evinced by those whose faith has always rested upon the authority of God speaking. It is not intellectual laziness or blind faith to accept the solemn word of the Church, since God has promised to guide the Church in communicating his Word, and since God intends for individual believers to receive his Word through the Church. When individual believers do so, they are acting in good faith; they are allowing God to instruct them. As Newman puts it, "A ready and easy acceptance of the apparent novelty, and a cordial acquiescence to its promulgation, may be the very evidence of a mind, which has lived, not merely in certain doctrines, but in those doctrines as revealed,—not simply in a Creed, but in its Giver,—or, in other words, which has lived by real faith."[128] In sum, not only did Newman intellectually affirm the doctrine of

126. Here Newman and Henry Cardinal Manning are in full agreement. In the mid-1860s, with Pusey's *Eirenicon* in view, Manning wrote: "It is not the believing of isolated doctrines, but the act of Divine Faith, terminating in its formal motive, the veracity of God through the living voice of the Church, that makes us Catholic Christians" (Manning, *England and Christendom* [London: Longmans, Green, 1867], lxxxii–lxxxiii). This passage is cited by James Pereiro's "Crossed Visions—The Anglican Manning's Opinion of Rome and the Catholic Manning's Thoughts on Canterbury," in *By Whose Authority? Newman, Manning and the Magisterium*, ed. V. Alan McClelland (Bath: Downside Abbey, 1996), 204–243, at 234.

127. Newman, 351.

128. Newman, 351. Notably, Newman goes on to make a point rich with ecumenical

papal infallibility prior to 1870, but he also praised assenting to, even without yet understanding, a dogma taught by the Church as part of faith's assent to God's speaking—an assent based not on our own reasoning but on the authority of the God who speaks.[129]

In a letter to Richard Littledale on September 15, 1872, Newman rejects Littledale's supposition that the dogma of papal infallibility means that Catholics must deem Pope Gregory XIII's stance on the Massacre of St. Bartholomew to be the infallible enunciation of divine truth. Against this unwarranted maximalism, Newman remarks that it is illogical to suppose that everything said or written by a pope stands as "a dogmatic *statement* on morals, such as constitute a definition ex cathedra."[130] He makes a similar point in a letter to Arthur Arnold on September 20, 1872. Papal infallibility does not mean that the pope is "infallible in his acts or his commands."[131]

---

consequences: "While, then, I think it plain that the existence of large Anti-Catholic bodies professing Christianity are as inevitable, from the nature of the case, as infidel races or states, except under some extraordinary dispensation of divine grace, while there must ever be in the world false prophets and Antichrists, standing over against the Catholic Church, yet it is consolatory to reflect how the schism or heresy, which the self-will of a monarch or of a generation has caused, does not suffice altogether to destroy the work for which in some distant age Evangelists have left their homes, and Martyrs have shed their blood. Thus, the blessing is inestimable to England, so far as among us the Sacrament of Baptism is validly administered to any portion of the population. . . . We may entertain most reasonable hopes, that vast multitudes are in a state of invincible ignorance; so that those among them who are living a life really religious and conscientious, may be looked upon with interest and even pleasure, though a mournful pleasure, in the midst of the pain which a Catholic feels at their ignorant prejudices against what he knows to be true. Amongst the most bitter railers against the Church in this country, may be found those who are influenced by divine grace, and are at present traveling towards heaven" (Newman, 353–355).

129. For further discussion of Newman on the assent of faith, see for example Avery Dulles, "From Images to Truth: Newman on Revelation and Faith," 51, no. 2 (1990): 252–267; John R. Connolly, "Newman on Human Faith and Divine Faith: Clarifying Some Ambiguities," *Horizons* 23, no. 2 (1996): 261–280; Thomas Norris, "Faith," in *The Cambridge Companion to John Henry Newman*, ed. Ian Ker and Terrence Merrigan (Cambridge: Cambridge University Press, 2009), 73–97; and Reinhard Hütter, *John Henry Newman on Truth and Its Counterfeits: A Guide for Our Times* (Washington, DC: The Catholic University of America Press, 2020), chapter 2.

130. John Henry Newman, Letter to Richard Frederick Littledale, 15 September 1872, in *The Letters and Diaries of John Henry Newman*, vol. 26, 169–170, at 169.

131. John Henry Newman, Letter to Arthur Arnold, 20 September 1872, in *The Letters*

This is how to understand the error of Pope Honorius. Divine providence prevents a pope from formally and solemnly teaching an error in faith and morals, but Newman thinks that a pope can err in all other ways. He concludes, "We can blame a Pope's actions, while we believe in his formal enunciations of Christian doctrine."[132]

In a second letter to Littledale on September 17, Newman offers a more detailed account of his views. He emphasizes that when not solemnly teaching doctrine, the pope is perfectly fallible and may well be egregiously sinful or misguided. Infallibility is not a habitual power that characterizes a pope's mind and ensures that his thoughts and words never err. Even when a pope teaches infallibly, the process or research by which the pope reaches his conclusion is not infallible, and in fact may be filled with errors. Moreover, the pope, in his solemn teaching, is not inspired or filled with truth, but rather is simply protected from error.[133]

Recall that in his *An Essay on the Development of Christian Doctrine*, Newman had already insisted that "a revelation is not given, if there be no authority to decide what it is that is given."[134] God has spoken authoritatively; but the inspired books of Scripture cannot interpret themselves, since God did not give them for that purpose. Given that the Church is the indefectible "pillar and bulwark of the truth" (1 Tim. 3:15; cf. Isa. 59:21), the Church interprets Scripture faithfully. Without here settling the matter of the infallibility of the pope, Newman in his *Essay* explains that "in the

---

and Diaries of John Henry Newman, vol. 26, 172–173, at 173.

132. Newman, 173. For background, see Page, *What Will Dr. Newman Do?*, 227–228. See also Matthias Joseph Scheeben, *Handbook of Catholic Dogmatics*, Book 1: *Theological Epistemology*, Part 1: *The Objective Principles of Theological Knowledge*, trans. Michael J. Miller (Steubenville, OH: Emmaus Academic, 2019), 144: "It is possible, notwithstanding the continuing operation of his authority, that the pope *extra iudicum* [i.e. not *ex cathedra*] should profess, teach, or attest something false or heretical."

133. John Henry Newman, Letter to Richard Frederick Littledale, 17 September 1872, in *The Letters and Diaries of John Henry Newman*, vol. 26, 171. In this regard, in a later letter to Arnold (September 22), Newman cites the authority of Giovanni Perrone, whose writings he often cites. For background see Joseph Carola, "Newman and the Roman College," *Nova et Vetera* 18, no. 3 (2020): 741–756.

134. Newman, *An Essay on the Development of Christian Doctrine*, 89.

course of time, first the power of the Bishop displayed itself, and then the power of the Pope"; since the latter, in its full form, was not yet needed in the early centuries for the purpose of holding together the Church.[135] Just as Trinitarian doctrine developed under the stimulus of controversy, so also doctrine regarding the Petrine office developed under the stimulus of events and needs. According to Newman, then, "St. Peter's prerogative would remain a mere letter, till the complication of ecclesiastical matters became the cause of ascertaining it."[136] Newman adds that the antecedent probability that God would provide his Church with a unifying center is matched and confirmed by the presence of biblical texts that show Christ bestowing upon Peter an office of primacy—texts that arguably have the marks of prophecies, which receive a partial fulfillment in the early centuries (as Newman shows in detail) and a fuller fulfillment from the medieval period onward.

In 1872, therefore, Newman found himself standing firmly between the Ultramontanists on the one hand and Döllinger and his followers on the other. Ian Ker remarks, "He was sure that it was divine intervention which had prevented the extreme Ultramontanists, including the Pope, from getting through a much stronger definition. It was a pity that Döllinger and others persisted in exaggerating what actually had been defined, however scandalous the proceedings."[137] Newman did not intend to publish anything further on the topic, but things changed in October 1874 when Gladstone—who between 1868 and 1894 served twelve years as prime

135. Newman, 149. For discussion, see Stephen Morgan, *John Henry Newman and the Development of Doctrine: Encountering Change, Looking for Continuity* (Washington, DC: The Catholic University of America Press, 2021), 256–258.

136. Newman, *An Essay on the Development of Christian Doctrine*, 150. As Newman goes on to say, "A political body cannot exist without government, and the larger is the body, the more concentrated must the government be. If the whole of Christendom is to form one Kingdom, one head is essential; at least this is the experience of eighteen hundred years. As the Church grew into form, so did the power of the Pope develope; and wherever the Pope has been renounced, decay and division have been the consequence. We know of no other way of preserving the *Sacramentum Unitatis*, but a centre of unity" (Newman, 154–155).

137. Ker, *John Henry Newman*, 660.

minister—published an article criticizing the dogma of papal infallibility as necessarily obstructing the duties of a Catholic citizen, followed on November 5 by a lengthy pamphlet titled *The Vatican Decrees in Their Bearing on Civil Allegiance: A Political Expostulation*.

The timing of Gladstone's pamphlet coincided with the high-water mark of Otto von Bismarck's notorious anti-Catholic *Kulturkampf* in Germany.[138] After Gladstone's pamphlet appeared, he received an appreciative letter from Bismarck, and he discovered with delight that Bismarck was avidly distributing the pamphlet in Germany. Like Bismarck, Gladstone favored a "coalition of state and church for the project of constructing the nation as a Christian moral order," and Catholicism had no place in such a coalition.[139] In addition, Gladstone's sister Helen had some years earlier converted from Anglicanism to Roman Catholicism. Gladstone knew that the declaration of the dogma of papal infallibility had shaken her allegiance to the Catholic Church, and when she died in 1880 (identifying herself as an "Old Catholic"), he ensured that she was buried with Anglican rites.[140] To attack the dogma, then, served Gladstone's purposes on multiple levels.

In letters to the editor published on November 9 in *The Times*, both Cardinal Manning and Acton replied briefly to Gladstone.[141] Newman had

---

138. Archbishop Manning had earlier published *Caesarism and Ultramontanism* (London: Burns and Oates, 1873), a pamphlet that had rightly decried the *Kulturkampf* and Gladstone's silence about it. See Jeffrey P. von Arx, "Archbishop Manning and the *Kulturkampf*," *British Catholic History* 21, no. 2 (1992): 254–266; as well as—in the midst of a broader examination of English anti-Catholicism—Walter L. Arnstein, *Protestant versus Catholic in Mid-Victorian England: Mr. Newdegate and the Nuns* (Columbia, MO: University of Missouri Press, 1982), 186–188. Yet Manning went too far, arguing that "the Church cannot err or mislead either men or nations" (*Caesarism and Ultramontanism*, 56) and therefore that the solution to all problems regarding matters of faith and conscience is for the State to obey the Church.

139. John E. Toews, "Church and State: The Problem of Authority," in *The Cambridge History of Nineteenth-Century Political Thought*, ed. Gareth Stedman Jones and Gregory Claeys (Cambridge: Cambridge University Press, 2011), 603–648, at 633. See also McElrath, *The* Syllabus *of Pius IX*, 297.

140. See Hill, *Lord Acton*, 271.

141. Lord Acton emphasized that there was good reason to be confident that, in the actual event, British Catholics would be loyal to Great Britain in political matters: see Acton, "Reply of Lord Acton," in W.E. Gladstone, *The Vatican Decrees in Their Bearing on Civil*

begun in October to write a response to Gladstone's article, and the publication of Gladstone's pamphlet in November further stimulated his writing. Ker comments, "He finished on 21 December after a month's continuous writing, and the 'pamphlet,' which was actually 150 pages of close print, was published on 14 January 1875."[142]

Let me note at the outset that Gladstone, in replying to Newman's *Letter to the Duke of Norfolk* in *Vaticanism*, begins by expressing appreciation for Newman's assurances regarding Catholic citizens. Yet Gladstone continues to fear that, *de iure*, "the Vatican Decrees do, in the strictest sense, establish for the Pope a supreme command over loyalty and civil duty."[143] In response to Newman's insistence that the dogma requires no political allegiance to the Vatican, Gladstone claims to believe that, today, "the loyalty of our Roman Catholic fellow-subjects in the mass is evidently untainted and secure."[144] However, he deems that this present loyalty only "means that the poison which circulates from Rome has not been taken into the system"—which bodes ill for the future, just as Bismarck likewise concluded in promoting his liberal *Kulturkampf*.[145] In Gladstone's view as expressed in *Vaticanism*, even the most reassuring Catholic protestations of civic loyalty would, if Rome deemed fit, "be qualified or retracted or reversed."[146] He points out that in various assurances given publicly in 1661, 1757, 1783, 1793, 1810, and 1825–1826, Catholics who were seeking

---

Allegiance: A Political Expostulation, with the Replies of Archbishop Manning and Lord Acton (New York: D. Appleton, 1874), 80–86, at 84.

142. Ker, *John Henry Newman*, 680. Manning also published an extensive reply to Gladstone in 1875. Ker adds that a few days after Newman's work appeared, Newman's confrere and close friend Ambrose St. John published a translation of Bishop Joseph Fessler's *True and False Infallibility*, a book notable for the fact that it "maintained a strictly moderate interpretation of papal infallibility" and "had received the official approval of Pius IX" (*John Henry Newman*, 680). Fessler had served as Secretary General of the Vatican Council. Ambrose St. John died shortly after completing the translation; for a superb account of his work and his friendship with Newman, see Cornwell, *Newman's Unquiet Grave*, 203–206.

143. William E. Gladstone, *Vaticanism: An Answer to Reproofs and Replies* (New York: Harper & Brothers, 1875), 7.

144. Gladstone, 11.

145. Gladstone, 11–12.

146. Gladstone, 14.

enhanced or full citizenship rights pledged to British politicians that "papal infallibility was no part of the Roman Catholic faith, and never could be made a part of it," and such promises have come to nothing.[147]

While Gladstone affirms that "every Christian must seek to place his religion even before his country in his inner heart," then, his intractable fear is that the pope, as a political actor, will in due time demand sedition on the part of British Catholics.[148] He argues that the absolute obedience now required by the pope includes not only faith and morals but also the governance and discipline of the Church, much of which "lies within the domain of the State."[149] Thus, he finds that the Vatican Council has ended any pretense that Catholics can be loyal citizens of a non-Catholic State.

As Gladstone puts the challenge: "Will it be said, finally, that the Infallibility touches only matter of faith and morals? Only matter of morals! Will any of the Roman casuists kindly acquaint us what are the departments and functions of human life which do not and cannot fall within the domain of morals?"[150] He insists that whatever might be said today by Catholic apologists such as Newman, there is no *real* limit to the obedience demanded by the pope. After all, in the third chapter of the dogmatic constitution, it becomes clear that "even . . . where the judgments of the Pope do not present the credentials of infallibility, they are unappealable and irreversible: no person may pass judgment upon them; and all men, clerical and lay, dispersedly or in the aggregate, are bound truly to obey them."[151] Unsurprisingly, in a private letter to Döllinger, Gladstone caustically dismissed Newman's *Letter*

147. Gladstone, 36.

148. Gladstone, *The Vatican Decrees in Their Bearing on Civil Allegiance*, 63.

149. Gladstone, 44.

150. Gladstone, 37. He adds: "I submit that [religious] Duty is a power which rises with us in the morning and goes to rest with us at night. It is co-extensive with the action of our intelligence. It is the shadow which cleaves to us, go where we will, and which only leaves us when we leave the light of life. So, then, it is the supreme direction of us in respect to all Duty, which the Pontiff declares to belong to him, *sacro approbante concilio:* and this declaration he makes, not as an otiose opinion of the schools, but *cunctis fidelibus credendam et tenendam*" (Gladstone, 38).

151. Gladstone, 39.

to the Duke of Norfolk: "I have never read a controversial tract containing more damaging admissions, nor one containing more of transparent sophistry with which the writer had imposed upon himself in order to avoid admissions."[152]

As noted above, the final edition of the *Letter to the Duke of Norfolk* contains a Postscript written in February 1875 in reply to Gladstone's *Vaticanism*. Newman begins with the common-sense point that if one exaggerates the dogma, then one inevitably will face far more difficulties, in a completely unnecessary way. He bemoans Gladstone's (and implicitly Döllinger's) "exaggerated notion of the force, drift, and range of the Vatican definition of the Pope's infallibility and supremacy."[153] In defense of the historical roots of papal infallibility, Newman appeals to a providentially guided development of doctrine in response to the growth of the Church. Gradually, for all sorts of reasons, the political situation changed in a way that increasingly revealed the necessity both of a primacy in the Church and of the bishop of Rome as the one who exercises the primacy promised to Peter.[154] This shift took place already in the patristic period, as is quite evident by the time of Pope Leo the Great. At the same time, Newman repeatedly cites the contention of Bishop Joseph Fessler and others to the effect that "the Pope cannot, by virtue of his infallibility, reverse what has always been held"[155]—the point being that

152. Gladstone to Döllinger, 21 February 1875, *BM, add.mss, 44,140*, f° 374, quoted in McElrath, *The* Syllabus *of Pius IX*, 299.

153. Newman, *A Letter Addressed to His Grace the Duke of Norfolk on Occasion of Mr. Gladstone's Recent Expostulation*, in *Certain Difficulties Felt by Anglicans in Catholic Teaching Considered*, vol. 2 (London: Longmans, Green, 1896), 171–378, at 350.

154. See Newman, 356.

155. Newman, 377. See Joseph Fessler, *The True and the False Infallibility of the Popes: A Controversial Reply to Dr. Schulte*, trans. Ambrose St. John (London: Burns and Oates, 1875). See also Vincent Gasser, *The Official Relatio on Infallibility of Bishop Vincent Gasser at Vatican Council I*, ed. James O'Connor (Boston: St. Paul Editions, 1986), as well as Kristin M. Colberg's helpful discussion of Gasser (whose viewpoint accords with Fessler's) in her *Vatican I and Vatican II: Councils in the Living Tradition* (Collegeville, MN: Liturgical, 2016), 59–67. Colberg remarks, "Gasser is careful to describe three distinct ways in which the pope's infallibility is limited—in relation to its *object*, its *active subject*, and its *act*. In regard to the *object* of infallible teachings, the pope's prerogative is explicitly restricted to instances where he 'defines a doctrine of faith and morals' (PA [*Pastor Aeternus*] 4). The text is clear that the

Catholics have never envisioned "blindly" obeying the pope to the detriment of Christian truth.[156]

Regarding whether a doctrine solemnly taught by a pope becomes infallible only once it has been received by the Church, Gladstone had interpreted Newman to say that if the doctrine were not received, then it would not be absolutely binding. Newman corrects this point, explaining that in fact (in accord with *Pastor Aeternus*) he holds that a pope can define doctrine on his own—from his own authority—in an infallible and binding manner.[157] Again, however, the key for Newman is that the great majority of papal teachings are not infallible, even if they are to be received with a reverential obedience at the time of their promulgation. He argues, for example, that the *Syllabus of Errors* is not dogmatically infallible. Catholics should avoid holding the (negative) propositions condemned by Pope Pius IX, but Catholics are not thereby committed to affirming in faith a set of (unstated) positive affirmations regarding the matters treated in the *Syllabus*.[158]

---

guarantee of infallibility does not apply to the pontiff's every act or utterance but is in effect only when he defines a teaching that is part of the apostolic tradition and the common faith of the church" (Colberg, 63). This point is crucial for my emphasis on doctrinal corruption: The pope, too (indeed perhaps more than anyone!), must worry about doctrinal corruption. The "apostolic tradition and the common faith of the church" are not a mere wax nose, but rather have evident content, traceable over the centuries.

156. Drawing upon Ultramontanist sources, Newman adds here that if a pope *did* solemnly teach a heresy, then of course a heretical pope should not be obeyed, and he also notes that a heretical pope may thereby immediately cease to be pope—presuming it were possible that a pope could solemnly teach a heresy.

157. See Newman, *A Letter Addressed to His Grace the Duke of Norfolk on Occasion of Mr. Gladstone's Recent Expostulation*, 371.

158. See Newman, 366. Newman devotes a chapter of his *Letter to the Duke of Norfolk* to the *Syllabus*, since Gladstone had made much of it. For a summary of the reasons Newman gives against the infallibility of the *Syllabus*, see McElrath, *The* Syllabus *of Pius IX*, 279–281; and for Newman's responses in his *Letter to the Duke of Norfolk* to Gladstone's particular criticisms of the *Syllabus'* propositions, see McElrath, 282–284. In his Postscript, Newman replied to Gladstone's ongoing misunderstandings of the *Syllabus* as found in *Vaticanism*; for discussion see McElrath, *The* Syllabus *of Pius IX*, 300–315, especially 313–315. See also McElrath's helpful summation of Newman's chapter in *Letter to the Duke of Norfolk* on *Quanta Cura*, in McElrath, 276–279. McElrath adds a note on the ensuing exchange between Propaganda and Bishop Ullathorne, in which Propaganda observed that since the *Syllabus*

In the main body of *A Letter Addressed to His Grace the Duke of Norfolk*, Newman observes that one reason for the necessity of the pope's unifying authority is that otherwise Erastianism will prevail: the Church will become ruled by the State in each land, which, of course, is exactly what Gladstone preferred (de facto), and which also fits with Bismarck's project and with Döllinger's repeated praise of the Germanic races over the Latin races (especially the Italians).[159] In the patristic Church, many bishops suffered exile and oppression at the hands of the State, both before and after Constantine. In the contemporary Church, the papacy ensures the independence of the Church from particular States. Newman argues that in this regard,

---

"contained many articles which were of faith, it would have to be received with something more than a simple act of obedience" (McElrath, 322–323). McElrath comments: "His [Newman's] interpretation of the *Syllabus* despite the letter from Propaganda could hardly have been too unorthodox, in view of the fact that he was created a cardinal some four years later. . . . I fail to find much difference between Newman's position and the conclusion of the article on the *Syllabus* in the *DTC* in which it is stated that though the *Syllabus* is probably not infallible, the faithful still owe to it respect and obedience" (McElrath, 328–329). For Gladstone, as McElrath says, "the decree of Infallibility was directed to the end of endowing Rome with the powers and instruments she required to confirm and ensure obedience to the condemnations contained in the *Syllabus* respecting the relations between Church and State and the rights of the Church" (McElrath, 324). McElrath replies by charging Gladstone with Erastianism: "There is no doubt that Gladstone refused to recognize in the Church a free and completely independent society, *equal* to, and by reason of its final end, even *superior* to the State. A Church of such definition and endowed with such a nature flatly rejected the notion that the Church and State should be so completely divorced that, according to the principle of naturalism condemned in the *Quanta Cura*, human society ought to be governed as if religion were of no account" (McElrath, 324–325).

159. Citing an as example a 1874 letter of Döllinger's to a former student, Chapman notes that for Döllinger, "Nations, both ancient and modern, had thus to cast off the Roman yoke in pursuit of a truth which had become more apparent to the Teutonic nations than to the Latins," and Chapman concludes that "a northern national catholicism could easily go hand in hand with racial superiority over the southern Europeans" (*The Fantasy of Reunion*, 241). In his *Antikatholizismus: Deutschland und Italien im Zeitalter der europäischen Kulturkämpfe* (Göttingen: Vandenhoeck & Ruprecht, 2010), 107–108, Manuel Borutta reports: "In essays, newspaper articles, and lectures, Döllinger depicted the conflict between liberal and Ultramontanist Catholics as both nationally and racially motivated. In 1861 he wrote of the 'Roman element,' in principle hostile to 'German Catholic science.' . . . In some cases, Döllinger's Italian opponents employed identical images of the enemy with an inverse application. In 1867 *L'Osservatore Romano* prophesied a final battle between Catholic Romanism and the anti-Latin, rationalistic German culture. The Vatican Council sharpened the dichotomization of 'Roman' and 'German' forces and led to a militarization of rhetoric."

"Rome is now the one faithful representative, and thereby is heir and successor, of that free-spoken dauntless Church of old."[160] As he points out, the Oxford Movement was founded precisely in opposition to Erastianism. Throughout the nineteenth century, Newman says, the Catholic Church has continued to assert its rights against those of any State. There have also been notable instances, both in the patristic age and in later periods, in which the rulers of the State have shown their submission to the Church "as far as the domain of religion extends, and that domain is a wide one."[161]

Newman emphasizes that in the patristic period, the Church claimed to be a unified body (though spread throughout the Roman Empire), and the State never managed to dominate the Church in that era. In this sense, says Newman, "the Pope is the heir of the Ecumenical Hierarchy of the fourth century, as being, what I may call, heir by default. No one else claims or exercises its rights or its duties."[162] Both in the Orthodox East and in Anglicanism, the bishops are under the sway of State power, and their Churches act as local Churches rather than as universal ones. Notably, it follows that either "there was a radical corruption of Christianity from the first, or Christianity came to an end, in proportion as the type of the Nicene Church faded out of the world"—or else there still remains a visible Church that claims and exercises a universal authority and that refuses to be subject to a particular State.[163] In fact, Newman avers, that visible Church is the

160. Newman, *A Letter Addressed to His Grace the Duke of Norfolk on Occasion of Mr. Gladstone's Recent Expostulation*, 198.

161. Newman, 201.

162. Newman, 207. T.S. Gregory aptly calls this argument "horse-sense" and adds that it is "an argument that would have passed the standard of Dr. Johnson. It can be refuted only by abolishing or eviscerating the Creeds, which are and claim to be statements of fact, of supernatural history" (Gregory, "Newman and Liberalism," in *A Tribute to Newman*, 84–115, at 109).

163. Newman, *A Letter Addressed to His Grace the Duke of Norfolk on Occasion of Mr. Gladstone's Recent Expostulation*, 207. See Avery Dulles, "Authority in the Church," in *The Cambridge Companion to John Henry Newman*, 170–188, at 180, summarizing Newman's position in his *Letter to the Duke of Norfolk*: "By default the papacy has taken over the authority that formerly belonged to bishops such as Athanasius, Basil, Gregory Nazianzus, and Ambrose. The pope today is the sole heir of the ecumenical hierarchy of the fourth century. This concentration of power has been providential." Newman's position is not that the bishops no

Catholic Church, with the bishop of Rome exercising the unique Petrine office. For Newman, it is a historical fact that with respect to continuity between the patristic Church and today, "We must either give up the belief in the Church as a divine institution altogether, or we must recognize it at this day in that communion of which the Pope is the head."[164] Only in the Church led by the pope do we find a clear representative of the patristic Church's claims to universality and autonomy from the State. It is here that we find "the claims, the prerogatives, and duties which we identify with the kingdom set up by Christ."[165]

Repeating arguments made in *An Essay on the Development of Christian Doctrine*, Newman grants that the patristic Church—the Church of Nicaea—did not know of the papacy as it now exists. He argues therefore that such passages as Matthew 16:18 have a prophetic import that develops in the Church.[166] Thus, it is correct to say—as a matter of historical fact—that the

longer have authority; rather, it is that the unity of the Church—its ability to act universally—now depends upon the role of the pope, whereas in the fourth century this was not the case (even though in the fourth century the bishop of Rome certainly did not lack a role, as Newman had shown in more detail in *An Essay on the Development of Christian Doctrine*).

164. Newman, *A Letter Addressed to His Grace the Duke of Norfolk on Occasion of Mr. Gladstone's Recent Expostulation*, 208.

165. Newman, 208.

166. Nicholas Lash responds, understandably but in my view unpersuasively: "The claim that the 'whole idea' of Christianity (of which later doctrines and institutions are 'realised aspects') has been present from the beginning would seem to be strengthened in proportion to the plausibility of the claim that these later doctrines and institutions may be regarded as the fulfilment of 'prophetic' words and gestures in the new testament. Discussing the early history of the papal primacy, Newman observes that 'The *regalia Petri* might sleep . . . as an unfulfilled prophecy' (*Dev* 4.3.3 . . .). Throughout *Dev* 4.3.1–3, Newman is attempting to draw a distinction between the 'existence' of the papacy and its 'operation' (*Dev* 4.3.1, both *1845* and *1878*, despite alterations). But if the only sense in which the papacy can be said to have 'existed' in the world in the early centuries was as an 'unfulfilled prophecy,' would it not be simpler to say of the papacy what Davison said of Christianity as a whole: 'There was a time when Christianity was not in the world, but only foretold: a time when it had no being, but in prophecy'?" (Lash, *Newman on Development: The Search for an Explanation in History* [London: Sheed & Ward, 1975], 112; the citation is from the seventh edition of John Davison's 1824 *Discourses on Prophecy, in Which Are Considered Its Structure, Use, and Inspiration* [Oxford: J.H. and J. Parker, 1861], 278). In the same vein, see Paul Misner, *Papacy and Development: Newman and the Primacy of the Pope* (Leiden, NL: Brill, 1976), 95–96,

claims and universal power of the Nicene Church, which was ruled by bishops, are now claimed solely by the pope, in the sense that no other bishop or group of bishops dares to claim them. Newman reiterates, "That which in substance was possessed by the Nicene Hierarchy, that the Pope claims now."[167]

The main fourth-century prerogative consists in the ability to define dogma for the whole Church. The Council at Nicaea had such an ability; the Vatican Council had such an ability; and, as the Vatican Council showed, the pope has such an ability, in accord with Christ's word in Matthew 16:18 as interpreted over the centuries. If the pope had no such ability, Newman argues, the result would quickly be the collapse of the Church into regional domains controlled by States, along the Erastian model. Christ himself recognized that "no large community could be strong which had no head"—that is, no vicar on earth. Christ ensured through the Spirit that this papal role would develop over the centuries, as the Church spread throughout the world and as Erastianism in various lands threatened the Church.[168]

---

where Misner argues that Newman's "treatment of the papacy is . . . the most striking example of Newman's oscillation between the aspect of continuity in development and the aspect of historical novelty. Again, his view of the papacy as a fulfillment of prophecy helps to account for this. If the prophecies apply as he is sure they do, then there is little or no need to establish any continuity between their announcement and their fulfilment—one can treat the three intervening centuries simply as a period of 'unfulfilled prophecy.' On the other hand he is anxious to assimilate this case also to his idea of development with its strong emphasis on perduring identity. When this motif dominates, then the scarce and ambiguous testimonies from the first three centuries become 'a partial fulfilment.' The two motifs seem to me to be incompatible and to generate a tension in his picture of the historical development of the papacy that is never resolved. His historical sense tells him that there was a period when nothing of the papacy was discernible, unless you count certain disparate elements which later on will combine to form papal supremacy. His theory of development, however, leads him to postulate an existing supremacy in some dormant state right back to the beginning of the church." To my mind, however, doctrinal development (and thus continuity) is congruent with the emergence in the later patristic period of realities that, while possessing a biblical basis and patristic foundations, were not explicitly known to the early Fathers. See also Maurice Nédoncelle, "La suprématie papale d'après l'Essai sur le développement de Newman," in *Parole de Dieu et sacerdoce*, ed. E. Fischer and L. Bouyer (Paris: Desclée et Cie, 1962), 139–152.

167. Newman, *A Letter Addressed to His Grace the Duke of Norfolk on Occasion of Mr. Gladstone's Recent Expostulation*, 208.

168. Newman, 209.

Newman finds Gladstone to be essentially a complacent Erastian. He observes in this vein, "It is the powers themselves, and not their distribution and allocation in the ecclesiastical body which [Gladstone] writes against."[169] The Catholic Church claims powers that in England are reserved for the State or at least are not the possession of any one ecclesial body. As Damian McElrath puts the matter, Gladstone exemplifies an "attitude . . . toward religion which was patronized by the State, assisted and cared for by it . . . but only to ensure control and domination. The Church was relegated to a secondary and soon helpless dependency. What angered Gladstone was that the Church of Rome did not find the role of a dependency to her liking and refused to play it."[170] Newman cites a Church historian who observes that the popes took over the autocratic privileges that had previously belonged to the other bishops. This point, so bemoaned by Döllinger, is for Newman evidence that the powers of the patristic Church have remained somewhere in force. Döllinger and Gladstone are mortified that the powers of the patristic Church are now in force largely in the papacy. Newman appreciates that the powers of the patristic Church are *still* in force at all.

Newman undertakes a thought experiment: What if the patristic Church's structure remained in place today, with the result that the Church was spread over almost two thousand bishoprics in diverse countries, and not unified in any concrete way under the bishop of Rome? Newman's question is whether such a Church would be less fit for dealing with the State or more so. He thinks that the State might actually find such a Church more troublesome. Rather than having to deal with the Vatican, each State would have to deal with its own local pope. Instead of one pope, "there would be a legion of ecclesiastics, each bishop with his following, each independent of the others, each with his own views, each with extraordinary powers, each with the risk of misusing them."[171] Each of the local bishops

169. Newman, 210.

170. McElrath, *The* Syllabus *of Pius IX*, 327.

171. Newman, *A Letter Addressed to His Grace the Duke of Norfolk on Occasion of Mr.*

would challenge the State for supremacy in the religious domain. Each would be stalwartly defending his own local interests. Arguably, the State should find it easier to deal with one universal pope who, while not backing down in the religious domain, nevertheless has more than local interests in view.

Newman denies that the popes, by their use (or abuse) of power, have been the real source of the concentration of power in papal hands. He thinks instead that this concentration of power arose due to certain vicissitudes of history under the providence of God. If the Muslims had not conquered Alexandria and Damascus and Jerusalem, or if the Vandals had not conquered Carthage, or if Constantinople had not come under imperial domination, who is to say that the bishop of Rome would ever have been able to concentrate power? Indeed, if England and much of Germany had not separated from Rome during the Reformation, who is to say that the bishop of Rome's power would not have become much less concentrated? Newman does not deny that the popes were ambitious and at times unscrupulous. But, as he points out, others were sometimes ambitious and unscrupulous on behalf of the bishop of Rome. Bishops from other countries actively sought to concentrate power in Rome in order to enable the Church to have a fighting chance against the rapacious "great and little tyrants of the middle age."[172]

Nor can the story boil down to a few figures, such as Leo or Gregory the Great or Gregory VII, who happened to seize the moment and ride to victory, supposedly ruining the patristic Golden Age in the process. Newman observes that even Protestant historians today often grant that "the concentration of ecclesiastical power in those centuries was simply necessary for the civilization of Europe."[173] In the past, Europe reaped benefits from centralization of ecclesiastical power. Ultimately, the responsibility for this centralization belongs to the providence that oversees doctrinal

---

Gladstone's Recent Expostulation, 210–211.

172. Newman, 212.

173. Newman, 212.

development and oversees the course of history so as to lead all things to Christ. During Gregory the Great's time, for example, Roman civilization had crumbled, and Western civilization needed a center that only the Church could provide—a point that Newman draws from Henry Hart Milman. Absent the centralization of power in the Church of Rome, Milman says, there never would have been a unified and educated Europe; instead, vastly different tribes and feudal castes, each with its own priesthoods, would have held sway.

Milman's words of praise for the centralized papacy apply to the six-hundred period between Gregory the Great and Innocent III. Newman knows plenty about papal corruption during this period, but he is aware that the popes had no monopoly on corruption. Many civilizing influences came to be during this period, thanks to the strong papacy. He remarks in this vein, "The right to warn and punish powerful men, to excommunicate kings, to preach aloud truth and justice to the inhabitants of the earth, to denounce immoral doctrines, to strike at rebellion in the garb of heresy, were the very weapons by which Europe was brought into a civilized condition."[174] Gladstone is critical of these as "rusty tools," but they can be looked at from a more positive angle: perhaps they are rusty because they served their purpose; or perhaps they are rusty because the pope and the Church do not need to resort to extraordinary measures regularly. Within Newman's own lifetime, Pius VII excommunicated Napoleon, thereby suggesting that these tools still serve an important purpose in the struggle against Erastianism. Newman quotes a Protestant historian who sees in Napoleon's fall the hand of providence, and Newman is glad to agree.

Yet Newman immediately adds: "I am far from saying that Popes are never in the wrong and are never to be resisted."[175] Without being one-sidedly negative as are Gladstone and Döllinger, he knows that popes have been corrupt and have erred in word and deed. Newman considers

174. Newman, 214.
175. Newman, 216.

that Pope Pius IX has made a number of mistakes, and Newman does not have an especially high view of the probity of the Vatican. He observes that the popes have misjudged Great Britain at various points in history. He therefore refuses "to defend the policy or the acts of particular Popes, whether before or after the great revolt from their authority in the 16th century."[176] Thus, as noted above, he is not denying the kind of accusations characteristic of Döllinger. He is simply making clear that Döllinger's perspective (and Gladstone's) is not the full story by any means. That there has been corruption, as well as seizure of power, Newman does not doubt; but the papacy can also be looked at from quite a different perspective. Papal centralization of ecclesiastical power has been a providential development of doctrine, rooted in Christ's prophetic teachings in Matthew 16:18 and elsewhere.

For Newman, all the corruption in the world, *pace* Döllinger (although Newman does not explicitly mention Döllinger), need not "at all affect, not by an hair's breadth, the validity of the resulting definition."[177] He grants that he had some doubts at first about how to receive the definition. His doubts arose from the question of whether a moral unanimity among the council fathers was necessary for a conciliar definition of a dogma. On July 27, 1870, he wrote to a friend in this vein, but he added the point that since 1845 he had always accepted, as a private theological opinion, the doctrine of papal infallibility. The council's dogmatic definition contains nothing that, in his view, contradicts Scripture or Tradition, or, for that matter, history. In this letter, he concludes that he is willing to receive the dogma as valid simply insofar as it comes from the pope and a majority of the bishops, whether or not a conciliar definition requires moral unanimity and whether or not the definition was a prudent action (he thinks it was not).

Commenting on this July 1870 letter in his *Letter to the Duke of*

176. Newman, 216–217. Newman goes on to use an image of a rock jutting up above malarial swamps: "The Rock of St. Peter on its summit enjoys a pure and serene atmosphere, but there is a great deal of Roman *malaria* at the foot of it" (Newman, 297).

177. Newman, 300.

Norfolk, he observes that it was written prior to the minority melting away. As he points out, rejecting the Vatican Council on procedural grounds would cast into profound doubt the Council of Ephesus on the same procedural grounds. He also expresses his belief that the weight given to the pope will be balanced, though certainly not reversed, by a future council. He quotes a passage from Luis de Molina to the effect that conciliar dogmatic definitions, while never in error, are generally interpreted and defined with more precision and breadth by later councils.

Gladstone holds that the Catholic Church is now openly and brazenly in rupture with the patristic age due to the recent dogmas of the Immaculate Conception and papal infallibility. By accepting excommunication, Döllinger made clear that this is his view as well. With Döllinger surely in view, Newman notes that "Gladstone . . . insists on the duty of 'maintaining the truth and authority of history, and the inestimable value of the historic spirit'; and so far of course I have the pleasure of heartily agreeing with him."[178] However, Newman crucially argues that the Protestant understanding of "the relation of History to Dogma" differs from the Catholic one.[179]

What then is the Catholic understanding of the relation of history and dogma? Gladstone, like Döllinger, holds that the Catholic Church, by dogmatically defining papal infallibility, has "repudiated ancient history."[180] The charge is not simply the neglect of history, or the garbling of the historical evidence, or even the contradicting of "certain ancient usages or doctrines to which it bears witness."[181] If any of these were the charge, then Newman himself likely could sign onto the charge at least in significant part. By holding that the Catholic Church has in fact now repudiated any continuity with the historical patristic Church, Gladstone (with Döllinger) goes beyond the notion that the Church has simply neglected or misused

178. Newman, 309.
179. Newman, 310.
180. Newman, 310.
181. Newman, 310.

history in formulating and defending the dogma of papal infallibility. Newman remarks that Gladstone "could not have used a stronger term," since the term "repudiated" suggests that the Vatican Council has, "by a formal act, cut itself off from early times, instead of professing, as it does (hypocritically, if you will, but still professing) to speak, 'supported by Holy Scripture and the decrees both of preceding Popes and General Councils,' and 'faithfully adhering to the aboriginal tradition of the Church.'"[182]

Newman well knows that the charge derives from Döllinger. Without mentioning Döllinger's name, he indicates that Döllinger is the source by whom Gladstone "is corroborated and sanctioned" on this point.[183] Newman makes clear that he does not want to critique Döllinger on Döllinger's own grounds. He puts it this way: "There are authors . . . of so commanding an authority from their learning and their honesty, that, for the purposes of discussion or of controversy, what they say may be said by anyone else without presumption or risk of confutation."[184] He states that he intends "never to say a word against" the persons of such authors (meaning Döllinger), and he makes a sorrowful implicit reference to Döllinger's refusal to accept the dogma: "Their present whereabout, wherever it is, is to me a thought full of melancholy. It is a tragical event, both for them and for us, that they have left us. It robs us of a great *prestige*; they have left none to take their place."[185]

Does Newman then respect Döllinger so much that he can only mourn, and cannot respond? No. He sets forth his position firmly: "I think them [i.e., Döllinger, although Newman mentions no names in this section] utterly wrong in what they have done and are doing; and, moreover, I agree as little in their view of history as in their acts."[186] The fundamental problem

182. Newman, 310.
183. Newman, 311.
184. Newman, 311.
185. Newman, 311.
186. Newman, 311. For background to what Newman means by a "view of history," see Nicholas Lash, *Newman on Development: The Search for an Explanation in History*. Lash remarks, "For Newman, the term 'view' refers to that synthetic, personal grasp of concrete

with Döllinger is not so much his historical insights—which Newman is willing largely to grant even if they are one-sided—but his "view of history" which has led him to abandon the Church.[187] As Newman observes, Catholic theologians give a particular place to history within the task of theology; an important place, but not the whole place. But Döllinger has given the whole place to "history." As Newman asks: "Why should Ecclesiastical History, any more than the text of Scripture, contain in it 'the whole counsel of God'? Why should private judgment be unlawful in interpreting Scripture against the voice of authority, and yet be lawful in the interpretation of history?"[188] Döllinger has shown himself to be an advocate of private judgment. When a Catholic teaching conflicts with his interpretation of Church

---

reality which was his educational and intellectual ideal. . . . A true 'view' incorporates and synthesizes data laboriously gained while, at the same time, it 'breaks through' the techniques of 'technical history and historical research.' . . . [Newman's] criticism of historians such as Gibbon was not that they interpreted their data from a coordinating philosophical viewpoint, but that the viewpoint adopted was incorrect, or the use made of it illegitimate" (Lash, 35–36).

187. See Mary Catherine Tillman, "The Definitive Third Edition of 1872: An Introduction," in *Fifteen Sermons Preached before the University of Oxford between A.D. 1826 and 1943*, ed. Mary Catherine Tillman (Notre Dame, IN: University of Notre Dame Press, 1997), vii–lii, at xxvi–xxvii, where (without reference to Döllinger or to the controversy over papal infallibility) she writes that for Newman, "one can develop a narrow, unphilosophical mind that is stuck in one view forever, like the inflexible bigot rigidly riding but one hobbyhorse. . . . Distortion becomes fixed when a single view is mistaken for the whole. Taking one abstracted aspect for the whole concrete reality or one method of approach as the only correct one is like worshipping the tabernacle or icon as the god."

188. Newman, *A Letter Addressed to His Grace the Duke of Norfolk on Occasion of Mr. Gladstone's Recent Expostulation*, 312. For background, see John Henry Newman, "Private Judgment," originally published in 1841, in Newman, *Essays Critical and Historical*, vol. 2 (London: Longmans, Green, 1895), 336–374, as well as various remarks in John Henry Newman, *Apologia Pro Vita Sua* (New York: Doubleday, 1989). In private correspondence, Gladstone accuses Newman of being the very epitome of "private judgment." Gladstone says of Newman: "He was trained (as I was) in the Evangelical School, which is beyond all others . . . the school of private judgment. By private judgment he excogitated the scheme of doctrine and thought which he taught in his Anglican works. By private judgment he grew sore with the manifold abuses and defects of the English Church; but then, also by private judgment, he measured the corruptions of the Roman, and recoiled from them" (quoted in Short, *Newman and His Contemporaries*, 238–239, citing the *Correspondence on Church and Religion of William Ewart Gladstone*, vol. 1, ed. D.C. Lathbury [London: 1910], 406). Gladstone has here misunderstood what Newman meant by "private judgment," since Newman never supposed that the rejection of private judgment entails rejecting theological interpretation.

history, he decrees that the teaching is false. Newman maintains, "They seem to me to expect from History more than History can furnish, and to have too little confidence in the Divine Promise and Providence as guiding and determining those enunciations."[189]

For Döllinger, as we have seen, the dogma of papal infallibility can only be true if it can be proven to be a patristic doctrine. Newman responds that historical tests have a place but cannot be determinative with regard to matters of Catholic truth, precisely because doctrinal development takes place under divine providence. History is important, because the Church's dogmas are not mere inventions; and yet the historical past is not the only thing, because the Church's dogmas are real developments. Newman therefore comments, "I would simply confess that no doctrine of the Church can be rigorously proved by historical evidence: but at the same time that no doctrine can be simply disproved by it."[190]

Newman goes on to specify in more detail how he conceives of the relationship of history and dogma. If biblical or patristic history clearly ruled out the possibility of a particular dogma, then Newman would not embrace the dogma. But he argues that in no case, and certainly not in the case of papal infallibility, does the study of history clearly rule out the truth of a dogma that the Catholic Church has defined. Here is how he puts the matter: "Historical evidence reaches a certain way, more or less, towards a proof of the Catholic doctrines, often nearly the whole way; sometimes it goes only as far as to point in their direction; sometimes there is only an absence of evidence for a conclusion contrary to them; nay, sometimes there is an apparent leaning of the evidence to a contrary conclusion, having to be explained."[191] In the last-named case, Newman thinks that suitable explanation can indeed be given, just as we have seen him do with regard to the gradual centralization of power by the bishop of Rome, as distinct from the

189. Newman, *A Letter Addressed to His Grace the Duke of Norfolk on Occasion of Mr. Gladstone's Recent Expostulation*, 311–312.

190. Newman, 312.

191. Newman, 312.

early Church's governance by relatively equal Apostolic Sees with Rome having a certain primacy. Divine providence has willed that the papacy and the doctrine of the papacy develop as it has done.

Emphasizing his concern about the use of private judgment in matters that pertain to divine revelation, Newman remarks, "He who believes the dogmas of the Church only because he has reasoned them out of History, is scarcely a Catholic."[192] For a Catholic, historical research is but one tool in the task of dogmatic inquiry, and it is not the results of historical research per se but rather "the Church's dogmatic use of History in which the Catholic believes."[193] This does not mean that the Catholic Church affirms dogmatic truths that are contradicted by history; Newman is not granting that Döllinger has found a real contradiction. The dogma is not nearly as maximalist as Döllinger says it is, and given that Döllinger exaggerates the solemnity of papal error. But in arriving at dogma, the Church does not solely employ history, or even primarily employ history. Certainly Athanasius did not do so in the fourth century! The Church employs historical reasoning but also, at the same time (and even more), employs "Scripture, tradition, the ecclesiastical sense or *φρόνημα*, and a subtle ratiocinative power, which in its origin is a divine gift."[194]

Does this mean that Catholic faith is not defensible and reasonable evangelization is at an end, because Catholicism is not grounded in the most up-to-date historical-critical research? Newman dismisses this suggestion as absurd, given that the Apostles themselves, when teaching new converts out of the Scriptures of Israel, did not see fit to undertake historical research into Israel's Scriptures. Just as it was perfectly rational to believe the apostolic preaching, so it is perfectly rational to believe the Church's preaching—although in both cases such assent is based not solely on reason (though reason does not contradict it), but rather comes from the gift of faith. Newman explains that "in all cases the immediate motive in the mind

192. Newman, 312.
193. Newman, 312.
194. Newman, 313.

of a Catholic for his reception of [dogmas] is, not that they are proved to him by Reason or by History, but because Revelation has declared them by means of that high ecclesiastical *Magisterium* which is their legitimate exponent."[195]

At this stage, Newman observes that there are truths that, while not easily traceable in the apostolic deposit itself, flow from truths that are more apparent in the apostolic deposit. Such truths, including papal infallibility, are recognized by the Church not simply because they can be "logically deduced in their fulness and exactness from the belief of the first centuries."[196] If this is what one supposes the theory of doctrinal development to require—logical proof on the basis of the witness of the early Church—then one has misunderstood the theory of doctrinal development.

Instead, the theory of doctrinal development begins with faith in the infallibility of the Church as part of a faith in the givenness of a divine revelation. Such faith allows for development of doctrine, so long as the "development" is not "a contradiction in thought."[197] A "development" cannot be the opposite of, or the reversal of, something that the Church has solemnly taught to be true—since if it were so, the assumption of the Church's infallibility could no longer stand and the whole edifice of "development" would collapse. A mark of the true Church is that it develops doctrine and has the capacity for doing so in a definitive, universal way. Newman agrees with Gladstone (and thus also with Döllinger) that, in the dogmas of 1854 and 1870, the Church proceeded in a manner that could raise eyebrows. But he insists that neither in 1854 nor in 1870 did the Church repudiate or pervert "the testimony of history."[198] History testifies to a developing papal office, rooted in Scripture and the Fathers, and concretized from the outset in the bishop of Rome.

Newman ends this section with a brief discussion of the case of Pope

195. Newman, 313.
196. Newman, 314.
197. Newman, 314.
198. Newman, 314.

Honorius, condemned as a heretic by the Sixth Ecumenical Council. He clearly thinks that this case is the most concerning of all the ones brought forward by Döllinger. In letters in response to Patriarch Sergius of Constantinople, Pope Honorius approved an opinion favored by Sergius, the very opinion condemned by the Sixth Ecumenical Council some forty years later. Newman observes that Pope Honorius' letters would violate the Vatican Council's definition of papal infallibility only if these letters were instances of solemn, *ex cathedra* dogmatic teaching. An examination of Honorius' letters indicates that he had no such intention; rather, he was contributing to an ongoing discussion. Honorius may have been a heretic, but, since he died before the matter was decided, he never displayed the obstinacy of a heretic and so we cannot determine what he would have decided on this matter.[199]

In the same context, Newman also makes a brief reference to the validity of the scriptural argument in favor of papal infallibility, which, as will be recalled, Döllinger opposed on the grounds that the Church Fathers did not interpret verses such as Matthew 16:18 as a reference to the primacy of the bishop of Rome. Citing Joseph Butler, to whom he is so often indebted, Newman argues that, though the Fathers are privileged witnesses, their testimony does not exhaust the truth of Scripture. There can be further enhancement of the understanding of Scripture beyond what the Fathers perceived. Newman concludes, "What has the long history of the contest for and against the Pope's infallibility been, but a growing insight through the centuries into the meaning of those three texts [Matt. 16:18; Luke 22:32; John 21:15–17]?"[200] Döllinger's critique takes too rigidly the principle of interpreting Scripture according to the mind of the Fathers. Petrine primacy and the infallibility of the Church—to which both the New

199. See also John Page's assessment of Newman's treatment of the case of Pope Honorius, in Page, *What Will Dr. Newman Do?*, 313.

200. Newman, *A Letter Addressed to His Grace the Duke of Norfolk on Occasion of Mr. Gladstone's Recent Expostulation*, 319.

Testament and the early Church testify—serve firmly to ground, as the history of the Church unfolds, the developed doctrine of papal infallibility.

Conclusion

Although more could be said—since Newman proceeds to devote a final chapter of his *Letter to the Duke of Norfolk* to interpreting and further defending the Vatican definition of the dogma of papal infallibility—I will stop here. As we have seen, Newman finds in Döllinger's perspective both the principle of private judgment and a polemical one-sidedness according to which every development in papal primacy from the past thousand years is simply a further demonstration of papal rapacity. The result is theological rationalism: Döllinger accepts only the contents of faith that he thinks can be demonstrated by historians to have been present and valuable in the early patristic period. For Döllinger, the development of doctrine does not really continue after the early patristic reception of the apostolic deposit.[201]

201. Howard explores Döllinger's relationship to the "Old Catholic" movement, with which Döllinger strongly sympathized but did not formally join (see *The Pope and the Professor*, 189). As Howard notes, "Anglicans were arguably the most smitten by the movement" (Howard, 187; cf. 200–202). Edward Pusey, however, decisively rejected the two Bonn ecumenical conferences of 1874 and 1875, due in part to their repudiation of the *filioque*, although Döllinger and Pusey agreed in rejecting the dogmas of Mary's Immaculate Conception and papal infallibility (even if Pusey wished to allow the Immaculate Conception to be held as a theological opinion). See Pusey, *On the Clause "and the Son" in Regard to the Eastern Church and the Bonn Conference: A Letter to the Rev. H.P. Liddon* (London: J.H. Parker, 1876), and Chapman, *The Fantasy of Reunion*, 251–260. Chapman discusses at length the two Bonn conferences, with special attention to the role of Pusey's disciple Henry Parry Liddon as well as to Gladstone's "prominent role behind the scenes" (*The Fantasy of Reunion*, 226). For further background, see the *Report of the Union Conferences, Held from August 10 to 16, 1875, at Bonn, under the Presidency of Dr. von Döllinger*, ed. Heinrich Reusch, trans. Samuel Buel (New York: T. Whittaker, 1876). In his preface to this volume, the Episcopalian Robert Joseph Nevin (son of the well-known Mercersburg theologian John Williamson Nevin) charged the Roman Catholic Church with doctrinal corruption: "The Roman Catholic Church has, in the most profoundly real sense, been made a *new Church* [by the Vatican Council]. Its very name now may well be felt to be something almost obsolete. . . . The Vatican Council gave the *coup de grace* to the long-tortured constitution of the old Church, and formally committed the Roman Communion to the new Latin creation. It has cut the Roman Church

Newman rejects this viewpoint, insisting that the very same principle that allows for doctrinal development in the patristic era must allow for it up to the present day. In fact, only a Church that has clear mechanisms to enable such development to take place, within the context of theological controversies and cultural shifts, can be the true continuation of the patristic Church. Papal infallibility is thus both a development of doctrine and one that helps to ensure that the patristic Church's ability to teach universally continues today.

In a footnote appended in 1871 to his 1840 Anglican essay on "The Catholicity of the Anglican Church," Newman allows that it is possible to imagine *theoretically* a future in which the pope, for whatever reason, was no longer able to exercise his proper role in the Church at least for a time, so that the early patristic model would be revived de facto; and in such a situation, he says, the Church would remain the Church.[202] Paul Misner makes much of this supposition, which he finds to be an "unabashed appeal to *fact* apart from dogmatic considerations."[203] In Misner's view, Newman's

loose from all obligation to historical descent from Christ and the apostles and has added as well heresy to her former guilt of schism" (Nevin, "Preface," in *Report of the Union Conferences*, iii–xlix, at iv–vi, ix, xiv). See also the discussion in Owen Chadwick, "Döllinger and Reunion," in *Christian Authority: Essays in Honour of Henry Chadwick*, ed. G.R. Evans (Oxford: Oxford University Press, 1988), 296–334.

202. In response to a point made in "The Catholicity of the Anglican Church"—"Why should it not be the intention of divine Providence, as on the one hand, still to recognize His Church when contracted into a monarchy, so also not to forsake her when relaxed and dissolved again into a number of aristocratic fragments?"—Newman appends the following footnote: "'Why not?' because, in fact, it is *not* so dissolved; doubtless, were it so dissolved, were the Pope, as indistinct a power as he was in the first centuries, and the Bishops as practically independent, the Church would still be the Church" ("The Catholicity of the Anglican Church," in *Essays Critical and Historical*, vol. 2, 1–73, at 44).

203. Misner, *Papacy and Development*, 126, emphasis added. Misner rejects the "imperial scheme" of the Church and argues that Newman, too, undermines it powerfully in his 1877 Preface to the third edition of his *Via Media*, thereby opening "the door in principle to the thoroughgoing revision of ecclesiology which is now underway with the aid of the whole modern instrumentarium of historical and theological scholarship" (Misner, 173). For Misner, "Newman held the Christian church to be a continuation of the Jewish in an extraordinarily uncomplicated sense" (Misner, 91), and Misner complains about "Newman's extreme and all too realistic kingdom ecclesiology" and "ecclesiological imperialism" (Misner, 179). I think Misner is mistaken here. Newman's ecclesiology, precisely as an ecclesiology of the inaugurated

point amounts to an admission that historical "fact" can override (both in the past and in the future) the dogma of papal infallibility, so that the Church could today choose to return to its pre–Vatican I form.

Newman, however, takes care not to set history (or "fact") *against* dogma. Under God's providence, the two go hand in hand. Just because the dogma of papal infallibility is related to specific, providential historical circumstances, its enduring truth is not thereby insecure. Whatever might happen to the Catholic Church in the future, Catholics will know that the bishop of Rome—the successor of Peter—teaches infallibly when he speaks *ex cathedra* about faith and morals.

In a letter of 1874, Newman told Döllinger's friend Alfred Plummer that Döllinger's actions since the council, including his support for the "Old Catholics" and for their effort to create a new Church, filled Newman with deep dismay.[204] No wonder, since what is at stake—as both Newman and Döllinger believed—is nothing less than whether there today exists an heir to the Church of the Fathers.[205] Döllinger believed that because the

---

kingdom, is astutely biblical and patristic. As Misner rightly observes, "It was to him inherently implausible that this vast church should not be the [inaugurated, but not consummated!] Kingdom whose features he found already in Old Testament prophecy" (Misner, 180).

204. Cited in Howard, *The Pope and the Professor*, 204. In a letter to Pastor Widmann of Todtnau, 18 October 1874, published in Ignaz von Döllinger, *Declarations and Letters on the Vatican Decrees 1869–1887*, authorized translation (Edinburgh: T.&T. Clark, 1891), 117–120, Döllinger states, "I belong by conviction to the Old Catholic Community"—although he did not formally become a member (Döllinger, 117). Toward the end of the letter, he protests vigorously against "the solemn proclamation of Alphonse Liguori as *Doctor ecclesiae*, consequently classing him with Augustine, Ambrose, etc.,—a man whose false morals, perverse worship of the Virgin, constant use of the grossest fables and forgeries, makes his writings a storehouse of lies. In the whole range of Church history I do not know a single example of such a terrible and such a pernicious confusion" (Döllinger, 119–120).

205. I agree with Misner, therefore, when he observes that "Newman continued . . . to recur first and last to the total church, treating the position of the pope as a question of secondary importance" (Misner, *Papacy and Development*, 178). Yet "secondary importance" can still be high importance. For Misner's perspective (shaped by his own historical context in the immediate postconciliar period), see also his "Newman and Theological Pluralism," in *New Dimensions in Religious Experience*, ed. George Devine (Staten Island, NY: Alba House, 1971), 233–244; Misner, "Newman's Concept of Revelation and the Development of Doctrine," *Heythrop Journal* 11 (1970): 32–47. Misner's own perspective is well expressed in the description of Newman with which he concludes his book: "His overriding concern at the end

Church of the Fathers knew no infallible pope with universally recognized jurisdiction (even though papal primacy was present), the dogma was a corruption. Newman believed that the dogma was a valid development of papal primacy (or the Petrine office), coextensive with the continuance of the very same Church of the Fathers beyond the patristic period. On this point, Newman the Anglican—who long held that the papacy was the Antichrist—and Döllinger the Catholic changed places. Indeed, upon his excommunication in 1871, the University of Oxford awarded Döllinger an honorary doctorate.

of his career was that none of the functions of the church should atrophy through the overbearing, perhaps pathological, vitality of the office of supreme direction given in the papacy" (*Papacy and Development*, 181).

CONCLUSION

How is it that a Church that deems itself able to develop doctrine does not end by corrupting it? It seemed evident to Gibbon and Francis Newman that the whole Catholic dogmatic system was just one doctrinal corruption after another, and their solution was to get rid of the whole thing. By comparison, Pusey and Döllinger believed that almost all Catholic doctrines were true. They believed that it was only in the nineteenth century that the (Roman) Catholic Church really began corrupting doctrine in a major way, even if the seeds of the Catholic Church's demise had been sown in earlier centuries.

By 1845 and for the remainder of his life, John Henry Newman believed that the doctrines of the Catholic Church—about the Trinity, Christ, the Church, Mary, the seven sacraments, the papacy, purgatory, and so on—are faithful and ontologically true developments of the Gospel given by Jesus Christ and handed on by the Apostles. Ever since his death, however, some Catholics have interpreted Newman's developmental theory along religiously liberal lines. In the introduction, I discussed the fact that for some Catholics today, Newman's theory insists far too strongly on the ontological truth of all solemnly taught Catholic doctrine. But a significant number of Catholic theologians do what they can to claim Newman for religious liberalism. Some theologians, for example, find the needed leeway in his 1859 *On Consulting the Faithful in Matters of Doctrine*, which they understand to teach the view that the laity can, by their lack of consent, nullify a solemnly taught Catholic doctrine—a view that Newman himself eventually explicitly repudiated, but not without first considering.

As noted above, against the emerging Ultramontanist movement, Newman made the point in *On Consulting the Faithful* that the doctrinal heritage of the Church is not solely enunciated by councils and popes but also is handed on in the Church "by liturgies, rites, ceremonies, and customs, by events, disputes, movements, and all those other phenomena which are comprised under the name of history."[1] Newman explains that it follows from this richer understanding of Tradition that "the body of the faithful is one of the witnesses to the fact of the tradition of revealed doctrine," and indeed also that "their *consensus* through Christendom is the voice of the Infallible Church."[2]

On the one hand, Newman's meaning is plain: among the "witnesses to Tradition," along with councils and papal teachings, stands the "consensus" of the faithful.[3] Not only the clergy but also the laity participates in the

1. John Henry Newman, *On Consulting the Faithful in Matters of Doctrine*, ed. John Coulson (Lanham, MD: Sheed & Ward, 2006), 63.

2. Newman, 63. Given the clarification that Newman makes in his 1875 *Letter to the Duke of Norfolk*, Newman is not contending here that dogma is only true and binding if and when it is received by the consensus of the whole Church. Richard F. Costigan provides helpful context here with respect to Vatican I and Gallicanism: "The dogmatic constitution *Pastor Aeternus*, in its finished form, states that the definitions of the Roman Pontiff are irreformable 'ex sese, non autem ex consensu Ecclesiae' (of themselves, and not from the consensus of the Church). This phraseology is clearly calculated to counter Article 4 of the Declaration of the Gallican Clergy of 1682. That article asserts that the pope does indeed have the leading role ('praecipuas partes') in teaching the faith to the whole Church but stipulates that his judgment is not irreformable 'unless the consensus of the Church is present with it' (nisi Ecclesiae consensus accesserit). The determination to prevent any possible revival of this idea associated with Gallicanism, with its evident nonacceptance of a totally monarchical papacy, was the reason why the majority refused to allow any mention of the episcopate in the text of the definition. It might somehow provide a possible opening to future 'Gallicans'" (Costigan, *The Consensus of the Church and Papal Infallibility: A Study in the Background of Vatican I* [Washington, DC: The Catholic University of America Press, 2005], 2). Costigan's book firmly favors the Gallican view, as does Klaus Schatz, *Papal Primacy: From Its Origins to the Present,* trans. John A. Otto and Linda M. Maloney (Collegeville, MN: Liturgical, 1996). If I understand him correctly, Costigan holds that popes can and do err in solemn teaching on matters of faith (see Costigan, 204). For further discussion of Vatican I as a response to Gallicanism, see Shaun Blanchard, "Settling Old Scores: *Pastor Aeternus* as the Final Defeat of Early Modern Opponents of Ultramontanism," *Newman Studies Journal* 17, no. 1 (2020): 24–51.

3. In his *On Divine Tradition* (second edition 1875), Johannes Franzelin addresses this topic at length and argues, "Although the faithful, whether individually from their ranks or the whole people, do not possess the faculty of authentically teaching (*docendi*), on the other hand they do possess the office of learning (*discendi*). . . . The 'Catholic sense' of the whole Christian people and a consensus on a dogma of Christian faith ought to be considered one of the criteria of divine Tradition" (Franzelin, *On Divine Tradition*, trans. Ryan Grant, ed.

authoritative handing on of divine revelation. Thus, focusing on the people with power in the Church—popes and bishops—does not suffice for understanding what is meant by a living Tradition; indeed, a focus on power distorts the matter.

On the other hand, Newman's concerns about doctrinal corruption are hardly set to the side here. Newman does not mean that when the consensus of the faithful becomes difficult to perceive—as for instance during the Reformation period, when a large portion of Catholics (led by the Reformers) rose up against many Catholic doctrines in the name of *sola scriptura*—the solution is to get rid of the contested doctrines, so that only doctrines most clearly supported by a supposed "consensus of the faithful" remain in place. Instead, Newman is aware that one has to ask who counts as "the faithful" and what it means to have faith.

Newman drew his Catholic understanding of the *consensus fidelium* from those theologians who sought to defend the truth of the doctrine of the Immaculate Conception by appeal to centuries of devotion and liturgical practice.[4] On this view, the *consensus* or *sensus fidelium* is "distinct (not

---

Chad Ripperger [n.p.: Sensus Traditionis, 2016], 147). Franzelin does not discuss Newmanian doctrinal development, but instead argues that by the Apostles "the whole revealed doctrine was transmitted to posterity. . . . The innate nature and proper principle of the Church was so constituted by its divine founder, that faith and discipline divinely handed down first by Christ himself and with the dictation of the Holy Spirit by the Apostles, was propagated from generation to generation through the ministry and the always authentic vigorous and living Magisterium" (Franzelin, 137–139).

4. For further analysis, see Benjamin J. King, "*Sensus Fidelium*," in *The Oxford Handbook of John Henry Newman*, ed. Frederick D. Aquino and Benjamin J. King (Oxford: Oxford University Press, 2018), 264–283. King observes that for Newman, *sensus fidelium* signifies Church members' "'instinct' or 'sense'—in Greek, *phronēma* (as in Philippians 3:15)—rather than a full understanding of what the Church believes. . . . To put it colloquially, the faithful 'get' the faith even though they may not be able to articulate it" (King, 264). King adds that Newman's approach is "part of a long history [going back to the days of the Church Fathers and earlier] of claiming more 'agreement of the faithful'. . . in matters of doctrine than in fact existed" (King, 264). For Newman, according to King, the first "*consensus*" of the faithful is their consent to be taught. King shows the dialectical significance of Newman's conversations in 1859 with Bishop Ullathorne in light of the latter's *The Immaculate Conception of the Mother of God: An Exposition* (London: Richardson and Son, 1855). Toward the end of his essay, King explores both the issue of the contemporary Catholic laity's general non-reception of traditional Catholic sexual teachings, and the fact that Newman's notion of a doctrinal

separate) from the teaching of their pastors" and indeed mirrors it.[5] The infallibility of the Church, under the Holy Spirit's guidance, depends as much on the laity as on the powerful clergy, but the laity's role does not mean that the laity of any particular era (or the clergy either) is empowered to overturn solemnly taught doctrine of prior eras.

Another issue that sometimes arises today with respect to doctrinal corruption comes from Newman's 1877 "Preface to the Third Edition of *The Via Media of the Anglican Church*." In this work, Newman addresses a variety of issues, but the pertinent one here is whether the sin of simony renders null and void all sacramental acts of a person who has been raised to the episcopacy or papacy by simony.[6] The question is a significant one because some eminent theologians over the centuries have claimed that simony has this effect. If so, then given the extent of simony in the history of the Church, it would follow that valid apostolic succession in the Catholic Church has long ago come to an end. If the efficacy of the sacraments

---

"consensus" among the faithful is an instance of idealized history. See also King, "The 'Consent of the Faithful' from *1 Clement* to the Anglican Covenant," *Journal of Anglican Studies* 12, no. 1 (2014): 7–36; Roderick Strange, "Newman on Consulting the Faithful: Context, Content, and Consequences," *New Blackfriars* 98, no. 1074 (2017): 134–146; and the highly optimistic perspective—presuming the relative ease of possessing a "common faith" and "common witness"—of Samuel D. Femiano, *Infallibility of the Laity: The Legacy of Newman* (New York: Herder and Herder, 1967), though Femiano offers a generally helpful discussion of Newman's theology of the laity.

5. Newman, *On Consulting the Faithful in Matters of Doctrine*, 66; cf. 71. Jan Hendrik Walgrave comments in 1985, "Through the all-pervading influence of the modern media the principles and opinions of a world which on the whole is no longer Christian are as efficaciously 'introjected' (Marcuse) in the minds of professed Catholics than in those of others. If there is in the Catholic world still a minority of 'faithful' in Newman's sense, the majority is actually more worldly minded and may be said to be inwardly estranged from their traditional faith" (Walgrave, "Newman's *On Consulting the Faithful in Matters of Doctrine*," in *The Teaching Authority of Believers*, ed. Johann Baptist Metz and Edward Schillebeeckx, English language ed. Marcus Lefébure [Edinburgh: T&T Clark, 1985], 23–30, at 29).

6. For discussion of Newman's "Preface," whose significance is greater than I can show here—though its richly nuanced argument can easily be misunderstood—see Ian Ker, *John Henry Newman: A Biography* (Oxford: Oxford University Press, 1988), 701–707; Andrew Meszaros, *The Prophetic Church: History and Doctrinal Development in John Henry Newman and Yves Congar* (Oxford: Oxford University Press, 2016), 152–157; Eamon Duffy, *John Henry Newman: A Very Brief History* (London: SPCK, 2019), 67–72.

depended upon the purity of the ministers—as logic may sometimes seem to dictate—then the sacramental system would not last long.

Newman notes therefore that the Catholic Church has fittingly made judgments about such matters, not by application of theoretical principle, but by practical reflection or "generous expediency," trusting in Christ's promise to preserve his Church.[7] In distinguishing the "Regal" from the "Prophetical" office of the Church, he observes for example that the papal acceptance of the validity of sectarian baptism was a minority position, rejected by various Synods and by Church Fathers including Clement of Alexandria, Tertullian, Cyprian, Athanasius, Basil the Great, Ambrose, and others. Newman concludes that "whatever is great refuses to be reduced to human rule [i.e., strict logic]," and so we must not be surprised to find the Church "presenting to us an admirable consistency and unity in word and deed, as her general characteristic, but crossed and discredited now and then by apparent anomalies which need, and which claim, of our hands an exercise of faith."[8]

---

7. See John Henry Newman, "Preface to the Third Edition," in Newman, *The Via Media of the Anglican Church*, vol. 1 (London: Basil Montagu Pickering, 1877), xv–xciv, at lxxxix.

8. Newman, xciv. For what happens when no apparent anomalies are allowed, see John Henry Newman, "Sermon 14: Wisdom, as Contrasted with Faith and with Bigotry," in Newman, *Fifteen Sermons Preached before the University of Oxford between A.D. 1826 and 1943*, ed. Mary Katherine Tillman (Notre Dame, IN: University of Notre Press, 1997), 278–311, at 310–311: "Persons of narrow views are often perplexed, and sometimes startled and unsettled, by the difficulties of their position. What they did not know, or what they knew but had not weighed, suddenly presses upon their notice. Then they become impatient that they cannot make their proofs clear and try to make a forcible riddance of objections. They look about for new arguments and put violence on Scripture or on history. They show a secret misgiving about the truth of their principles, by shrinking from the appearance of defeat or from occasional doubt within. They become alarmists, and they forget that the issue of all things, and the success of their own cause (if it be what they think it is), is sealed and secured by Divine promise; and sometimes, in this conflict between broad fact and narrow principle, the hard material breaks their tools; they are obliged to give up their principles. A state of uncertainty and distress follows, and, in the end, perhaps, bigotry is supplanted by general scepticism. They who thought their own ideas could measure all things, end in thinking that even a Divine Oracle is unequal to the task." I note that this bigotry or dogmatism is not synonymous with systematic thinking, in Newman's view, although systematizers *can* be rationalists: see Frederick D. Aquino, *An Integrative Habit of Mind: John Henry Newman on the Path to Wisdom* (Dekalb, IL: Northern Illinois University Press, 2012); and Mary

Newman may be misunderstood here to be saying that sometimes—though rarely—there is in fact acceptable doctrinal corruption. In fact, he holds the opposite. As we saw above, his point is simply that it will not always be possible for either the theologian or the historian to tie up all loose ends. The theory of doctrinal development, in other words, is not another form of rationalism that answers to the fallen human desire to prove everything in matters of faith, as though faith were so uncomplicated as to allow for logical demonstration. In his fourteenth University Sermon, preached in 1841 when he was beginning to move toward his theory of doctrinal development, Newman bemoans rationalistic Christians who have "clear and decisive explanations always ready of the sacred mysteries of faith," and who accept no divergence from their own private explanations.[9] Such Christians have substituted the product of their own minds for the inexhaustible word of God—whereas dogmas not only provide light and truth, but also leave room for the "darkness" of divine mysteries that far exceed our finite capacity to understand.[10]

The point is that for Newman, firm adherence to the dogmatic principle and to the intelligibility of the doctrinal development of the apostolic deposit of faith must be distinguished from *dogmatism*. Newman has no problem with the fact that doctrinal developments such as papal infallibility, while intelligibly grounded in Scripture and Tradition, do not have such logical force as to countermand absolutely every concern or problem. As Andrew Meszaros observes, the doctrinal development of the Church "shows its conditioning, its historical life, its meandering, searching, and reacting—its experimentation and its error."[11] Doctrinal development displays this historical life without thereby negating the "absolute and

Catherine Tillman, "The Definitive Third Edition of 1872: An Introduction," in *Fifteen Sermons Preached before the University of Oxford between A.D. 1826 and 1943*, vii–lii, at xxvi–xxxvi.

9. Newman, "Sermon 14," 306.

10. See Marial Corona, "Newman and Ratzinger on Mystery," forthcoming.

11. Meszaros, *The Prophetic Church*, 156.

normative status" of the Church's solemn doctrine.[12] Historians may not be able to demonstrate with strict logic this or that element pertaining to doctrinal development, but, in the case of solemnly taught doctrines, historians (and theologians) will be able to make a reasonable case for the presence of a development rather than a corruption. A clear contradiction or rupture in solemn doctrine would be doctrinal corruption. Such a contradiction is perfectly imaginable: for instance, one could imagine that (were it not for the Holy Spirit's guidance) the Catholic Church could eventually teach that confirmation's status as a sacrament is uncertain, or that a valid and consummated sacramental marriage between two Catholics is not absolutely indissoluble, or even that Jesus did not rise bodily from the dead but instead "rose" in the hearts of the disciples. Such a rupture would make all Catholic dogmas to be fundamentally reversible under new circumstances—the very opposite of Newmanian doctrinal development.

When faced with the messiness of history, religious liberalism adopts the solution of identifying as "development" what could only be a chain of doctrinal corruptions, if indeed (as religious liberalism denies) there ever was a divinely revealed apostolic deposit to be corrupted.[13] For religious liberalism, there is nothing but an ever-changing doctrinal expression of a universal religious experience grounded in Jesus. The other extreme is taken by religious traditionalism, which shies away from the often-messy historicity of doctrinal development, including the historical context of Jesus

12. Meszaros, 156.

13. Owen Chadwick presents Lord Acton ultimately taking this view of Newman's theory of development: "Acton took this unrevolutionary thinker to have a revolutionary force in one idea. The Church is more profound than hierarchs. It is the vessel of a people's prayers. . . . What the idea of development did for the Church was to allow it to grow out of error; it meant that the consensus fidelium could slowly correct what Popes and councils of bishops had decreed" (Chadwick, *Acton and History* [Cambridge: Cambridge University Press, 1998], 134). To his credit, Chadwick recognizes that this judgment about Newmanian doctrinal development does not "stand up to critical inquiry. Acton was not getting these doctrines out of Newman but using Newman as a peg on which to hang . . . things he thought vital for the progress of human thought" (Chadwick, 134). Chadwick appears to side here with Acton, whom he considers to have been "far more learned than Newman" (Chadwick, 135).

himself. For both religious liberals and religious traditionalists (as distinct from those who recognize the historicity of doctrine without falling into a historicist view of doctrine), Newman's writings are suspect, even if occasionally useful.

As an example of religious traditionalism as Newman perceived it, one might mention Henry Manning's 1861 remark (prior to succeeding Cardinal Wiseman, who died in 1865): "The one truth which has saved me is the Infallibility of the Vicar of Jesus Christ, as the only true and perfect form of the Infallibility of the Church, and therefore of all divine faith, unity, and obedience."[14] In fact, the infallibility of the pope hardly preserves Catholics from all difficulties, since, as history shows, not all the words of the pope are true or helpful. The pope has a significant role, but Manning exaggerates it.[15] No doubt, a form of Ultramontanism can equally affect those who style themselves "progressives," depending upon who holds the papal office.

14. See Edmund Purcell, *Life of Cardinal Manning*, 2 vols., (London: Macmillan, 1896), 2:160, cited in Kenneth L. Parker, "Henry Manning and Neo-Ultramontanism: The Anglican Context for an Oxford Movement Convert's Faith in Papal Infallibility," in *Authority, Dogma, and History: The Role of the Oxford Movement Converts in the Papal Infallibility Debates*, ed. Kenneth L. Parker and Michael J. Pahls (Bethesda, MD: Academica, 2009), 95–113, at 97. See also Adrian Lüchinger, *Päpstliche Unfehlbarkeit bei Henry Edward Manning und John Henry Newman* (Freiburg, CH: Universitäts Verlag, 2001); and Eamon Duffy, *Saints and Sinners: A History of the Popes*, 2nd ed. (New Haven, CT: Yale University Press, 2001), 299: "Manning and his associates wanted history without tears, a living oracle who could short-circuit human limitation. They wanted to confront the uncertainties of their age with instant assurance, revelation on tap." For the argument that "Manning is more accurately described as holding a 'moderate' view of infallibility similar to the one defined at the First Vatican Council and held by Cardinal John Henry Newman," see Christian D. Washburn, "The First Vatican Council, Archbishop Henry Manning, and Papal Infallibility," *Catholic Historical Review* 102, no. 4 (2016): 712–745, at 712. Washburn grants that Manning appears to imply a maximalist understanding of papal infallibility in Manning, *The Vatican Decrees in Their Bearing on Civil Allegiance* (London: Longmans, Green, 1875), 14; and Manning, *The Centenary of Saint Peter and the General Council: A Pastoral Letter to the Clergy* (London: Longmans, Green, 1867), 33–34. See also James Pereiro's *Cardinal Manning: An Intellectual Biography* (Oxford: Clarendon, 1998).

15. See, however, James Pereiro's "Crossed Visions—The Anglican Manning's Opinion of Rome and the Catholic Manning's Thoughts on Canterbury," in *By Whose Authority? Newman, Manning and the Magisterium*, ed. V. Alan McClelland (Bath: Downside Abbey, 1996), 204–243, where Pereiro describes the Anglican Manning's concern about the Roman Catholic doctrine of the Magisterium: "The Church would, thus, be a living and infallible

Catholic religious liberalism has many adherents today, and its worldview is articulated well by Peter Hünermann as follows: "Those who believe and who affirm the eschatological truth of Christ are called to accept a radical openness, a theological ignorance, the radical impossibility of complete self-determination, the impossibility of turning history into a straight line."[16] In light of what he deems to be the post–Vatican II awareness of "ambiguity in the authority of the Catholic Church," Hünermann insists upon "emphasizing the Spirit, and not the letter."[17] On this view, Newman's denial of doctrinal corruption in the Catholic Church could only be the result of a lack of historical consciousness. Hünermann suggests that whatever "continuity" there may be in Catholic teaching will come about through an embrace of "radical openness" and "theological ignorance," grounded upon the ever-new "Spirit" that moves the Church forward into the "eschatological truth of Christ." One thing is certain: this is not Newmanian doctrinal development but instead is an embrace of doctrinal corruption that, when all is said and done, renders Christianity devoid of truth-content prior to the eschaton. Indeed, if we are being "radically open" and practicing "theological ignorance," we cannot really know that there *is* a distinct divine "Holy Spirit," let alone a real "eschatological truth of Christ."

In *John Henry Newman on Truth and Its Counterfeits*, Reinhard Hütter provides an appropriate response to such perspectives. While recognizing the presence of significant change as part of the development of doctrine,

judge of interpretation. Manning saw an obvious danger in this principle: when doctrine is 'tied to follow the utterance of a *living* voice . . . [it] must vary with its living expositor'" (204). For the Anglican Manning, says Pereiro, such variation had happened with the result that "doctrinal corruptions had found their way . . . into the Roman Church; corruptions that Rome had tried to impose on other churches as points of necessary belief for salvation" (Pereiro, 204–205).

16. Peter Hünermann, "Jewish-Christian Relations: A Conciliar Discovery and Its Methodological Consequences for Dogmatic Theology," in *The Catholic Church and the Jewish People: Recent Reflections from Rome*, ed. Philip A. Cunningham, Norbert J. Hofmann, and Joseph Sievers (New York: Fordham University Press, 2007), 113–126, at 121.

17. Hünermann, 123.

Hütter criticizes those whom he terms "ecclesial presentists."[18] He sums up their perspective succinctly: "Ecclesial presentism holds the church to be a self-actuating and self-norming body empowered by the Spirit. Rupture is an inbuilt moment in this dynamic. It is the Spirit-granted liberation from a past that once was the self-actuation of what is now the church of the past."[19] Hütter offers an equally sharp criticism of religious traditionalism or "antiquarianism."

Recall that in repudiating religious liberalism, Newman insisted that doctrinal development means that *every* "new truth which is promulgated, if it is to be called new, must be at least homogeneous, cognate, implicit, viewed relatively to the old truth."[20] At the same time, Newman was firmly associated with the "liberal" side of English Catholicism, at least by comparison with many of his fellow converts.[21] The key to

---

18. Reinhard Hütter, *John Henry Newman on Truth and Its Counterfeits: A Guide for Our Times* (Washington, DC: The Catholic University of America Press, 2020), 134. For a study of Newman that ultimately is more in accord with Hünermann's perspective than with Hütter's, see Roman Siebenrock, *Wahrheit, Gewissen und Geschichte: Eine systematisch-theologisch Rekonstruktion des Wirkens John Henry Kardinal Newmans* (Sigmaringendorf, DE: Glock und Lutz, 1996).

19. Hütter, *John Henry Newman on Truth and Its Counterfeits*, 134. Hütter recognizes that contemporary theologians often appeal to a utopian eschatological future that stands as "the blueprint for the self-actualization of the emergent church of the present and the criterion by which the outgoing church, now the church of the past, is purged, corrected, and remodeled" (Hütter, 134). As Hans Urs von Balthasar succinctly defines religious liberalism or "modernism": "The central presupposition of modernism . . . is that every objective dogmatic proposition must be measured in terms of its suitability to the religious subject," who is ever changing (Balthasar, *Love Alone Is Credible*, trans. D.C. Schindler [San Francisco: Ignatius Press, 2004], 40).

20. John Henry Newman, *Apologia Pro Vita Sua* (New York: Doubleday, 1989), 329–330.

21. For helpful background to the *Syllabus* and to the infallibility debate—placing both in the context of the broader politics of the day—see Nicholas Atkin and Frank Tallett, *Priests, Prelates and People: A History of European Catholicism since 1750* (Oxford: Oxford University Press, 2003), 101–141, including the discussion of the role of Count Charles de Montalambert, who argued at an 1863 conference that "the Church in any particular country should no longer depend upon state power and financial wherewithal to sustain its activities. Catholics should especially dissociate themselves from reactionary regimes. Instead, they should be prepared to argue their case on equal terms with other denominations and those of no denomination at all. Tolerance, even when this allowed error to exist, was preferable to intolerance [i.e., the Inquisition]" (Atkin and Tallett, 134–135).

understanding Newman's perspective both as an Anglican and as a Catholic, then, is to begin with his sense of the Church's Spirit-guided mediation of divine revelation in Jesus Christ. Christopher Cimorelli observes, "One of the goals of the Oxford Movement was to ensure the church's autonomy from the state, at the very least in doctrinal matters," since the Tractarians perceived that the ongoing "pattern of secularization . . . was indicative of a failure to understand that God had entered history and revealed divine truths to humanity."[22] The Oxford Movement recognized that if one believes there is a God whose presence and action undergird all finite and historical realities (the "sacramental principle"), then the case for real continuity or identity-in-difference in the handing on of the apostolic deposit of faith (the "dogmatic principle") becomes plausible—without the need for a reactionary or defensive response to historical research or natural science.

In this light, the significance of Newman's early Oxford period becomes fully apparent with respect to his lifelong concern regarding doctrinal corruption. In the *Apologia Pro Vita Sua*, as we saw, Newman highlights two things that he learned from Joseph Butler and John Keble. The first was the doctrine of cumulative probabilities, and the second was the sacramental principle, the doctrine that "material phenomena are both the types and instruments of real things unseen."[23] The latter doctrine was confirmed for Newman through his reading of the early Alexandrian Fathers in the late 1820s. He remarks that their writings "were based on the mystical or sacramental principle and spoke of the various Economies or Dispensations of the Eternal. I understood them to mean that the exterior world, physical and historical, was but the outward manifestation of realities greater than itself."[24] In this way, the Church can be

22. Christopher Cimorelli, *John Henry Newman's Theology of History: Historical Consciousness, Theological 'Imaginaries,' and the Development of Tradition* (Leuven, BE: Peeters, 2017), 15, 18.

23. See John Henry Newman, *Apologia Pro Vita Sua*, 139; cf. 132–133.

24. Newman, 145–146.

profoundly immersed in historical change, even while communicating unchanging divine realities in history.

Gibbon assumed that there is no God behind historical and natural phenomena, and therefore he interpreted all history as being about intraworldly power relationships. Gibbon deemed paganism to be good because it supposedly resulted in religious harmony and tolerance in the political sphere, whereas Judaism and Christianity fostered the political disorder of fanatical violence and persecution. Gibbon supposed that the proclamation of Jesus' divinity diverged from the original teaching of the Jewish Jesus, and thus all Christian dogma is a corruption. By contrast, Newman began with the sacramental principle, which makes plausible a belief in divine revelation. Much more than Gibbon, he was aware of the violence and persecution built into the Roman Empire itself, but he did not reduce everything to politics. He viewed Athanasius as a defender of the truth of the Gospel, and contemporary biblical scholars have vindicated him by showing that the proclamation of Jesus' divinity was present from the outset of Jewish Christianity.

Against Erastian threats to the integrity of the (Anglican) Church, Newman joined Froude in seeking to insist upon the limits of State power vis-à-vis the Church. Cimorelli points out that although "Froude . . . was more favorably disposed toward the revolutionary spirit" with respect to disestablishment, Newman and Keble were deeply influenced by Froude's anti-Erastian arguments, since "the constitutional reforms of 1828–33 revealed the impossibility of maintaining the status quo, and called for something more than a mere conservative response."[25] This "something more" was a revival, in Anglican minds and hearts, of belief that the Church was founded by Jesus Christ and endowed with gifts that neither the State nor Church leaders have a right to alter or negate. In appealing to the patristic witness to the doctrinal and sacramental gifts given the Church, the Oxford Movement maintained that only a reaffirmation of such "Catholic"

25. Cimorelli, *John Henry Newman's Theology of History*, 20–21.

principles could preserve the Church from doctrinal corruption.[26] As a Catholic, Newman retained this concern about the ways in which power can be abused within Christian communities, but now with a focus upon powerful clergy.

Francis Newman's ideas are representative of the broad tendencies of the nineteenth century, even if the Victorian era was hardly as skeptical as scholars often imagine. Francis concluded that historical criticism of Scripture and of the Church's dogmatic Tradition has demonstrated that both are false. In John's view, the problem is that Francis' understanding of the transmission of divine revelation in Scripture and Tradition was flimsy and misdirected from the outset. For John, Francis was bound to find doctrinal corruption where in fact there is doctrinal development.

Edward Pusey considered that he had good reason to suppose that the (Roman) Catholic Church in the nineteenth century was rushing headlong into doctrinal corruption. Newman, having shared Pusey's views in the 1830s, ended up rejecting them. For Newman, attention to the teachings of the Church Fathers and Mary as the New Eve and Mother of God exhibits the plausibility of affirming that Catholic teachings about Mary are true developments, not corruptions.

Lastly, Döllinger insisted that the Catholic Church's understandings of the papacy since the end of the patristic period have been a dreadful mistake, one that the Vatican Council turned into a flagrant doctrinal corruption. Against this perspective, Newman underscored that in the patristic period, the Church was able to speak with one voice across all nations and to define dogma in a universally binding way. The only Church with a plausible claim to do this now is the Church in communion with the bishop of Rome. This fact indicates the presence of a development: God

26. See the remark of James Pereiro, *'Ethos' and the Oxford Movement: At the Heart of Tractarianism* (Oxford: Oxford University Press, 2008), 182, summarizing Newman's position both as an Anglican and as a (Roman) Catholic: "Revealed doctrines generate Catholic principles, at least some of them, in 'absolute terms.' They are doctrines (facts) beyond human reach, and, consequently, their principles cannot be generated by any human agency."

always intended for the Petrine office to receive universal jurisdiction, so as to preserve the Church's ability to function as a vibrant unity.

Did Newman's effort to respond to the threat and challenge of doctrinal corruption succeed? My answer at the end of this book is, yes and no. Yes, insofar as Newman shows that Gibbon's reading of the history of the early Church as a history of doctrinal corruption is no more objectively historical (indeed less so) than is the very opposite reading of the early Church as a history of doctrinal development. Yes, insofar as Newman shows that Francis Newman's argument that rational inquiry necessitates skepticism about Christian doctrine is a false argument. Yes, insofar as Newman shows that an overemphasis on power, whether from the side of liberal Whig Anglicans or from the side of Ultramontanists, opens up the Church to the threat of doctrinal corruption. Yes, insofar as Newman shows that the dogmas of Mary's Immaculate Conception and of the infallibility of the pope can reasonably be interpreted as doctrinal developments rather than doctrinal corruptions.

Yet, in another sense, the answer is no—at least in the eyes of the contemporary world. Newman understood this situation well. In a Catholic sermon, he asks what the "world" is likely to make of the notion that Mary is ever virgin and that she lives today as "the great Intercessor of the faithful."[27] The answer of course is that the world today is skeptical of such claims. Newman perceives that the "world" approves of Catholics when they hold their faith at arm's length. The "world" tells itself reassuringly, "The Catholic doctrines are now mere badges of party. Catholics think for themselves and judge for themselves, just as we do."[28] In Catholicism that is assimilated to the "world," the sacramental and dogmatic principles are downplayed or negated.

In his sermon, Newman concludes that the "world," in encouraging

27. John Henry Newman, "Discourse VIII: Nature and Grace," in *Discourses Addressed to Mixed Congregations*, ed. James Tolhurst (Notre Dame, IN: University of Notre Dame Press, 2003), 145–168, at 167.

28. Newman, 166.

doctrinal corruption, is the same world about which Christ says in the Gospel of John: "If the world hates you, be aware that it hated me before it hated you. If you belonged to the world, the world would love you as its own" (John 15:18–19). Newman therefore exhorts his hearers: "Be not seduced by this world's sophistries and assumptions."[29] Instead, he urges his hearers to imitate and "follow the Saints, as they follow Christ."[30] Standing against the world's "sophistries and assumptions" means recognizing that there is a living Creator and Redeemer God present and active in history. Of course, one law of the "world" is that humans make a mess of all institutions, generally sooner rather than later. The dogmatic principle thus expresses how radically Christ and the Holy Spirit are at work in the Church, which bears the liberating truth of the Gospel.[31]

As Newman well understood, non-Catholics are unlikely to agree with Newman about the fidelity of Catholic doctrinal development. For instance, the Orthodox theologian David Bentley Hart has recently described *An Essay on the Development of Christian Doctrine* as "Newman's splendid speculative fantasia."[32] Hart suggests that the source of the "fantasia" is wishful thinking in the service of ecclesiastical conservatism. The problem with Newman's approach to doctrinal development, Hart says, is that "he trained his gaze on only one horizon . . . the receding horizon of the past."[33] Hart considers that Newman overlooked the apocalyptic dimension of Christianity, in the light of which radical doctrinal ruptures can be

29. Newman, 168.

30. Newman, 168.

31. As Newman says in "Discourse IX: Illuminating Grace," in *Discourses Addressed to Mixed Congregations*, 169–191, at 171: "You ask, what it is you need, besides eyes, in order to see the truths of revelation: I will tell you at once; you need light. . . . Now, though your mind be the eye, the grace of God is the light; and you will as easily exercise your eyes in this sensible world without the sun, as you will be able to exercise your mind in the spiritual world without a parallel gift from without."

32. David Bentley Hart, "Tradition and Authority: A Vaguely Gnostic Meditation," in *The Idea of Tradition in the Late Modern World: An Ecumenical Conversation*, ed. Thomas Albert Howard (Eugene, OR: Cascade, 2020), 56–76, at 66.

33. David Bentley Hart, *Tradition and Apocalypse: An Essay on the Future of Christian Belief* (Grand Rapids, MI: Baker Academic, 2022), 18.

justified. Going further, Hart deems that in reality, there is no doctrinal development of the kind Newman opposes to doctrinal corruption; there is a "continuous Christian tradition," but not of the kind that Newman's seven notes wish there might have been.[34]

When one looks closely, however, Hart's critique of Newman can be seen to arise from religious liberalism. For example, while praising "the wonderfully rich theological heritage of the council [of Nicaea]," Hart maintains that "the historical record gives no evidence for or against the correctness or incorrectness of any doctrinal synthesis," and he concludes that the most that can be said is that the Nicene tradition is "handed over to future elaboration, adaptation, and reconceptualization."[35] In his own pushing beyond Newmanian doctrinal development, Karl Rahner said something similar. Along lines that resonate with Rahner's essay "Yesterday's History of Dogma and Theology for Tomorrow," Hart continues, "It would be foolish, moreover, to suppose that one could foresee the forms it

34. See Hart, 65–66. For an instance of Hart's rather delightful critique of Newman's seven notes—a critique that rejects (mistakenly in my view) the apologetic and explanatory value of Newman's effort to discern plausible paths and probabilities—see Hart's critique of the fourth note: "There is, after all, an obvious impediment to any practical application of Newman's fourth criterion: to wit, the 'discovery' of an implicit logical coherence in the historical unfolding of any conceptual transition is, almost by definition, indistinguishable from the retrospective fabrication of some abstract principle that is merely reconcilable with—or simply not repugnant to—the two distinct moments of the disjunction; this principle, once found or fabricated, can then be adduced as the subtle, perhaps even invisible bond uniting two phases of a single conceptual shift. Principles, as articles of historical judgment, can be delightfully pliable things. But, as deeply problematic as Newman's *principia ex machina* are, of even greater concern is the defectiveness of the analogy in its own terms. Newman may talk here of logical sequences or processes of ratiocination, but what he is describing might every bit as well be characterized—just as before—as mere evolutionary adaptability. If anything, his reasoning suggests that tradition advances precisely by way of the *absence* of any seamless logical necessity in the unfolding of its basic premises. After all, a genuinely logical sequence of propositions or principles or even sound intuitions, however various they may be, must still terminate in only *one* possible conclusion. If more than one is possible, then all that can be demonstrated is the logical non-repugnance of any given stage of development to what either precedes or succeeds it. Once again, then, nothing more has been established than a kind of mechanical determinism—the mere momentum of a stream of thought or of eventualities, continuous in a more or less trivial sense, discontinuous in another sense, and channeled into new configurations by external pressures" (Hart, 56–57).

35. Hart, 129–130.

might yet assume, the accords it might yet strike, the discoveries it might yet make—both within and beyond itself."[36] Thus, everything that we think we know in faith (as received and handed on in tradition) might change. Hart bemoans the fact that traditionalists, following a Newmanian path, will inevitably exercise their "inhibiting influence" against "any healthy developments" by resisting "the living tradition's often chaotic and disruptive vitality" as inaugurated by the interruptive apocalyptic prophet Jesus.[37]

Somewhat like Newman in *The Arians of the Fourth Century*, but from a perspective shaped not by romanticism but by Loisy, Hart has some critical words to say about dogma. He observes that "Christian dogma has always had some quality of disappointment about it, some impulse to anger, some sense that a creed is a strange substitute for the presence of the Kingdom."[38] Indeed Hart goes on to say that Loisy was right: Jesus preached the kingdom but the Church arrived, in "its often almost comically corrupt and divisive form," ever needing to be sustained by a defensive and fear-filled propositional orthodoxy whose function is to ward off the "shadows of doubt" fueled by the "history of defeated expectations."[39]

The solution that Hart proposes is a religiously liberal Christianity that retains the doctrine of eschatological hope and a confidence in the creative fruitfulness of the liberated tradents. On this view, Tradition is "the constant creative recollection of a promise whose fulfillment and ultimate meaning are yet to be unveiled. Tradition thus must be seen as history's

36. Hart, 130.

37. Hart, 130–131. Hart adds, "The alloy of apocalyptic longing and historical continuity was never entirely stable. The Christian event proved to be far more refractory to be contained within institutions, even institutions of its own devising. At the very heart of its spiritual rationale there always remained an impulse to rebellion. . . . Christianity is filled with an indomitable and subversive ferment, an inner force of dissolution that refuses to crystallize into something inert or stable, but that instead insists upon dispersing itself into the future ever again" (Hart, 136–137).

38. Hart, 138. In *The Arians of the Fourth Century*, Newman argued that the formulation of dogma was a declension from the earlier, more innocent time in which the Gospel did not need such propositional support.

39. Hart, 138.

secret, redemptive rationale."[40] Hart cautions against smuggling Newmanian doctrinal continuity through the back door. He argues that healthy Tradition "is possible only so long as faith is able to descry a future apocalyptic horizon where the tradition's ultimate meaning is to be found, and is able also to refuse any reduction of that final revelation to whatever formulations of belief happen to be available at any given stage of doctrinal development."[41] Such a "reduction" prior to the eschaton would assert the ontological truth and irreversibility of all the Church's solemnly taught doctrines. Preempting such a stance, Hart argues that dogmatic "formulations of belief" are at best "dim prefigurations" that can point us toward the eschaton in which everything will become clear; prior to this end, every formulation is in principle open to rupture and reversal, so long as our trust in the doctrine of the Kingdom does not itself succumb to the solvent.

Rahner's updating of Loisy's apocalyptic religious liberalism—or, indeed, Loisy's own updating of Newmanian development—is perfectly echoed by Hart's conclusion:

> If Christian tradition is a living thing, it is only *as tradition*—as a "handing over," a passage through time, a transmission, the impartation of a gift that remains sealed, a giving always deferred toward a future not yet known—that the secret inner presence can be made manifest at all. And that gift must remain sealed until the very end. . . . Once that vital force has moved on to assume new living configurations, the attempt unnaturally to preserve earlier forms can achieve nothing but, at the very best, the perfumed repose of a cadaver bedizened by mortuary cosmetics. True fidelity to whatever is most original and most final in a tradition requires a positive desire for moments of dissolution just as much as for passages of

40. Hart, 139.
41. Hart, 139.

> recapitulation and refrain. . . . Even the act of reverently looking back through the past to the tradition's origin is also an act of critique, a judgment on the past that need not be a kind one, as well as an implicit act of submission to a future verdict that might be equally unkind with regard to the present, and even submission to a final verdict in whose light all the forms the tradition encompasses can be understood as at best provisional intimations of something ineffable and inconceivable. The tradition's life, it turns out, is an irrepressible apocalyptic ferment within, beckoning believers simultaneously back to an immemorial past and forward to an unimaginable future. The proper moral and spiritual attitude to tradition's formal expressions, if all of this is correct, would not be a simple clinging to what has been received, but also a relinquishing, even at times of things that had once seemed most precious: *Gelassenheit*, to use Eckhart's language, release.[42]

Loisy could not have said it better. Yet I note that one of the first things that will be relinquished or released is belief in the apocalyptic future in any specifically Christian sense.

Ultimately, Hart is merely repackaging the familiar notion that there is a fundamental intuition or non-conceptualizable religious experience that is the real core of everything toward which Christians have been striving—the real meaning (if we could only speak it) of everything that the Church's faltering words seek to express. On this view, Christianity in its essence is a non-expressible religious experience, and "faith is the will to let the past be reborn in the present as more than what until now had been known, and the will to let the present be shaped by a future yet to be revealed."[43] Yet, as

---

42. Hart, 139–40, 145.

43. Hart, 188. I note that for Hart, "The doctrinal past can never be abandoned" (Hart, 188), but this does not mean that the doctrines of the past will not be reversed or ruptured by new syntheses emerging from the experience of apocalyptic hope. Hart holds that tradents

always, the theologians proposing this view have dogmas to which they are wedded—in Hart's case the universal salvation of humans and angels/demons. Hart elsewhere makes clear that anyone who does not believe in this dogma is (objectively speaking) a worshiper of an evil "god" and that any Church that denies this dogma is proclaiming not God but an idol.[44] Liberal theologies are as enmeshed in absolute dogmatic truth as are any other theologies, but on different grounds.

As we have seen, Newman understood the religiously liberal vision and he deemed it to be unreal, lacking adequate connection to the Gospel. For to say that Jesus is Lord, that Jesus is the divine Son, that Jesus died for our sins, that Jesus rose from the dead, that the Holy Spirit is divine, that God is Trinity, that the Church is Christ's Mystical Body, that the Eucharist is Christ's Body and Blood, that faith and Baptism unite us to Christ, that Mary is Theotokos, and so on, is not merely to profess "provisional intimations of something ineffable and inconceivable," let alone merely to profess "precious" things that Christians should be prepared to "release" or that may be radically revised. Newman knew well that these truths are

within the living Tradition must recognize the possibility of "a radical revision of much that the faithful think they have been taught to believe" (Hart, 187), and he argues that the future of Christian faith is radically unknowable in terms of its cognitive content: "As the final intentional horizon of the tradition is nothing other than the final apocalyptic horizon of historical and cosmic time, the intrinsic final causality of the tradition's rational unity may in fact also be the intrinsic final causality of far more than we can see at present, including many things we now understand as being merely outside the faith. As yet, that last end is perceived in shadows, glimpsed in a glass darkly, in an enigma, as Paul says—in doctrines only partly understood, in premonitions and prophecies and visions, in omens, mysterious promises, inexhaustible symbols, works of art, above all in faith and hope—and no one has the ability to discern from the vantage of this present moment within the life of the tradition just how much more than end may encompass, and how many local truths it may summon into existence and embrace within itself" (Hart, 183). Hart contends that he has not fallen into "the seductions and preposterous certitudes of either dogmatism or historicism" (Hart, 187), and this is correct given a certain definition of "dogmatism" and "historicism." But Hart has fallen into a form of religious liberalism with respect to the ontological truth-claims of doctrine (whether Eastern Orthodox or Catholic).

44. See David Bentley Hart, *That All Shall Be Saved: Heaven, Hell, and Universal Salvation* (New Haven, CT: Yale University Press, 2019), as well as his *The New Testament: A Translation* (New Haven, CT: Yale University Press, 2017).

inadequate expressions of inexhaustible mysteries, while at the same time being ontologically true in their reference to realities. In this light, Newmanian doctrinal development is not a mere cover for "a radical diffuseness and pliancy native to Christian belief from its inception."[45] There exists an intelligible divine revelation, an apostolic deposit of faith. It can be and has been "developed" rather than "corrupted."

Recall that the Newmanian theory of development of doctrine does not demand a rationalistic proof from history, but only accumulated probabilities. Hart exaggerates when he says that "as an object of historical scrutiny . . . tradition has all the appearances of a chance emergence from material forces, determined more by the power of natural selection than by any intrinsic rational necessity."[46] But Newmanian doctrinal development accepts that the path of doctrinal development is not determined by an "intrinsic rational necessity" but instead relies upon the providential course of the Spirit-guided Church in history.

From Hart's perspective, sharing Newman's concern about doctrinal corruption entails a defensive attitude, in which one looks out upon other Christians from a stance of "We've got it, they've lost it" and in which one embodies an absurd (and ugly) "overweening confidence" in one's own orthodoxy and a corresponding confidence that "other communions have distorted or occluded or betrayed" the true orthodoxy.[47] Let me close, then, by differentiating Newman on doctrinal corruption from such entailments of dogmatism. Newman does believe that Christ has given a revelation that is truly known and believed in the Catholic Church. He thinks that doctrinal controversy between Christian communions is possible on the ground of truth and he engages in such controversy. But, given the inexhaustible character of the dogmatic mysteries and the ease with which sin creeps into the human breast, he does not think that the truth of Catholic faith and sacraments warrants a sense of superiority on the part of Catholic believers.

45. Hart, 41.
46. Hart, 41.
47. Hart, 42.

On the contrary, maturity in faith bears with it an ever-increasing humility and a corresponding reliance upon the divine mercy, not only for oneself but also for others. As Newman has the dying Gerontius say in "The Dream of Gerontius" (1853), "Lover of souls! great God! I look to Thee/. . . Help, loving Lord! Thou my sole Refuge, Thou."[48]

Far from trusting in his own advantages, whether intellectual or ecclesiastical, the mature Newman recognizes that all human boasting falls flat: "Opinions change, conclusions are feeble, inquiries run their course, reason stops short."[49] He perceives, in other words, that a dogmatic faith differs from dogmatism.[50] The Church's solemn doctrines are true and their corruption would be a terrible thing for all humankind. But this does not mean that Newman arrogantly imagines himself or other Catholics to be the apogee of divine wisdom in a world filled with lesser men and women. He is always open to seeing further and more profoundly thanks to the insights of others who disagree with him. Yet he holds, as a Catholic believer, to what he has received "concerning the word of life" (1 John 1:1).[51]

---

48. John Henry Newman, "The Dream of Gerontius," in Newman, *Selected Sermons, Prayers, and Devotions*, ed. John F. Thornton and Susan B. Varenne (New York: Random House, 1999), 352–383, at 353.

49. Newman, "Discourse IX: Illuminating Grace," 190.

50. Thus, Newman's understanding of doctrinal development allows for what Robert Barron calls a certain "perspectivalism" that nevertheless is not relativism. Barron notes that today, a primary reason young Catholics give for leaving the faith is that "claims to absolute truth are exclusive and aggressive"—in other words, a narrow dogmatism (Barron, *Renewing Our Hope: Essays for the New Evangelization* [Washington, DC: The Catholic University of America Press, 2020], 267). But while affirming the absolute truth of dogma, "Newman teaches that an idea does not present itself univocally and one-sidedly. Rather, it discloses itself gradually and through the process of lively thought and conversatoin. It is a bit like a diamond that is thrown repeatedly in the air, allowing various aspects to present themselves. . . . This notion of doctrinal development not only allows for but positively demands steady dialogue, debate, and openness to new perspectives" (Barron, 267).

51. Consider for example Newman's Sermon 33 (No. 398), "Slavery Allowed Not Encouraged under the Gospel," preached on December 27, 1835 and again on September 22, 1839, which Newman rightly did not include among his published sermons, but which Francis McGrath and Placid Murray have published for the benefit of scholars, and to which Kenneth Parker (indebted to Benjamin King's forthcoming "John Henry Newman: Scholar, Sage, and Slavery Anti-Abolitionist") has drawn my attention. Unfortunately, Newman holds that according to St. Paul, slaves do not have a right—lamentable though the condition of

For Newman, it is the incarnate Lord, known in the Church's liturgy, in prayer, and in the midst of our lives through faith and charity, who is the ground of our apocalyptic hope. To know this Jesus requires a faith shaped by repentance, humility, mercy, and love—a dogmatic faith, but not an arrogant dogmatism.

In sum, not least in his lifelong reflection on doctrinal corruption in light of Christ's promises to his Bride the Church, Newman recalls us to the need to devote ourselves in faith and love to the one "head of the church" (Eph. 5:23), Jesus Christ. As Newman asks his fellow theologians:

> What will it avail us then, to have devised some subtle argument, or to have led some brilliant attack, or to have mapped

enslavement is—to be freed from their bondage (no more than poor persons have a right to be made wealthy). Newman affirms that "the influences of Christianity in the course of many years tend to destroy slavery—merely because its *spirit* is that all men should be equal, all brethren. In the course of centuries it will imperceptibly change the face of society and by degrees, by little and little, no one knows how slavery will disappear. And in like manner Christianity will effect many other changes. . . . Did the gospel extend all over the earth in its fullness, there would doubtless be no slaves, but then how many other things would there not be—there would not be any war—there would be no army—swords would become plowshares—there would not be this insatiable trafficking and thirst after gain which at present prevails among us—we should not have such large unwieldy wealth in some persons and such abject poverty in others. . . . Doubtless—but for all this it would be a sin for any of us to take away the wealth of these worldly rich persons. God suffers these things—we must suffer them. God suffers slavery—slaves must endure it" (Newman, Sermon 33, "Slavery Allowed Not Encouraged under the Gospel," in Newman, *Sermons 1824–1843*, vol. 3, *Sermons and Lectures for Saints' Days and Holy Days and General Theology*, ed. Francis J. McGrath and Placid Murray [Oxford: Clarendon, 2010], 239–253, at 248–249). What is missing here is the fact that slavery makes it impossible for a Christian slaveowner truly to treat a Christian slave as a "beloved brother," as Paul commands (Philem. 16)—because one would never enslave, or control as property, or force to live in slave-quarters, a real "beloved brother." Much better is Newman's argument in *Grammar of Assent*: "The iniquity . . . of the slave-trade ought to have been acknowledged by all men from the first; it was acknowledged by many, but it needed an organized agitation, with tracts and speeches innumerable, so to affect the imagination of men as to make their acknowledgment of that iniquitousness operative" (Newman, *An Essay in Aid of a Grammar of Assent* [Westminster, MD: Christian Classics, 1973], 77). The Catholic Magisterium of Newman's day condemned the slave trade but not slavery itself. I have discussed this topic in relation to doctrinal development in my *Engaging the Doctrine of Revelation: The Mediation of the Gospel Through Church and Scripture* (Grand Rapids, MI: Baker Academic, 2014).

> out the field of history, or to have numbered and sorted the weapons of controversy, and to have the homage of friends and the respect of the world for our successes—what will it avail to have had a position, to have followed out a work, to have re-animated an idea, to have made a cause to triumph, if after all we have not the light of faith to guide us on from this world to the next?[52]

Faith in Christ through the Spirit's illuminating work, and not anything merely our own, is the great thing. The true sorrow of doctrinal corruption consists in its undermining our ability to relate to Jesus Christ in the full and rich way to which he calls us, which involves not pride in our own knowledge but rather cruciform humility, through which the Church manifests the love of the crucified Christ for the world. As Jude exhorted an earlier generation of Christians: "Now to him who is able to keep you from falling, and to make you stand without blemish in the presence of his glory with rejoicing, to the only God our Savior, through Jesus Christ our Lord, be glory, majesty, power, and authority, before all time and now and forever. Amen" (Jude 24–25).

52. Newman, "Discourse VIII: Nature and Grace," 190–191.

BIBLIOGRAPHY

Abraham, William J. "Revelation." In *The Oxford Handbook of John Henry Newman*, edited by Frederick D. Aquino and Benjamin J. King, 304–317. Oxford: Oxford University Press, 2018.

Acton, John. "Conflicts with Rome." *Home and Foreign Review* 4 (1864): 667–690.

———. "Döllinger's Historical Work." *English Historical Review* 5 (1890): 700–744.

———. "Munich Congress." *The Home and Foreign Review* 4 (1864): 209–244.

———. "Reply of Lord Acton." In *The Vatican Decrees in Their Bearing on Civil Allegiance: A Political Expostulation*, by W.E. Gladstone, 80–86. New York: D. Appleton, 1874.

———. *Sendschreiben an einen deutschen Bischof des Vaticanischen Concils.* Nördlingen: C.H. Beck, 1870.

Adler, Curtis. "John Henry Newman on Edward Gibbon: Indebted to the Infidel." *The Classical Bulletin* 69, no. 1 (1993): 17–20.

Alfeyev, Hilarion. *Orthodox Christianity*, Vol. 2, *Doctrine and Teaching of the Orthodox Church.* Translated by Andrew Smith. Yonkers, NY: St. Vladimir's Seminary Press, 2012.

Allchin, A.M. "The Theological Vision of the Oxford Movement." In *The Rediscovery of Newman: An Oxford Symposium*, edited by A.M. Allchin and John Coulson, 50–75. London: Sheed & Ward, 1967.

Allen, Louis. "Introduction." In *John Henry Newman and the Abbé Jager: A Controversy on Scripture and Tradition*, 1–32. Oxford: Oxford University Press, 1975.

Altholz, Josef L. *The Liberal Catholic Movement in England: The "Rambler" and Its Contributors, 1848–1864.* London: Burns & Oates, 1962.

Andrews, Robert M. *Apologia Pro Beata Maria Virgine: John Henry Newman's Defence of the Virgin Mary in Catholic Doctrine and Piety*. Dublin: Academic, 2017.

Aquino, Frederick D. *An Integrative Habit of Mind: John Henry Newman on the Path to Wisdom*. DeKalb, IL: Northern Illinois University Press, 2012.

Arjakovsky, Antoine. *What Is Orthodoxy? A Genealogy of Christian Understanding*. Translated by Jerry Ryan and Penelope Cavill. Brooklyn, NY: Angelico, 2018.

Arnold, Claus. "Newman's Reception in Germany: From Döllinger to Ratzinger." *Newman Studies Journal* 18, no. 1 (2021): 5–23.

Arnold, Thomas. "The Oxford Malignants and Dr. Hampden." *Edinburgh Review* 63, no. 127 (1836): 225–239.

———. "Principles of Church Reform." In *Miscellaneous Works of Thomas Arnold, D.D.*, edited by A.P. Stanley, 73–130. London: B. Fellowes, 1845.

Arnstein, Walter L. *Protestant Versus Catholic in Mid-Victorian England: Mr. Newdegate and the Nuns*. Columbia, MO: University of Missouri Press, 1982.

Arx, Jeffrey von. "Archbishop Manning and the *Kulturkampf*." *British Catholic History* 21, no. 2 (1992): 254–266.

———, ed. *Varieties of Ultramontanism*. Washington, DC: The Catholic University of America Press, 1998.

Asveld, Paul. "Newman and Wiseman in the Days of the Oxford Movement." In *From Oxford to the People: Reconsidering Newman and the Oxford Movement*, edited by Paul Vaiss, 286–298. Leominster, UK: Gracewing, 1996.

Atkin, Nicholas, and Frank Tallett. *Priests, Prelates and People: A History of European Catholicism since 1750*. Oxford: Oxford University Press, 2003.

Atkins, Gareth. "Evangelicals." In *The Oxford Handbook of John Henry Newman*, edited by Frederick D. Aquino and Benjamin J. King, 173–195. Oxford: Oxford University Press, 2018.

Barnes, Michel René. "De Régnon Reconsidered." *Augustinian Studies* 26, no. 2 (1995): 51–79.

Barraclough, Geoffrey. *The Medieval Papacy*. New York: W.W. Norton, 1979.

Barron, Robert. *The Priority of Christ: Toward a Postliberal Catholicism*. Grand Rapids, MI: Brazos, 2007.

———. *Renewing Our Hope: Essays for the New Evangelization*. Washington, DC: The Catholic University of America Press, 2020.

Barth, Karl. *Church Dogmatics*. Vol. 1, *The Doctrine of the Word of God*, Part 2. Edited by G.W. Bromiley and T.F. Torrance. Translated by G.T. Thomson and Harold Knight. Peabody, MA: Hendrickson, 2010.

Batiffol, Pierre. "The Gospel and the Church." In *Defending the Faith: An Anti-Modernist Anthology*, edited and translated by William H. Marshner, 27–37. Washington, DC: The Catholic University of America Press, 2017.

Beaumont, Keith. "The Reception of Newman in France at the Time of the Modernist Crisis." In *Receptions of Newman*, edited by Frederick D. Aquino and Benjamin J. King, 156–176. Oxford: Oxford University Press, 2015.

Benn, Alfred W. "Introduction to the Present Reprint." In *Phases of Faith, or, Passages from the History of My Creed*, 2nd ed., 11–14. London: Watts, 1907.

Bennett, James. *Justification as Revealed in Scripture, in Opposition to the Council of Trent and Mr. Newman's Lectures*. London: Hamilton, Adams, 1840.

Benson, Robert Hugh. *Confessions of a Convert*. Notre Dame, IN: Ave Maria, 2016.

Berlis, Angela. “Ignaz von Döllinger and the Anglicans.” In *The Oxford Movement: Europe and the Wider World 1830–1930*, edited by Stewart J. Brown and Peter B. Nockles, 236–248. Cambridge: Cambridge University Press, 2012.

Biemer, Günter. *Newman on Tradition*. London: Burns & Oates, 1967.

———. “Newman on Tradition as a Subjective Process.” In *By Whose Authority? Newman, Manning and the Magisterium*, edited by V. Alan McClelland, 149–167. Bath: Downside Abbey, 1996.

Bischof, Franz Xaver. *Theologie und Geschichte: Ignaz von Döllinger in der zweiten Hälfte seines Lebens. Ein Beitrag zu seiner Biographie*. Stuttgart, DE: Kohlhammer, 1997.

Blanchard, Shaun. “Settling Old Scores: Pastor Aeternus as the Final Defeat of Early Modern Opponents of Ultramontanism.” *Newman Studies Journal* 17, no. 1 (2020): 24–51.

Blehl, Vincent Ferrer. “Newman and the Church of England.” In *By Whose Authority? Newman, Manning and the Magisterium*, edited by V. Alan McClelland, 41–48. Bath: Downside Abbey, 1996.

———. “Newman’s Conversion of 1845: A Fresh Approach.” In *By Whose Authority? Newman, Manning and the Magisterium*, edited by V. Alan McClelland, 123–135. Bath: Downside Abbey, 1996.

Blondel, Maurice. *The Letter on Apologetics & History and Dogma*. Translated by Alexander Dru. Grand Rapids, MI: Eerdmans, 1994.

Boeve, Lieven. *Interrupting Tradition: An Essay on Christian Faith in a Postmodern Context*. Louvain, BE: Peeters, 2003.

Bokenkotter, Thomas S. *Cardinal Newman as an Historian*. Louvain, BE: Publications Universitaires de Louvain, 1959.

Borutta, Manuel. “Anti-Catholicism and the Culture War in Risorgimento Italy.” In *The Risorgimento Revisited: Nationalism and Culture in Nineteenth-Century Italy*, edited by Silvana Patriarca and Lucy Riall, 191–213. London: Palgrave Macmillan, 2012.

Borutta, Manuel. *Antikatholizismus: Deutschland und Italien im Zeitalter der europäischen Kulturkämpfe*. Göttingen: Vandenhoeck & Ruprecht, 2010.

Bouyer, Louis. *Newman's Vision of Faith*. San Francisco: Ignatius Press, 1986.

Brady, Ciaran. *James Anthony Froude: An Intellectual Biography of a Victorian Prophet*. Oxford: Oxford University Press, 2013.

Brendon, Piers. *Hurrell Froude and the Oxford Movement*. London: Paul Elek, 1974.

Brent, Richard. *Liberal Anglican Politics: Whiggery, Religion, and Reform 1830–1841*. Oxford: Clarendon, 1987.

Brilioth, Yngve. *The Anglican Revival: Studies in the Oxford Movement*. London: Longmans & Green, 1933.

———. *Three Lectures on Evangelicalism and the Oxford Movement*. Oxford: Oxford University Press, 1934.

Broker, Ralph H. *The Influence of Bull and Petavius on Cardinal Newman's Theory of the Development of Christian Doctrine*. Rome: Gregorian University Press, 1938.

Brown, David. "Pusey as Consistent and Wise: Some Comparisons with Newman." *Anglican and Episcopal History* 71, no. 3 (2002): 328–349.

Bull, George. *A Defence of the Nicene Creed, out of the Extant Writings of the Catholic Doctors Who Flourished during the Three First Centuries of the Christian Church*. London: James Parker, 1851.

Bullivant, Stephen. "Newman and Modernism: The *Pascendi* Crisis and Its Wider Significance." *New Blackfriars* 92, no. 1038 (2011): 189–208.

Burrow, John W. *A Liberal Descent: Victorian Historians and the English Past*. Cambridge: Cambridge University Press, 1983.

Butler, Joseph. "The Analogy of Religion." In *The Works of Joseph Butler, LL.D.*, new ed., 1–280. London: William Tegg, 1867.

Butler, Perry. *Gladstone: Church, State and Tractarianism: A Study of His Religious Ideas and Attitudes, 1809–1859*. Oxford: Oxford University Press, 1982.

Butler, William Archer. *Letters on Romanism in Reply to Mr. Newman's* Essay on Development. Edited by Thomas Woodward. Cambridge: Macmillan, 1854.

Cannadine, David. *Victorious Century: The United Kingdom, 1800–1906.* London: Penguin, 2017.

Carlton, Clark. *The Truth.* Salisbury, MA: Regina, 1999.

Carola, Joseph. "Newman and the Roman College." *Nova et Vetera* 18, no. 3 (2020): 741–756.

Carter, Grayson. *Anglican Evangelicals: Protestant Secessions from the Via Media, c. 1800–1850.* Oxford: Clarendon, 2001.

Chadwick, Owen. *Acton and History.* Cambridge: Cambridge University Press, 1998.

———. "A Consideration of Newman's *Apologia Pro Vita Sua.*" In *From Oxford to the People: Reconsidering Newman and the Oxford Movement,* edited by Paul Vaiss, 163–185. Leominster, UK: Gracewing, 1996.

———. "Döllinger and Reunion." In *Christian Authority: Essays in Honour of Henry Chadwick,* edited by G.R. Evans, 296–334. Oxford: Oxford University Press, 1988.

———. *From Bossuet to Newman.* 2nd ed. Cambridge: Cambridge University Press, 1987.

———. "Introduction." In *The Mind of the Oxford Movement,* 11–64. London: Adam & Charles Black, 1960.

———. "The Limitations of Keble." In *The Spirit of the Oxford Movement: Tractarian Essays,* 54–62. Cambridge: Cambridge University Press, 1990.

———. "The Mind of the Oxford Movement." In *The Spirit of the Oxford Movement: Tractarian Essays,* 1–53. Cambridge: Cambridge University Press, 1990.

———. *Newman.* Oxford: Oxford University Press, 1983.

———. *The Secularization of the European Mind in the Nineteenth Century.* Cambridge: Cambridge University Press, 1975.

Chandler, Michael. "The Significance of the Friendship between William E. Gladstone and Ignaz von Döllinger." *Internationale Kirchliche Zeitschrift* 90, no. 2 (2000): 153–167.

Chapman, Mark D. *Anglicanism: A Very Short Introduction*. Oxford: Oxford University Press, 2006.

———. "Ecumenism, Mariology, and the Papacy." In *The Oxford Handbook of John Henry Newman*, edited by Frederick D. Aquino and Benjamin J. King, 355–372. Oxford: Oxford University Press, 2018.

———. *The Fantasy of Reunion: Anglicans, Catholics, and Ecumenism, 1833–1882*. Oxford: Oxford University Press, 2014.

———. "Temporal and Spatial Catholicism: Tensions in Historicism in the Oxford Movement." In *The Shaping of Tradition: Context and Normativity*, edited by Colby Dickinson with Lieven Boeve and Terrence Merrigan, 17–26. Leuven: Peters, 2013.

Chenu, M.-D. "La raison psychologique du développement du dogme d'après saint Thomas." *Revue des sciences philosophiques et théologiques* 13, no. 1 (1924): 44–51.

———. "Vérité évangélique et métaphysique Wolffienne à Vatican II." *Revue des sciences philosophiques et théologiques* 57, no. 4 (1973): 632–640.

Chillingworth, William. *The Works of William Chillingworth*. London: A. & J. Churchill, 1704.

Church, R.W. *The Oxford Movement: 1833–1845*. London: Macmillan, 1891.

Cimorelli, Christopher. *John Henry Newman's Theology of History: Historical Consciousness, Theological 'Imaginaries,' and the Development of Tradition*. Leuven: Peeters, 2017.

Clark, J.C.D. *English Society 1688–1832: Ideology, Social Structure and Political Practice during the Ancien Régime*. Cambridge: Cambridge University Press, 1985.

Cleenewerck, Laurent A. *His Broken Body: Understanding and Healing the Schism between the Roman Catholic and Eastern Orthodox Churches.* Washington, DC: Euclid University Consortium Press, 2007.

Colberg, Kristin M. "'Not Undone, but Completed': John Henry Newman and the Reception of Vatican I." *Newman Studies Journal* 17, no. 1 (2020): 5–23.

———. *Vatican I and Vatican II: Councils in the Living Tradition.* Collegeville, MN: Liturgical, 2016.

Collins, Kenneth J., and Jerry Walls. *Roman but Not Catholic: What Remains at Stake 500 Years after the Reformation.* Grand Rapids, MI: Baker Academic, 2017.

Congar, Yves. "Saint Thomas Aquinas and the Infallibility of the Papal Magisterium (*Summa Theologiae*, II-II, q. 1, a. 10)." *The Thomist* 38, no. 1 (1974): 81–105.

Conn, Walter E. *Conscience and Conversion in Newman: A Developmental Study of Self in John Henry Newman.* Milwaukee, WI: Marquette University Press, 2010.

Connolly, John R. "Newman on Human Faith and Divine Faith: Clarifying Some Ambiguities." *Horizons* 23, no. 2 (1996): 261–280.

Conway, Michael A. "Maurice Blondel and *Ressourcement.*" In *Ressourcement: A Movement for Renewal in Twentieth-Century Catholic Theology*, edited by Gabriel Flynn and Paul D. Murray, 65–82. Oxford: Oxford University Press, 2012.

Conzemius, Victor. "Ignaz von Döllinger und die Viktorianische Kirche." In *Kirche, Staat und Gesellschaft im 19 Jahrhundert. Ein Deutsch-Englischer Vergleich*, edited by Adolf M. Birke and Kurt Kluxen, 121–152. Munich: K.G. Saur, 1984.

Conzemius, Victor. "Lord Acton, Ignaz von Döllinger und John Henry Newman: Lebenssituationen und Kirchenkonflikte." In *Newman-Studien* 12, 83–102. Nüremberg: Glock und Lutz, 1988.

Cornwell, John. *Newman's Unquiet Grave: The Reluctant Saint*. London: Continuum, 2010.

Costigan, Richard F. *The Consensus of the Church and Papal Infallibility: A Study in the Background of Vatican I*. Washington, DC: The Catholic University of America Press, 2005.

Coulson, John. "The *Apologia* Revalued." In *Newman: A Portrait Restored*, edited by John Coulson, A.M. Allchin, and Meriol Trevor, 27–61. London: Sheed & Ward, 1965.

———. *Newman and the Common Tradition: A Study in the Language of Church and Society*. Oxford: Clarendon, 1970.

———. "Was Newman a Modernist?" In *John Henry Newman and Modernism*, edited by Arthur Hilary Jenkins, 74–84. Sigmaringendorf, DE: Glock und Lutz, 1990.

Craddock, Patricia. *Edward Gibbon: Luminous Historian, 1772–1794*. Baltimore, MD: Johns Hopkins University Press, 1989.

Cummings, Owen F. *John Henry Newman and His Age*. Eugene, OR: Cascade, 2019.

Daley, Brian E. "The Church Fathers." In *The Cambridge Companion to John Henry Newman*, edited by Ian Ker and Terrence Merrigan, 29–46. Cambridge: Cambridge University Press, 2009.

Darby, John Nelson. *The Irrationalism of Infidelity: Being an Analysis of "Phases of Faith."* London: Groombridge and Sons, 1853.

Davis, Hudson Russell. "William George Ward, the Dublin Review and Neo-Ultramontanism." In *Authority, Dogma, and History: The Role of Oxford Movement Converts in the Papal Infallibility Debates*, edited by Kenneth L. Parker and Michael J. Pahls, 129–155. Bethesda, MD: Academica, 2009.

Davison, John. *Discourses on Prophecy, in Which Are Considered Its Structure, Use, and Inspiration*. Oxford: J.H. & J. Parker, 1861.

———. *An Inquiry into the Origin and Intent of Primitive Sacrifice, and the Scripture Evidence Respecting It*. London: John Murray, 1825.

Dawson, Christopher. *Spirit of the Oxford Movement.* London: Sheed & Ward, 1933.

D'Costa, Gavin. "Between Doctrine and Discernment: The Question of the Jewish People and the Development of Doctrine Arising from Vatican II." In *The Past, Present, and Future of Theologies of Interreligious Dialogue*, edited by Terrence Merrigan and John Friday, 64–80. Oxford: Oxford University Press, 2017.

Dechamps, Victor. *L'Infaillibilité et le concile général.* Paris: Magnin, 1869.

de La Soujeole, Benoît-Dominique. *Introduction to the Mystery of the Church.* Translated by Michael J. Miller. Washington, DC: The Catholic University of America Press, 2016.

Delio, David P. *'An Aristocracy of Exalted Spirits': The Idea of the Church in Newman's Tamworth Reading Room*. Leominster, UK: Gracewing, 2016.

Demacopoulos, George E. *The Invention of Peter: Apostolic Discourse and Papal Authority in Late Antiquity*. Philadelphia: University of Pennsylvania Press, 2013.

Denzinger, Heinrich. *Compendium of Creeds, Definitions, and Declarations of the Catholic Church on Matters of Faith and Morals*. Revised and enlarged and edited by Peter Hünermann, Helmut Hoping, Robert Fastiggi, and Anne Englund Nash. 43rd ed. San Francisco: Ignatius Press, 2012.

Dessain, Charles Stephen. "Cardinal Newman and the Eastern Tradition." *Downside Review* 94, no. 315 (1976): 83–98.

———. "The Reception among Catholics of Newman's Doctrine of Development." In *Newman-Studien* 6, 179–191. Nüremberg: Glock und Lutz, 1964.

Döllinger, Johann Joseph Ignaz von. *Christentum und Kirche in der Zeit der Grundlegung*. 2nd ed. Regensburg: G.J. Manz, 1868.

Döllinger, Johann Joseph Ignaz von. "Considerations for the Bishops of the Council Respecting the Question of Papal Infallibility." In *Declarations and Letters on the Vatican Decrees, 1869–1887*, edited by F.H. Reusch, 1–32. Edinburgh: T&T Clark, 1891.

———. *Die Papst-Fabeln des Mittelalters. Ein Beitrag zur Kirchengeschichte.* Munich: J.G. Cotta'schen Buchhandlung, 1863.

———. "Die Vergangenheit und Gegenwart der katholischen Theologie." In *Kleinere Schriften: Gedruckte und Ungedruckte*, edited by F.H. Reusch, 161–196. Stuttgart, DE: J.G. Cotta'schen Buchhandlung, 1890.

———. "Döllinger to Archbishop von Scherr (January 28, 1871)." In *Declarations and Letters on the Vatican Decrees, 1869–1887*, edited by F.H. Reusch, 74–77. Edinburgh: T&T Clark, 1891.

———. "Döllinger to Archbishop von Scherr (March 28, 1871)." In *Declarations and Letters on the Vatican Decrees, 1869–1887*, edited by F.H. Reusch, 82–104. Edinburgh: T&T Clark, 1891.

———. "Döllinger to Lady Blennerhasset, 20 February 1875." In *Ignaz von Döllinger Briefwechsel mit Lady Blennerhassett, 1865–1886*, edited by Victor Conzemius, 4:597–598. Munich: C.H. Beck, 1963.

———. "Döllinger to Professor Michelis (May 1, 1879)." In *Declarations and Letters on the Vatican Decrees, 1869–1887*, edited by F.H. Reusch, 122–123. Edinburgh: T&T Clark, 1891.

———. "Erwägungen für die Bischöfe des Conciliums über die Frage der päpstlichen Unfehlbarkeit." In *Briefe und Erklärungen über die Vaticanischen Decrete, 1869–1887*, 1–28. Munich: C.H. Beck, 1890.

———. *Fables Respecting the Popes in the Middle Ages: A Contribution to Ecclesiastical History*. Translated by Alfred Plummer. London: Rivington, 1871.

———."A Few Words on the Address Presented to the Pope by Certain Members of the Vatican Council, Urging Him to Declare His Own Infallibility." In *Declarations and Letters on the Vatican Decrees, 1869–1887*, edited by F.H. Reusch, 33–45. Edinburgh: T&T Clark, 1891.

Döllinger, Johann Joseph Ignaz von. *The First Age of Christianity and the Church*. Translated by Henry Nutcombe Oxenham. 4th ed. London: Gibbings, 1906.

———. "Letter to J. H. Newman, 19 March 1870." In *The Letters and Diaries of John Henry Newman*, edited by Charles Stephen Dessain and Thomas Gornall, 25:84. Oxford: Oxford University Press, 1973.

———. "The New Order of Business in the Council, and Its Theological Significance." In *Declarations and Letters on the Vatican Decrees, 1869–1887*, edited by F.H. Reusch, 46–64. Edinburgh: T&T Clark, 1891.

———. *The Pope and the Council.* Boston: Roberts Brothers, 1870.

Duffy, Eamon. *John Henry Newman: A Very Brief History*. London: SPCK, 2019.

———. "The Reception of Turner's Newman: A Reply to Simon Skinner." *The Journal of Ecclesiastical History* 63, no. 3 (2012): 534–548.

———. *Saints and Sinners: A History of the Popes*. 4th ed. New Haven, CT: Yale University Press, 2015.

Dulles, Avery. "Authority in the Church." In *The Cambridge Companion to John Henry Newman*, edited by Ian Ker and Terrence Merrigan, 170–188. Cambridge: Cambridge University Press, 2009.

———. "From Images to Truth: Newman on Revelation and Faith." *Theological Studies* 51, no. 2 (June 1, 1990): 252–267.

———. *Newman*. London: Continuum, 2002.

———. "Newman on Infallibility." *Theological Studies* 51, no. 3 (September 1, 1990): 434–449.

Dupuy, B.D. "Newman's Influence in France." In *The Rediscovery of Newman: An Oxford Symposium*, edited by A.M. Allchin and John Coulson, 147–173. London: Sheed & Ward, 1967.

Egner, G. *Apologia Pro Charles Kingsley*. London: Sheed & Ward, 1969.

Erskine, Thomas. *Remarks on the Internal Evidence for the Truth of Revealed Religion*. Edinburgh: Waugh & Innes, 1821.

Evans, Richard J. *The Pursuit of Power: Europe 1815–1914*. London: Penguin, 2016.

Evdokimov, Paul. *Orthodoxy*. Translated by Jeremy Hummertone. Translation revised by Callan Slipper. Hyde Park, NY: New City Press, 2011.

Faber, Geoffrey. *Oxford Apostles: A Character Study of the Oxford Movement*. London: Faber & Faber, 1933.

Faber, George Stanley. *The Primitive Doctrine of Justification Investigated: Relatively to the Several Definitions of the Church of Rome and the Church of England, and with a Special Reference to the Opinions of the Late Mr. Knox, as Published in His Remains with an Appendix, Containing among Other Matters, a Notice of Mr. Newman's Lectures on Justification*. 2nd ed. London: R.B. Seeley & W. Burnside, 1839.

Fairbairn, Andrew Martin. *Catholicism: Roman and Anglican*. 2nd ed. London: Hodder and Stoughton, 1899.

———. *The Place of Christ in Modern Theology*. London: Hodder and Stoughton, 1893.

Femiano, Samuel D. *Infallibility of the Laity: The Legacy of Newman*. New York: Herder & Herder, 1967.

Fessler, Joseph. *The True and the False Infallibility of the Popes: A Controversial Reply to Dr. Schulte*. Translated by Ambrose St. John. London: Burns & Oates, 1875.

Fiedrowicz, Michael. *John Henry Newman und die Kirchenväter: Anti-Liberalismus im Geist der frühen Kirche*. Fohren-Linden, DE: Carthusianus Verlag, 2020.

Finsterhölzl, Johann. *Ignaz von Döllinger*. Graz, AT: Verlag Styria, 1969.

Fitzmyer, Joseph A. *The One Who Is to Come*. Grand Rapids, MI: Eerdmans, 2007.

Fitzsimons, Robert. "The Church of England and the First Vatican Council." *Journal of Religious History* 27, no. 1 (2003): 29–46.

Franzelin, Johannes. *On Divine Tradition*. Edited by Chad Ripperger. Translated by Ryan Grant. n.p.: Sensus Traditionis Press, 2016.

Franzen, August. *Die katholisch-theologische Fakultät Bonn im Streit um das Erste Vatikanische Konzil.* Cologne: Böhlau, 1974.

Frappell, Leighton O. "John Henry Newman: History and the Two Systems of Providence." *Journal of Religious History* 15, no. 4 (1989): 470–487.

———. "'Science' in the Service of Orthodoxy: The Early Intellectual Development of E. B. Pusey." In *Pusey Rediscovered*, edited by Perry Butler, 1–33. London: SPCK, 1983.

Friedel, Francis J. *The Mariology of Cardinal Newman.* New York: Benziger, 1928.

Friedrich, Johann. *Die Wortbrüchigkeit und Unwahrhaftigkeit deutscher Bischöfe. Offenes Senschreiben an W. E. Freiherr von Metteler in Mainz.* Constance: Ammon, 1873.

Fries, Heinrich. "Die Dogmengeschichte des fünften Jahrhunderts im theologischen Werdegang von John Henry Newman." In *Das Konzil von Chalkedon: Geschichte und Gegenwart*, edited by Aloys Grillmeier and Heinrich Bacht, 3:421–454. Würzburg: Echter-Verlag, 1954.

———. "J. H. Newmans Beitrag zum Verständnis der Tradition." In *Die mündliche Überlieferung*, edited by Michael Schmaus, 33–122. Munich: Max Hueber Verlag, 1957.

———. "Newmans Bedeutung für die Theologie." In *Newman-Studien* 1, 181–199. Nüremberg: Glock und Lutz, 1948.

Fries, Heinrich, and Karl Rahner. *Unity of the Churches: An Actual Possibility.* Translated by Ruth C.L. Gritsch and Eric W. Gritsch. New York: Paulist, 1985.

Froude, James Anthony. *Lectures on the Council of Trent.* London: Longmans & Green, 1896.

———. *The Nemesis of Faith.* London: J. Chapman, 1849.

———. "Reminiscences of the High Church Revival: Six Letters." *Good Words* 22, no. 1–6 (1880): 18–23, 98–102, 162–167, 306–312, and 409–415.

Froude, Richard Hurrell. *Remains of the Late Reverend Richard Hurrell Froude*, edited by John Keble and John Henry Newman. Vol. 1. London: J.G. & F. Rivington, 1838.

———. "Remarks on State Interference in Matters Spiritual." In *Remains of the Late Reverend Richard Hurrell Froude*, edited by John Keble and John Henry Newman, 2:184–269. London: J.G. & F. Rivington, 1838.

Gaffney, James. "Preface." In *John Henry Newman: Roman Catholic Writings on Doctrinal Development*, v–xx. Kansas City, MO: Sheed & Ward, 1997.

Garnett, Jane. "Joseph Butler." In *The Oxford Handbook of John Henry Newman*, edited by Frederick D. Aquino and Benjamin J. King, 135–153. Oxford: Oxford University Press, 2018.

Garrard, James. "Archbishop Howley and the Oxford Movement." In *From Oxford to the People: Reconsidering Newman and the Oxford Movement*, edited by Paul Vaiss, 269–285. Leominster, UK: Gracewing, 1996.

Gasser, Vincent. *The Official Relatio on Infallibility of Bishop Vincent Gasser at Vatican Council I*, edited by James O'Connor. Boston: St. Paul Editions, 1986.

Gauthier, Pierre. "Richard Hurrell Froude's Influence on Newman and the Oxford Movement." In *From Oxford to the People: Reconsidering Newman and the Oxford Movement*, edited by Paul Vaiss, 255–268. Leominster, UK: Gracewing, 1996.

Giarrizzo, Giuseppe. *Edward Gibbon e la cultura europea del Settecento*. Naples: Istituto Italiano per gli Studi Storici, 1954.

Gibbon, Edward. *The Decline and Fall of the Roman Empire*. 6 vols. New York: Alfred A. Knopf, 1993–1994.

———. *Memoirs of My Life and Writings*. Edited by Betty Radice. New York: Penguin, 1984.

Gilley, Sheridan. "The Ecclesiology of the Oxford Movement: A Reconsideration." In *From Oxford to the People: Reconsidering Newman and the Oxford Movement*, edited by Paul Vaiss, 60–75. Leominster, UK: Gracewing, 1996.

———. *Newman and His Age*. 2nd ed. London: Darton, Longman & Todd, 2003.

Gittens, Peter. *Mary More or Less: Anglican and Catholic Mariology of John Henry Newman*. Saarbrucken, DE: Scholar, 2013.

Giustino, David De. "Disconnecting Church and State: Richard Whately's Ideas in the 1830s." *Albion* 35, no. 1 (2003): 53–70.

———. "Finding an Archbishop: The Whigs and Richard Whately in 1831." *Church History* 64, no. 2 (1995): 218–236.

Gladstone, William E. *Correspondence on Church and Religion of William Ewart Gladstone*. Vol. 1. Edited by D.C. Lathbury. London: Macmillan, 1910.

———. *Remarks on the Royal Supremacy as It Is Defined by Reason, History, and the Constitution*. London: John Murray, 1850.

———. *The State in Its Relations with the Church*. 3rd ed. London: John Murray, 1839.

———. *Vaticanism: An Answer to Reproofs and Replies*. New York: Harper & Brothers, 1875.

Goode, William. *The Divine Rule of Faith and Practice*. 2 vols. London: J. Hatchard & Son, 1842.

Graef, Hilda. *Mary: A History of Doctrine and Devotion*. Notre Dame, IN: Ave Maria, 2009.

Grafton, Anthony. *What Was History? The Art of History in Early Modern Europe*. Cambridge: Cambridge University Press, 2007.

Greenfield, Robert Harvie. "'Such a Friend to the Pope'." In *Pusey Rediscovered*, edited by Perry Butler, 162–184. London: SPCK, 1983.

Gregoris, Nicholas. '*The Daughter of Eve Unfallen': Mary in the Theology and Spirituality of John Henry Newman*. Mount Pocono, PA: Newman House, 2003.

Gregory, T.S. "Newman and Liberalism." In *A Tribute to Newman: Essays on Aspects of His Life and Thought*, edited by Michael Tierney, 84–115. Dublin: Browne and Nolan, 1945.

Griff, J.R. "The Anglican Politics of Cardinal Newman." *Anglican Theological Review* 55, no. 10 (1973): 434–443.

Gross, Michael B. *The War against Catholicism: Liberalism and the Anti-Catholic Imagination in Nineteenth-Century Germany*. Ann Arbor, MI: University of Michigan Press, 2004.

Guarino, Thomas G. *The Disputed Teachings of Vatican II: Continuity and Reversal in Catholic Doctrine*. Grand Rapids, MI: Eerdmans, 2018.

———. *Revelation and Truth: Unity and Plurality in Contemporary Theology*. Scranton, PA: University of Scranton Press, 1993.

———. *Vincent of Lérins and the Development of Christian Doctrine*. Grand Rapids, MI: Baker Academic, 2013.

Gurney, Archer. *'Visible Unity': The Price to Be Paid for It. A Letter to Christopher Wordsworth D.D., Archdeacon of Westminster, from Senex, on Reading Dr Pusey's Eirenicon*. London: Hatchard, 1865.

Gwynn, Aubrey. "Newman and the Catholic Historian." In *A Tribute to Newman: Essays on Aspects of His Life and Thought*, edited by Michael Tierney, 279–306. Dublin: Browne and Nolan, 1945.

Hammond, Jay M. "The Interplay of Hermeneutics and Heresy in the Process of Newman's Conversion from 1830 to 1845." In *Authority, Dogma, and History: The Role of Oxford Movement Converts in the Papal Infallibility Debates*, edited by Kenneth L. Parker and Michael J. Pahls, 45–75. Bethesda, MD: Academica, 2009.

Hampden, Henrietta, ed. *Memorials of Renn Dickson Hampden, Bishop of Hereford*. London: Longmans & Green, 1871.

Hampden, Renn Dickson. "The Work of Christ and the Work of the Spirit." In *Sermons Preached before the University of Oxford, in the Cathedral of Christ Church, from 1836 to 1847*, 462–463. London: B. Fellowes, 1848.

Hanson, R.P.C., and Reginald H. Fuller. *The Church of Rome: A Dissuasive*. 2nd ed. London: SCM, 1960.

Harris, Wendell V. "Newman, Peel, Tamworth, and the Concurrence of Historical Forces." *Victorian Studies* 32, no. 2 (1989): 189–208.

Harrison, Nonna Verna. "The Relationship between Apophatic and Kataphatic Theology." *Pro Ecclesia* 4, no. 3 (1995): 318–332.

Harrold, Charles F. "John Henry Newman and the Alexandrian Platonists." *Modern Philology* 37, no. 3 (1940): 279–291.

Hart, David Bentley. *The New Testament: A Translation*. New Haven, CT: Yale University Press, 2017.

———. *That All Shall Be Saved: Heaven, Hell, and Universal Salvation*. New Haven, CT: Yale University Press, 2019.

———. *Tradition and Apocalypse: An Essay on the Future of Christian Belief*. Grand Rapids, MI: Baker Academic, 2022.

———. "Tradition and Authority: A Vaguely Gnostic Meditation." In *The Idea of Tradition in the Late Modern World: An Ecumenical Conversation*, edited by Thomas Albert Howard, 56–76. Eugene, OR: Cascade, 2020.

Hasler, August. *How the Pope Became Infallible: Pius IX and the Politics of Persuasion*. Translated by Peter Heinegg. Garden City, NY: Doubleday, 1981.

Hays, Richard B. *Echoes of Scripture in the Gospels*. Waco, TX: Baylor University Press, 2016.

———. *Echoes of Scripture in the Letters of Paul*. New Haven, CT: Yale University Press, 1989.

Headley, John M. *Luther's View of Church History*. New Haven, CT: Yale University Press, 1963.

Healy, Nicholas J., Jr. "*Dignitatis Humanae.*" In *The Reception of Vatican II*, edited by Matthew L. Lamb and Matthew Levering, 367–392. New York, NY: Oxford University Press, 2017.

Heering, Gerrit J. *The Fall of Christianity: A Study of the Relationship between Christianity, the State, and War.* Edited by J.W. Thompson. London: George Allen & Unwin, 1930.

Henrici, Peter. "Blondel und Loisy in der modernistischen Krise." *Communio: Internationale Katholische Zeitschrift* 16, no. 6 (1987): 513–530.

Hergenröther, Joseph. *Anti-Janus: An Historico-Theological Criticism of the Work Entitled "The Pope and the Council."* Translated by J.B. Robertson. New York: Catholic Publishing Society, 1870.

Herring, George. *What Was the Oxford Movement?* London: Continuum, 2002.

Heyck, Thomas William. *The Peoples of the British Isles: A New History.* 3 vols. Belmont, CA: Wadsworth, 1992.

Hill, Harvey. "Historical Consciousness and the Controversy over *Essays and Reviews.*" In *The Rise of Historical Consciousness among the Christian Churches*, edited by Kenneth L. Parker and Erick H. Moser, 123–140. Lanham, MD: University Press of America, 2013.

Hill, Roland. *Lord Acton.* New Haven, CT: Yale University Press, 2000.

Hinchliff, Peter. *God and History: Aspects of British Theology 1875–1914.* Oxford: Clarendon, 1992.

Hines, Mary E. *The Transformation of Dogma: An Introduction to Karl Rahner on Doctrine.* Mahwah, NJ: Paulist, 1989.

Holmes, J. Derek. "Cardinal Newman and the First Vatican Council." *Annuarium Historiae Conciliorum* 1, no. 2 (1969): 374–398.

———. "Cardinal Newman on the Philosophy of History." *Tijdschrift vor filosofie* 32 (1970): 521–553.

———. "How Newman Blunted the Edge of Ultramontanism." *Clergy Review* 53 (1968): 353–362.

Holmes, J. Derek. "Newman, History and Theology." *Irish Theological Quarterly* 36, no. 1 (1969): 34–45.

———. "Newman's Reactions to the Development of Scientific and Historical Criticism in England." *Clergy Review* 64 (1979): 280–290.

Holyoake, George Jacob. *Christianity and Secularism: Report of a Public Discussion between Rev. Brewin and G. J. Holyoake*. London: Ward, 1853.

———. *The Principles of Secularism*. 3rd ed. London: Auston, 1870.

———. *Rationalism: A Treatise for the Times*. London: J. Watson, 1845.

Howard, Thomas Albert. *The Pope and the Professor: Pius IX, Ignaz von Döllinger, and the Quandary of the Modern Age*. Oxford: Oxford University Press, 2017.

———. *Religion and the Rise of Historicism: W. M. L. de Wette, Jacob Burckhardt, and the Theological Origins of Nineteenth-Century Historical Consciousness*. Cambridge: Cambridge University Press, 2000.

Hügel, Friedrich von. "Du Christ éternel et de nos christologies successives." Translated by Henri Bremond. *La quinzaine* 58 (1904): 285–312.

Hünermann, Peter. "Jewish-Christian Relations: A Conciliar Discovery and Its Methodological Consequences for Dogmatic Theology." In *The Catholic Church and the Jewish People: Recent Reflections from Rome*, edited by Philip A. Cunningham, Norbert J. Hofmann S.B.D., and Joseph Sievers, 113–126. New York: Fordham University Press, 2007.

Hütter, Reinhard. *John Henry Newman on Truth and Its Counterfeits: A Guide for Our Times*. Washington, DC: The Catholic University of America Press, 2020.

———. "Progress, Not Alteration of the Faith: Beyond Antiquarianism and Presentism. John Henry Newman, Vincent of Lérins, and the Criterion of Identity of the Development of Doctrine." *Nova et Vetera* 19, no. 2 (2021): 333–391.

Hutton, Richard H. *Cardinal Newman*. London: Methuen, 1891.

Ignatius of Antioch. "To the Trallians." In *The Epistles of St. Clement of Rome and St. Ignatius of Antioch*, translated and edited by James A. Kleist, 75–79. Westminster, MD: Newman Bookshop, 1946.

Ih-Ren, Ambrose Mong. *The Liberal Spirit and Anti-Liberal Discourse of John Henry Newman*. Bern: Peter Lang, 2011.

Imberg, Rune. *In Quest of Authority: The "Tracts for the Times" and the Development of the Tractarian Leaders, 1833–41*. Lund, SE: Lund University Press, 1987.

———. "Who, Then, Was Dr. Newman?—The Man and the Myth." In *From Oxford to the People: Reconsidering Newman and the Oxford Movement*, edited by Paul Vaiss, 198–202. Leominster, UK: Gracewing, 1996.

Irenaeus. "Against Heresies." In *The Apostolic Fathers: Justin Martyr and Irenaeus*, The Ante-Nicene Fathers, edited by Alexander Roberts and James Donaldson, 1:315–567. Peabody, MA: Hendrickson, 1995.

Jaki, Stanley L. *Newman's Challenge*. Grand Rapids, MI: Eerdmans, 2000.

Jasper, David. "Pusey's 'Lectures on Types and Prophecies of the Old Testament.'" In *Pusey Rediscovered*, edited by Perry Butler, 51–70. London: SPCK, 1983.

Jebb, John. *Sermons on Subjects Chiefly Practical; with Illustrative Notes, and an Appendix Relating to the Character of the Church of England as Distinguished Both from Other Branches of the Reformation, and from the Modern Church of Rome*. London: T. Cadell, 1815.

Jelf, Richard William. *Via Media, or the Church of England Our Providential Path between Romanism and Dissent*. Oxford: John Henry Parker, 1842.

Jewel, John. *The Works of Bishop John Jewel*. Edited by Richard William Jelf. 4 vols. Cambridge: Cambridge University Press, 1845–1850.

Jodock, Darrell. "D. F. Strauss's *Life of Jesus*, F. C. Baur, and Modern Historical Consciousness." In *The Rise of Historical Consciousness among the Christian Churches*, edited by Kenneth L. Parker and Erick H. Moser, 65–88. Lanham, MD: University Press of America, 2013.

Johnson, Luke Timothy. *Among the Gentiles: Greco-Roman Religion and Christianity*. New Haven, CT: Yale University Press, 2009.

Jones, Tod E., ed. *The Broad Church: A Biography of a Movement*. Lanham, MD: Lexington Books, 2003.

Jones, William. *A Course of Lectures on the Figurative Language of Holy Scripture, and the Interpretation of It from Scripture Itself*. London: G. G. G. and J. Robinson, 1789.

Keble, John. *The State in Its Relations with the Church: A Paper Reprinted from* The British Critic, *October, 1839*. London: James Parker, 1869.

———. "Unpublished Papers of Bishop Warburton." In *Occasional Papers and Reviews*, 108–147. London: James Parker, 1877.

Kemp, Anthony. *The Estrangement of the Past: A Study in the Origins of Modern Historical Consciousness*. Oxford: Oxford University Press, 1991.

Ker, Ian. *John Henry Newman: A Biography*. Oxford: Oxford University Press, 1988.

———. *Newman and the Fullness of Christianity*. Edinburgh: T&T Clark, 1993.

———. *Newman on Vatican II*. Oxford: Oxford University Press, 2014.

———. "What Kind of Book Is the *Apologia*?" In *From Oxford to the People: Reconsidering Newman and the Oxford Movement*, edited by Paul Vaiss, 186–197. Leominster, UK: Gracewing, 1996.

Kertzer, David I. *Prisoner of the Vatican: The Popes' Secret Plot to Capture Rome from the New Italian State*. Boston: Houghton Mifflin, 2004.

Ketteler, Wilhem. *Die Minorität auf dem Concil. Antwort auf Lord Actons Sendschreiben an einen deutschen Bischof des Vaticanischen Concils*. Mainz: 1871.

King, Benjamin J. "The 'Consent of the Faithful' from *1 Clement* to the Anglican Covenant." *Journal of Anglican Studies* 12, no. 1 (2014): 7–36.

———. *Newman and the Alexandrian Fathers: Shaping Doctrine in Nineteenth-Century England*. Oxford: Oxford University Press, 2009.

King, Benjamin J. "The Protestant Reception of the *Essay on Development*, 1845–1925." In *Receptions of Newman*, edited by Frederick D. Aquino and Benjamin J. King, 9–29. Oxford: Oxford University Press, 2015.

———. "*Sensus Fidelium*." In *The Oxford Handbook of John Henry Newman*, edited by Frederick D. Aquino and Benjamin J. King, 264–283. Oxford: Oxford University Press, 2018.

Kingsley, Charles. *Hypatia, or New Foes with an Old Face*. London: John W. Parker, 1853.

Klausnitzer, Wolfgang. *Päpstliche Unfehlbarkeit bei Newman und Döllinger: Ein historisch-systematischer Vergleich*. Innsbruck: Tyrolia, 1980.

Klaver, Jan Marten Ivo. "The Apologia." In *The Oxford Handbook of John Henry Newman*, edited by Frederick D. Aquino and Benjamin J. King, 454–474. Oxford: Oxford University Press, 2018.

Klawans, Jonathan. *Purity, Sacrifice, and the Temple: Symbolism and Supersessionism in the Study of Ancient Judaism*. Oxford: Oxford University Press, 2006.

Küng, Hans. *Infallible? An Unresolved Enquiry*. Translated by John Bowden. Rev. ed. New York: Continuum, 1994.

Lagrange, Marie-Joseph. *La méthode historique: Surtout à propos de l'Ancien Testament*. Paris: Victor Lecoffre, 1903.

———. "Review of Alfred Loisy, *L'Évangile et l'Église*." In *Defending the Faith: An Anti-Modernist Anthology*, edited and translated by William H. Marshner, 38–70. Washington, DC: The Catholic University of America Press, 2017.

Larsen, Timothy. *Crisis of Doubt: Honest Faith in Nineteenth-Century England*. Oxford: Oxford University Press, 2006.

Lash, Nicholas. "Newman and 'A. Firmin.'" In *John Henry Newman and Modernism*, edited by Arthur Hilary Jenkins, 56–74. Sigmaringendorf, DE: Glock und Lutz, 1990.

———. *Newman on Development: The Search for an Explanation in History*. London: Sheed & Ward, 1975.

Lattier, Daniel J. "The Orthodox Theological Reception of Newman." In *Receptions of Newman*, edited by Frederick D. Aquino and Benjamin J. King, 177–194. Oxford: Oxford University Press, 2015.

Lawson, Stephen D. "'To Be Deep in History': The Role of History in the Conversions of John Henry Newman and Erik Peterson." *Newman Studies Journal* 16, no. 2 (2019): 5–33.

Levering, Matthew. "Development." In *Engaging the Doctrine of Revelation: The Mediation of the Gospel through Church and Scripture*, 175–216. Grand Rapids, MI: Baker Academic, 2014.

———. *Did Jesus Rise from the Dead?* Oxford: Oxford University Press, 2019.

———. "Introduction: Doctrine and Ecumenism." In *Joseph Ratzinger and the Healing of Reformation-Era Divisions*, edited by Emery de Gaál and Matthew Levering, ix–xxvii. Steubenville, OH: Emmaus Academic, 2019.

———. "Mary and Grace." In *The Oxford Handbook of Mary*, edited by Chris Maunder, 289–302. Oxford: Oxford University Press, 2019.

———. *Mary's Bodily Assumption*. Notre Dame, IN: University of Notre Dame Press, 2015.

———. *Participatory Biblical Exegesis: A Theology of Biblical Interpretation*. Notre Dame, IN: University of Notre Dame Press, 2008.

———. "Temple." In *Engaging the Doctrine of Israel: A Christian Israelology in Dialogue with Ongoing Judaism*, 262–321. Eugene, OR: Cascade, 2021.

———. *Was the Reformation a Mistake? Why Catholic Doctrine Is Not Unbiblical*. Grand Rapids, MI: Zondervan Academic, 2017.

Levine, Joseph M. *The Autonomy of History: Truth and Method from Erasmus to Gibbon*. Chicago: University of Chicago Press, 1999.

Lingard, John. *Remarks on a Charge Delivered by the Bishop of Durham to the Clergy of His Diocese*. London: Keating & Brown, 1807.

Lisowski, R. James. "A Fitting Glory: Newman and Mariology." *Newman Studies Journal* 15, no. 2 (2018): 21–38.

Loisy, Alfred. "The Development of Christianity According to Cardinal Newman." In *Prelude to the Modernist Crisis: The "Firmin" Articles of Alfred Loisy*, edited by C.J.T. Talar, translated by Christine Thirlway, 3–16. Oxford: Oxford University Press, 2010.

———. *The Gospel and the Church*. Translated by Christopher Home. London: Isbister, 1903.

Lothar, Kuld. "Evangelical Patterns of Conversion in Newman's Autobiographical Writings." In *By Whose Authority? Newman, Manning and the Magisterium*, edited by V. Alan McClelland, translated by Michael Payant, 112–122. Bath: Downside Abbey, 1996.

Loudovikos, Nikolaos. *Church in the Making: An Apophatic Ecclesiology of Consubstantiality*. Translated by Norman Russell. Yonkers, NY: St. Vladimir's Seminary Press, 2016.

Louth, Andrew. *Discerning the Mystery: An Essay on the Nature of Theology*. Oxford: Clarendon, 1983.

———. *Introducing Eastern Orthodox Theology*. Downers Grove, IL: IVP Academic, 2013.

Lüchinger, Adrian. *Päpstliche Unfehlbarkeit bei Henry Edward Manning und John Henry Newman*. Freiburg, CH: Universitäts Verlag, 2001.

Lukacs, John. *At the End of an Age*. New Haven, CT: Yale University Press, 2002.

Macaulay, Ambrose. *Dr Russell of Maynooth*. London: Darton, Longman, and Todd, 1983.

MacDougall, Hugh A. *The Acton-Newman Relations: The Dilemma of Christian Liberalism*. New York: Fordham University Press, 1962.

Machin, G.I.T. *Politics and the Churches in Great Britain, 1832 to 1868*. Oxford: Clarendon, 1977.

Maher, Anthony M. *The Forgotten Jesuit of Catholic Modernism: George Tyrrell's Prophetic Theology*. Minneapolis, MN: Fortress, 2018.

Mallock, W.H. *Doctrine and Doctrinal Disruption: Being an Examination of the Intellectual Position of the Church of England*. London: Adam & Charles Black, 1900.

Manning, Henry. *Caesarism and Ultramontanism*. London: Burns & Oates, 1873.

———. *The Centenary of Saint Peter and the General Council: A Pastoral Letter to the Clergy*. London: Longmans & Green, 1867.

———. *England and Christendom*. London: Longmans & Green, 1867.

———. *The Rule of Faith: Appendix to a Sermon*. 2nd ed. London: J.G.F & J. Rivington, 1839.

———. *The Vatican Decrees in Their Bearing on Civil Allegiance*. London: Longmans & Green, 1875.

Mansini, Guy. "Experience and Discourse, Revelation and Dogma in Catholic Modernism." *Nova et Vetera* 17, no. 4 (2019): 1119–1143.

———. "Saint Thomas and the Development of Doctrine." *Nova et Vetera* 19, no. 2 (2021): 393–422.

Margival, Henri. *Essai sur Richard Simon. La critique biblique au XVIIe siècle*. Geneva: Slatkine Reprints, 1970.

Marlé, René, ed. *Au coeur de le crise moderniste. Le dossier inédit d'une controverse. Lettres de Maurice Blondel, Henri Bremond, Friedrich von Hügel, Alfred Loisy*. Paris: Aubier, 1960.

Mather, F.C. *High Church Prophet: Bishop Samuel Horsley (1733–1806) and the Caroline Tradition in the Later Georgian Church*. Oxford: Oxford University Press, 1992.

Mazio, Giacomo. "Liturgia Anglicana." *Annali Delle Scienze Religiose*, 2nd Series, 5, no. 13 (July/August 1847): 181–192.

McCarren, Gerard. "Development of Doctrine." In *The Cambridge Companion to John Henry Newman*, edited by Ian Ker and Terrence Merrigan, 118–136. Cambridge: Cambridge University Press, 2009.

McCarren, Gerard. "'Tests' or 'Notes'? A Critical Evaluation of Criteria for Genuine Doctrinal Development in John Henry Newman's *Essay on the Development of Christian Doctrine*." Ph.D. Dissertation, The Catholic University of America, 1999.

McCready, David. *The Life and Theology of Alexander Knox: Anglicanism in the Age of Enlightenment and Romanticism*. Leiden, NL: Brill, 2020.

McElrath, Damian. *Lord Acton: The Decisive Decade 1864–1874. Essays and Documents*. New York: Humanities, 1970.

———. *The* Syllabus *of Pius IX: Some Reactions in England*. Louvain, BE: Publications Universitaires, 1964.

McGuckin, John Anthony. *The Path of Christianity: The First Thousand Years*. Downers Grove, IL: IVP Academic, 2017.

McInroy, Mark. "Before Deification Became Eastern: Newman's Ecumenical Retrieval." *International Journal of Systematic Theology* 20 (2018): 253–268.

McIntire, C.T. *England against the Papacy 1858–1861: Tories, Liberals, and the Overthrow of Papal Temporal Power during the Italian Risorgimento*. Cambridge: Cambridge University Press, 1983.

McLeod, Hugh. *Religion and Society in England: 1850–1914*. New York: St. Martin's, 1996.

Merrigan, Terrence. "Newman and Theological Liberalism." *Theological Studies* 66, no. 3 (2005): 605–621.

—. "'One Momentous Doctrine Which Enters into My Reasoning': The Unitive Function of Newman's Doctrine of Providence." *Downside Review* 108, no. 373 (October 1, 1990): 254–281.

———. "Revelation." In *The Cambridge Companion to John Henry Newman*, edited by Ian Ker and Terrence Merrigan, 47–72. Cambridge: Cambridge University Press, 2009.

———. "The 'Theological Imaginary' in History: John Henry Newman and the Catholic Theological Imagination." *Louvain Studies* 34, no. 2 (2009): 185–208.

Meszaros, Andrew. "Cardinals Newman and Scheffczyk on the Development of Dogma." *Rivista Teologica di Lugano* 25 (2020): 411–437.

———. "John Henry Newman and the Thomistic Tradition: Convergences in Contribution to Development Theory." *Nova et Vetera* 19, no. 2 (2021): 423–468.

———. *The Prophetic Church: History and Doctrinal Development in John Henry Newman and Yves Congar*. Oxford: Oxford University Press, 2016.

Milman, Henry Hart. *The History of Christianity, from the Birth of Christ to the Abolition of Paganism in the Roman Empire*. 3 vols. New York: A.C. Armstrong, 1887.

———. *History of Latin Christianity; Including That of the Popes to the Pontificate of Nicholas V*. 9 vols. 4th ed. London: John Murray, 1867.

———. "Newman on the Development of Christian Doctrine." *Quarterly Review* 77, no. 3 (1846): 404–465.

Milner, Joseph. *The History of the Church of Christ*. Vol. 1, *The First Three Centuries*. 4th ed. Revised by Isaac Milner. London: T. Cadell and W. Davies, 1812.

Misner, Paul. "Newman and Theological Pluralism." In *New Dimensions in Religious Experience*, edited by George Devine, 233–244. Staten Island, NY: Alba House, 1971.

———. "Newman's Concept of Revelation and the Development of Doctrine." *Heythrop Journal* 11, no. 1 (1970): 32–47.

———. *Papacy and Development: Newman and the Primacy of the Pope*. Leiden, NL: Brill, 1976.

Mitchell, Sally. *Daily Life in Victorian England*. Westport, CT: Greenwood Press, 1996.

Möhler, Johann Adam. *Unity in the Church, or, The Principle of Catholicism Presented in the Spirit of the Church Fathers of the First Three Centuries*. Translated by Peter C. Erb. Washington, DC: The Catholic University of America Press, 1996.

Momigliano, Arnaldo. "Gibbon's Contribution to Historical Method." *Historia: Zeitschrift für Alte Geschichte* 2, no. 4 (1954): 450–463.

Montagnes, Bernard. *Le Père Lagrange (1855–1938). L'exégèse catholique dans la crise moderniste*. Paris: Cerf, 1995.

———. *The Story of Father Marie-Joseph Lagrange: Founder of Modern Catholic Bible Study*. New York: Paulist, 2006.

Montalembert, Charles de. *A Letter Addressed to a Rev. Member of the Camden Society, on the Subject of Catholic Literary Societies, on the Architectural, Artistical, and Archaeological Movements of the Puseyites*. Liverpool: Booker, 1844.

———. *The Political Future of England*. 2nd ed. London: John Murray, 1856.

Morgan, Stephen. *John Henry Newman and the Development of Doctrine: Encountering Change, Looking for Continuity*. Washington, DC: The Catholic University of America Press, 2021.

Morris, Jeremy. "'Separated Brethren': French Catholics and the Oxford Movement." In *The Oxford Movement: Europe and the Wider World 1830–1930*, edited by Stewart J. Brown and Peter B. Nockles, 203–220. Cambridge: Cambridge University Press, 2012.

Mozley, J.B. *The Theory of Development: A Criticism of Dr. Newman's* Essay on the Development of Christian Doctrine. London: Rivington, 1878.

Murphy, Martin. *Blanco White: Self-Banished Spaniard*. New Haven, CT: Yale University Press, 1989.

Nédoncelle, Maurice. "La suprématie papale d'après l'Essai sur le développement de Newman." In *Parole de Dieu et sacerdoce*, edited by E. Fischer and L. Bouyer, 139–152. Paris: Desclée et Cie, 1962.

———. "Le développement de la doctrine chrétienne: J. B. Mozley, critique Anglican de Newman." In *Tradition in Lutheranism and Anglicanism*, edited by G.V. Gassmann and V. Vajta, 156–172. Minneapolis, MN: Augsburg, 1972.

Nédoncelle, Maurice. "Newman et Blondel. La théologie des développements doctrinaux." In *Newman-Studien* 6, 105–122. Nüremberg: Glock und Lutz, 1964.

Nevin, Robert Joseph. "Preface." In *Report of the Union Conferences, Held from August 10 to 16, 1875, at Bonn, under the Presidency of Dr. von Döllinger*, edited by Heinrich Reusch, translated by Samuel Buel, iii–xlix. New York: T. Whittaker, 1876.

Newman, Francis William. *Contributions Chiefly to the Early History of the Late Cardinal Newman*. London: Kegan Paul, Trench, and Trübner, 1891.

———. *A History of the Hebrew Monarchy*. 3rd ed. London: N. Trübner, 1865.

———. "Letter to J. H. Newman, 6 August 1845." In *The Letters and Diaries of John Henry Newman*, edited by Francis J. McGrath, 10:745. Oxford: Oxford University Press, 2006.

———. *On the Defective Morality of the New Testament*. Ramsgate: Thomas Scott, 1867.

———. *Phases of Faith, or, Passages from the History of My Creed*. 2nd ed. London: Watts, 1907.

———. *A Plea for Catholic Union: Essays towards a Church of the Future as the Organization of Philanthropy*. London: J. Chapman, 1854.

———. *The Soul, Its Sorrows and Aspirations: An Essay Towards the Natural History of the Soul, as the True Basis of Theology*. London: George Manwaring, 1849.

———. *Theism, Doctrinal and Practical; or Didactic Religious Utterances*. London: J. Chapman, 1858.

Newman, John Henry. *Apologia Pro Vita Sua*. New York: Doubleday, 1989.

———. *Apologia Pro Vita Sua and Six Sermons*. Edited by Frank Turner. New Haven, CT: Yale University Press, 2008.

———. *The Arians of the Fourth Century*. 6th ed. London: Longmans & Green, 1890.

Newman, John Henry. "Biglietto Speech," 1879. http://www.newmanreader.org/works/addresses/file2.html.

———. "The Catholicity of the Anglican Church." In *Essays Critical and Historical*, 2:1–73. London: Longmans & Green, 1895.

———. *Certain Difficulties Felt by Anglicans in Catholic Teaching Considered.* Vol. 1. London: Longmans & Green, 1897.

———. "Discourse VIII: Nature and Grace." In *Discourses Addressed to Mixed Congregations*, edited by James Tolhurst, 145–168. Notre Dame, IN: University of Notre Dame Press, 2003.

———. "Discourse IX: Duties of the Church Towards Knowledge." In *The Idea of a University*, edited by Martin J. Svaglic, 161–181. Notre Dame, IN: University of Notre Dame Press, 1982.

———. "Discourse IX: Illuminating Grace." In *Discourses Addressed to Mixed Congregations*, edited by James Tolhurst, 169–191. Notre Dame, IN: University of Notre Dame Press, 2003.

———. *An Essay in Aid of a Grammar of Assent.* Westminster, MD: Christian Classics, 1973.

———. *An Essay on the Development of Christian Doctrine.* 6th ed. Notre Dame, IN: University of Notre Dame Press, 1989.

———. *An Essay on the Development of Christian Doctrine [1845].* Edited by Stanley L. Jaki. Pinckney, MI: Real View Books, 2003.

———. *Elucidations of Dr. Hampden's Theological Statements.* London: J.H. Parker and Messrs. Rivington, 1836.

———. "Faith and Doubt." In *Discourses Addressed to Mixed Congregations*, edited by James Tolhurst, 214–237. Notre Dame, IN: University of Notre Dame Press, 2002.

———. "Fall of De la Mennais." In *Essays Critical and Historical*, 1:138–178. London: Longmans, Green, 1897.

———. *Fifteen Sermons Preached before the University of Oxford between A.D. 1826 and 1843.* Edited by Mary Katherine Tillman. 3rd ed. Notre Dame, IN: University of Notre Dame Press, 1997.

Newman, John Henry. "A Form of Infidelity of the Day." In *The Idea of a University*, edited by Martin J. Svaglic, 286–303. Notre Dame, IN: University of Notre Dame Press, 1982.

———. "Holy Scripture in Its Relation to the Catholic Creed." In *Discussions and Arguments on Various Subjects*, edited by Gerard Tracey and James Tolhurst, 109–235. Notre Dame, IN: University of Notre Dame Press, 2004.

———. *The Idea of a University*. Edited by Martin J. Svaglic. Notre Dame, IN: University of Notre Dame Press, 1982.

———. "John Davison." In *Essays Critical and Historical*, edited by Nicholas Schofield, 2:445–494. Leominster, UK: Gracewing, 2019.

———. "John Keble." In *Essays Critical and Historical*, edited by Nicholas Schofield, 2:499–536. Leominster, UK: Gracewing, 2019.

———. "A Letter Addressed to His Grace the Duke of Norfolk on Occasion of Mr. Gladstone's Recent Expostulation." In *Certain Difficulties Felt by Anglicans in Catholic Teaching Considered*, 2:171–378. London: Longmans & Green, 1896.

———. "A Letter Addressed to the Rev. E. B. Pusey, D.D., on Occasion of His Eirenicon." In *Certain Difficulties Felt by Anglicans in Catholic Teaching Considered*, 2:1–170. London: Longmans & Green, 1896.

———. "Letters to Arthur Osborne Alleyne, 30 May 1860, 15 June 1860 and 17 June 1860." In *The Letters and Diaries of John Henry Newman*, edited by Charles Stephen Dessain, 19:346–347, 361–370. Oxford: Oxford University Press, 1969.

———. "Letters to Richard Frederick Littledale, 15 September 1872 and 17 September 1872." In *The Letters and Diaries of John Henry Newman*, edited by Charles Stephen Dessain and Thomas Gornall, 26:169–171. Oxford: Oxford University Press, 1974.

———. "Letter to Alfred Plummer, 3 April 1871." In *The Letters and Diaries of John Henry Newman*, edited by Charles Stephen Dessain and Thomas Gornall, 25:308–310. Oxford: Oxford University Press, 1973.

Newman, John Henry. "Letter to Arthur Arnold, 20 September 1872." In *The Letters and Diaries of John Henry Newman*, edited by Charles Stephen Dessain and Thomas Gornall, 26:172–173. Oxford: Oxford University Press, 1974.

———. "Letter to Bishop William Ullathorne, 28 January 1870." In *The Letters and Diaries of John Henry Newman*, edited by Charles Stephen Dessain and Thomas Gornall, 25:18–20. Oxford: Oxford University Press, 1973.

———. "Letter to E. B. Pusey, 24 January 1836." In *The Letters and Diaries of John Henry Newman*, edited by Thomas Gornall, 5:214. Oxford: Oxford University Press, 1981.

———. "Letter to H. A. Woodgate, 17 April 1833." In *The Letters and Diaries of John Henry Newman*, edited by Thomas Gornall and Ian Ker, 3:297–300. Oxford: Oxford University Press, 1979.

———. "Letter to His Mother, 13 March 1829." In *The Letters and Diaries of John Henry Newman*, edited by Thomas Gornall and Ian Ker, 2:130. Oxford: Oxford University Press, 1979.

———. "Letter to Hugh James Rose, 23 May 1836." In *The Letters and Diaries of John Henry Newman*, edited by Thomas Gornall, 5:301–304. Oxford: Oxford University Press, 1981.

———. "Letter to J. M. Capes, 23 August 1850." In *The Letters and Diaries of John Henry Newman*, edited by Charles Stephen Dessain, 14:48–49. Oxford: Oxford University Press, 1963.

———. "Letter to Jemima [Newman] Mozley." In *The Letters and Diaries of John Henry Newman*, edited by Charles Stephen Dessain and Thomas Gornall, 28:121. Oxford: Oxford University Press, 1975.

———. "Letter to Johann Joseph Ignaz von Döllinger, 9 April 1870." In *The Letters and Diaries of John Henry Newman*, edited by Charles Stephen Dessain and Thomas Gornall, 25:85. Oxford: Oxford University Press, 1973.

Newman, John Henry. "Letter to R. F. Wilson, 18 March 1833." In *The Letters and Diaries of John Henry Newman*, edited by Thomas Gornall and Ian Ker, 3:257–258. Oxford: Oxford University Press, 1979.

———. "Letter to Robert Whitty, April 12, 1870." In *The Letters and Diaries of John Henry Newman*, edited by Charles Stephen Dessain and Thomas Gornall, 25:93–95. Oxford: Oxford University Press, 1973.

———. "Letter to T. W. Allies, 3 September 1854." In *The Letters and Diaries of John Henry Newman*, edited by Charles Stephen Dessain, 16:244. Oxford: Oxford University Press, 1965.

———. "Letter to the Editor of *The Guardian*, 12 September 1872." In *The Letters and Diaries of John Henry Newman*, edited by Charles Stephen Dessain and Thomas Gornall, 26:166–168. Oxford: Oxford University Press, 1974.

———. "Letter to the Editor of *The Standard*, 15 March 1870." In *The Letters and Diaries of John Henry Newman*, edited by Charles Stephen Dessain and Thomas Gornall, 25:54–55. Oxford: Oxford University Press, 1973.

———. "Letter to the Editor of *The Times*, 9 September 1872." In *The Letters and Diaries of John Henry Newman*, edited by Charles Stephen Dessain and Thomas Gornall, 26:163–164. Oxford: Oxford University Press, 1974.

———. "Letter to Walter John Trower, 16 April 1833." In *The Letters and Diaries of John Henry Newman*, edited by Thomas Gornall and Ian Ker, 3:293. Oxford: Oxford University Press, 1979.

———. "Letter to William Wilberforce, 9 December 1860." In *The Letters and Diaries of John Henry Newman*, edited by Charles Stephen Dessain, 19:437–438. Oxford: Oxford University Press, 1969.

———. *Loss and Gain*. Edited by Trevor Lipscombe. San Francisco: Ignatius Press, 2012.

Newman, John Henry. "The Memorandum on the Immaculate Conception." In *Meditations and Devotions of the Late Cardinal Newman*, edited by William P. Neville, 115–126. London: Longmans & Green, 1893.

———. "Milman's View of Christianity." In *Essays Critical and Historical*, edited by Nicholas Schofield, 2:224–293. Leominster, UK: Gracewing, 2019.

———. "Note A.: Liberalism." In *Apologia Pro Vita Sua*, edited by Charles F. Harrold, 259–269. New York: Longmans & Green, 1947.

———. "Note on Essay X." In *Essays Critical and Historical*, 2:74–111. London: Longmans & Green, 1895.

———. *On Consulting the Faithful in Matters of Doctrine*. Edited by John Coulson. Lanham, MD: Sheed & Ward, 2006.

———. "Preface to the Third Edition." In *The Via Media of the Anglican Church*, 1:xv–xciv. London: Basil Montagu Pickering, 1877.

———. "Private Judgment." In *Essays Critical and Historical*, 2:336–374. London: Longmans & Green, 1895.

———. "Reformation of the Eleventh Century." In *Essays Critical and Historical*, edited by Nicholas Schofield, 2:294–377. Leominster, UK: Gracewing, 2019.

———. "Religious Faith Rational." In *Parochial and Plain Sermons*, 121–128. San Francisco: Ignatius Press, 1987.

———. "The Self-Wise Inquirer." In *Parochial and Plain Sermons*, 137–144. San Francisco: Ignatius Press, 1987.

———. "Sermon 14: Wisdom, as Contrasted with Faith and with Bigotry." In *Fifteen Sermons Preached before the University of Oxford between A.D. 1826 and 1843*, edited by Mary Katherine Tillman, 3rd ed., 278–311. Notre Dame, IN: University of Notre Dame Press, 1997.

Newman, John Henry. "Slavery Allowed Not Encouraged under the Gospel." In *Sermons 1824–1843*, Vol. 3, *Sermons and Lectures for Saints' Days and Holy Days and General Theology*, edited by Francis J. McGrath and Placid Murray, 239–253. Oxford: Clarendon, 2010.

———. "The Tamworth Reading Room." In *Discussions and Arguments on Various Subjects*, edited by Gerard Tracey and James Tolhurst, 254–305. Notre Dame, IN: University of Notre Dame Press, 2004.

———. "The Theory of Developments in Religious Doctrine." In *Fifteen Sermons Preached before the University of Oxford between A.D. 1826 and 1843*, edited by Mary Katherine Tillman, 3rd ed., 312–351. Notre Dame, IN: University of Notre Dame Press, 1997.

———. "Tract 20: The Visible Church: Letters to a Friend, No. III." In *Tracts for the Times*, edited by James Tolhurst, 68–73. Notre Dame, IN: University of Notre Dame Press, 2013.

———. "Tract 41: Via Media II." In *Tracts for the Times*, edited by James Tolhurst, 116–128. Notre Dame, IN: University of Notre Dame Press, 2013.

———. "Tract 71: On the Controversy with the Romanists." In *Tracts for the Times*, edited by James Tolhurst, 140–179. Notre Dame, IN: University of Notre Dame Press, 2013.

———. "Tract 73: On the Introduction of Rationalistic Principles into Religion." In *Tracts for the Times*, edited by James Tolhurst, 180–243. Notre Dame, IN: University of Notre Dame Press, 2013.

———. "Tract 90: Remarks on Certain Passages in the Thirty-Nine Articles." In *Tracts for the Times*, edited by James Tolhurst, 383–475. Notre Dame, IN: University of Notre Dame Press, 2013.

———. *The Via Media of the Anglican Church*. 3rd ed. London: Basil Montagu Pickering, 1877.

Newsome, David. "The Evangelical Sources of Newman's Power." In *The Rediscovery of Newman: An Oxford Symposium*, edited by A.M. Allchin and John Coulson, 11–30. London: Sheed & Ward, 1967.

Newsome, David. "Newman and Oxford." In *Newman: A Man for Our Time*, edited by David Brown, 35–51. London: SCK, 1990.

———. *The Parting of Friends: The Wilberforces and Henry Manning*. London: John Murray, 1966.

Newton, Thomas. *Dissertations on the Prophecies, Which Have Remarkably Been Fulfilled and at This Time Are Fulfilling in the World.* 2 vols. New York: William Durrell, 1794.

Nguyen, Theresa Marie Chau. "Encountering Truth: Newman's Theological Method in *An Essay on the Development of Christian Doctrine*." *Newman Studies Journal* 8, no. 1 (2011): 40–55.

———. "Preservation of Type and the Continuity of Patristic Principles in the Legacies of Saint John Henry Newman and Henri de Lubac." *Newman Studies Journal* 17, no. 2 (2020): 22–40.

Nicholls, David. "Newman's Anglican Critics." *Anglican Theological Review* 47, no. 4 (1965): 377–395.

Nicholls, Guy. *Unearthly Beauty: The Aesthetic of St John Henry Newman*. Leominster, UK: Gracewing, 2019.

Nichols, Aidan. *From Newman to Congar: The Idea of Doctrinal Development from the Victorians to the Second Vatican Council.* Edinburgh: T&T Clark, 1990.

———. "Littlemore from Lucerne: Newman's *Essay on Development* in Balthasarian Perspective." In *Newman and Conversion*, edited by Ian Ker, 100–116. Edinburgh: T&T Clark, 1997.

Nockles, Peter B. "'Church and King': Tractarian Politics Reappraised." In *From Oxford to the People: Reconsidering Newman and the Oxford Movement*, edited by Paul Vaiss, 93–123. Leominster, UK: Gracewing, 1996.

———. "'Lost Causes . . . and Impossible Loyalties': The Oxford Movement and the University." In *The History of the University of Oxford.* Vol. 6, *Nineteenth-Century Oxford,* Part 1, edited by M.G. Brock and M.C. Curthoys, 195–267. Oxford: Clarendon, 1997.

Nockles, Peter B. "Newman and Early Tractarian Politics." In *By Whose Authority? Newman, Manning and the Magisterium*, edited by V. Alan McClelland, 79–111. Bath: Downside Abbey, 1996.

———. "Newman, Tract 90 and the Bishops." In *John Henry Newman: Reason, Rhetoric and Romanticism*, edited by David Nicholls and Fergus Kerr, 28–87. Bristol: Classical Press, 1991.

———. "The Oxford Movement and Evangelicalism: Parallels and Contrasts in Two Nineteenth-Century Movements of Religious Revival." In *Perfecting Perfection: Essays in Honour of Henry D. Rack*, edited by Robert Webster, 233–259. Cambridge: James Clarke, 2016.

———. "The Oxford Movement in an Oxford College: Oriel as the Cradle of Tractarianism." In *The Oxford Movement: Europe and the Wider World 1830–1930*, edited by Stewart J. Brown and Peter B. Nockles, 11–33. Cambridge: Cambridge University Press, 2012.

———. *The Oxford Movement in Context: Anglican High Churchmanship, 1760–1857*. Cambridge: Cambridge University Press, 1994.

———. "Pusey and the Question of Church and State." In *Pusey Rediscovered*, edited by Perry Butler, 255–297. London: SPCK, 1983.

———. "Revelation." In *The Oxford Handbook of John Henry Newman*, edited by Frederick D. Aquino and Benjamin J. King, 304–317. Oxford: Oxford University Press, 2018.

———. "Sources of English Conversions to Roman Catholicism in the Era of the Oxford Movement." In *By Whose Authority? Newman, Manning and the Magisterium*, edited by V. Alan McClelland, 1–40. Bath: Downside Abbey, 1996.

Norris, Thomas. "Faith." In *The Cambridge Companion to John Henry Newman*, edited by Ian Ker and Terrence Merrigan, 73–97. Cambridge: Cambridge University Press, 2009.

Oakely, Frederick. *The Subject of Tract XC Examined*. London: J.G.F & J. Rivington, 1841.

O'Connell, Marvin R. *Critics on Trial: An Introduction to the Catholic Modernist Crisis*. Washington, DC: The Catholic University of America Press, 1994.

———. *The Oxford Conspirators: A History of the Oxford Movement 1833–45*. London: Macmillan, 1969.

O'Connor, Benjamin. "The Oxford Movement." In *Authority, Dogma, and History: The Role of Oxford Movement Converts in the Papal Infallibility Debates*, edited by Kenneth L. Parker and Michael J. Pahls, 9–43. Bethesda, MD: Academica, 2009.

O'Gara, Margaret. *Triumph in Defeat: Infallibility, Vatican I, and the French Minority Bishops*. Washington, DC: The Catholic University of America Press, 1988.

O'Malley, John W. *Vatican I: The Council and the Making of the Ultramontane Church*. Cambridge, MA: Harvard University Press, 2018.

O'Regan, Cyril. "Newman's Forensic Classic of Development: Its Uniqueness and Its Agon with Gibbon and Surrogates." *International Journal of Systematic Theology* 20, no. 2 (2018): 225–252.

Overton, John Henry, and Elizabeth Wordsworth. *Christopher Wordsworth, Bishop of Lincoln, 1807–1885*. London: Rivington, 1888.

Oxenham, Henry N. *Dr. Pusey's Eirenicon Considered in Relation to Catholic Unity: A Letter to the Rev. Father Lockhart*. London: Longmans, Green, 1866.

Page, John R. *What Will Dr. Newman Do? John Henry Newman and Papal Infallibility, 1865–1875*. Collegeville, MN: Liturgical, 1994.

Pahls, Michael J. "Canterbury's Rejoinder: Pusey, Gladstone, and the Neo-Ultramontanism of Manning." In *Authority, Dogma, and History: The Role of Oxford Movement Converts in the Papal Infallibility Debates*, edited by Kenneth L. Parker and Michael J. Pahls, 115–128. Bethesda, MD: Academica, 2009.

Pakaluk, Michael. *Mary's Voice in the Gospel according to John*. Washington, DC: Regnery, 2021.

Palmer, William. *The Doctrine of Development and Conscience Considered in Relation to the Evidences of Christianity and of the Catholic System*. London: France and John, 1846.

Parker, John W. *Essays and Reviews*. 2nd ed. London: John W. Parker, 1860.

Parker, Kenneth L. "Henry Manning and Neo-Ultramontanism: The Anglican Context for an Oxford Movement Convert's Faith in Papal Infallibility." In *Authority, Dogma, and History: The Role of Oxford Movement Converts in the Papal Infallibility Debates*, edited by Kenneth L. Parker and Michael J. Pahls, 95–113. Bethesda, MD: Academica, 2009.

———. "Historical Consciousness and the First Vatican Council: Manning, Döllinger, Newman, and Acton's Uses of History in the Papal Infallibility Debates." In *The Rise of Historical Consciousness among the Christian Churches*, edited by Kenneth L. Parker and Erick H. Moser, 89–122. Lanham, MD: Rowman & Littlefield, 2013.

———. "Historiography." In *The Oxford Handbook of John Henry Newman*, edited by Frederick D. Aquino and Benjamin J. King, 557–577. Oxford: Oxford University Press, 2018.

———. "Newman's Individualistic Use of the Caroline Divines in the *Via Media*." In *Discourse and Context: An Interdisciplinary Study of John Henry Newman*, edited by Gerard Magill, 33–42. Carbondale, IL: Southern Illinois University Press, 1993.

———. "Re-visioning the Past and Re-sourcing the Future: The Unresolved Historiographical Struggle in Roman Catholic Scholarship and Authoritative Teaching." In *The Church on its Past*, edited by Peter D. Clarke and Charlotte Methuen, 389–416. Rochester, NY: Ecclesiastical History Society, 2013.

———. "Tractarian Visions of History." In *The Oxford Handbook of the Oxford Movement*, edited by Stewart J. Brown, Peter B. Nockles, and James Pereiro, 151–165. Oxford University Press, 2017.

Parker, Kenneth L., and C. Michael Shea. "Johann Adam Möhler's Influence on John Henry Newman's Theory of Doctrinal Development: The Case for a Reappraisal." *Ephemerides Theologicae Lovanienses* 89, no. 1 (2013): 73–95.

———. "The Roman Catholic Reception of the *Essay on Development*." In *Receptions of Newman*, edited by Frederick D. Aquino and Benjamin J. King, 30–49. Oxford: Oxford University Press, 2015.

Parker, Kenneth L., and The Contributors. "The Converts and the Council." In *Authority, Dogma, and History: The Role of Oxford Movement Converts in the Papal Infallibility Debates*, edited by Kenneth L. Parker and Michael J. Pahls, 1–9. Bethesda, MD: Academica, 2009.

Parker, Thomas M. "The Rediscovery of the Fathers in the Seventeenth-Century Anglican Tradition." In *The Rediscovery of Newman: An Oxford Symposium*, edited by A.M. Allchin and John Coulson, 31–49. London: Sheed & Ward, 1967.

Pastor Aeternus. In *Decrees of the Ecumenical Councils*, edited by Norman P. Tanner. 2:811–816. Washington, DC: Georgetown University Press, 1990.

Pattison, Robert. *The Great Dissent: John Henry Newman and the Liberal Heresy*. Oxford: Oxford University Press, 1991.

Paz, D.G. *Popular Anti-Catholicism in Mid-Victorian England*. Stanford, CA: Stanford University Press, 1992.

Peel, Robert. *An Inaugural Address Delivered by the Right Hon. Sir Robert Peel, Bart. M.P., President of the Tamworth Library and Reading Room on Tuesday, 19th January 1841*. 2nd ed. London: James Bain, 1841.

Pelikan, Jaroslav. *The Christian Tradition: A History of the Development of Doctrine*. Vol. 5, *Christian Doctrine and Modern Culture (since 1700)*. Chicago: University of Chicago Press, 1989.

———. *Development of Christian Doctrine: Some Historical Prolegomena*. New Haven, CT: Yale University Press, 1969.

Pereiro, James. *Cardinal Manning: An Intellectual Biography*. Oxford: Clarendon, 1998.

———. "Crossed Visions: The Anglican Manning's Opinion of Rome and the Catholic Manning's Thoughts on Canterbury." In *By Whose Authority? Newman, Manning and the Magisterium*, edited by V. Alan McClelland, 204–243. Bath: Downside Abbey, 1996.

———. *'Ethos' and the Oxford Movement: At the Heart of Tractarianism*. Oxford: Oxford University Press, 1991.

———. *Theories of Development in the Oxford Movement*. Leominster, UK: Gracewing, 2015.

Peterburs, Michael. "Newman and the Development of Doctrine." In *By Whose Authority? Newman, Manning and the Magisterium*, edited by V. Alan McClelland, 49–78. Bath: Downside Abbey, 1996.

Peterson, Linda H. *Victorian Autobiography: The Tradition of Self-Interpretation*. New Haven, CT: Yale University Press, 1986.

Pius IX, Pope. *Iam Vos Omnes*. September 13, 1968. In *Compendium of Creeds, Definitions, and Declarations of the Catholic Church on Matters of Faith and Morals*, 43rd ed, Revised and enlarged and edited by Peter Hünermann, Helmut Hoping, Robert Fastiggi, and Anne Englund Nash, 2997–2999. San Francisco: Ignatius Press, 2012.

———. *Qui Pluribus*, November 9, 1846. https://www.papalencyclicals.net/pius09/p9quiplu.htm.

———. *Singulari Quidem*, March 17, 1856. https://www.papalencyclicals.net/pius09/p9singul.htm.

Pocock, J.G.A. "An Overview of *The Decline and Fall of the Roman Empire*." In *The Cambridge Companion to Edward Gibbon*, edited by Karen O'Brien and Brian W. Young, 20–40. Cambridge: Cambridge University Press, 2018.

Poston, Lawrence. *The Antagonist Principle: John Henry Newman and the Paradox of Personality*. Charlottesville, VA: University of Virginia Press, 2014.

Purcell, Edmund. *Life of Cardinal Manning.* 2 vols. London: Macmillan, 1896.

Pusey, E.B. *The Articles Treated on in Tract 90 Reconsidered and Their Interpretation Vindicated.* Oxford: J.H. Parker, 1841.

———. *An Eirenicon, In a Letter to the Author of "The Christian Year."* London: John Henry and James Parker, 1865.

———. *First Letter to the Very Rev. J. H. Newman, D.D., in Explanation Chiefly in Regard to the Ever-Blessed Theotokos, and the Doctrine of Her Immaculate Conception.* London: James Parker, 1869.

———. *Is Healthful Reunion Impossible? A Second Letter to the Very Rev. J. H. Newman, D.D.* London: James Parker, 1870.

———. *On the Clause "and the Son" in Regard to the Eastern Church and the Bonn Conference: A Letter to the Rev. H. P. Liddon.* London: J.H. Parker, 1876.

———. *The Royal Supremacy: Not an Arbitrary Authority, but Limited by the Laws of the Church, of Which the Kings Are Members.* Oxford: J.H. Parker, 1850.

———. *Scriptural Views of Baptism.* London: J.G. & F. Rivington, 1836.

Rahner, Karl. "Considerations on the Development of Dogma." In *Theological Investigations.* Vol. 4, *More Recent Writings*, translated by Kevin Smyth, 3–35. New York: Seabury, 1974.

———. "Pluralism in Theology and the Unity of the Creed in the Church." In *Theological Investigations.* Vol. 11, *Confrontations 1*, translated by David Bourke, 3–23. New York: Seabury, 1974.

———. *The Shape of the Church to Come.* Translated by Edward Quinn. New York: Seabury, 1974.

———. "Yesterday's History of Dogma and Theology for Tomorrow." In *Theological Investigations.* Vol. 18, *God and Revelation*, translated by Edward Quinn, 3–34. New York: Crossroad, 1983.

Ratzinger, Joseph. *Milestones: Memoirs 1927–1977.* Translated by Erasmo Leiva-Merikakis. San Francisco: Ignatius Press, 1998.

Read, Donald. *England 1868–1914*. London: Longman, 1979.

Rechtenwald, Michael. *Nineteenth-Century British Secularism: Science, Religion and Literature*. New York: Palgrave Macmillan, 2016.

Reusch, Heinrich, ed. *Report of the Union Conferences, Held from August 10 to 16, 1875, at Bonn, under the Presidency of Dr. von Döllinger*. Translated by Samuel Buel. New York: T. Whittaker, 1876.

Richardson, Ann Margaret Schellenberg. "Brothers." In *The Oxford Handbook of John Henry Newman*, edited by Frederick D. Aquino and Benjamin J. King, 70–89. Oxford: Oxford University Press, 2018.

Robbins, William. *The Newman Brothers: An Essay in Comparative Intellectual Biography*. Cambridge, MA: Harvard University Press, 1966.

Roberts, Charlotte. *Edward Gibbon and the Shape of History*. Oxford: Oxford University Press, 2014.

Roberts, Clayton, and David Roberts. *A History of England*, Vol. 2, *1688 to the Present*. Englewood Cliffs, NJ: Prentice-Hall, 1991.

Roe, W.G. *Lamennais and England: The Reception of Lamennais's Religious Ideas in England in the Nineteenth Century*. Oxford: Oxford University Press, 1966.

Rowell, Geoffrey. "'Church Principles' and 'Protestant Kempism,' Some Theological Forerunners of the Tractarians." In *From Oxford to the People: Reconsidering Newman and the Oxford Movement*, edited by Paul Vaiss, 17–59. Leominster, UK: Gracewing, 1996.

Rowland, Tracey. "John Henry Newman on the Development of Doctrine: A Via Media between Intellectualism and a Voluntarist-Historicism." In a forthcoming essay collection, edited by Juan Velez. Washington DC: The Catholic University of America Press, 2022.

Rowlands, J.H.L. *Church, State and Society: The Attitudes of John Keble, Richard Hurrell Froude, and John Henry Newman, 1827–1845*. Worthing, UK: Churchman, 1989.

Rule, Philip. *Coleridge and Newman: The Centrality of Conscience*. New York: Fordham University Press, 2004.

Sabatier, Auguste. *De la vie intime des dogmes et de leur puissance d'évolution.* Paris: Fischbacher, 1890.

Sandius, Christopher. *Nucleus Historiae Ecclesiasticae.* Cologne: J. Nicholas, 1676.

Schatz, Klaus. *Papal Primacy: From Its Origins to the Present.* Translated by John A. Otto and Linda M. Maloney. Collegeville, MN: Liturgical, 1996.

———. *Vaticanum I, 1869–1870.* 3 vols. Paderborn: Schöningh, 1992.

Scheeben, Matthias Joseph. *Handbook of Catholic Dogmatics.* Book 1, *Theological Epistemology.* Part 1, *The Objective Principles of Theological Knowledge.* Translated by Michael J. Miller. Steubenville, OH: Emmaus Academic, 2019.

Scherr, Gregor von. "Archbishop von Scherr's Pastoral Letter." In *Declarations and Letters on the Vatican Decrees, 1869–1887,* edited by F.H. Reusch, 105–110. Edinburgh: T&T Clark, 1891.

———. "Letter to Pastor Widmann of Todtnau, 18 October 1874." In *Declarations and Letters on the Vatican Decrees, 1869–1887,* edited by F.H. Reusch, 117–120. Edinburgh: T&T Clark, 1891.

Schillebeeckx, Edward. *Church: The Human Story of God.* Translated by John Bowden. New York: Crossroad, 1990.

———. *Jesus: An Experiment in Christology.* Translated by Hubert Hoskins. New York: Seabury, 1981.

Schleiermacher, Friedrich. *On Religion: Speeches to Its Cultured Despisers.* Edited and translated by Richard Crouter. 2nd ed. Cambridge: Cambridge University Press, 1996.

Schoenig, Steven A. *Bonds of Wool: The Pallium and Papal Power in the Middle Ages.* Washington, DC: The Catholic University of America Press, 2016.

Schultenover, David G. *George Tyrrell: In Search of Catholicism.* Shepherdstown: Patmos, 1981.

Scott, Thomas. *The Force of Truth: An Authentic Narrative*. London: J. Keith and J. Johnson, 1779.

Shea, C. Michael. "Doctrinal Development." In *The Oxford Handbook of John Henry Newman*, edited by Frederick D. Aquino and Benjamin J. King, 284–303. Oxford: Oxford University Press, 2018.

———. *Newman's Early Roman Catholic Legacy, 1845–1854*. Oxford: Oxford University Press, 2017.

Sheridan, Thomas L. "Justification." In *The Cambridge Companion to John Henry Newman*, edited by Ian Ker and Terrence Merrigan, 98–117. Cambridge: Cambridge University Press, 2009.

Short, Edward. *Newman and His Contemporaries*. London: T&T Clark International, 2011.

———. *Newman and His Family*. London: Bloomsbury, 2013.

———. "Newman and the Liberals." In *Newman and History*, 135–202. Leominster, UK: Gracewing, 2017.

———. "Newman, Gibbon and God's Particular Providence." In *Newman and History*, 3–80. Leominster, UK: Gracewing, 2017.

———. "Newman, Superstition and the Whig Historian." In *Newman and History*, 83–115. Leominster, UK: Gracewing, 2017.

Sidenvall, Erik. *After Anti-Catholicism? John Henry Newman and Protestant Britain, 1845–c.1890*. London: T&T Clark International, 2005.

Siebenrock, Roman. *Wahrheit, Gewissen und Geschichte: Eine systematisch-theologisch Rekonstruktion des Wirkens John Henry Kardinal Newmans*. Sigmaringendorf, DE: Glock und Lutz, 1996.

Sieveking, Isabel Giberne. *Memoirs and Letters of Francis W. Newman*. London: Kegan Paul, Trench, and Trübner, 1909.

Söhngen, Gottlieb. *Kardinal Newman: Sein Gottesgedanke und seine Denkergestalt*. Bonn: Götz Schwippert, 1946.

Staniloae, Dumitru. "The Orthodox Conception of Tradition and the Development of Doctrine." *Sobornost* 5, no. 9 (1969): 652–662.

Stanley, A.P. *The Life and Correspondence of Thomas Arnold, D.D.* London: Ward, Lock, 1846.

Steinsdorfer, Helmut. “Gladstone—gehörte mit Lord Acton zum Döllinger-Kreis.” *Internationale Kirchliche Zeitschrift* 90, no. 2 (2000): 123–131.

Strange, Roderick. *Newman 101: An Introduction to the Life and Philosophy of John Cardinal Newman*. Notre Dame, IN: Ave Maria, 2008.

———. “Newman and Hampden.” In *John Henry Newman and Modernism*, edited by Arthur Hilary Jenkins, 29–40. Sigmaringendorf, DE: Glock und Lutz, 1990.

———. “Newman on Consulting the Faithful: Context, Content, and Consequences.” *New Blackfriars* 98, no. 1074 (2017): 134–146.

———. “Reflections on a Controversy: Newman and Pusey’s ‘Eirenicon.’” In *Pusey Rediscovered*, edited by Perry Butler, 332–348. London: SPCK, 1983.

———, ed. *John Henry Newman: A Portrait in Letters*. Oxford: Oxford University Press, 2015.

Strauss, David Friedrich. *The Life of Jesus Critically Examined*. Philadelphia: Fortress, 1972.

Strong, Rowan, and Carol Engelhardt Herringer, eds. *Edward Bouverie Pusey and the Oxford Movement*. London: Anthem Press, 2012.

Sullivan, Francis. “Newman on Infallibility.” In *Newman after One Hundred Years*, edited by Ian Ker and Allan Turnbull, 419–46. Oxford: Clarendon, 1990.

Svaglic, Martin J. “The Revision of Newman’s *Apologia*.” *Modern Philology* 50, no. 1 (1952): 43–49.

Sykes, Stephen W. “Newman, Anglicanism and the Fundamentals.” In *Newman After a Hundred Years*, edited by Ian Ker and Alan G. Hill, 353–374. Oxford: Clarendon, 1990.

Talar, C.J.T. “Newman and the ‘New Apologetics.’” *Newman Studies Journal* 6, no. 2 (2009): 49–56.

Talar, C.J.T. "Rehabilitating Richard Simon, Legitimating Alfred Loisy." In *The Rise of Historical Consciousness among the Christian Churches*, edited by Kenneth L. Parker and Erick H. Moser, 47–64. Lanham, MD: Rowman & Littlefield, 2013.

Théobald, Christoph. "L'exégèse catholique au moment de la crise modern-iste." In *Le monde contemporain et la Bible*, edited by Claude Savart and Jean-Nöel Aletti, 387–439. Paris: Beauchesne, 1985.

Thirlwall, Connop. *Letters Literary and Theological of Connop Thirlwall*. Edited by John J.S. Perowne and Louis Stokes. London: Richard Bentley & Son, 1881.

Thomas, Stephen. *Newman and Heresy: The Anglican Years*. Cambridge: Cambridge University Press, 1991.

Tierney, Brian. *The Origins of Papal Infallibility, 1150–1350: A Study of the Concept of Infallibility, Sovereignty and Tradition in the Middle Ages*. Leiden, NL: Brill, 1972.

Tillman, Mary Katherine. "The Definitive Third Edition of 1872: An Introduction." In *Fifteen Sermons Preached before the University of Oxford between A.D. 1826 and 1843*, edited by Mary Katherine Tillman, vii–lii. Notre Dame, IN: University of Notre Dame Press, 1997.

———. *John Henry Newman: Man of Letters*. Milwaukee, WI: Marquette University Press, 2015.

———. "Newman: The Dialectic of 'Liberalism' and 'Conservatism.'" *Josephinum Journal of Theology* 9, no. 2 (2002): 181–195.

Toews, John E. "Church and State: The Problem of Authority." In *The Cambridge History of Nineteenth-Century Political Thought*, edited by Gareth Stedman Jones and Gregory Claeys, 603–648. Cambridge: Cambridge University Press, 2011.

Toon, Peter. *Evangelical Theology, 1833–1856: A Response to Tractarianism*. London: Marshall, Morgan, and Scott, 1979.

Trocholepczy, Bernhard. "Newman's Concept of 'Realizing.'" In *By Whose Authority? Newman, Manning and the Magisterium*, edited by V. Alan McClelland, 136–148. Bath: Downside Abbey, 1996.

Troeltsch, Ernst. *Religion in History*. Translated by Walter F. Bense and James Luther Adams. Minneapolis, MN: Fortress, 1991.

Turner, Frank. "The Victorian Crisis of Faith and the Faith That Was Lost." In *Victorian Faith in Crisis: Essays on Continuity and Change in Nineteenth-Century Religious Belief*, edited by Richard J. Helmstadter and Bernard Lightmand, 9–38. London: Macmillan, 1990.

Turner, Frank M. *John Henry Newman: The Challenge to Evangelical Religion*. New Haven, CT: Yale University Press, 2002.

Turner, James. *Philology: The Forgotten Origins of the Modern Humanities*. Princeton, NJ: Princeton University Press, 2014.

Tyrrell, George. *Christianity at the Cross-Roads*. London: Longmans & Green, 1910.

Ullathorne, William. *The Immaculate Conception of the Mother of God: An Exposition*. London: Richardson & Son, 1855.

Vaiss, Paul. "Newman's State of Mind on the Eve of His Italian Tour." In *From Oxford to the People: Reconsidering Newman and the Oxford Movement*, edited by Paul Vaiss, 203–222. Leominster, UK: Gracewing, 1996.

Varley, Elizabeth A. *The Last of the Prince Bishops: William Van Mildert and the High Church Movement of the Early Nineteenth Century*. Cambridge: Cambridge University Press, 1992.

Vaughan, Robert. *The Causes of the Corruption of Christianity*. 2nd ed. London: Jackson and Walford, 1852.

Von Balthasar, Hans Urs. *Love Alone Is Credible*. Translated by D.C. Schindler. San Francisco: Ignatius Press, 2004.

———. *The Office of Peter and the Structure of the Church*. Translated by Andrée Emery. San Francisco: Ignatius Press, 1986.

Von Balthasar, Hans Urs *Theo-Drama: Theological Dramatic Theory.* Vol. 3, *The Dramatis Personae: The Person in Christ*. Translated by Graham Harrison. San Francisco: Ignatius Press, 1992.

Walgrave, Jan Hendrik. "Newman's *On Consulting the Faithful in Matters of Doctrine*." In *The Teaching Authority of the Believers*, edited by Johann-Baptist Metz and Edward Schillebeeckx, English volume edited by Marcus Lefébure, 23–30. Edinburgh: T&T Clark, 1985.

———. *Newman the Theologian: The Nature of Belief and Doctrine as Exemplified in His Life and Works*. Translated by A. Littledale. New York: Sheed & Ward, 1960.

———. "'Real' and 'Notional' in Blondel and Newman." In *John Henry Newman and Modernism*, edited by Arthur Hilary Jenkins, 142–156. Sigmaringendorf, DE: Glock und Lutz, 1990.

———. *Unfolding Revelation: The Nature of Doctrinal Development*. Philadelphia: Westminster, 1972.

Walsh, John D. "Joseph Milner's Evangelical Church History." *The Journal of Ecclesiastical History* 10, no. 2 (1959): 174–187.

Warburton, William. *The Alliance between Church and State: Or the Necessity and Equity of an Established Religion and a Test-Law Demonstrated.* 4th ed. London: A. Millar and J. and R. Tonson, 1766.

Ward, William. *Essays on the Church's Doctrinal Authority*. London: Burns & Oates, 1880.

Ware, Timothy. *The Orthodox Church*. London: Penguin, 1997.

Washburn, Christian D. "The First Vatican Council, Archbishop Henry Manning, and Papal Infallibility." *Catholic Historical Review* 102, no. 4 (2016): 712–745.

———. "Three Sixteenth-Century Thomist Solutions to the Problem of a Heretical Pope: Cajetan, Cano, and Bellarmine." *The Thomist* 83, no. 4 (2019): 547–588.

Whalen, Brett. *The Medieval Papacy*. New York: Palgrave Macmillan, 2014.

Whately, Richard. *Easy Lessons on Christian Evidences*. London: John W. Parker, 1838.

———. *Elements of Rhetoric*. 2nd ed. Oxford: John Murray, 1828.

———. *The Errors of Romanism Traced to Their Origin in Human Nature*. London: B. Fellowes, 1830.

———. *Letters on the Church*. London: Longman, Rees, Orme, Brown, and Green, 1826.

———. *Remarks on Some Causes of Hostility to the Christian Religion*. Dublin: Milliken and Son, 1838.

Wheeler, Michael. *The Old Enemies: Catholic and Protestant in Nineteenth-Century English Culture*. Cambridge: Cambridge University Press, 2006.

White, Joseph Blanco. *The Life of the Rev. Joseph Blanco White, Written by Himself, with Portions of His Correspondence*. Edited by John Hamilton Thom. 3 vols. London: J. Chapman, 1845.

———. *Observations on Heresy and Orthodoxy*. London: J. Mardon, 1835.

White, Thomas Joseph. *The Incarnate Lord: A Thomistic Study in Christology*. Washington, DC: The Catholic University of America Press, 2015.

———. *Wisdom in the Face of Modernity: A Study in Thomistic Natural Theology*. 2nd ed. Ave Maria, FL: Sapientia, 2016.

Willey, Basil. *More Nineteenth Century Studies: A Group of Honest Doubters*. London: Chatto & Windus, 1956.

Williams, Rowan. "Newman's *Arians*." In *Newman After a Hundred Years*, edited by Ian Ker and Alan G. Hill, 263–285. Oxford: Clarendon, 1990.

Wilson, A.N. *God's Funeral*. New York: W.W. Norton, 1999.

Wilson, James Matthew. "Doctrinal Development and the Demons of History: The Historiography of John Henry Newman." *Religion and the Arts* 10, no. 4 (January 1, 2006): 497–523.

Wiseman, Nicholas. *Lectures on the Principal Doctrines and Practices of the Catholic Church*. London: J. Booker, 1836.

Wiseman, Nicholas. *A Letter Respectfully Addressed to the Rev. J. H. Newman upon Some Passages in His Letter to the Rev. Dr. Jelf.* London: C. Dolman, 1841.

———. *A Sermon Preached at the Opening of St. Mary's Catholic Church in Derby*. London: James Storer, 1839.

Wood, Jacob W. "The Five-Hundredth Anniversary of the Reformation: A Catholic Perspective." In *Reformation Observances: 1517–2017*, edited by Philip D.W. Krey, 69–93. Eugene, OR: Cascade, 2017.

Wordsworth, Christopher. *Union with Rome: Is Not the Church of Rome the Babylon of the Book of Revelation?* London: Rivington, 1850.

Wormersley, David. "Afterword: A New Gibbon Manuscript." In *The Cambridge Companion to Edward Gibbon*, edited by Karen O'Brien and Brian W. Young, 219–232. Cambridge: Cambridge University Press, 2018.

Young, Brian W. "Gibbon and Catholicism." In *The Cambridge Companion to Edward Gibbon*, edited by Karen O'Brien and Brian W. Young, 147–166. Cambridge: Cambridge University Press, 2018.

———. "Gibbon, Newman, and the Religious Accuracy of the Historian." In *The Victorian Eighteenth Century: An Intellectual History*, 70–102. Oxford: Oxford University Press, 2007.

Zuijdwegt, Geertjan. *An Evangelical Adrift: The Making of John Henry Newman's Theology*. Washington, D.C.: Catholic University of America Press, forthcoming.

———. "Richard Whately." In *The Oxford Handbook of John Henry Newman*, edited by Frederick D. Aquino and Benjamin J. King, 196–216. Oxford: Oxford University Press, 2018.

INDEX

(Works of John Henry Newman appear in bold type)